Ma

Moral Apologetics

P R E S S

ISBN: 978-1-7359363-4-5 (Paperback)

www.moralapologetics.com

CASTING BREAD 2021

——

A History of HBU's Center for the Foundations of Ethics

David Baggett

Casting Bread

A History of the Center for the Foundations of Ethics at HBU, 2021

Volume 2

"Cast your bread upon the waters, for after many days you will find it again."
Ecclesiastes 11:1

Friday, January 1, 2021: First day of the year, although it started on a somber note—some 77,000 people dying from covid in the States in December. Horrific. Still in the throes of this thing; hopefully the vaccine will circulate quickly. Feeling a bit overwhelmed with work to do during break. I need to do one thing at a time and not indulge the sense of inundation. I'm both excited at the prospects of 2021 and find them daunting. Marybeth and I should probably schedule a prayer session, season, or even mini-retreat soon. Sent in last year's journal to Jonathan to publish through Moral Apologetics Press.

It is now late evening and I am about to go to bed—hoping that fireworks don't keep me up half the night like they did last night. For as much work as I have to do, today I did nothing particularly productive—a bit groggy from the bad sleep. Made it a lazy day. Found I needed a bit more leisure before getting back to work. I did listen to a chapter of *Washington Square*, and read a swath of pages from the Ginsburg book, but that's about it. Soon I need to share a few reflections from that book. Otherwise it was playing with my cat, watching *Cobra Kai* and *Frasier*. One of these days soon I'll get busy again. Jerry didn't come over this evening, because he had some football to watch—including a Notre Dame game featuring the prospect of their going up for the national championship.

Saturday, January 2, 2021: I hope to listen each day this year to the Daily Audio Bible, and near the beginning of Genesis, right after creation, comes the warning not to partake of the tree in the garden dubbed the Tree of the Knowledge of Good and Evil. I'm always fascinated by that. I should read up on some biblical commentary on it. Goodness as a topic also comes up during creation—everything God made was good. Since I'm not steeped in Hebrew, I don't know all the significance of the word used for 'good' there. I do wonder if it means less morally good than somehow valuable. Which reminds me of the piece on metaethics I'm reading from a guy named Danaher. Following Murphy, I think, he uses as a paradigm example of a potentially necessary truth that "pain is bad." But surely, I find myself thinking, pain is not morally bad. What's morally bad is, for example, intentionally inflicting pain on someone for no good reason. But pain itself strikes me as morally neutral, though nonmorally bad, no doubt—horrific even. But this subtle confusion or conflation of the moral and nonmoral leads people to infer it's easier than it is to derive ethics from natural properties alone.

The thought occurred this morning that perhaps I should ask Murphy to write on concurrentism in the anthology.

Great chat and prayer time with TJ, and chat this morning with Elton. One interesting part of the Elton exchange: Why do Protestants, generally less than Roman Catholics, not emphasize the Day of Judgment? Elton conjectured it was because of an overly sentimental view of God's love, whereas retaining a stronger rationalist component in our faith reminds us of the need to obey God's commands (even though some of them might be hard to make full sense of rationally), not to sin that sin might abound, and to take moral maturity seriously as believers.

I finally got around to answering a FB friend's question this morning; here's my reply, which embeds his question:

> Jeremy, I know we haven't met in person, but I want to tell you, once again, what a blessing you are to me. You have such a kind and irenic and generous spirit. I just love you! I am confident God is going to use you mightily!
>
> Sorry for the delay in getting to your question. Let me say a few words about it at least, though you probably have more to say to me than I to you on the topic.
>
> Can a moral saint be a systematic philosopher?
>
> I suspect God calls all of us as Christians to be saints. Moral saints, well, not so sure; we're called to be holy as God is holy, to love God with all of our hearts, souls, minds, and strength, and our neighbor as ourselves. Perhaps that's enough to make one a moral saint? The power of God that raised Jesus from the dead is at work within us, enabling us in him to find deliverance from the power of sin and to fulfill our vocations—so maybe? Just not entirely sure what being a moral saint amounts to (as you admitted the same). But we are surely supposed to allow God's Spirit to live in and through us—the very life of God is to be expressed in how we live. I am speaking of course as a Christian—but I have a hard time separating the present question from that.
>
> Might a person be totally committed to the Good, as you put it? In light of our sinful condition, I doubt anyone could do so without God's grace. I take original sin seriously, as I'm sure you do, and think God's grace is necessary for us to become wholly oriented to the good. As a Wesleyan, I'm inclined to emphasize the role of God's Spirit in sanctification—including entire sanctification, which might fruitfully be thought of in terms of complete orientation to the good.
>
> In terms of what that looks like, I am inclined to think it looks different for different people, for reasons not unrelated to the multifarious nature of the good.

3

Since each of us is unique, sui generis, called to inhabit particular parts in the body of Christ, I find myself averse to thinking of any "one-size-fits-all" depiction of how it looks. We are called to love our neighbor, but what does love look like? It looks different for Mister Rogers from what it looks like for you or me—despite some commonalities. A robust doctrine of vocation helps remind us that God's love can be at work in us and through us in a wide variety of different ways—from being a janitor to an ambassador. Doing it for God's glory, in his strength, and in the right spirit of selflessness is the key.

I think you're right to see giving as central, though I'm not sure about focusing on the limiting case of giving away everything (you yourself recognize a potential limitation of that). The reason for my hesitation is, again, related to what one's called to do. I tend to be a divine command theorist, so more tend to suspect there are more than just general principles to guide our action, I believe God's Spirit can, does, and will lead us in very specific ways. And in some cases, I imagine, that might not involve great financial (or other sorts of) sacrifice (though it will always involve elements of sacrifice, but the degree of sacrifice, I suspect, will fluctuate). In other cases it would.

Some of what you characterize as a saintly life strikes me as unsustainable over the long term. Morality is meant for rich relationships, a flourishing life, and freedom from guilt and shame, legalism and moralism. This notion that we are to be preoccupied every waking minute with maximizing our effect seems inordinately rigid to me. Perhaps this owes to my lack of saintliness, of course. ☺

Let's take an example. I think reading can be part of the vocation of some (a vocation that has lots of long-term indirect effects of building up others, potentially anyway), but it would be hard to fit that in on too rigid a model. Or take sleep. I'm inclined to think we should sleep exactly as much as we need—for most people that's about 8 hours a night. Over the long term, such a habit is most sustainable.

Similarly, I doubt I see the same tension as you may between asking what I most want to do and what is best for others. I think there is greater intended congruence in these matters. My view of vocation is that God can and does inculcate a desire within us to do (or at least eliminate too great an aversion to doing) what we are called to do.

Of course on occasion we may be called to do something to which we are genuinely averse, but I think we can and should pray for God's grace on those occasions for our desires to be changed and for us to learn better how to love and see what God loves and sees. And we shouldn't wait for our desires to change before obeying our call.

4

All of this is too brief, I know, but regarding your question of whether a moral saint would pursue philosophy, I see no compelling reason why not. Again I think some are called to such a vocation, and that we're all called to something like moral saintliness, so some are called to both.

You mentioned the power of ideas, and I think this is one of the ways in which our trying to figure out in advance how best to, say, maximize utility are bound to be limited and often mistaken. There is often a paradox in this life; what seems natural to assume is the best means to produce an outcome turns out not to be the best way at all. As a Christian, once again, I am strongly inclined to think that the most good gets done by each of us as we hear and heed God's call—and, for some, that likely means becoming a good philosopher. There are of course dangers of self-delusion and dishonesty, but there's also the prospect, which isn't risk-free, of hearkening to what we think is God's actual voice.

Well, as I say, I don't think this begins to do justice to your question, but those are a few of my thoughts anyway. Blessings, my friend, Dave

Sunday, January 3, 2021: Been a good day save for some excruciating lower back pain that's proven to be well-nigh immobilizing. I seem to have periodic bouts with back trouble. Last time it happened I muscled through without pain medication; but not this time!

Marybeth and I are both keeping up on the daily audio Bible readings; we hope to stick with that this year.

On other fronts: Received yesterday Mary Jo Sharp's book *Why I Still Believe*. Started reading it today, and hope to interview her at the site. I feel a strong desire to read the work of my colleagues and make it more visible. Enjoying it so far a lot. Listened to several more chapters this morning of Washington Square, and read a nice piece today by David French on *Ted Lasso* focusing on Ted's forgiving heart. He memorably called the show a countercultural masterpiece. And got caught up with an old Michigan friend this morning on the phone; we hope to chat about once a month from now on.

I also wrote Manuel back this morning like this:

Manuel, hey there, my friend. Sorry for my delay. Break's been crazy! Hope you have a great new year!

Allow me to respond to your ideas in this paragraph of yours:

> I ask what the foundation for objective moral values and duties might be, and then say that one way to answer this question would be to establish certain criteria for said foundation. In other words, what would something have to be in order to qualify as the ultimate foundation for

objective moral values and duties? So far, I have come up with the following characteristics. First, the foundation should exist **outside of, and independent of, human beings**. This is so that it may be objective, for if morality was determined by human beings, it would no longer be objective. Second, it must **transcend the universe**. This is building off of the previous video on the Cosmological Argument. If the foundation for objective morality were a part of the universe, that would mean that it began to exist (for the universe began to exist). Hence, it would depend on some other thing (the first cause, for example) for its own existence, meaning that, whatever that other thing is, that is the ultimate foundation for morality. It seems, then, that the foundation should exist outside of the universe. Similarly, for the same exact reason, the foundation should be **eternal**. Lastly, the foundation should be **personal**, for morality (based on our experience and what we know of the universe) only exists in persons. A lion may kill a zebra, but it does not murder a zebra. Moral qualifications like that are exclusive to persons (human beings). This need not imply that certain animals do not or cannot display certain behavior that human beings can classify as moral (such as empathy or helping another fellow animal). But, moral values and duties themselves seem to be found only in persons. As such, the foundation for morality should be personal.

Okay, so you're after establishing the foundation for objective moral values and duties. First do recall that this is just one set of moral phenomena in need of explanation. There are other moral facts—rights, moral freedom, regret, etc. Plus there's moral knowledge, the two dimensions of Kantian moral faith, etc. Anyway, just to say my approach is four-fold—and objective moral values and duties are just the first of the four parts. I know you know that, but I like to repeat myself. ☺

I like your approach here, but I might note that logically prior to establishing criteria for foundations is close attentiveness to the evidence. So what ARE objective moral duties and values? What are their features and properties? I argue, especially in the history book, that relative inattentiveness to these matters contributes a great deal nowadays to folks not seeing the need for robust foundations.

On the matter of criteria, your approach reminds me of Zach Breitenbach's approach. He wanted to retain a deductive methodology, and he figured the way he could do it was to talk about criteria of adequacy or something along such lines, such that theism would provide them and nothing else would. I suppose what is more distinctive about your approach is its intentionality to build a cumulative case by conjoining the moral argument with the other arguments from natural theology.

Regarding your first criterion, to say the standard should exist "outside" human beings, some might say there's an ambiguity there. Perhaps morality is a function of aspects of human beings, but just not a matter of consensus among them. This would mean that the criterion isn't outside humans at least in every sense. I think you can fix this pretty easily, though, by using language like "the first criterion is that the moral foundation isn't determined by human consensus."

Regarding the second criterion, to say it must transcend the universe will likely strain credulity for many. Some might say if this is required this gives us reason to be skeptical about moral realism. Others would say they're okay with moral foundations coming into existence—especially if such standards aren't independent of human beings in every sense. Others would say Platonism works well enough. I'm not suggesting these are effective refutations; just some ideas of things to anticipate.

Regarding eternality, Platonism would again satisfy that requirement, and plenty would deny it's a good criterion, but largely, I think, because they're too quick looking at the nature of the evidence.

Regarding the personal requirement, plenty of folks will suggest that morality is personal in virtue of being a function of that which conduces to harmonious human interaction and flourishing.

Again, not pointing this out because I disagree with you, but this is the sort of thing we encounter. Personally I think a richer moral argument is needed—one that talks about a wider array of evidence than duties and values. But I also find myself often thinking of this whole project of trying to succinctly summarize the moral argument as almost bound to fail. As a moral apologist this is making me rethink how to get people onboard. I am increasingly drawn to more implicit, imaginative, and literary ways of doing it. But that's a topic for another day.

I do encourage you to follow God's lead on this. I think God wants to use you, especially among those you can reach with your knowledge of the Spanish language. Proud of you!

Do try to read Shafer-Landau's book on moral realism if you get a chance.

Blessings, djb

Monday, January 4, 2020: Today was a good day. I'm up to about a quarter through Mary Jo's book, and am looking forward to interviewing her about the book once I'm done. The latest chapter was on doubt, and she used Habermas's distinction to distinguish between volitional doubt and other forms. One of the questions I want to ask her about is the way some nowadays seem to exalt doubt as a great virtue. My friend Bill Irwin does this, and some former students, often a big fan of Peter Enns, who writes about doubt and the evils of seeking or claiming certainty. Marybeth and I decided to order one of his books so we can read it together to be better prepared to engage in conversation those drawn to his work. I'm sure it's not without insights, but I also suspect it's overblown at points.

Marybeth and I are reading together a few other books at the moment. *A Tale of Three Kings* and *The Steward Leader*. The former is about three biblical kings and the problems associated with autocratic leads. The dangers of bad leadership, of authoritarianism, and of autocracy, even in the church—and our previous school—have sensitized us to think about better models and find additional healing from the past, which led us to the latter book. Since we both have small administrative roles at HBU, it's a good book for us for that reason, too. The way we leave authoritarianism and autocracy behind as leaders in the church—or a Christian school—is to be reminded that the biblical model of leaders is as servants.

Continuing to read the book about Ginsburg. It fills me with a certain desire at some point to reflect on the trend toward liberalism over the last few hundred years. In lots of ways I think it's been healthy—giving women the right to vote, ending segregation, addressing various injustices, etc.—but I also fear it leads to crossing certain lines that we shouldn't. Lots of interesting issues to explore.

I finished at long last Fraser's first two chapters and got those back to him. His literature review on debunking objections has been tremendously good and helpful. This is going to help with my own chapter on the subject in my upcoming book with OUP. I really need to get serious about that work very soon. As far as John's concerned, I'm confident he'll be able to defend by around the end of March.

Marybeth and I listened to scripture and spent good time in prayer and conversation today. It was a lovely day, despite my lower back pain, which is still rather acute but gradually improving.

Also decided today that I'm really going to try to exhort and encourage my colleagues. I'll be systematically writing all of them in the SCT to encourage them to write for MA and the WB.

Tuesday, January 5, 2021: I wrote TJ yesterday with an idea for his dissertation. He's convinced that the four-fold moral argument has a lot of potential to be applied in a number of different areas. So I suggested he might try something like writing an explanation, defense, and application of a four-fold moral apologetic philosophically, theologically, and exegetically, with particular emphases in preaching, pastoring, counseling, leading, and teaching. TJ just recently got over a bout with covid, and I found out today that my colleague Mary Jo Sharp, whose book I'm reading, has also contracted it. Marybeth and I will pray for her today.

Jonathan sent me a potential book cover for the first volume of this Journal. Looks sharp! A few tweaks, but it's going to be very nice. Just a self-published piece, not for wide consumption, but it will keep a solid chronicle of the history of the Center.

I wrote my old dean at Liberty today, who recently suffered and recovered from the coronavirus. He'd written a nice letter to the local paper thanking the hospital workers for their help. I told him I was relieved he'd recovered, and I talked a bit about why we came to Houston Baptist and about the Center. He had stepped down by the time I got really exasperated with SOD leadership there, so he wasn't the target of any my earlier ire. I respected his leadership. I'm still in the process of coming to terms with some of what was lost and sacrificed by leaving there; I don't miss the bad stuff, but there are certainly aspects and people of the place I miss horribly. And Lynchburg was a lovely place to live. But life moves on; sometimes we need to try to forget what's behind and just strive forward, let go of the comfortable and launch into the risks and uncertainties of the future.

Marybeth and I also dropped 20,000 dollars on the principal of the house today, getting us to within about $5700 of owning the Texas house outright. Very exciting. We had taken the money from our retirement. The prospect of paying the house off promises an extra thousand a month freed up, which should alleviate the financial pressures we have been feeling since taking a much smaller salary here. A sacrifice well worth the freedom it furnished—freedom both *from* and *to*.

In the evening Jonathan and I finalized the cover; he also asked me to write a paragraph for the back cover, and here's what I came up with:

The Center for Moral Apologetics at Houston Baptist University got underway in 2020, a year for the ages—a most trying and tumultuous time whose vagaries and vicissitudes could hardly have been predicted in advance, and which seem almost surreal in retrospect. The inaugural director of the Center kept, almost accidentally, a journal through much of the year, intermittent at first, and later in earnest. Jacqueline Woodson once wrote, "The more specific we are, the more universal something can become. Life is in the details. If you generalize, it doesn't resonate."

These pages chronicle personal, local, and national events of this remarkable time—the context culminating in the Center at long last transforming from marinating dream to concrete reality. During the pilgrimage the author has occasion to talk about his vision for the Center, steps toward its inception, and his family's transition from Virginia to Texas in the throes of a pandemic. They capture the opening pages of a fresh, exciting chapter: the first fledging steps and humble beginnings of an ambitious new initiative fraught with pitfalls and rife with potential.

Perhaps a bit dramatic, admittedly; but after all, if *I* don't think we're building a cathedral here, rather than merely a wall, who will? Precursive faith, baby!

Wednesday, January 6, 2021: Today was a sad day in American history, with rabid Trump supporters attempting to put a stop to Congress handing the presidency to Biden. Armed resistance penetrated the Capitol Building; shots were fired; there was likely loss of life. We are in a lamentably bad place as a society. After a great deal of left-inspired violence all over the country all summer, now a dose is coming from the right. Substantive discourse seems to be breaking down. Sadly many in the church don't seem to offer much of an alternative to the rabid partisanship and zealous advocacy that are so deleterious to civility. Nothing but a significant revival will salvage this situation; what a cultural mess.

On a more theoretical level—since the practical challenges of the moment seem almost intractable—the study of law would be simply fascinating. Reading a book about Ruth Bader Ginsburg over the last few months has been enlightening and eminently thought-provoking. Numerous issues have recurred in the reading that have led me to imagine it would be worthwhile to devote more thought to them. For example, it makes sense that in a culture such as ours there would, over time, be a liberalizing tendency. In many ways this strikes me as a good thing. It becomes harder and harder, on secular grounds, to justify fundamentally different treatment of persons—men and women, black and white, etc.

It's natural that some would extend this liberalizing tendency to other categories like gay versus straight. A worldview like Christianity, which has deeply immersed itself into the consciousness of the nation, emphasizes the inherent dignity and worth, equality and value of human persons, and it's thus, at least in a general sense, profoundly congruent with the essential thrust of Christian ethics to see a trajectory toward, first, justice and, second, more and more classical liberalism according primacy to equal consideration under the law, rooting out injustices, measures to ensure equity, and the like.

It is also easy to see how such equalizing and liberalizing attitudes could, over time, be construed along the lines of moral sanction on behaviors formerly thought morally suspect. The way in which taboos against inter-racial marriages have gone away, and rightly so, is a good example; and of course many would suggest that it would be an equally good thing if homophobia went away too. In fact, many suggest that retaining moral qualms about gay sexual practices is tantamount to racist or chauvinist attitudes that demean and devalue others.

10

Traditional attitudes about the propriety and normative nature of heterosexual marriages are increasingly cast as repressive, homophobic, and the rest. They get cast as (unprincipled) moral convictions that have no place in the law but are getting illegitimately imposed and foisted on others, and unless arguments for them can be found that don't appeal to personal religious convictions, they don't seem to have much of a chance to be enforced by law; even if they do, they will eventually come to be thought of as repressive and retrograde. This is undoubtedly why someone like Robert George attempts to cast a case against the legalization of gay marriage in terms of general revelation—an appeal to an essentialist construal of marriage as intrinsically involving a man and a woman. But such essentialist appeals nowadays seem unlikely to be effective. I myself find myself wondering if it's as appropriate to appeal to essentialism when it comes to an institution like marriage as it is when it comes to understanding human beings.

Well, I'm not resolving anything here—just spit-balling a bit on a day when the cultural divide seems well-nigh irreparable. Can't help but think of the biblical passage, "If my people, who are called by my name, will humble themselves and pray, seek my face, and turn from their wicked ways, then will I hear from heaven, forgive their sin, and heal their land." The problem we're facing isn't at root a partisanship issue, but a far deeper sin issue.

Thursday, January 7, 2021: I have been extending invitations to members of the SCT of late, one at a time, to contribute to MoralApologetics.com and the *Worldview Bulletin*. I am also in the process of expressing interest in doing podcasts with them on some aspect of their work. E-mails are slow in reply, but I need to set that aside and just keep with it. Yesterday, owing to all the chaos in DC, was definitely one of those reminders not to grow weary in well-doing.

Yesterday a friend mentioned, with the horrific events in DC, that all the mess and chaos, contention and acrimony drive home the importance of ethics. True enough, but a complicating factor, it seems to me, is that this isn't an ethics versus no-ethics sort of situation, but rather more about competing ethical visions. Those doing even the worst of the worst yesterday were animated by their own abiding sense of right and wrong—however misguided. This, needless to say, complicates the task of being a moral apologist nowadays.

The political and worldview tensions of this fraught moment are not just out there, but have found their way into our own house. Trump clearly triggers Marybeth, and I get that. Lots of flawed character traits there on his part. Still, however much I may agree with the Democrats historically on numerous issues, and some issues today, the most progressive elements of the party nowadays strike me as really hideous. Critical race stuff, abortion support, the equality act, transgender agendas, and more lead me to think that they are radically off base. In a conversation with MB, though, it became clear that at the forefront of her mind remain Trump's faults, more than the issues with the left.

11

I knew we had voted differently in the election, and it was never much of an issue. But this morning my frustration with the direction of the country, and the rage it momentarily caused me, boiled over and I made it personal, saying unkind and mean-spirited things to her about how she voted. She and I, in all of our years of marriage, have had very few fights, but today we did. I let my negative emotions get the better of me and I said several regrettable and hurtful things. I was horrible, and I feel awful about it. I have told her so.

She went for a drive afterwards and we texted back and forth. I apologized, but she said we can't ignore what happened, and she's right. I found myself unsure what to do, however; I know what *not* to do, namely, what I did: lash out in anger. But what am I to do with this pent-up rage I'm feeling about the abysmal trajectory of our nation? I told MB as much, and she suggested I speak with TJ.

So I called him and told him what happened, and he shared some insights he had included in his teaching on Psalm 31 last night. There David laments, rawly and transparently, before God. He honestly shares what's bothering him, what's getting to him, what angers him, what terrifies him. And opening up about one issue lends itself to opening up to another, and the whole process gives the Holy Spirit a chance to minister to us. Lament can be a means of grace for us, taking the edge off the rage, and culminating in worship.

There is even scientific foundation for this process, concerning neuroplasticity; laments can open up new neural pathways to help defuse our anger and frustration, our disappointments and rage. TJ suggested practicing this discipline, allowing myself to hear the words that are prayed. Even if I write out my prayers, he suggested I then go back and speak them out loud; apparently the act of *hearing* them is helpful to the process. So I will do this, making it a regular practice.

He also rightly reminded me that the enemy's strategy is always to attack our most important relationship, and that relationship, for me, is my marriage to Marybeth. In that sense this machination of hell is par for the course. Undermining or sabotaging our marriage is the perfect way that forces of darkness can undermine and vitiate the ministries for which God intended us, both individually and together. It's also an effort to make us think we have less in common, fewer shared convictions, than we actually do. As TJ also pointed out, when it comes to our most basic core values, she and I are deeply simpatico, even if, by the time they bubble to the surface, they might occasionally take on differing political manifestations. Our foundation remains secure.

TJ is a wise man.

After MB got home, we had a long talk in which I apologized for what I had said. It was a good chance for us to process and get to the bottom of what was really going on there. Although it wasn't good, I'm confident God can and will bring good out of it.

Later in the day I finalized the syllabus for the May course with WLC on the moral argument and sent it to him for approval—or silence, which works as well. He'll teach the first week, and I'll teach the second. There will be two discussion boards and one big final exam with some rigorous writing requirements. Really looking forward to it.

Friday, January 8, 2021: My mind raced a lot last evening and I couldn't get to sleep until very late. So now I'm feeling a bit lethargic today. But I need to fit in more reading of Mary Jo's book, and Jerry is coming over this evening. I definitely don't want the conversation to move into politics; Marybeth and I are feeling a bit burned out on all of that at this point. Glad we have one more week off before the spring starts; hope to finish Mary Jo's book and get a few additional items checked off my to-do list by then.

I was fascinated to find out that a gal I'd met at a theistic ethics conference five years ago has been hired by my alma mater Wayne State. I think I'm going to reach out to her and she if she'd like to write a chapter on forgiveness in the Ted Lasso & Philosophy project if MB and I are able to secure a contract for it. This gal, named Jada, does very good work in philosophy generally and on forgiveness particularly. Her view is that the essence of forgiveness is openness to reconciliation. This does raise interesting questions, though—for example, what about a situation of abuse? But at least regarding divine forgiveness, she's certainly on to something, I suspect, as she rightly points to the story of the Prodigal Son as a paradigmatic example of such forgiveness. I might wonder, though, what she'd say if something suggested that this is an implication or general benefit of forgiveness rather than its essential nature.

This morning Jonathan Pruitt informed me that the proofs for the journal book have been sent off and I should be getting a copy next week. I'll look it over and make any last adjustments, then we'll print up several copies. Again, I think it will prove helpful in time to come if, say, anyone ever wanted to write a history of the Center. I hope to keep a journal every day of the Center's history for at least as long as I'm in charge of it. Of course the journal includes some stuff not directly relevant to the Center; but speaking for myself, my vocation and my life often seem inextricably intertwined, so I don't feel particularly, well, apologetic about it.

I put a Facebook status out there about the upcoming course on the moral argument with William Lane Craig, telling anyone interested in signing up for it, either for credit or audit, to jot me a personal note and I'd be happy to send the syllabus along. Really hoping for a healthy dose of auditors. This could be a significant push to get people interested in the upcoming Certificate program.

Saturday, January 9, 2021: Last night was lots of fun. Jerry came over and we watched his son Johnny's film *All About the Afterglow*. Heady, thoughtful film; among other things I liked how the interplay of the characters demonstrated the variety of impulses we as humans have—from the rational to the aesthetic, from the relational to the affective, from the poetic to the imaginative, from the scientific to the magical. Jerry called Johnny and we were able to encourage and affirm him, which he seemed to appreciate.

Appreciation is the topic that William James lamented not having discussed in his magnum opus *Principles of Psychology*. I need to be more consistently intentional to express appreciation for others.

This morning more folks asked for the syllabus for the May course, which I sent along; then MB and I went to Toasted Yolk, where we had a wonderful breakfast. We know it's the last time we're going there in a while; financial limits preclude going again in January. So it was most enjoyable! I found it interesting how she said one of the aspects of this journal I'm keeping that she likes is the way it doesn't separate out the personal from the activities pertaining to the Center. She thinks a virtue of that approach is that it reminds us that the Center, and the task of moral apologetics, are inextricably related to life itself in all of its various aspects and concrete realities. It's no mere dry academic exercise.

After getting home I had a delightful conversation with Elton Higgs. We talked about numerous things, including Lewis's background in both philosophy and literary criticism. Regarding literary criticism, I shared my view that it involves using different lenses by which to accentuate various aspects of a text, some more revelatory than others. Then, at best, having gleaned an assortment of disparate insights, they can be gathered back together for an overall greater perspective and appreciation of the text—not unlike the way in math we first differentiate, then integrate. And again, it seems that some lenses are better than others at furnishing insight, and the insistence on one all-consuming lens can detract seeing what's really there and perhaps make us think things are there that actually are not.

I asked Elton what he thought of my take, and he had some good ideas to share, starting with the observation that my approach rather presupposed what Elton considers to be the highest function of literature, namely, getting at the core of a work of art. For example, if any interpretation of *Hamlet* were to miss that it's primarily a powerful presentation of a soul in anguish because of tensions between what he feels compelled to do and what his own sensibilities make him apt to do, it's not good literary criticism. Elton is a firm believer in the existence of limits on how literary criticism can deal with a text—contra a relativistic or postmodern approach that might wish to suggest a text is infinitely malleable. That said, though, he freely admits a text will look differently to different cultures, persons, etc.

At this juncture of the conversation we took a brief foray into considering the potentially related issue of where appeals to essentialism stand in our cultural moment. I mentioned Robert George's appeal to an essentialist consideration of what marriage is. Elton, too, is skeptical that such appeals to something like general revelation, natural law, or civic religion are likely to hold as much sway in our society as they once did. One like Ginsburg, in *Obergefell*, made it clear that she simply thought the meaning of marriage had changed—that this is both obviously possible and perfectly permissible—which led me to broach a question to Elton about the seemingly Christian, or at least Judeo-Christian roots of liberal thought. What seemed historically to drive so much of the liberalizing trends—women's suffrage, opposition to slavery, equal considerations under the law—were Christian convictions about the value and equality, dignity and worth of human persons. But somewhere along the way such humanizing and liberalizing elements started crossing certain lines that seem to be mistaken.

Elton suggested that without transcendent foundations and strictures, this is the likely outcome—when legitimate humanistic concerns start morphing into something potentially grotesque. If such considerations are thought to spring merely from humans alone, the case could be made, and is made, by the ultra-liberals that the agenda getting pursued is just the natural, logical progression of Enlightenment thought. This is where the church has a role to play in being the church, reminding the societies in which they function of the transcendent foundations of ethics, but without falling prey to the mistake of expecting a political utopia. The perfidy of men makes a measure of corruption inevitable. The church needs to accord primacy to the kingdom of God without allowing their notion of a heavenly kingdom to be corrupted by expecting it to be made manifest in a heaven on earth.

Generally, then, Elton's response to my reflections on literary criticism was to point out two important functions of good literary criticism: (1) Read a text closely and carefully, using one's training to be sensitive to its nuances, in an effort to get at the core meaning of the text; and (2) do additional thinking to ask how such a core meaning can contribute to and fit into our overall understanding of the world. Ask, in other words, for what insights the literature affords us through an exercise of our imagination into matters on which we needed insight. This can be paradoxical, of course, since on the one hand we're using our insights and skills to read and interpret a text, and on the other allowing the text to teach us something new.

This led to my asking where philosophy fits, to his thinking, on a continuum with scientific reasoning at one point and literary criticism at another. He suggested philosophy resides at an interesting nexus of the imaginative and logical. In that connection I mentioned some of my frustrations with the way philosophical apologetics gets taught at HBU, and my draw to the imaginative approach—the other tier in the program. The distinction between the two approaches—philosophical and imaginative—as much as I understand and can appreciate what it's after, also strikes me as sad and regrettable in certain ways. For surely the imaginative types need more practice in discursive reasoning, and the stricter philosophers shouldn't be discouraged from exercising their imaginations to augment their rigor. Moral apologetics, not to mention the Bible itself, seem invariably, to me anyway, to be examples of a nice balance between the conceptually distinct but organically connected approaches.

After the conversation with Elton, Marybeth mentioned a Twitter discussion of which she was a part in which some in our "tribe" are outraged over the removal of Trump from Twitter—claiming we're quickly approaching a dystopian nightmare rife with censorship and such. Though I'm not unmindful of the need to be vigilant to protect essential freedoms—I hope I'm not, anyway—I also can't help but suspect that those most exercised over this are often, at root, less animated by evidence for dystopia than evidence that our efforts at securing a political or legal utopia are falling short—which, again, is invariably so. And why on earth would we as Christians imagine otherwise? As MB put it today, when did rage and despair gain such a foothold in conservative Christian circles? Cannot help but wonder if the mistake is related to forgetting that it is not with flesh and blood we wrestle.

Sunday, January 10, 2021: A damp, dank morning here in Stafford. Still a week to go before the spring terms starts. Marybeth and I are having a relaxing time of it, about to have some tea and listen to the daily audio Bible. I've enjoyed green tea of late with a generous dousing of cinnamon and topped off with some heavy cream. It doesn't get too cold in Texas, but after the long, outrageously hot summer, even when it is 50 degrees here it feels bone-chilling, and a hot cup of tea is the perfect antidote. This is one of those mornings. Plan to spend a fair bit of time today continuing to read Mary Jo's book and Ward's *Planet Narnia*. Enjoying them both immensely.

How can the church function as a reminder of the need for transcendent moral foundations? One way that Americans at any rate can do so is to remember that we are country that was born out of a set of ideals—universal truths—never before invoked among the nations of the world. "We hold these truths to be self-evident, that all men are created equal, that they are endowed by their Creator with certain unalienable Rights, that among these are Life, Liberty and the pursuit of Happiness. — That to secure these rights, Governments are instituted among Men, deriving their just powers from the consent of the governed."

This excerpt of course comes from the Declaration of Independence. We are *all* equal in the eyes of God, our Creator. Our self-evident rights flow freely from the intrinsic value imbued in us by God. Governments do not grant us rights. Rather, governments are created to protect these natural rights. Governments do not, nor ever will, have the authority to grant them. To suggest otherwise is to place power where it does not belong—and such power is invariably abused. How easy and tempting to fall into the trap of thinking our rights come from government, but that's just not a big enough story.

Similarly, as Michael Ward's *Planet Narnia* reminded me this morning, Lewis didn't think reason could be made sense of simply within the confines of our heads. On a naturalistic order of things, there are no good reasons to think that our reason would possess the capacity to put us in touch with reality. This is why Lewis was drawn to aspects of Idealism (like A. E. Taylor and others)—in its assignment of primacy to Mind. Our reason puts us in touch with a divine Logos, a cosmos infused with rationality. This, perhaps *only* this, is what enables a practicable epistemology, including a moral epistemology. Interesting the way Lewis gives his argument from reason in ch. 3 of *Miracles* and an analogous variant of the moral argument in ch. 5.

In the evening we watched a live, streamlined conversation with the cast members of *Ted Lasso*. As I write this it's coming up in about fifteen minutes. If MB and I get a chance to edit a book on Lasso and Philosophy, this should prove helpful. Looking forward to it. If, though, we get that contract and Hare and I get the anthology contract, I'll be under four book contracts. Yikes. Great opportunities, but plenty daunting.

Monday, January 11, 2021: Unsure why I'm feeling down today, but can't seem to shake the feeling. This morning Marybeth and I listened to scripture and prayed, read from *A Tale of Three Kings* and a book on servant leadership, and after that I've been reading more of Sharp's and Ward's books. But I can't shake my melancholy feelings. MB admitted this morning in prayer that she has yet to feel like she's a good fit at HBU, which was a bit of a bummer to hear. She and I both are still getting acclimated to the new environment. Maybe that's related, not sure. Adam Harger got back to me with some interest in doing a podcast with me; so the first three I should do are Mary Jo, Lou, and Adam. Maybe just knowing Christmas vacation is winding down is a bit depressing; it's nice to carve out my schedule as I like.

Tuesday, January 12, 2021: Today 4400 people died of the coronavirus, a new record, breaking the record from a day or two before. This tragedy just keeps growing worse.

I finally got to work trying to figure out how to do podcasts. Three colleagues have agreed to let me interview them, so I need to get on it. Jonathan offered me this advice:

Well, if I was going to do "remote" podcasts, I would use this free program called "OBS".

https://obsproject.com/

This has the ability to record your audio and the incoming audio. It can also record the screen if you wanted to do video podcast.

I would also get a mic.

For in person interviews, I would get something like this:

https://www.amazon.com/Alesis-MultiMix-Four-Channel-Integrated-Effects/dp/B00IPF9DX2/ref=sr_1_2?dchild=1&keywords=usb+mixer&qid=1610490121&sr=8-2

I would get a couple of these:
https://www.amazon.com/Audio-Technica-AT2020PK-Microphone-Streaming-Podcasting/dp/B07JM5FLVF/ref=sr_1_7?dchild=1&keywords=AT2035PK&qid=1610490225&sr=8-7

These look like the best "mid range" microphones for this purpose.

For remote podcasts, you just need 1 mic, and you can get a cheaper, USB powered one. But these nicer ones will work for both.

So, about 500 bucks for some good in-person equipment. This would be much better than the setup we used for our podcasts, which used no mixer and a single, 50 dollar mic.

If you are doing the remote podcast, then you are limited by audio signal you get from the other person. This shouldn't really be a problem. Most computers have decent built in microphones. You also don't need a mixer for remote podcasts.

It's basically two different procedures for in person versus remote.

For remote podcasting, here is what you would do.

1. Download and install OBS
2. Download and install zoom (or other video conferencing software)
3. Plug in microphone
   a. If you get the midrange ones I suggested, you will need xlr to usb cable like this one: https://www.amazon.com/Microphone-HOSONGIN-Converter-Connector-Microphones/dp/B07ZBZ62X9/ref=sr_1_5?crid=2CZYP0H50C D56&dchild=1&keywords=xlr+to+usb&qid=1610490305&spref ix=xlr+to+us%2Caps%2C229&sr=8-5
4. Start OBS and set up (I can show you how via zoom or send you a tutorial video; it's not hard, but hard to explain)
5. Call the person you are interviewing
6. Press record on OBS
7. Once done, press stop recording

At the end of that, you've got a file you can then turn into a podcast.

For in person, here is what you would do.

1. Download and install the free program "audacity" https://www.audacityteam.org/
2. Plug in USB mixer
3. Plug mics into USB mixer
4. Set up audacity to record those channels (I can show you how, not hard)
5. Press record when ready
6. Stop recording when done

In person will give you better audio quality with more chance to fix things that go wrong in the recording.

But once you have the audio file, then you have to edit it. This was sorta hard for our podcasts because we would have several sections that we wanted to cut, but if you don't have to cut anything, it can be pretty simple.

You would do this edit through audacity. I can do this part If you'd like. This isn't really that hard, but it's the most fiddly and complicated.

The other option is that you can just release the audio with no bumper, no edits, no sound leveling and so on.

Anyway, I know you're not a tech person and this might seem overwhelming. I promise it is not as hard as it seems and I am 100% you can do it. Most of it is fairly intuitive.

Blessings, Jonathan Pruitt '08

I also made an exception from my usual practice of not arguing politics in order to respond to a friend who was enthusiastically advocating my colleague Robert Gagnon's take on Trump and the recent riots in DC. Listening to John Searle lecture on philosophy of language today helped inspire it; I wrote this:

Robert's a smart guy and a friend here at HBU, but I have my doubts about the starkness with which he puts it here. JL Austin distinguished between illocutionary speech acts and perlocutionary speech acts. What Trump literally said was his illocutionary act, but the effects of one's words—which admittedly are a bit out of our control—is one's perlocutionary act. Incitement to violence is one potential perlocutionary act. In a situation this volatile, this potentially explosive, with feelings running so high, couldn't a case be made that Trump's words were imprudent and potentially dangerous? It's not a matter of his words entailing or explicitly endorsing the violence that ensued, but the standard of proof, so to speak, for incitement is not as high as that. For pretty much the first time in American history, we saw a serious risk of losing a peaceful transfer of power. And of course in retrospect we can plainly see that five lives were lost. We know from inside sources that Trump rather relished seeing what was unfolding, at least before it crossed a certain line. But the fact that the whole country was worried that just such a tragedy was a potential contingency shows, at the very best, that Trump's imprudence bespoke a lamentable absence of judiciousness and discernment. Or so it seems to me. So though I'm not generally a fan of the left-wing media, the depiction of Trump's words as culpable of a measure of incitement seems plausible to me—and even if, in principle, it's mistaken, I doubt it's anything like 100% wrong. I think he should have definitely known better, and I suspect conservatives would be best served by just admitting as much. Not all the mistakes here are on the left.

Wednesday, January 13, 2021: Early in the morning I at long last finished De Hart's book on Ginsburg. It was wholly uncritical and overly fawning, but a worthwhile read, at times greatly enjoyable. It reminded me that on some issues I am conservatives, and on others much more liberal. Seems unlikely at any rate that either major political party platform would be sacrosanct. And in fact recent events and partisan tensions have convinced me all the more that a rigid de facto two-party system is likely to offer rather poor options.

Meanwhile the US House of Representatives today is in the throes of figuring out whether or not to impeach Trump for a second time. I'm leaning toward thinking it's a good thing—the more bipartisan the better. Rabid partisanship is seemingly ubiquitous nowadays, but some things transcend politics, and this is one of them. Trump's behavior was beyond the pale and should be officially recognized as such. I say this as someone with no shortage of conservative convictions; at present that just isn't the point. But I wonder if the nation is capable of expunging the partisanship from this decision and its aftermath; have my doubts.

I got around today to responding to a friend who will be teaching a course on the moral argument at a seminary. I won't include my full letter here, but I did include a recent repost from MoralApologetics.com on book suggestions on the moral argument (to a guy named Lucas):

Hi, Lucas! Love that you want to spend time sinking into the moral argument. I think that too often nowadays arguments like this are treated as just a tool in the arsenal, rather than the rich resource they are for reflection, enjoyment, beauty, insight, spiritual formation, etc. The moral argument has it all going on.

There are five major components to the moral argument as I think about it. One is the history of the argument; another is a critique of secular ethics; another is a defense of theistic ethics; another is a defense of the moral realism on which it is all based; and another is an extension of the argument beyond theism to Christianity.

Regarding its history, Jerry Walls and I wrote _The Moral Argument: A History_, which directs you to folks like Kant, Newman, Taylor, Sorley, Rashdall, and others. Some of that's really rich reading—especially Newman's _Grammar of Assent_ and Taylor's _Faith of a Moralist_. Classics. Anyway, lots of recommendations in that book.

In terms of a critique of secular ethics, we wrote *God and Cosmos*, but just a start and promissory note. Linville's piece on the moral argument, easily accessible online, is well worth reading. The debate between Craig and Wielenberg is coming out this year; that's quite good. Edited by Adam Johnson. In terms of defending theistic ethics, that was the main goal of our *Good God*. But there are lots of possibilities here, including Zagzebski's *Divine Motivation Theory*, Evans' *God and Moral Obligations*, Hare's *Moral Gap*, Adams' *Finite and Infinite Goods*, Ritchie's *From Morality to Metaphysics*. Most of these cover more than just one aspect of the moral argument—both defending theistic ethics and critiquing alternatives, for example. Wielenberg's *Robust Ethics* offers criticisms of theistic ethics and an effort at a more secular account of ethics. Wielenberg and I have a written debate on Lewis's moral argument in a book edited by Greg Bassham.

In terms of defending moral realism, see Cuneo's *The Normative Web*, Shafer-Landau's *Moral Realism*, and Enoch's *Taking Morality Seriously*; all are important. Jerry and I aim to write our fourth book on the moral argument on this topic, finishing our planned tetralogy.

For extending the moral argument to Christianity, that is cutting-edge stuff. We need to see more books on this—especially using, say, Trinitarian resources. Adam Johnson wrote his dissertation on this recently at Southeastern, and Brian Trapp did about a decade ago at Southern. There may be more resources along such lines but I'm not as familiar with this literature. I have some doctoral students working on such topics in their dissertations. My guess is great work is coming here as the community of moral apologists builds and the momentum of the movement grows.

Incidentally, several of the folks mentioned—Hare, Adams, Evans, etc.— have done more than one book that's important for the moral argument.

Important folks who are more secular to consider can be found when you look at rival ethical accounts. I mentioned Wielenberg, Enoch, and Shafer-Landau (though he aims for more neutrality on the God question than most), but as you get into error theory, expressivism, constructivism, sensibility, theory, and nontheistic moral realism (either natural or non-natural), you run into a host of thinkers: McDowell, Blackburn, Wiggins, Mackie, R. M. Hare (John's father), Joyce, Korsgaard, Brink, Harman, Boyd, Foot, Parfit, etc.

There's a four views book on God and morality edited by Loftin, and a nice anthology on God and ethics edited by Garcia and King called *Is Goodness without God Good Enough?* that's eminently worth reading.

Of course avail yourself of this website, MoralApologetics.com, for a host of resources related to the moral argument from a wide array of disciplines. (The site will soon come under the auspices of the Center for Moral Apologetics we get to start at Houston Baptist this fall, as we are joining all the exciting things already happening there.) Recently the site's begun a new series about recent developments in the moral argument—which reminds me, I have hardly mentioned contemporaries working on the moral argument; we've seen a real resurgence of work and interest on the topic over the last several decades.

Mark Murphy is an important thinker who has written some serious books on ethics from a theistic perspective although he is more reticent than many to make it into an apologetic matter. Still, though, quite worth reading, rife with trenchant insight and philosophical rigor. Kevin Kinghorn is a friend and good philosopher who studied with Swinburne and has written some important and germane books: *A Framework of the Good,* & (with Travis) *But What About God's Wrath?* Much recommended.

In taking on alternative moral theories, of which there are a plethora, one might also be interested in taking on not just nonreligious alternatives, but non-Christian religious perspectives. Brian Scalise has done nice work using the Trinity to contrast an Islamic conception of love with that of Christianity's; Ronnie Campbell has contrasted a Christian perspective on the problem of evil with those of several worldviews (pantheism, panentheism, etc.); TJ Gentry is finishing up a dissertation at North-Western using resources from moral apologetics to critique Mormonism; etc.

Paul Copan has penned a widely anthologized piece on the moral argument, and my wife and I have done a more popular level book that incorporated elements of *Good God*, *God and Cosmos*, and the history of the moral argument called *Morals of the Story*.

Sorry I can't give you a more exhaustive list for now, but this is at least suggestive. You can find more resources in the notes and bibliographies of these books. I encourage you in your study! I am excited you have the interest; please keep in touch and let me know how it goes.

Thursday, January 14, 2021: What an exciting day this has been! This morning we had some HBU meetings, which we attended remotely. HBU has decided to make the first two weeks of the term online, which is probably smart.

Afterwards MB and I spent some time thinking about the impeachment of Trump. We think it was a good thing—feeling that Trump clearly crossed lines he shouldn't have. I sympathize with those who stress the way plenty of Democrats went after Trump from day one, but I don't think that means impeaching him now isn't the right thing to do. I think it clearly is, but plenty of our friends disagree. Their prerogative, I suppose; I respect their mental freedom, and would ask them to do the same.

Then something truly exciting happened! Adam Johnson, who earned his doctorate at Southeastern, wrote a good dissertation there on Wielenberg's ethics and Trinitarian theology. (He is also the guy who edited the book featuring the debate between Wielenberg and Craig.) I was on his committee, along with Greg Welty and Ross Inman, very good philosophers. The dissertation passed muster with all of us, and Adam has been trying to get it published. I did what I could to encourage and support his efforts. He wrote me this e-mail today:

Dr. Baggett,

I'm pressing forward looking for a publisher for my dissertation (Trinitarian Metaethical Theory) that you helped supervise last year at Southeastern Baptist Theological Seminary. I've sent my book proposal to about 40 publishers now, have gotten 11 official declines, and one offered contract (but I'd have to buy 250 copies up front at a reduced price so I'm holding back on this one for now). A few publishers have indicated they're interested and are continuing to evaluate it – B&H, P&R, Crossway, Kregel, and AMG Publishers.

I wanted to ask you about the "Moral Apologetics Press, LLC" that I read about on your website. Here's the blurb I'm referring to:

"The Center recently started its own publishing arm, creating "Moral Apologetics Press, LLC." A precursor to these efforts was Elton Higgs' *The Ichabod Letters*, an electronic copy of which is available to subscribers by signing up here. The first book officially published by the press, Brian Melton's *The Wrackturn Letters*, will be available before the end of the year. Inspired by C. S. Lewis's *The Screwtape Letters*, this book records the devious schemes of a pair of demons assigned to sabotage Christian higher education. The next book will be theological and philosophical exploration of the thinking of Thomas Aquinas. *A Moral Way* by T. J. Gentry will be available in early 2021. Finally, there are plans for a collaboration with *The Worldview Bulletin* for a third book, yet to be titled, but likely to release in the Spring of 2021."

Do you think the Moral Apologetics Press would be interested in publishing my book?

Your servant,
Adam Lloyd Johnson

I have to confess that this was and is an exciting prospect for me. Heretofore I hadn't thought much about our publishing a book that, to my thinking, had this high of a chance to be published elsewhere. I'd love if we did this, and I think it would have the possibility of selling some serious copies while advancing the mission of the Press and Center and of putting us on the map as a serious publisher of substantive books, at least some of which hold serious prospects of generating some revenue for the author, for Jonathan as remuneration for the work he'll put into it, and perhaps even a bit extra for the Center itself.

I realize at this point none of this is guaranteed. We are trading more in possibilities than probabilities, but I'm thrilled Adam approached us first, and I can't help but get excited at the possibilities. We are not to despise small beginnings, nor let those humble beginnings hem in God's freedom to bless and exceed our expectations. God's honored more by our dreaming big than cultivating pessimism. God has blessed the moral apologetics venture in all sorts of ways already, and I think we can trust him to bless this. I don't presume to know exactly what forms the blessing will take, but I definitely think we can trust him—spoke with Jonathan on the phone about all this, and he agrees on that point.

So, very excited today. Who knows—maybe one day, if God provides a generous increase, this entry will be the point at which it all began, the day an e-mail from Adam changed our paradigm a bit, opening us to new possibilities not imagined before. I think Aslan's on the move. Praying for your will to be done here, dear God. By coincidence, today the proof copy of the Journal book should be arriving in the mail. Marvelous day! A day of brilliant light during an otherwise dark time, a day of hope in a context filled with such despair.

Just as I typed that, Marybeth told me Joanne Rogers—the wife of Mister Rogers—died. Which makes me sad, though thinking she has been reunited with him is a sweet thought. In my mind's eye is the little family mausoleum there in Latrobe, PA where MB and I visited the summer before last—where her body will go, near that of Fred's. I had tried to arrange a meeting with her when we did research at the Rogers Center at St. Vincent's, but to no avail. Alas. I'll look forward to meeting her when all things have been made new.

I ended last year's journal by making reference to the way we live in the best and worst of times, a Dickensian convention. Still true here in 2021. Perhaps appropriate a few weeks ago there was in the sky the conjunction of Saturn and Jupiter. Reading Ward's book about Lewis's invoking of medieval imagery, I learned that Saturn represents death, and Jupiter life and joy. A rather apt juxtaposition at the culmination of 2020—and the start of 2021.

Friday, January 15, 2020: Friday was a fruitful enough day. I enjoyed some leisure time playing some online chess; what a remarkably interesting and complex game. So many contingencies and strategies and nooks and crannies. I've enjoyed every movie I have ever watched on chess. If I could, I might like to read some more. Jerry came over Friday evening, and we watched the first half of the first season of Ted Lasso. He enjoyed it, as I figured he would. At the end of the evening I tried to show him how to do something in his course online, but ran into unexpected and exasperating hitches. I also heard my sister Sandra was enduring a painful kidney stone, and without medicine until morning. Between the frustration of helping Jerry and worry over Sandra, I had a very hard time sleeping Friday night. One other feature of note about Friday was that I got a hard copy of *Humble Beginnings in a Whirlwind* in the mail. Looks good.

Saturday, January 16, 2020: After bad sleep Friday night, I slept very late on Saturday. Before even getting to sleep, I went with MB to Toasted Yolk for a yummy breakfast. Took it easy the rest of the day, playing some chess, listening to some scripture, and praying and fellowshipping with Marybeth. Got a sweet note back from the author of the Ginsburg book, expressing her appreciation that I'd written her a note of thanks for her good book. Also received an e-mail from an old PhD student who's writing on the moral argument at Liberty, Dale Kratt. I need to write him back tomorrow. Speaking of students in that program, another one, named Chad Fultz, we received word today, died from covid. I didn't know him, but he seemed like a great guy. What a heart-wrenching loss. MB and I spent some time praying for his family and friends, who must be reeling from so tragic a loss.

Sunday, January 17, 2020: Last day of Christmas vacation. Tomorrow morning begins the first 8 week class for HBU, an online course on apologetic methodology. I will also be serving on the defense of Conway's thesis around 8 am my time, 2 pm for those in Birmingham, England. Today MB and I read some more from Peter Enns' book *The Sin of Certainty*. It seems deeply confused to me—conflating, for example, conviction with dogmatism or certainty. There's some truth in the book, but it's mixed in with lots of error. NT Wright's book on Christian ethics is a book we are enjoying quite a bit more.

Monday, January 18, 2020: Got up early to write an orienting introductory e-mail to the HBU class. Only four students are enrolled. Have to keep praying that God blesses the program and draws in more students. At 8 am my time was Bobby Conway's defense. He did a fine job, and the Birmingham guys were a delight. Bobby's biggest challenge in his version of the moral argument based on our experience of moral guilt was putting all his eggs in that one basket to argue for moral realism when likely we need a broader case of which guilt is just a piece. But with just minor revisions, he passed. Great guy!

Later in the day I felt inspired to write my WB piece on "The Work of Prayer," and it went like this:

The Work of Prayer

It is a fascinating and frequent observation to note that work was not a result of the fall; work was around first, and will likely be around after all things have become new. Perhaps something like *unproductive* work—the "sweat of the brow" stuff—was a result of the fall, but not work per se. In fact, work understood as a sacred calling of sorts has been a prominent part of certain Christian theologies. And we have all likely had those moments when doing what we feel called and especially equipped to do is among the most satisfying of human experiences.

As I write this today, it happens to be Martin Luther King Day, and King occasionally talked about how all sorts of work can be meaningful and worthwhile—if we do them excellently and for God's glory. You may remember this famous passage of his: "If a man is called to be a street sweeper, he should sweep streets even as a Michelangelo painted, or Beethoven composed music, or Shakespeare wrote poetry. He should sweep streets so well that all the hosts of heaven and earth will pause to say, 'Here lived a great street sweeper who did his job well.'"

As gratifying as work can be, doing what we are supposed to do will often involve real work. Sometimes it is a genuine chore and slow-going, unglamorous and tedious. On occasion it is altogether challenging.

Just a few days ago we lost Joanne Rogers, the wife of Mister Rogers, another loss among so many recently. Well, Fred Rogers used to talk about the arduous work of learning to love our neighbors as ourselves, especially those hard to love. As easy as he made it look, it's not easy at all; sometimes it proves very hard, even impossibly difficult—at least without a miracle of sorts. Yet it is work to which we are called, by God's enablement, since loving our neighbors is the second most important command of all, and organically tied to the first—love of God with all of our heart and soul, mind and strength.

Perhaps part of our having been made in God's image is our identity as purposive and teleological creatures. We constantly wonder about our purpose, our mission, our meaning, our telos—the work to which we are called. And those missions and vocations among us can vary widely; each of us has a particular and irreplaceable place to inhabit in the body of Christ.

Yet despite our distinctive individual vocations, we also share certain common missions in our humanity and in our identity and high calling in Christ—to love our neighbor, for example. And another is to be a praying people. In times past I have thought of prayer as involving petitioning and praise, attentiveness and intercession, but I haven't much thought about the work of

26

prayer. But lately I have begun to do so, and as a result I am beginning to become convinced of something.

When we face daunting challenges, feel oppressive burdens, or encounter profound feelings of helplessness, as this life is wont to ensure, these all provide us opportunities to engage in the work of prayer. In fact I suspect we are confronted with a rather stark choice: either take these things to God in prayer, spending time lamenting and mourning, processing and relinquishing, or end up feeling overwhelmed and defeated, depressed and ineffectual.

Think about the passage of scripture from Ephesians that says we don't wrestle against flesh and blood, but against principalities and powers, against the rulers of the darkness of the air, against spiritual wickedness in high places. Negatively the passage teaches us that we are misled if we mistake fellow persons as our true enemies—a point worth pondering especially in the throes of acrimonious cultural conflicts in a charged partisan climate. Positively, though, it tells us with whom our real fights rage. There are spiritual forces at work in this world against which we are to do battle. And that takes work—even if the deepest work is appropriating the finished work of Christ.

I do not bring this up to get us sidetracked articulating or arguing about the specifics of what spiritual warfare involves or looks like, but to emphasize that there really is work to be done in prayer, work we neglect to our detriment. This is not the only function of prayer, of course, but it's a part of it that, for too long, I neglected—even while paying it lip service.

After all the recent political turmoil in our country, I was feeling down—unsure what to do with my negative emotions that had, unbidden, welled up within me. I'm sure I wasn't alone. My wife knew I was flummoxed, struggling to process the whole situation, and she encouraged me to speak with a pastor friend, T. J. Gentry. So I called him, and he shared some insights that, as providence arranged it, he had included in his teaching on Psalm 31 the night previous. There David laments, rawly and transparently, before God. He honestly shares what's bothering him, what's getting to him, what angers him, what terrifies him. Lament, T. J. reminded me, can be a means of grace for us all, culminating in worship.

There is even scientific foundation for this, concerning neuroplasticity; laments can open up new neural pathways to help defuse our anger and frustration, our disappointments and rage, our indignation and incredulity. My friend suggested practicing this discipline, allowing myself to hear the words that are prayed. Even if I write out my prayers, as he knew is my habit, he suggested I then go back and speak them out loud. Apparently the very act of *hearing* the words is helpful to the process. So I have been doing this, making it a regular practice. Opening up about one issue lends itself to opening up to another, and the whole process gives the Holy Spirit a chance to minister to us, and through us.

I submit that this is one way in which we should be proactive to pray. Indeed, praying against systemic evils, pleading for God's intervention, admitting our confusions, viscerally sharing our deepest frustrations, claiming God's promises in the face of discouraging circumstances, honestly sharing our feelings of abject helplessness, lamenting our losses, confessing our rage and our weaknesses, acknowledging our utter dependence on God—all of these are paradigmatic biblical examples of the work of prayer, work to which each one of us is called, work that God hard-wired us to do. Although it can be extremely hard to do, I am convinced that ultimately it is a far easier yoke and lighter burden than *not* doing it. Weeping may endure for the night, but joy comes in the morning (Psalm 30:5).

We also got back to Adam Johnson today about his book proposal. Here's what Jonathan wrote him:

Hi Adam,

I hope you are well!

We had the chance to review the proposal this weekend and based on that and Dr. Baggett's knowledge of your dissertation, we would like to offer to publish your book under Moral Apologetics Press.

Please take a look at the attached agreement and let us know if you would like to move forward on this project together.

Regards,

Jonathan Pruitt
Managing Editor

Adam responded: "Thank you. Two other publishers have offered me contracts and I'm waiting to hear back from a few more. So I'll need some time to make my decision. But I'm very excited about the idea of publishing with Moral Apologetics Press because you specialize in this topic that my book is about. How could I learn more about Moral Apologetics Press? Is there a website for it? Your servant, Adam Lloyd Johnson"

To which I responded like this:

Well, we are just getting up and running, Adam, so if you decide to go with a more established press, I'll understand. But I'm excited at the possibility of putting out your book, too; I think it's quality work, and right up our alley. Of course because we're just getting started, that might be a disincentive for you. So far we've printed up the journal I kept about the start of the Center for Moral Apologetics in 2020; we're in the process of printing a collection of essays from the Worldview Bulletin and a Screwtape Letters-like book from an old colleague. We don't yet have a website up and running; it's one of many projects in the works. But I can say this: we would do everything we could to push and promote it—everything the website and Center can muster. Every press had a starting point, I figure, and this just happens to be ours. My mantra the past several months has been a personal reminder to me: not to despise humble beginnings. What I think we have, though, is enthusiasm and purity and clarity of vision. I believe in the ministry of moral apologetics passionately, and in the new Center we're starting at HBU; and I think the Press will be an important aspect of this ministry. We have hopes and designs on printing and pushing high-quality works in moral apologetics particularly. This is what makes your book such a good fit. But I realize all this sounds a bit like an elaborate promissory note. I would suggest you see what offers come in and then seriously just pray about it; I have confidence God will be a light to your path, whether that path leads you to us or not. Blessings, brother,

Dave Baggett

Tuesday, January 19, 2021: Today Marybeth decided to get a covid test over at HBU. We doubt she has it, but it might help her rest more at ease. It's been getting to her that Liberty student died from covid; seemed like such a great guy, just heartbreaking. At any rate, on the way over and back we noticed the bumpy road, and she mentioned that the reason for bad roads in Texas is different from that in Michigan. Up there it's all the salt in the winter, plus Michigan's financial struggles. Here's it's the shifting ground, which reminded me of the biblical warning to avoid building a house on shaky foundations. Which reminded me of what I want to call the podcast once it's up and running: On Ancient Foundations.

This morning Marybeth and I read from several books, then I read the chapter on Good and Evil in Mary Jo's book. It was good. She related her conversation with Clay Jones, who's done quite a bit of work on the problem of evil. He has read numerous books about genocides and other atrocities committed by human hands, and he thinks the case can be made quite effectively that human beings aren't particularly good. We're bad. We really do horrible things to each other; in fact, genocide tend to be carried out by very average, typical people. If people become convinced that some atrocity is in their interest and they can get away with it, there are few limits that constrain their behavior. Original sin make sense of such brokenness within us, and it's not just others, it's ourselves.

Wednesday, January 20, 2021: Today was a delightful day. First I went through the third chapter in Stephen Jordan's dissertation. Good stuff! Then I had two protracted phone conversations, first with Bobby Conway about needed tweaks in his thesis, then with TJ as we reflected on the state of the church and nation, and more locally, our own lives and ministries. Later I answered an e-mail from the interim chair of the apol department about steps taken to increase residential enrollment. Here's what I wrote him:

Hi Jason,

Allow me to answer your questions. They were these:

1. What tasks have I done?
2. Where could I give incorporate HBU Apologetics into my social networks?
3. What kind of material could I produce that could be used on the HBU Apologetics pages?
4. What students could I involve in promotion (e.g. getting short quotes/testimonials from)?

In terms of what tasks I have done, here's a list: (a) I'm in the process of encouraging my fall residential students to do what they can to push and promote the residential program; (b) we sent out the first newsletter for the Center for Moral Apologetics; (c) we set up a mechanism by which folks can donate to the Center, and we're planning on part of such gifts going toward scholarships for students; (d) we're including in the newsletter an "HBQ" section featuring SCT faculty (mainly) answering questions about theology, the Bible, apologetics, etc.; (e) Moral Apologetics Press published my journal from 2020 highlighting the start of the Center, and we're in the process of putting out a few more books; (f) we're pushing for students and auditors in the course on the moral argument I'm co-teaching with William Lane Craig in May; (g) my wife and I are making ourselves available to speak either in person or remotely to churches to share the vision of HBU and the Center; (h) I've been sharing a lot of content from MoralApologetics.com and the Worldview Bulletin on the HBU apologetics page on FB; (i) I'm intentional to "like" everything HBU related on FB; (j) I pushed HBU and the Center through the Worldview Bulletin; (k) I'm in the process of inviting HBU SCT faculty to contribute to MoralApologetics.com and the Worldview Bulletin; and (l) I've arranged to do three upcoming podcasts for the Center with HBU faculty, including two from the SCT and one from the apol dep't. This will be a regular feature of the Center.

In terms of question (2), I've already been incorporating HBU Apologetics into the Worldview Bulletin and MoralApologetics.com, and vice versa.

In terms of (3), I've been consistently sharing what I can on HBU Apologetics pages. (Already explained.)

In terms of (4), a few students seem especially keen on helping with promotion, namely, Bill Scott and Taylor Neil. Bill's involvement with Ratio Christi can help quite a bit.

Best, Dave

Thursday, January 21, 2021: The reading Marybeth and I did this morning was touching. The book on steward leadership provided a timely reminder that more important than building our own little kingdoms is participation in the kingdom of God. We shouldn't inordinately fret about our own fulfillment or satisfaction in a job, but rather to be wholly committed to following the path God reveals to us, entrusting our happiness into his hands. The Wright book used the various vignettes of Mark 10 to illustrate that at the foundation of questions of happiness and holiness is something even more basic: following Christ. This is what enables those two tributaries to come together—a rich biblical insight rife with relevance to what I call the rational variant of the moral argument. Now I am spending time in Morley's *Mapping Apologetics* for class.

The chapter on presuppositionalism in Morley was interesting. Seems to me that such an apologetic approach has some truth in it, but it overplays its hand at numerous points. Not altogether unlike the way Enns does so on the rather opposite end of the spectrum.

Jotted my dean a text encouraging him to consider HBU starting a PhD in Philosophy & Apologetics. Might be a nice way to carve out unique niche, providing a program at once rigorous and practical.

Marybeth and I enjoyed watching *When Harry Met Sally* this evening, and afterwards I found out that my Uncle Cecil's son Brent died from covid. Sad. The losses keep piling up. Cecil and his wife are still alive; my dad was Cecil's brother.

A fellow named Chad McIntosh sent me this work he'd done compiling notes on variants of the moral argument; good stuff!:

MORAL ARGUMENTS

Arguments which take particular or general facts about morality to support the existence of God.

From Objectivity of Morality Generally	
(1) Morality is objective only if God exists. (2) Morality is objective. (3) So, God exists.	• **Morality:** Moral propositions, duties, obligations • Re (2): common sense, experience - This includes evil

	- Re (1): If God does not exist and naturalism is true, morality is just the byproduct of evolution, so can't be objective.
	- Re (1): Moral Platonism?
	  - Oddly anthropocentric
	  - Epistemological objection
	  - Vulnerable to anti-realist critiques
	  - Vulnerable to other theistic arguments

An abductive version:
 	
(1) Morality is objective.
(2) If morality is objective, then God is the best explanation for its being objective.
(3) So, God is the best explanation for its being objective.
(4) So, (probably) God exists.
	- Re: (2). God best ground for morality because:
	  - Like explains like: morality is personal, so is God
	  - Like explains like: God is a person with an objective moral nature. Hence, objective morality reflects God's objective moral nature.
	  - There are no comparably good naturalistic explanations. If anything, we'd expect morality to *not* be objective if naturalism were true.

From Evil in Particular **The Normative Implications of Evil**[1] (1) Evil contrastively implies that there is a way the world *ought* to be. (2) There is a way the world ought to be only if there is an intention or goal or purpose behind it. (3) So, there is an intention or goal or purpose behind the world. (4) There is an intention or goal or purpose behind the world only if God	- Re: (1). Some come close to *defining* evil this way, as a deviation, distortion, or corruption of the way things are supposed to be. - Another aspect of this argument is that it implies goodness is primary, or more fundamental than, evil, which makes perfect sense on theism but not naturalism.

---

[1] Gregory Ganssle, "Evil as Evidence for Christianity," in Meister and Dew, *God and Evil* (IVP, 2013), ch. 15.

exists.
(5) So, God exists.
 	
Horrendous Evils[2]
 	
(1) Some evils are so bad that they seem to have a non-naturalistic dimension to them.
(2) If (1), we are justified in thinking they do have a non-naturalistic dimension to them.
(3) There can be evils so bad that they have a non-naturalistic dimension to them only if something like theism is true.
(4) So, something like theism is true.
	• Re: (1). Some evils are so objectively appalling and horrendous that they seem to have cosmic or spiritual significance.
	  - They seem Satanic, or to require Hell
	  - They provoke existential outrage, "Shaving one's fist at heaven".
	• Re: (2). Phenomenal conservatism.
	• Re: (3). If theism is true, reality has a *deep* moral dimension.
	  - Horrendous evils are deep defiance of a morally perfect being and the goodness of his creation.
	• Re: (3). If naturalism is true, there is no more to human evil than the human-analogue of animal savagery. But this just doesn't seem to capture all there is to evil.

From Universal Belief[3] (1) Certain moral beliefs are shared by all of humanity. (2) If certain moral beliefs are shared by all of humanity, God is the best explanation for that. (3) So, God is the best explanation for there being certain moral beliefs are shared by all of humanity. (4) So, (probably) God exists.	• Re: (1): Although there is disagreement about the application of certain moral beliefs, there is a stable core across cultures. • Re: (2): Why God would instill morality: - God, as a moral agent, creates moral agents in his likeness, being a trace or clue to His own nature.

---

[2] Alvin Plantinga, "Two Dozen (or so) Theistic Arguments," in Walls and Dougherty (eds.), *Two Dozen (or so) Arguments for God* (Oxford, 2018), pp. 476-477. See also Lewis, discussed in Baggett and Walls, *The Moral Argument* (Oxford, 2019), p. 167.

[3] Such an argument can be gathered from C. S. Lewis, *Abolition of Man.*

	- God would want creatures to come to know him via conscience. - Moral law is "written on our hearts" (Rom 2) - Moral behavior has world-enhancing value. - Moral beliefs are good for the cooperation and flourishing of humanity, which God wants. • Re: (2): There are no comparably good naturalistic reasons explaining there being certain moral beliefs are shared by all of humanity.
Arguments from the Practical Rationality of Morality **Sidgwick and Kant**[4] (1) Acting morally is always rational only if it's always what's ultimately best for me. (2) Acting morally is always what's ultimately best for me only if God exists. (3) So, acting morally is always rational only if God exists. (1, 2 HS) (4) Acting morally is always rational. (5) So, God exists. (3, 4 MP) **Oderberg's Argument from Cosmic Justice**[5] (1) We live in a rational moral order. (2) If we live in a rational moral order, there is cosmic justice. (3) So, there is cosmic justice. (1, 2 MP)	• Sidgwick thought the central problem of ethics was showing how (1) could be true. It must be rational for me to act morally. Otherwise noble deeds like self-sacrifice and altruism might be irrational! But it seems true that it's never irrational to be altruistic. • (2) is equivalent to: if God does not exist, acting morally not always what's ultimately best for me. Seems true—morality and self-interest come apart, leaving us with the question of why I should be moral in times where I'd personally be worse off for doing so. It *is* irrational to act altruistically. • **Cosmic justice**: all virtue is

[4] This argument is gathered from David Baggett and Jerry Walls' discussion of Sidgwick and Kant in *Good God: The Theistic Foundations of Morality* (Oxford, 2011), pp. 12-15.
[5] David Oderberg, "Morality, Religion, and Cosmic Justice," *Philosophical Investigations* 34/2 (2011), pp. 189-213.

34

(4) If there is cosmic justice, there must be a cosmic judge who administers it. (3, 4 MP). (5) So, there is a cosmic judge who administers it.	rewarded, all vice punished. • Rational moral order: where it always makes rational sense to behave morally. • Oderberg thinks the argument works without assuming an afterlife is necessary for administering cosmic justice.

Layman[6]
 	
(1) In every actual case, one has most reason to do what is morally required.
(2) If there is no God and no life after death, then there are cases where morality requires that one make a great sacrifice for only modest benefits.
(3) If in a given case morality requires that one make a great sacrifice for only modest benefits, then one does not have the most reason to do what is morally required.
(4) So, if there is not God and no life after death, then in some cases one does not have most reason to do what is morally required. (2, 3 HS)
(5) So, it's false that there is no God and no after life (1, 4 MT).
	• (1) just says that there is overriding reason to perform one's moral duty.
	  - E.g., slapping a fork out of the president's hand.
	• Re: (2), Layman gives "Ms. Poore case."
	  - Given that there is no God or afterlife, there are no overriding reasons not to steal the money.

From the Need for Divine Aid in Being Moral **Linda Zagzebski:**[7] (1) It is rational to try to be moral only if it's rational to believe the attempt would likely be successful. (2) But it's not rational to believe the attempt would likely be successful if all we have is our own human faculties to go on.	• Not "Why be moral?" but "Why try to be moral?" • Re: (2). Because if all we have is our own faculties, we can't be confident that - we have genuine moral knowledge, given the depth and diversity of moral disagreements.

---

[6] C. Stephen Layman, "God and the Moral Order," *Faith and Philosophy* 19/3 (2002), pp. 304-316.
[7] Linda Zagzebski, "Does Ethics need God?" *Faith and Philosophy* 4/3 (1987), pp. 294-303.

(3) But it is rational to try to be moral.	- or that we can to overcome moral weakness and bring about good in the world.
(4) So, it's rational to believe the attempt would likely be successful. (1, 3 MP)	- or that our moral efforts won't be in vain in the end.
(5) So, we have more than just our own human faculties to go on. (2, 4 MT)	

(6) If a theory postulates exactly what more we need to be rational in believing the attempt at being moral would likely be successful, then its rational to believe that theory.

(7) Christian theism postulates exactly what more we need to be rational in believing the attempt at being moral would likely be successful.

- Re: (7). On Christian theism, we have divine revelation, assurance and guidance, and grace, and providence—exactly what we need to be confident that
  - we have genuine moral knowledge
  - can to overcome moral weakness and bring about good in the world, and that our moral efforts won't be in vain in the end

(8) So, it's rational to believe Christian theism.

John Hare:[8]

(1) If one ought to *x*, one can do *x*.

(2) One ought to live up to the demands of morality.

- The moral gap is between the demand that morality places on us and our natural capacity to live by it.

(3) One can live up to the demands of morality. (1, 2)

(4) One can live up to the demands of morality only if one has the requisite "extra-human assistance."

- But morality essentially demands that we be perfect!
- The gap can be filled only with "extra-human assistance."

(5) So, one has the requisite "extra-human assistance."

(6) If a theory postulates exactly the "extra-human assistance" needed to live up to the demands of morality, it is rational to believe that theory.

(7) Christian theism postulates exactly the "extra-human assistance" needed to live up to the demands of morality.

- Re: (7). The requisite "extra-human assistance" to live up to the demands of morality are found in Christianity's doctrines of atonement, justification, and sanctification.

(8) So, it is rational to believe Christian theism.

---

[8] John Hare, *The Moral Gap* (Oxford, 1996).

Kant on Duty to Promote the Highest Good[9] (1) We ought (morally) to promote the realization of the highest good. (2) What we ought to do must be possible for us to do. (3) It is not possible for us to promote the realization of the highest good unless there exists a God who makes that realization possible. (4) So, there exists such a God.	• **Highest good**: "Perfect proportionment of happiness to virtue." I.e., You are happy (in the eudaimonistic sense) to the extent that you are virtuous. • Re: (2) only God can ensure "perfect proportionment of happiness to virtue."

Obligations and Duties in general[10]
 	
 (1) We have objective moral obligations.
 (2) If we have objective moral obligations, they are best understood as divine commands.
 (3) So, objective moral obligations are best understood as divine commands.
 (4) If objective moral obligations are best understood as divine commands, God exists.
 (5) So, God exists.
	• Re: (2). Objective obligations are:
	   - Like *authoritative imperatives*, not descriptives
	   - They are *impositions*, we ought to obey even when we don't want to. They have "umph"; they are *intrinsically motivating*.
	   - They seem deeply *social*, such that disobedience incurs objective guilt and offense to a person.
	 • The alternative is Platonsim, but Platonica
	   - Don't have the above features, and
	   - Would be exceedingly odd on naturalism
	 • The best explanation of this is that they are the imperatives of a personal, good God, who has the power authority to impose them on

---

[9] In *Critique of Practical Reason*. Defended in Robert Adams, "Moral Arguments for Theistic Belief," in Adams, *The Virtue of Faith and Other Essays in Philosophical Theology* (Oxford, 1987), ch. 10.

[10] George Mavrodes, "Religion and the Queerness of Morality." Robert Adams, *Finite and Infinite Goods* (Oxford, 1999). C. Stephen Evans, *God and Moral Obligation* (Oxford, 2013).

	all of humanity.
Newman's Argument from Conscience[11] (1) Guilt, shame, responsibility, etc. are only appropriately felt in relation to other moral agents. (2) But sometimes we appropriately feel guilt, shame, responsibility, etc. for deeds done in secret (that harm no others). (3) So guilt, shame, responsibility, etc. for deeds done in secret are appropriately felt only if there's another moral agent that's privy to deeds done in secret. (From 1) (4) So, there's another moral agent that's privy to deeds done in secret. (2, 3 MP) (5) The best explanation of there being another moral agent that's privy to deeds done in secret is that a God-like being exists. (6) So (probably) a God-like being exists.	

Dore on the Intrinsic Harmfulness of Wrongdoing
 	
(1) Wrongdoing is intrinsically harmful to the wrongdoer.
(2) Wrongdoing is intrinsically harmful to the wrongdoer only if that harm is punishment from a God-like being.
(3) So, there is a God-like being.
	• **Harm**: not pain or suffering, or guilty conscience, or having bad character.
	  - But objective well-being.
	  - Metaphorically, wrongdoing is soul-withering
	• Re: (1). Morality is "overriding" in that one's well-being is affected by one's moral deeds. E.g., Plato, Gyges ring.
	• Re: (2). Wrongdoers never intend to harm themselves when they commit wrongs, and can escape punishment

[11] John Henry Newman, *A Grammar of Assent* (1870), ch. 5. My own reconstruction based on discussion of Newman in Mackie, *The Miracle of Theism* (Oxford, 1982), pp. 103-106 and Oppy, *Arguing About Gods* (Cambridge, 2006), pp. 369ff.

	from men. • Only a God-like being has the knowledge and power to inflict *intrinsic* harm on wrongdoers whenever they commit wrongs.

Moral Knowledge[12]
 	
 (1) We have moral knowledge.
 (2) If naturalism is true, then we (very probably) don't have moral knowledge.
 (3) If theism is true, then we (very probably) do have moral knowledge.
 (4) So, if we have moral knowledge, that is strong evidence for theism and against naturalism.
 (5) So, moral knowledge is strong evidence for theism and against naturalism.
 	
 Ritchie[13]
 	
 (1) We have capacity to apprehend objective moral norms.
 (2) If (1), the best explanation for that is that our cognitive faculties are intended to apprehend objective moral norms.
 (3) So, (probably) our cognitive faculties are intended to apprehend objective moral norms.
 (4) If (3), theism is the best explanation for that.
 (5) So, theism is the best explanation for our having the capacity to apprehend
	• Re: (2). If naturalism is true, the faculties we use to form moral beliefs aren't aimed at truth, but fitness.
	   - If naturalism is true, it's possible that we have true moral beliefs, but we shouldn't trust them.
	   - Stopped clock analogy.
	 • Re: (3). If theism is true, God, as a moral being keen on us being moral too, likely wired our moral belief-forming faculties to aim at truth.
	   - So, if theism is true, we should trust our moral faculties tell us the truth just as we should trust a properly functioning clock tells the time.
	
	 • The argument differs from previous ones in two ways:
	   - Concerned more with *explaining* moral cognition rather than justifying it.
	   - Even if there can be a naturalistic account of objective moral truths, there is still the difficulty of explaining how, on naturalism, we can apprehend such truths.

---

[12] Mark Linville, "The Moral Argument," in Craig and Moreland (eds.), *The Blackwell Companion to Natural Theology* (Blackwell, 2012), ch. 7. Philip Swensen and Dustin Crummett, "God and Moral Knowledge," in Rasmussen and Vallier (eds.), *The New Theist Response to the New Atheists* (Routledge, 2020), ch. 3.

[13] Angus Ritchie, *From Morality to Metaphysics* (Oxford, 2012).

objective moral norms.	• Naturalism leaves us with an explanatory gap between moral ontology and moral epistemology. • The best way to fill the gap is if our cognitive faculties are *intended* to apprehend moral truths. • Theism closes the gap, since on theism our cognitive are intended by God to apprehend moral truths.

Altruism
 	
Schloss[14]
 	
(1) If evolutionary naturalism is true, genuine altruism either doesn't exist or is irrational.
(2) Genuine altruism does exist and is rational.
(3) So, evolutionary naturalism is false.
(4) If there are good theistic explanations for the existence and rationality of genuine altruism, then that is evidence for theism.
(5) There are good theistic explanations for the existence and rationality of genuine altruism.
(6) So, the existence and rationality of genuine altruism is evidence for theism.
 	
Pruss[15]
 	
(1) Moral altruism is irreducibly normative.
(2) There can be no naturalistic explanation for moral altruism if moral altruism is irreducibly normative.
	• **Genuine altruism**: sacrificial behavior *exclusively* for another; it incurs *no* benefit to oneself, kin, or group.
	• Re: (1). Is true virtually by definition. Natural selection entails that genuine altruism doesn't exist, or if it does, it is irrational.
	• Re: (2). Common sense, and some empirical literature.
	  - E.g.s, adoption of non-relatives, acts of supererogation, saints.
	  - Altruistic behavior seems natural and instinctual.
	
	• Re: (5). If theism is true, humans would be how a good God intends, which would likely include being altruistic.
	• Re: (5). If Christian theism is true, humans are created in the image of a God who is *agape* (self-giving love) and therefore altruistic.
	
	• Normative vs. Nonnormative facts
	  - "Sheep are four legged" vs.
	  - "Most sheep are four legged."

[14] Jeffrey Schloss, "Evolutionary Accounts of Altruism and the Problem of Goodness by Design," in Dembski (ed.), *Mere Creation* (IVP, 1998), ch. 10. See also Colin Grant, *Altruism and Christian Ethic* (Cambridge, 2001).

[15] Alexander Pruss, "Altruism, Normalcy, and God," in Nowack and Coakley (eds.), *Evolution, Games, and God* (Harvard, 2013).

(3) So, there can be no naturalistic explanation for moral altruism.
(4) If there are good theistic explanations for moral altruism, then moral altruism is evidence for theism.
(5) There are good theistic explanations for moral altruism.
(6) So, moral altruism is evidence for theism.
	• Naturalistic, scientific explanation is always in terms of nonnormative facts.
	• **Moral altruism** = morally praiseworthy, sacrificial action for another's good.
	
	• Re: (1). Moral altruism is irreducibly normative, being about what is praiseworthy and good.
	• Re: (2). Even if there can be a naturalistic explanation for moral altruism (i.e., how it evolved, why we have a tendency toward it), there cannot be a naturalistic explanation for why moral altruism is normal/appropriate.
	• Re: (5). Good theistic explanations of moral altruism:
	  - Proper function: moral altruism is normal because proper functioning humans will be morally altruistic.
	  - Human nature: moral altruism is normal because God created human nature to reflect his own, morally altruistic nature.

Friday, January 22, 2021: Wrote a letter of recommendation for Joe Swanner, an old student. Love him and his siblings I've met; what a wonderful family. He's applying to law school; I know he'd perform wonderfully. Miss him. Touching base with him is always a little bit of heaven.

Signed up for a series of two-hour discussions about John Hare's new yet-to-be-published book. Fun!

This morning's reading with MB was great fun. Enns is reliably disappointing; *The Three Kings* has something to offer, though so far not quite as much as I'd hoped; but Wright's and Roden's books are a triumph, as far as I'm concerned.

Bible reading from this morning featured, among other things, the passage where Jesus walked on water. Peter did for a bit, too, before becoming fearful based on the wild winds. It was an inspiring passage; hope this day I can metaphorically walk on water, doing what in my own strength I can't, but by keeping my eyes on Jesus I can. This is especially important for me to remember when I feel overwhelmed. Between all the requirements of my position—including duties associated with my directing the Center—I can easily feel like it's too much: the research, the reading for class, the discussion boards, the lectures, the podcasts, the reading of colleagues' books, the speaking in churches (soon), the promotion of HBU apologetics, etc. But this is when I have to remember that I can do all things through Christ who strengthens me. Sometimes it feels like I'm trying to do *all* things! ☺

Answered a WB question: "What do you believe is the most compelling evidence or argument for Christianity, and what is the most challenging objection to Christianity?" Here's what I wrote:

I am always struck with what Paul said in Acts 17, namely, that the hour of ignorance was over because of the resurrection of Jesus. That was a game-changer, Paul insisted, rendering ignorance culpable. Fascinating he said this in Athens, of all places, where Socrates several centuries before had made professions of ignorance his veritable mantra. I doubt the irony was lost on Paul's audience.

For a long while I have thought the case for the resurrection to be the centerpiece of Christian apologetics, but there's another piece of evidence I intend to discuss momentarily that, at an existential level, is profoundly compelling.

First, though, what's the most challenging objection to Christianity? Again, the most obvious answer is the problem of evil. It's at least likely to be the deal-breaker for most of those who resist Christianity. Even more existentially pressing than the theoretical challenge of evil, though, is the personal or psychological struggle with evil. We may have perfectly adequate reasons to think that the sufferings of this world don't preclude a good God, but that's a far cry from being able and willing to emotionally cope with real instances of heart-wrenching loss and grief.

But this is where I might make a Copan-like maneuver and emphasize ways in which the evils of this world provide, in their own way, a pointer toward Christianity. Evil is a morally thick term, and it usually means more than suffering alone. There's a moral component; the world is not as it ought to be. This basic assumption resides at the heart of the problem of evil, and gives it much of its punch. But why think the world should be any different from what it is? Christianity provides a good reason for thinking the world is broken and yet will be set right, but a view like naturalism offers nothing of the kind.

Taking seriously the moral thickness of a notion like evil, too, reminds us that the right worldview should be able to provide a robust foundation for morality. This is the topic on which I have devoted the bulk of my professional work. I am convinced that a vast swath of moral phenomena—objective moral values, binding moral duties, unalienable human rights, moral regret, moral freedom, moral knowledge, moral transformation, moral rationality, etc.—are best explained by theism generally and Christianity particularly.

Finally, what is best characterized as good or evil are not states of affairs, but persons. Accidentally smashing my thumb with a hammer is bad, but nonmorally bad, not morally bad. But someone intentionally smashing my thumb with a hammer is morally bad. Moral goodness and badness are categories most fitting of persons. And the fact is, if God were to immediately obliterate the evils in this world, as some suggest any loving God would have to, that would mean the destruction of you and me. We ourselves are part of the problem.

Clay Jones has read a great deal about various historical atrocities and genocides, and he is struck by the fact that those carrying out such evil deeds tend to be average, normal people who find themselves in a situation in which they think doing so will serve their own interests and they will get away with it. History has revealed that human beings are desperately, well, sinful—and not just others, but you and me, too. As Clay puts it, we're all born "Auschwitz-enabled." Something is broken within us and a doctrine like original sin explains just what it is.

Unless we see ourselves as having fallen short of an unbending moral standard, as people in need of both radical forgiveness and transformation, the Christian message doesn't come alive and speak to us. So much of the force of the problem of evil derives from taking moral badness seriously. So it is finally confused when the problem of evil is taken as decisive evidence against Christianity, when, in fact, it is Christianity that ultimately offers principled hope for its deepest solution.

Saturday, January 23, 2021: I didn't feel like working much today; I had stayed pretty busy all week and found myself in need of rest more than anything today. Marybeth and I watched a fun documentary later in the day on *Back to the Future*. Chatted with Bill Irwin about a variety of matters, including the prospect of doing a book on Ted Lasso and Philosophy—much might ride on catching Sudeikis's attention. I also managed to write up a draft of a short blog on Ted Lasso.

Sunday, January 24, 2021: MB and I had a mini-prayer-retreat today, which was wonderful. Prayed at length about a long list of needs/desires/concerns. Much needed. It was a year ago this month we had a prayer retreat during which I sensed the need to reach a wholly fresh audience with the message of moral apologetics. Today we prayed about the Center, HBU, our health and habits, our new callings here in Houston, our families, our projects, our nation, the pandemic, etc. Important to spend time doing such work in prayer. Convinced it yields important dividends. In the evening we watched a documentary on Jeffrey Epstein. Also received Fraser's third chapter of his dissertation, which goes fairly long; fortunately the fourth (and last) shouldn't be nearly as long. Looks like we're on track for him to defend by late March or so.

Monday, January 25, 2021: After sending my weekly e-mail to my class, I went to breakfast at Toasted Yolk with MB. Then we came home and read from our books and prayed. The *Three Kings* book continues to mystify us certain respects. I know there's stuff to gain from it, especially from its innovation and creativity, but some of the content strikes us as suspect. For example, he crafts this distinction between a King like Saul vs. a King like David, and how we don't ever know the difference. Really? Can't we on occasion have the discernment to know? I'm not sure why that wouldn't be the case. And he suggests we shouldn't go after a King Saul because, for all we know, it's a King David. But if we think of Christian leaders in charge of organizations today, wouldn't this mean there's little to no accountability for them if nobody feels like they should be challenged? And didn't Nathan confront David himself? And leaders of Christian outfits aren't kings! So there's that. The worse problem today among evangelicals than holding its leaders to too much account seems to be treating them like the kings they aren't! So we—MB and I— are not quite sure what to do with any of this. The Enns books continues to be hard to listen to, though, but the Roden and Wright books are marvelous, reminding us that our main call is joyful obedience, and that more than valuing what God does *through* us we should prize what he's doing *within* us, first and foremost.

Last night I was awake for a long while, and couldn't stop thinking about the possibilities of a radio show with me and Jerry. Not sure if this idea is of God, but I'm open to it. I found it interesting that my thoughts were preoccupied with it after a full day of prayer. It potentially resonates with that message from last January's prayer retreat where I felt impressed by the notion that our ministry had a wholly fresh audience to reach. I know I need to get over my fear of figuring out this podcast stuff very soon. A good place to begin to move in this direction.

Lord, if a radio venture is your will for me and Jerry, I pray that you would provide confirmations of this in your way and time, and in the meantime I intend to proceed confidently in the direction of the podcast and whatnot, casting the vision and proclaiming the truth as you enable me to, entrusting into your hands my desire to see that new, fresh audience materialize. Time to trust you.

It dawns on me today that perhaps my problem is less that my desires are too strong, but rather that certain ones among them are too weak. God, make my desire to love you a ravenous, craving, insatiable, all-controlling passion. Make me passionate about holiness, serving you, loving others as I ought, esteeming others better than myself, putting others first, glorifying you in all I say and do and think.

I did what I could on Fraser's dissertation today but didn't get as far as I wanted. At 4 in the afternoon I zoomed into a lecture by a colleague on the atonement. Then, in quick succession, I got a *Ratio Christi* speaking invite, Hare's chapter we'll be zooming to discuss, a request by a friend to peruse a manuscript of his, and a meeting invite for Wednesday about funding for the Center (I'm assuming anyway; details weren't provided; hope they're not firing me). Feeling distinctly overwhelmed! Just trying to stay positive and take one day at a time. Good problem to have, I suppose. But I don't like feeling like there's just too much on me. Seriously need to get up early every day and stick with it!

Need to get a good night's rest tonight and experience more peace. God will keep him in perfect peace whose mind is stayed on him.

Tuesday, January 26, 2021: A remarkable day! God really blessed. I awoke in the middle of the night and found the inspiration and strength to finish the big chapter of Fraser's and give him feedback—John is knocking it out of the park!—plus then to read the Hare chapter in its entirety. A wonderful and moving chapter, by the way. That made a big difference emotionally. I actually wrote John Hare this little letter afterwards:

Hi John,

I hope this e-mail finds you well.

No word yet from OUP, but hopefully soon!

I have read the first chapter of your new book and am quite excited by it. Greatly looking forward to the first group chat about it via zoom. Such an honor to be part of that.

I was up during the night, after being unable to sleep for a while, reading your chapter, and I found it brilliant, insightful, and deeply moving. The story of your child's pilgrimage with gender issues was profoundly poignant. Wow! Your analysis and transparency just impressed me mightily. I never had any idea that this was an issue that had touched your family. I so appreciate your willingness to share. You are such a blessing.

For what it's worth, I jotted down a few suggestions about typos and such, as follows:

Page 2: you probably need semi-colon before "in my opinion" 9 lines from bottom

Page 3: third line, "liked" should be "like"

Page 7: in penultimate line, "what" perhaps should be "that"

Page 11: line before note 24 (the superscript), cut extra space between "morally" and "wrong"

Page 11: note 22, "Edwards" spelled wrong

Page 13: Yes Kant seems wrong on a few points, including perhaps such a strong emphasis on duties; duties are important, but ultimately they seem an early step down the path of morality. So, assuming this is right, to say "morality withers away" in heaven seems wrong to me. I prefer Mavrodes' picture as teh much more compelling picture, where things like rights and duties pave the way to things like gift and sacrifice, but I don't see this as morality withering away, but coming to its intended fulfillment. Seeing as how you often talk about various phenomena coming to their intended destination or final form in heaven, it seems a mistake not to suggest as much about the enterprise of morality itself. Surely the perfect love in heaven isn't morality going away as much as it's morality finding its perfect fulfillment, right? I see rights and duties as the anteroom (or something like that) in a great cathedral, the love, gift, sacrifice, etc. to come making up its towering spires.

Page 21: last line, "send" should be "sends"

Page 24: is "movement" in heaven perhaps a better understanding of what Kant was getting at in seeing eternal movement toward the good?

Page 27: first full paragraph, fourth line, "as" should be "at"

Page 28: paragraph starting "In the…" is a little bigger than usual

Blessings, Dave

Then I caught some more shut eye and woke up feeling altogether better. After waking up I had a chance to go see a prospective student at HBU, a kid who's graduating from Union in TN. That was fun, and I ended up taking him back to the airport. Enjoyable experience. Praying God directs him; he's also considering Palm Beach Atlantic. Could hardly go wrong going to study with the Pauls!

MB and I did some wonderful reading. The *Three Kings* book was powerful in depicting the vulnerability of good leaders; the Roden book on the need for joyful obedience; the Wright book on the process of moral maturation and transformation.

Wright's book is a neat weaving together of Hellenistic and Hebraic elements. Perhaps at some point I should devote more thought to the four cardinal (hinge) virtues of courage, justice, prudence, and temperance and their centrality to human flourishing. Wright suggests that Paul would say of such things something similar to what he said about the Mosaic law—good as far as it goes, but alone they can't quite deliver what they promise. Christ completes and transforms this process of character formation.

Wednesday, January 27, 2021: Today promises to be a lovely day. Closer to dinner time I have a zoom session with some folks at HBU about the Center. Still not entirely sure what it's about, but my guess would be funding. Trusting God to bless our fundraising efforts. I've also agreed to referee a journal article within the next week on Railton's ethical theory. It is not very long so I figured it would be a neat thing to do.

It's a bit later and I'm now done with reviewing the piece. I suggested publication. The author argues that Railton's constructivism is susceptible to Euthyphro-like objections—especially the prior obligations objections—and that he needs realism, perhaps even divine command theory, to salvage his account and evade the force of the objection(s).

The zoom meeting is now over; it was a good discussion of the Center. I got to share my vision for it with Sharon Saunders from Placement and Sandy Mooney, the CFO. It will be particularly important to keep Sharon in the loop—with names of Board officers, copies of newsletters, donor lists, etc. Eventually we'll have to work a bit more, too, with Jay Spencer and Steve Peterson since they do a lot of targeted marketing for grad classes. There's also the prospect of the Center being made more prominently a part of the new Ten Pillars initiative. I always worry that I end up oversharing a bit in these meetings, but MB listened in and thought it went well. Very supportive folks—Phil, as always, along with both Sharon and Sandy—the names of my two sisters, as it happens!

Thursday, January 28, 2021: Bible reading this morning included Pharaoh's heart hardening, which reminded me of a Mailbag Question at the website that went like this: **Question**: Can you offer any insight into God's hardening of Pharaoh's heart? If God is good, why would he do that?

> **Answer**: Eleonore Stump, in her magisterial *Wandering in Darkness: Narrative and the Problem of Suffering* (and an older article on sanctification, freedom, and the hardening of Pharaoh's heart), offers some very useful insights that may shed some light on this topic. In a nutshell, we're as human beings all of us, to one degree or another, internally fragmented, double minded, and in a real sense our deepest freedom is compromised when there's a fundamental disconnect between our (1st order) *desires* and our (2nd order) *desires about our desires*. So if I have an

overwhelming desire to gamble but a desire not to have that desire, I'm in that sort of dissonant state and my deepest agency is somewhat compromised.

Suppose I ask God for help and to take away my desire to gamble, and in an act of miraculous deliverance he does. He has not thereby vitiated my freedom by this gift of sanctification; to the contrary, he has enhanced it, by enabling my first order and second order desires to move into alignment and for me to live more effectively as the person I want to be.

An inverted example is a case like Joseph Goebbels, Hitler's Nazi propagandist, who wanted his own heart to harden so he wouldn't feel compassion for the suffering Poles when he saw a graphic account of the hideous atrocities they were suffering at the hands of German soldiers. "Be hard, my heart, be hard," he told himself. On reflection his choice was to be *that* kind of uncompassionate person. His first order desire, at least fleetingly, was one of compassion, but his second order desire, which more accurately reflected who he wanted and deliberatively chose to be, was not to have those compassionate desires.

If God, suppose, were to intervene and harden Goebbels' heart, taking away some of that compassion, he would be bringing Goebbels' lower and higher order desires into alignment, making him a more internally integrated person. Rather than detracting from his free will, in a real sense he would be enhancing it a bit. He certainly wouldn't be making Goebbels *less* free. God would be giving Goebbels what he really wanted down deep, what he chose when, presumably he could and should have done otherwise. (For all we know, God doing this might help Goebbels see the horror of his choices and choose to repent and change course.)

So when Pharaoh hardened his own heart and God hardened it even more, God was actually honoring Pharaoh's choice, not detracting from his freedom. God loves us, and desires that none would perish; love isn't just what God does, it's who he is. But God will also honor our choices if we decide to hold on to sin tighter than we hold on to him; if we renounce the only ultimate source of Joy there is, we may just get what we want.

That's the basic idea, and I think it is a helpful analysis to get our minds, at least a little, around what's going on in the Pharaoh passage that, for many, poses quite the *bête noire* of OT stories. Of course the clearest picture we have of the immeasurable love of God is the cross; the Pharaoh passage is

48

one of those challenging ones we have to think about a bit more to understand—in light of the cross.

I am trying to stay positive and motivated to do my work, feeling a bit inadequate, finding it hard to keep up with everything. No time to waste any by being negative, but I'm not letting that stop me! MB gave me a pep talk about that. Part of what I'm experiencing is probably what Lewis dubbed the Law of Undulation, which rears its head even when I'm spending time in prayer and Bible reading each day. Just an inexorable part of life, it seems. Another part of my emotional struggle, I imagine, is the ongoing pain of transition; in the process of forming new neural pathways—new life, new context, new home, new job, new house, new routine, new students, new expectations. But like learning virtue, a new language, or a musical instrument, I just need to persevere in the face of the newness, knowing that at first it is difficult in various, and sometimes surprising, respects. It will get easier. New patterns need to become second nature, and my faith needs to grow. I believe, but the Lord needs to help my unbelief.

Our reading was good this morning. The servant leadership book has begun comparing and contrasting five models of leadership: the Great Man or Charismatic model, the Transactional model, the Transformational model, a New Science model, to a Servant Leadership model. I used to find talk of leadership uninteresting until some recent evangelical debacles drove home its importance. I've also been spending more time again today back in Sharp's book, which is good. Prayer coming up with TJ as well.

The dates have been set for the zoom discussions of Hare's book, once about every three weeks on a Wednesday from 9-11 am. The last date is on the Wednesday of the first week of the course I am co-teaching with Craig. Speaking of Hare, one aspect of his writing I love is the way it's so wide-ranging—from analytic philosophy to gender studies, from literature to music, from contemporaries to Medievals to Ancients. Much to emulate there. Erudite and learned; proficient at drawing out all sorts of novel connections. Love him!

Friday, January 29, 2021: The day got off to a marvelous start. Listened to scripture, and was touched and moved once more. I decided to jot Brian there at the Daily Audio Bible a note of appreciation. I also posted the sign up e-mail to the HBU Apologetics website—the sign-up for the Center's newsletter. The day just seemed to get off on the right foot; it's still early in the day, but I'm filled with hope.

Received recently by the way the schedule of classes I'll be teaching next school year. Exciting stuff. In the fall, it will be this:

APOL 5320: Phil of religion: Faith and Reason, online first 8 weeks
APOL 5340: Medieval Philosophy and Culture, online second 8 weeks
APOL 6323: Frameworks and Issues, online second 8 weeks

In the spring 2022, it will be this: Theistic Ethics and Moral Apologetics (online) and Ancient Philosophy & Culture (online). That leaves me needing one more class to make load. So, the proposal is that I would be listed as professor of record for Bill Craig's two 1-credit hour classes. He teaches one in the fall and one in the spring. Basically, as I understand it, I would handle normal professor duties for the two classes. This would make my fall a little busier, but the spring lighter. Hopefully this can both help make Craig's class grow plus benefit the Center as well. I feel like I hit pay dirt coming here!

Still morning time—since it's payday, I paid the monthly mortgage bill on the house and we're now down to owing just $4400 on the house. Close! Thankful!

At breakfast MB and I discussed the political situation in the country. The divisiveness is disheartening. With Jerry Walls and Robert Gagnon coming over tonight, two ultra-partisans (so it seems to us), it's on our minds how the conversation will go. They are both tremendously gifted—and between them they went to Harvard, Princeton, Yale, and Notre Dame—not too shabby! Rob is especially adept at whipping his followers into a frenzy on social media. But MB and I entertain some reservations about some of the culture war stuff, thinking prophetic voices in the church are more needed to rise above it than mobilize the troops. Such voices need to call the church to repent— including of its public acrimony, besetting sins, and chronic idols—and remind her that we wrestle not against flesh and blood, but against principalities and powers. Some are called to have a voice in the public square, no doubt, and it's not that I always disagree with these friends of mine, one old, one new. I often agree with them, truth be told, and viscerally so. But the one-sidedness and stridency and starkness with which they tend to paint their positions and those of their political foes strikes me as dubious. Still, these words of John Adams continue to ring true: "Our Constitution was made only for a moral and religious People. It is wholly inadequate to the government of any other."

Saturday, January 30, 2021: Last night was great fun. Had both Robert Gagnon and Jerry Walls over. Robert is perhaps the world's leading biblical expert on homosexuality. All evening Jerry kept ripping into Gagnon about forgetting the earlier appointment. Gagnon wrote this on FB today: "I had a delightful time with dinner and movie at colleague David Baggett's home yesterday with other colleague Jerry Walls. David and his wife Marybeth were very gracious but I was repeatedly the victim of Jerry's microaggressions. I also had to agree to David's demand that I not 'incite to violence.' I don't know if I was successful because we ended up watching the movie *Gladiator*. In spite of all this (or maybe because of it) I had a great hilarious time."

Exceptionally tired today. Nice chat with Elton, then a long nap, then MB and I enjoyed a movie. The chat with Elton was wide-ranging, including whether morality

50

continues in heaven. Elton and I locked horns on that one. The nap was unusually long and intense. Perhaps as an introvert I'm recovering a bit from all the socializing from last night. Great fun but exhausting. I also tend to get tired by Saturday afternoons as weeks come to a close.

Received tough news about my sister Sandra last night. She has numerous health issues, not just kidney stones, some fairly serious and a few horribly pain-inducing. Spine issues, missing cartilage in her knees and discs, bursitis in her hips and knees, severe digestive issues. Very concerning.

Nathaniel is giving consideration to moving to Texas. A large part of me would like him to. His willingness to think seriously about effecting serious changes in his life is a good sign. Change isn't easy for anyone; for him it's virtually traumatic.

Marybeth and I, in addition to reading from the four books we're going through, also spent some time discussing which covid vaccines are best to use; preferably we want to take a vaccine, when the time comes, that didn't use embryonic stem cells in its various stages of development and confirmation. Pfizer and Moderna look like pretty good possibilities so far. I think Mark Foreman is going to write up something on this for the website.

Stan Key wrote me back; we've been reflecting in correspondence a bit about how God leads us to unexpected places. We recently moved to TX, he and Katy to MI, my old stomping grounds (I had assured him as a native that he was a welcome honorary Michigander). Here's what Stan wrote back:

Yes, the pillar of fire leads us places we never expected to go! (Michigan, Texas, Mara, etc.). Do you know the poem by C. S. Lewis "Pilgrim's Problem"?

> By now I should be entering on the supreme stage
> of the whole walk, reserved for the late afternoon.
> The heat was to be over now....
> I can see nothing like all this: Was the map wrong?
> Maps can be wrong. But the experienced walker knows
> that the other explanation is more often true.

Oh that's good....

Anyway... he leads. We follow.
In his will is our peace (who said that?).

Blessings, Stan

I ended up sending this poem in an e-mail to Rob Gagnon, Jerry Walls, and Marybeth, for all of us came to HBU after a negative experience elsewhere. Jerry faced unjust accusations at Asbury years ago, a situation that has never resolved. Robert had to leave Pittsburgh Theological Seminary under unfortunate conditions. In both of those cases certain colleagues appear to have had it out for them. Marybeth and I of course felt we needed to leave Liberty for the sake of our mental health, and if ever the Center was going to get underway, it wouldn't have been there. And even if it had been there, I don't think it would have ever reached its potential. Liberty simply doesn't have the right context for it to thrive. Too much of the stench of fundamentalism hangs in the air. At any rate, it's heartening to be reminded that in God's providence we can trust how path unfolds, even if some of the twists and turns along the way owe initially to regrettable unfortunate circumstances. It's a picture of God's redeeming grace and a source of great comfort.

Marybeth and I are also about to give our permission for our correspondence from back in March with Elizabeth Williamson from the *New York Times* to be made public in the lawsuit Liberty is bringing against her, the NYT, and a photojournalist from Roanoke the NYT hired. Seems like the right thing to do; praying it doesn't result in too many deleterious repercussions for us—but even if it does, seems like the right to do to battle injustice. Liberty's leadership consistently lied through its teeth back around March and someone needs to stand up against it.

Sunday, January 31, 2021: Rested today; Marybeth did fit in Bible reading and reading from our four books; good stuff. And I wrote this little FB comment in a discussion of the moral argument: "What I find unpersuasive about the sanguine acceptance that objective moral values and duties would plausibly obtain even in the contingency of God's nonexistence is that it seems to assume that God's existence is contingent. That there could be a non-null world in which God doesn't exist assumes God's existence isn't necessary. And since I think there are good reasons to take God's existence as necessary, I don't find persuasive the notion that an atheistic world would feature objective moral values and duties. This isn't even yet to consider the challenges of an atheistic world to make sense of robust moral properties (owing to Mackie's 'queerness' notion, for example). I think what usually happens when folks casually express confidence in an atheistic world featuring objective moral values and duties is that the thought experiment goes something like this: Let's just assume a world like the actual world, and then imagine God doesn't exist; when we do, we'd still wish to affirm promise keeping is right, friendship is morally good, etc. I get that, but again, on either classical theism or theistic personalism a world like the actual world wouldn't actually be so much as possible without God as the ground of its existence. I don't mean to beg the question from the other direction here by assuming God's existence and God's necessary existence; I'm not, in other words, trying to say that these considerations show the moral argument to be sound. All I'm saying for now is that the casual depiction of it as obviously flawed (or 'widely refuted') strikes me as unprincipled—and likely viciously circular."

I was largely responding to my FB friend Jeremy Huntington, who replied like this:

> David, it's of course humbling to interact with you on this topic, because you are such a master! As I've shared with you before, I look forward to reading your work on this subject and I know I will learn a ton.
>
> For now I'll just share that whether or not I find coherent the notion of God as a "necessary" being depends on what "necessary" means. I think the non-existence of God is a fully coherent notion, such that I don't see any detectable contradiction, or inherent impossibility, in the idea that God doesn't exist. Again, I find myself, on this point, in agreement with Swinburne. I also agree with, e.g., van Inwagen's modal skepticism, in that I don't even know, a priori, if God is metaphysically possible.
>
> If, by necessary, one means that God has the power to exist, without needing to be sustained by anything external to Godself, and that God has in some sense (e.g. an A or B view of Time) "always" existed and "will always" exist and that nothing can cause God to cease to exist, including God, then I find that sort of necessity coherent.
>
> Or, one might mean that all concrete being, other than God, is such that it must be sustained in existence by God, then, again, I find that notion coherent. But I also find it coherent that nothing exists, including God. I just don't think these sorts of questions can be settled, a priori. (I also don't find persuasive arguments to the affect that necessary truths depend on God, e.g. mathematical propositions. If those arguments succeeded, they'd show that a concrete being is, after all, logically necessary).
>
> But even if God is a necessary being, I still don't think that moral truths would depend on God. (Wasn't it van Inwagen who wrote an essay with a title something like, "God and Other Necessary Beings"?)
>
> I regard the thought experiment concerning moral truths existing, even if God ceased to exist, as a helpful way of bringing out that I just don't think moral truth depends on God. Thought experiments don't always have to be possible, to be helpful. Einstein, for example, didn't think it was actually possible for us to travel along, with a light beam, at the speed of light, but he could still use such a thought experiment in a helpful way.
>
> Even if God is a necessary being, we could still ask, "But what would happen, to assume the impossible, if God ceased to exist?" I'm sure open to the view that all concrete Reality, other than God, would cease to exist, if God ceased. But, in my view, if God and all concrete Reality ceased to exist, there would still be moral truths, just as there would still be, e.g., mathematical truths. For me that thought

experiment is a helpful way of bringing out the notion that there are inherent moral truths.

I also don't find Mackie's view persuasive. I don't think there's anything queer about inherent value. I find few things more plausible, as a matter of fact.

For me, the big question, when it comes to metaethics, isn't whether God grounds moral truths, but whether there is a plausible answer to epistemic skepticism, since, in my view, all moral realism rests, ultimately, on a priori intuitions that can't be proven. In my view, the question of God in no way helps to solve that problem. Should I trust my intuition that, say, it's inherently wrong to pluck out a little girl's eyes, without pain meds, in front of her wailing mother (as a Nazi did, to a little girl and her mother), or should I be skeptical that such a thing is inherently wrong, or positively disbelieve that it's wrong?

That said, I find moral non-realism *unthinkable*. The little girls name was Zosia and I stand with her: what was done to her was objectively evil. I think the notion of inherent value is quite coherent and I'm content to trust that I'm seeing, via a priori intuition, inherent moral truths, including the truth that what was done to Zosia was a horrendous evil.

For me paradigmatic evils (and goods) settle the truth of moral realism. I think there's a lot of hard work to do, when it comes to working out a theory that best accounts for the paradigms and quite plausible principles--in search of Rawls' "reflective equilibrium"--but that hard work simply doesn't lead me to doubt the existence of Good and evil.

In this connection, I love what Dr. Johnson said:

"The existence of twilight is no argument against the noonday sun."

Anyway, despite our differences, I greatly respect both the immensity of your learning as well as you, as a person. I look forward to continuing to learn from you. Blessings!

To which I responded like this: "So much to unpack here! Thanks for the thoughts. I can't do them justice in short compass. Just a few points, and we can talk more about it later: I entirely agree we can apprehend the truth of certain moral principles, but that recognition underdetermines their ontological foundations. The notion that necessary truths can't be undergirded by others depends on conflating dependence and control, which Morris and others have called into question. Regarding Mackie, what he characterized as queer was the authoritative nature of moral obligations in particular, and I see little hope for something like naturalism to make sense of compelling reason-conferring capacities. I think what tends to happen is that duties, for lack of attentiveness to their distinctive nature, get watered down and domesticated, or explained away, rather than explained by naturalism in any sort of robust fashion. I am in complete agreement with the impulse to take as axiomatic certain moral facts, but again, that doesn't show them to exist ontologically independently of God. It is rather what gets the discussion started about what constitutes their most plausible explanation. Personally I'm inclined to think a theistic picture makes better sense of necessary truths than does naturalism (à la Plantinga's 'How to be an Anti-Realist'). It's not at all intuitively clear to me that mathematical truths are independent of God, but that discussion would take a lot of time. In general, my point is simply this: assuming that God is irrelevant to ethics doesn't make the case; it just strikes me as question begging. The evidence typically adduced for such independence isn't enough; that there are axiomatic moral truths doesn't show it, or so much as suggest it; that there are necessary truths (true in every possible world) doesn't show it without assuming what's not in evidence, and actually, to my thinking, invites us to account for how this could be so, to which theism provides a very good answer. I agree considering implications of counteressentials can be useful, but a situation in which God, traditionally thought of as the ground of being itself, is assumed for the purpose of argument not to exist is a particularly problematic counteressential. Again, failing to recognize this treats in too sanguine a fashion its implications, to my thinking, resulting in what I consider to be the aforementioned circularity. Again, here I'm not making the case that the moral argument goes through; I'm simply pointing out that your assumption it is refuted or implausible strikes me as hasty. Looking forward to discussing this more with you down the line, friend!"

Then Jeremy replied:

Great thoughts, as always 😊! What I'll particularly want to explore with you sometime is the question of relevance.

When I think about what was done to Zosia, the reason I think it's wrong is because of the sort of thing it is. Suppose we imagine that state of affairs, involving Zosia, as existing within a "circle."

It's what's in that circle that makes it wrong, in my view. *Nothing* outside of the circle is relevant, including God. In my view nothing about God--no property or set of properties, whether properties are, e.g., understood univocally or analogically (as those terms are understood by analytic theists), or as classical theists understand "properties"--is relevant to why what was done to Zosia was wrong. There are things inherent, or intrinsic to, that state of affairs that are the reasons for its wrongness--things inside the circle, so to speak.

Because that's the case, if such a state of affairs exists, it's necessarily wrong, whether or not God exists.

I don't see anything about God that could possibly help to ground or explain why such a thing is wrong. What property or set of properties are relevant, to the existence of inherent Goodness? I don't think there are any. Again, to look outside of the circle is, in my view, to look away from what matters.

In my view, seeking to ground Goodness in God seems to undercut what I mean, by moral realism. It seems to suggest that what was done to Zosia wasn't wrong because of the sort of thing it is. Instead, it's wrong because of something about God, something outside the circle. But, again, the very reason that I think it's wrong is because of what's in the circle. To say that it could only be wrong if such and such obtained outside the circle is, in my view, to shift away from what really matters, when it comes to the question of moral realism.

It's sort of analogous to how I felt when I first heard about compatibilism. I was reading an essay by Joel Feinberg in which he was saying that free will is compatible with determinism and at first I thought that I wasn't understanding his view! But then I realized that he was just using "free will" in a different way. That's what grounding Goodness in God seems like to me. I thought that what was done to Zosia was evil because some kinds of things just are evil and what was done to her is a paradigm of such evil. But then I'm told that that's not sufficient. There has to be something outside the circle to ground Goodness, and hence the evil of what was done to Zosia. Again, the reason I think it's wrong is because of the sort of thing it is. If I'm told that's not right, my grounds for thinking there is Good and evil in the first place feel as though they've been undercut.

As for duties, I think they naturally arise from the inherent value of certain beings and probably also from certain actions we perform, e.g. making promises. I think God gives the commands S/He does because of our inherent value and because of certain actions that God has performed. Here I'd agree with Swinburne to a sort of modified divine command theory, in that, e.g., God may have the right to command that we meet together on a certain day, because, as our great Benefactor, we owe such obedience to God. But the principle that we owe to our benefactors would be necessary, if true. Yet, God has no right to command us to torture babies for fun and God commands us to care for babies because of their inherent value. But these are, of course, big topics!

Anyway, I know life is busy! It's fitting for me to give you the last word, if you'd like to take it. You are, on this topic, Gandalf, and I'm Frodo ☺. I look forward to more discussion. Blessings!

To which I replied like this: "Thanks, Jeremy! I usually don't do long FB discussions on this topic. ☺ I definitely want to discuss with you more down the line, though. I'll say just a few quick things. I get where you're coming from and I think it's a good place. But I do see things a bit differently. When someone is subjected to horrible pain, morality isn't yet in the picture. If I inadvertently hit my thumb with a hammer, for example, we could say the pain is "bad," but it's not morally bad. It's just dang painful. It's nonmorally bad. But someone intentionally bashing my thumb with a hammer makes the decision by that person bad--the motivation of that person, perhaps the person's character. Now we've moved into the province of morality. So even when it comes to the good/bad distinction, I don't see empirical properties alone as sufficient to account for objective value. And this is why, to my thinking, it's not as unnatural as some may imagine that the personal One in whose image we've been made is centrally relevant to the foundations of ethics. It's why I think Lewis was exactly right that the existence of inviolable moral standards and our invariably falling short of them provide a key clue to the nature of reality and the human condition. Too often what happens, I think, confusion of moral and nonmoral goodness or badness obfuscates a vision of the distinctive and evidential attributes of morality. Regarding moral duties, to me again the issue is whence comes their authority? That we can adduce what we would all agree are certain moral reasons to do something is necessary but not sufficient for the sort of authority that I think moral obligations instantiate. We have Kant most particularly to thank for highlighting the binding authority of duties. So often what seems to me takes place is inattentiveness to their remarkable features (that folks like Newman and A. E. Taylor are incredibly adept at accentuating) is what makes folks think their explanation is garden variety or as good a fit with naturalism as with theism. Two other quick matters, and I'll refrain from covering any of the same material: I'm a staunch critic of radical voluntarism, but its patent falsehood is something that can be shown not to undermine a practicable and plausible theistic metaethic; and regarding my earlier concerns about the intractable counteressentials discussed, this is why I shy away from a deductivist account of moral apologetics and talk about 'better' or 'best' explanation rather than 'only' explanation. I consider the latter initiative rather beyond my pay grade. (I won't elaborate on this for now, but also relevant to note is that there's a range of moral arguments to consider, of which Craig's is just one narrow variant—versions pertaining to a variety of moral facts, moral knowledge, moral rationality, performative issues, etc. Mainly I want to encourage folks not to be overly dismissive too hastily before thinking them through; personally I think this is one of the best clues God's given to us—a clue that speaks to head and heart, educated and uneducated, young and old. But it may take a serious investment of time, I think, to apprehend their power. Keeping an open mind is vitally important.)"

Monday, February 1, 2021: Wasn't much in the mood for work today. Did some cleaning of the house, watched some television with Marybeth, and sent my weekly e-mail to my online class, but that's about it. Played chess against the computer. Hopefully tomorrow I'll be more in the mood to work again. Just one of those days. Tomorrow I hope to write a letter of recommendation for my friend Mark Foreman's book on bioethics to be picked up by a publisher; grade discussion boards; prepare for the Hare zoom talk on Wednesday; and finish Jordan's fourth chapter. I also did do about a quarter of that chapter today. But not a banner work day! Some days I find myself worrying about fund-raising. Other than praying hard for the funds, I feel wholly ill equipped to actually raise it. Dawned on me today I never heard back from my Lilly Foundation inquiry letter. That we ourselves are struggling financially a bit until the house is paid off isn't instilling great confidence on fiduciary matters. Feeling bummed about my sister, and of course perpetually a bit overwhelmed with the work before me. Anyway, on other fronts, a week from today I'm slated to do an online lecture on the moral argument for HBU's *Ratio Christi*.

Tuesday, February 2, 2021: Much better day today. Wrote the letter for Mark's book, got caught up on my Bible reading/listening, then MB and I did our reading. Roden's and Wright's books continue to be great; the Enns and *Three Kings* book not so much. After this I need to turn to Jordan's chapter and grading DB's. The next chapter from Fraser will be in by this weekend so I need to get done with Jordan's first…. Later in the day now, and I wasn't able to get quite as much work done today as hoped. Only about two thirds through Jordan's chapter, which is on moral values. Oh well. One does what one can. Need to quit for the day and relax a bit with MB.

Wednesday, February 3, 2021: The highlight of today was the two hour period of time I was able to spend with John Hare and about a dozen other folks in a zoom session about the first chapter of his new book. It was really wonderful! Save for me, I think everyone else was associated with Yale, most if not all former or present students of Hare's. Each and every one seemed so extremely bright, but also warm, collegial, and personable. Among the ones I remember were Matt, who graduated with a Masters from Yale and is now working on his PhD at the University of Texas, Kaylie (I think a current Masters student at Yale), Kyler (student at Yale), Chet (a 2020 grad from Yale awaiting news on PhD applications), Neal (a prof at Notre Dame, former student of John's), Jamie (student at Yale), Karen (former student of John's), Layne (Yale grad who's now working on his doctorate at Notre Dame), and Sarah (PhD student at Yale). It was really just so inspiring to be involved in a chat with such sharp folks; definitely makes me want to be a little better prepared next time. I had three or four contributions, but these people were wonderful. And seeing Hare again always warms my heart. So deeply grateful for the opportunity!

John started it off by welcoming everyone and letting each person briefly introduce themselves. Then he talked about the a few general features of the book. He noted that it's different from his other books in three ways: (1) it's more personal; (2) it's more theological, making a greater use of scripture; and (3) it's normative rather than meta-ethical, asking what kind of life we ought to lead. It was originally four lectures at Cambridge. He admitted that his previous books have been much helped by a discussion group like this, and knows this one will be too. Doing philosophy with friends, he said, is the best way to do philosophy. I loved his humility and teachability.

Neal started with some macro comments about the first chapter and project, noting the personal tone and wondering if John would get into the matter of people claiming to have heard things from God directly. John had taken that up elsewhere, so made it clear that instead he's taking up a set of examples. It's comprehensive in its way, though, by providing examples of the four main kinds of unity—with the world, life, other people, and God. (Later Neal pointed out that this four-fold structure happens to correspond perfectly to the four relationships that are broken and that God is restoring according to standard theology about hamartiology rooted in Genesis 3 and 4.)

Layne, I think, noted the way the book claims to be philosophy, but doesn't swear off using the resources of special revelation, to which John said the book wasn't either philosophy or theology, but a third thing: philosophical theology, which takes the givens of special revelation and using the tools and skills of philosophy to understand them. This is a helpful reminder for me to bear in mind as I work on the book with Ronnie.

John admitted that it's odd to put so much by way of anticipation of chapters to come into the first chapter; the biggest danger is redundancy. What he emphasized the subsequent chapters don't have, though, is the personal element. Later I pointed out that I think the strong personal element, though a little unorthodox, is a refreshing departure and can make more accessible some of the intimidation and distance of recondite philosophy. Chapter 1 is largely autobiographical. With this particular subject matter— the Holy Spirit—Hare is convinced that it matters how we get to our conclusions; it's inherently personal. Some of the sections, in fact, we seemed to come to think, could be more personal. John is going to talk more about his working in DC, his coming to this country as an immigrant, and his struggle with the "America First" sloganeering and the election of 2016, without making the book partisan.

John approach to the Holy Spirit will of necessity leave much out, and it's more bottom up than top down. He won't primarily be focusing on the role of the Spirit for the regenerate, but other things, like the important work of the Spirit in creating beauty and special nonsalvific work the Spirit, as in accounting for the heroic virtues and the special graces given to poets.

John strongly objects to accounts of the ground of human dignity that make it unavailable to impairments of certain kinds.

The main reason lists of things that make a good life are brought up early on is to point out important items left out.

In response to what I'd written him and to something that someone else brought up in discussion, John agreed he should stop saying morality "withers away" in heaven. Rather, there's something analogous to morality that survives, but it's not morality as Kant defines it, which features centrally oughtness that requires contrary dispositions. Whatever it is in heaven, it's not Kant's morality. There is, though, something analogous to motion, which he thinks Kant gets at least partially right. (Yes, we keep drawing ever closer to God; I've talked about this in class!) And this gets us closer to the sublime. John wants to say more on what the analogue of morality in heaven may be, but he recognizes it's difficult.

John emphasizes that our experience of the deep pleasure beauty gives us as something need of an explanation. His view of beauty is that it gives us a foretaste of the highest good. One person suggested the Edwards sermon "Excellencies of Christ." The same student, following Edwards, distinguished the Holy Spirit as *being* the Beauty, and *communicating* the Beauty. John agreed the latter is probably right for the Spirit, and the former for Jesus. (Filioque doctrine: the Spirit issues from Father and Son.)

A gal commended John's reflections on gender transition as a useful middle ground.

Personal notes I need to give John: connections between personal and universal; Newman on special revelation, and correction in note 21.

Regarding the gender transition stuff, another raised the concern it might smack of the arbitrary choice often connected to voluntarism. To which John responded by saying nature can mean different things. Kant gave three accounts of nature. John tends to use nature mostly in terms of what survives into the next life, and he doesn't think male and female do, but maybe something analogous.

John strongly resists as confused the conflation of voluntarism and anti-realism. Scotus is talking about natures!

Something is discovered about gender, John affirms; not altogether arbitrary choice. But he's open to what's discoverable being different from what was given at birth. I thought this stuff fascinating. He's read widely in the area and is clearly a brilliant man and philosophy, and a father, who's struggling to understand all this.

In general he thinks we should trust the "inner picture" more than the "outer picture" in general because that's how the Spirit works. We should look to interior illumination first, not, though, because it's infallible; it isn't.

Thursday, February 4, 2021: The morning got off to a lovely start as I listed to scripture. This morning's passage was about God showing up at Mount Sinai. Incredible story. Good insight from Brian about the mention of slavery. All of these folks had been born into slavery; it was all they knew. But the guidelines represented a huge step forward. This is one of those occasions where we really need to use our imaginations to put ourselves into the mindset of the people at that time.

Thinking some more about Hare's first chapter…he notes that the four main influences on him were Aristotle, Scotus, Kant, and his father, R. M. Hare. He'd done his dissertation at Princeton on Aristotle—on substance, essence, and eudaimonia. From Scotus he picked up the notion of individual essence and the priority of will over the intellect. From Kant the centrality of moral theology. And his dad's early unpublished work most resembles John's own work and in that work his dad called himself a Christian. These are the figures John discusses in *God and Morality*; I should reread that! And I should definitely reread the first chapter of this new book now that we've discussed it.

While MB and I did our reading today, an inspiration hit for a piece at MoralApologetics.com:

Moral Apologetics & Christian Theology

For some while now I have had the thought that it would be worthwhile to explore the connection between moral apologetics and theology. I have had occasion to touch on this matter here and there, but never anything remotely exhaustive. It remains in my mind a project to pursue for later—resonances of the moral argument(s) with such theological categories as ecclesiology and Christology, eschatology and soteriology, pneumatology, theological anthropology, and theology proper. In this short piece today, I'm going to just tip my toe in such a project by using something of a traditional four-fold distinction that cuts across a variety of theological concerns.

From the earliest chapters of Genesis we find that what gets broken and is need of being set right are the following facets of our existence: ourselves, the creation, our relationship with others, and our relationship with God. John Hare's forthcoming book on theistic ethics—the third in his trilogy (after *The Moral Gap* and *God's Command*)—is structured in a similar four-fold way: specifically, the unity we seek in life, with the creation or environment, with other people, and with God. And R. Scott Rodin's excellent book on the steward leader similarly couches the discussion in terms of four areas in which leaders foster robust health: in the self, with others, with creation, and with God. Categories of self and life might seem different, but since I see the biblical discourse of life primarily in terms of the abundant, kingdom life for which God designed each one of us, it seems to me that they are inextricably linked. So let's quickly canvass each in turn.

In terms of the self, and the sort of life for which we were made, there are three conceptually distinct aspects to our salvation. There is *justification*, which puts us right with God; this largely involves our forgiveness for falling short. C. S. Lewis said the key to understanding the universe resides in recognizing that there's a moral standard and that we fail to meet it. This introduces the need, first, for our forgiveness, and according to Christian theology God has made provision for our forgiveness in the death and resurrection of Jesus. The second dimension of salvation is *sanctification*, the gradual process by which we are not just forgiven, but actually changed and transformed into the likeness of Christ. This introduces what John Hare calls the performative dimension of moral apologetics—how we can cross the gap between the best we can do, morally speaking, and the moral standard. If we are obligated to meet the standard, but are unable to do so on our own, Augustine thought that this was to show us our need for God's grace to be changed. The culmination of salvation is *glorification*, the point at which, by God's grace, we are entirely conformed to the image of Christ; we are made perfect, altogether delivered from sin's power and consequences. Christian theology thus makes sense of our need for forgiveness, our need to be changed, and ultimately even our desire to be perfected.

Immanuel Kant's argument for the afterlife was predicated on his thinking that a "holy will" was the province of God's alone, and that it would forever reside beyond our reach. We would thus need eternity to approach it asymptotically (ever closer but never there)—because it's a process that will never be completed. He was both right and wrong, I think. Contra Kant, Christian theology says that we will indeed by God's grace be entirely conformed to the image of Christ, so there is a destination at which the regenerate will arrive. But I suspect he was right in an important sense to think of our eternal state as involving more of a dynamic picture than a static one. Once glorified, our growth won't cease; indeed, completion of "the good work within us" will mark the chance for us to live as we were fully intended with all the obstructions removed.

Sometimes there is debate over whether morality will go away in heaven. My guess is that morality in Kant's sense certainly will; talk of rights and duties will pass away. But they will be replaced by something far grander—gift and sacrifice, as George Mavrodes would say. Or think of rights and duties as the mere anteroom in a grand castle or cathedral that represents morality. Life in that place will be as it should be: life among its towering spires, where self-giving love is the norm. We are told, in fact, that the glory to come is something so wonderful we can scarcely imagine it.

Lewis sometimes likened the whole quest of morality to a fleet of ships. This fleet must consist of vessels that are individually seaworthy. It must function cooperatively, with all vessels navigating their ways without crashing into one another. And this fleet must have a destination. The first and third requirements—individual seaworthiness and reaching a destination—are closely connected to the individual's moral trajectory. By God's grace we are made seaworthy: we find forgiveness for our invariable shortcomings, grace to be radically transformed, grace by which to find meaning in life and our vocations of purpose, and grace ultimately to become the wholly distinctive expressions of Christ God designed us to be.

Lewis's middle requirement in the fleet example pertains to not bumping into others, and this is the second of the aforementioned four theological constraints. In fact, nowadays, morality is often deflated in the minds of many to pertain just to this feature of ethics, but in fact it is only one of the four parts. Morality rightly understood and practiced does indeed lead, in general, to more harmonious relations with others; this is one reason why Christ followers are called to be ministers of reconciliation. Indeed, this is arguably also part of the goal or telos of humanity: that the barriers of fellowship between people would be removed and we would learn to love another and forge deep relationships of mutual care with one another. Indeed, in Christian theology, after the most important commandment, which we'll get to in a moment, the second most important command is that we love our neighbors as ourselves. And we are pretty much told that we can't discharge the most important command without taking the neighbor-love command with dreadful seriousness. The communal aspects of sanctification remind us that the implications of morality are not a simply individualist affair; waging war on systemic evils, promoting justice, feeding the poor, opposition to slavery—all of these are aspects of the moral life expansively and communally construed. Paul Copan is especially effective at highlighting this historical dimension of the moral argument by chronicling a myriad of ways in which Christians have traditionally led the way in women's suffrage, building orphanages, opposing foot-binding, and the like.

In terms of the third theological category—unity with creation—two salient connections with moral apologetics immediately come to mind, namely, moral duties we have to care for the creation of which we have been made stewards, and treatment of animals as the sacred creatures they are. In his *Lectures on Ethics* Kant tried to spell out how our duties to animals are rooted in our obligations to fellow human beings, writing that if a man treats his dog well, regularly feeding and watering it and taking it for walks, this man is probably going to be kinder in his dealings with human persons. This is why Kant says, "We can judge the heart of a man by his treatment of animals…. Tender feelings towards dumb animals develop human feelings towards mankind."

Although that is likely true, I can't help but be a bit dissatisfied by this analysis alone. It seems sounder to say we have an obligation to God to treat his creation properly, which includes animals, and it's even more pressing we treat animals well because they are capable of feeling pain. It's almost become cliché to remind us all that dominion isn't domination. Intentionally and needlessly inflicting pain on animals, for example, is cruel disregard for God's creation— and a sin against God. We should care about the experience of animals and want them not to suffer needlessly, and not just for instrumental reasons. I count the inability of a number of naturalist accounts to justify believing we have obligations toward animals a deficiency—even if it's true that animals don't have rights (a question on which I'm currently agnostic).

Elsewhere I have repeatedly made it clear that I'm eminently open—with N. T. Wright, John Wesley, and C. S. Lewis—to the idea that we will see animals in heaven. It's not a nonnegotiable conviction of mine, but it's a reasonable inference, I think, if we take seriously the notion that the work of Christ redeemed the entirety of the created order, of which animals are a vital part. It is actually quite illuminating to peruse the full range of biblical teachings about the animals.

Fourthly, finally, and most centrally, Christian theology gives pride of place to reconciliation with God—and not just reconciliation, but a relationship of all-consuming love for and relationship of intimacy with God. Since there are principled reasons to think of the ultimate good in personalist terms (as nothing less than God himself) and the ultimate good *for us* in such terms as well (nothing less than the beatific vision), I can't help but think of the telos of humankind and the culmination of salvation in the Christian order of things through the lens of Goodness itself. The deontic family of terms, discourse about what's obligatory or permissible, might well pass away when all things are made new, but the Good and the Beautiful will be on full display and to be enjoyed forever. That Christianity teaches that the most important commandment of all— a necessary and eternal truth—is love of God with all of our heart and soul, mind and strength, puts this dimension, this unity, this relationship at the core of reality.

Morality here and now involves just the first, fledgling lessons in learning the dance steps of the Trinity. For this reason Lewis once wrote these words: "Mere *morality* is not the end of life. You were made for something quite different from that…. The people who keep on asking if they can't lead a decent life without Christ don't know what life is about; if they did they would know that 'a decent life' is mere machinery compared with the things we men are really made for. Morality is indispensable: but the Divine Life, which gives itself to us and which calls us to be gods, intends for us something in which morality will be swallowed up."

Friday, February 5, 2021: Went to the doctor's office early for my blood to be taken; appointment Tuesday next week. Then MB grabbed a little breakfast and then made in home on time for me to talk and pray with TJ. After that I finished Mary Mo's book, which was an enjoyable experience from cover to cover. Now I hope to write in my journal, prepare some discussion questions for Mary Jo, and grade some reflection papers for my online course.

The conversation with TJ was delightful, always is. Wanted to capture some of its aspects before they slip my mind. I had told him of the zoom session with Hare and his various students, including the personal nature of Hare's latest book. There's a bit of an irony regarding that, I think, since Hare's Calvinism seems to me and TJ to be more theoretical than practical, more formal than personal, more abstract than concrete. In this way it perhaps fits his persona as an aloof academic, but the new book is anything but that. It's intensely personal. It canvasses, or at least is motivated by, among other things, his relationship to his dad, the time he spent working for the US government, and his child's gender transition. TJ mentioned that the more personal something is to us, the better able we become to use passional reason, an integration of our heads and hearts. I definitely think John is moving in that direction in some areas. A personalist approach has lots of virtues; it's something we want to capture in the Center.

We also discussed my evening with Jerry and Rob, and the pitfalls of a belligerent social media presence in standing up for the truth. I definitely think Rob is talented and called to have an important voice in the public square, but I still can't help but think he could tone it down on occasion. At the same time, the time I spent with him challenged me to consider what public stances I'm willing to take, especially if they would cost me. I don't want to delude myself into thinking cowardice is commitment to being irenic.

TJ also mentioned that he's convinced my keeping this journal can function cathartically in my life. Sort of a pressure valve to release pent up energies as I continue to heal from my time at Liberty and launch into all that God has for us here.

He also mentioned one Daniel McCoy, a friend of his who wrote his dissertation on Buddhist ethics and Christianity. Perhaps this may be a project we will consider at the Press.

Finally, regarding the gender stuff Hare's working through, we came to a shared conclusion that there are some difficult questions and messy situations that aren't always easy to work through here. And that's okay. We should be reconciled to acknowledging some messiness. A good line in the last pages of Mary Jo's book read, "The answers on this side of resurrection are going to be messy." Undeniably certain nonnegotiables and absolutes exist, but we probably delude ourselves when we think that every question admits of easily accessible, tidy answers. I suspect, though, that the popularity of some is largely attributable to their adeptness at projecting the impression that there are.

Mary Jo ends her book by encouraging folks to tell their own stories. I suppose this journal I'm keeping is, in its own (unwieldy and tedious) way, doing just that.

Saturday, February 6, 2021: Didn't accomplish a great deal today. After getting up early and listening to scripture, I was feeling rather tired. So after I chatted with Elton and MB and I hung out for a while we decided to take a nap, and mine extended longer than usual. By the time I got up I could only work a little while before shifting gears to Jerry's visit tonight. He usually comes on Friday, but we changed it up this week. Among the few things I did today, besides laundry, was I gave some thought to the chapters I need to write for my book with Ronnie Campbell on philosophical theology. My chapters cover faith and reason (including setting the tone of the book with a God-as-good motif); creation, fall, redemption; evil, hell, and suffering; and heaven, resurrection, and the future. I generated a few more questions to ask Mary Jo in our upcoming podcast, and I also came up with a few ideas of what I can talk about on Monday for the Ratio Christi meeting on the moral argument. I suspect I'll talk about the performative variant of the moral argument. Father—Son—Spirit; Adams on guilt; stuff from WB piece on guilt; justification; transformation/sanctification/Holy Spirit; quote Oswalt; social transformation; Habermas and Copan; glorification and Kant. I'll try to write this out by Monday and then I'll include that here in the journal. Tonight: salmon and *Casablanca*. (As it happened, before quitting work, MB and I were able to effect a few revisions on our Lasso blog; hopefully we're getting close.)

Sunday, February 7, 2021: Largely rested today except for some work MB and I did to bring home the final version of the Lasso blog. We also watched several episodes of *The Morning Show*, which is rife with fascinating observations about the human condition: appearances versus reality, journalism versus entertainment, dangers of self-deception, and more. Some gripping television!

Here's our final draft of Lasso:

Why We Need *Ted Lasso and Philosophy*

The growing popularity of Apple TV's *Ted Lasso* is a bit of a surprise, given its inauspicious beginnings as a satirical NBC Sports promotion back in 2013. Premiering last August, this breakout hit has now garnered two Golden Globe nominations—for the show and lead actor—and has continued gaining fame through word of mouth.

But those who have watched the show, featuring biscuits-with-the-boss and exorcisms of training rooms, will find its defiance of expectations more than fitting. Like a candy bar little Ronnie Fouch might offer you on the playground, it is so much more than meets the eye.

Ted Lasso is a comedy about a cheerful, charming, and eminently optimistic amateur American football coach (played by SNL alum Jason Sudeikis) enlisted to coach AFC Richmond, a professional soccer ("football") team in England—the land of garbage water, hazardous street crossings, boots and chips and crisps. Along with his friend and sidekick, the aptly named Coach Beard, Ted embraces the challenge with characteristic enthusiasm. The game, like the grass on the pitch, is "the same yet different."

"A metaphor?" Beard asks.

"You know it, baby," Ted replies. The quip, we soon learn, has serious implications, as the show challenges viewers to look beyond surface differences and misleading appearances that too often divide or prove destructive.

For a show in so many ways easy to watch—usually light and lots of fun—*Ted Lasso* features far more nuance, depth, and philosophical resonance than one might expect. The nature of true success, sportsmanship, revenge versus justice, the importance of friendship, the imperative of respect for persons, humility, leadership, identity, virtue ethics, courage, journalistic ethics, and what love looks like: these are all topics broached by the show, and a whole lot more.

David French is particularly struck by the forgiveness motif, particularly Ted's forgiveness of team owner Rebecca—played by the enchanting and magnificently talented actress/singer Hannah Waddingham (known for her role as the Wicked Witch of the West both in London and on Broadway). For Michaela Flack, a different aspect of Ted's character comes to the fore. As she puts it, Ted believes in you.

This issue of *belief* functions as a central motif of the show, a notoriously rich philosophical concept. What exactly constitutes belief? What we honestly assent to verbally? What our actions reveal? Our dispositions? Can we believe a proposition without accepting it, or vice versa? Fine questions all, but the show usually approaches belief from the angle of "believing in" oneself or others.

Ted is adamant about believing in the best of people, without being blind to corruption or cruelty. Facing much resistance, even from his own team members, Ted is undaunted. Early on, in response to Captain Roy Kent's meanspirited barbs, Ted confides in Beard, "If he's mad now, wait until we win him over." Beard offers a signature cryptic reply: "He'll be furious." The question is not *if*, but *when*.

Ted is an unpretentious, easy-to-underestimate coach who has a singular brilliance for building community, and he cares about more than winning. In his unorthodoxy and prodigious emotional intelligence, he refuses to think of sports as a zero-sum game. He thinks of winning in terms other than scoring more than the opponent, and sees his job as helping his players become the best versions of themselves on and off the field. His coaching style is as holistic and his personality as winsome as his character is wholesome.

Watching Ted is a little like watching Mister Rogers as a soccer coach—an intentional decision by Sudeikis—and how can you go wrong with that? From the first episode, the importance of believing in oneself is on full display. This took a quiet self-assurance and laudable courage in the face of chronic condescension and a chorus of derogatory epithets from "wanker" to "Ronald McDonald."

In the locker room Ted posts a sign emblazoned "BELIEVE," and when asked if he believes in ghosts, Ted immediately replies, to Rebecca's stymied response of incomprehension, "I do. But more importantly they need to believe in themselves."

This playful equivocation on *belief-that* and *belief-in* brings to mind a funny exchange from our friend Jonny Walls' movie script <u>Couch Survivor</u>: one character, hoping for a bit of affirmation, asks another, "Do you believe in me?"

"Of course!" comes the gentle, sympathetic reply. "But I can also see you."

Some might suppose that *believing in* another person, or a particular outcome, or oneself, is more a psychological matter than a philosophical one, but we suspect this is a rather false dichotomy. William James, for example, had a penchant for sharing insights with both philosophical and psychological import. In his discussion of "precursive faith," he challenged the notion that all of our beliefs need to be based on adequate prior evidence. Precursive faith, as he understood it, involves believing *ahead of* the evidence, which on occasion seems permissible, even important.

Take social coordination cases, where a group acting in unison (and only acting in unison) can, say, stop a single terrorist (or, to use his example, train robber). Such united action requires boldly acting without the assurance of cooperation ahead of time.

Or in the logic of personal relations, we often recognize the need to function as more than strict evidentialists. Starting romantic relationships, for example, may require taking an initiative to grow a relationship before knowing for sure that our advances will be reciprocated.

Such dynamics remind us of the need to qualify our accounts of belief—and what justified beliefs call for—depending on the nature of the context. This certainly has psychological implications, but it is also interesting for philosophers.

Some of the best examples of James's precursive faith come from sports. AFC Richmond's believing in themselves, that they stood a chance against Everton, despite their decades-long track record of losses against them, is just such an example. To have a chance at winning, a team may well have to believe they can do it, on at least some level or to at least some small degree—and believe before having decisive evidence that they can. Such "belief" will not ensure the desired result, but it may well be needed for its very possibility.

Such *belief in* is closely related to *hope*, one of the classical theological virtues, another recurring theme of the show. Rather than embracing the pessimistic mantra cynically repeated by Richmond's fans that "it's the hope that kills you"—and thus lowering expectations and expecting the worst—Ted's irrepressible optimism retains faith in faith and soaring hope, a hope that may or may not disappoint. Soccer, like life itself, involves risk, and to avoid risk by not playing is too steep a price to pay.

Those are just a few of the many rich philosophical dimensions of a show that, of all years, came out in 2020, a rather ignominious moment, most would agree. When anti-intellectualism and public acrimony, rampant pessimism and ubiquitous grudges held sway, a show like this was just the countercultural antidote we needed.

Like Ted would say, it's like we fell through a lucky tree, hit every limb, and landed in a pile of money and Sour Patch Kids.

Monday, February 8, 2021: Today was a pretty good day. I gave a talk on the moral argument via zoom to HBU's Ratio Christi. It was fun that my old pal Mark Foreman showed up—on a Monday night, appropriately enough, when we used to always get together for dinner and a movie. Here are the notes I jotted down in preparation; it has a few new aspects, but it's largely a collation of previous work in different places:

The Moral Argument(s)

Pleasure to be here with you today. Thanks for taking the time out of your schedules to learn a little more about the moral argument. It's an argument that's been a source of encouragement and fascination to me for quite a number of years now, and I'm happy to talk a little about it today. You may know that one of the reasons I came to HBU was to start a Center for Moral Apologetics—a whole Center dedicated to equipping students with the tools and resources of the moral argument. What we envision is making HBU a central hub of research on all things related to the moral argument—arguments for moral objectivity, arguments defending theistic ethics against a variety of objections, critiques of secular efforts to make full sense of morality, the rich history of the moral argument, extending the moral argument beyond generic theism to Christianity specifically, explorations of the relative adequacy or lack thereof of nonChristian religious ethical foundations, the devotional and spiritual formational aspects of moral apologetics, exploration of resonances between moral apologetics and Christian theology; and so on. In time we hope to generate curricula for home schoolers, for churches, for chaplains, for Christian schools; we run the website MoralApologtics.com and we'll be starting a new website through HBU on the Center for Moral Apologetics; we put out a bimonthly newsletter; you can write me and I'll let you know how you can sign up for that. We hope in time to offer scholarships for folks who want to become premier moral apologists, lectures and conferences, a Certificate program in moral apologetics is in the middle of getting established now, and lots more, including a physical space eventually at the university where students and scholars can come and visit; we'll have places people can work, and talk, and a library of relevant resources, files of materials on the moral argument, and so on. We are excited about the possibilities, and I'm very happy to be here at HBU to get it underway. In May WLC and I will be co-teaching a course on the moral argument; I hope to see some of you there; should be lots of fun.

Before I begin, do you have any questions about the Center? (4 classes corresponding to 4 books with Jerry Walls.)

So when I say "the moral argument," I'm using that phrase in a general sort of way. In truth there's more than one moral argument. There's a whole range of them; or, I suppose, if you prefer, you can think of one moral argument with lots of different parts. At least most of the time that works since the different variants of the argument tend to be rather consistent with one another. The specific formulation of the argument I'll look at today is what I'll call the "performative" version of the moral argument, but again, as I say, you can give lots of other versions of the argument. One reason I chose to go in this direction today is because it lends itself to drawing some connections to Christian theology, which I thought might be a worthwhile thing to do.

Do y'all remember in Book 1 of *Mere Christianity* what C. S. Lewis says are the two things that are at the heart of our understanding of reality? He says, first, there's a moral law, and second, that we all fall short of it. That's a good place to start to lay out the version of the moral argument I'll discuss today. There's a moral standard that's objective and universal, and it's binding and authoritative on us, and we invariably fall short of meeting it. This results in what John Hare calls a "gap" between the best we can do and what morality requires. And this gap needs addressing. How can we close it? We find ourselves as having fallen short, and we know it. And we recognize we've got a problem on our hands.

How do we know we've got a moral problem on our hands? One way, you might say, is by our moral sense, which even plenty of secular thinkers recognize as in some way significant. Take Charles Darwin, for example, who thought it's our moral sense that best distinguishes human beings from the animals. Indeed he begins chapter 5 of *Descent of Man* with this admission: "I fully subscribe to the judgment of those writers who maintain that of all the differences between man and the lower animals, the moral sense or conscience is by far the most important." He even says he considers the moral sense, our sense of "ought," to be "humankind's finest quality." Elsewhere in the same book he casts both "ought" and "disinterested love for all living creatures" as the noblest attribute of man.

Darwin intuitively felt the importance of morality, even if he ended up embracing a deflationary analysis of its import. Similarly with Sigmund Freud. To Freud's thinking, the problem of guilt is so severe that he diagnosed it in *Civilization and Its Discontents* as the single most important development of civilization—a problem so acute that it is the thing most responsible for our unhappiness. Perhaps what helps explain Freud's conviction is that what he found in his analytic work, to his surprise, was that nearly every neurosis conceals an unconscious sense of guilt, which in turn "fortifies the symptoms by making use of them as punishment."

For both Darwin and Freud, the phenomenon of guilt was both interesting and important, even revelatory. Recall their depictions: Darwin thought our capacity for experiencing the moral sense and a painful conscience is by far the most important distinction between us and the animals, and our sense of ought and disinterested love for all creatures is the noblest virtue of man. And Freud took the problem of guilt to be the single most important development of civilization. But they mistook its import, I suspect, embracing reductionist analyses and taking guilt itself as the essential problem, rather than the deeper malady of which guilt is but the symptom. Rightly construed guilt is semiotic, pointing beyond itself.

That we intuitively sense there to be a moral standard of which we fall short leaves us with a condition of guilt in need of fixing. And if we take our feelings of guilt as more than *mere* feelings, and something like a real objective condition of guilt, we're left wondering if there's a solution. We need forgiveness for having fallen short of the moral standard—and not just falling short in the past, but continuing to fall short all the time. Forgiveness is a basic existential human need.

I rather doubt Freud was wrong about guilt creating quite a bit of unhappiness, which makes it understandable that our secular friends see the need to deal with it and usually by trying to deny that we're really guilty. Unaddressed guilt eats us up. And sometimes people do have an overactive superego and feel guilty for all sorts of things that they're not really guilty of. But at other times, most of us intuitively recognize, our guilt isn't a mistake, but a real insight into ourselves. We don't need our guilt explained away, in those cases, but taken away, forgiven.

And of course this is one way that the moral argument serves as the perfect segueway to the gospel of Christ—indeed we have fallen short, and are in need of forgiveness. And God offers us that forgiveness. Not only, then, does God offer us forgiveness, we as his forgiven children can extend forgiveness to others. This is why it's so imperative we maintain a stance of forgiveness toward our neighbors, modeling the grace God has shown us. And of course you all recognize this broaches the whole theological topic of justification.

So you might wish to approach this philosophically—talking about guilt and our need for forgiveness, and then showing how philosophy leads you to the brink of theology. Or start with a theological discussion of justification, and then show how it comports with what we learned from our moral experience and what we might call general revelation. Or take the deliverances of theology like justification and use insights from moral apologetics to spell out part of what's going on—that's doing philosophical theology. All sorts of ways to discuss this, depending on your interests and your audience.

So now let's move on from the issue of forgiveness, because we're still left with the moral gap—the best we can do and what morality requires. We need more than our sins to be forgiven; we need our sin to be taken away. A documentary concerning the issue of nutrition and physical health I saw a few years ago made several interesting points that are relevant here by way of analogy. One of its initially startling claims is that doctors do not really produce health. About the best they can do is remove some barriers that impede and stand in the way of health. What actually produces health is the properly functioning body—a healthy immune system, a body, properly treated and fed, doing what it was meant to do.

This is most clearly seen when it comes to chronic diseases. Doctors and pharmaceutical companies cannot fix such problems; the best they can do is provide medicines that help alleviate and manage certain symptoms and make life more comfortable for the patient, even while the affliction persists. Although medical practitioners are rather limited in what they are able to do, the body is remarkably resilient in its ability to ward off diseases, recover from various injuries, and heal itself. This is why proper nutrition and exercise are so important, because they enable the body to do what it does best. Chronically undernourished or sedentary bodies eventually become impaired in their ability to perform their proper functions.

The point of the documentary was well made: there is a crucial difference between genuine health, on the one hand, and merely treating conditions, on the other, however much a blessing the latter can be. Another fitting analogy would be the distinction between pulling out a dandelion versus killing its root.

A similar distinction holds in the arena of morality. One option is merely to deal with symptoms, settling for marginal moral improvements, avoiding hurtful consequences by our actions. True achievement of integrity, virtue, and holiness, though, requires considerably more. In light of what seem to be some deeply entrenched patterns of selfishness and moral weakness endemic to the human condition, we need profound resources to meet the moral demand and effect the needed change in our character.

Benjamin Franklin once tried to do this on his own, setting himself to the formidable task of achieving moral perfection. In "Arriving at Perfection," an excerpt from his *Autobiography*, he wrote about his plans to conquer all imperfections that either natural inclination, custom, or company might lead him into, but "I soon found I had undertaken a task of more difficulty than I had imagined. While my care was employ'd in guarding against one fault, I was often surprised by another; habit took the advantage of inattention; inclination was sometimes too strong for reason."

Immanuel Kant, like Lewis, recognized that we fall short of what morality requires, and so he said we need to have moral faith: the belief that the moral life is *possible*. But in light of our moral malady, this requires radical transformation. Can we be transformed? This is a second great existential moral need, after forgiveness. Perhaps as a vestige of his Lutheran upbringing, Kant was quite sure that human beings have a deep moral problem, a tendency to be curved inward on themselves, an intractable ethical taint, a deeply flawed moral disposition in need of a revolution. Kant saw clearly that the moral demand on us is very high, while also recognizing that we have a natural propensity not to follow it.

{Babylonbee laugh.} A famous line from Malcolm Muggeridge says that depravity of man is at once the most empirically verifiable reality but at the same time the most intellectually resisted fact.

In both Kant and Lewis, the suggestion seems to be not just that we happen to fail to meet the moral demand, but that our failure is inevitable. We have a problem, one too deep for us to solve on our own. Humans are not essentially good. We are broken, deeply broken. Like Clay Jones says, all of us are born Auschwitz-enabled—the people responsible for the atrocities of history weren't particularly bad people; they were garden variety human beings who, when certain circumstances presented themselves, behaved deplorably. There's something in need of fixing deep within us. We need radical surgery.

But of course there is soaring hope, even without sugarcoating our brokenness. Christianity says the needed resources for transformation are available. Although we can't meet the moral demand on our own, God himself has made it possible, if we but submit and allow Him to do it through us. It will require a painful process, but it is possible.

Having started his book *Mere Christianity* with talk of the moral gap between what we are and what we ought to be, Lewis then explained his reason for doing so, and his explanation is a telling one. The passage is his concluding paragraph of Book 1 and it goes like this:

> My reason was that Christianity simply does not make sense until you have faced the sort of facts I have been describing. Christianity tells people to repent and promises them forgiveness. … It is after you have realized that there is a real Moral Law, and a Power behind the law, and that you have broken that law and put yourself wrong with that Power— it is after all this, and not a moment sooner, that Christianity begins to talk. When you know you are sick, you will listen to the doctor. When you have realized that our position is nearly desperate you will begin to understand what the Christians are talking about. They offer an

explanation of how we got into our present state of both hating goodness and loving it. They offer an explanation of how God can be this impersonal mind at the back of the Moral Law and yet also a Person. They tell you how the demands of this law, which you and I cannot meet, have been met on our behalf, how God Himself becomes a man to save man from the disapproval of God.

God can do more than merely ameliorate the symptoms of our chronic moral malady. In the face of our urgent need to become not just *better* men, but *new* men, for a revolution of the will, for radical moral transformation, the death and resurrection of Christ is indeed "good news." Of course this issue of transformation you'll recognize as the theological category of sanctification. So just as justification answers our need for forgiveness, God's grace in sanctification answers our need for radical moral transformation.

By the way, biblical holiness is not just *individual*, but *social*. And here one like Paul Copan has done us a great service by bringing a historical twist to the moral argument. He's shown how historically it's been Christ followers who were largely responsible for such significant social advances as building orphanages, arguing for the inherent dignity of the handicapped and infirmed, fighting for women's suffrage, standing against footbinding, and so forth. This gets into historical and empirical matters, a little outside my wheelhouse, but it's a neat thing to consider, and there have been several books written on this topic. It also brings to mind John Wesley's refrain that there's no holiness without social holiness.

Finally to wrap up—we have a deep need for forgiveness and transformation, but for something else too. Not just to be radically transformed, but for the process to culminate. For the good work that's begun within to be completed. And of course now we're talking about the Christian category of glorification, when we are entirely conformed to the image of Jesus. This answers to a deep intuitive recognition of a third basic moral drive or need, or maybe aspiration—yet one, once more, beyond the reach of our own capacities without divine grace—the hunger to be perfected, turned into the best versions of ourselves, delivered entirely from the power and consequences of sin. And Christianity assures this is no Pollyannaish pipe dream, but a reality we can look forward to with hope.

The last thing I want to say goes back to the first topic of guilt. Just as we share the good news that by God's grace guilt need not be the final word, because there is forgiveness and transformation available, we ourselves, as believers, need to be continually reminded that God's grace is available for us as well. There is no condemnation for those in Christ Jesus, despite our many stumbles in our earthly trek and travail. Far too many Christians, in my experience, seem needlessly riddled with guilt for falling short and weighed down by feelings of spiritual or ethical inadequacy. Real guilt can and should lead us to repent, of course, but then we can and must walk in the freedom and forgiveness that God graciously bestows. Merely stewing in guilt for its own sake is worse than indulgent, predicated on the ridiculous subtext that our standards are higher than God's.

So please take this to heart and let this sink in: the same truths that we proclaim to our unbelieving friends, truths that liberate and speak to their deepest needs, are also the same truths that still speak to our own deepest needs. God's grace is still sufficient for us. God's love is still greater than our sin. We can still be filled with a hope that won't disappoint. God still wishes to do unique good works through each one of us. God can still empower us to live as we ought. God can still change us into the people he wants us to be, despite however many times we have fallen. We are still infinitely valuable, and not only does God still love each and every one of us, he even likes us.

One of the issues that came up during discussion (from Riz) was the way guilt isn't thought of in Japan the same way it is in the west. This is an interesting issue that needs further exploration. Perhaps it's a project we can undertake at the Center. This sort of east versus west issue has arisen before. Ben Galindo mentioned the book *Misreading Scripture with Western Ideas*, which I should read. I suspect much of the purchase of the moral argument can be salvaged employing categories of shame instead of guilt, but it's an issue I need to think about some more.

Tuesday, February 9, 2021: A student who attended last night's talk wrote me today with ideas about a new moral argument. It's heavier on metaphysics than I'm accustomed to, but here it is (his name is Nathan):

I don't recall if I mentioned yesterday that I have been working on my own argument. I am more than happy to share it! This preliminary argument of mine has three parts which begin by subsuming moral goodness under love, and working out how that infers a personal source:

P1: If moral goodness is derivative from love, then love is the foundation of moral realism.
P2: Moral goodness is derivative from love.
C1: Hence, love is the foundation of moral realism.

P3: Love is a state of intentionality.
P4: Intentionality has its ontological basis in consciousness.
C2: Therefore, love has its ontological basis in consciousness.

P5: Moral realism is true.
P6: Moral realism does not derive from contingent minds.
P7: Consciousness is a property of mind.

P8: Since the foundation of moral realism is love, and love is ontologically based in consciousness,
C3: From this, it follows, moral realism derives from a non-contingent mind.

Here are some implications I've considered regarding this metaethical argument:

1). Morality ultimately derives from a Mind (or, at least, a 'Mind-like' source?).
2). Since this Mind is not contingent, it exists necessarily. And, is arguably not materially based since physical matter is plausibly contingent. Hence, it's immaterial.
3). This Mind has, at least, two centers of consciousness since love involves the existence of the 'other'.

I have been considering the possibility of whether this Mind might have three centers of consciousness rather than simply two. The reasoning goes as follows:

Let's call non-derivative love, 'primal love'. Since primal love is fundamental and non-contingent, whatever possible manifestations it can exhibit on a fundamental level, it will exhibit. What are the possible manifestations of primal love? At least two are reciprocation and cooperation. Two subjects are sufficient to instantiate reciprocal love. Cooperative love, on the other hand, involves love to, or towards, 'another' by at least two subjects. Let's consider two *imaginable* worlds:

W1: Only two subjects, *S1* and *S2*, exist in a reciprocal relationship.
W2: Subjects *S1* and *S2* direct their love towards subject *S3*, but *S1* and *S2* do not reciprocate love towards each other.

Both worlds describe two distinct manifestations of primal love. W1 does not involve the form of cooperative love of W2, and W2 does not involve the reciprocation of W1. However, as mentioned above, since primal love is non-contingent, it will manifest all possible aspects of fundamental love. This will involve a combination of the loving relations in W1 and W2:

W3: *S1* and *S2* are in a reciprocal relationship and are involved in a cooperative relation towards *S3*.

As mentioned above, two subjects are necessary and sufficient to instantiate reciprocal love. With regards to cooperative love, three subjects are both necessary and sufficient. Can it be argued that S3 must also engage in a reciprocal relationship with both S1 and S2? Perhaps? I have an idea of a possible answer, but what I have tried to argue so far is that this Mind, which is the source of Love, has at least three centers of consciousness.

So that's my argument in a nutshell. I'm most confident about the second part of my argument (P3-C2). This is based on the growing literature among philosophers of mind who within the past few years have argued for the plausibility of grounding representational states (including intentional states) in phenomenal consciousness. I find myself in this camp as well.

I'm not as confident in the first part however (P1-C1). A problem might arise if there's a contrast between love and justice. Both are arguable goods, but how would justice be subsumed under love? I know Kevin Kinghorn makes some insightful comments on this issue. I also plan to eventually look into Wolterstorff's book *Justice in Love* to gain better insight.

So that's what I have for now Dr. Baggett!

God bless!

Wednesday, February 10, 2021: Very productive day. I wrote some folks familiar with Chinese culture and asked them about the guilt/shame question. I read a lot of Swinburne's *Existence of God* in preparation of grading discussion boards. Appreciate his distinction between P-inductive and C-inductive arguments! I also read and commented on the last two chapters of Jordan's dissertation. He's getting close.

Here's what one of my friends said about the guilt question: "Anyway, one book is called *Biblical Encounter with Japanese Culture* by Charles Corwin from 1967, but there's probably newer books. One thing I would try to explain about sin is that it's not just external actions or 'crimes', but sin is an internal mindset. Sin begins with the mind, the heart, our thoughts. Japanese people are very good at hiding their true thoughts and feelings and they think if they just act good or appropriately that they are 'sinless'. But Christ came to cleanse our hearts and free our minds, hearts from evil, selfish, sin. That's how I remember explaining guilt...that it's our inner selfish and lack of love and forgiveness that God sees, even if no one else can see it. You might be able to hide the truth of your sin from everyone else, but you can't hide it from God. Hope that helps."

I received an e-mail again about the need for more residential students in the apologetics programs. I find this a tad trying, as it raises the specter or Liberty's modus operandi—unreasonable demands on faculty to do what it isn't their job to do. I'm trying to follow the lead of the *Steward Leader* book and not get derailed from trusting God and getting my marching orders from him—for the classes, the Center, for HBU, etc.

Thursday, February 11, 2021: Today's off to a good start. Hope to read more Swinburne, grade the DB's, and I've already gotten started reviewing a manuscript for IVP called *Atheism on Trial*, written by a lawyer. Just a few pages in but liking it a lot.

I quit working around 3:30 in the afternoon. Have about 20 pages left of Swinburne to read before grading the DB's, but I've grown weary from working for the day. Yesterday was an unusually long work day and I feel like I'm still recovering a bit from it. MB doesn't seem too much into her work today; perhaps she and I can spend some time together, which would be good.

Friday, February 12, 2021: Very productive day! Wrote 1000 words in the fourth book of the tetralogy; finished reading Swinburne; graded discussion boards and wrote the class a longish e-mail; made progress on the IVP book I'm reviewing and Fraser's chapter; attended an interview with Phil for the deanship; and now I'm getting ready for Jerry to come over for the evening. Getting started at 1:30 in the morning certainly helped. Feeling a tad ragged, but not too bad considering. TJ's been diagnosed with covid for the second time. Likewise our friend Ginny from LU. Prayers needed for these dear folks! I asked Phil a few questions at the interview: besides theological liberalism, what other vulnerabilities might HBU have? And does he sometimes fall prey to the temptation to think in terms of solving problems in his own strength? I encouraged those there to read Rodin's excellent book on steward leadership.

Saturday, February 13, 2021: Woke up very early, too early, so decided to fit in some work. It's currently just after 5 am and I've made some progress on the IVP book I'm reviewing. Hope before long to get drowsy again and catch some more shut-eye. The IVP book by the lawyer isn't bad, but needs some editing and could use to take on better atheistic arguments. Seems a bit preoccupied with low-hanging fruit. I suspect the book would have benefited quite a bit had the author teamed up with a philosopher to write it.

Sunday, February 14, 2021: Woke up early in the morning and spent time praying and listening to scripture, then went back to bed but couldn't sleep. A few thoughts kept recurring, so I got up and wrote this e-mail to Phil Tallon:

Hey Phil!

I don't typically work on Sunday, but I woke up this morning with some ideas I'd like to pass along.

First, I thought you did a terrific job in the interview the other day. I'm sure you're the one for this deanship, and I can't think of anyone better.

I appreciated your answers to the various questions, including mine. My experience at Liberty gives me a bit of a different perspective on occasion, I imagine. I don't think we should ever think, "Yeah, we've got plenty enough of students," but what happened at Liberty was a real shame. There was something rapacious and ravenous about their desire for bigger and bigger profits, and it was altogether acidic to morale. In lots of ways they really seemed to lose their way. Over time, the better they did financially, the more deleterious it was spiritually and academically. There was great emphasis on never "going liberal," but they got off track in all sorts of other ways—like inordinate love of money. I don't anticipate such a thing happening at HBU, but it can't help but come to mind occasionally. I mean, with a two billion dollar endowment, veritably flush with cash, they discontinued the philosophy department because it wasn't lucrative enough. That is seriously messed up. Here's something I published on it a while back: https://worldviewbulletin.substack.com/p/the-business-of-a-university

Anyway, as I say, thanks for taking my questions seriously, and I am praying for God's will in this dean decision. I suspect it's you! Know I'll always be in your corner.

But the main thing I wanted to tell you about was this: I'd mentioned to you that one of our initiatives is that we've started Moral Apologetics Press, and we're putting out about our fourth or fifth book at this point. We went through a bunch of hoops, purchasing ISBN numbers and the whole shot. We have done a couple of Screwtape Letter-like books, published my journal from 2020 chronicling that portion of the history of the Center (I'm planning on doing that every year, writing a bit each day), and a few more books are in the pipeline. Marybeth and I have noticed that between us we have about 30 pieces on popular culture, so we're thinking of getting relevant permissions and publishing the collection as something like Moral Apologetics and Popular Culture with the press, all proceeds going directly into the Center.

This morning I was in bed thinking and praying and something dawned on me. I wonder if HBU would be interested in starting HBU Press. They could basically take over Moral Apologetics Press, and perhaps it could generate a revenue stream for the school. Seems to me that we could start a series like "Apologetics and Popular Culture," along the lines of the Phil and Pop Culture series—and HBU could benefit financially. I think it could both do good and make money.

Anyway, that was my main thought this morning I wanted to share with you. HBU Press! I'd be interested in your thoughts.

Blessings,

Bag

Monday, February 15, 2021: Productive but weird day. Record low temps; water is out, has been all day. Lots in the area have lost power, though we haven't. Jerry Walls lost power but hasn't responded to our invitation to come stay with us. Despite the craziness I had a productive day—writing my class the Monday e-mail; reading a chapter in Swinburne; reading a chapter of the IVP book; reading a few sections in Fraser's chapter.

The IVP book has lots of potential, but strikes me, when doing moral apologetics, as overly zealous and ambitious at points. It's not that he's wrong, necessarily, but I question the rhetorical wisdom of some of his approaches.

The whole day, at any rate, had a weird and surreal feel to it. Today was the due date for the updates from the Moral Apologetics team for the upcoming newsletter. And oh, paperback copies came of Elton's *Ichabod* Letters and Melton's *Knockturn*. Both look good. Melton is pressing us on what we're going to do by way of promotion. Jonathan wrote this in reply: "My marketing strategy at the moment has two main elements. We would offer to send review copies to influential people in the sphere of apologetics/literature/philosophy. The idea here is that folks would review it and post it on social media or their own blog to raise awareness of the book. The other strategy would be more traditional marketing. We are planning to run paid advertisements on Facebook and other places."

Tuesday, February 16, 2021: Today was a very challenging day. The water remained off at the house, though we never lost our electricity. But lots of people lost one or both, including Jerry Walls, who lost both. Robert Gagnon lost his electricity, and so needed to find a warm place to stay. The night before he stayed at a neighbor's of Phil Tallon's, but then they lost their heat in the middle of the night. So he came over our place today and will be staying the night tonight. Jerry had a pipe burst later in the day, so he has that to contend with. Despite all the craziness, I was able to read through another chapter in the IVP book. We had good conversation and fellowship with Rob in the late afternoon and evening. I still need to look at some sections of Fraser's chapter, then head to bed. Crazy times we're living in!

Wednesday, February 17, 2021: Today I worked hard and finished up the IVP book. I think it's a good book. Written by a lawyer, it has a number of insights that comes from his background. I did think, though, that at points it would have benefited by greater exposure to the philosophical literature. On other fronts, we had a leak in the house from the bad weather that caused the ceiling in a closet to collapse. Contacting the insurance now to see if we may be able to get our expenses in a hotel covered while the repairs are done. For the third or fourth day running, we have no running water in the house. I got an invitation to do a podcast on some philosophical comedy show, which I'm happy to do, but I'd prefer to wait until after things settle here. In reply to a friend's question about it all, I wrote, "Very cold, for here, but the place just isn't able to handle it. Things are not insulated properly, the energy grid is vulnerable (doesn't help that TX has its own and is outside a number of federal regulations), water system easily vulnerable once pipes start bursting, etc. Just a mess down here. They need to fix a number of infrastructural issues and pervading mentalities to address this stuff, I imagine."

Thursday, February 18, 2021: Gagnon stayed a second night, and we enjoyed a fund morning of food and fellowship. Then MB and I were determined to find a hotel, in desperate need of a shower. Tried contacting numerous plumbers but so far to no avail. Started reading Peter Kreeft's *Between Heaven and Hell* in earnest to do a blurb for a reissue through IVP. We ended up staying at a Sleep Inn in Stafford. Over the next few days we've got to get our pipe fixed and our water back up and running in the house. Water is a nonnegotiable, easily taken for granted.

Friday, February 19, 2021: Up early at the hotel, I was able to text back and forth a great deal with my sister Sandra. It was fun as we did a lot of reminiscing about various matters, including some childhood memories—like waking up in TN when visiting our grandmother to the smell of eggs and sausage and biscuits. It is with only a few in this world I share such precious memories, and of those few, it's only Sandra I'm likely to talk much about them. We agreed, once covid has passed, to meet up at the Grand Ole Opry. Our parents used to talk about going there but never did. Two-day drive for me, but much shorter for Sandra. This ice storm, I saw on the news, is likely to be the single biggest insurance event in Texas. On top of covid, it continues to fill the air with the feel of the apocalypse. We skated through relatively unscathed, despite the broken pipe and collapsed closet ceiling. Lots of others had it quite a bit worse. The morning also began with an encouraging note from an old student who had enjoyed the Kant chapter in the history of the moral argument book; a nice way to start the day! Words of encouragement, affirmation, and appreciation buoy spirits and sustain the soul. Later in the day we figured out how to turn off the water heater, and was able to have Jerry over for a Friday night dinner and movie—after we were able to stock up with water.

Saturday, February 20, 2021: Our efforts to procure water today have not been particularly successful, but it does look likely a plumber should show up before long, maybe as soon as tomorrow. We're heading out near the Woodlands this afternoon for me to get my first vaccine shot. Older than MB, I'm getting mine first, it would appear. We may just stay at a hotel out near there rather than coming home. A shower will be nice, and perhaps we can have a relaxing time. No running water really makes everything so much harder—kitchen cleanup, the dishwashing, running toilets, showering, etc. MB and I are hoping and praying that the lessons of all this challenge and discomfort—which for us is mild by comparison to the suffering of many others—won't be lost on us. Among them greater sensitivity to the plight of the poor, more gratitude for our many blessings, and the like.

The chat with Elton this morning was good. Among the insights was an application from *Pride and Prejudice*: Darcy and Elizabeth often misjudge one another, thinking they know more about each other than they do. We can easily make the same mistake about God, thinking we know more about him than we do. Another was an aphoristic way to capture I Cor 13: loveless words have no power; loveless knowledge has no meaning; loveless belief has no saving power; loveless giving has no benefits. Elton and I also discussed book promotion, since that's an issue that will be on increasing importance for Moral Apologetics Press.

Sunday, February 21, 2021: We spent the night in Spring, Texas, catching dinner at a small local rural-feeling restaurant. Nice night away. Home now, nearly 2 in the afternoon. Hopefully the plumber will be here soon and we can get our water fixed. Really need to get beyond this; everything's harder without water. We've been relaxing a bit by watching a show called "Billions." Though just a show, it captures the elevated view of money many have, and we're all tempted to have. It brought to mind on our drive home the fundraising I need to do for the Center. Oh, how I wish I just had the money myself to give to the Center. Having to motivate others to give is so utterly outside my wheelhouse and comfort zone, quintessential awkwardness. I shared this with Marybeth, but she suggested I remember what we often remind ourselves of—our money is God's, not ours. And that goes, too, for those I'll try to encourage to give. Perhaps God's Spirit is already at work within them, priming them to give.

It is now past 6 in the evening and the plumber has yet to arrive, which is disappointing. But on a positive note, I received a warm note from the fellow at Lincoln who runs "Reasons for Doubt," and he asked me to write an endorsement for a short book he's put together called *Truth about God*, and floated the possibility of a speaking engagement there at Lincoln. I told him I would definitely be interested. Good sign!

Monday, February 22, 2021: So grateful that at long last the plumbers got here late last night and repaired the broken line above the back closet. We have running water again! So glad we will be able to resume a more normal life—and just in time, because our plates are full with work. I need to finish the Kreeft blurb, the blurb for the fellow at Lincoln, do two weeks' worth of grading for my online course, get clarity on the Auten podcast, zoom with a student about his thesis project, prepare for the Hare zoom session on Wednesday, write a WB piece within the next three days, finish Fraser's chapter, finalize my questions for MJ, and more! Should be a busy but productive week. God's grace will make it possible!

Jerry came over in the late afternoon for a shower, and then we shared some dinner and watched some John Adams mini-series. Around the same time I accepted an invitation to do a podcast with an outfit in Toronto that's interviewed some big names in the past, including Noam Chomsky and Graham Oppy.

I wrote this for the WB in the afternoon:

Cascading Crises and Robust Apologetics

Along with plenty of other Texans, my wife and I just went through something of a perfect storm. In what was likely to be the biggest insurance event in Texas history to date, the ice and freezing cold spell featured the convergence of a number of calamities. The death toll in Texas has already reached multiple dozens. A vulnerable energy grid, inadequate insulation, ubiquitous burst pipes in both power plants and private residences, and more systemically, infrastructural issues, regulatory failures, and a host of other factors contributed to the catastrophe. There is bound to be no shortage of finger-pointing, recriminations, and demands for accountability for quite a while.

Described as a "cascading crisis" in which one problem led to another, and then another, and yet another, low temperatures led to burst pipes and equipment failure (spanning solar, coal, and nuclear energy sources), resulting in compromised water pressure, loss of power, and rolling blackouts designed to prevent an already horrible situation from becoming even worse. Despite the valiant efforts of many, this downward spiral continued relatively unabated for days, until experts now say the actual number of deaths, many from hypothermia, won't be known for some time.

These depressing and eminently stressful events could provide the fodder for all sorts of reflections, but I would briefly like to use them, sad and lamentable as they are, for a hopeful and redemptive purpose—as an analogy of sorts for the way robust apologetics can and ought to be done. The relevant narrative needs some inverting, but there's an underlying principle at work here worth noticing and salvaging. Rather than a cascading crisis or escalating emergency, think about the power of an expansive, cumulative apologetic, where its different parts reinforce one another and combine to powerful effect.

One way to get our minds around the possibility here is by thinking about what Richard Swinburne calls C-inductive arguments and P-inductive arguments. C-inductive arguments *add to the probability of their conclusions, without necessarily showing them to be more likely true than false.* Swinburne is notorious for examining a cumulative case argument for God's existence that features a number of C-inductive arguments, each incrementally adding to the likelihood of theism. Then, cumulatively, their combination results in a P-inductive argument—an argument designed to show that the conclusion is actually *more likely true than false.*

Of course this is nothing new, but I would like to make a specific application in light of a hopeful trend we have seen in apologetics. We have seen a range of books in recent years that have emphasized aspects of apologetics that go beyond philosophical arguments alone; we have seen arguments rooted in science, in history, in existential aspects of our existence. Appeals have been made to cultural apologetics, literary apologetics, moral apologetics, imaginative apologetics. At Houston Baptist, I am in the apologetics department, where our MA in apologetics has a philosophical track, and a cultural track. Each track has its own emphasis, but both feature a rich mix of the rational and imaginative. It's this blending or mixture that I wish to discuss, because this synthesis of cascading approaches features tremendous potential—not unlike how aerobic and cardio exercise combined intensify the effects of each.

A perfectly legitimate conceptual distinction—such as between philosophical and cultural apologetics—doesn't mean they have nothing to do with one another, either ideally or in practice. To the contrary, they are more akin to the two legs with which we walk. But rather than merely pay lip service to their rapprochement, I want to offer three quick illustrations of their juxtaposition and integration.

First, drawing from my own wheelhouse, what careful study of the history of the moral argument(s) shows is that, to a person, all the great luminaries of moral apologetics exhibited an expansive epistemology. None were mere logic choppers; all were committed to buttressing their philosophical and ethical analysis with illustrations drawn from the literary, the aesthetic, the imaginative, the relational, or the affective. This is why some of the greatest moral apologists have been great poets or novelists or dramatists, rather than just philosophers.

Second, consider my friend and fellow Worldview Bulletin colleague Paul Gould's terrific book *Cultural Apologetics*. Paul is a premier philosopher, but this book of his is a breath of fresh air. He writes with the fertile mind of a philosopher, the capacious heart of a poet, the vivid imagination of an artist, and the nimble hands of a passionate practitioner. I have said before that this book is essential reading for every actual or budding apologist; in fact, the book deserves a very wide readership among believers and skeptics alike.

Culturally informed and sensitive, embodying what it extolls, eclectic in numerous respects, and punctuated with clever and telling illustrations—both verbal and visual—this remarkable book makes a powerful case for an expansive apologetic true to a good anthropology. It's just the corrective to reawaken the imagination of a disenchanted age. Every page crackles with insight and erudition. At moments it is veritably sublime and enchanting; as inspiring, persuasive, and moving as it is eminently practical. He never leaves his philosophical talents or insights behind, but combines them with other aspects of our humanness to give us all a compelling read and roadmap for powerful apologetics.

Third, recall C. S. Lewis's depiction of the resurrection of Jesus as the "true myth." In short compass we see both the rational and imaginative, the true and the mythical, in perfect synthesis, any hint of competition or tension between them excised and expunged forever. As the remarkable work of such historical apologists like Gary Habermas and Mike Licona shows, there's nothing in solid historiography standing in the way of embracing in the most principled way as established historical fact the bodily resurrection of Jesus. The event happened, and we can and should argue discursively and evidentially that it has.

Yet Lewis also saw that the event, though true, is no less mythical, stirring our imaginations, speaking to our deepest needs, enchanting the world around us, appealing to our affective and aesthetic sides. Lewis was able to see Christianity not as a set of doctrines or moral principles, but a controlling grand narrative, a myth in the true sense of the term. As Alister McGrath puts it, the story of Christ is to be understood as God's myth, whereas the great pagan narratives are merely those of men. Lewis, like Tolkien, knew that myth can speak to both our hearts and minds in a way that simple fact cannot.

Lewis was trained in both philosophy and literary criticism. This is arguably a big reason he was the preeminent apologist he was. You might say he took plenty of courses in both tracks of apologetics—philosophical and cultural. In his case, and potentially our own as the Holy Spirit animates and anoints our outreach, doing so didn't just help him to walk, or even run. It enabled him to dance, if not to fly.

Tuesday, February 23, 2021: Finished Fraser's fourth chapter and Hare's second today, the latter in preparation for tomorrow morning's zoom session. Felt burdened much of today about the Center, so wrote this letter to the leaders of the ministry:

Hi folks,

I'm writing today to ask for prayer for the Center. We are quickly approaching some crossroads regarding the Center and I want us to really bathe it all in prayer.

First off, y'all know that TX just went through a horrific cold spell that resulted in a great deal of suffering and no small number of deaths. Marybeth and I lost water for a week, but not our power. A water pipe busted above a back closet in our home, but we were finally able to get that fixed, which was a great relief. Amazing how much we need water!

Do be praying for TJ, who's recently been diagnosed with covid for the second time. Most are content with getting it once. Sort of like one PhD. Not TJ! ☐

Marybeth is in the process of putting together the second newsletter for the Center, which is exciting. Prayers coveted for that.

And more...

I have zero background in business, fundraising, tax law, book promotion, and publishing. Yet one of our outreaches is Moral Apologetics Press, which will raise tax questions and issues pertaining to business and challenges associated with, say, promoting books. We will be speaking with a tax guy and learning more; we're on a big learning curve with all of this. I wish I knew how to promote books that we wish to publish, but it's altogether outside my wheelhouse. I don't have a clue how to raise money, yet it's one of my jobs as Director of the Center. Etc.

All of this to say: there's a lot to learn, a lot to do. All of this of course is on top of doing the research and writing on moral apologetics. It's logistics and advertising and business and taxes and fundraising. All of which leaves me feeling wholly ill-equipped to handle it. Jonathan has been handling the book stuff most ably, but I hate just putting more and more on him.

What I need to ask from you guys is that you pray. We need wisdom and guidance. I know I do. I need opportunities to cast the vision for the Center and get more people excited and onboard. I need help from various directions, and grace to learn more on my own.

There's no shortage of book ideas for the Press. Just today a friend of TJ's contacted me who's written a manuscript on Buddhist ethics and how it contrasts with Christian teachings on love--a perfect extension of our work into the arena of comparative religion. I'll be speaking with him soon.

But the experience with Brian Melton makes me a little gun shy. After he couldn't find a publisher for his Screwtape Letters-type book, we said we'd do it. We were excited, and Jonathan worked really, really hard to make Brian happy with it all. The final product looks amazing. But Brian now seems to be needling us on what we plan to do to promote and advertise the thing. We have precious little infrastructure set up for this. Jonathan has a plan, but again, so much is getting put on him. And Jonathan, you never, ever complain; you're awesome! But I hate seeing so much of the burden always falling on you. I just don't know how to fix it. I want to pray that some folks with business experience or advertising experience catch a vision for the Center and volunteer to help. Or we can get speaking engagements after this covid thing and we're able to raise some money so we can outsource some of these jobs so it's not all on JP.

I don't entirely how best to pray. These are good problems, in lots of ways. Doors are opening. Things are beginning to happen. But with those developments come more challenges and questions. Pray that God's provision is adequate; that God enables us to do what needs to be done; that we'll have wisdom about which doors to go through.

Adam Johnson approached us about printing his book with us. It was a good dissertation he wrote for Southeastern. Right up our alley. I was on his committee. Would have loved to, but we can't offer a guy like that what an established press can. I'd love to see us eventually to be able to, but we're just starting out. We're not to despise humble beginnings, but sometimes it's tempting!

So feeling a bit overwhelmed. I've been mentioning the Press outreach a lot, but that's just one of many things we're beginning to do in earnest. Hoping for a devoted space to be allocated to us soon at HBU. Praying for the right one. Of course there's the work itself--I've got the fourth in the tetralogy to write, which I often feel is enough to keep me plenty busy apart from all the other tasks that go beyond my skill set. Again, another reason I'm asking for your prayers. And Hare and I are waiting to hear back on the Collection proposal.

So please, please pray about all of this. MB and I are continuing to adjust to our new life here. I've gotten nearly a half dozen podcast appointments on tap, so things are happening. The May course with WLC should be fun. But feeling, at the same time, nervous and stressed. Pray for peace, for God's will to be done, for God's blessing to rest on the venture, for wisdom to know how best to proceed. If you feel motivated to fast and pray, I wouldn't mind! ☐

Blessings, friends, thanks for listening,
Dave

Pastor Tom replied with some words of encouragement: "…There is a world of stuff flying around in your head which is stimulating and rich. Since you're just starting – just a few months into it - you can only take baby steps. Prioritize; think what absolutely must happen first, then second, then third…. You may have to tell the people you want to publish you're just not there yet. Spirit is willing but the flesh is weak – at the moment. Relieve your mind – you just can't do all you want now…in time. Concentrate on the most important few and desirous things at the heart of your mission.

"…Thank you so much. I think of you with joy. I feel for you and Marybeth for the stress you are under. I hear Jesus say to you, 'Let not your heart be troubled'; 'cast your anxieties upon the Lord for he cares for you.'"

Wednesday, February 24, 2021: This morning I was able to participate in the second zoom session discussing Hare's book. I jotted down these notes afterwards: John said he had revised the first chapter based on the first zoom meeting—in order to avoid being redundant. Regarding the second chapter, he opened by asking if folks without the same background in music will be able to appreciate it. Most seemed to think that, even if we didn't follow all the details of his analysis, the general thrust of his points was clear.

Most in attendance had taken him for his course on theological aesthetics at Yale. I would have really enjoyed the chance to do so. He admitted that the prevailing view today, including among many of his students, is that beauty is altogether subjective, in the eye of the beholder, as they say. Even Kant, he points out, thinks beauty is subjective in a way—involving the free play of our imagination and understanding *in us*, but grounded in the object.

Hare mentioned that he was pointing to an aesthetic argument for the existence of God featuring the same structure as the moral argument, but rooted in aesthetic experience. I asked a question about this. The "gap" in our aesthetic experience (analogous to the moral gap) is our experience of a great deal of ugliness. What God does is bring nature and our capacities together to produce blessing. We need an explanation for how it is we feel such extraordinary pleasure as human beings when we experience beauty. John considers the extension of the moral argument to aesthetic experience rather new.

Morality itself is beautiful, by the way. We find such an emphasis in Augustine and Edwards. So there's moral beauty we can come to see, along with physical beauty. But seeing moral beauty depends on who we are. Might we come to see beauty better by getting beyond the uncanny sublime to the optimistic sublime because of our awareness of the author of nature?

Hare wants both to applaud Kant for connecting beauty and religion but also condemn him for reducing this connection to making beauty a vehicle. He admitted it's hard to do both. For much of the twentieth century Kant scholars said God in Kant's writings functions only as a regulative principle, but Hare thinks this has changed and God has come to be seen as constitutive—not merely "as if"—because of the unity of reason and the coming together of the theoretical and practical—and priority of the latter. Spinoza said Kant had too much trust in theoretical reason, yet in his life that Kant demonstrated belief in God; he just couldn't say it. Interestingly, Hare suggests the same about his father—after positivism he couldn't say he believed in God, but he lived as if he did. (John says his dad would mention Ps. 75:3—God as pillar of the world.)

Both moral and aesthetic arguments feature an experiential starting point. In the moral case the starting point is the fact of reason that we are conscious of being under the moral law. In the aesthetic case the starting point is the extraordinary pleasure we feel at beauty. There is also, though, a potential disanalogy: morality requires us to say every person is capable of virtue. It's not clear that aesthetic pleasure is similarly essential to human beings. From Rousseau Kant learned trust in ordinary persons' moral sense; maybe not so with the beautiful.

John thinks Beethoven gives us a sonic picture of Kantian's notion of the sublime, which he calls "optimistic," but he may change that to "hopeful." John wants to say there's something universal about our capacity for aesthetic experience, but that there are different levels of its analysis possible. It can take serious and important work to be prepared to hear or see how God's using beauty to draw us to himself.

Hare admitted a tension within himself on questions of universalizability. His intellectualist and democratic impulses were at odds.

There was a brief discussion of how God's under no obligations because, unlike us, he isn't constrained by the desire to be happy.

Regarding the negative uses of Beethoven's music, John said, following Cicero I think, that the worst is the corruption of the best. Nazi appropriation, for example, comes about from the combination of triumphalism with our anxiety.

Thursday, February 25, 2021: A friend was told yesterday by HBU that his contract won't likely be renewed in a year and a half. Ostensible reasons financial, but it can't help but raise the specter a bit of traumatic memories of Liberty. This morning MB and I are headed out for her to get her first vaccine shot, about five days after I got mine. Jerry came over last night and we commiserated about our colleague, ate some salmon, he took a shower, and we watched some of the John Adams mini-series. MB currently trying to scan the OUP contract for the fourth book in our tetralogy to resend to Drew Anderla in New York. Got an e-mail question from an old student from Liberty asking about my moral epistemology. I suggested a principled integration of internalist and externalist components.

A different old student wrote today and asked me what I thought about the young earth debate—not really my thing, but here's what I wrote back: "I'm probably not the best guy to ask about the young earth question, as I've never devoted a great deal of thought to it. I tend to be an old earther, thinking it prudent to follow the best scientific evidence to determine something like the age of the earth and universe. I think science largely came about as a result of convictions rooted in classical theism that we live in a stable, orderly world. Since God created the world and imbued it with its features, and gave us the cognitive capacities to figure things out about it, it's a sacred sort of endeavor to do science in recognition of such facts. I suspect many are called to the vocation of theoretical and empirical investigation of the natural world, and that the work is intended of God and can serve to bring glory to him. When I consider the expanse of the universe, for example—far bigger than I can begin to get my mind around—I'm bolstered in believing that the heavens declare the glory of God. The notion that it all came about within the last six thousand years is predicated on a particular reading of the Bible, and I figure if such an interpretation exists in too great a tension with what the best science has to say, and if there's another interpretation of the Bible possible that's entirely consistent both with sound principles of exegesis and hermeneutics and deliverances of scientific investigation, the rational course of action for me is to opt for the alternative reading. This isn't a failure, to my thinking, to take the Bible seriously enough; I think it's rather interpreting or dividing the word of truth rightly. Lots of early Christians interpreted the early chapters of Genesis in nonliteral ways, thinking that an insistence on wooden literalness misses out on a lot. NT Wright more recently has suggested the same. I suspect this is right. Walton's work on Genesis can be helpful along these lines. Another reason I resist a young earth interpretation is that it would seem likely to implicate God in a sort of systematic deception, making the world appear much older than it actually is. Is that an epistemic possibility? Sure. But are there reasons to think it plausible? I doubt it. And are there reasons, both scientific and theological, to think it implausible? I'm inclined to think so. So for such reasons I tend to be an old earther, and don't consider that provisional commitment in any way to constitute a challenge to my orthodox faith. Does any of that help?"

Been reading Habermas and Licona on the resurrection. In these days of ubiquitous conspiracy theories believed in by too many Christians, it dawns on me a certain irony: one practically has to be a conspiracy theorist to *doubt* the historicity of the resurrection.

Friday, February 26, 2021: HBU is about to break ground on new building to house a Center on Law and Freedom, or something like that. The building(s) look beautiful. What a marvelous thing it would be eventually if we could do the same with the Center for Moral Apologetics! We will see what God has in store. This morning I was filled with a great deal of excitement about the prospects of many good things to come regarding the Center—publications, classes, podcasts, etc. I like some of what this other Center does and I think we should emulate aspects of it—talks to faculty, for example.

This morning I have a zoom conversation with Mark Dunn about his thesis; I'd been meaning to speak with him. He reminds me of TJ. He already has his PhD in NT. I want to make sure he's welcome to contribute to the website. Later tonight Jerry will be coming over, and I've invited Rob Gagnon to join us if he's like. In between I hope to get as close as I can to wrapping up the Habermas/Licona book and grade some discussion boards. I also need to e-mail and write some handwritten notes to prospective students in the MA in apologetics program.

The chat with Mark Dunn was delightful. Such a kindred spirit. He's thinking of writing his thesis on a perceived need for grace among lots of folks he's talked with around the world. I connected it to the performative variant of the moral argument and offered a few suggestions. I also invited him to contribute to the website. Such a delightful guy and encouraging conversation!

Jordan Hampton sent me the link to a video he did yesterday with Eric Sampson giving four positive reasons for moral realism. Great stuff! https://youtu.be/9KICGOHpz7A. Going up at the site soon.

Saturday, February 27, 2021: Talked to Elton in the morning. I asked him how to approach conversations about homosexuality with those who don't take biblical teachings as authoritative. He shared some good ideas, including the following: (1) Our discussions must be shaped by our audience; it's an emotionally loaded subject. (2) Whereas some might think about it dispassionately as a right or wrong matter, for others, it's a deeply emotional issue and the discussion needs to be conducted in a different way. (3) Even without scripture, some rational considerations can be brought to bear. For example, no great world religion endorses the practice. Also, (4) common sense, biology, and experience point to the propriety of heterosexual practice and family structures, departure from which produces huge sociological repercussions. (5) A number of physical dangers attend the practice, especially for men. Books he mentioned are *The Crisis of Homosexuality*, *Sexual Sanity*, and *The Sexual Christian*. He also stressed how churches need to be intentional in not harping nearly exclusively on this one sin, and in reaching out to those struggling in this area. (By coincidence my friend Rob Gagnon, along with Jerry, was over last night. We prayed, chatted, laughed, and watched some John Adams mini-series.) On a different note, Elton gave me his nephew's name and number who might help us promote books: Stephen Alexander: (512) 277-4563. Afterwards I touched base with Jonathan about this matter; it's a work in progress.

In the afternoon I did more reading, grading, getting caught up in Bible reading, and doing some tasks for the apologetics department—reaching out to new and prospective students in the MAA. Marybeth and I are now done with our work for the day and looking forward to praying, eating a bit, and catching an episode or two of a show before going to bed.

Sunday, February 28, 2021: The big thing today was a podcast, that ended up lasting about an hour and a half, with Brian Auten and his friend from Apologetics 315. It was a nice time; they were very cordial and fun. They asked about HBU, my background, the Center, the MA in apologetics (both tracks), and more. I tried to mention most all the faculty who teach in the program, but I think I inadvertently neglected mentioning Mary Jo. I could have also said a few more things about the cultural apologetics track had I been a little better prepared, but overall I think it went okay. Jerry came over for dinner and a shower, then we watched another John Adams episode—the one in which he became vice president, then president. Beginning to pray in earnest for speaking engagements, especially in churches, so I can cast the vision of the Center.

Monday, March 1, 2021: Good day. Not having been able to rest much yesterday, I didn't overdo it today. After sleeping in, I listened to scripture, sent out the weekly announcement to my online class, answered some e-mails, and made a cash withdrawal from our retirement. It was a small withdrawal of just two thousand dollars with which we'll be able to pay off our Texas house later this week; exciting! Hoping doing so marks the occasion of our really being able to turn our money more outward for good purposes. After Marybeth got home from teaching, she and I spent some time praying and relaxing. Then I read more Licona and Habermas, then some Knopp. Knopp's little book is succinct, but insightful. I like his unapologetic apologetic, some of his incisive analysis of the relationship between modernism and postmodernism, and certain of his biblical insights concerning truth. The blurb is due this Friday. This morning the second newsletter for the Center also went out. These were Marybeth's opening words in the newsletter:

> As I write this, Houston is coming out from under the aftermath of February's news-making deep freeze and its attendant power and water outages. It was a difficult time for everyone in the city and across Texas, and prayers are appreciated for clean up, repairs, and recovery. We ourselves had comparatively little damage, but we now feel fully christened as Houstonites (Houstonians?). It was heartening to see our fellow citizens and especially HBU come together to support and help one another. We do not relish reliving such an experience, but we are grateful to be part of a community that clearly cares for one another.
>
> The experience was also a crucial reminder that so much of life is beyond our control and that our trust, therefore, must be in God, not our plans or personal resources (Proverbs 16:9). Whatever strategies we devise, whatever projects we envision, whatever dreams we aspire to: all of these must be bathed in prayer and consistently surrendered to God's leading. That attitude is absolutely key to the mission of the Center for Moral Apologetics, and it is in that spirit we lay out below the tasks we are currently undertaking and the programs that are in the works.
>
> As with our initial newsletter, this one covers the various facets of the ministry, with updates from each member of the team. We also have an HBQ contribution from Dr. Chris Kugler, with the School of Christian Thought at Houston Baptist and links to some recent articles at the site. Do feel free to share this newsletter with anyone who might be interested in the work we are undertaking. They can also sign up for the mailing list here.
>
> We are honored and humbled that you have come alongside us to support in whatever way you are able and feel led. Of course we need much prayer, especially for the undertakings noted below. And if you would like to support the work of the Center financially, you may make a tax-deductible gift through the HBU online giving form (select "Additional Giving Opportunities" and designate Center for Moral Apologetics from the pop-up list). You may also mail contributions to the following address (with Center for Moral Apologetics in the memo line): HBU Advancement Lockbox, PO Box 4897, Dept #527, Houston, TX 77210.

And this was my little contribution: "Three quick matters: first, we are gearing up for the two-week May course that William Lane Craig and I will be teaching on the moral argument(s). Folks can register to take it either as an HBU student or as an auditor, from anywhere in the world with internet access. It appears that Dr. Craig will be teaching remotely because of the pandemic, but it will still be a great time. Second, the Center will hopefully soon be allocated a dedicated space on the campus of HBU, and in preparation for that, we are collecting philosophy and theology, ethics and apologetics books for the Center's library resources. If anyone would like to donate any such books, it would be much appreciated. You can send them to this address: 11510 Pagoda Drive, Stafford, TX 77477. And third, we are asking for regular concerted prayer support as the Center gets underway with the aim of becoming the definitive cutting-edge community of research on all things related to moral apologetics—from theology and the arts to philosophy and literature, and plenty more besides. We are acutely mindful as we get underway that it will be God alone who brings the increase, and so to that end we covet your intentional and faithful prayer support."

Tuesday, March 2, 2021: Today I read through another chapter in the Knopp book. It's pretty good, though it raises a few questions in my mind. For example, he rightly emphasizes we don't have much Cartesian certainty, but then argued on this basis that doubts are natural and okay. But I think this isn't quite right, or at least not fine-grained enough. I don't have Cartesian certainty that Marybeth exists, but doubts about her existence strike me as pernicious. Knopp's operative account of doubt is objectionably capacious. One of a few reservations; generally it's pretty good, though.

I also spoke on the phone with Daniel McCoy, who's written a manuscript contrasting Buddhist compassion with Christian love. A kindred spirit! We may wish to publish it with Moral Apologetics Press. He and I have a similar vision of ministry, and both see the increasing emerging importance of this topic. It was fun sharing our visions for outreach and apologetics. Very nice time. His work fills an important niche in the ministry of the Center. A joy to welcome into the growing community. I'll be speaking with Jonathan soon about the prospect of taking on this project.

Another highlight of the day was that my dean floated the possibility of Marybeth becoming the chair of the apologetics department. If this happens, it might be just the ticket to scratch where she's been itching. Like I shared with the dean afterwards: "Phil, I know you didn't solicit my opinion, but if I may presume to volunteer this information: After Marybeth was offered the chance to direct the Masters in English program at Liberty her last year, I saw her navigate some remarkably challenging terrain with great deftness. I remember being so impressed I told her on numerous occasions that she seemed to possess real leadership skills. When we then ended up leaving after just one more year, it's been a nagging question in her mind what all of that meant, since no leadership roles at HBU seemed likely to present themselves for her—until your call today. I know you're still in the process of deciding, but for what it's worth, I'm convinced you wouldn't be disappointed with this choice; quite to the contrary. And the prospects, as she said, of our collaborating to grow the department and the Center are exciting and bright."

I also communicated with the committees for Jordan and Fraser in an effort to nail down defense times later in the month. Stephen's will be March 26th; maybe we'll set the date for Fraser's by tomorrow.

Tom Thomas also reached out about a Houston business man and lawyer who might be able and willing to help us think through some things with the Center. Here is what the fellow replied to Tom, the most relevant section of which highlighted in bold:

1. I'm getting ready to cut off this e-mail address, so please note the new one:

anthonyrbenedetto@gmail.com

A nuisance to type the first time, but auto-complete is a wonderful feature for future uses!

2. Thank you for the kind words! My wife and I have been spared COVID and have received both doses of the Moderna vaccine. Now, if Canada will just open the border for our August golf trip!

3. The good news: I am willing to be a shoulder to cry on if Dr. Baggett can't find a closer one.

4. The less-than-good news: I doubt I can be of much help in getting the Center up and running. I've never helmed such an entity, and they are special animals in the academic world; I can imagine there are even greater issues in the private university world. Since we moved to The Woodlands in 1999, I have had no significant contacts with the city of Houston and all of its varied institutions, except the Texas Medical Center, where I briefly worked as a Six Sigma consultant. My only "contact" with Houston now is Andy Nixon, former pastor at The Woodlands UMC and now Senior Pastor at First UMC downtown. He was our Loft pastor, and my wife and I are Sanctuary folks, so we had only limited contact with him. I'm not sure he remembers me much, if at all, since he's been gone from TWUMC for some time.

My recommendation for Dr. Baggett is to dig around at HBU and Rice to look for organizations similar to his, then to make friends with the Center directors and, more importantly, their administrative leader(s). They will have much better insight into HBU as an institution and into the various issues you raised. Though I have a law degree, my primary practice after law school was child protection mediation, so the law as it applies to academic institutions and to religious institutions is something of an enigma to me and a specialty of its own within the legal community. Andy Nixon may have been at First Church long enough to have identified parishioners with these skill sets, so Dr. Baggett would do well to take Andy to lunch and become good buddies with him. ;)

Again, thank you for thinking of me. I'd be glad to help in any way I can, but I think I'm not likely to be much help beyond the suggestions in this message. You are welcome to share this message with Dr. Baggett.

Wednesday, March 3, 2021: My sleep was fitful last night. It's now nearly six in the morning. Feeling a bit groggy, but it's going to be a big day. I hope nearly to finish the Knopp book and close in on that endorsement, and Jerry Walls is coming over around noon so we can take him for his covid vaccine shot. We are also hoping today is the day we can wire the remaining money we owe on the TX house to pay it off completely. Today I also hope to get to the bottom of the hitch we've experienced in the committee getting all of Fraser's chapters in a timely fashion.

It's the evening now. Good day indeed! Jerry got his shot, and the house is paid off. It was a year ago today that Marybeth put this announcement on FB:

> David and I are excited to share the news that next academic year we will be joining the faculty at Houston Baptist University.
>
> This move involves a welcome development for David especially, who will see the fulfillment of a longtime dream of building a Center for Moral Apologetics. As most of you know, research and writing on the moral argument has been a passion and calling of his for, well, decades, and we look forward to this work finding a fitting institutional home in which it can best flourish. HBU will house MoralApologetics.com, and in time the Center aspires to feature a weekly podcast, generate curricula, put on workshops, conferences, classes, and eventually even subsidize a Chair of Moral Apologetics in honor of Jerry Walls, David's co-author and our soon-to-be colleague in Houston. In addition to helping David with the Center, I will be teaching English and literary apologetics.
>
> We couldn't be more pleased that HBU found fit to offer us both positions to join a school where such exciting things are happening. Under the leadership of Dr. Robert Sloan, HBU has the sort of academic vision that we wholeheartedly believe in and for which we'll happily expend ourselves in service, hopefully for many years to come. Our hearts are full as we reflect on God's goodness in mapping out this new stage of our careers.
>
> We leave Liberty grateful for our wonderful colleagues. Those folks are truly the best, and we are better people and scholars for having known them. We leave behind a great number of dear and lifelong friends and many fond memories—among them (for Dave) Monday night movies with Mark Foreman, racquetball and billiards with Jim Nutter, and collaborations with Ronnie Campbell. As for me, I think about the education I've earned here—both in undergrad and more recently in seminary. And irreplaceable was the time spent with Nathaniel as a student, especially through his master's program. It was pure joy to watch him learn from those for whom I have the utmost respect.

Additionally, in the 14 and 17 years (respectively) that David and I taught at LU, we have been blessed with amazing students too numerous to mention by name and enriching career opportunities. It has been an honor to serve those students and do what we can to help them grow intellectually and spiritually. Best of all, of course, is that David and I met each other at Liberty; for that reason alone if none other, the school will retain a special place in our hearts.

As our days at Liberty are few, we look back with gratitude at this marvelous chapter of our lives and wish all and only the best for Liberty. We also look forward to our new possibility-filled season at HBU with hopeful expectation, and we covet your prayers.

Thursday, March 4, 2021: This morning around 9 am Marybeth has a phone interview with Houston Christian High School. She had a great time when we visited with them in the fall, and there's an AP English teaching position open. She thought she'd throw her hat in the ring, largely because leadership positions at HBU didn't seem likely, especially in the English department. But a day or two ago my dean called and floated the possibility of making her the apol dep't chair, so what we're praying for is that one of these doors opens, the other closes, so God's direction is clear. I definitely think she has prodigious leadership skills and a real hunger to exercise those gifts, so I'm looking forward to seeing how he directs.

I'm looking to set the defense date for John Fraser on March 31, a Wednesday. I have suggested as much to him, and to Ed and Jerry. Hopefully that can get sealed into place before long.

Still basking in the joy of paying off the house yesterday. Almost too hard to believe; what a blessing! To be completely debt free we have some student loans to finish paying off, but now that the house payment is out of the way, that task becomes considerably more doable.

Today I hope to wrap up Knopp's book and give him both an endorsement and a bit of feedback. If I have the time, perhaps I can do the grading for my online course as well. Book orders for the May course on the moral argument are also due today.

Spent time chatting and praying with TJ, and much of the conversation was geared around his contribution to the Moral Apologetics ministry. His foci are chaplaincy, campus ministry, and church ministry. We came to a meeting of the minds eventually that his efforts are likely best directed toward the church ministry to start with.

One of these days this first installment in a new series I'm doing at the site will go up:

The Moral Argument(s) and Christian Salvation, Part I: Forgiveness

Over the next three installments, we will extend the discussion of moral apologetics and Christian theology by connecting the moral argument—particularly one version of it—with three deep moral needs we as human beings display: our need to be forgiven, our need to be changed, and our need to be perfected. Each of these profoundly existential needs we possess as human beings corresponds to an important aspect of Christian salvation.

When I say "the moral argument," I'm using that phrase in a general sort of way. In truth there's more than one moral argument. There's a whole range of them. If you prefer, you can think of one moral argument with a number of different parts. At least most of the time that works pretty well since the different variants of the argument tend to be rather consistent with one another. The specific formulation of the moral argument we will consider today is what John Hare calls the "performative" version or, for reasons that will become clear, an "argument from grace."

You might remember in Book 1 of *Mere Christianity* C. S. Lewis says two things are at the heart of our understanding of reality: First, there's a moral law, and second, we all fall short of it. On his claim we can start to build a performative moral argument. There is a moral standard that's objective and universal. It's binding and authoritative on us, but we invariably fall short of meeting it. This results in the "gap" between the best we can do and what morality requires. And this gap needs addressing. We find ourselves as having fallen short, and we know it.

How do we know we've got a moral problem on our hands? One way, you might say, is by our moral sense, which even plenty of secular thinkers recognize as in some way significant. Take Charles Darwin, for example, who thought it's our moral sense that best distinguishes human beings from the animals. Indeed, he begins chapter 5 of *Descent of Man* with this admission: "I fully subscribe to the judgment of those writers who maintain that of all the differences between man and the lower animals, the moral sense or conscience is by far the most important." He even says he considers the moral sense, our sense of "ought," to be "humankind's finest quality." Elsewhere in the same book Darwin casts both "ought" and "disinterested love for all living creatures" as the noblest attribute of man.

Darwin intuitively felt the importance of morality, even if he ended up embracing a deflationary analysis of its import. Similarly Sigmund Freud. To Freud's thinking, the problem of guilt is so severe that he diagnosed it in *Civilization and Its Discontents* as the single most important development of civilization—a problem so acute that it is the thing most responsible for our unhappiness. Perhaps what helps explain Freud's conviction is that his analytic work found that nearly every neurosis conceals an unconscious sense of guilt, which in turn "fortifies the symptoms by making use of them as punishment."

For both Darwin and Freud, the phenomenon of guilt was both interesting and important, even revelatory. Recall their depictions: Darwin thought our capacity for experiencing the moral sense and a painful conscience is by far the most important distinction between us and the animals; our sense of ought and disinterested love for all creatures, he believed the noblest virtue of man. And Freud took the problem of guilt as the single most important development of civilization. But they mistook its import, I suspect, embracing reductionist analyses and taking guilt itself as the essential problem, rather than the deeper malady of which guilt is but the symptom. Rightly construed guilt is semiotic, pointing beyond itself.

That we intuitively sense there to be a moral standard that we fall short of leaves us with a condition of guilt in need of fixing. And if we take our feelings of guilt as more than *mere* feelings, and something like a real objective condition of guilt, we are left wondering if there's a solution. We need forgiveness for having fallen short of the moral standard—and not just falling short in the past, but continuing to fall short all the time. Forgiveness is a basic and chronic existential human need.

I rather doubt Freud was wrong about guilt creating quite a bit of unhappiness, which makes it understandable that our secular friends see the need to deal with it, usually by trying to deny that we are really *that* guilty. Unaddressed guilt eats us up. And sometimes people do have an overactive superego and feel guilty for all sorts of things that they're not really guilty of. But at other times, most of us intuitively recognize, our guilt isn't a mistake, but a real insight into ourselves. We don't need our guilt explained away, in those cases, but taken away, forgiven.

And of course this is one way that the moral argument serves as the perfect pathway to the gospel of Christ—indeed we have fallen short, and are in need of forgiveness. And God offers us that forgiveness through the death and resurrection of Christ. Not only does God offer us forgiveness, but we as his forgiven children can extend forgiveness to others. This is why it's so imperative we maintain a stance of forgiveness toward our neighbors, modeling the grace God has shown us. And of course many will recognize that all of this broaches the whole theological topic of *justification*.

So you might wish to approach this philosophically—talking about guilt and our need for forgiveness, and then showing how philosophy leads you to the brink of theology. Or start with a theological discussion of justification, and then show how it comports with what we learned from our moral experience and what we might call general revelation. Or take the deliverances of theology like justification and use insights from moral apologetics to spell out part of what's going on—that's doing philosophical theology.

However we approach it, the moral argument, from this angle, functions as an ideal way to introduce the good news of the gospel. We have a problem, yes, but God offers the solution.

In the next installment we will discuss the moral argument and moral transformation.

Friday, March 5, 2021: Finished the Knopp blurb today, and not much else to report; sometimes tasks are time-consuming but show little sign afterwards of much accomplishment: "Motivated by a practitioner's heart and informed by decades of teaching philosophy and apologetics, Richard Knopp's handy primer is an eminently useful roadmap for navigating the thorny terrain of whether and what we can know about God. Crackling with both biblical and philosophical clarity, these pages can serve to embolden and equip prospective defenders of the faith. With rigor and winsomeness, perspicacity and orthodoxy, Knopp's work, in impressively short compass, by turns resonates with the likes of Charles Taylor and John Henry Newman, C. S. Lewis and A. E. Taylor, impeccably helping fill the dire need for such substantive and streamlined treatises." (Cameron Bertuzzi shared the interview ad for the upcoming chat with Craig about the moral argument class; meh.)

Saturday, March 6, 2021: Marybeth and I did a function in late morning at HBU, speaking with prospective students about the School of Christian Thought and the apologetics department. That went very well. It was nice to have a chance to speak in person to folks; that hadn't happened in a while. Hoping and praying for more opportunities soon. We continue to pray that God opens one door and closes another for Marybeth—either the high school job or the chair of the apol dep't. I'm inclined to think the latter is the better of the two scenarios. Nathaniel is getting some interview requests for jobs he's applied to in Texas; he is hoping to move here this summer, which I think would be good for both him and MB. Families aren't meant to be so widely separated.

I didn't mention it yesterday, but I had expressed some reservations to Cameron about his labeling his chat with me and Craig as "What moral argument is the best?" To me this sets an entirely wrong tone and hits a completely wrong note. I'd have much preferred a more straightforward "The Moral Argument(s) for God's Existence." Iconoclastic clickbait strategies don't tend to build the best bridges.

Jonny Walls called what I put on FB the other day "sticking to the bit." It doesn't have anything to do with the Center, but it's a story I like to tell from time to time, and I suppose it certainly does have something do with love:

> Right near the end of my dad's life, a cute thing happened. My mom loved this story, so I'll share it since it's so heartwarming to think they're together again. My dad was home, working in the garage, and my mom at the big shopping

center. She called him, he answered, and she said, "I hear your wife is out." "Yeah, she is," he said. "Well, wanna slip away for little while? She'll never know." "Sure," he said. A short while later he showed up, all spiffied up in fancy clothes, and they walked the mall hand in hand, the whole time acting as if they were doing something altogether wicked, and then he finally said he'd better get home before his wife did. They kissed, he left. When she got home, he was in the garage, wearing his greasy work clothes again, and she walked on by, asking as she did, "Anything go on when I was gone?" "No, no," he said, a little too insistently. And they never mentioned it again.

Sunday, March 7, 2021: Marybeth and I turned this day into a mini-prayer-retreat, covering a wide range of concerns and topics. Regarding HBU, we prayed for the leaders, for an influx of students, for donors both big and small, for middle management, for the situation regarding MB becoming chair of the apol dep't, and God's blessings on the Center in various ways. I also sent this note to Jonathan to put on FB:

> Houston Baptist University's Center for Moral Apologetics is undertaking a new initiative to form a community of prayer warriors committed to interceding for God to do with and through the Center as he desires. We are hoping for a group of 300 people who will commit to pray for the Center on a regular basis—that God's will would be done through the ministry. Everything at the Center is just starting to get underway, but our hopes for its various efforts of outreach are high. We are praying that God directs our steps, makes clear his path, and brings the increase. Among the agendas of the ministry are Moral Apologetics Press, MoralApologetics.com, an upcoming Masters level Certificate program in moral apologetics at HBU, outreach to local churches, the development of curricula for Christian schools and homeschoolers, and more. It's our hope that the Center makes HBU the preeminent place for those who wish to become immersed in and engage in cutting-edge, world class scholarship on the moral argument(s) to find a community of scholars with which to do so. In time we hope to offer workshops for faculty, lectures, conferences, and eventually to underwrite a permanent Chair in moral apologetics at HBU. From our earliest days we want to bathe all we do in prayer and remain in the center of God's plan. If you would like to be put on the list of intercessors, please jot a note to David Baggett at dbaggett@hbu.edu and he will add you to the list.

Monday, March 8, 2021: Last week of this term's first eight weeks. I need to get through Fraser's fifth chapter in very short order this week, as well as wrap up the course on Apologetic Frameworks. I have an online philosophy course starting next week, which is also spring break, and a very busy week with a number of other commitments—an online alumni gathering of HBU apol students, a Hare zoom meeting, and the Craig discussion of the moral argument with Bertuzzi. I had written him briefly the other day to discourage him from framing the discussion in terms of which moral argument is "best." I just wrote him a follow-up e-mail to elaborate, especially since I haven't heard back:

Hi Cameron,

I haven't heard back from you, which might mean nothing at all, but just in case, I glanced back at the note I jotted you and realized it was rather brusque. In all honesty, at the time I hadn't intended it to be. It was something I dashed off in the middle of a busy day without giving it much of a second thought. I could and probably should have been much more delicate, circumspect, and felicitous in my wording. Sorry, man!! On occasion I'm an inadvertent idiot!

But just to explain the concern a bit more, and do with it what you will, the way I see it, the various moral arguments fit together into a coherent whole. Perhaps some analogies could help. Think of it as a body—where the different parts all work together. Or a puzzle, where the removal of any one piece means the puzzle is incomplete. Or the process of walking, requiring both legs, not just one or the other.

As soon as we ask which moral argument is the BEST argument, it trains the mind to focus on just the one best one, and accords primacy to a needlessly comparative mentality, rather than cultivating the view that something like a cumulative case might be the goal, motivated more by integrating than dividing and conquering.

There's no real competition between an argument that says morality, to be fully rational, needs to feature an ultimate correspondence between happiness and holiness, on the one hand, and an argument that says the authority of moral obligations needs to be adequately explained, or the great intrinsic value of human beings accounted for, on the other. Just to adduce a few examples.

Not only is there no competition, there's no real way, so far as I can see, of saying one is any "better" than another. Better by what metric? Sometimes this seems nothing less than comparing incommensurables. Broaching the question of the "best" moral argument practically strikes me as a category mistake.

It's useful to bear in mind that there should be a unity between our various commitments, and surely a unity when it comes to our commitments in just one area, like ethics. The evidence, rightly construed, should all, collectively at any rate, push in the same direction, even if in disparate ways and from different perspectives.

Finally, though it seems that framing the question in terms of the BEST moral argument might catch attention and garner some interest, it's likely to catch best the attention of those looking to have a fight about this, folks taking sides and feeling like they've got a stake in it or skin in the game, when rather I'd suggest that folks would be better served, and would better serve the cause of truth, by fostering an attitude of genuine interest in apprehending the evidential force of morality per se.

It was for such reasons I urged you to change the name of our chat. But of course it's your call, and I appreciate your willingness to do this. Thanks for reading!

Blessings, Dave

Cameron replied like this, which seems fair enough: "Hello David! Sorry I didn't respond to the other email. It seems I'm getting worse at that these days. I hear what you're saying. The reason that I went with this title is because it seemed in line with what Phil said we'd talk about. Moreover, terms like 'BEST' are strong keywords that have potential to make our discussion visible to many more thousands of people. This is no trivial matter! Someone that really needs to watch this stream could end up seeing it simply due to the addition of a single word. My thought on your competition concern is that you can clarify at the very beginning what your view is, namely, that the best moral argument is a cumulative one. The title in question and what you intend to say are actually a great combination! Let me know your thoughts."

To which I responded, "I got ya, Cameron, appreciate it. I figured something like that might be the case. And I suppose you're right that I can say I think the cumulative case is best. Thanks for the thoughts, which help. And thanks again for your willingness to conduct the discussion. Should make lots more aware of the upcoming class we're teaching, and the Center we're getting underway at HBU in moral apol. Looking forward to it!"

In the afternoon I read through and extensively commented on Fraser's last chapter, then sent that back to him. And I responded more briefly to the changes Jordan had effected on his last chapter. So I think I'm largely done giving feedback to those guys and I'll let the committee do its work. The main job left will be the defenses in each case. Feels good!

Tuesday, March 9, 2021: Today has been a very difficult day for me. It's been very productive, funny enough. I was able to finish reading the book and then write a blurb for a re-issue of Peter Kreeft's *Between Heaven and Hell*: "So often reason and imagination are seen in tension or conflict, but Kreeft's classic piece of posthumous fictional dialogue powerfully illustrates the prospect of their seamless integration. Rife with no-nonsense uncommon common sense, not to mention unapologetic apologetics, it explores timely and timeless questions—from the nature and primacy of reality to the power and purpose of evidence, argument, and even debate—in an utterly charming, engaging way. Eminently readable and a veritable delight to relish, it takes truth with sober seriousness yet also with playfulness, creativity, and a winsomely light touch. Its longevity and enduring impact is no mystery."

Still, though, it's been a painful day. Two Bible verses come to my mind today: not to grow weary in well-doing, and not to despise humble beginnings. I suspect we're given both of these injunctions because God knows our default is easily doing otherwise: growing weary in well-doing and despising humble beginnings. Today I feel the full force of both temptations. My work at HBU seems ineffectual and fruitless and futile; my teaching seems to be stymied and well-nigh silenced; the work for the Center seems slow and incremental at best. My efforts to get prayer partners signed on yesterday have produced precious few results. At breakfast I broke down in tears as I confided to Marybeth that I feel altogether out of my depth, utterly ill-equipped to get this Center up and running. It seems altogether beyond my abilities, outside my wheelhouse. I have the wrong skill set for it. I yearn for someone else to do this work so that I can just set myself to do the work in moral apologetics I feel called to do. Publicly crying like a baby admittedly, though, helped a little.

I suppose that moments like this are a reminder not to rely on ourselves. Down deep I'm sure there is a great deal of fear I'm feeling—fear I will fail, the various efforts to garner interest will yield no dividends, that I'll fall flat on my face. Marybeth suggested we should spend more time reading Rodin's book on servant leadership, and she's probably right. I have to let God do the work within me that needs to be done, and somehow I have to more fully appropriate the unalterable fact that God's the one responsible for generating the increase and blessing our efforts. It's just so easy for me to imagine that the seeming failures are my fault, even if any success we see is God's.

I have been hoping and praying since this morning for a word of encouragement, or perhaps a hopeful sign. So far nothing of the sort has been forthcoming. Just obstinate steely silence. I continue to wait. About to go for a walk, in the hopes that a modicum of bodily exercise might help lift my spirits. Otherwise I seem quite incapable by dint of mental effort to extricate myself from these oppressive doldrums and an unrelenting sense and fear of failure. I know that it's easy to overestimate what can be done in a short interval, and to underestimate what can be done in a longer one; perhaps I need to take this lesson more to heart at times like this. All I know is that today I feel defeated, discouraged, despondent, depressed. Dispirited. I'm sure there are more D words.

It's a bit later; I'm back from my walk. Sat on a bench in the park for a while, figuring the sun and wind would do me good. I suppose a few steps I need to start taking include writing pastors to express an interest in speaking at their churches about the Center, and contacting the Director of the Center for Law and Justice at HBU, a Center that's seemed to have fared well in recent years, attracting some major donations. Really not sure why today was my emotionally hardest day since getting to Houston—relating to matters of being in Houston and at HBU. Skipped the afternoon meeting the SCT had for the sake of my mental health. I can also begin personally asking folks to become prayer partners with us—I just started by writing Shane O'Neill and Ginger Asel. I'm feeling embarrassed we made a public appeal and got such little feedback. I suppose I need to just get over it, but I'm reeling a bit.

Wednesday, March 10, 2021: Woke up this morning with a much brighter disposition. TJ had written me back last night: "So sorry to hear of the low point, but I am reminded that weeping may endure for the night but joy will come in the morning. I suspect there is sometimes a necessary albeit painful dark night of the soul that attends to beginnings of important works like the Center's stepping off out of the shadow of Liberty and into its fuller light at HBU. I am reminded that this is a bit of a spiritual battle, and that the enemy is most keen to attack you, the director, in particular. While your being discouraged is real, so also is the promise that God's grace is at work and He has not for one minute stopped making good on His promise to not only give you vision but to see that all resources of heaven are brought to bear in fulfilling it. Love you, brother. Let's definitely plan to pray on Thursday."

I think today is going to be a great day! Regarding the prayer team I'd like to build, I figure I can just keep adding to it. It can be something we emphasize if we get speaking opportunities.

Todd Starnes is now doing his radio show on the campus of Liberty. One more reason I'm glad we've largely severed ties with that school. Starnes is a piece of work. Enough said, other than that truth is not a priority of the man; as MB puts it, he has a quite casual relationship with it. The choice to partner with him speaks volumes.

It's still just after 9 am, but we just sent a contract to Daniel McCoy about his book comparing and contrasting Buddhist compassion and Christian love. Excited about that. And another exciting project is in the works. Marybeth and I were discussing what her summer project would be, and I think she's leaning toward spearheading a book we'd planned to do—collecting together a whole range of pieces we've done, some articles, some blogs, on popular culture. I had done a number of the articles for various books in the philosophy and pop culture series, but the nature of my work often blends philosophy and apologetics. So our collection or anthology will basically be on Apologetics and Popular Culture. And not only that, but the book will serve as the springboard to launch a whole series on apologetics (or perhaps even moral apologetics) and popular culture. (Maybe just apologetics generally to appeal to a broader audience, though I suspect most of the focus will broach matters of ethics in one way or another.) Marybeth will serve as editor of the series, and we can consider proposals as folks send them in. Same idea as Irwin's regarding philosophy, but geared to apologetics specifically. It is genuinely surprising but perhaps providential nobody has done this yet. We think it has the potential both to do good and to generate a revenue stream for the Center.

I wrote the moral apol team this morning and shared this, and a few other things, then finished it like this: "Sometimes I fantasize about having a whole building on the HBU campus for the Center, and a healthy office and salary for each one of you—as we write and edit books, generate curricula, do teaching workshops, zoom sessions, teach classes to students, run the site, train pastors, organize conferences, host lectureships, etc. But maybe that expects this world to be more like heaven than I can hope for."

Thursday, March 11, 2021: Contemplative today. Need to wrap up penultimate grading assignments in the Foundations course, and Matthew from Houston Christian wrote me back, not having written in a while. I'll share his e-mail and my response in a bit. In the early afternoon MB and I went to Barnes and Noble for the first time in quite a while to do some work. That's where I am as I write this. On the way over I shared with MB I'm coming to the conviction that my main job as director of the Center is to pray it in.

In the late afternoon I wrote my first local pastor to express interest in sharing a word about the Center; I wrote the pastor of Sugarland United Methodist Church:

Hi Pastor Nicholas. You don't know me, and I'm sorry for e-mailing you out of the blue. I hope and trust you and yours are doing well, and faring with all the challenges of this pandemic with relative success.

My wife and I moved to Stafford TX, just a few miles from your church, this past summer in order to teach at Houston Baptist. We are United Methodists, and hope to attend your church. We have only done online services during the pandemic, but have finally each gotten our first vaccine shot and are hoping to start attending in person soon. We have had our eyes on your church for quite some time.

As for why I'm writing, one of my jobs is as Director of the newly formed Center for Moral Apologetics at HBU. This has been a longtime dream or vision of mine, and HBU has given me the chance to launch this initiative here. This was why we left our previous school where we had taught for seventeen and fourteen years, respectively, to come to HBU. My wife teaches English and I teach philosophy.

I have been praying for months for opportunities to share the vision for the Center, and I've decided to touch base with local pastors to express my interest in doing so. If you were open to such a possibility, I would relish the chance to speak to your church, whether for a few minutes or an hour, or whatever suits your schedule best. I would mainly talk about a particular sort of "argument" for God's existence, namely, an argument based on such realities as the dignity and value and equality of human persons, the authority of moral obligations, and the like.

I would do my level best to make the talk, of whatever length, suitable for a lay congregation, and if it were done in an informal setting, I'd be happy to have a discussion afterward. At my previous school I trained a lot of pastors, and I am confident the time would be well spent, equipping your folks with some tools they can use in their evangelistic outreaches. I'm not a heavy-handed apologist;

mine is a dialogical and gentle approach. My website is MoralApologetics.com, which could give you an idea of my approach, including that it tends to be team-based and interdisciplinary.

I've also published several books on the subject, including three with Oxford University Press (*Good God*, which won a *Christianity Today* book award in 2012, and my wife and I also wrote a book called *The Morals of the Story* that won another CT book award in 2019; *God and Cosmos*; and *The Moral Argument*). I don't say any of this except to let you know that I've worked for many years on this topic and would love the chance to share some of my thoughts with local churches.

So that's about it. Wanted to introduce myself and let you know of my interest in speaking at your church if ever you might be interested. Thanks for taking the time to read this.

Blessings, Dave Baggett

Friday, March 12, 2021: The morning featured a nice chat and prayer time with TJ, who volunteered to help me with some of the chores I'm tasked with as Director that are outside my wheelhouse. He's more the organizational and logistics guy than I, and he volunteered to do some of that work so I could be freed up to do more of what I feel specifically called to do in moral apologetics. I will definitely pray about this and think on it some more, because to me it sounds right. He also said he would like his *Good Reasons* outfit to come under Moral Apologetics more explicitly, so I'll direct JP to start doing that through the website. I also need to get JP to set up a Press tab at the site.

TJ and I also discussed and prayed about the Ravi piece I need to write for the WB. I intend to use Rodin's book on steward leadership in the short piece, and as it happens MB and I just now, a little after noon, spent time reading a section from his book. We were at a section that talked about how a leader shapes culture, which is interesting because, following Crouch, I have often tended to think of the start of the Center as an intentional effort to do some culture building. Rodin emphasized in today's selection for a leader neither to underestimate his role in shaping the culture of his or her organization, nor to overestimate it, especially after they leave. This is a good reminder to me that the ultimate direction of the Center may go in unanticipated directions after my tenure ends, and that this is perfectly okay. God is likely to use the next leader to set a new tone and trajectory, and I need to be okay with that. This thing is far bigger than I.

Marybeth got a call in the afternoon from the high school. They decided to go in a different direction. So one door closed. Now let's see if the other one opens! Exciting stuff.

Saturday, March 13, 2021: Encouraging day! Marvelous breakfast at Toasted Yolk, and Jonathan got up the Moral Apologetics Press tab at our site. Looks great; this is the mission statement of the Press he asked me to write: "Moral Apologetics Press has for its primary purpose the publication of books that advance the mission of the Center for Moral Apologetics at Houston Baptist University. This mission has six crucial ingredients: (1) defending theistic ethics against various objections and offering positive evidential reasons in its favor; (2) critiquing secular ethical theories and demonstrating their relative inadequacy in accounting for the full range of moral phenomena in need of explanation; (3) defending moral realism on which the enterprise of moral apologetics is predicated; (4) extending the moral argument to a positive moral case for Christianity in particular; (5) highlighting the rich and fertile history of the moral argument; and (6) encouraging dialogue with non-Christian religious approaches by comparing and contrasting their ethical foundations with those from the Judeo-Christian tradition."

Also received Daniel McCoy's signed contract for his book, so I electronically signed it as well. Great fun. Most encouraging. I also got a FB message from a fellow who is part of the Hare book discussion group: "David (if I may), I am in the manuscript review group with you for Prof. Hare's upcoming book. I wanted to say how much I've appreciated your work through the years (both the work in Phil. & literature and moral philosophy). *Good God* was one of those books that stuck with me in college and sparked my interest in moral philosophy, more broadly." His name is Chet; what a marvelous encouragement!

Heard from Matthew at Houston Christian a few days ago. He wrote this:

Hi Dr. Baggett,

Thanks for reaching out. I have a few thoughts I'd like to run by you if that's okay. Over the past few months I have been consuming as much of the literature on supererogation and the relevant issues in metaethics as I can. I have read some of Aquinas and Scotus as well as several contemporary DCT, natural lawyers, and virtue ethicists. As I have been thinking about the argument I will present in my mock thesis as well creating an outline and writing the introduction section, I have come to some interesting considerations and potentially successful arguments about supererogation. I have also come to several difficult questions that I imagine will still need much thinking.

My argument is for a sort of quasi-supererogatory act that relies heavily on the idea of vocation. If the three classical conditions for supererogatory acts are 1. The performance of the act fulfills no moral duty or obligation; 2. The performance of the act is morally praiseworthy; and 3. The omission of the act is not morally blameworthy, then I will contend that no such acts exist for one individual agent, but they do exist when comparing agents.

The metaethical framework that I argue for grounds questions of value in the nature of God and questions of obligation in human nature, both the haecceity and quiddity. I argue that the essence of an individual is what that individual is without flaw, and, though humans are presently flawed, we must (in the obligatory sense) use practical rationality to attain this fully actualized version of ourselves. For questions of the good I am still hesitant to make a highly specific claim and I don't think it is particularly necessary for my argument for me to do so. All I know about the good is that I can't be a nominalist and I can't be an Aristotelian. I have some concerns about classical divine conceptualism and I am looking into William Lane Craig's version of anti-realism. Currently I am writing the section of my paper where I try to substantiate the claims I have made about the nature of the good and right. Then I will write about how this broader metaethical view seems to lead to the existence of something like supererogation.

What my view allows me to do is explain the phenomenon of supererogation rather than the actual existence of supererogatory acts. Under my teleological view of obligation it seems inconceivable that someone could actually go beyond their end. If some action is morally good and the person is physiologically capable to do the act at that time, then I think it is both Biblical and potentially metaphysically arguable that the person has a moral obligation to perform that action. If this is what truly constitutes moral obligation, then I think it is obvious that different people have different obligations. A man in a wheelchair that cannot swim does not have a moral obligation to save a drowning child, but a physically capable person does have that obligation. Nevertheless, saving a drowning child is both good and praiseworthy. Thus, between the two people, the action fulfills all three conditions for supererogatory acts. Saving a drowning child is morally praiseworthy to perform, not blameworthy not to perform for the injured person, and it fulfills the obligation of the capable person. Although I think my view leads to anti-supererogationism, I think it successfully explains the apparent existence of acts of supererogation.

At this point, I must, over the next couple of months, compile all the research I have done into a complete document and then prepare a presentation. I have written some of the sections, including the introduction section. I have attached the introduction to this email and would appreciate any critiques you have of it. I really appreciate all your help!

Sincerely,
Matthew

To which I responded like this today:

Matthew:

Thanks for this! Let me respond piece by piece.

First, there's a good dissertation on supererogation you might want to look at by Claire Brown (at least that's her maiden name; she married a guy named Peterson, so not sure if her name now is Claire Peterson—first I'd check Brown). Well worth reading if you get a chance. Supererogation is certainly an interesting topic!

Okay, so the view you wish to take, if I read you right, is that there's a kind of appearance of supererogation, but not really supererogation. Is that right? By the way, if so, this reminds me (especially the denial of supererogation) of the way lots of Calvinists, Lutherans, and Methodists have historically been skeptical of supererogation. By coincidence I wrote about this yesterday in a piece that's still a work in progress about the fall of Ravi Zacharias for the *Worldview Bulletin*:

> As an ethicist I have occasionally pondered why certain theologians dismiss the idea of *supererogation*—a big word that refers to actions we are praiseworthy for doing but not blameworthy for not doing. It's the idea of going above and beyond the call of duty. Lutherans and Calvinists, in particular, are skeptical of such a notion, tending to stress that the demands of God are so extensive and prohibitive that human beings don't have the slightest chance of ever satisfying them, let alone going beyond them.
>
> Although I retain the category of supererogation as an ethicist, I have come to see a real measure of wisdom in the aforementioned theological reticence. A particularly heartbreaking revelation that came out of the Ravi story was how he seems to have seen his ministry as entitlement for wrongful indulgence, perhaps even predation. When a leader falls into the trap of thinking that his sacrifice and service entitles him to partake of some proverbial forbidden fruit, he is forgetting that it's by God's grace alone we stand and breathe. When we have expended ourselves entirely in outreach, ours should be an attitude that says only this: This was merely my duty to God. The occupational hazard or pitfall of leadership to do otherwise poses a continual temptation, and we can and sadly do succumb to it in a variety of ways, big and small.

So I include that just to let you know from the start that I'm inclined to think the category of supererogation makes good philosophical sense, even if there's an eminently understandable theological rationale for resistance to or reticence about it in a distinct and real sense.

Okay, so you cite as the "classical conditions" for a supererogatory act that it isn't dutiful, it's morally praiseworthy, and its omission isn't blameworthy. And you wish to argue that no such acts exist for one individual agent, but they do exist when comparing agents, as you put it. On the surface of it, of course, this raises a number of challenges, including of course what exactly it means. (I'm proceeding through your e-mail piece by piece, so you're hearing me think out loud, as it were.)

Regarding value, you find its locus in the nature of God; I am drawn to that. Regarding obligations, you find its locus in human nature, both haecceity and quiddity, both the *thisness* of persons and *whatness* of persons. Okay, you're not alone, I suspect, though I move in a bit of a different direction on the latter, but this is interesting stuff.

So you argue that the essence of an individual is what that individual is without flaw. Since our sinful conditions are contingent and thus not essential features of ourselves, this makes very decent sense, in my estimation.

Then you say that though humans are presently flawed, we must use practical rationality to attain this fully actualized version of ourselves. Okay, though wondering what this looks like, so I continue....

Regarding the good, though you tie it to God's nature, you're still trying to find the right detailed story. You're potentially drawn to Craig's personalism rather than, say, theistic Platonism. That's fine. Ultimately to affirm that God, in one sense or other, is the ultimate Good makes good sense to me. Seems like either a personalist or a theistic activist or a theistic Platonist or a conceptualist approach can affirm something in the neighborhood. But I also agree you needn't settle that matter here; given the size and complexity and inherent difficulty of the question, delimiting your thesis is crucial anyway, so good call. You really have to take this delimitation constraint seriously if you hope to make this a manageable project within the time and space strictures.

Though you can but gesture toward the good and various possible fine-grained accounts of it, you will need to spell out your account of the right (in the sense of the dutiful) more carefully in light of your subject of supererogation. I'd say get to that as soon as you can. Time is of the essence.

Now, when you say you want to explain the phenomenon of supererogation rather than the existence of such acts, you need to clarify a bit. Do you mean the concept of supererogation? Or do you mean the (mere) appearance of such acts? "Phenomenon" is too vague a term in this context. Try to clarify that, it's important.

You then make reference to your "teleological view of obligation," but be sure, as I said a moment ago, to spell that out clearly and cleanly. In what sense do obligations derive from our nature—be it our human nature generally or individual essence particularly or some combination thereof? I'm also wondering where the authority of such obligations derives on your view. Simply because an action might help fulfill our nature doesn't seem adequately to account for the requisite binding authority of moral obligations—and our blameworthiness for failing to discharge them. Thinking otherwise seems objectionably predicated on conflating moral and nonmoral goods. This is why I tend to be skeptical, in general, of thinking an appeal to practical rationality alone suffices to undergird the moral authority of our obligations, which to my thinking is one of the most important moral phenomena in need of adequate explanation—and thus a crucial litmus test for a good moral theory.

At any rate, on your view it strains credulity that one could "go beyond their end." This conviction or perspective of yours might reside in close proximity to the aforementioned theological rationale for resisting supererogation. Perhaps you could strengthen your case by making explicit this alignment yourself. Calvin, Luther, Wesley, use them; at least worth a note or something so your view doesn't seem free-floating, unmotivated, or largely unconnected with the literature.

But I'm wondering at this point about the connection between the three conditions of supererogation and your notion of "going beyond one's end." If I were to volunteer at the soup kitchen five days a week, it seems to me that goes beyond my duty, I wouldn't be blameworthy for not doing it (most likely— though in principle on my view I could be if God specifically called me to do it), and it's plausible to say I'm praiseworthy for doing it at least in a rough-and-ready colloquial sense (surely not praiseworthy the way God's praiseworthy). I wouldn't say the behavior "goes beyond my end," but I'd still say it's supererogatory. If you wish to deny that, which of the three conditions isn't being fulfilled, on your view? Or is there a fourth condition for supererogation you're assuming? If so, what is it?

You remind me a little of Kant. Remember his distinction between the phenomenal and noumenal? If we were purely noumenal creatures, we wouldn't be concerned with something like happiness; virtue alone would be enough. But since we inhabit both spheres, it's the conjunction of happiness and virtue that's our highest good. There's a certain concession he wants to make to our being more than purely noumenal creatures. You, too, seem to recognize a certain bifurcation: our best, idealized, actualized self on the one hand, and our contingently fallen condition on the other. And you use this distinction to do some work. It remains to be seen if your distinction can do the work you want it to.

As to whether you're right in your conceivability claim concerning going beyond our end, much will depend on what "going beyond" our end *means*. If you don't want to spell that out in terms of the three conditions for supererogation, the reader needs to know why. If you do, be as explicit as you can be.

Now, this may be your attempt: "If some action is morally good and the person is physiologically capable to do the act at that time, then I think it is both Biblical and potentially metaphysically arguable that the person has a moral obligation to perform that action." But surely this needs qualification. For one thing, we have to choose from among which good acts to perform. For another thing, various nonmoral goods presumably wouldn't be morally obligatory. It might be a good thing to become a dentist; it seems odd to say one is morally obligated to do it. But most importantly, it seems intuitively implausible that we're obligated to do each and every good action we're capable of. That would actually make us morally blameworthy for ever doing something other than morally good things, except insofar as taking a break is required for us to gather our strength to continue. This leads to a prohibitively, simply impossibly rigorous regimen of good works in this life. It sets the bar way too high, at least in a practical way and likely in a moral way, because as human beings we're, well, more than noumenal creatures alone. Rather than enhancing freedom, it would severely restrict it, among other problems. This is where I think you could take a lesson from Kant. If your intuition is that the claim is right, I'm in no position to insist you're wrong, of course; and you're potentially in good company with some major theologians, but as an ethicist I find that such a claim strains credulity beyond the breaking point.

Much will ride on how you think obligations derive from our natures, of course, so I'll look forward to hearing that story.

Now, you say your story entails that folks will have different obligations. Perhaps. But from what I'm seeing so far, there's something else that bears emphasis: this account so far is very open ended. It's a formal-looking approach that doesn't tell people what their obligations are. Again, how do we decide which of the good actions at our disposal are the ones we should choose to do? Should I go help out at the soup kitchen or make money to send to famine relief?

By the way, I think some of this rings a bell with aspects of Hare's book *God's Command*, where he talks about the way in which utilitarianism at times sets impossibly high moral demands on us. Might be worth a look.

Now, regarding the child-saving scenario, I'd agree a person has a duty to do so if he's able. Such a thing isn't supererogatory, but dutiful. But in light of the fact that there's more, to my thinking, to morality than doing our duties, there are ever so many instances of, say, loving actions that go beyond our moral duties. Here again you remind me of Kant, but I might disagree with you both; I think conducting moral discussions in terms inordinately shaped by obligation discourse leaves too much out. This is one of my critiques of Calvinism, as you know: does God have an obligation to save anyone? Perhaps not. But so what, I'm inclined to say. For God's motivated by things like love, which goes far beyond duties. It's practically obscene to speak in terms of a mother's sacrifice of herself for her child as a duty; it may well be a duty, but I would hope and suspect in the vast swath of cases that's not the reason she would do it, and without hesitation. In God's case, since there are no conflicting desires or contrary impulses, I agree with Kant that he has no obligations, but still we can speak of his moral nature—his goodness, his grace, his love, etc. All of this to say that duties are but one (relatively small) aspect of ethics, and we overemphasize their importance to the detriment of our analysis, I think. I suspect they're like training wheels at this early stage of our moral maturation and eventually we'll leave them far behind and matters like gift and sacrifice will replace them.

I agree that saving the drowning a child is good, and it's also praiseworthy, but on the standard model of supererogation, that doesn't preclude its being a duty. Praiseworthiness is *necessary* for supererogation, not *sufficient*. What's sufficient, presumably, is the simultaneous or several fulfillment of all three conditions, each individually necessary.

I think your account of the mere appearance of supererogation fails exactly because of your comparative component. The disabled man isn't obligated to save the drowning child, the able man is obligated. In the latter case, he would have been blameworthy not to do it. The fact that someone not similarly situated or equally capable wouldn't have been blameworthy isn't relevant. (But I see now how you're tying it to the three conditions, but I think that analysis fails for just the reason you think it works.)

Part of your analysis might be predicated on the idea that moral duties have to be universal, but DCT'ists who believe in what Evans calls the "discretionary hypothesis" (like I do—basically, the idea that some of God's commands are contingent) don't believe a duty has to apply across the board. (This is why I may have an obligation you don't, or vice versa, on my view.) Yes, at least some are likely necessary, but other duties are relativized to persons and their capacities, situations, callings, divine commands to persons, etc. A general command might apply to you but not to me in a particular situation; some specific commands might be issued to me but not you; etc. I don't see any of this helping anti-supererogationism.

So I'm left rather unconvinced by your argument, but still, intrigued; I think it's a clever attempt! Of course you can always make your case, and then make a case against it—that might be a good thesis! At the very least I hope this can help you anticipate some robust objections or concerns you might wish to address.

Thanks for letting me take a look at this. Even if I'm right that your analysis doesn't quite work, at least at this stage of the game, none of your mistakes strike me as dumb ones. Quite to the contrary! It's a very good start!

But chop chop, my friend; don't let the clock run out before you've churned this baby out! You can do it; I'm rooting for you!

Blessings, and keep in touch,
Dave B.

Sunday, March 14, 2021: Largely a day of rest. Phil Tallon, the new permanent dean, intends to meet with each member of the SCT over the next few weeks to discuss its future. It should be a good chance to discuss space for the Center, the Press, contact information on donors, the website for the Center, and PhD ideas (apologetics, phil rel). Jonathan Pruitt also added information to the Press tab at the site to let prospective writers know the procedure of how to submit proposals. Felt discouraged a bit today, reminding me of last Tuesday. Perhaps occasional bouts with doubts and worries and fears are something I need to expect from time to time. Wish I knew what victory in such circumstances looked like. It's after 8 in the evening now; lost an hour with daylight savings time this weekend, so headed to bed. Hope I feel better in the morning. Thankful that God's mercies are new every morning. No word from Matthew after I e-mailed him yesterday; he apparently doesn't feel much obligation to acknowledge my messages. Fair enough!

Monday, March 15, 2021: Woke up feeling much today than I did yesterday. Mindful of the need each day to put on the full armor of God before going forth to do battle. No news yet from Fraser; I should be getting the revision of his fifth chapter soon. When I do, I'll get Jerry a copy. The rest of the day I hope to work some more on the Ravi piece, wrap up grading for my Foundations course, re-read more from Fraser's dissertation, and start my preparation for the Thursday chat with Craig. Could really use to get back on my low-carb regimen and go for a walk as well. This evening there's a zoom alumni reunion meeting I am somewhat obligated to attend.

Weird sometimes to think about how life might have gone differently. Had I stayed at King's, I'd be in my 19th year. Had I stayed at Liberty, I'd be in my 15th year. Instead, I'm in my first year at HBU, feeling like a rookie. It's humbling. Trusting God uses all of this. HBU is just filled with people—fallible folks with their own insecurities, foibles, agendas, limitations one would find anywhere else. Just like me. But this is where I have been called, and where I am to expend myself in service—sometimes seemingly fruitless service, sometimes glorious, at other times frustrating or flummoxing, on occasion even dispiriting or depressing, even more than humbling very occasionally, almost humiliating. Sometimes I almost have the sense that I was called to Houston to die—not physically, but the way a seed has to die to prepare for a crop. Sometimes it feels more than a little like dying, some of what's transpired and still to come. My prayer is that God's life manifests in the death, God's glory in the humiliation, God's power in my weakness, God's beauty in my uncomeliness.

Spent most of the afternoon reading Oliphint; have lots of ideas about how to articulate my numerous reservations about presuppositionalism (or covenant apologetics, as he calls it, or transcendentalism; hope to find some time soon to write some of those out). In the morning I wrapped up my revision of a second blog for my site on the moral argument and Christian theology:

The Moral Argument and Christian Theology, Part II: Sanctification

The first installment of this series covered forgiveness. To be made right or reconciled with a holy God involves forgiveness for the many ways in which all of us fall short. More than this is required, but such forgiveness is an ineliminably important part of this process. Mercifully, because of God's provision in Christ, forgiveness is available for those who seek it.

Another part of a reconciled relationship with God has to do with the next step or stage of salvation—still tied to the theology of "justification," but usually more associated with what theologians call "sanctification." Intimate and organic connections obtain between justification and sanctification, but rather than offering an exegetical analysis, we are using these categories as a way to connect the parts of Christian salvation with aspects of the moral argument. After our conversion to Christ, we are still left with a moral gap—the space between where we are morally and spiritually, on the one hand, and where we need to be, on the other. We have a long way to go. That gap needs to be closed. To be forgiven without being changed leaves too much undone.

Another way to put it is like this: we need more than our sins to be forgiven; we need our sin problem itself to be taken away. A documentary concerning the issue of nutrition and physical health I saw a few years ago may be helpful here by way of analogy. One of its basic claims is that doctors do not really produce health. About the best they can do is remove some barriers that impede and stand in the way of health. What actually produces health is the properly functioning body—a healthy immune system, a body, properly treated and fed, doing what it was meant to do.

This is most clearly seen when it comes to chronic diseases. Doctors and pharmaceutical companies cannot fix such problems. What they can do is provide medicines that help alleviate and manage certain symptoms and make life more

115

comfortable for the patient, even while the affliction persists, managed to one degree or another. Although medical practitioners are rather limited in what they are able to do, the body is remarkably resilient in its ability to ward off diseases, recover from various injuries, and heal itself. This is why proper nutrition and exercise are so important, because they enable the body to do what it does best. Chronically undernourished or sedentary bodies eventually become impaired in their ability to perform their proper functions.

The point of the documentary was well made: there is a crucial difference between genuine health, on the one hand, and merely improving conditions, on the other, however much a blessing the latter can be. Another fitting analogy would be the distinction between pulling out a weed versus killing its root. The former is at best a temporary fix; the underlying problem will recur until the latter step is taken.

A similar distinction holds in the arena of morality. One option is merely to deal with symptoms, settling for marginal moral improvements, avoiding hurtful consequences by our actions. True achievement of integrity, virtue, and holiness, though, requires considerably more. In light of what seem to be some deeply entrenched patterns of selfishness and moral weakness endemic to the human condition, we need powerful resources to meet the moral demand and effect the needed change in our character.

Benjamin Franklin once tried to do this on his own, setting himself to the formidable task of achieving moral perfection. In "Arriving at Perfection," an excerpt from his *Autobiography*, he wrote about his plans to conquer all imperfections that either natural inclination, custom, or company might lead him into, but "I soon found I had undertaken a task of more difficulty than I had imagined. While my care was employ'd in guarding against one fault, I was often surprised by another; habit took the advantage of inattention; inclination was sometimes too strong for reason."

Immanuel Kant recognized that we fall short of what morality requires, and so he said we need to have moral faith: the belief that the moral life is *possible*. But in light of our moral malady, this requires radical transformation. Can we be transformed? This is a second great existential moral need, after forgiveness. Perhaps owing to his Lutheran upbringing, Kant was quite sure that human beings have a deep moral problem, a tendency to be curved inward on themselves, an intractable ethical taint, a deeply flawed moral disposition in need of a revolution. Kant saw clearly that the moral demand on us is very high, while also recognizing that we have a natural propensity not to follow it.

Malcolm Muggeridge once said that the depravity of man is at once the most empirically verifiable reality but at the same time the most intellectually resisted fact. In Kant, the parallel suggestion seems to be not just that we happen to fail to meet the moral demand, but that our failure is inevitable. We have a problem, one too deep for us to solve on our own. Humans are not essentially good. We are broken, deeply broken, and need to be healed at the root, not merely the symptoms removed. Like Clay Jones puts it, all of us are born Auschwitz-enabled—the people responsible for such unspeakable atrocities of history were not, as human beings go, preternaturally bad people. They were garden variety human beings who, when certain circumstances presented themselves, behaved deplorably. All of us have that hideous potential. Moral ugliness lurks in each of our hearts. There is something in need of radical fixing deep within us. We need major moral surgery.

The moral standard remains obstinately in place, but because of our moral weakness, corrupt characters, irremediable selfishness, intractable egoism, and the like, we are unable to meet that standard. An axiomatic deontic principle is that "ought implies can" in some sense, and yet we seem to be obligated to do what we simply cannot. How can this make sense? Augustine offered the crucial insight: God bids us to do what we cannot, in order that we might learn our dependence on Him. We cannot live as we ought in our own strength alone, but we can by God's grace, with divine assistance.

So, even without sugarcoating our brokenness, there is great hope. Christianity says the needed resources for transformation are available. Although we cannot meet the moral demand on our own, God himself has made it possible, if we but submit and allow Him to do it through us. It may well require a painful process, but it is possible.

Having started his book *Mere Christianity* with talk of the moral gap between what we are and what we ought to be, Lewis then explained his reason for doing so. His explanation is telling. The passage can be found in his concluding paragraph of Book 1:

> My reason was that Christianity simply does not make sense until you have faced the sort of facts I have been describing. Christianity tells people to repent and promises them forgiveness. … It is after you have realized that there is a real Moral Law, and a Power behind the law, and that you have broken that law and put yourself wrong with that Power— it is after all this, and not a moment sooner, that Christianity begins to talk. When you know you are sick, you will listen to the doctor. When you have realized that our position is nearly desperate you will begin to understand what the Christians are talking about. They offer an explanation of how we got into our present state of both hating goodness and loving it. They offer an explanation of how God can be this impersonal mind at the back of the Moral Law and yet also a Person. They tell you how the demands of this law, which you and I cannot meet, have been met on our behalf, how God Himself becomes a man to save man from the disapproval of God.

God can do more than merely ameliorate the symptoms of our chronic moral malady. In the face of our urgent need to become not just *better* people, but *new* people, and our desperate need for a revolution of the will and for radical moral transformation, the death and resurrection of Christ is indeed "good news." This issue of transformation, again, is the theological category of *sanctification*. Just as God answers our need for forgiveness, God's grace in sanctification answers our need for radical moral transformation.

By the way, biblical holiness is not just *individual*, but *social*. And here one like Paul Copan has done us a great service by bringing a historical twist to the moral argument. He has shown how historically it has been Christ followers who were largely responsible for such significant social advances as building orphanages, arguing for the inherent dignity of the handicapped and infirmed, fighting for women's suffrage, standing against foot-binding, and so forth. This investigation gets into historical contingencies, but it remains an important empirical consideration, one that brings to mind John Wesley's refrain that there is no holiness without social holiness.

Having discussed our need for and God's gracious gift of both forgiveness and transformation, next time we will discuss a third deep existential and spiritual need, namely, to be morally healed *completely*, saved to the uttermost.

Tuesday, March 16, 2021: Read most of ch. 3 of Hare's new book today; seven pages left to read in the morning before our zoom session. Fascinating stuff! Mind-blowing at points; need to think more about a line like this: "But a principle that is within the theoretical use of reason merely 'regulative' (telling us that we should conduct our thinking as if it were true) can be within the practical use of reason 'constitutive' (telling us what we should think is actually the case)." [Which reminds me of a line from a FB message from Chet Duke some days ago with which I tend to concur: "I think the works of Dr. Hare, Chris Firestone, Stephen Palmquist, etc. represent a sea-change in Kant studies regarding the significance of religion in Kant's thought."]

Thought a bit today about story or narrative; the issue came up in the Hare chapter, and he adduced the work of several who have touched on it, including Charles Taylor. I suppose in a real sense this journal I keep is gradually telling my story, in addition to the story of the Center. The process of laying such a story (or stories) out is a useful one, I think. It helps crystallize a measure of clarity about what is it about the story that's genuinely central. Hopefully what I increasingly think of as central is what God himself intends to be central. If I were to hazard a guess about what's central, and meant to be central, in my life I would surely say, after my family relationships, is my vocation as a moral apologist. I aim to do philosophy well and right, on ancient foundations, using the phenomena of moral reality to point people to God and to Christ. This is what I hope to expend myself in service to do, until God calls me home.

Jonathan whipped up contracts for TJ's two books he wants to do with MAP; TJ wants to donate all of their proceeds to the Center. I wrapped up my first eight-week online class today, turning in grades and offering a few reflections on presuppositionalism (transcendental or covenantal apologetics). Here is what I wrote the class about the latter, though it's just a start of the reflections I would eventually like to articulate:

First, a presuppositionalist approach seems highly tied to Calvinist theology, and not just Reformed theology more generally. Olson has rightly distinguished these two. Calvinism is one among other significant Reformed traditions, and it's a tradition about which I entertain a number of reservations. Numerous times while reading Oliphint what he had to say struck me as heavily Calvinist in tone, and since I find Calvinism deeply unpersuasive, and predicated on a picture of God I have a hard time recognizing as essentially loving, some of my skepticism carries over to presuppositionalism. Some might suggest I'm wrong to let that happen, but there are aspects of this apologetic approach that make good sense on Calvinism but are far less intuitive for someone like me. Who we think God is does and rightly should shape the way in which we do evangelism and apologetics.

Second, presuppositionalism always strikes me as problematically circular. We have seen this issue earlier in the term, but it invariably rears its head. It's true that not every circularity is a "vicious circularity," but Oliphint's view *does* strike me as viciously circular. And if persuasion is what he's after, as he claims (and I have great respect for the discipline of rhetoric), the transparent circularity of the approach detracts, it seems to me, from this ostensible motivating purpose.

Third, I think Oliphint is right to see apologetics and evangelism or preaching as related, but I think he tends to blur the distinction between them altogether. Sometimes apologetics can do important pre-evangelistic work, it seems to me. Sometimes it's time to evangelize, sometimes it's time to answer various questions and do apologetics as a preliminary to evangelism. Sometimes it's right to proclaim, and other times it's more appropriate to converse and dialogue.

Fourth, the approach strikes me as deductivism on steroids. Personally I tend to gravitate more to cumulative cases and nondeductive argument forms, since they strike me as more dialogical and bridge-building. Oliphint, following Van Til, seems not to be much of a fan of building bridges with unbelievers. I disagree. I think this is a highly effective way to reach people. Implicating people in contradictions might appeal to some; I tend rather to talk about what better explains various phenomena (order, existence, mind, consciousness, beauty, duties, goodness, rationality, etc.), rather than the *only* or *only possible* explanation. I know some like to think of apologetics as giving people no wiggle room, backing them into a corner, going for the jugular, etc. I don't.

Fifth, I agree that apologetics should aim toward the case for Christ, but I find unpersuasive the way the presupps aim to do that. I think often it's best to argue for theism first and Christianity later. Lewis first became a theist, then became a Christian. Some are ready to do it all at once, but I don't like what I consider to be cookie cutter approaches predicated on the notion that there's just one best way to go about this. Sensitivity to the guidance of the Holy Spirit likely suggests otherwise.

Sixth, Oliphint thinks apologetics is mainly about answering challenges to Christianity. I don't see it that way. I think there are lots of positive reasons we can give for theism and Christianity—apart from the defensive task of answering objections. And the positive case is, to my thinking, the more important job. There are important phenomena in need of robust and excellent explanation, and I think theism and Christianity best explain them in a way that speaks to us imaginatively, creatively, affectively, relationally, aesthetically, and ethically—in short, holistically.

Wednesday, March 17, 2021: This morning we did the third zoom session with John Hare and his group of Yalies. Bright folks. The discussion was interesting. John has a child who went through gender reassignment surgery. It's fascinating to see a profound Christian ethicist struggle with something so intensely that's so personal to him. It's hard not to think there's some capitulation to secularity, but it would also be extremely difficult to suggest as much to him personally. I will likely have occasion to write about this soon, as I took copious notes and will probably be recording them on the computer before long.

Other than that I largely took it easy today, although MB did our taxes and discovered that our refund should be just big enough to get us out of debt completely within about three weeks. Good news! And a good feeling! Trusting the God really enables us to use our extra resources to bless others.

Thursday, March 18, 2021: It's very early in the morning as I write this. I may go back to bed for some more sleep before long. But up early because an upcoming event is on my mind. In the afternoon, around 2 pm I think it is, I have an hour and a half video scheduled with Cameron Bertuzzi and William Lane Craig to discuss the moral argument and our upcoming class in May. This is quite an honor, but a bit nerve-wracking. Hope to spend the morning hours reviewing various versions of the argument, as Cameron cast the discussion in terms of which moral argument is the best. Mainly I want to emphasize their cumulative power and the chance to audit the upcoming class, in an effort to garner more and more interest in this important topic. Grateful for the opportunity and praying that God prepares my heart and mind.

It's now after dinner. The chat with Cameron and Craig was lots of fun! Most enjoyable! Very grateful it's over and overall went pretty well. The comments on YouTube about it, though, are predictably critical for the most part. Something about the culture generally or the culture of certain apologetic discussion forums weighs heavily in that direction, sadly.

Friday, March 19, 2021: I woke up this morning with this e-mail in my inbox: "Dear Dr. Baggett, [y]ou do not know me, I recently came across your work through viewing the *Capturing Christianity* episode where you present a moral argument with William Lane Craig, and while I acknowledge that this might be a bit out of the ordinary, I thought I'd ask you if you could direct me at some work on metaethics done by Christian philosophers. You see, I am a Christian research Master student at a secular university in the Netherlands, i.e. Groningen University, and I'm having some difficulty finding cutting edge papers on metaethics from a Christian perspective. Now that I know of your work I will be spending some time reading it, but if you know of anyone who is explicitly working in meta-ethics, perhaps even as a critic of error-theory, then I'd really like to familiarize myself with their work as well. I hope this wasn't too forward of me. Kind regards, Johan Rodenburg."

To which I responded, "Hi Johan, so nice to hear from you! Thank you for the note. Terence Cuneo from the University of Vermont, I think it is, is a Christian philosopher who works in metaethics. He's a great place to begin. He has a number of articles on it, and also some books. I would encourage you to start there. He does not tend to make his theism too explicit in his writings; he is a nonnaturalist, but much of what he writes is consistent with a religious metaethic. Mark Murphy at Georgetown has done interesting work on God and ethics. I tend to disagree with some of how he goes about things, but he's very bright and worth reading. Robert Adams' work on metaethics from a theistic perspective is crucial. See especially his Finite and Infinite Goods, which includes portions of articles he had written on the topic over a twenty-year period. Steve Evans from Baylor has done some good work, including a few books and recently an article critiquing Peter Railton's constructivism for falling prey to Euthyphro-like objections that theism could solve. Yale's John Hare has a number of important works on God and ethics you might wish to look at, and he's currently wrapping up a trilogy on it. That's a start anyway. Personally I wish more Christian philosophers were actively involved in and contributing to the literature of metaethics. It could do real good and it is one of my real hopes and dreams. Jerry Walls and I are now writing a book on moral realism, and we will have a chapter on error theory. Although I have done some work on the chapter, it is not yet complete. But basically my argument will be that theism solves every alleged problem with moral realism that Mackie identifies (a few by Mackie's own admission). Hope this helps a bit! Blessings! Dave"

That was a nice piece of fruit that came from yesterday's event. Almost makes worth it some of the acerbic critiques offered. It's actually an oft'-discussed phenomenon that the comment section on things like YouTube videos are something to avoid for the

121

sake of one's mental health. But the truly ugly nature of so many of such comments does make one wonder where it comes from. It certainly bolsters one's convictions about a deep-rooted depravity in the human heart.

TJ and I had a good chat and prayer time. One of the things we discussed is that we probably need to dissolve the Moral Apol LLC and instead begin a 501c3. Live and learn!

Saturday, March 20, 2021: Fun evening last night with Rob and Jerry. Rob had written a challenging piece on FB critiquing the way Catholics refuse to allow Protestants at Table. I deeply concur. We discussed that, and had great fun, usually at one another's expense, throughout the course of the evening. Today I'll be chatting with Elton in an hour and a half, and not long after that MB and I are going to go away for the day and spend tonight in a hotel—out near where I'll be getting my second vaccine shot at around 1 pm near the Woodlands.

I need to speak to the Director of that other Center at HBU before too long.

Sunday, March 21, 2021: Got my shot yesterday, about 24 hours ago now. The only side effect seems to me some extra tiredness. It made my sleeping more difficult last night in the hotel, ironically. I was both especially tired and had a hard time getting to and staying asleep. We're home now, a little afternoon. I have a video chat with my African friend about *Good God* around 3:30 my time, so I think I have a chance to fit in a nap beforehand.

By the way, this was an interesting FB exchange on TJ's page. He shared about my chat with Craig, and a friend of his asked him a few questions, as follows: His friend Matthew first wrote that "C. S. Lewis's moral argument from *Mere Christianity* is my favorite though I don't know if it is the best." TJ responded, "What I appreciate most about Dave's approach is the emphasis on abduction in making a moral argument." Matthew asked, "What is abduction in making a moral argument?" And TJ's answer was this:

> Abduction is concerned more with method than anything. When Craig makes his argument he generally follows a deductive method which seeks to affirm, based on premises, an outcome that is logically necessary. Abduction, especially through the lens of Dave's four-fold approach (moral facts, moral knowledge, moral transformation, moral rationality) has a teleological sense to it that morality is pointing toward a goal, a cumulative sense that morality gives so many deliverances about life and meaning that there is this building, mounting explanatory power that leads to its outcome. Basically it's an outcome that concludes God is a very likely explanation for morality--possibly/probably the best explanation. But it doesn't insist on the type of certainty that deductive

structuring does. As an apologist I find abduction much more conducive to ongoing discussion and a sense of epistemic humility.

Monday, March 22, 2021: Feeling completely recovered from my second vaccine shot, and glad to be in this place. Up early to start the day, and just listened to the scriptures. In the OT passage the Israelites are on the move, going from place to place, closer and closer to the promised land. I love the journey imagery, as it's so true to life for us all.

The conversation yesterday afternoon with Kedric was fun. He has a good mind, and I think the time invested with him should be well spent. He lives in New Zealand. I appreciate his interest in the material of moral apologetics.

Starting to teach a new eight-week online class today, an introduction to philosophy. The first course I'm doing at HBU outside apologetics. Should be interesting. Pretty full class of 30 folks or so. I need to get into Bb and set things up and start getting oriented to it all.

Got to work in earnest today rereading Fraser's dissertation. It's really good stuff on the debunking argument against moral realism and/or moral knowledge, and since I'm doing a chapter on it in the new book, this will prove most helpful.

Finally churned out my Ravi response for the WB:

I had intentionally refrained from entering the fray of the Ravi Zacharias situation, for a number of reasons, not the least of which that there has been no shortage of vocal commentators. But our fearless leader Chris Reese charged us with the task of responding, so with tremulous trepidation I will venture a few brief thoughts, knowing full well in advance that there are pitfalls aplenty all about. I will limit my general points or observations to five.

First, I hope the church sees this as a general call for repentance. Unless we see the larger picture and feel the call to repent generally, the temptation will be to scapegoat one fellow, and that would be a shame. Judgment begins in the house of God, the Bible tells us, and God's people are called to seek God's face and turn from their wicked ways and to pray; then, we are told, God will hear from heaven, forgive their sin, and heal their land.

Second, among what that biblical injunction implies is that God's people are quite capable of wickedness. Even people doing powerful ministry can get caught up in entrenched patterns of sin. Moses' face shone with the presence of God at Mount Sinai, yet he didn't enter into all that God had for him (the promised land). Peter identified Jesus as God's Chosen One, insight given him by the Spirit of God, but almost immediately served as the mouthpiece for the enemy in denying the need for the cross. We all of us remain profound admixtures of light and darkness, and so this is a powerful teachable moment for us all. Let's remember, before building ministries or reputations or platforms, to seek first the kingdom of God and his righteousness.

Third, this call to holiness and radical repentance trumps even the need for greater strictures of accountability. External measures of accountability for Christian leaders are vitally important—and one ineliminable step to address the crisis of leadership in the evangelical world—but infinitely more important is allowing God to do the work within us that he wants to do. It appears sadly true that Ravi did not find some of the victory over certain besetting sins that he could and should have. The lesson is not to finger wag, pontificate, or think ourselves better, but to realize that we too are vulnerable to whatever our own areas of weakness may be. Either we avail ourselves of God's deliverance and path of escape, or our sins will find us out.

Fourth, regarding sexual sin in particular, marriage alone isn't the answer. It can help, but married or single, all of us as Christian believers need to realize that a ceremony different from marriage is called for. What's needed is a funeral. Certain lustful desires have to die for they have no legitimate satisfaction in the Christian life. The power that raised Jesus from the dead is at work within us, and we can trust God's grace to forgive us as we repent, to change us as we trust and obey him, and ultimately to save us to the uttermost. All of us have to remain sensitized to those areas of our lives where we refuse to relinquish total control to Christ. I was raised in the holiness tradition, and remember many a camp meeting sermons encouraging "total submission to the kingship of Christ," and I wondered where I could find the "total commitment" button to push. It is here: let's turn to God next time we are tempted to indulge a besetting sin instead.

Fifth, if all things work together for good for those who love God and are the called according to his purpose, how might we think of this tragedy in redemptive terms? In short, let's learn the right lessons. More prayer and metaphorical sackcloth and ashes, less sanctimony and soapboxes. That some took the occasion to disparage the value of apologetics was as appalling as it was opportunistic. I submit that all of us should instead take from this heart-wrenching saga a newfound passion to renounce the works of darkness and lean heavily into God to live worthy of the vocations to which we are called. Then great good can come out of this—and what the enemy intended for evil, God will use for good.

Tuesday, March 23, 2021: It's just after noon as I write this. This morning some advising activities filled my time. A student from PA needed some help figuring out which classes to take this summer and fall, and then I interacted with a few other advisees, one of them needing help withdrawing from a course this term. I'm on a learning curve with a number of these matters, but it feels good to learn some of the procedures. That should give me confidence moving forward. Marybeth as always is such a great help to me when it comes to such logistical matters. She's a wizard. I suggest everyone marry someone smarter than them like I did. About to turn back to Fraser's dissertation.

It's now nearly dinner. Just finished going through the first chapter of Fraser's dissertation, which surveys the literature on the empirical premise of the debunking argument that says our evolutionary history shaped in some significant way our moral beliefs. The next chapter will get into the epistemic premise that says that, if the empirical premise is true, then this entails we should lose a great deal of confidence in the truth of our moral commitments and intuitions.

Wednesday, March 24, 2021: It's early Wednesday. My sleep last night was pretty good. MB and I are both up early. She has to teach in a few hours, and is leading a discussion of a chapter in a book by Rita Felski in the afternoon at HBU. In between we're taking Jerry Walls to his second Pfizer vaccination shot. I just wrote my student Jay from last term, a lawyer, to ask his advice about seeking the help of a lawyer to transition MAP from an LLC to a 501c3. Marybeth and I are about to drink a coffee and then spend time praying and listening to scripture, then I'm going to turn back to the Fraser dissertation. I'm getting excited about inching closer to the summer and working in earnest on the fourth in the tetralogy.

We just listened to the daily scripture and I was heartened to remember the verse that says it's not a good thing when everyone speaks well of you. This was a nice reminder after that YouTube event from a few days ago with WLC and several commenters indeed didn't speak well of us. The verse says it's the false prophets everyone speaks well of.

Thursday, March 25, 2021: The big thing today, I suppose, was that I wrote this month's WB piece, on an issue pertaining to moral apologetics. Here it is:

Why Believe that God is Good?

Some days ago William Lane Craig and I did an interview with the amiable Cameron Bertuzzi that then went up on YouTube. In the comment section beneath the video there were of course various and sundry comments— some complimentary, some riddled with delightful derogation and charming condescension. But embedded among the accolades and diatribes were some questions worthy of serious consideration. One question in particular was especially important: Why think that God is good? This is a question of the utmost concern to us all. It is not just a question about God's *existence*, but about God's *nature*.

The Bible tells us that even Satan believes that God exists. Merely believing in God's existence is no particularly mean feat. *Who God is* can't be avoided; it is not merely God's *existence* but his *character* that makes him worthy of worship and of our deepest adulation. So the question of whether God is good is of ultimate importance.

Addressing this question requires that we first emphasize the sense in which we mean "good." I suspect, following one like Robert Adams, that God's goodness involves more than *merely* the ethical good. God is good in every sense—moral, aesthetic, metaphysical, and more. But for present purposes let's confine our attention to moral goodness.

Asking whether God is (morally) good also requires that we disambiguate or differentiate between *partially* good and *wholly* good. If God were to have a fundamental capricious mean streak inconsistent with perfect goodness, for example, he perhaps could still be said to be good in certain specifiable respects, but not in every way. I suspect the question most are really driving at, the question of the most central existential concern, is whether God is *wholly* morally good.

Now, scripture seems to teach that God is indeed wholly good. When someone called Jesus good, recall how he replied, "Why call me good? Only God is good." And we are told explicitly that God is holy, impervious to sin and temptation; that in him there's no shadow of turning. The scriptural witness is clear, but of course that won't much move many or most of those who don't accept scripture as an axiomatic starting point. So what might we say to such folks to make a case for God's goodness?

One approach might be to say that God is good by definition. The fancy way of putting this in philosophical parlance is to say that the proposition "God is good" is necessarily true *de dicto*. It is a proposition that is true in virtue of how we define God. God, by definition, is perfectly good; if any particular being were to lack the quality of perfect goodness, such a being would not qualify for the office of deity, as it were. Or again, if a being were not worthy of worship (by, for example, having a capricious character, nasty mean streak, etc.), then such a being would not be God.

All of this, though, seems to be something that an atheist could agree with entirely. She could say, "Yes, this is true; by definition God is worthy of worship, and by definition God is perfectly good; but I don't think anyone actually inhabits the office of deity."

So another way of asking the question about God's perfect goodness is this: does the actual inhabitant of the office of deity—God, in other words—have

126

the quality of perfect moral goodness? And moreover, does God have this quality essentially, not merely contingently or accidentally? This is to ask whether "God is good" is necessarily true *de re*. Putting the question this way makes it about God himself, not merely propositions about God whether God exists or not. Is God essentially or necessarily perfectly good? That is the question, and again, how might we go about addressing it if we don't rest content simply affirming the biblical answer?

The notion that God might be less than perfectly good might seem odd, but recall, as one example, the Greek pantheon of gods, according to which, according to their legends, the gods were capricious and flawed to the core. One of the best initial answers to the Euthyphro Dilemma is to distinguish such theology from that of Christian theology, according to which God is impeccable. At first go this is a strong way to begin dispelling otherwise intractable arbitrariness concerns.

Various arguments for God's existence don't effectively answer the question of God's nature. Even if there is a first cause, for example, what would make that first cause morally good? It is not immediately clear. Likewise with a great designer; perhaps God is the perfect artist but without being morally perfect. Those arguments are helpful and fascinating, but for reasons other than addressing our present question. Is there any help from natural theology to point to a morally perfect God?

Two possibilities immediately present themselves. One is the ontological argument, according to which God can be known to exist in virtue of possessing all the great-making properties, including omnibenevolence. Some quite sophisticated versions of the ontological argument have been advanced—Plantinga's modal variant comes to mind—but I will point instead to the moral argument(s), according to which a God of a particular character exists.

Moral arguments come in a number of forms, and by this I don't mean to emphasize different logical forms—inductive, deductive, abductive, transcendental, etc.—but contrasting versions in virtue of different aspects of morality receiving emphasis. Personally I tend to make a four-fold moral case that encompasses (1) various moral facts, including but not limited to objective moral values and duties; (2) moral knowledge; (3) moral rationality; and (4) moral transformation.

If such moral phenomena as intrinsic human value, essential human equality, authoritative moral obligations, moral knowledge, moral regret, moral freedom, moral forgiveness, individual and cultural transformation, ultimate perfection, and moral rationality are taken seriously, they have as their best explanation, I have argued at length elsewhere, a perfectly good God. This explanation enables all of the moving parts and disparate pieces of a cumulative moral argument to cohere and constitute a compelling piece of reasoning. I am not asserting this without argument; these are the conclusions for which I have devoted, successfully or not, whole books to arguing.

Supposing God does provide such an explanation, does that give us reason to think, then, that God both exists and is wholly good? This raises various questions about the nature of this argument, which happens to be an abductive argument, an inference to the best explanation. If someone, for example, were to insist a priori that the explanation candidate of a perfectly good God is too intrinsically implausible—the "bad lot" objection—then such a person could reject the argument. But then I would wonder on what basis they are making this claim? To me it seems ad hoc.

Someone else might insist that we first have to show that God's existence is possible before we include it among the potential explanation candidates. But this seems unconvincing to me. If we have an argument that, predicated on a number of phenomena that require an explanation, gives us principled reasons to think a particular explanation is the best, this itself provides reason to take the explanation seriously. Especially if the explanation can't be shown to be logically or metaphysically ruled out, it should be at least on the table as a contender to be considered. Insisting otherwise seems unmotivated.

Another objection might come from thinking the moral evidence is *too strong*, for the suggestion might be that we are more sure of *it* than we are of God's existence. But here it helps to bear in mind that any good argument needs to be based on solid premises, so this is a virtue, not a vice, of the argument. And the objection is also slightly confusing epistemology and ontology. Our moral convictions are constructed bottom up, but they leave open the question of their ontological foundations. And if the moral evidence points to God as their ultimate source, this is just another example of the way in which the order of being differs from the order of knowing, as certain Medievals put it.

Another objection might go like this: even if we have reason to postulate God's existence to make sense of the moral law and the like, as Kant argued, that gives us at most *practical* reason to act like God exists, but not *theoretical* reason to argue that such a God in fact exists. But in recent years the works of John Hare, Chris Firestone, Stephen Palmquist, and others have represented a sea-change in Kant studies regarding the significance of religion in Kant's thought. As Hare puts it, "a principle that is within the theoretical use of reason merely 'regulative' (telling us that we should conduct our thinking as if it were true) can be within the practical use of reason 'constitutive' (telling us what we should think is actually the case)."

So if the moral argument(s) work, providing us grounds to postulate the existence of a perfectly good God in order to explain a range of important moral phenomena veritably crying out for robust and adequate explanation, I would suggest that this gives us compelling reasons to think both that God exists and that God is good. The suggestion is not that nearly enough has been said here to back all of this up—that would be a neat trick in 1500 words. Nor is the contention that enough has been said to render the conclusion so obviously clear that anyone unconvinced is irrational. It is rather simply a sketch of the sort of answer I might offer to the question with which we began.

Friday, March 26, 2021: Stephen Jordan defended his dissertation late morning. That was fun, and he did a fine job. Marvelous to call him Dr. J! He offered a variant of the moral argument that has for its focus the personal nature of God. Eventually he should publish it as a book after some augmentation and muscular revision. MB and Ronnie Campbell were the other committee members. Only a few hours before Jer and Rob arrive, so I had better get cracking on my Fraser reading for the day.

Here was a full set of questions I had for Stephen, just a few of which I touched on:

There are various arguments for God's existence—ontological, cosmological, teleological, moral, and so forth. You argue that the moral argument provides evidence of God's personal nature. What of those others? Let's go through in turn—the ontological? Cosmological? Teleological?

A question of personal curiosity—based on your study of the moral argument, do you think it's more accurate to say there's one moral argument with lots of interrelated parts, or a number of different moral arguments?

Why do you think the moral argument really came into its own because of the work of Immanuel Kant?

You didn't pick up the fourth strand of the moral argument—the so called argument from providence, as Hare calls it. Or the argument from rationality—pertaining to the ultimate correspondence of happiness and holiness. If you were to wish to turn the dissertation into a book, might you consider adding that bit to your analysis? Do you think that that argument points to God's personal nature? (Think about the names of the argument!)

More on the issue of evil and suffering? Wouldn't some say this makes the moral evidence more ambiguous? Maybe God is personal, but is there enough evidence to suggest he's good?

In the Greek *prosopon* and Latin *persona*, personhood seems connected to a role one plays. Any thoughts on the significance of that? Is it just a quirky historical linguistic factoid, or potentially indicative of something important? Connected to that, the face is important—you have a note on this. Any thoughts on that?

Our personhood and God's---is God a person, relative to our personhood, univocally, equivocally, or analogically?

Might Ward and Davies, in their skepticism about God's being a person, be confusing epistemology and ontology?

What did you learn from the process of writing a dissertation—not in terms of the content, but in terms of writing a project this big?

Other changes or additions that you might wish to effect if you decide to turn this into a publishable book? (I might suggest more on Newman, especially his personalism—see John Crosby's work. A touch of William James and what he says of relationality.)

Is God rightly said to be a person, or three persons, on your view?

By using the Trinity, you seem to be extending the moral argument beyond generic or bare or merely classical theism to something distinctively Christian. How much of this work, this step into Christianity, in your estimation, is via philosophy, and how much is it more something like theology? (Is it that the philosophical analysis made the step natural?)

Regarding Kant's argument from grace, the focus is much on transformation. In Christian terms, this is the issue of sanctification. Do the theological categories of justification and glorification also point to God's personal nature, and if so, how?

Do you think that the personal nature of God is a resource we can use in dialogue with folks from other worldviews and religions in which the personality of God is less pronounced?

Is Beck's conclusion at end of resurrection book adequate?

When Jer and Rob came over, largely thanks to Jerry's incessant pushing, Rob seemed to finally come to think that writing a book on the Lord's Supper was a good idea. We both then encouraged him. I joked that the evening would become famous for birthing the book; I actually do think Rob will do an amazing job with it, and it's important. The exclusion of folks who are not Roman Catholics from the Lord's Table, which is supposed to be a covenant meal celebrating our oneness in Christ, does indeed strike me as rather horrific. It is as if the tacit suggestion is that the atonement is not enough; what really matters is the magical transformation of the bread and wine into the literal blood and body of Christ—as if early Jews for whom the consumption of blood would have enthusiastically embraced such a thing. Fat chance.

Saturday, March 27, 2021: Good chat with Elton and prayer time with TJ, and then a productive day reading Fraser's dissertation. Now I can take tomorrow off from work. If I read through one more chapter Monday and another Tuesday, I'll be ready for his defense on Wednesday.

Sunday, March 28, 2021: Started the day with some prayer and Bible listening, then tweaked my third blog on Christian theology and the moral argument—this one was on sanctification:

The Moral Argument and Christian Theology, Part III: Glorification

In earlier installments we discussed our deep need for forgiveness and moral transformation—justification and sanctification, respectively—but there is one more step: Not just to be wholly forgiven and radically transformed, but for the process to culminate. We need the good work that has been begun within us to be completed, which God promises to do at the day of Christ Jesus for those who trust him. And so what we are talking about now is the Christian category of glorification, when we are entirely conformed to the image of Jesus, morally beautified to the uttermost, every last vestige of sin having been excised and expunged.

This answers to a deep intuitive recognition of a third basic moral drive or need, or maybe aspiration—yet one, once more, beyond the reach of our own capacities without divine grace—the hunger to be perfected, turned into the best versions of ourselves, delivered entirely from the power and consequences of sin. Christianity assures us, and we have principled reasons to believe, that this is no Pollyannaish pipe dream, but a reality we can look forward to with a hope that will not disappoint.

Interestingly, Immanuel Kant thought that human beings would never achieve a "holy will," which he considered reserved for God alone. The process of moral perfection was thus something at best approached asymptotically—we get closer and closer throughout eternity but never fully arrive at it. It is a process that is never completed, he thought, so this served as the basis of his argument for immortality, since the process must continue forever.

Christian theology, I suspect, suggests that Kant was both right and wrong. He was wrong to think we will not be perfected. The Christian doctrine of glorification is about the process of sanctification reaching an end point. Ultimately sin will be completely defeated within us, and we will find complete deliverance from its power and consequences. That is a glorious hope.

Still, Kant was also likely right that there will remain a movement, a dynamism, even after the point of glorification. For one thing, the prospect of beholding the glory and beauty and goodness of God is an unending process. For another, once full deliverance from sin comes is when the fullest life for which we were created can really begin, which even the present life already intimates at.

A. E. Taylor wrote eloquently about this in his Faith of a Moralist. Here is just one example:

> The moral life does not consist merely in getting into right relations with our fellows or our Maker. That's only preliminary to the real business: to live in them. Even in this life we have to do more than unlearn unloving. We have to practice giving love actual embodiment. This is continuous with what is morally of highest importance and value in our present life.... Heaven must be a land of delightful surprises. We should have learned to love every neighbor who crosses our path, to hate nothing that God has made, to be indifferent to none of the mirrors of His light. But even where there is no ill-will or indifference to interfere with love, it is still possible for love to grow as understanding grows.

Combining all the discussions of our last three installments, what we have here is a three-pronged moral argument based in God's grace. It is by God's grace we can find the forgiveness we desperately need for having fallen short of the moral standard, which we all do. It is by God's grace we can be set free from both our subjective feelings and objective condition of guilt, and it is by God's grace that we will be eventually entirely conformed to the image of Christ and delivered completely from sin's power and consequences. From first to last, what answers our deepest moral needs—for forgiveness, for change, and for perfection—is the astounding grace of a good God perfect in holiness and perfect in love.

After that, something unexpectedly fell in my lap. David Ochabski last week had written me about a chaplain who wanted to talk about his work in conjunction with mine in moral apologetics. So I wrote that fellow and said I'd like to chat before long. And then I was reminded that Brian Chilton had asked about chaplaincy a few days back, so I did a follow up with him, and he wrote me back this:

Dr. Baggett,

To be honest, it was not until I began working as a hospice chaplain that I realized just how many people did not realize that God loved them. Most people I encounter have only heard about the wrath of God. They have been led to believe in an ultra, or hyper, Calvinistic interpretation of God, where God is viewed as an angry, malevolent overlord who wants to strike them down when they do something wrong. When I mention the goodness of God, they are overwhelmed with emotion. Most of my work has involved active listening--being in the moment and allowing the person the ability to work through their emotions. I normally ask the patient if I can read Scripture to them. When they permit me, the combination of Psalm 23, the Lord's Prayer, with Romans 8:35-39 has proven powerful. They hear about the goodness of the Lord coming from the pages of Scripture. On more than one occasion, I have been asked about why a good God would allow the sickness of their loved one, or their own personal terminal illness, to occur. The tools you provided in the moral apologetics class at Liberty have proven to be the most helpful of all the apologetic tools in my tool chest. The chaplain must deal with moral apologetics and the problem of evil more than nearly any other profession. I even used the issue of utilitarianism that you taught us when asked by a high-ranking leader in our organization concerning how the organization should proceed with the COVID-19 vaccines. Moral apologetics/PoE is an underutilized yet extremely critical aspect of chaplaincy work. Thus, chaplains trained in moral apologetics will prove to be highly effective when shaping questions and leading people to the goodness of God's personal, holy nature. Patients will find that God is their loving, heavenly Father rather than the angry tyrant they have been led to believe. For patients at the end of life who are ready to pass, it is shocking how this information gives them the peace to transition into eternity where they were previously struggling. I have witnessed firsthand the power that the love of God has on individuals. It is overwhelming.

Training would include at least the basics on moral apologetics, the importance of active listening, creating a sacred space in the place of transition, training on the problem of evil, how to shape questions that lead the patient to own the information for oneself, working through the chaplain's own hurts (so that he/she will not allow personal demons to hinder the loving work of God), and approaching each patient with the love of God while removing personal judgments. The last two are areas where God has really had to work with me. I did not realize how much the hurt from my own past was hindering the way I interacted with people.

This definitely put chaplaincy ideas into my head, and then I was reminded of a student of Marybeth's who had served in the military and her reaction to the moral argument. Here is a portion of what she had written MB:

Hi, Dr. Baggett,

I had a *journey* last week in philosophy class on the moral argument for God. It was a wonderfully challenging, healing, consuming week.

All that to say, by the end of the week I realized that moral injury stood in the way of my accepting the moral argument for God. Not many people will have the blessing of Dr. Travis directing their learning and an open-hearted class to talk to while they pray and study their way through the process of embracing the argument, which got me thinking.... how are apologists in the wider world breaking down this barrier? How are we talking about moral injury in today's landscape, especially with people who have dealt or are dealing with moral injury?

I spent a fair amount of time on the moralapologetics.com website, but don't know what search terms to use beyond "moral injury," so I'm coming up a little dry. Is there somewhere more specific you might direct me on the site, to continue learning?

Thank you!

Hope your rainy Houston day is a happy one!

With gratitude,
Jan

And this was a subsequent e-mail Jan wrote to my wife:

Thank you so much, Dr. Baggett, and to your husband, as well. I ordered these books and have the articles tee'd up to read (on breaks between essay writing, of course!) I also ordered his *Good God*, and your joint *The Morals of the Story*.

I have wonderful pastors in Simonton Community Church and will not move from them during the course of this degree for just that reason - they've known me and my daughters for 8 year and have loved us unconditionally. It is a classical Christian congregation very rooted in Scripture and committed to the value of apologetics.

I had never heard of the moral argument until last week in philosophy class, and my initial skepticism surprised me. Dr. Travis directed me to *Mere Christianity*, and some incredible classmates walked through the week with me. I was determined to get to a place of faith in this argument because Lewis was there and he has experienced way worse than me - if he can believe in universal moral values, I can get there, too. Also, the class was united in feeling that the moral argument is among the strongest for God, as you said. One of Lewis's points hit me like a freight train - that all of the evil in the world we've seen *still* amounts to a small percentage of humanity. Therefore humanity is fundamentally good, God's creation is good, God is good. I cannot describe how profoundly healing last week was. I didn't even know I carried anything that needed healing, but the lightness and relief I continue to feel at accepting the moral argument is undeniable.

I shared my experience last week with several people I know who have suffered moral injury as a result of exposure to violence. Once started crying immediately but wants to talk more. One grunted responses but called me back a few days later to say they couldn't stop thinking about it. Two spent more than an hour on the phone asking questions and walking through the argument; both said it bolstered their faith. That's what drove me to your website - I'm looking for materials that address the role of moral injury in accepting the moral argument for God, with an emphasis on moral injury incurred as a result of deliberately

134

violent events (i.e., a woman who was raped by a stalker; some combat scenarios; law enforcement professionals who encounter the same patterns of behavior in humanity over and over). It sounds like the biography series by (the other) Dr. Baggett is working on the same subject matter, and I am grateful for the timing.

I'm going to start a notebook on this issue, as well, to keep my arms around it as God continues to walk me down the road..... thank you to both you and your husband for walking with me.

With gratitude,

Jan

I don't agree with Jan that humanity is fundamentally good, not by any stretch of the imagination. Fundamentally valuable, but not good! But that issue aside, all of this correspondence today has bolstered my conviction that this chaplaincy issue has come to me unbidden, and perhaps it should be one of the topics I broach in conversation with Phil on Tuesday.

Monday, March 29, 2021: Yesterday I also received a note back from David Ochabski about the possibility of his doing more for the moral apologetics initiative. Dave is a very bright doctorate student at Liberty—with strong interests in both the social sciences and epistemology. Here was his reply:

I'm honored to be under your consideration. I wanted to see how I could best be of use, so I purchased *Humble Beginnings* to get a better picture. The stories were illuminating, especially around the time of the Mister Rogers class. It's awesome to see how many amazing people you've already gotten on board. I did skim through quite a few entries, so I'll have to go back.

I would love to say I was part of the formation of this 10 years from now. If you have any positions in mind, I'll be all ears. As of now, I'll keep promoting the Center through my outlets in Ratio Christi and Liberty. You can call me a liaison to the everyday apologist. I'll think of something more formal later, haha.

I'm making an outline from the interview with *Christian Post*, meeting notes with Dr. Napper, and the Moral Apologetics Outline at the end. I'll use it in the national training for RC chapter directors and put links to the Moral Apologetics website and donation page of HBU. My favorite quote (that I'll use to vision cast for others) was: "It's a privilege and joy when our God-given vocations and our spiritual lives go hand in hand, and that's certainly been true for me." I also really liked the wording related to the great command and commission. Looking for onboarding words to get people excited.

Btw, an apologist is willing to help with the sound engineering side of audiobooks and podcasts. I've asked him if he'd be willing to do anything for Moral Apologetics. He said he'd love to. His name is Nick Henretty. Let me know if you'd like the help and I'll send you his email (or I can facilitate however you need). I thought it would be great for *Humble Beginnings* to be an audiobook as a vision casting tool.

And speaking of Dave, he's the one who had told me of the chaplain who had expressed interest in getting in touch with me. I never did share some of the e-mail exchanges between the two of them, so let me do that now:

David … can you connect me with David Baggett? I've looked at the website and see that you are correct, I may be able to assist and offer ideas for them doing chaplaincy work and moral apologetics thought in general.

I think some of the work we are doing in Naval Special Warfare, and specifically the work I am beta testing, will be an interesting conversation to have with him and others. I am beta testing a spirituality assessment that looks at the intersection of spiritual beliefs (worldview) and morality/ethics or an operators character. It's some fascinating stuff!

We also teach a five-day Force Development Course for newly graduated SEAL's and SWCC's where I teach three lectures (Warrior Worldview, Warrior Identity, and Warrior Purpose) where we expose many of them for the first time to worldview. We ask them to reflect on how worldview forms their sense of morality, identity, purpose and value. Additionally, we teach a course called Just Warrior Training. It's a course on ethical moral reasoning, moral resiliency, and exploring the many potential ethical dilemmas and issues they will find themselves in during deployment and combat.

Let me know your thoughts, and please connect me with Dr. Baggett.

Blessings, Billy Hardison
773-936-4249

It's before 8 in the morning, and I've already listened to the scripture for the day. So I'm about ready to dive into the Fraser reading for the day.

Just before 11 am I received this e-mail from someone I don't know with a question:

Good morning Dr. Baggett,

I hope all is well with you, but I wanted to ask you a question as it pertains to Moral ontology. Now bear with me Dr. Baggett I am a novice and am just throwing thoughts out there so i may sound silly at times. However, when it comes to moral ontology I know many people who aren't theist will argue morality exist in this platonic state. That moral truths exist necessarily and we can ground them in moral Platonism therefore there is no need for God as the grounding.

My question is this: do you think the foundation of morality (its ontology) needs to be a personal source? The reason I ask this is because when I think about morality it seems to only make sense between personal agents. Take for example humans When I kick another human for no reason that is considered immoral, however when I kick say a rock or a tree no one looks at that and says I'm being immoral. As a matter of fact we would say that the relationship between a rock and me is more morally apathetic, to even speak of morality between us is absurd.

So if that's the case and morality only seems to really make sense between Personal agents. Why should we believe that Moral Platonism (a non-sentient or personal object) can even ground morality?

Thanks for the reply and sorry for the long question Dr. Baggett. Joshua

Here was my reply: "For a self-professed novice you ask an excellent question, and I think your intuition is exactly right. How we might choose to couch it could be either (among other possibilities) to say that the personal source is the ONLY explanation or the BEST explanation. It may well be both but it's a bit less ambitious to argue the latter. This is what I do. A personal source of morality makes better sense of the relevant moral data than an impersonal source. After all the truths of morality don't merely seem abstract, but intimately tied to personhood. Many of the great luminaries in the history of the moral argument have shared this conviction, which inspired them to look for a personal source. Platonism is perhaps, to my thinking, the second-best account out there, and it has more than a little going for it. For example, a committed secular Platonist would agree with the thorough-going theistic ethicist on moral realism, moral cognitivism, error theory, expressivism, constructivism, and even non-naturalism. It's just the final fork in the road where they part ways: Platonism or theism. And this is where the personal nature of theism has a definitive advantage, it seems to me. But as George Mavrodes puts it, the Platonic man rightly sees morality as deeply rooted in reality, which is absolutely right. This means there's lots of common ground shared by the theist and Platonist. And even though theism posits an additional entity, as it were, there are principled reasons for doing so because the personal explanation is the better, more robust explanation, so parsimony alone can't be used to give the nod to Platonism. Besides, if Swinburne is right, a theistic explanation can often prove simpler than secular ones. We can also choose, if we wish, to be something like theistic Platonists, as Robert Adams does, which may well be the way to go. This way the eternal verities are thoughts in God's mind, or something like that, rather than existing in metaphysical limbo, as John Rist puts it. So those are a few thoughts anyway! Thanks so much for the note, and I

137

encourage you to keep thinking these matters through, Joshua. You might peruse MoralApologetics.com for additional resources, all free. Blessings, Dave"

Ironically, Jordan's dissertation we just wrapped up was all about pushing just such a line. And as I was putting this entry into the journal, the Nick Henretty mentioned earlier e-mailed me, expressing his enthusiasm at helping the Center and MAP. Exciting stuff! I jotted him a note back saying I'd get back to him later in the week. Now I need to do that with Nick, Jan, and Billy! And probably I need to follow up some more with Brian; good stuff!

Tuesday, March 30, 2021: Today we began to advertise Melton's book, the latest MAP project, and I also encouraged Jonathan to wrap the *Good Reasons* initiative of TJ's into the moral apologetics outreach, which should help provide more content at the site and add some texture to our ministry. Working now on finishing up my reread of Fraser's dissertation on debunking objections. I have gotten to the last chapter, which looks at a theistic solution.

In the evening now. I feel like I broke my brain finishing Fraser's dissertation again. I'll go to bed early tonight and get up early to organize my thoughts before the defense at 9. My afternoon chat with Phil went fine; we discussed a number of issues related to the Center, though I still have work to do to help him grasp the extent of the vision. I need to contact Advancement and get some information to Celeste to get a Moral Apologetics Center website up and running. Today JP also reached out to TJ to discuss ways to create more synergy between MoralApologetics.com and his *Good Reasons* initiative.

Wednesday, March 31, 2021: Got up just after midnight to work on preparations for John's defense. I've reread the dissertation but now want to collate my salient observations and insights so I'm good to go come 9 am. I've already written a note I intend to put on FB:

> Over the course of about the last year, I was privileged to serve on four dissertation committees at three different institutions. The four persons with whom I worked were all eminently impressive and my appreciation for each of them grew exponentially through the process. It was also exciting to see that all four dissertations touched on issues of moral apologetics.
>
> In chronological order, first there was Adam Johnson, who earned his doctorate at Southeastern, and he was expertly directed by Greg Welty. Philosopher extraordinaire Ross Inman and I rounded out the committee. Adam wrote a simply brilliant dissertation that spelled out the relevance of Trinitarian theology to a theistic and Christian metaethic; he also raised some trenchant criticisms of contemporary secular ethicist Erik Wielenberg. Even while a

graduate student Adam orchestrated and edited a book on a debate on God and ethics between William Lane Craig and Wielenberg: *A Debate on God and Morality*.

Next was the dissertation of the *One-Minute Apologist* Bobby Conway, one of the sweetest and humblest people I have ever had occasion to meet. Standing on the shoulders of the likes of John Henry Newman and A. E. Taylor, Bobby wrote on a distinctive variant of the moral argument, one focused on the issue of *guilt*—both guilt as a subjective feeling and an objective condition. By delimiting his work in this way, he was able to accentuate aspects of the phenomenology of guilt that made a real contribution to the literature of moral apologetics. Working with Bobby and his committee at the University of Birmingham was an unmitigated joy.

More recently was Liberty's Stephen Jordan, who caught a vision for moral apologetics some years ago and plays an important part at MoralApologetics.com and the Center for Moral Apologetics at HBU. Stephen directed the focus of his work on the personal nature of God, mining the rich literature from the history of the moral argument to make his case in compelling fashion. The personalist focus enabled him to add some texture to his analysis and eventually extend it beyond generic or bare theism to something more distinctively Christian. It was also a joy to serve alongside my wife Marybeth and my dear friend Ronnie Campbell on Stephen's committee. Adding to the special occasion was that Ronnie's was the first dissertation I directed some years ago, and it culminated in the excellent book *Worldviews and the Problem of Evil*.

And just today I oversaw an excellent dissertation defense by a fellow Free Methodist, Asbury Seminary grad, and kindred spirit, John Fraser, alongside the other committee members of current colleague Jerry Walls and former colleague Ed Martin. John wrote a masterful work on debunking objections against moral realism/knowledge. John may have been my student, but I learned more from him on this project than he learned from me. What a truly remarkable privilege to work with this brilliant fellow, and how exciting to see yet more top-notch, cutting-edge work by emerging Christian thinkers on metaethics and the moral argument.

I am confident that all of these guys will publish their work and thus benefit the wider philosophical and apologetic community. Their insights and arguments are important, and they deserve accolades for putting in the time, living with these ideas, allowing them to marinate, not rushing things, and backing up their findings with serious thought and effort and research. I am deeply grateful for the chance to have played a part in their exciting intellectual, vocational, and spiritual journeys. Hats off to all of these good men and freshly minted Doctors!

Here are some notes I jotted down in preparation for John's defense:

1. Connects to an epistemic version of the moral argument.
2. When you refer to theism, are you speaking of Christian theism in particular for the most part? What do you think is minimally required when it comes to theism to emphasize, say, the valuings of God as central to the issue of moral goodness?
3. Divine value theory of the good? How would you respond to Euthyphro question on that issue? Does God value it because it's valuable, or is it valuable because God values it? Is the locus of value in something God does, or is, or doesn't it matter (or is there no practical difference)?
4. If the former, isn't that Platonism? If the latter, what is it about God's valuing that makes something valuable?
5. Forms of coincidence: "Theism not only explains the cosmic coincidence between our moral beliefs and moral facts, but it also explains the deeper cosmic coincidence between universal benevolence and human flourishing." The latter seems close to Reid's coincidence thesis.
6. In the abstract you say that some EDAs aim at undermining moral realism in general, but in numerous places you suggest that EDAs don't have as their target moral realism, but moral knowledge, even if moral realism is true. Which is it? Another way of putting it: Do EDAs in general try to provide a rebutting defeater for moral realism by showing it's false, or an undercutting defeater for moral realism by showing it's not rational to believe, or an undercutting defeater for moral knowledge that suggests we don't have moral knowledge even if moral realism is true?
7. Often found myself remembering Plantinga's point about the distinction between evolution and theological add-ons. Your points about the assumption of methodological naturalism and materialism were quite similar.
8. I like how John navigates the wider literature, which forms the larger context of the discussion. Gives it robustness, richness, and texture.
9. Huemer also says we should be suspicious of intuitions that align with strong feelings. Seems quite wrong to me! Entails suspicion about beliefs of deepest ingression.
10. Do you see an epistemic part built into the definition of moral realism—like such truths are accessible to us somehow. If an epistemic component is part of moral realism, then the dichotomy here is false that says moral realism could be true but we just might not have access to them—for moral realism itself would be false for their inaccessibility. If an epistemic component isn't built into the account of moral realism, then why think that the debunkers pose a challenge to moral realism? Probably shouldn't—and just say pose a challenge to moral knowledge.
11. You seem to be skeptical of the idea that moral truths are knowable a priori. A big reason seems to me the analogy with mathematical truths—and how moral truths are importantly distinguishable, especially in terms of prescriptivity. But couldn't we say that some a priori truths carry a greater degree or quality of prescriptivity than others, and allow for the possibility of at least some moral truths remaining knowable a priori? If a theistic ethicist did think at least some

moral truths are knowable a priori, would he have a theoretical advantage over nontheistic moral realists who did as well?

12. Both Skarsaune and Vavova attempt to subvert the debunking challenge by appealing to the badness of pain, with Skarsaune also postulating the goodness of pleasure as a premise. My question: doesn't it seem like a mistake to treat these as good or bad in a moral sense? I know this isn't uncommon nowadays, but it always strains my credulity. Sure pain is nonmorally bad and highly unpleasant, but it's not it's morally bad, is it? It's morally bad to inflict it, but the pain itself seems morally neutral—just seems to me like a confusion of categories otherwise. Notice the subtle conflation by some of well-being and intrinsic value, which is likely an important underlying culprit in confusing moral and nonmoral goods.

13. The notion of a special moral faculty is often thought nowadays as epistemically indulgent. Of course Newman thought it less a faculty than a voice. Do you think there's a special moral faculty we possess? You seem to suggest it's not precluded by science as long as we don't take methodological naturalism and physicalism as sacrosanct—and that what morality is for is related to what sort of faculty is needed to apprehend moral truth. But I was still left wondering just where you stood on this whole score.

14. What I have attempted to show is more than this relatively bland conclusion. I have argued that realist responses to the debunking challenge that begin from non-theistic premises do not adequately meet that challenge. The strongest such arguments either result in a stand-off, or else they point toward theism as a better explanation for moral knowledge. (3 parts to moral argument.)

I also woke up with a desire to touch base with Phil about a few matters pertaining to the Center. Here is what I just wrote him:

Phil, hey man. Thanks for the chat yesterday. I appreciated the chance to discuss several items that had come up briefly but we'd said we'd talk about some more.

I do hope that something like the publication initiative of our moral apologetics team doesn't give you the impression I'm not about seeing happen at HBU what needs to happen. I'm taking the fundraising seriously, despite that it's entirely outside my wheelhouse and something I have never done before. I've been praying about this thing daily—and I'm not just throwing those words out there; we literally spend time every day praying about this—and sending feelers to churches, waiting for the pandemic to lift, and trusting for doors to open up speaking engagements at which I can cast a vision for the Center. I'm not sure what else at this point I can do on that score.

The publication initiative is something we're intending to pursue with or without HBU; I was just mentioning that collaboration under the auspices of HBU as a possibility. But we're doing it either way. My managing editor Jonathan Pruitt is pursuing it. It takes little of my time. I only brought it up to give HBU a chance to participate more fully. But I've got a whole team at work on this stuff, have for years. What's happening at HBU is just one part of a multi-pronged initiative.

This summer my main job is to work on the fourth book in the tetralogy in moral apologetics. And there are several other book projects in the works. My first job as director of the Center is to be a top scholar in this field.

The Certificate will be up and running a year from this summer, and hopefully that will take off. If there's more by way of classes on moral apol you'd like me to offer, just say the word. I'm veritably champing at the bit. I really miss the chance to teach this stuff. I feel like I've largely been bridled in my teaching since getting here, grading discussion boards and sending weekly announcements to students.

And in terms of events, the two things that have stopped me have been covid and lack of resources. The lack of resources doesn't bother me, as we can use the HBU faculty, but the covid has been a bit of a deal breaker. What I don't want to do is burn through any cash we get for an event that's a one off. I'd rather save the money for things like scholarships for students who have a passion to come and study moral apol. And I don't just want to add my more busy-ness to people's schedules. The faculty lecture series has helped ensure regular lectures, which has been a great thing.

Anyway, just wanted to add those things because I want to emphasize some of the breadth of the vision—and I have hardly mentioned curriculum ideas, pastoral training, chaplaincy possibilities, etc. I'm profoundly mindful that I have a limited opportunity to get something up and running before my time is through. I'm trying very hard to follow God's lead on this matter. It's a vision that's gestated in my heart for 15 years, and I'm grateful for HBU's offer to give me a chance to build it.

Thursday, April 1, 2021: As if yesterday wasn't a big enough day with Fraser's defense and MB and I getting entirely out of debt, it was also the day I received in an e-mail my second contract with HBU. The salary remains the same, and the workload too. Officially it's a 4/4, but in a subsequent letter inviting me to continue directing the Center, that decreases to 3/3. Once the Certificate program is up and running, it'll be a 4/4 again in essence, which is fine as far as I am concerned. Last night, before realizing that the load would be reduced (as it was this year with the directorship), I was worried about time for writing. But my dean assures me all is well, although it's a departure from what we had originally been told—that after the first year there would no longer be a course release. The person who told us that, though, I think is no longer in that position.

When I was discouraged last night, though, one big consoling factor was remembering how we had prayed a year ago about HBU. Our prayer was that God would open the door if we were meant to come here, and that he would absolutely shut it otherwise. So a year ago around this time when we received the offer, we took it as a reliable sign this was God's will. And I have to remember that God knows exactly what he's doing. He knew what he was doing when he opened this door, and he knows what he's doing still.

Having just wrapped up John's dissertation, yesterday I also received the first chapter of Pruitt's dissertation. No rest for the weary!

After a conversation with Fred Smith, I chatted with Taylor Neill, a grad student in apologetics at HBU. After Taylor and I chatted, I wrote him this e-mail: "Taylor, my conversation with you got me thinking about something I had thought about before and started thinking of again. I am thinking of beginning a Moral Apologetics Student Fellows initiative. It would involve some events at which aspects of the moral argument(s) are discussed, though nothing by way of prohibitive time commitments. Largely about equipping folks to use the resources of the moral argument in their outreach and evangelism and such, and some exposure to some of the more theoretical aspects of the discussion, appropriate for students. Perhaps some undergrad and some grad. Do you think such an idea would have potential? If so, would you be interested in participating in such a thing?"

I wrote this in response to a DB question about Euthyphro in my online course:

Hey Class, I have now had a chance to review your submissions on the Platonic dialogues. I plan to reply to your essays individually, but allow me to talk about the discussion boards. This week I pretty much gave you full credit if you participated, but I'll apply more rigorous stands in the weeks to come, so be sure to do a good job on them. You had different options of what you wanted to write about, so I'll choose one of them and talk a bit about it by way of an example of what you are to do. Just a few of you chose to write about the early dialogue of *Euthyphro*, so I'll choose that one as the model.

So this is an interesting dialogue. Just two characters: Euthyphro and Socrates. Euthyphro is a religious fellow and is suing his own father for being responsible for a man's death. Socrates is taken aback a bit by Euthyphro's intentions and asks Euthyphro to explain to him the nature of piety. After all, if Euthyphro has such confidence in his own judgments on the matter, he must know what it's all about. To which Euthyphro says that piety is what he himself is doing: punishing a wrongdoer. Socrates says, though, that he doesn't want merely an example of it, but its underlying general principle, so Euthyphro replies it's a matter of what the gods desire. Euthyphro believed all the Greek lore about the pantheon of gods. Socrates then notes that, according to those legends, the gods don't always agree, so that answer seems problematic. So Euthyphro finally, in his third attempt to answer Socrates, says the pious or the just is what *all* the gods love, and the impious or unjust is what *all* the gods hate.

Obviously the context was polytheistic. Euthyphro didn't believe in one God, but many, and he took as authoritative all the legends about them. Somehow Euthyphro wanted to tie the foundations of piety or justice (morality, we might say nowadays) to the will or the loves of the gods. Socrates was skeptical, so he asked one more centrally important question, which has come to be known as the Euthyphro Dilemma. Expressed in its original context it went like this: Is the pious pious because all the gods love it, or do the gods love it because it is pious?

Now, folks nowadays tend to shift gears when applying this Dilemma and speak of God rather than the gods, commands rather than loves, and morality rather than piety or justice. Expressed in contemporary terms, you might ask the question like this: Is something moral because God commands it, or does God command something because it is moral? If one were to affirm the first horn of the dilemma and say something is moral because God commands it, a question that might arise is something like this: If God were to tell us to torture people, would that make it morally okay, or perhaps even our moral duty? This understandably makes people nervous, and it's often called the "arbitrariness" challenge to divine command theory (the theory that what God commands is moral in virtue of his commanding it). If, on the other hand, we were to say that God commands something because it is moral, this seems to render God practically irrelevant to ethics. At most he's filling us in about the content of morality but isn't responsible for its content in any ultimate sense, and many might think this seems unlikely because God is, well, God, after all.

The idea is that either way you go, the theistic ethicist (the one who grounds morality in God) has a problem: either morality is arbitrary, or God is ultimately irrelevant to the content of ethics. This is a fun puzzle to think about. I've written a whole book on it. It's called *Good God*. It's one of those enduring philosophical puzzles, and worthwhile to think about at great length. It caught my own attention when I was an undergraduate and I found myself thinking about it for years afterwards.

You may have an intuition about how best to try resolving the Dilemma. Personally I would emphasize that there is a world of difference between Euthyphro's morally defective gods and, say, the God of Christianity. I also distinguish between the good and the right, and take what's called a divine nature approach to accounting for the good and a divine command theory with respect to moral obligations.

But rather than just jumping to the conclusion, I encourage you to think about the Dilemma for yourself and struggle with it a bit. That's doing philosophy. It involves some real struggle and mental labor, but that's what's needed to develop insight and wisdom, rather than quick, easy, knee-jerk responses that show an allergy to thinking hard. Part of becoming educated is being willing to put in the time and effort to think hard. This is a class that all about encouraging you to do

144

so, and all of us to do so together. It is a class that celebrates that childhood impulse we all had to ask "Why?"

Later in the day I wrote my dean to give him a heads up: "So I'm thinking on moving on a new initiative for next school year that wasn't so practicable this year. It's the formation of a group of Moral Apologetics Fellows among students at HBU, both undergrad and grad. Haven't decided on whether they need to be residential. I'm not averse to folks at a distance participating remotely in events, but folks who are local would have the benefit of getting together and chatting in person. Thinking of putting Taylor Neill somewhat in charge of it. He seems to have a pretty big interest in such things. He could arrange meetings two or three times a term, and maybe one or two of those MB and I could attend. And any faculty who'd like to, and I'm thinking about Faculty Fellows for the Center, too, but am undecided on the wisdom of that. Anyone and everyone would be welcome, pf course, but I'm weighing the pros and cons of naming Faculty Fellows explicitly. Events could be both social occasions and opportunities to learn about aspects of moral arguments for purposes of equipping folks to use the resources in their own outreach and evangelism, and also to familiarize folks with some of the more theoretical aspects of the arguments, appropriate for students, of course."

Suffice it to say that today was one of those days when I realized that there's a price to pay to get something like this Center up and running at an institution with its own structure and infrastructure. It's got its advantages, but it certainly has its drawbacks. Some days feel like dying more than others. Today had the distinct aroma of formaldehyde.

On a more positive note, I wrote this for a short collection of tributes to my friend John Morrison for his retirement:

John Morrison and I were colleagues at Liberty University for fourteen years. If ever the phrase "a scholar and a gentleman" had a clear referent, it was John. From my earliest days in Lynchburg he was nothing but supportive, generous, and a source of incessant joy. He couldn't see someone without dropping a word of encouragement, a witty line, a literary reference, or some other helping of edification of one sort or another.

Unless he couldn't avoid it, he usually didn't settle for a quick hello, but was always intent on a little conversation in which he found out what I was up to or working on, and then usually share a litany of disparate and relevant references from the literature that would prove useful to my research. He really was and is an unmitigated delight, one of those whose name can't help but make me smile.

Like so many would say, John was more than just a neighbor or colleague, but a friend—one of those Aristotelian friends able and willing to make you better for the friendship, by just exuding his joy, modeling his character, living his life, and sharing both his head and heart. He simply couldn't not be inspirational.

Everyone knows his delightful idiosyncrasies—his fondness for multi-colored highlighters, his meticulous care of his books, his loquacious phone messages whose interval was never quite able to fit the time limit (and replete with benedictions and doxologies), his allergy to e-mail, his exacting standards as a teacher that struck fear in the hearts of his students, his remarkable erudition and vast reservoir of knowledge, his unquestionable genius. When I think of John, I can't but think of a unique, distinctive, and eminently lovely reflection of Jesus in this world, a Christian brother I am privileged to call dear friend and cherished colleague.

In recent years he endured a series of difficulties, but he never lost his joy or his elegant but unassuming style. He seemed to never complain, he showed grace in suffering and loss, and his unflappable essence persisted. His body declined but not his spirit, and through it all he retained his outward orientation—always asking questions, as insatiably curious as ever, and never failing to ask for specifics on how he could intercede for you better.

Then he would invariably follow up—*numerous times*—to hear the results, as he did after my wife's and my move to Houston during a pandemic while we tried to sell two houses elsewhere. If I missed his call, I would hear his sweet voice asking about the status of the houses and where we were in the transition. And I'm sure I would have heard lots more, but, well, the answering service ran short of time.

It is such a pleasure and privilege to extend my heartiest congratulations to the distinguished Dr. John Morrison on the occasion of his retirement—marking yet another of those pesky artificial limitations that impose themselves well before he is done.

Friday, April 2, 2021: Today is Good Friday. A dark day on the Christian calendar, but a reminder of the great hope we have as believers. When I think of the little deaths I'm called to experience in this life, the little humiliations, the little offenses, the little sacrifices, I'm reminded of the abject humiliation, the unspeakable offense, the ultimate sacrifice Jesus was willing to pay for us. And I am appalled at myself for thinking anything I might be called to endure remotely compares to what Jesus was willing to take on for me. Thank you, Lord Jesus, for the great gift of your suffering and death for our sake, for my sake, and thank you that though it's Friday, Sunday is coming.

In early afternoon I wrote this to a group of about a dozen friends who care about the Center: "Blessed Easter weekend, dear folks. I'm spending several hours on this Good Friday writing local churches. So far I've written three UM churches, one Baptist, and one Anglican. Sort of fanning out from where I live. I've decided to throw caution to the wind and put myself out there—hoping to elicit invitations to go to churches in the area and speak about the Center for Moral Apologetics at HBU. As of tomorrow it'll be two weeks since my second vaccine shot, so feeling better about attending church in person. The idea is to cast the vision for the Center, and entrust the results to God. If I might ask, would you please remember to keep this initiative in your prayers? I have no confidence in myself to generate any interest, but if the vision for the Center is of God, as I truly believe it is, I think we can pray boldly that God accomplish this work. As an officially credentialed bona fide introvert, doing this is a bit outside my comfort zone. I'm not used to speaking to lay audiences as much as college students, and in recent years mainly graduate and seminary students. So I myself need all the prayers you can muster. And beyond that, please pray that the vision for the Center can be found compelling, and that those intended to catch the vision would have ears to hear. Who knows, the next William Lane Craig might be some kid sitting in the pews of one of these churches. Please pray, as God inspires you."

Very cool thing later in the afternoon; I got an e-mail from a former student who leads an apologetics club in his church in Dallas. He asked if I would do a presentation on the moral argument on April 16 for them via zoom. Marvelous!

In the early evening I received this e-mail from a Masters student from Biola:

Greetings,

I am a student in the Apologetics program at Biola University. I heard your interview on the podcast Apologetics 315 and I have a question regarding your discussion of the Euthyphro Dilemma. William Lane Craig likes to push back on the idea that the two options typically presented by the Euthyphro Dilemma are really the only two valid options. Craig claims that there is a "third option" which he states as "God is the good." I think you are familiar enough with Craig for me not to have to go into too much detail. Why did you pass over this during the interview? Do you see problems with this? I realize you are busy, but hope you can find time to respond. References or links to recommended articles would be most particularly appreciated.

Doug

To which I replied like this:

Hi Doug! I think God is indeed the good, but I'm not sure this is a third option. Not much rides on this, most likely, but it seems to me I can endorse a nonvoluntarist account of the good and a voluntarist account of the right, and thus stick to the categories furnished by the ED. The nonvoluntarist account of the good basically says God commands stuff that's good. That then raises an additional question: what's my account of the good? If one has sympathies with a theistic Platonic account (like Adams, Craig, me, etc.), that account tends to go along the lines of suggesting that God himself is the ultimate good, and lesser or finite goods are good in virtue of something like relevant resemblance to God.

So my thinking that God is the good doesn't commit me to saying the ED doesn't exhaust the alternatives, to my thinking. It seems to me I can affirm that God commands something because it's good--or perhaps on rare occasions because it's the least bad, or something like that. But this doesn't pose any challenge to God's freedom, because goodness itself is rooted in God's own essence. This is the sort of thing I've argued in *Good God*, and it's close to what Adams argues in *Finite and Infinite Goods*.

Perhaps it's just my stubbornness, but I resist saying the horns of the ED aren't exhaustive. It often strikes me as motivated by a tacit claim of cleverness that suggests the person doing it is privy to some great additional insight that shatters the categories of the ED. I'm not saying that's Craig's motivation, and he's surely not the only one who couches it in these terms. I love Craig, and have no intention to criticize him. But you asked me why I do it the way I do, and that's the reason. I'd rather just hammer things out according to the categories of the ED if I can, and I think I can without losing anything important. At any rate, it adds a little diversity to how theists can answer the question so we don't sound like we're reading the same talking points.

Saturday, April 3, 2021: I woke up very early and finished grading last week's assignments for the online course I'm teaching for HBU. I found interesting how so few of the students could much distinguish between Socrates' view of the soul and that of Christian theology. They also seemed not to have much appreciation for principled civil disobedience. And they had a fair bit of trouble deciphering the main lines of argument in the Euthyphro. Ah well.

I spent the rest of morning and into the early afternoon carefully going over Pruitt's first chapter of his dissertation. Decent work, though too often he seems to cast in needless tension a theistic explanation and a distinctively Christian one.

Had a thought earlier, as I've been anticipating speaking at a variety of churches, that a little book or at least article on moral apologetics and different Christian traditions might be useful. At different churches I can emphasize denominational distinctives, which amount to their strengths. Anglican, Methodist, Roman Catholic, Baptist, etc. Fun project.

Sunday, April 4, 2021: Easter Sunday! MB and I attended the 9:45 service at the Sugarland United Methodist Church. Good time! Later in the day I did a quick journal article review; I was unimpressed. I also sent Celeste some information so we can get the Center's website up and running.

Something that dawned on me today was the way the challenge of building the Center is exacerbated by my emotions. Unbidden they can discourage me at times, especially when I sense that those around me—Jerry or my dean or my provost—don't believe in me and/or the vision of the Center. I cannot anticipate my negative feelings when this happens, and so they are hard to figure into the calculations ahead of time. Perhaps if I knew how better to navigate my emotions, they wouldn't pose such a hindrance at such times; but as Kant would say, I'm not just a noumenal creature, but also a phenomenal one, subject to garden-variety physical and psychological susceptibilities like emotional fluctuations. As an ineliminably emotional creature I stand vulnerable in this regard; at times the challenges I am already facing as I try to build this thing—and all the initiatives I have to undertake to that end—are made the considerably worse by having to contend with negative emotions that threaten debilitation, sapping my confidence. Building anything new, enduring humble beginnings, persevering in doing good, staying true to one's vision, patiently awaiting the fruit—all of these things are hard enough. The added layer of negative emotions intensifies the difficulty, at times smothering me in oppression. I need to know what's important and stick to my guns, getting everything in place before God gives the increase, before the tipping point(s) I'm hoping will come—with a hope, I hope, that won't disappoint.

I wrote a former president of Asbury and CBN Vice President, David Gyertson, a Free Methodist, this note today:

> Dr. Gyertson, hello. You and I have met before, briefly. You spoke at my home church in MI years ago—the Dearborn Free Methodist Church. I've followed your career with interest for a long time—your years at CBN, Asbury, etc. I'm a graduate of Asbury Seminary. In 2002 I finished my doctorate (in MI, like you, but at WSU rather than MSU)—in philosophy. I then taught for four years at King's College in northeast PA (a small Catholic school), then for fourteen years at Liberty in VA, and then my wife and I this past summer moved to TX to teach at Houston Baptist. She teaches English and cultural apologetics, and I teach philosophy and philosophical apologetics. She's about to be installed as the chairperson of the apologetics dep't here, and one of my jobs when I was hired was to direct the newly formed Center for Moral Apologetics. I had had the vision for such a thing for about 14 years and could never motivate Liberty to start it, but Robert Sloan, the president of HBU, caught the vision for the Center when I wrote him a few years ago and a year ago offered us jobs and the chance to come and build it.

> I have never before had a chance to do anything like this. I have just been an academic. I don't have administrative experience to speak of. So though I have a great deal of passion for moral apologetics (different aspects of the moral argument(s) for God's existence and goodness), and having written several books on it, I'm really on a learning curve as I work to build this Center. Basically I want to see it become a hub of cutting-edge research on aspects of the argument, getting folks involved from an array of disciplines, offer some coursework in it and the chance for folks to study at HBU to become premier moral apologists. Maybe in time build curricula for younger students, train pastors, hold workshops, do lecture series, host debates, etc.

Well, I'm writing just to pick your brain for a moment. As I'm just starting out trying to get this thing off the ground, and everything from motivating colleagues to get onboard to raising money for the Center seems new to me, I was wondering if you have any quick words of advice or counsel as to how to proceed. If nothing occurs, please don't spend any more time on this. But if your reservoir of experience and leadership yields any words of advice or counsel, I'm all ears. Thanks, and blessings to you! I hope you are enjoying your research and writing and other activities in which you're engaged!

Blessings, Dave

The WB published this older piece of mine in the last day or two:

Easter and Moral Apologetics

Easter is the most important holy day for Christians; it's the day we celebrate the resurrection of Jesus. Christianity is unapologetically historical. If the resurrection didn't happen, and happen literally, then Christianity is false; and anyone and everyone is perfectly within their prerogative to heap scorn on Christianity to their heart's content. If Jesus wasn't raised from the dead, then Christians are of all men most miserable, for their hopes are in vain and their faith vacuous. But if Jesus was raised from the dead, scarcely anything could be more important, more revelatory of ultimate reality, more hopeful for the world and human beings.

When I think of the resurrection, my mind goes to Antony Flew, who had three debates with my friend and former colleague Gary Habermas on the resurrection. Flew, perhaps the most famous philosophical atheist of the twentieth century, underwent a huge change of mind near the end of his life.

Having argued forcefully but respectfully his whole career that the evidence led in the direction of atheism, he came to believe that the preponderance of evidence pointed instead to the existence of God—though more the deity of Aristotle than the God of Abraham. On the strength of scientific arguments for theism, especially biological and fine-tuning ones, Flew left atheism behind, but only to become a deist, not a classical theist.

Interestingly enough, he remained unmoved by the moral argument, C. S. Lewis's variant as the salient example in his mind. Since a deist does not believe in an interventionist God, arguments for the historicity of the resurrection of Jesus never quite brought Flew around, despite his having said that, if he became a theist, he would probably become a Christian because of the power of the case for the resurrection.

Flew's resistance, it would seem, was primarily rooted in his inability to affirm God's moral attributes, and his difficulty overcoming this challenge explains his resistance to the moral argument for God's existence. Moral arguments have the distinctive advantage of accentuating God's moral nature: his omnibenevolence, his impeccability, his goodness. If such arguments work, they make sense of a God who does more than merely contemplate himself; indeed, they dovetail and resonate perfectly with a God who pursues, who would deign to intervene, become involved, stoop to save, die to bring life. Flew could not bring himself to believe this, as far as we know.

Flew was a firm moral realist and, later on, a believer in libertarian free will. Belief in moral regrets, moral responsibilities, moral rights, and moral freedoms, one would have hoped, might have enabled him to see the power of theism to explain such realities. He came to see the inadequacy of a naturalistic perspective when it came to the laws of nature, the existence of something rather than nothing, human consciousness, the efficacy of reason, and the emergence of life. He took all of these to be sound evidential considerations in favor of a divine Mind. Why not moral experience and the existence of a moral law as well?

As far as I can tell, the reasons for his resistance to the moral argument(s) were four-fold. One issue was that he was convinced biblical exegesis led to the view that God inexplicably predestines some to an eternal hell for lives they could not have avoided. A second issue was that if morality were to depend on God, God would be its justification, which would lead, at most, to prudential reasons to be moral, based on the prospects of punishment for failure to comply. A third issue was his concern over the equation of goodness and being, originally deriving from the teachings of Plato. One like Gottfried Leibniz, Flew argued, used this equation to derive a system of ethics on theistic foundations that is irremediably arbitrary. Things not at all recognizably good are to be called good anyway. This concern basically sounds like the classical arbitrariness and vacuity problem rooted in Ockhamistic voluntarism.

And a fourth issue was perhaps the biggest of all, and in a sense the culmination of all of the above: the problem of evil. Flew's resistance to the moral argument makes good sense thus construed, and it was inevitable that until he thought of God as personal and moral, rather than merely intellectual and impersonal, his resistance to special revelation would remain intact and he would continue to be convinced by the teleological and cosmological arguments but not the moral one. Of course his resistance to the case for the resurrection would persist as well.

Flew's story underscores the need for moral apologetics, because all of Flew's worries can be effectively answered. The historical, biblical, and philosophical evidence weighs heavily against the problematic predestinationist soteriology that worried him, and most recent theistic ethicists, especially since Locke, have focused on the ontological grounding of moral facts in God, not the motivational and prudential incentive for morality provided by divine threats. A theistic ethic that avoids Ockhamistic voluntarism can be defended, and moral apologetics and the problem of evil are locked in a zero-sum battle; only one can survive, and I think the evidence for the success of moral apologetics is strong. This is not to say the problem of evil lends itself to any simple solution; certainly it doesn't. In fact, the way the problem of evil *remains a problem* for Christianity, though not an intractable one ultimately, is one of the distinctive strengths of this worldview; it's the worldview that lacks the resources to offer a robust account of evil in the first place that suffers from explanatory inadequacy.

What all of this shows is that the case for the resurrection of Jesus—likely the strongest argument for Christianity (even more so than the moral argument!)—goes hand in hand with moral apologetics. They are not in competition; they are rather two star players on a very talented team.

Moreover, the resurrection shows the inauguration of God's kingdom life; resurrection living, free from the fear of death and sin, is the sort of life for which we were designed. Resurrection represents God's work of re-creation; the power that raised Jesus from the dead can be at work within us, renewing us, transforming us, making us into the people God intended us to be. The resurrection shows that our hope is not in vain, that the moral gap can be closed by God's transforming grace, and ultimately that there is no tension or conflict between the dictates of morality and rationality. The resurrection shows that the grain of the universe is good; that God intends to redeem the entirety of the created order, making it teem with life according to his original plan; that the worst of evils can be redeemed and defeated; that life is a comedy, not a tragedy; that the day will come when all our tears will be wiped away.

Monday, April 5, 2021: Early in the morning I finished working on a list of things I've done in my capacity as director of the Center this first year. A few are by way of anticipation (for example, I've reached out to about six churches so far, but I put my goal for the year into the list); here it is:

1. Published my journal about the Center from 2020 (*Humble Beginnings in a Whirlwind*), Brian Melton's *Knockturn Method*, Elton's *Ichabod*, signed contract with McCoy and agreed to write foreword, published book by TJ Gentry on Aquinas and the moral argument, signed another with TJ on his leaving Calvinism, all with MAP, our newly established publishing arm of ministry—applying for 501c3
2. Wrote over fifty local churches introducing myself and expressing interest in coming to speak about apologetics and the Center; taped a short introductory video to facilitate this

3. Did Zoom or Microsoft Teams session in May for former student Mark Dunn's apol club at his church in Dallas, Apol 315, Cameron Bertuzzi and WLC, with Khaldoun Sweis, with TJ Gentry's church group, with Tim Stratton, the HBU Ratio Christi group, with Parker Settecase, and with Mike Jones' ethics class at LU

4. Did class with WLC in May, with close to forty auditors, and was the teacher of record

5. Wrote script and did video promotional with Marybeth for the May course

6. Served as Executive Editor of MoralApologetics.com

7. Directed two doctoral dissertations in moral apologetics—by John Fraser and Stephen Jordan

8. Procured OUP book contract for fourth book in tetralogy

9. Procured OUP book contract with John Hare for my fifth OUP book, a collection of essays on the moral argument. Hope to arrange a major conference at HBU with contributors

10. Procured B&H Academic contract for intro to philosophical theology with Ronnie Campbell with moral apol emphasis

11. Arranged to do book with wife on moral apologetics and popular culture called *Telling Tales: Intimations of the Sacred in Popular Culture*

12. Tutored Kedric Kwan in moral apologetics via zoom on issues related to the moral argument

13. Planning launch of book series on apologetics and popular culture to be edited by Marybeth

14. Applied for Lilly grant for either interreligious conference and monograph on ethical foundations, and/or a series on luminaries from the history of the moral argument, but did not get it

15. Applying for $30,000 grant for the Center

16. Certificate in Moral Apologetics program in the works—filled out all the relevant paperwork

17. Taught moral apologetics course in the fall in innovative hybrid format at HBU

18. Arranging Student Fellow program in the fall with Taylor Neill as Senior Student Fellow

19. Started Center website at HBU

20. Used my voice at the WB to push HBU, HBU Apologetics, and the Center

21. Started Center's bimonthly newsletter, including HBQ

22. Began to compile file cabinet of resources for the space for the Center, enlisting Jan Shultis to add materials on moral injury. Invited Jan to contribute to MoralApologetics.com with blogs relevant to her therapeutic work in which morality plays such a central role

23. Started journal for 2021, writing something each day, and recording all things relevant to the development of the Center

24. Wrote fundraising letter Christmas Eve Eve and approached some prospective individual donors

25. Prayed daily for the Center and its various initiatives, and for HBU and its leadership, asking for God's blessings in terms of wisdom, donors, students, etc.
26. Explored possibility of MA outreach to chaplains
27. Enlisted a chaplain to write regularly for the site
28. Invited Adam Johnson to contribute regularly to the site
29. Conferred the title of Senior Contributor to Brian Chilton
30. Spoke at HBU's apologetics conference in a breakout session in May 2021
31. Refereed about six journal articles, wrote about a dozen blurbs for books, and wrote two book forewords (for Zach and Adam)
32. Participated with John Hare's once-every-three-week Yale zoom sessions about the third in his trilogy on God and ethics.
33. Hatched idea of moral apologetics student writing contest for 2021-2022
34. Published article in Licona and Beck book on the history of the moral argument
35. Published article on A. E. Taylor written with Michael Obanla in a history of apologetics book edited by Alister McGrath
36. Co-authored with Marybeth Baggett the lead chapter in *The Good Place and Philosophy* on the moral argument from rationality.
37. Came up with idea for book on moral apologetics and church traditions
38. Agreed to direct one more dissertation on moral apologetics—with my right-hand men at MoralApologetics.com: Jonathan Pruitt
39. Wrote blog for AndPhilosophy.com on Ted Lasso, hoping to procure contract to co-edit book on Philosophy and Ted Lasso with Wiley Blackwell
40. Published chapter in Adam Johnson's edited book about the debate between Craig and Wielenberg on the moral argument
41. Came up with idea for brochures for Center for Moral Apologetics
42. Came up with idea for book on moral apologetics and the Bible
43. Read Mary Jo's book in preparation of interviewing her for my site
44. Told Adam Harger and Lou Markos I hope to interview them, too
45. Invited everyone in the SCT to consider contributing to MoralApologetics.com (and to the WB)
46. Learned how to do podcasts for the purpose of doing them for the Center—a series called "On Ancient Foundations" and started taping them
47. In the process of looking into the possibility of starting an online show with Rob Gagnon and Jerry Walls called "Two Philosophers and a Bible Guy"
48. Checked into the possibility of putting MAP books on tape
49. Discussed with Billy Hardison chaplaincy outreaches
50. Re-acquired rights to *Lewis as Philosopher* with plans for MAP to reissue third edition with new chapters commissioned for Lou Markos, Andrew Lazo, and Michael Ward. We also wish to include the Addison's Walk "transcript" written by Reno, Ward, Tallon, and Walls.
51. WLC and I combined our work for the May course into a 100,000-word manuscript we are going to try to publish.
52. Will be getting some training in fundraising summer of 2021

53. Agreed to write article on debunking objections to moral knowledge for upcoming issue of *Perichoresis*

Tuesday, April 6, 2021: Yesterday I received a list of donors for the Center. Looks like we have just over a thousand dollars so far. Phil gave $100, Dave Ochabski $500! Jerry Bogacz and his wife $250, and Jeremy Huntington $100. $100 more was due to be given out of the budget for books that came from excess auditing money, mainly from Gagnon's class, but it wasn't there. Trying to get that matter resolved. But getting that list was nice yesterday, along with starting the Center's website at the HBU site. Piece by piece, things are coming into shape.

Taylor Neill also agreed to be the Senior Student Fellow of the Center, and so we are now intending to launch the Student Fellows program in the fall. I think that has a great deal of potential. Each meeting will have a prayer, fellowship, teaching, and service component. Lord God, I pray your blessing on this venture. This morning, then, at breakfast, I got some clarity on another piece. I wrote this e-mail when I got home:

Hey folks!
I hope you're all well. I have been kicking an idea around for a while now, and I'm ready to roll it out. It involves YOU!
A new initiative of the Center starting the fall will be a Student Fellows program. A graduate student here named Taylor Neill has a lot of interest in moral apologetics and has agreed to be the Senior Student Fellow. He'll lead meetings when Marybeth and I do not, and those meetings will start in the fall. The Student Fellows will be residential undergrad and grad students at HBU. The meetings will have four components: fellowship, teaching, prayer, and service. The service component is designed to illustrate that morality for us isn't just a theoretical matter, but something of profound practical import. We may do things like distribute water bottles to folks in need of it—that sort of thing. (Houston is HOT! Why didn't anybody tell me?!?)
I had been ambivalent on something like Faculty Fellows; it didn't seem quite right to me. But finally this piece came together at breakfast with MB this morning. What I need are Senior Research Fellows for the Center. And guess what? You're it!
Here's my list: David Ochabski, TJ Gentry, Marybeth Baggett, Jerry Walls, Jonathan Pruitt, and Stephen Jordan.
So this letter is to extend to you an official invitation to become a Senior Research Fellow in the Center for Moral Apologetics at Houston Baptist. We just got a website for the Center up and running on the HBU site. https://hbu.edu/school-of-christian-thought/related-student-organizations/center-for-moral-apologetics/ We will put the list of Senior Research Fellows there when it's ready (I will be putting together a brief

description of each of you and the work you do germane to interests of the Center).

In terms of duties, we ask, of course, that you remember the Center in prayer on a regular basis. That is the MOST IMPORTANT thing—that we continually bathe the Center in prayer and ask for God's blessing on this whole venture. It's only God who can give the increase to any of this. Your second duty is to be encouraged to contribute blogs to MoralApologetics.com. It would be great if you did a little something once a month, but I'm not requiring it. Contributions need not be full-fledged 1000 word blogs—sometimes just a paragraph or two might be perfect.

Your third duty is less a duty than the joy to keep doing what you're doing—you're all already hard at work in researching aspects of the moral argument. Stephen just defended his dissertation giving a moral argument for God's personality; JP is extending the moral argument to Christianity in his dissertation; TJ is going to write his dissertation on the moral argument and a range of topics: chaplaincy, counseling, preaching, teaching, etc. Keep this work up. It's vitally important! We are in your corner, and here to encourage you and cheer you on. We're a team, my friends—this is a job for a community. We have been saying this for years, and now more than ever we are about to see it come to fruition. Your fourth and final duty is closely connected: you have developed and are continuing to cultivate your research expertise in aspects of the moral argument, and now I would ask that you be available to the Student Fellows if any occasionally might wish to pick your brain. This expands the scope of resources we would have at our disposal for those with questions they might wish to pursue. On certain occasions we may ask that you do a zoom session with the full group of Student Fellows—but we promise we will never ask you to do this more than once per year (at most).

I ask that each of you would give this invitation your prayerful consideration. I love each and every one of you more than I can say, and am deeply appreciative of your co-laboring with us and your abiding friendship. So grateful for your hearts, minds, and hands in this shared work!

Blessings, Dave Baggett

A few days ago I asked Jonathan to dream big about the Center and tell me what he came up with; he just wrote me this back (right after I sent the previous e-mail out):

Here we go! Put my dreaming hat on for this one.

Center for Moral Apologetics: DREAM EDITION
By JP

The mission of the CMA, stated as simply as possible, would be to develop the moral argument for the existence of God.

This development has multiple dimensions. These can be broadly categorized as academic and popular.

Academically, CMA should be a sort of catalyst that 1) helps to improve existing moral arguments and 2) expands the scope of moral arguments.
Ideas for developing this dimension:

a) Small academic conferences on the moral argument, aimed at producing new scholarship.

> Example: Conference topic "Linville's MA." Invite Linville and several respondents, some big names, like Copan/Craig, but some new guys like Adam Johnson, to respond to Linville's argument with the aim of revising and extending his argument.

b) Issuing of grants for research and publication in needed fields.

> Possibly Moral Apologetics Press can provide some gas on this, by offering contracts on needed books, like the Buddhism book.

c) Interdisciplinary round table discussions

> Example: These would be exploratory and creative exercises where integration between disciplines was sought. We might, for example, invite a Christian biologist to discuss the role of evolution (or lack of) in the development of a moral sense (I suspect that biology has little to do with it, but getting feedback and insight from a scientist is the whole point). Or "Neuroscience and the Moral Argument" could be a theme. Topics include the practical limits of free will according to neuroscience and the implications for moral transformation, for example. Other fields of interest would be sociology, anthropology, laws, business. As we know, virtually all human disciplines have something to say.

d) Expansion and deepening of current integrative model

> Already, the CMA has had significant success in terms of integrating three disciplines, philosophy, theology, and literature. These should be expanded and deepened, and creativity should be a priority.

The other dimension would be on the popular level. The CMA would an entry point for people wanting to explore the moral argument. This would be accomplished through podcasts, animated YouTube videos, public debates/discussions, church events, campus events, and so on. I do not foresee something like the local chapters of Reasonable Faith, but I think their accessibility level and multimedia elements are something to strive for.

More CMA dreams:
- Dedicated, physical location. I picture something like the Honors Office in the LU Library.
- Full time administrative staff

- Plan and manage events
- Maintain media and online presence
- Schedule and cater to "talent," ie the people we might bring in for round tables and conferences
- Copy-editors for journal (see below)

- An annual *Journal of Moral Apologetics*
  - Interdisciplinary
  - Peer-reviewed
  - Creative
  - Can be rolled into Moral Apologetics Press
- Establishment of MAP as a credible press with aprox 4 significant works in moral apologetics being published each year
- Raising the profile of CMA director
  - This is not for the sake of fame or anything like that.
  - The development of recognizable representatives of Christian apologetics is a boon, especially in terms of expanding the reach of our audience.
  - As people think of "kalam" and connect that to Craig, we should try to associate "abductive moral argument" with Baggett. The implicit idea is that you go to Baggett (or his center/website) to get reliable and authoritative information on the moral argument.
- Full time staff apologists
  - Think of someone like TJ heading up the popular level/pastoral level events.
  - Maybe two or three staff apologists (could potentially do admin work as well) who would anchor academic and popular level conferences, produce multimedia content, write for journal, and so on.

Another thought: The CMA should seek also to have a prophetic voice to culture. I am thinking here specifically of Robert Gagnon. In my dream CMA, part of the mission of the CMA would be to develop a Christian conscience and moral sense. It would seek to preserve that moral sense that is foundational to the moral argument and so there would be some sort of emphasis on responding to immorality in culture, at least insofar as such challenges pose an implicit objection to the moral argument. Example: "Christian ethics is hateful and arbitrary in its view on homosexuality."

CMA distinctives:

Creative yet rigorous
Interdisciplinary but ultimately philosophical
Integrative but ultimately biblical
Producer of moral apologetic content, but equally a catalyst for others

I really appreciated JP's ideas there. Very cool. A bit later Rob Gagnon called and told me he'd shared with President Sloan the idea of starting an Institute for Biblical Ethics here at HBU. He's been told that he won't be renewed beyond next year. This may be a way to salvage a position for him, though funding is always a challenge. I told Rob what JP had written, and floated the possibility that perhaps we could dovetail and conjoin our efforts between his Institute and the Center. Lots of intriguing possibilities there! I grow so weary of financial constraints and stultifying strictures. I only half-jokingly broached with Jerry and Rob the notion of the three of us doing a radio show a bit ago. If it could take off, maybe it could generate some needed money to support worthy causes. But even risking it would take courage, including the willingness to risk failure, and I feel like a cowardly weasel.

Wednesday, April 7, 2021: I had to skip the Hare chapter discussion today. Was just too tired and needed the break—from both reading the 40-page chapter and devoting the two hours to discuss it. The internet apologist sensation Tim Stratton has asked me to discuss the moral argument with him in a podcast, so hope to do that in a little over a week.

Yesterday or so New York pastor and famed Christian writer Tim Keller wrote a FB status that went like this: "No one can prove any moral values to be true—they are in the end all matters of faith. Much of the rage on Twitter is because we are holding others to moral values they don't own and we can't prove. Saying "we all know this moral to be true" is not an argument, it's an assertion that can't be proven. Interestingly, the Christian sex ethic has been embraced and practiced by billions of people for centuries across more cultures than any other faith. It is agreed upon by all branches of Christianity—orthodox, Roman Catholic, and Protestant. It overturned the older Greco-Roman shame and honor sex ethic that privileged males and the aristocracy. It introduced the idea of consent that many say "we all just know this is true"—but history shows for centuries this simply wasn't the case. So even if you disagree with this great and historical ethical tradition, we must contend with it since worldwide it is growing, while the secular understanding is decreasing."

I decided to write this in reply after someone shared it critically: "Thanks for sharing this AJ. I have derived some real benefit from some of Keller's work, but I definitely think some of the wording here is at the least infelicitous. Of course the term 'prove' is such a vexed notion nowadays—does he mean merely evidence or some sort of knock-down argument that will convince everyone, or something in between? It's largely a non-starter without his clarifying what he's getting at. And his use of 'faith' makes it seem, potentially, that faith has for one of its salient features epistemic disadvantage, which in one way is true, but not in the way it often gets construed nowadays as tantamount to fideism. What's also the case, it seems to me, is that he's saying it all with a sort of authority he doesn't possess except insofar as he's been dubbed one of those Christian celebrities whose every word gets treated as sacrosanct until it becomes obvious, as it already should be, that doing so is a grave mistake. Any salvageable and

159

legitimate insights here are shrouded in needless overreach and unfortunate wording. My two cents' worth, anyway, for what it's worth (probably something less than two cents)."

A few days ago I wrote the dean of the Houston campuses of DTS, offering my services if ever there's an opportunity to promote the moral argument for local DTS students. Today I wrote Charles Mickey, who runs the Lanier library here in Houston. They put on a number of good events, and I wanted him to know the Center would like to promote their good work. I also told him I appreciated Mark Lanier's work in apologetics. His forthcoming book with IVP was the one I reviewed a few months back. Trying to cast my bread on the waters—not knowing what will yield fruit and what will not.

Today we've made a useful find! The Crazy Coffee Café in Richmond! Good place to work, good food. Delightful time. Fantastic get-away.

Thursday, April 8, 2021: Marybeth has a meeting with Phil Tallon today, dean of the SCT, largely about her upcoming role as chairperson of the apologetics department. Personally I hope she's able to communicate a few concerns about HBU we have—like how a few things seem to have changed between our negotiations and now. What was our offering our services freely has occasionally felt more recently like HBU insisting on taking from us, and holding our feet to the fire to do what it was originally our idea to do, and do so gladly.

HBU is no Liberty, but still there are little trouble spots; to cite one example, in a meeting with Stan he characterized our jobs as a "shared position." In light of the fact that we have full-time positions, in truth, the only sense in which it's a shared position is the reduced salary. We are content with what we make, and are grateful for the chance to serve, but can't help but feel like a bit more honesty is called for. Failing that, at least that they would back off a bit on foisting demands. A new initiative getting put into place will require of faculty (the year after next) a form detailing how they spend their time, allocating it between different tasks. Bad idea. Whatever benefits will accrue, precious few to my thinking, will come at the expense of a much more valuable commodity— faculty morale and their conviction that they are working for God, not men.

I prayed hard about two things today, both of them a bit of a psychological block for me: getting help from a CPA on the LLC matter and getting set up for podcasts. Then I got busy. Two folks showed interest in helping after I posted about the former on FB, and the IT folks at HBU let me make an appointment in my office for tomorrow at 12:30 pm. Progress! God is faithful! Both will be crucial steps forward for the Center.

Found out that Robert Sloan was the one who had turned down Marybeth's and my request that the original $75,000 request we made for remuneration at HBU be given to us, rather than the 70K they offered. That was disappointing to discover. But trying to trust God with it all. We also found out today that with Marybeth's taking over the apologetics department next school year she'll make $7,777.77 more, which is nice. That will put our joint income at $77,777.77. Easy to remember. Having eliminated all of our debt, that's a fine amount to live on. If 7 is the biblical number of perfection, for obvious reasons I suppose I could think of such a salary as well-nigh perfect.

Jokingly put this up as a FB status today to poke fun at how well I have avoided the office at school (adapting a famous John Adams quote): "Tomorrow I will make an appearance at my school office. I am apt to believe the occasion will be celebrated, by succeeding Generations, as the great anniversary Festival. It ought to be solemnized with Pomp and Parade, with Shews, Games, Sports, Guns, Bells, Bonfires and Illuminations from one End of this Continent to the other from this Time forward forever more."

Marybeth was interviewed by a *New Yorker* writer doing a story about Liberty, and I added a few comments of my own. One of them was this, regarding Falwell Jr.'s claim to have no regrets: "Without regrets there's no repentance, and restoration without repentance is easy believism and what Bonhoeffer called 'cheap grace.'"

Friday, April 9, 2021: Went to the office at school and the IT gal came by and set me up for podcasts. Exciting! Hopefully by next week or so Jonathan and I can begin exploring possibilities. The afternoon featured a celebration party of Phil becoming dean. In the evening at dinner I broached the idea of a radio show with Jerry and Rob and neither nixed the idea. The possibility lives. We watched *Some Like It Hot*. In the morning I am scheduled to do a Husky Preview, and then MB and I are planning a getaway for the day and tomorrow night.

Saturday, April 10, 2021: Woke up this morning feeling pretty good. Exciting prospects for an online and maybe later a radio show with Rob and Jerry. Things are really happening. A conversation with Nancy Pearcey yesterday sealed the wisdom of our redoing the apologetics program, and with MB as department chair we will have the opportunity. Podcasts are getting closer. Help with dissolving the LLC is on the way. God is blessing, I'm confident. Scripture reading today was the start of Joshua, as God's people move into the promised land. All sorts of promises are given them if they remain faithful to God. It's hardly a mechanistic assurance; God's people may have to endure all manner of loss and suffering. Still, through it all, God promises to be with them, accomplishing his purposes through them. After a Husky event later this morning, MB and I are doing a getaway and looking forward to that.

Sunday, April 11, 2021: Marybeth enjoyed a hotel near the Woodlands last night, and a nice lunch at Landry out that way today. Came home in the afternoon, when I took a nap, then discussed with Jonathan Pruitt the prospect of his going to work with TJ in Illinois. Jerry Walls sent his revised bio, we wrapped up our list of bio's for the senior research scholars for the Center; Marybeth sent the list of the Center's Board members and the senior research scholars to Celeste at HBU to add to the Center's website. Here are the senior scholars:

Marybeth Baggett: Marybeth is Professor of English and Cultural Apologetics, and chairperson of the Apologetics Department, at Houston Baptist University. She is co-author of *The Morals of the Story: Good News about a Good God*, which won the *Christianity Today*'s 2019 Honorable Mention in the category of Apologetics/Evangelism. She is also the editor of Moral Apologetics Press's forthcoming series on Popular Culture and Apologetics, and is currently working on a book on Kurt Vonnegut in an attempt to find common ground with a writer and thinker whose worldview is significantly different in key respects from her own.

TJ Gentry: TJ currently serves as Senior Minister at First Christian Church, West Frankfort, IL. He holds several doctoral degrees (in Counseling, Leadership, New Testament, and Theology), has authored books on evangelism, theology, and preaching, and is an Associate Editor at MoralApologetics.com. With Tony Williams, he also runs the *Good Reasons* online initiative. He is currently working on a book that discusses the convergence of moral apologetics and pastoral ministry, counseling, evangelism, and preaching. Two of his books are slated for publication by Moral Apologetics Press (MAP)—one on his journey out of Calvinism and the other on Aquinas's Fourth Way and the moral argument.

Stephen Jordan: Stephen currently serves as a high school Bible teacher at Liberty Christian Academy, a Bible teacher and curriculum developer/editor at Liberty University Online Academy, and he oversees the curriculum development arm of The Center for Moral Apologetics at Houston Baptist University. Prior to these positions, he served as a youth pastor in North Carolina for several years and taught courses at a local Seminary Extension for a year. He possesses four graduate degrees (MAR, MRE, MDiv, ThM) and a PhD in Theology and Apologetics. His doctoral dissertation was on the moral argument, where he argued for the existence of a personal God from morality. Stephen and his wife, along with their children, reside in Goode, Virginia. In his spare time, he enjoys spending time with his family, being outdoors, fitness, sports, and good coffee/tea.

Jonathan Pruitt: The Managing Editor of MoralApologetics.com, Jonathan has been a vital part of the Moral Apologetics team since its inception. Currently, he serves as adjunct instructor of philosophy for Grand Canyon University and Liberty University. Prior to these positions, he was ordained as a minister and served as spiritual life director. He is the author or co-author of several articles on metaethics, theology, and history of philosophy. With a Master's in Global Apologetics and a graduate of Biola's Master's program in philosophy, he is currently in the throes of finishing his doctoral dissertation in which he extends a four-fold moral argument from mere theism to a distinctively Christian picture of God. Jonathan, his wife Sara, and their two children presently live in Lynchburg, Virginia.

David Ochabski: David is wrapping up his doctoral work in theology and apologetics at Liberty University, and has strong interests in both social science and epistemology. He serves as a national training and area ministry director of Ratio Christi in the Virginia, Maryland, and Delaware areas. He is also managing editor of *Eleutheria*, the Rawlings School of Divinity journal at Liberty. He intends to write his dissertation on abduction and verification in the use of apologetic and theological methods.

Jerry Walls: Jerry is a seasoned philosopher and the author or editor of over a dozen books. He currently serves as Research Professor of Philosophy at Houston Baptist University. Among his works are his ground-breaking trilogy on eschatology and his tetralogy on the moral argument, co-authored with David Baggett, the fourth volume of which is currently being written.

MB and I also finished up a draft of the script for the commercial we are taping over at HBU for the upcoming course on the moral argument in May:

Black screen

MB: Okay, everyone, quiet on the set. This is a promo for Houston Baptist University's upcoming course on the moral argument in May, taught by Dr. William Lane Craig. We have Dr. Craig here with us. So Dr. Craig, whenever you're ready.

Screen is Dave.

Dave: Oh, there might have been a miscommunication. I'm Dave Baggett, and I'll be doing this today. I'm the guy co-teaching the class with Dr. Craig, you see.

MB: Cut! Mike, was Dr. Craig not available? [Slight pause]

MB: Okay, Mr. Baggett, co-teaching? What does *that* mean?

Dave: Yeah, no need for scare quotes around "co-teaching." And so Dr. Craig will teach the first week, and I'll teach the second week. And it's not a big deal, but it's Dr. Baggett.

MB: Okay, Dr. Budget, we know about Dr. Craig; maybe you can talk about your work. What are your PhD's in?

Dave: Well, I have a PhD in philosophy. And it's Baggett.

MB: So just the one PhD, then, Dr. Badger? Because Dr. Craig has two.

Dave: It's Baggett, and right, just the one. You might say Craig has a paradox— see what I did there? A little philosophy humor.

MB: Uh huh, let's not. Alright then, Dr. Bag End—why don't you go ahead and talk about the class a bit.

Dave: I think Bag End is that little town for hobbits, it's just Baggett. So yes, I'm really excited about the class. It will run from May 17th to May 28th, those two weeks, five days a week, from 3 to 5:30 Central time each day. It will also be taped so students can watch it anytime. I'm especially excited about teaching the class with my dear friend Dr. William Lane Craig.

MB: Excuse me, Dr. Bunion, your *dear friend* William Lane Craig. *Really?*

Dave: Well—and it's Baggett—I mean, we've met, and I really like him. He is a little intimidating, truth be told; I mean, he's got two PhD's for crying out loud. But we've done stuff together—we did an interview with Cameron Bertuzzi a few weeks ago, for example.

MB: That rings a bell. How did people respond to that?

Dave: Great! Well, it could have been better. One YouTube commenter said we were charlatans and insane, so there's that. It sort of hurt my feelings a little, to be honest.

MB: That sounds really unfair [pause], to Dr. Craig. Maybe let's not mention that. Anyway, let's try to wrap this up, Dr. Baggins.

Dave: Again, a Tolkien thing—that's the name of the hobbit. But as I say, it should be a great class. HBU students can take it for credit, and auditors can take it for just 300 bucks—280 if they catch the early bird special. And students can either take it in person or from anywhere in the world online.

MB: Well, I think that's a wrap, everybody. This is our promo for Houston Baptist University's class on the moral argument, May 17th to 28th, with Dr. William Lane Craig….and Dr. David Banner.

Black Screen

Dave: David Banner is the Incredible Hulk.

Monday, April 12, 2021: Today's scripture covered both the crumbling of the walls of Jericho and the story of the Prodigal Son. Each is a remarkable story of God's salvation, yet both carries a cautionary tale. Some took some of the riches of Jericho to themselves, bringing judgment on themselves. And the Prodigal Son narrative, a wonderful story of redemption, also featured the older brother who resented it.

In the late afternoon I got my zoom account up and running and did a test session with MB. All went well, so I e-mailed JP to see if he might be willing to help me tomorrow do the final steps in setting up what I need to do podcasts.

My brother Gary hasn't much spoken to me since our mom died. The details don't matter for now, but I would like to see a measure of reconciliation. Last week I thought I would try some humor to move things forward. I found an advertisement he put out on the internet to hire some folks who work in clean energy for his company. He invited those interested to write him, so I wrote this e-mail:

Dear Mr. Baggett,

I noticed your recent online communication with Hello Energy Pro's on behalf of Zehnder North America. I see that you are putting out a request for 3rd party QA/commissioning agents across North America. You are looking for Home Energy Raters, HERS raters, and Passive House raters who already own powered hoods for measuring low velocity airflows—among folks looking for occasional work commissioning your systems. I see that training for commissioning is provided and fees paid on a "per system" basis.

Well, I don't mean to brag or anything, but this is your lucky day, amigo, because I definitely think I'm exactly (*exactly*!) what you're looking for. I'm more than a little happy to say I'm something of a bona fide, certified, credentialed "expert" on all such matters. Yeah, that's right—Home Energy Raters, Passive House raters, Active House raters, HERS raters...covered, nailed it! HIS raters, THEIR raters, got those too under my belt. That's right, you name it. Extensive experience with all such various and sundry raters and, you know, whatnot. And do I already own powered hoods for measuring low velocity airflows? Oh yes. I own them in spades. I've got them coming out of ears.

At this point you're undoubtedly wondering why, with my technical proficiencies and admirably extensive experience in such matters, I'm looking for a side job. Well, truth be told, the wife is spending money like it grows on trees. My bank account is like a friggin' sieve once she gets my debit card in hand. Buying things left and right, she's gonna drive me to the almshouse before long. Love the gal, but man alive! You know what I'm talking about, right?! So cash is a definite need in this household, I'll be honest with ya—**lots** of it, and fast.

But again, good thing I've got a bead on the "codes" and the "standards" and the "QA whole-house ventilation for tight homes." So I for one am enthusiastic to get ahead of the "curve" and "train with the industry leader in heat recovery ventilation systems." It's not just the dollar signs I see; I love this stuff! I mean, I live and breathe it. One look at me and you'll immediately think whole-house ventilation for tight homes; if I had a dollar for every time someone has told me that!

I see you are looking for agents in Canada, Maine, Massachusetts, Rhode Island, Connecticut, Maryland and the DC area, Michigan, Illinois, Wisconsin, Iowa, Colorado, Minnesota, Utah, Oregon, and New Mexico. Although i don't really "live" in any of those "states"—though I used to live in Michigan, a decent place, but cold winters and awfully flat—I'm happy to relocate. Just say the word. My wife can hold down the fort here in Texas; besides, she has a job. She probably won't notice I'm gone for a few weeks anyway.

I see that many of your projects are Passive House or Net Zero homes and verifying raters are on those jobs already. Personally I prefer the Coke Zero Active House situations, but again, I'm not picky. Just need gobs of cold cash which I will happily earn by using my extensive knowledge of the, you know, code/standard Passive tight industry ventilation HERS/THEIRS paradigm. I mean, you know what I'm talking about—us experts.

I think it's pretty obvious we are on the same page here.

So, definitely interested on this end! I am geeked and all about it! I'll be waiting at my phone; I mean, whatever, if you want to call, I might be available.

Thanks for your time (and you're welcome!), djb

Interestingly, I thought I was ready for bed when a bit of inspiration hit this evening. We have to discuss a divine attribute for the upcoming WB roundtable, and I figured I'd write about aseity. And the piece came quickly this evening:

God's Aseity

More of a philosopher than a theologian, I am not altogether comfortable or in my element venturing into a matter of theology like this. But if I am going to discuss one of God's attributes, I am most inclined to discuss either God's omnibenevolence or aseity (and inch toward apologetics). The former is a divine trait central to my work in moral apologetics, and it really is in many ways the central-most characteristic of God. God is not just largely good, or pretty good, loving for the most part, or merely contingently or accidentally righteous or just. Unlike, say, the fickle, capricious gods of Euthyphro's Greek pantheon, God is essentially good, altogether loving, wholly upright, and perfectly just—in him there is no shadow of turning—which means, among other things, that the ease with which some might contrast God's love with his other features, like his holiness or justice, seems largely predicated on a mistake.

To say "God is love *but* God is also holy" casts, however unwittingly, God's love and holiness, to some measure, as standing in tension with one another. What God's perfection and impeccability instead suggests is that God's love and holiness, or God's love and justice, are perfectly congruent and coherent, without the slightest bit of tension or dissonance between them. Likewise God's love and sovereignty, God's love and wrath, God's love and every other attribute that he has. Love functions primordially and foundationally, coloring and conditioning every other of God's attributes. Simplicity theorists are surely right at least in the minimal suggestion that God's various attributes never stand at odds or in variance with one another, and love is who and what God is most essentially of all. God's Trinitarian nature, which Paul Copan earlier discussed, is a big reason why this is so.

God's aseity is the other divine attribute that has mesmerized my attention for a great long while, for organically connected reasons. For God to possess aseity, or to exist a se, means that God is absolutely independent, ontologically speaking. It is often closely associated with God's sovereignty— Alvin Plantinga, of course, referred to the "aseity/sovereignty intuition" in *Does God Have a Nature?* There's a positive and a negative aspect of this, because, on the one hand, God possesses such a feature—exists in this way—and, on the other hand, nothing and nobody else does. This axiomatic, fundamental truth about God has rich implications, among them that God is dependent on nothing and nobody else for his existence. His existence alone is ontologically independent, entirely and completely.

In my work in ethics and metaethics, for example, convictions about divine aseity render it practically impossible for me as a serious theist to entertain the hypothesis that something so important as the realm of ethical truth can exist and obtain out from under the provenance and providence of God. Such a notion has always seemed to me predicated on too small a view of God. If an atheist is a firm moral objectivist, I can well understand his or her desire to make sense of morality apart from God. I respect those honest, assiduous, and intelligent efforts and always find fascinating serious efforts by secularists to lay out the foundations of morality as they see them—particularly if they are as averse as I to resorting to reductionist or deflationary accounts of ethical truth to make their tasks more palatable and practicable.

What I have always had a much harder time respecting, however, is the insistent attitude that *even if God does exist*, he is still largely irrelevant to ethics. For if God exists a se, then to my thinking there is little principled reason to suspect that something as important as ethical truth itself would not depend on God in some important way, and every reason to think that moral realism evidentially points to God. If God *doesn't* exist, I am the first to pack it up and stop from pontificating about what the world is like. If God *does* exist, though, those who refuse to believe it, or those with paltry, wispy conceptions of what God is like, should, in all honesty, have the decency to return the favor and graciously vacate the lectern.

In the meantime, inhabiting the same epistemic boat, we find ourselves with robust evidence calling for rigorous explanation. Saddled as we are with our cognitive limitations, all we can do is our best. Recall some of the moral phenomena in need of robust explanation: the essential equality of human beings, the intrinsic worth of every person, the binding authority of moral obligations, the rationality of the moral enterprise, an objective condition of guilt for

167

wrongdoing, coincidence between moral facts and our epistemic faculties, adequate resources to undergird moral forgiveness, transformation, and ultimately perfection, to name but a few—all of which are arguably better explained by a God who is morally and metaphysically good and is *the* good, and who alone exists a se, than by anything on offer by our secular interlocutors, thus pointing to a vital (asymmetric) dependence relation of morality on God.

The precise, fine-grained details of that dependence relation is the cause of plenty of debate. However, the fact that theistic natural lawyers, divine will, divine command, divine desire, and divine motivation theorists all affirm such a dependence relation in one form or another, for a range of compelling considerations, is highly significant. To get off the ground, what something like the moral argument requires of its proponents is not unanimity on the precise shape of the dependence relation, but the simple principled agreement that some such essential dependence relation obtains of even necessary moral truths on God. Nothing less than a God with aseity, and who created and upholds this world each moment by his sustaining power, can furnish so robust an explanation. This is one among other important ways in which the moral argument(s) gesture not just to God's existence, but to his character and nature.

Tuesday, April 13, 2021: Jonathan and I worked together for over an hour online so I could learn how to podcast. Huge stride forward, even if I still have a little way to go. Hopefully soon I'll be up and running. This is an important piece coming into place. Today was also the ten-year anniversary of MB's and my first date. I just put this into a FB status:

> I had not realized it until Marybeth just told me, but our first date was ten years ago this very day. I had asked her out some months before, after some colleagues conspired to get us together, but she had said no. After some time passed she finally told me that if I asked her out again, she'd give a different answer.
>
> So on that first date we met at Barnes and Noble in Lynchburg and drank some coffee, shared a sugar cookie and good conversation, and quickly discovered that we were kindred spirits. It was a tad dicey dating a colleague; if it didn't work out, after all, that could have been more than a little awkward. But any misgivings were quickly alleviated on my end; heck, I ended up buying her engagement ring the next month. Of course I was getting old fast and figured I had little time to waste.
>
> It's remarkable when I think about the last ten years and all the life MB and I have had the chance to experience together. What could have been a casual date that changed nothing was instead an occasion that changed the whole trajectory of our lives. I'm deeply grateful that in his timing God orchestrated events in such a way that enabled our paths to cross; my life became exponentially better as a

result; he who finds a wife finds a good thing, and obtains favor from the Lord. Happy Coffee-versary, my precious wife.

Wednesday, April 14, 2021: Got a number of little things done in the morning, and in the afternoon MB and I took some time off to go see a few movies and have a nice dinner at Red Robin. Needed break. When I got home I see that I had heard back from Jan Shultis, an HBU student, a Naval Academy graduate, who is interested in connections between moral injury and the moral argument. I had written to ask if she would help me bolster a file on this issue for the Center. Here's her response (I italicized the most important part; I really need to consolidate this chaplaincy stuff!):

Hi, Dr. Baggett,

Thank you for this exciting email, and for including me. It is a privilege to be part of the vision for the Center in any way helpful, and I would love to start compiling resources on moral injury. Thank you!

Your note is also an answer to prayer lifted just this week ☐ I have so enjoyed this year in the Apologetics program, and I do not want to lose the valuable momentum gained in writing and research in the gap year between MAA graduation and starting a full course load for the DMin (I have Greek and more theology for leveling over the next 12 months, which will be great). On Monday I started praying for God to bring me to projects that are in alignment with His will for and use of me, that would keep me fully engaged. And here we are, discussing a project.... how cool is that?! Thank you!

Thank you, too, for your kindness and encouragement. I am humbled daily by the team at HBU, and any of my thought patterns that prove fruitful to the Kingdom over time are truly a reflection of shaping that has occurred here.

I will talk your ear off about moral injury, please just let me know in what format and when is best for you. I work in Sugar Land, so it's easy to get away for an hour or two if you ever have availability for an office visit or coffee. I'm told my personal experiences are unique, but more than that, I've had the privilege of leading teams all over the world, walking with more than 2,000 individuals in the context of the ministry (which took several years to openly become a ministry, that's another story!), and looking at humanity through a camera lens for twenty years now. That last thing, I think, is more formative than it sounds.... everyone looks the same through a camera, Dr. Baggett, no matter where in the world you go. And when you study them, waiting for the perfect shot, they act the same, too. Their faces hold the same hopes and fears. They are children of the One True God, every one of them belongs to our God. It is a privilege to see people in this way, because to some extent they have to allow it, and in that moment, they are vulnerable.

I'm musing..... *I would go so far as to say that based on what we've experienced at the non-profit and what I learned teaching a 3-day Leadership and Ethics course all over the country on behalf of the Navy Leadership and Ethics Center, at the ministry we now approach all trauma first as moral injury. There are other physiological things, of course, and more scientific things to consider, but in the spiritual is where both healing and resilience are found. Modern society doesn't want to talk about that, because then you have to admit that God exists, that the relationship with God or lack thereof is what's causing the pain, that it can go away and may not require a handful of pills, and that nothing else will work until the hurting individual gets the God part right. If you admit that moral injury is real, you admit that there are moral standards.*

I fear I am shifting from musing to rambling, but please do let me know the best way to continue the moral injury conversation and when, and it is a priority. In the meantime, I just thought of the first book to add to our reading list ☐

Thank you, Dr. Baggett! Hope your day is progressing wonderfully.

With gratitude,
Jan

Thursday, April 16, 2021: Spent time chatting and praying with TJ today. He's experiencing some reservations about the HBU connection to the Center, since he's averse to seeing them potentially begin micromanaging what we do. I hear his concerns, and am trusting that God makes all these things clear. I appreciated his transparency.

About to head over to HBU to tape the promo for the upcoming class with Craig. I also hope to do a short video introduction I can send to pastors when I reach out to churches—TJ's idea, and a good one—just something along these lines: "Hi Pastor, my name is Dave Baggett, and I'm a philosophy professor at Houston Baptist University. I am contacting local churches to share a bit of my vision for the Center for Moral Apologetics here at HBU. I'm privileged to be the director of the Center. We envision it becoming a hub of cutting-edge work on the moral argument for God's existence and goodness. I know you have a lot on your plates as you lead your congregations, and get pulled in lots of directions. So I'm sending this short introduction in the hopes of letting you know what I'm about. I would love to forge connections with you and your church. If you have any interest in having me come to speak there at your church—on apologetics, or moral apologetics, or the Center for Moral Apologetics here at HBU—I'd relish the chance to do it. The resources of moral apologetics are not just for folks in academia—it's vital we train and equip folks in the pew with these resources, and I want to make myself available to help in any way I can. My wife is also a professor—in her case, of English and cultural apologetics—and she's about to head up the apologetics department here at HBU. She too could come along and speak if you'd like. Thanks for listening to this, and I hope that we can become better acquainted. Every blessing as you continue your work in ministry."

Jan Shultis wrote back with an enthusiastic response to my invitation to write for the site. She seems to follow the site closely and to enjoy the newsletters a lot. I am beginning to think our paths crossing was quite providential. She half-jokingly volunteered to work for the Center in whatever capacity we need her.

Friday, April 16, 2021: So the week winds down. I have to turn to grading today, before dinner tonight with the guys. I also need to write a few checks and perhaps listen to the second big lecture by the St. Andrews prof who's currently lecturing at HBU (via zoom). Went yesterday and it was great, really fascinating. Leviticus gives several features that shaped the Jewish understanding of sacrifice. Using that framework helps inform our understanding of the sense in which Jesus was our sacrifice. Included is not just his death, but his resurrection and his ascension, a prelude to his continuing to intercede for us. Per impossibile, if Jesus didn't continue to intercede for us (a high priestly image that harkens back to Leviticus), we wouldn't experience the fullness or completion of our salvation. I was almost left wondering if there's at least a rough correlation between justification, sanctification, and glorification, on the one hand, with death, resurrection, and ascension/intercession, on the other. The intercession is key both to covenant maintenance and its culmination, the completion of the good work that's begin within us.

We are trying to transfer our membership from the Heritage United Methodist Church in Lynchburg to the Sugarland UM Church here in TX, but for some reason the secretary at Heritage is under the impression we transferred our membership to Thomas Road in 2017. Weird. I think I attended Thomas Road once in all my years in Lynchburg, the first week I got there in 2006. There was talk of transferring to Bethany, but it never happened officially. Anyway, hope to get all this resolved before too long. We want to be settled in a local church home now that the pandemic is dying down and the vaccine more widely distributed.

I had to write a follow-up e-mail to TJ about yesterday's conversation. The angst he's experiencing about the Center's connection to HBU is reminiscent of some tension between us a few years back when we had a prayer meeting in VA we invited Pastor Tom and his wife, Jonathan, Stephen, and TJ to. It was largely a prayer meeting about the Center we hoped to start eventually at HBU, and something got to him that night. Something again seems to be bothering him. I know TJ is a born leader, and it may be hard for him not to be able to be at the helm of the moral apologetics initiative. I know he has a burning heart for ministry, but I hate the thought that he be perpetually afflicted with angst. Praying that God answers his concerns and gives him peace, but I also wanted him to know he's got freedom to do as he feels God leads. Love him like a brother, and it would break my heart to lose him, but here's what I wrote him:

> TJ, as I've reflected more on our talk, it dawns on me that I should ask you a question. If the answer is no, I'll be happy (though I know more work is needed navigating these issues), but you have to feel the freedom to say yes if that's how you feel led. I'll be fine either way, and our friendship won't be threatened.
>
> So the question is just this: Do you want to be released from your "responsibilities" you have with Moral Apologetics in light of your reservations concerning the connections with HBU? Is this where you see this going?
>
> Again, I'm not here to dictate how God is leading you. I'd hate to lose your energy and passion, but if you can't find peace continuing (and I'm not sure you are there; I just know you're experiencing some real angst about it all), know that I'll respect your freedom to go your own way.
>
> I'd hate it, if so, but again, do know that this co-ministry is one thing, and our friendship is another, and nothing regarding the former will detract from the latter.
>
> Love ya, Dave

Later I did a short follow-up: "TJ, part of me wants to plead with you to reconcile yourself with the HBU piece so we can keep on keeping on. I felt like God really gave you to me to be a partner in this ministry, and of course you have been such a supreme source of encouragement all along. I'm not inclined to think that God's changed his mind. I know we have to be open to fresh marching orders, but I hadn't sensed the need for a big change here. BUT, I think my thinking, nevertheless, has been this: You need to think and pray through this on your own. By which I don't mean I'm not willing to talk or pray about it with you—but you have to come to your own conclusion. I'm respecting your 'Kantian autonomy' on this—as you personally appropriate whatever God is doing here. I'm hoping God gives you his peace and we can go on ... but I also know that the reason it's so important for you to get to that place—or peace in a different direction—is for you not to be riddled with angst over this. I don't want that—first and foremost I don't want it _**for you**_. So I'm refraining from the pleading, because that's too external a thing right now, where you're concerned; I'm mainly continuing to hope for the right solution here and to pray for you that you'll find his perfect peace as God chooses to furnish it. I believe God can and will use this to further his purposes, but I'm giving you all the mental space you need right now. Love ya! Dave"

Saturday, April 17, 2021: We're looking to the fall before we try something like the radio idea—me, Jerry, and Rob. They were over last night and it was a good time, as always. Rob and I prayed for Jerry's right foot and for his desire for a wife. Food was good; I departed from the salmon plan and we had steak instead. Today I need to wrap up grading, talk to Elton, and start thinking about Monday's podcast with Tim Stratton.

Just wrote TJ yet another e-mail:

TJ, speaking with Elton Higgs this morning, I mentioned to him your concerns about HBU and we chatted about them a bit. Two thoughts occurred as a result:

First, if you would like for me to arrange a conversation between you and either my dean or provost (or both) to talk about your concerns about the Center's connection with HBU, I'll be happy to do that. Nothing like allaying concerns by facilitating communication, I figure. It might be helpful for you, but also for them to help them understand that we're about more than just the HBU stuff— including outreach to churches, which I think they would claim to care about and certainly should.

Second, I see the moral apol ministry as involving two distinct tracks: the part connected with HBU's programs and such, and the outreach to laity and pastors and the like—outside the purview of HBU in large part. I'm overseeing the first part, and though I'm not uninvolved in the latter part, I see you as very much at the forefront of that initiative. Most specifically I see your potential powerful presence on our website, on the internet, and in outreach to churches and pastors. A thought I have had is you and I spearheading something like an online outreach to pastors (and perhaps interested lay people) who want training in moral apologetics. HBU wouldn't have to be involved in that at all, and if, say, we were eventually to generate a revenue stream from it by offering the training for a small fee or something, we could make sure that those resources would be directed toward this aspect of the ministry and not put into the coffers of HBU. It seems to me we could easily enough arrange something of a division of labor like that with the requisite bifurcation of organizational structures.

Just a thought! Love ya! Dave

Sunday, April 18, 2021: Feeling a bit weary at this stage of the term and school year, and really the whole last year has been insane—the Liberty debacle, selling houses, moving cross country, learning a new school routine, etc. Just want to rest. Bb was down yesterday so couldn't finish grading. It's not Sunday and I have a podcast with Tim Stratton tomorrow but feel little energy to prepare. Tough time. Hearing very little from TJ, which is a bummer. Can't help but feel like I'm losing him.

I had a bit of a back-and-forth with a YouTube commenter on my dialogue with William Lane Craig. Here's what I just sent—which summarizes the relevant stuff that came before:

Thanks, Theo, for spelling out some of your views in more detail. Okay, so you're referring to the authority of the individual making moral judgments or determinations. And you seem to punt to a notion of "appropriateness" for assessing the quality of those determinations. And you also include in the notion of the "sole arbiter" that each person is solely responsible, accountable, etc. for the intentions, decisions, and actions based on those moral assessments. With respect to beliefs, you think we exert little to no volitional control; either we find ourselves convinced of the truth of a claim or not; what we do exert volitional control over is whether to acquire new information, become better educated, etc., but our beliefs are based on what we're convinced of by the evidence we consider. Is that pretty accurate?

There's much there I don't find objectionable. I doubt we have direct volitional control over our beliefs, but I suspect we either have indirect volitional control or at least volitional control over the sorts of evidence we expose ourselves to (the latter is closer to your view, I think). And I suspect you think the latter is enough to imbue our judgments, determinations, and actions with the aforementioned "authority." Perhaps one addition I'd make comes from virtue epistemology— whether a certain piece of evidence convinces seems likely to me a function, to some extent, of the right epistemic virtues—such as being sufficiently attentive to the evidence and being willing to follow it unflinchingly if it's clear enough. One form of excellence is sensitivity to good arguments and evidence. I suspect, in the Flat Earth case, there is likely a lack of epistemic virtues (perhaps among other intellectual deficiencies).

All of this is on the epistemic end of things, and again, I find most of that fairly unobjectionable, for what it's worth. ☺

But you interject at the end of your first comment this line: "There is no objectivity in issues of morality." None of that seems determined or even implied by the epistemological ideas that you have. It seems to be an independent conviction of yours. It's of course not an uncommon view, even if it's a minority view (at present, though I've been predicting for years that it will be an increasingly common view), but it's clearly where the big fork in the road is that divides us. I'm not convinced that there is no objectivity in issues of morality. It's a view that has never appealed to me; it just doesn't have the ring of truth, to my thinking. I suppose one way of putting it is that I'm more convinced that, say, child torture for fun is wrong than I am of any reasons I've heard to be skeptical of it. To the extent that there are standards of appropriateness in assessing folks' convictions, behavior, etc., an important consideration for me is that it's inappropriate and indeed deeply culpable for one to believe something that seems false—like "it's not wrong to torture children for fun." So I gravitate, it would seem, toward moral objectivity much more than you do.

174

So all in all, you and I are somewhat close in epistemology, as far as I can tell, but differ rather markedly on the question of moral objectivity. What I'd say regarding the moral argument is that it's not surprising that such an argument does not move you since you are not inclined to grant the moral realism on which it is predicated. This of course only means the moral argument is flawed if you're right about rejecting moral realism, and I'm not inclined to think you are—that's not an argument, just an observation. Jerry Walls and I are currently working on a book defending moral realism; lots to discuss on that score, of course. But in the meantime, thanks for taking the time to clarify your views for me.

And then a different commenter claimed to be at theist skeptical of the moral argument, so I asked him why, and he claimed to be a Platonist, so I wrote him this back: "Thanks LeBron. I think Platonism is the second best view out there. I agree with the Platonist on nearly everything; in fact, I'm a theistic Platonist, following Robert Adams, thinking it makes sense that the necessary truths of which Platonism speaks are thoughts in God's mind, or something along those lines, as Plantinga put it. But I agree with the Platonist on the issues of cognitivism, error theory, expressivism, constructivism, realism, and even non-naturalism. The only disagreement comes after all that shared ground: which is the better explanation, theism or Platonism? I think Platonism leaves moral truths in metaphysical limbo, as John Rist argues; that something like theistic activism enables us to have principled reasons for thinking even necessary truths have their locus in God's noetic activity; that a personalist explanation of moral phenomena, for a variety of reasons, trumps a nonpersonalist one; and that theism provides the more robust account of authoritative obligations. (A few of those issues came up briefly in the chat with WLC.) I respect someone who sees this differently, like yourself, but to my thinking the theistic component enhances the robustness of the explanation—and I think a really attentive look at the nature of the moral evidence on offer—intrinsic human value, binding obligations, the personalist nature of morality, the possibility of moral knowledge, the coincidence of happiness and holiness, and worldview resources required for moral forgiveness, transformation, and ultimate perfection—points more in the direction of theism than Platonism. As a theistic Platonist, I'd actually say, more accurately, that it points not just to Platonism but to theism as well. Thanks for letting me know where you're coming from on this! Keep in touch, LeBron, if you'd like."

Monday, April 19, 2021: Received another marvelously encouraging e-mail from Jan Shultis this morning:

Good morning, Dr. Baggett,

Looks like the systems are back up, yay! Those poor IT folks, I bet they had a very long weekend....

Thank you, thank you, THANK YOU for letting me be part of Team Moral Apologetics (caps so necessary). I cannot wait to see what unfolds, starting with the library project on moral injury and the blog. I shared with your wife during our weekly call last week that when I took her Apol Research & Writing Class las August and was exposed to the website and your joint work, I sent this kind of half-prayer to God, as I think of them - you know when you're not formally praying, you're just kind of existing and talking to God and going about things? It's a half prayer. At any rate, I thought to God, "God, it would be so cool to be part of this Center... this is the future, the work that is going on now and will go on there. It would be *so cool* to work for You, with them." And here we are, how incredible is that?! ▢ We need a better work than "amazing" to describe God, but perhaps not, because I am continually amazed.

Thank you for the movie reviews! Yes, I have an 8 year old daughter, and she is the absolute coolest ▢ That is another way that Team Baggett spoke life into me this year - about midway through Apol Research & Writing, I and another single mom ended up in a rather personal conversation on a forum about how we see God show up in this journey as a single parent, unorthodox though that sounds to some. Dr. Baggett wrote us an email that simply shared a word of encouragement and her own testimony that we *can* pursue higher ed, we *can* become better equipped to serve Him, and be single parents, and He can change our story and bless us with a partner in that journey if and when He chooses. It was very inspiring.

I cannot wait to see the class promo! You already opened a book on apologetics with a shout out to zombies, the bar is set pretty high for engaging content ▢

Hope your day and week get off to a wonderful start!

With gratitude,
Jan

Around noon I did a podcast with Tim Stratton. That was a great deal of fun. I felt a tad out of sorts, but it went alright. Was wiped out much of the rest of the day. The situation with TJ came to a head in the evening, and it appears we have agreed he'll step down from his leadership roles with the moral apologetics outreaches. Sad, but perhaps for the best. He's such a born leader; it was hard for him to see me make certain leadership decisions with which he disagreed. Praying that God uses the separation, and that TJ's own work is mightily blessed. Still, hard.

One of Tim's questions today was about the Center, and this was my answer: "My wife and I came to HBU this past summer in large part because we had the chance to start this thing. It's been a dream of mine for about 15 years, and it's finally coming to fruition. We envision building it into a hub of cutting-edge work and training and research on aspects of the moral argument. We want to reach chaplains and laypeople and counselors and preachers and teachers with the resources of the moral argument. We want to encourage people to be attentive to the moral evidence, to inculcate intellectual virtues like sensitivity to excellent evidence and the distinctive evidential power of morality, we want to encourage people to explore that aspect of the moral argument to which they're drawn in a special way, because we think God might well have plans for that person to make a distinctive contribution to the discussion in a way that nobody else could, we want to train the next generation of Christian thinkers to see how central God's love and goodness is to all that we say and do as Christians, and we want to do all of this important, cutting-edge work in community. There's a website on the HBU portal for folks interested, and as always MoralApologetics.com has lots of resources on all of this, all free."

Tuesday, April 20, 2021: After a fitful night of sleep occupied with concerns about the TJ situation, I awoke this morning with an intention to ask Jan to replace TJ in leadership, so I wrote her this morning with that invitation. Then at 10 am I spoke with Nick Henretty, a guy trained in music and sound. We discussed the possibility of his generating audio books for what Moral Apologetics Press puts out. He's going to do a sample chapter from Elton's book, and crunch some numbers to give us an idea of the cost to generate an audio book. I also got an e-mail back from the Asbury grad who's on staff at Sugarland UM Church, where MB and I are now official members, from what I understand. And as I type this, Nathaniel is in a remote interview with a local insurance agency for a position. Lots of things happening!

Just heard back from Jan with her customary enthusiasm:

Dr. Baggett,

Wow.... I have a grin so wide my face literally hurts. Thank you for blessing me and yes, yes, YES!!!!! It would be an incredible privilege to come onboard as a Senior Research Fellow and Associate Editor. (I literally cannot diminish this grin ☐)

I feel like I say this about every time I speak with you, but this invitation is a direct response to prayer. I've been researching the historical development of moral injury by modern definition, and after two days remain shocked by how little is out there. This is exciting because I believe this topic area constitutes an incredible opportunity for the Center to lead research, dialogue, and training, if it be God's will. I was drafting up a working plan that is larger than one blog and praying on whether submitting it to you would be too bold, and.... here we are. Wow!

Please let me know next steps. I'm just going to keep grinning over here...

Hope you are enjoying this beautiful day!

With extreme gratitude,

Jan

That is definitely a silver lining in this situation regarding TJ. I don't know all the details, but it seems that Paul and Barnabas parted ways in their ministry; perhaps God used it to multiply their ministries somehow. I do hope and pray the best for TJ and his outreach, but getting Jan onboard definitely seems like a God thing. As if more confirmation is needed, Jan and I just wrote some more e-mails. First her:

Hi, Dr. Baggett,

I'm so excited about your most recent email that I'm truly giddy and apologize if anything here lacks coherence as a result. Hurrah, let's work for the Kingdom! THANK YOU □

Thank you, too, for your prayers. They are felt, and much appreciated. I am praying for both of you individually and as a unit, as well. I pray that the peace that surpasses understanding, that you freely illuminate for others, is received by you instantly and in lasting ways during this tough time. You are high value targets for the enemy, and I can only imagine how you might experience those attacks as the Center gains momentum and its impact is felt in ever-increasing ways, in addition to the incredible body work already underway. Let these prayers guard the entrance to more days in movie theatres, full of love, companionship, and rejuvenation.

It is in His name that we pray, and worship and glorify Him on such an incredibly, breathtakingly gorgeous day.

Hugs for continued strength and encouragement,

Jan

P.S. I'm working on calling both of you something other than "Dr. Baggett," because I realize that is confusing and your email signatures suggest that would be alright, but I'm downright starstruck by both of you, so..... I'm working up to it. Thank you for your patience and incredibly kind welcome □

And my response:

Oh my, how both edifying and hilarious!

Feel free to call me Dave, and Marybeth says call her MB, or Marybeth, whatever you'd like! I was just typing up my update for the upcoming newsletter in which I will introduce you in your new roles. I can sense God's clear providence in all of this, not a doubt in my mind.

Don't feel pressured to do anything beyond what you're already doing. The research you're doing on moral injury is exactly what I want you to keep doing. What makes this fit so impeccable is that all you need to do is continue in the same direction; the Center will help give you a voice and showcase your vitally important research. It really is just perfect! Seamless. You can dovetail any blogs you might wish to do for the site with the writing you want to do for your research and eventual thesis—hopefully anything and everything you do for the Center will just propel you along toward the very goals God's already laid on your heart.

At some point I'll replace TJ in the list of Senior Research Fellows with you. That will involve a paragraph summing up your background and work. I'll let you write that at your convenience, but no rush at all.

What you need to know is that we are here to cheer you on and contribute to giving you a platform. We're so happy you are part of the team!! And it really is a team, a community we're building here, and you are now an essential part of it, as far as MB and I are concerned. You're a gift. We want to do everything we can to maximize your impact, give you a voice, and enable you to function and thrive in all your obvious gifts and callings. We'll never hand you a muzzle, only a megaphone. ☐

Thanks for your encouragement!!

Blessings, Dave

After a long while, I heard again from Matthew at Houston Christian High School. His oral defense is tomorrow night, so we're planning on attending. He sent me the first fifteen pages or so of his work. I still tend to think it's confused. He conflates reasons for action with moral duties; or reasons for action with moral authority. He also doesn't recognize that sometimes "ought" captures notions of moral obligations and sometimes it does not—a failure perhaps owing to Gewirth's watered-down notion of prescriptivity. He also thinks the fact that X can be obligatory for you but not for me is going to help his case against supererogation, but it doesn't. And finally, he seems to confuse belief in biblical inerrancy with belief in inerrancy in our biblical interpretations, not to mention that he seems to think the Bible provides an answer to every metaethical question under the sun we might wish to raise, and he exploits the ambiguity inherent in claiming we "can't go beyond our duties." Generally my preference, admittedly, would be for him to inject a bit more epistemic humility in his suggestions, rather than treating things as a slam dunk that are not.

Wednesday, April 21, 2021: In the next fifteen minutes or so Jerry Walls should be getting to the house, then he and MB and I are heading to Galveston to celebrate his birthday with some red fish and shrimp kisses! Should be great fun. The promo commercial for the upcoming May course came in. It's good; MB and I suggested a few tweaks, but it should be available soon.

Thursday, April 22, 2021: So I'm going to spend the day with Bill Scott at the Lanier Library today, then have dinner with him and a representative of the place. Going to meet Bill in a little while. Tim Stratton put up the video of him and me discussing the moral argument. And when I got home from the library there were two great pieces of news: Marybeth just got a new piece on LU accepted to be run by the Religious News Service, and OUP's reader reports on the book proposal Hare and I sent in back in December came back very positive. More tomorrow!

Friday, April 23, 2021: Great conversation today with a Navy chaplain—more on that tomorrow. For now I want to share Cynthia Read's e-mail from yesterday and the two reader reports. First Cynthia:

> Dear David and John,
>
> I am horrified to see how long ago you sent me your proposal. We have FINALLY obtained two readers' reports. Happily, both readers recommend publication enthusiastically. Not surprisingly both have a few questions/suggestions as well as praise. It would be helpful now to have your response to the readers' comments. With that in hand, I am confident that I will shortly be in a position to offer you a contract. It seems clear that this will be an important book that OUP should be proud to publish. I hope to have the pleasure of working on it with you.
>
> All the best,
>
> Cynthia

First reader report:

> Reader #1
>
> How would you describe the rationale, purpose, or thesis of the work? In this proposal on the Moral Argument for God's existence, Baggett and Hare describe what could become a very welcome publication, one sorely needed in the field at this time. Why needed? Because there are several classes for which such a text would be a welcome textbook—where there is currently no such text. Their rationale is sound: to bring together, in one volume, a comprehensive synthesis of the current thoughts regarding what may seem (or be, except, perhaps, for the expert in the moral argument) the disparate field of theories, concepts, arguments, and monographs devoted to various facets of the moral argument and allied topics.

Do you approve of the scholarship, the writing style, and organization? The proposed chapters and their authors are excellent and some of the best people to write these chapters. The organization seems sound; my only misgivings are explained below (e.g. at least one issue that should be more prominently discussed that isn't here—as far as I can see).

Does the work make a significant contribution to the field? I agree with Baggett and Hare that this book would be a most welcome addition. Also intriguing is the promise that this work will be written so that the 'non-specialist' should be able to follow the points. This is a tall order, but these authors seem altogether committed to this outcome, and such a book would be doubly-welcome. If such were achieved, then their claims that the readership could range from undergraduate all the way to graduate-level instruction is warranted.

Do you have any suggestions for ways in which it could be improved? Some possible suggestions: Expand on POE section, or have Copan include address both of two questions: 1) the one under chapter 9's explanation, 'The Problem of Evil', viz., the zero-sum game problem; but also 2) The 1989 *Nous* article by Paul Draper, where the HI (Hypothesis of Indifference) is the best explanation for moral phenomena—not moral Theism. Dan Howard-Snyder would be a good author for a separate chapter, if such were desired or found needful or helpful.

I would like to see, in a theistically-heavy text such as this proposed here, an answer to Walter Sinnott-Armstrong's argument that rape is wrong because it harms the other person (where the concept of 'harm' can apparently, he thinks, be cashed out completely and satisfactorily without reference to God simpliciter). Interestingly, Sinnott-Armstrong's argument is found in the Oxford University Press publication of the debate between Sinnott-Armstrong and W. L. Craig.

Rawlsian/Contractarianism is mentioned in the proposal, but with so many adhering to Rawls' general picture of justice these last 50 years, perhaps more focus/ a chapter might be devoted more clearly to answer how Rawls must import a tacit theistic assumption or the like?

Many theists hold to a moral realism based on a sort of G. E. Moorean argument for intrinsic value quite independent of Theistic moorings or grounding for moral reality, value, or authority. (I think here e.g. of William Wainwright, Keith Yandell (arguably), and William Alston. Alston had a piece called 'What Euthyphro Should Have Said,' in the Craig Philosophy of Religion anthology (Rutgers University Press), but in his problem of evil articles in (e.g.) Howard-Snyder (1996), he seems to toe the line of moral realism as a theist within an intuitionistic framework of ethics reminiscent of G. E. Moore's *Principia Ethica*. Where will this point be addressed in this proposal? Perhaps it easily will be; however, I wondered about this point.

Under the last section, 'Comparative Religion (Buddhism),' Buddhism is mentioned but then does not have a chapter devoted to Buddhism (from what I could tell). However, Harold Netland may be a very good name to suggest for such a chapter. Or, possibly Paul Griffiths.

I feel it is worthwhile to think about adding a chapter on what is the most central issue that is not, as far as I can see, addressed in this manuscript proposal: the problem of the moral argument and how it underdetermines the exact "God concept" that one gets from a sound argument of this ilk. Even the great C. S. Lewis, in his first conclusion on the matter, said the most we can say is that there is 'Something or Someone' behind the Law of Human Nature (i.e. the Moral Law). But what of the identity of that something or someone? Surely this problem might be addressed with a chapter? On the other hand, John Hare might treat this topic historically in chapter 1; however, I consider this the #1 weakness of the moral argument, so if I were to buy this book, I would expect that this #1 issue would be address front and center, yes?

A related issue might be addressed as well: How does the Moral Argument work cumulatively (to establish good reasons for believing in the Christian Theistic God) with the ontological argument? Cosmological? Teleological? Argument from personhood? Resurrection argument? Might these issues be explored in some of the chapters, also?

What do you perceive to be the market for the book? Do you recommend that Oxford offer to publish it? I do agree with Baggett and Hare that there will be a significant demand for this book. The moral argument has become a hot field in apologetics, and this book speaks directly to a need in the market—and a want. As I said above, if the book is sculpted to be high on readability, this will augur well for marketing and sales, it seems to me. I recommend that Oxford definitely offer to publish this text. It is a wonderful proposal and fills such an important niche, just as the proposal claims. Bravo!

Any other comments you may have will be very welcome as well. Many of these chapters sound just wonderful, e.g., chapter 10 would be an excellent contribution and a real staple of this volume. Chapter 18 also sounds great: Have Prof. Zagzebski provide updates and replies to objections since the publication of her work. This sort of approach will make the volume all the more attractive, as it has made it attractive to me.

Second reader report:

Reader #2

How would you describe the rationale, purpose, or thesis of the work?

The aim of the work is to provide something that is both timely and sorely needed: a comprehensive discussion of the moral argument(s) for God's existence. There are many volumes on the moral argument but all of them are limited or idiosyncratic in scope. The moral argument is alive and well – perhaps more alive now than ever – and, not surprisingly, it has become increasingly interesting and variegated. As of yet, there is no volume that aims to cover this scope of this rich and important argument. So the rational for this proposed volume is very sound and convincing.

A related aim is to provide a discussion of the moral argument for a variety of audiences, and not merely for specialists. This is also a strong rationale, as there are several different audiences that will be interested in the volume: both scholars and students of religious studies, theology, and philosophy.

Do you approve of the scholarship, the writing style, and organization?

Yes, I approve of the organization:

The authors have organized the material in a very natural and logical way. The chapters clearly build upon each other.

I also approve of the scholarship:

Each of the editors has written major works on the moral argument. Each is known to be among the very best philosophers who have worked on this topic. In fact, in my view, you couldn't do better than Hare and Baggett for a volume like this. If I saw their names on a book like this, I would order it sight-unseen.

I was impressed with the list of potential contributors. They represent a very eminent group of scholars.

I was pleased to see that they have included a chapter on the problem of evil (Ch 9). It might seem to be out of place in a volume on the moral argument, but (in my experience) the topic almost always comes up in discussions of the moral argument. And it is not hard to see why: both the moral argument and the problem of evil begin with a near identical normative premise (say, certain acts are wrong and certain act are evil, respectively) and head to contradictory conclusions (i.e, God exists and God doesn't exist, respectively). So I think the inclusion of this chapter shows great insight on the part of the editors, and will make the volume especially useful for teaching.

I was also pleased to see that they hope to have a chapter (Ch 12) by Crosby on human value and personalism. I assume this will discuss a/the version of the moral argument that moves (very roughly) from the intrinsic value of human persons to the existence of God. This is an old line of thought that has somehow fallen off center-stage in discussions of the moral argument (though John Rist seems to be attempting to re-center it in his recent book, *What is a Person?*), so it is nice to see it here. And you couldn't do better than Crosby to write such a chapter!

I approve of the writing style:

The proposal is well written and organized. I have also read many things by both authors, and each has a clear and accessible style.

Does the work make a significant contribution to the field?

Yes, without question. The volume will have no-rivals: It will be the place to go to understand the history, nature, and future of the moral argument.

Do you have any suggestions for ways in which it could be improved?

The volume is very well designed as it stands, but towards improving the volume the editors might consider the following observations and comments:

· I was surprised to not see Erik Wielenberg in the list of potential contributors. Perhaps he declined their offer to contribute? At any rate, Wielenberg has several major books on the topic, especially his *Robust Ethics*, which defends moral realism from an atheistic framework. There is also a recent edited volume in which Wielenberg and Craig debate this topic. So, I would suggest that the editors consider him for a chapter on secular ethics.

· I was confused about the last section. The title is "Comparative Religion (Buddhism and Judaism)" but there are no chapters listed for Judaism or Buddhism. Did they forget to list those chapters?

· Relatedly, there is a version of the moral argument within Buddhism, and it would be great to see it discussed here. For details, see the essay by Siderits in the recent volume *Persons: A History*, ed. by Lolordo (OUP, 2019), esp. pg. 311.

What do you perceive to be the market for the book?

The book will be of interest to professional philosophers and theologians, both for their research and teaching. With respect to the former (research), the volume will represent the current state of the debate and will be a focal point for future work on the topic. For the latter (teaching), the volume would be perfect for use in undergraduate and graduate courses in ethics or philosophy of religion; it would make an ideal text for a graduate seminar that focuses on the relationship(s) between religion (the existence and nature of God, religious belief, etc.) and ethics (the basis, motivation, and rationality of moral action, etc.).

In addition, there is a significant market for books in Christian apologetics, and this volume would also be of great interest to that market.

Do you recommend that Oxford offer to publish it?

Yes, without question.

Saturday, April 24, 2021: Received news yesterday Elton won't be available to talk this morning. He had a heart attack and is recovering in the hospital. A stint was put in, but resting in the hospital is hard. MB and I have been praying for him. Will miss the chat today, but what a sober reminder of life's brevity and our physical precariousness.

I had shared with my dean yesterday the good news from OUP, and the way this may give us a chance to dovetail work on that book with an HBU moral apologetics conference. His excited reply bodes well for such a collaboration. We should really look into finding some funding to help subsidize such a conference. It would be great if we could pay for folks to come in to do their papers.

Don't feel like diving into the OUP proposal stuff, or much of anything. Feel dog tired again today; lots catching up with me. So relaxing today and trying to get caught up on my rest. Just wrote Rob Gagnon and Jerry Walls about my five favorite movies:

Rob's questioning Jerry last night about favorite movies got me thinking about mine, so here are my top five, in no particular order:

(1) *About Time*: a profoundly funny and poignant story with a simple but penetrating takeaway.
(2) *It's a Wonderful Life*: with the possible exception of *Christmas Carol*, the greatest counterfactual story ever, and has so much going for it; in a class by itself.
(3) *Shadowlands*: set in the most picturesque environment imaginable, my favorite place in the world (Oxford), featuring rare academic element well done, and an eminently well-crafted story impeccably interweaving Lewis's life and work.

(4) *Rocky*: taps into so many enduring universal themes; love the dream/hard work stuff; tremendously inspiring (I watched and re-watched it numerous times while writing *Good God*).

(5) *Back to the Future*. A well-nigh perfect movie as far as I'm concerned. Breaks all sorts of cinematic rules. Best time-travel movie I know of. I've lost count how many times I've seen it. Just pure fun.

Citizen Cane, *Casablanca*, *The Birds*, etc. are likely intrinsically greater than some of these, but this list of five captures the ones that have most touched me personally.

Sunday, April 25, 2021: Day of rest, and a needed one. Trying to do nothing but spend time relaxing, praying, and listening to some scripture. Wrote TJ this morning, but it seems he needs some more time to process. Marybeth made an insightful point in a prayer earlier—that this past week was both astounding and heartbreaking. Some really great things happened that made us feel like we're beginning to hit our stride here in Houston, but there was also the loss of TJ from leadership. Perhaps a takeaway is that we should remember God's involved in it. The good stuff is not of us, and the bad stuff doesn't leave us alone to handle it. TJ's struggle and Elton's heart attack were tough. The good things were definitely good, though: great trip to Galveston with Jerry, solid reception of our video promo, good news from OUP, progress on replacing the LLC with a 501(c)3, the acceptance of MB's commentary in the RNS, the floating of the possibility of moral apologetics conference next year or thereabouts.

Around mid-afternoon MB got corrections on her piece from the *Religious News Service*. Unfortunately they insisted on reducing the size of it to 1000 words, so here's the original and better version of what she wrote:

The Smoke and Mirrors of Liberty University's Suit against Jerry Falwell, Jr.

Self-preservationist spin is no substitute for the real work of repentance and revival essential to the institution's long-term flourishing.

To read the lawsuit Liberty University brought against Jerry Falwell, Jr. last week, you get the impression that their former president was a master manipulator who presented to everyone a faux Christian veneer that obscured a vulgar reality. Requesting upwards of $41 million in compensatory and punitive damages, Liberty's suit charges Falwell with breaching both his contract and fiduciary duties and with conspiring to secure an unjustly advantageous contract that would shield him from consequences for his grave transgressions.

In support of this case, the complaint details the school's fundamentalist bona fides, pointing to Liberty's roots in the Moral Majority founded by Falwell's televangelist father, highlighting the strict code governing student conduct, and underscoring the responsibility of all members of the community to hold others to account. The suit then proceeds to run down the many ways in which Falwell spurned the school's founding spirit and purported mission.

The filing catalogues Falwell's questionable dealings with Giancarlo Granda, the pool attendant he and his wife Becki met in Miami; it details his clubbing and lavish lifestyle; it notes his excessive alcohol consumption; and it spotlights his sordid social media activity. All in all, the suit tells the story of a man who flouted the rules and of a board lied to and defied, hoodwinked by some seasoned subversive.

Clutching their pearls, the board now cries foul, seeking restitution for Falwell's shocking misbehavior that "induced injury to Liberty's enrollment, impacted its donor base, disrupted its faculty, . . . and damaged Liberty's reputation." On the version of the story they tell, the board is the aggrieved party, victim of Falwell's machinations.

As charming as this narrative is, it is far from the truth. Oh, Falwell was a lamentable train wreck as president, don't get me wrong. Working for him the past decade took a toll on my soul. His behavior and character were steadfastly at odds with the stated mission of the school he was tasked with leading. All that the board stipulates in their lawsuit makes this fact plain, and their case is bolstered by so much more misbehavior left unmentioned.

Even still, what goes unacknowledged by the lawsuit is that Falwell has long been unworthy of the position with which he was entrusted. Nothing noted in the suit is new news. The board has long had ample evidence to question his fitness for office.

Falwell's Twitter feed alone demonstrates he was anything but the "spiritual exemplar" the board allegedly expected of their president. In fact, he explicitly disavowed that role in an infamous tweet from June of 2019. Earlier that year, he bragged in university-wide convocation that he liked to start Twitter fights when he got bored. And he's waged such fights against politicians and Christian ministers, even faculty and Liberty parents.

For the board to now act shocked that Falwell would treat others with disdain is culpably obtuse at best, willfully dishonest at worst. It's worth noting that many of them had first-hand experience with Falwell's mistreatment of board member Mark DeMoss who in 2016 was pushed out after having the audacity and temerity to express an opinion at variance with Falwell.

And Falwell's lawsuit against the school back in October 2020 should have come as no surprise, given that under his leadership, Liberty sued everyone from the Moorman family for daring to shield their ancestors' graves from Liberty's construction to landowners unlucky enough to own property adjacent to a lake donated to the university to the New York Times (including a reporter and freelance photojournalist) for exposing the folly of the school's COVID response.

As well, Falwell weathered numerous campaigns over the years that challenged his inappropriate behavior, of which the board cannot claim ignorance. Students and alumni have called into question his remarks about Muslim terrorists, his belligerent political activism wrapped in Liberty's imprimatur, his censorship of the student paper, his questionable entanglement of the Cinema Arts program with a propagandistic (and borderline heretical) film, and his racially insensitive attack on the Virginia governor, to name just a few.

Each of these situations (and many others) provided fodder for Liberty's "mockery and consternation in the media," which the board has only now suddenly taken an interest in. No matter that, prior to Falwell's contract renegotiation, nothing more than a cursory Google search would readily yield a litany of public relations debacles and nightmarish optics. Bombshell reporting from Brandon Ambrosino and Aram Roston from as early as 2017, for example, revealed the puzzle pieces that would later form the scandal that brought Falwell down.

Yet the board was remarkably incurious and conspicuously silent through that time.

Additionally, Liberty was getting plenty of other bad press: for students' outsized reliance on federal student loans, for a culture of fear on campus, for callously cutting crucial programs and loyal faculty that were not making money fast enough for the university.

Again, all of this information was readily available for anyone with eyes to see. Yet the board, which is charged with holding Falwell accountable, obstinately refused to look. For that reason, it is difficult to read their charges against the former president without a healthy dose of skepticism, if not a modicum of incredulity.

If their concern is truly with the reputation of the university, if they genuinely hope to restore the school's integrity and keep it on mission, they must reckon with their own culpability in Falwell's transgressions. For who else but the board, and specifically the executive committee, could hold him to account?

Such governance is the board's primary responsibility, and the stronger they make their case about Falwell's misbehavior, the more they incriminate themselves.

Either the board knew about Falwell's indiscretions, or they didn't. However, neither ignorance nor neglect absolves them. Both equate to dereliction of the board's duty, as they should have

kept a careful eye on Falwell and his management and were obligated to hold him to the code of conduct they now wield as a weapon against him.

Here's the crucial point that the lawsuit attempts to obscure: the board let Falwell behave egregiously and recklessly. They encouraged him even. Every time they ignored Falwell's blatant public misconduct, with every dismissal of legitimate stakeholder concerns, at every unspoken assent to his outlandish and prodigious boasts of his own achievements, he was emboldened to go further.

I am grateful that Liberty is attempting with this lawsuit to draw a clearer line between themselves and their former president. Falwell's recent gestures toward a comeback have left many faculty, students, and alumni uneasy.

That said, the damage to Liberty from Falwell's tenure is far more extensive than the lawsuit suggests. The former president consistently put profits over people leaving untold casualties along the way, he twisted Christian theology and biblical passages to suit his egotistical purposes, he ruled Liberty with an iron fist and made dissent analogous to disloyalty.

In the wake of his regime, he left the school compromised and corrupted, a legacy that carries on unabated in the structures he established (and in the Twitter feed of incoming board chairman Tim Lee). The full array of his henchmen and cronies remain in power and emulate his modus operandi.

The root of the rot at Liberty is far deeper than the complaint acknowledges. Falwell did not inflict this damage alone. Rather, the suit is an implicit attempt to advance a revisionist narrative, to scapegoat Falwell and cast the remaining administration as faultless and with altogether clean hands.

For the spiritual health of the school, this redacted narrative cannot stand. As such, projecting a mere appearance of godliness is insufficient to the high calling of the school's leaders. They must also embrace its power and surrender to the dictates of the faith they espouse. They must confess and own the roles they played in propagating and perpetuating the sin they now condemn with impunity and suffocating sanctimony.

Those who care about the name of Christ claimed by the institution simply must insist on real penitence, deep repentance, and sweeping reform at Liberty University.

Monday, April 26, 2021: MB's piece came out around noon in the RNS, and later in the day it was picked up by the *Washington Post*, which should lead to a great deal more circulation.

My contribution to the WB this month:

Book Suggestions on the Moral Argument

The moral argument(s) are sometimes treated just as just a tool in the arsenal, rather than the rich resource they are for reflection, enjoyment, beauty, insight, and spiritual formation. This month I thought I would offer some suggestions for resources on various aspects of the moral argument for those with an interest in pursuing this topic further. Of course nothing I do here is anything like exhaustive. That would be exhausting.

Although to date there is not, to my knowledge, an exhaustive single-volume collection of essays that cover the whole terrain of moral apologetics, John Hare and I intend to edit such a collection to fill that gap in the literature.

There are five major components to the moral argument as I think about it. One is the history of the argument; another is a critique of secular ethics; another is a defense of theistic ethics; another is a defense of the moral realism on which it is all based; and another is an extension of the argument beyond theism to Christianity.

Regarding the fertile history of the moral argument, Jerry Walls and I wrote *The Moral Argument: A History*, which directs you to folks like Immanuel Kant, John Henry Newman, A. E. Taylor, William Sorley, Hastings Rashdall, and others. Those luminaries provide some really rich reading—especially Newman's *Grammar of Assent* and Taylor's *Faith of a Moralist*.

In terms of a critique of secular ethics, Jerry and I wrote *God and Cosmos*, but it is just a start and promissory note. Mark Linville's piece on the moral argument, easily accessible online, is well worth reading. The debate between Craig and Wielenberg came out last year; edited by Adam Johnson, it is quite good. In terms of defending theistic ethics, that was the main goal of our *Good God*. But there are lots of possibilities here, including Linda Zagzebski's *Divine Motivation Theory*, C. Stephen Evans' *God and Moral Obligations*, John Hare's *Moral Gap*, Robert Adams' *Finite and Infinite Goods*, Angus Ritchie's *From Morality to Metaphysics*. Most of these cover more than just one or two aspects of the moral argument—defending theistic ethics and critiquing alternatives, for example. Erik Wielenberg's *Robust Ethics* offers criticisms of theistic ethics and an effort at a more secular account of ethics. Wielenberg and I have a written debate on Lewis's moral argument in a book edited by Greg Bassham.

In terms of defending moral realism, see Terence Cuneo's *The Normative Web*, Russ Shafer-Landau's *Moral Realism*, and David Enoch's *Taking Morality Seriously*; all are important. Jerry and I aim to write our fourth book on the moral argument on this topic, finishing our planned tetralogy.

For extending the moral argument to Christianity, that is cutting-edge stuff. We need to see more books on this—especially using, say, Trinitarian resources. Adam Johnson wrote his dissertation on this recently at Southeastern (which will be published), and Brian Trapp did as well about a decade ago at Southern. My guess is great work is coming here as the community of moral apologists builds and the momentum of the movement grows.

Incidentally, several of the folks mentioned—Hare, Adams, Evans, etc.— have done more than one book that's important for the moral argument.

Important folks who are more secular to consider can be found when you look at rival ethical accounts. I mentioned Wielenberg, Enoch, and Shafer-Landau (though he aims for more neutrality on the God question than most), but as you get into error theory, expressivism, constructivism, sensibility, theory, and nontheistic moral realism (either natural or non-natural), you run into a host of thinkers: McDowell, Blackburn, Wiggins, Mackie, R. M. Hare (John's father), Joyce, Korsgaard, Brink, Harman, Boyd, Foot, Parfit, etc.

There's a four views book on God and morality edited by Loftin, and a nice anthology on God and ethics edited by Garcia and King called *Is Goodness without God Good Enough?* that's eminently worth reading; the latter came out of a debate William Lane Craig had with Paul Kurtz.

Of course avail yourself of the website, MoralApologetics.com, for a host of resources related to the moral argument from a wide array of disciplines.

Recently the site ran a series about recent developments in the moral argument. This reminds me that I have hardly mentioned contemporaries working on the moral argument; we have seen a real resurgence of work and interest on the topic over the last several decades.

Mark Murphy is an important thinker who has written some serious books on ethics from a theistic perspective although he is more reticent than many to make it into an apologetic matter. Still, though, quite worth reading, rife with trenchant insight and philosophical rigor. Kevin Kinghorn is a friend and good philosopher who studied with Swinburne and has written some important and germane books: *A Framework of the Good*, & (with Travis) *But What About God's Wrath?* Much recommended.

In taking on alternative moral theories, of which there are a plethora, one might also be interested in taking on not just nonreligious alternatives, but non-Christian religious perspectives. Brian Scalise has done nice work using the Trinity to contrast an Islamic conception of love with that of Christianity's; Ronnie Campbell has contrasted a Christian perspective on the problem of evil with those of several worldviews (pantheism, panentheism, etc.); T. J. Gentry is finishing up a dissertation at North-Western using resources from moral apologetics to critique Mormonism; Daniel McCoy is writing a book contrasting Christian love and Buddhist compassion; etc.

Paul Copan has penned a widely anthologized piece on the moral argument, and my wife and I have done a more popular level book that incorporated elements of *Good God*, *God and Cosmos*, and the history of the moral argument called *Morals of the Story*.

This list is at least suggestive. You can find more resources in the notes and bibliographies of these books. I encourage you in your study!

Around 8:20 in the morning my time I did a Microsoft Teams meeting with Mike Jones's ethics class at Liberty to discuss moral apologetics. I spoke for about 30 minutes, then opened the floor to questions. It went pretty well, I think. Yet earlier this morning Jan wrote with her bio, so I sent it along to Celeste to replace TJ in the list of Senior Research Scholars on the HBU site for the Center. She also asked for permission to put her affiliation with the Center on her business card, and we said yes; in fact, this is a good idea for all the members of the team.

Here's Jan's bio: "Jan Shultis is a Naval Academy graduate, author of two books, and Associate Editor at MoralApologetics.com who plans to pursue her DMin at

Houston Baptist University. After 14 years in uniform serving around the U.S. and in Afghanistan, she founded a faith-based non-profit focused on veterans, law enforcement, first responders, and families that supports warriors in need throughout Texas, with a special focus on ministry in local courts and jails. Jan brings to the Moral Apologetics team additional professional experience in biotechnology, public relations, and ethics curriculum development. Jan shares that she is extremely excited to spearhead the Center's innovative exploration of the organic connections between moral apologetics and moral injury, including but not limited to military veterans. She is local to Houston and looks forward to contributing to the Center's robust on-campus presence at HBU."

Mike Jones wrote and thanked me for the time this morning, and elaborated on a question he'd raised. What follows is his e-mail and my response:

Thanks, Dave – both for speaking to and with my students, and also for this additional response to me question. Behind my question was a question about "divine nature theory" that's been in the back of my mind for some time. This isn't an original question: others have asked it, and probably someone has answered it, but I haven't come across that answer yet, nor have I thought one up on my own. If you have a few minutes, I'd like to run it by you. I think you probably have an answer.

We reject classical DCT because, among other reasons, it's arbitrary. From that point of view atheistic Platonism seems preferable. But such Platonism also seems a bit arbitrary: why are the extant moral truths the moral truths that exist? Why these moral truths rather than some others? Even if they're labelled "necessary moral truths" – why is it that they are necessary? What "made" them so? (That seems like a problematic question, but at the same time it seems to point toward something that needs to be addressed.)

A similar question can be asked of theistic Platonism, though. If God's character or God's thoughts or something like that is determinative of morality, we can still ask "why does God have the character that he has, or why does he think the thoughts that he does?" If the answer is that he has the character that he has because it's the most perfect character possible, and thus God, being perfectly perfect, must have it, then it seems like we're positing timeless moral truths that determine (rather than being determined by) God – we're back to the Platonic horn of the Euthyphro Dilemma, aren't we? But how else can we account for God's character being perfect without ending up in a sort of Occamist DCT?

Any thoughts?

Thanks,

Mike, this is about as big a question as they come! Ultimately it seems to me we're dealing with things that are very difficult for us to understand, very much at the limits of our understanding if not beyond—why is God the way he is, thinks the thoughts he thinks, etc.? That's huge.

I can't do it justice, but one thing that perhaps can at least help a little is that I endorse building our ethical theory bottom up. So we start with what's transparently good, morally speaking—predicated on the assumption that we're at least right, in broad outline, about such things. Then we begin to ask questions like what is the ultimate account of such moral facts and phenomena? To me nothing finally does justice except either Platonism or theism. Platonic truths would be free-floating and sort of brute facts. At least an appeal to God provides the sort of personalist account that seems to do justice to the personalist nature of morality. When it comes to the necessary truths of value, those seem best regarded to me as finding their locus in God's nature. Now, epistemically we go bottom up--we start with a rough-and-ready nonnegotiable set of value assumptions, but if we finally infer that they have God for their metaphysical foundation, we can affirm the metaphysics top down. As I see it, the necessary truths are aspects of God's unchanging and perfect character. Here's where Anselmianism helps—God possesses all the great-making properties. What accounts for their necessity, on such a view, except that they are a function of God (perhaps his noetic activity or something—those are deep waters) in this and all possible worlds, thus true in all possible worlds, i.e., necessarily true. They depend on God in some essential sense for their modal status, and perhaps ultimately for their truth value, since the propositions in questions wouldn't so much as exist at all without being thoughts in God's mind.

Anyway, this is one way of putting it—the theistic activist route. WLC instead rejects abstract objects altogether and simply speaks of God AS the ultimate good. I'm inclined to think of God as the ultimate good, too, though I'm less committed to eschewing abstract truths—but since I think they are thoughts in God's mind, the sort of theistic Platonism to which I'm drawn doesn't threaten God's sole aseity. Even though the necessary truths depend on God, on one of the other view, God doesn't control these truths—if he did, that would result in universal possibilism—the sort of intractable caprice associated with radical voluntarism. No, I think there really are necessary truths, but they have as their best explanation God himself, thus making them essentially dependent on him, even if God himself can't change them—for that would be tantamount to God's denial of himself, something he can't do, owing to his perfection, impeccability, and the like. All of this is to affirm a divine nature theory of the good, which still leaves some of your questions rather under-addressed, admittedly. Getting to the bottom of what you're raising here is a protracted work in progress! I'm not sure eternity itself will enable us to finish that task. □

Regarding moral duties, I gravitate toward divine command theory, predicated on God's essential goodness and indeed on an "is-of-identity" conflation of God and the ultimate transcendent good (despite "their" conceptual distinctions). This nicely avoids the concerns of radical voluntarism. I'm no Ockhamist, though I do affirm DCT appropriately qualified—as do Hare, Adams, and Evans. Here there is some variability with respect to at least some of God's commands, at least on my view, since I endorse what Evans calls the "discretionary hypothesis." God could have commanded us to tithe, say, 15 percent instead of 10—or God could issue a command to you, given your haecceity and vocation, that he doesn't give to me. That's my view anyway, which shows, if true, that some divine commands could be contingent without introducing intractable arbitrariness concerns.

Again, though, there remain unanswered questions. But this is my first go at it. Philosophy, as you know, goes quite slowly. Your questions are scary big; I want to approach them with caution and deliberately incremental steps.

Thanks again for the time today!

Blessings, friend, Dave

Tuesday, April 26, 2021: Today I have been trying to get caught up in my grading for my philosophy online course. Currently it's a little after 1 in the afternoon and MB and I are at a coffee house in Richmond. Grading these unrelenting discussion boards is veritably oppressive. Really just no fun at all, and honestly it seems like a huge waste of my time. So often I feel like I have ever so much more to offer than I'm able to give. MB and Phil had a long conversation about aspects of the apol dep't. I'm glad she's going to at the helm; I trust her to effect some needed changes to the program to help better to tap into the strengths of the faculty available.

Jan wrote some encouraging words to me and MB as she's wont to do:

Thank you, Dave and Marybeth! It's so exciting.... I'm still walking on air, but as I share the Center on a personal level with good folks in the area, the circle of people praying for the work and our team is growing. That feels very strong.

I wish I could talk to you in person on these subjects, but for today, I hope you both feel virtual hugs. I just read Marybeth's Liberty article, and first of all, can we all pause and appreciate her use of the phrase "clutching their pearls"?! Perfect, absolutely perfect □ With seriousness, though, it strikes me that this is a time of transformation for you both and for your work. I know that you know this and walk with eyes on the cross, but I am praying for peace and sustainment as God shapes the Center to His will, under your earthly leadership. It's always painful, I think, to lose a founding member of a team, no matter what their role or the circumstances. I am sorry that TJ has stepped away for now, and I hope that order is established in his household in accordance with God's will. I hope that your household continues to brim over with joy at these transformations, even when they are stressful - God is making it happen! The Center is growing, launching, morphing.... it's shimmering. That's a VERY cool thing to be around, and it's through God's energy pulsed into your labor, that it comes to life at HBU. So. Cool. But yes, lots of hugs during the process, especially on rough days, and prayers every day.

Yes, Sir, you've got it, I'll keep marching, then! I'm outlining blogs now, but it occurs to me that for the next two weeks I had better prioritize finishing out these classes and thesis because a) I've got to actually get this MAA degree to move on to the DMin and be of optimal use to the Center, and b) it's probably in poor form to turn in work for a project headed by one of the Dr.'s Baggett, when you owe work to the other Dr. Baggett ☺ What I'm doing now is taking that paragraph that you originally highlighted from one of my emails and breaking it down into a series of conversations; initial research is highlighting that the area of moral injury is a bit lacking in the "definitions" sense, so there's more than I knew to unpack there... the super exciting part is that I think by establishing definitions and then working from them, the Center is optimally poised to lead exploration of moral injury. So. Cool!

I will talk your ear off, with delight, about absolutely anything related to military experience, the chaplaincy, ethical training, etc., please just say when and how! I have the biggest grin to see this chunk of life become useful. I marvel at His plans.

I hope you both are enjoying a wonderful day!

With gratitude and more hugs,
Jan

Wednesday, April 28, 2021: Got up early to finish reading Hare's chapter for the zoom discussion at 9. Remarkable how well read he is; what an inspiration. It's approaching 7 and I'm about half through the chapter, so hopefully I can make it through.

Still reeling from TJ no longer being part of the ministry. Trying to find my equilibrium again.

Got an encouraging note from a Duke grad today, Matthew Hartman, with an interest in moral apologetics—he wrote his Master's thesis on DCT—and another e-mail from a student who had attended the LU class the other day. He asked a question:

> Dear Dr. Baggett,
>
> I am one of the students at Liberty University that you spoke to on Monday about Moral Apologetics in Dr. Jones class. I had a question after class that I hope you don't mind addressing. I really appreciate your work on the Moral Argument and I was pleasured to be able to have class with you. My question is,
>
> What underlying principle determines which moral principles should be accepted by the "gods"? Every religion is different and wouldn't one have to assume that all religions share a moral common ground? It seems to me that one has to first specify their metaphysics (perhaps even their epistemology) before arguing from morality.
>
> Thank you for taking the time out of your day to read this email. God bless!
>
> In Christ,
> Matthew Camacho

My reply:

> Hi Matthew,
>
> Thanks for the note.
>
> This sounds like a question of first principles. Here I tend think morality has a sort of primacy. A German philosopher named Hermann Lotze affirmed a principle that our metaphysics is rooted in morality. This is rather different from what often gets affirmed today—start with metaphysics and epistemology, and then fit everything else in and around those disciplines. Lotze thought it okay to start with morality, sensing that it is somehow fundamental. I'm inclined to agree. Following Mark Linville, I call this "Lotze's Dictum." I see something like such a principle at the heart of the moral apologetics enterprise.
>
> Then, following Robert Adams, I tend to think, based on basic credulity principles and such, that we are entitled to think that our moral convictions of the deepest ingression can be taken as generally reliable. Without some such assumption, there's not much hope of constructing anything like a moral argument. But again, if morality is considered for principled reasons a real indicator of reality, and evidentially significant in enabling us to figure out

aspects of the world, these starting points seem eminently reasonable to me. If someone demurs, they're perfectly entitled to, of course, but I don't find there to be compelling reasons for me to overly concerned with their skepticism on the matter. I simply don't think I'm surer of just about anything than I am that, say, torturing kids for fun is wrong. So to me this can function axiomatically. I don't have apodictic certainty, but such an aim is unrealistically high. As I said in class, putting it this way makes it seem like affirming moral objectivism is nothing more than an intuitive matter, but I think there's a lot more to it than that. That's more appearance than reality. But for a starting point, it's not bad.

Up until now religion and God haven't played any part in the conversation, you will note. We're just talking about a basic axiomatic moral principle or two. Once one becomes convinced of something like moral realism, the question then becomes, what worldview best accounts for the existence of objective moral facts (again, if such there be)? Now, there are two matters here: the *modality* of these truths, and the *content* of these truths. Some might simply wish to run a moral argument based on moral realism--the modality of these truths--their necessary truth or existence, for example. Others might wish to delve into the content.

As for me, I stay away from the content except a few general claims. I like the example of torturing kids for fun. It's not particularly controversial. It's something I suspect most every religion would agree on. And most every atheist. It's a likely contender for a synthetic necessary moral truth if there is one, something we're more sure of than most anything that could challenge it, perhaps even something that's properly basic (though it needn't be for the moral argument to get off the ground). In other words, its epistemic credentials are pretty impeccable, as far as I'm concerned.

At this point if one insists we must first lay out the metaphysics of such a truth before arguing from morality, I think I'd say I don't think so. The self-evidence of the proposition in question makes it such that it's more likely to be argued from than to. The moral argument is an effort to get at the metaphysics behind such a moral truth. Getting to the metaphysics is what the moral argument tries to do. If something like an Anselmian God provides the best explanation of such a moral truth, then I consider myself altogether justified and warranted to infer, at least tentatively, to God as the likely true explanation, which is to say, the metaphysical foundation, the ontological grounding, of such a truth.

Part of what's going on here, I think, is this: our epistemic faculties are such that we can hold our belief about child torture for fun with a high degree of assurance. This is good, since it's basically a premise in the moral argument, and the premises of an argument, if the argument is a good one, need to be strong. If you're convinced of the truth of realism, with at least this minimal content held in common across a broad array of worldviews and religious persuasions, the rest of the work the argument needs to do falls on how well theism generally (or perhaps Christianity particularly) provides the most robust explanation on offer.

When it comes to basic moral principles, I say I lean toward focusing on noncontroversial content (the vexed questions can be taken up later; this is a matter of ethical foundations)—but it's true that I also extend my four-fold approach to include matters of performance, knowledge, and rationality. But I at least start with minimal content and matters of metaphysics and epistemology—but with a high view of what morality has to say to us and a basic confidence in pre-theoretical moral convictions of a certain stripe. It has always seemed to me that we can know with great confidence the nonnegotiable truth of at least certain basic ethical principles, which is why I'm convinced they're as good a place as any to start doing natural theology. I figure if I'm wrong, well, I'm wrong, but it's where I feel good throwing my lot. People should not be sawn in two; dignity should be upheld; etc. (I'm not saying the rest of the moral argument is this obvious, but the starting point, at least, seems to be.)

This is all too brief, but in a nutshell, it gives you an idea of what I think. I encourage you to keep thinking about this stuff! I appreciate your note very much.

Blessings,
Dave B.

I also wrote an e-mail to the surveyors who have signed up for the May class—about 22 so far:

Hey Auditors/Surveyors,

I'm so happy to hear that you want to sit in on the May course with me and William Lane Craig on the moral argument. As you know, we'll be meeting from May 17th through May 28th, Monday through Friday, from 3 to 5:30 each afternoon, Central time. Originally it was going to be from 3-5 pm, but we decided to add on the extra half hour each day, likely for additional opportunities for questions and discussion.

Dr. Craig chose two books, each based on a debate that he had on the topic—one with Wielenberg and one with Kurtz. I chose two books as well—my wife's and my *Morals of the Story* and Steve Evans' *God and Moral Obligations*. I'll attach a copy of the revised syllabus so you can see the sorts of assignments that folks signed up for the class for credit will be doing.

The first week Dr. Craig will teach, and owing to covid he decided to do so via zoom, though I'll be there in person. The second week I'll then teach. I don't know exactly what he'll be covering that first week, though I suspect the two books he assigned would give you a fairly clear idea. Craig will introduce you, I'm sure, both to deductive and abductive variants of the moral argument.

The second week, when I teach, I'll cover a defense of moral realism (including a critique of meta-ethical theories like error theory, expressivism, and constructivism), a defense of and case for theistic ethics, and a critique of various secular ethical theories, both naturalistic and Platonic. There may be some occasion as well for a few quick critiques of non-Christian religious ethical theories and a bit of extension of the moral argument beyond theism to Christianity in particular.

We'll spend time on each of the four aspects of the moral argument I tend to focus on, based by turns on moral facts and phenomena (rights, duties, intrinsic human value, essential human equality, etc.); moral knowledge (including the so-called "debunking objections" to moral knowledge and the resources of theism to answer such objections); performative matters (including our deep existential moral needs for forgiveness, transformation, and ultimately perfection in the beatific state); and moral rationality (broaching issues like Reid's "coincidence thesis," Kant's recognition of our being both noumenal and phenomenal creatures that renders the juxtaposition of happiness and holiness our highest good, and Sidgwick's dualism of practical reason). I also have a penchant for singing the praises of an abductivist approach to these matters.

I think the two weeks will be well spent. Don't hesitate to let me know if you have any questions. Looking forward to getting to know each one of you better, either in person or online.

Blessings,

Dave B.

Thursday, April 29, 2021: I heard back from Heather and she sent me the Lewis book electronically. I wrote Cheryl Job at LU to inquire about re-acquiring rights to it, and she's going to check into it. Jonathan and I decided to offer a contract to Keith Loftin for his book on the humanities and education. And MB decided this morning to use our upcoming book on apologetics and popular culture in the writing class she's overhauling. Good stuff! I had a weird dream last night, but perhaps a useful one in making sense of some of the challenges I've had adjusting to HBU. I shared it in an e-mail to TJ in the hopes that it might enable us to discuss a bit more what's been bothering him. Here is what I wrote him after he told me I could send it along:

Thanks, man!

So, though you weren't in dream last night, it pertains to matters that are relevant to the move to HBU, and I thought could help inform the context of our recent discussions a bit. That said, though, I'm fully aware that this may be significant, and maybe not. Just open to the possibility.

In the dream I was in the SOD at Liberty and assigned a task by the leadership. It wasn't an academic exercise, but a manual task. The whole environment was dark and gloomy, if not sinister, truth be told. It was as if a dark, foreboding cloud hung over the place. The task assigned me was to clean something like a dark ink stain that was on the floor down at the end of a hallway. But it seemed the more I worked the worse it got. Either it kept growing or I'd realize that whatever little I had accomplished, in the context of the whole, was to little avail, and when I backed away from it and looked, it was as if nothing had been done at all. It was a frustrating job and one I was failing at spectacularly.

Worse still, the administration was peeved at me for failing to fix the problem, which seemed only to be spreading—this taint, this stain, it was intractable. And I was being held responsible by the leaders of the SOD for the problem—for not fixing it. Their attitude toward me was acerbic, and as the dream wore on— which I remember far more vividly than most—their attitudes toward me became more and more negative. So much so that the proverbial writing was on the wall that they were going to find a reason to get rid of me. I was not long for LU, it became increasingly clear.

The darkness and oppression felt throughout the dream were palpable. It was as if the growing floor stain almost represented it. But it felt futile to fix it. It was inevitable, I felt, that I was to move on. The administrators, especially Troy Temple, Gabe Etzel, and John Cartwright, were pulling out all the stops to undermine my tenure there, including launching a number of accusations against me. The experience, even in the dream, felt deeply traumatic. I remember having a conversation with Ed Hindson, who wasn't responsible for the nastiness, telling him that my departure was imminent. He seemed to try to help, but to no effect.

At some point I had left and was now at HBU. I don't remember as much about that part of the dream, and it was winding to a close. I do remember driving with Bruce Gordon and someone else in Houston looking for a Chinese restaurant. ☺ But there was one telling feature connected with the earlier stuff. The sinister and dark and oppressive stuff from earlier was still present, but what dawned on me was that it was not a function of HBU so much as a vestige of the earlier time at Liberty. It was as if what occurred to me was the danger of my interpreting things at HBU through the negative lens of Liberty, especially owing to how deeply traumatic was the tragically dysfunctional set of challenges at Liberty.

Well, that was mainly it. Maybe it means nothing. But I know that sometimes dreams in the Bible are significant, and in light of how vivid this one was, how

201

much I remembered afterwards, and especially viscerally dark and oppressive the chapter at Liberty was, I wanted to share it with you.

Love ya, Dave

At any rate, TJ hasn't responded. I think he's still processing stuff. MB and I are now, this early afternoon, at the Blockhouse, a small new coffee house in Richmond we're trying out. I have meant to get around to something for a while now, so now may be a good time. I wanted to type in a few notes from my conversation with Billy some days back.

Billy emphasized that the nature of the jobs of the military guys he teaches requires a lot of moral resiliency, including processing a lot of moral guilt. He trains his guys to realize that if they don't deal with these issues well, a number of problems can emerge later on, after years of compartmentalization. He emphasized that chaplains need much more training than they usually have. Much of this comes from a more recent initiative in the military to train their soldiers in thinking through issues of ethics. How prisoners get treated, how to think about the enemy, and the like raises issues of character and of worldview. Chaplains need training to prepare the soldiers better to think through their ethical battle space—their moral/ethical frameworks.

In his own teaching, Billy puts a lot of focus on the role of worldview in how we think about ethical questions. He's convinced that something much in the neighborhood of moral apologetics is prevalent in SOCOM. Much talk about morality and where it comes from, which leads to lots of good conversations. Spirituality and worldview are often the starting point of the conversation. Such issues are unavoidable if the soldiers are going to be holistically able to live their lives and do their duties well. In the process of recent changes, the role of chaplains is changing. They are taking on a bigger role in educating soldiers on these matters of spirituality, worldview, and ethics. An example is the issue of identity—is our essential identity something like having been made in God's image? Or something else? Divergent worldviews can imply very different things about an issue like human identity and value, and the wrong worldviews can generate quite a bit of cognitive dissonance.

Billy is planning to send me some power points on some presentations he gives on such matters. The presentations help soldiers think about identity, human value, moral dilemmas, purpose, and moral reasoning/thinking. Although he can't exactly preach, he can broach important matters and get the soldiers thinking more deeply and critically.

We're going to talk more about the possibility of something like the moral apol Certificate qualifying to train chaplains, and I encouraged him to write for MoralApologetics.com. He also encouraged me to make my students more aware of the possibility of finding a mission field in the military. He as well pointed me in the direction of the work of Bruce Ashford out of Cambridge, who writes a lot about just war and has a website called BruceAshford.net, I believe.

Friday, April 30, 2021: Spent the morning going through the revised version of Pruitt's first chapter in his dissertation. It's coming along. He still needs to trim some parts, but it's getting there. Step by step. Then worked on grading; nearly caught up in my online grading. In the evening we went to a School of Christian Thought function, which wasn't bad at all. In the morning I wrote this e-mail to the Moral Apologetics team:

Good morning, all! I woke up this morning with it on my mind to introduce everyone to everyone on the growing Moral Apologetics team. TJ has stepped down, having so much on his plate. Do pray for his wife; they're going to see a specialist today as they try to get to the bottom of what's been ailing her. Although TJ's departure makes me sad, I am tremendously excited about some new additions and what the future holds for the ministry and the team.

So starting with Associate Editors at MoralApologetics.com, we have Marybeth Baggett (aka "the Baggett lady") and Jan Shultis. Jan is new, and we are very excited to welcome her onboard. Here is her bio:

Jan Shultis is a Naval Academy graduate, author of two books, and plans to pursue her DMin at Houston Baptist University. After 14 years in uniform serving around the U.S. and in Afghanistan, she founded a faith-based non-profit focused on veterans, law enforcement, first responders, and families that supports warriors in need throughout Texas, with a special focus on ministry in local courts and jails. Jan brings to the Moral Apologetics team additional professional experience in biotechnology, public relations, and ethics curriculum development. Jan shares that she is extremely excited to spearhead the Center's innovative exploration of the organic connections between moral apologetics and moral injury, including but not limited to military veterans. She is local to Houston and looks forward to contributing to the Center's robust on-campus presence at HBU.

So welcome to Jan! Your irrepressible enthusiasm and excitement is veritably contagious! We are wholly confident that, in his providence, God orchestrated the intersection of our paths.

The Managing Editor at MoralApologetics.com continues to be my right-hand man, Jonathan Pruitt, who is finishing his dissertation on extending the moral argument to Christianity. Jonathan is also spearheading the publishing arm of the ministry. Moral Apologetics Press has done three books so far—Elton Higgs' *Ichabod Letters*, Brian Melton's *Knockturn Method*, and my first-year journal starting the Center at HBU called *Humble Beginnings in a Whirlwind*. (I have kept a journal every day since a week before my contract kicked in here at HBU on August 1 last summer, and intend to keep doing so until either I retire or shuffle my mortal coil. Perhaps after they plant me with the spring crops someone might wish to look at the whole history of the Center and the journals will help—they pretty much chronicle every fresh daily development with the

Center.) We have signed contracts to produce three more books, and may on the cusp to offer two more. Jonathan's doing a bang-up job on all of this, and we are very excited about this dimension of the outreach.

Brian Chilton just agreed to accept our offer for him to become a Senior Contributor to MoralApologetics.com. He has been a regular contributor for a while, and we figured it was high time to make it official. Brian has pastored and worked as a hospice chaplain, has written one book and is working on another, is wrapping up his PhD in theology and apologetics at Liberty, and runs his *Bellator Christi* outreach. We are so glad and privileged he is now part of the team.

Stephen Jordan continues to be in charge of generating curriculum using the resources of moral apologetics, and he is also one of the Senior Research Scholars at the Center. He just finished up his substantive dissertation on the personalist aspects of moral apologetics, and is a Bible high school teacher in Virginia. Such a kindred spirit, he has been an important team member for several years now.

Besides Stephen, other senior research scholars at the Center are Jan, Jonathan, Marybeth, Jerry Walls, and David Ochabski. David, as most if not all of you know, is wrapping up his doctoral work at Liberty, works as a regional director for *Ratio Christi*, and has strong interests in epistemology and social science. We were delighted to welcome him aboard the team just recently as well, after several telling indicators it was time to do so.

Of course Jerry Walls needs no introduction. He is my long-time friend and dear colleague here at HBU, the author or editor of no less than what will soon be eight books with Oxford University Press, likely the world's greatest expert on matters of eschatology, and my co-author on the tetralogy we are finishing up on the moral argument.

So, welcome, welcome, welcome to you all! So glad you are part of this exciting movement. Please remember to be in prayer for the ministry and for one another as we move forward, and know we are here to help encourage and support you in any way we can. Marybeth and I so appreciate each and every one of you!

Blessings, Dave

I also sent along to JP to put up this Editor's Suggestion at the site for Zach's book *Slipping through the Cracks*:

Over the course of my long friendship with Zach Breitenbach, he has consistently shown a remarkable willingness to keep struggling with an issue until clarity comes. I recall that he used to be a wrestler, and it would appear that he still is! Like many of the luminaries in the history of apologetics, he is willing to sit with an issue, live and wrestle with questions, and give a topic the time and effort required to do it justice.

This delightful book is a product of such laudable patience, tenacity, and labor, and the result does not disappoint. To the contrary, he has done the Christian, philosophical, apologetic, and theological community a wonderful service. Unafraid to tackle prohibitively difficult questions, the prodigiously gifted author has the expansive mind and requisite skill and aptitude to navigate their contours, often with penetrating profundity. He is unrelenting in his search for a theory that is at once both philosophically rigorous and biblically sound.

One of the significant challenges assailing those who believe in a wholly good and loving God is to make sense of the category of the "contingently lost" (i.e., those who are lost but would have been saved in other circumstances that God could have brought about). Indeed, this problem is intractable enough that some insist that no sense can be made of it at all, and that no one is ultimately unredeemed in the actual world if they are redeemed in some other world that is feasible for God to make. This deep existential issue of whether some people "slip through the cracks," as it were, can hardly be overstated, shedding light by turns on the human condition and questions of ultimate meaning and significance, the nature of reality and the very character of God.

Breitenbach's original theodicy offered here is both extremely thoughtful and eminently worthy of careful consideration. Canvassing and digesting, integrating and synthesizing an array of disparate discussions—from Reformed epistemology to Molinism, from exclusivism to theodicy—he makes accessible and brings to life wide, important, and difficult literatures, deftly navigating their nuances and generating real clarity in the process.

With lucid prose and crystal clear explanations, he has written a wonderful book that is both philosophically astute and historically informed, and both theologically sophisticated and biblically faithful. He does not make the job he carves out for himself an easy one. He aims to effect a rapprochement of nothing less than the conjunction of exclusivism and the possibility of some people being contingently lost, a God of perfect love (for all) and substantive doctrines of sovereignty—albeit decidedly non-Calvinist variants of election and predestination. His interlocutors may agree or disagree with his analysis, but they will be unable responsibly to ignore it.

Saturday, May 1, 2021: My dad would have turned 94 today. Haven't seen him now in 28 years. Hard to believe. Miss him.

TJ wrote to say Amy is struggling with a lot of pain. At yesterday's doctor appointment they took a lot of blood from her to get to the bottom of what's going on. MB and I will pray for her and them today in earnest.

Have a talk with Elton scheduled for this morning, and time with Jerry and Rob this evening—rescheduled because of yesterday's events. In between I want to finish my grading for the online course and write up a response to the reader reports so I can get back to OUP on the proposal with Hare.

Just got off the phone with Elton. He shared what had happened with his heart attack. He's doing well. He had received treatment quickly and the doctors are hopeful that what damage was done to the heart will repair itself. It was good to talk to him again. He told me of a Wall Street Journal article adapted from a book called *Reopening Muslim Minds*, by a fellow named Akyol, which bears on, among other things, the Euthyphro questions.

Sunday, May 2, 2021: I was finally able to draft a response back to Cynthia Read at OUP, after Hare approved it. Just sent this back to Cynthia.

> Hi Cynthia. Thanks again for sending along the reader reports for the Collection on the Moral Argument that John Hare and I submitted. We have read the reports and reflected on them, finding them eminently helpful as we tighten and augment the proposal a bit. I will quickly review how we have done so. A few changes remain tentative, and somewhat contingent on how many chapters OUP will allow. We are trying to remain within the original envisioned set of chapters as best we can, but think the addition of at least two or three chapters would be best.
>
> In terms of the problem of evil, which both readers mentioned, the first reader suggested we might expand it, or at least have Paul Copan address both of these questions: (1) the one under chapter 9's explanation—the zero-sum game problem, and (2) the 1989 *Nous* article by Draper, where the Hypothesis of Indifference, not moral theism, is the best explanation for moral phenomena. If we opt for a second chapter instead of the expanded chapter by Copan, the suggestion was for Dan Howard-Snyder to write it. We intend to speak with Copan on this matter and, depending on what he says, follow one of these two suggestions. Great idea.
>
> This reader also expressed the desire to see an answer to Sinnott-Armstrong's argument that rape is wrong because it harms the other person—without any reference to God needed. We will honor this desire and make sure that it is covered in one of the chapters already assigned discussing the relative merits of nontheistic ethical foundations.
>
> We are in the process of deciding on this reviewer's suggestion for a chapter devoted to how Rawls must import a tacit theistic assumption. We suspect it can be adequately addressed in an already existing chapter, perhaps the one on constructivism.

The point about realism without God is likely best covered when Platonist approaches are discussed; we will make sure that Moore's salient construal of such a variant of realism is sufficiently addressed in that chapter (ch. 20 in the original). (Perhaps it will also be covered when Platonism is not so much rejected as integrated within a theistic perspective. Both approaches remain live options for the theistic ethicist.)

Both reviewers noted that we mentioned Buddhism and Judaism in the Comparative Religion section without devoting chapters to them. This was because we had thought we might not be allotted enough chapters to do it, as we had originally planned. However, if we can add those two chapters, we would be very happy to. We appreciate the reviewers suggesting that we do, and even some specifics as to how, which we intend to heed, with permission from OUP.

On the issue of the "God concept," the operative conception of God the moral argument(s) introduce, we are in the process of deciding whether this will be handled within one of the current chapters or if it will call for a new chapter. Once we contact prospective contributors and discuss various chapters, we plan to make that final determination. We definitely appreciate the strong encouragement to take up this issue explicitly, and will do so for sure. The reader was quite right to point out its importance.

On how the moral argument might work in tandem with other arguments from natural theology and evidential apologetics, we think this matter will best be taken up at a few junctures within existing chapters. As we edit we will ensure this takes place.

The second reviewer's comments were wonderfully encouraging and appreciated. Several points have been mentioned already, but one last one remains. The reviewer thought that Wielenberg should be offered to write a chapter defending moral realism from an atheistic framework. This is a bit tricky.

On the one hand, Wielenberg's affirmation of realism makes him an ally of the moral argument, since it tends to be predicated on moral realism. Then again, Wielenberg's variant of Platonism offers an alternative to theistic ethics and thus counts against the moral argument.

Although we see value in such a contribution, we are not convinced allocating a chapter to Wielenberg would really help advance the aim of this book to showcase the resources available to the moral apologist to make the moral argument(s). Giving a chapter to, say, a Muslim thinker to spell out his or her theistic ethic makes sense in such a book, but not so much an atheist arguing, ultimately, that the moral argument simply fails.

Wielenberg has laid out his views in several books, and his views (and various criticisms of the moral argument) will be discussed and subjected to scrutiny, but in light of the limited number of chapters that we can commission, we are unconvinced that assigning one to him would be the best choice. This is not for lack of appreciation of what he has to offer, but owing to the specific goals of this Collection. So at this point, although we appreciate the suggestion, we are inclined to demur.

Again, we are strongly thankful for all of the encouraging and helpful insights and suggestions on offer from these terrific readers. We relish the prospect of moving forward with this project, the stronger for them.

Best,

Dave & John

In the evening Marybeth and I attended a Ratio Christi get-together at Lou Markos's house. We sat with Nancy Pearcey and, for a while, Lou. Eric Scott from RC also showed up for a while. Good conversation about a lot of things, including some talk about Calvinism. I shared my reservations about it and I had the sense that Nancy and Lou concurred, perhaps Eric not so much. But just guessing. I really like Eric, though, and we hit it off when talking about a lot of other topics. We all also discussed the erosion of moral foundations and the reigning commitment nowadays to be a change agent when it comes to morality rather than getting at the truth. Nancy quoted Marx along the lines of it's not about understanding but reform. I wish I could remember the exact words. It was insightful. I also mentioned to Lou the possibility of his adding a new chapter to the Lewis as Philosopher book. Nancy also talked about her time(s) at L'Abri, and the way so much of what appealed to her was Christianity as an all-encompassing perspective, including the arts—apologetics in the true cultural sense, much broader than the narrow and discursive. Seems to me that moral apologetics would be good if it could tap into this dimension.

Monday, May 3, 2021: Did my weekly announcements for my online phil course; penultimate week on that. Had hoped maybe to work on my upcoming apologetics conference paper and church apol presentation, but didn't get to them. I did, though, invite Michael Ward to write a chapter for the third edition of *Lewis as Philosopher*, and Lou got back to me excited at the prospect of contributing. Cynthia replied to my e-mail happy with what John and I had sent her. I also spent time zooming with Jonathan to nail down a few last things on how to do a podcast, so that's just about in place. So gradually lot of pieces are coming together.

I reiterated our interest to Keith Loftin in publishing his book on education with MAP. Apparently I used his old e-mail, so he wrote right back and acknowledged the note that I'd sent him through FB and gave me his new e-mail address. He's just accepted a new job as headmaster in Lubbock, and we were glad to hear that. Hopefully this book contract will be a blessing to him, us, and eventually to many more. Relatedly, I also wrote TJ and asked for clarification on whether he still plans for MAP to publish his two books.

Liberty informed us that they don't want MB on Jonathan's committee—she apparently has gotten under the skin of some of the admin there, which is more than a little humorous. The voice of the prophetess is silenced by those who propped up and did the bidding of the corrupt leader for over a decade. My goodness. Likely means they won't let me direct TJ's dissertation. Speaking of MB, she's leaning toward *Telling Tales: Intimations of the Sacred in Popular Culture* for our collection on apol and pop culture she's editing, which will introduce our series in that area. MB is also working on the new Moral Apologetics Newsletter.

The Lanier library got back to me with this nice note:

Hi, David!
I'm afraid your message below was lost in an email nightmare or storm in recent weeks. We're not sure what to call it, but we're digging out of it and it may take a while. Sorry for the delayed reply, but I am copying two other Davids whom you should meet. David Capes is our Senior Research Fellow, former professor at HBU, and David Fleming is our Director of the Lanier Foundation. Both will want to read your message below and know about your role at HBU, along with your wife's.

I'm anxious to get you to LTL so you can see the beauty and, more importantly, use the incredible resources we've gathered over the last 11 years. Just let me know when you might like to come and I will give you a brief tour. If the other Davids are available, I will gladly introduce you to them. Just let me know in advance so I can plan around your arrival.

You will want to know that registration will open soon for our N. T. Wright lecture on June 19. We also have a lecture scheduled for Oct. 16 by John Warwick Montgomery which I think may be especially interesting to you. I will add your email address to our list of those who receive our newsletter about such events here at LTL.
Grace and peace,
Charles

Charles G. Mickey
Director, Lanier Theological Library

Tuesday, May 4, 2021: Today has been a good day so far. I got both Michael Ward and Andrew Lazo onboard to write a chapter in the third edition of Lewis as Philosopher (Markos already agreed). Third edition is going to be epic. The third Newsletter ("On the Move") for the Center went out today; here it is:

It's hard to believe that the Center for Moral Apologetics is closing out its first academic year here at Houston Baptist University. And what a year it has been! Zechariah cautions against despising humble beginnings, and as I look back on this year, that admonition makes a lot of sense. When God places a burden the size of a Center on your heart, it can be hard to square small necessary steps with the bigness of the vision. And yet, those daily tasks add up to something substantial over time. We are seeing this come to fruition, especially as we look forward to next year. David has chronicled these activities (collected in this volume for last year) and will continue to do so going forward. This record promises to be a testimony to God's faithfulness and his ability to use human vessels despite our limitations.

A few of the initiatives underway include adding a slate of Senior Research Fellows who are engaged in projects centered on Moral Apologetics. The link above provides bios and descriptions of those projects. Additionally, we will be appointing Student Fellows, HBU students (both undergraduate and graduate) who will explore the moral argument(s) alongside the Senior Research Fellows and serve the Center in a variety of capacities. Also, we have brought Brian Chilton on board as a Senior Contributor to MoralApologetics.com. Brian has been a regular contributor for a while and has pastored and worked as a hospice chaplain. He has written a book on apologetics and is working on another. He is wrapping up his PhD in theology and apologetics at Liberty University, and runs an outreach called *Bellator Christi*. We are so glad and privileged to have him join our team.

Jonathan Pruitt will share news on the publication front below, but one other book in the works is a collection by me and David, of short pieces we have written using pop cultural artifacts for apologetic purposes. The collection will be entitled *Telling Tales: Intimations of the Sacred in Popular Culture*, and it should be available later this summer. All proceeds will go to the Center for Moral Apologetics. Even more exciting is that this volume will serve to kick off a series of edited collection devoted to Pop Culture and Apologetics. Once the series is in place, we will be accepting proposals for future volumes; be on the lookout for more details on this or reach out to me, as I will be the series editor (mbaggett@hbu.edu).

Additionally, we have some news regarding the HBU Apologetics department. As of June 1, I'll be stepping into the department chair position vacated by Dr. Phil Tallon who has taken on the role of the Dean of the School of Christian Thought. This move will allow me to work more closely with David in speaking to churches, planning events or other projects, and supporting the work of the department and the Center. Regarding the talks for churches: David and I are actively seeking such opportunities. Check out the video below for more info, and please reach out if you have interest in hosting us (mbaggett@hbu.edu or dbaggett@hbu.edu). We are available by Zoom anywhere or in person for churches in the Houston area.

Finally, David will be co-teaching a course at Houston Baptist University with Dr. William Lane Craig on the Moral Argument. The course runs from May 17 through May 28 (3:00 to 5:30 Central Time), and will meet either in person or by Zoom for those unable to attend live. The sessions will be recorded for those unavailable during those hours. It can be taken either for credit or as an auditor. Check out the video below to get a sense of what to expect in the course. You can find more information at this site, which also provides registration details.

We are honored and humbled that you have come alongside us to support in whatever way you are able and feel led. Of course we need much prayer, especially for the undertakings noted below. And if you would like to support the work of the Center financially, you may make a tax-deductible gift through the HBU online giving form (select "Additional Giving Opportunities" and designate Center for Moral Apologetics from the pop-up list). You may also mail contributions to the following address (with Center for Moral Apologetics in the memo line): HBU Advancement Lockbox, PO Box 4897, Dept #527, Houston, TX 77210.

- Marybeth Baggett, Associate Editor

Invitation to pastors to share a talk on the Moral Argument by David Baggett

The Moral Argument for God
with Dr. William Lane Craig

Commercial Promotion: Take 1

GO DEEPER with Houston Theological Seminary
hbu.edu/HTSGoDeeper

Promo for HBU class on the Moral Argument with Dr. David Baggett and

Publishing & Communications

At MoralApologetics.com, we are continuing the informative introductory series from R. Scott Smith, "Making Sense of Morality." This series provides concise overviews of key issues in moral apologetics and suggestions for those who would like to go deeper on a given topic. Other highlights include the creative and integrative series from David Baggett on "The Moral Argument and Christian Salvation."

Moral Apologetics Press (MAP) has now released two books: Elton Higgs's humorous and insightful *The Ichabod Letters* and Brian Melton's timely and imaginative *The Wrackturn Method*. The next book will be a theological and philosophical exploration of the thinking of Thomas Aquinas. *A Moral Way* by T. J. Gentry will be available in the first half of 2021. There are plans for a collaboration with The Worldview Bulletin for a third book, yet to be titled, but likely to release in the Fall of 2021. We are also excited to announce a newly contracted book with Daniel McCoy which contrasts Buddhism with Christianity in five crucial areas, namely, their viewpoints on ultimate reality, ultimate attachments, ultimate aversions, ultimate example, and ultimate purpose. Those interested can keep up with the Press at the new web page.

- Jonathan Pruitt, Managing Editor

Curriculum

Regarding curriculum development, work continues on developing content that will eventually be made available to Christian schools. Several introductory lessons on moral apologetics are still in the works. Each of these lessons will include everything that a teacher needs in order to instruct his or her students for an entire class period. The goal is for some of these lessons to become available over the next few months, perhaps even in time for the start of the 2021-2022 academic year.

- <u>Stephen Jordan</u>, Curriculum Coordinator

Director Update

Although T. J. Gentry has stepped down from his leadership roles for now at Moral Apologetics to focus his energies toward some other ministry outreaches—we will miss his passion and will be happy to welcome him back if circumstances change—we have added two dynamic new team members to the Center.

David Ochabski, whose research interests include both social science and epistemology, has come onboard as a Senior Research Fellow of the Center. He is wrapping up his PhD in theology and apologetics and serves as a national training and area ministry director of *Ratio Christi* in the Virginia, Maryland, and Delaware areas.

Jan Shultis, author of two books, a Naval Academy graduate, and seasoned speaker who plans to pursue her DMin at HBU, is joining us as both a Senior Research Fellow and Associate Editor of MoralApologetics.com. With her inimitable enthusiasm, she is spearheading an exciting initiative of the Center that explores the organic connections between moral apologetics and moral injury, including but not limited to military veterans. More broadly, exciting chaplaincy outreaches are in the works.

<u>The Fellows</u> will contribute regularly to MoralApologetics.com and make themselves and their research available to the Center's Student Fellows, an initiative that will begin at HBU this fall. We are thrilled to welcome both David and Jan!

- <u>David Baggett</u>, Executive Editor & Director of the Center for Moral Apologetics, Houston Baptist University

Recent Articles at <u>MoralApologetics.com</u>

"Mailbag: Does Morality Need a Personal Explanation" by David Baggett explores the distinctions between Platonism and theism to determine which provides the better explanation of the source of morality.

"Divining the Absence" by Tom Thomas uses Solomon to reflect on the question of life's meaning and the temptation we sometimes feel toward nihilism. Ultimately, Thomas concludes, only Jesus offers us life.

"How the Resurrection Impacts Theology" by Brian Chilton recalls the life and death of his beloved grandmother, in light of the promises of the Resurrection.

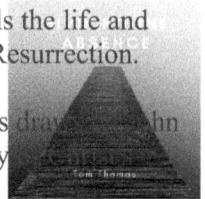

"Lord's Supper Meditation: Children of the Father" by Elton Higgs draws from John 14-17 to remind us that communion is meant to remind us not only of crucifixion but also of our union with God through him.

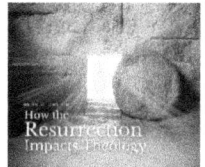

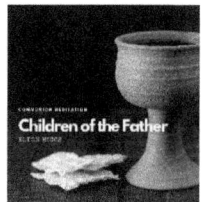

HBQ: HBU Faculty on Apologetics

How can a study of classical mythology conjoin the rational and imaginative arms of the apologetic endeavor?

Many theories exist as to why C. S. Lewis was the greatest apologist of the twentieth century. I think the most compelling of them is that Lewis found a way to hold reason and imagination together in a perfect balance that speaks to the mind as well as the heart.

For example, in *Mere Christianity*, Lewis makes his famous argument that Jesus was either a liar, lunatic, or Lord. Then, in *The Lion, the Witch and the Wardrobe*, he brings this rational, abstract argument to life by having the Professor argue that Lucy's insistence that she has been to Narnia suggests that she is either making it up, has lost her mind, or has actually been to another world. Since her siblings can see that she is not crazy, and since they know her to be a truth teller, they should remain open to the possibility that her story is true. This argument shocks Lucy's elder siblings (and readers of Lewis's fantasy novel) because they have unconsciously bought into a modern, materialist worldview of the nature of reality and so have dismissed Lucy's claims without giving them serious consideration.

Lewis was grounded in both Greco-Roman and Norse mythology and that grounding helped him to develop into an apologist who could draw equally from his logical mind and his imaginative heart. Indeed, the revelation that helped him to move from theism to Christianity was directly related to his love of mythology.

Lewis, guided by *The Golden Bough* of James Frazer and his own modern, materialist worldview, had taken for granted that, because the gospel story sounded so much like the myths of Osiris, Adonis, Mithras, and Balder, Jesus himself must have been little more than a myth. Then his friend J. R. R. Tolkien challenged him to interpret the data in a different way: what if the reason that Jesus sounded like a myth was because he was the myth that became fact?

Lewis's recognition of Jesus as a true myth empowered him to embrace the gospel; we, his apologetical heirs, can (and must) build bridges between Christianity and the secular world by referencing the classical myths that undergird so much of our art, music, and literature. Although young people today tend not to resonate with logical, rational arguments for God, they nevertheless yearn for meaning and purpose in their lives and are hungry to see themselves as part of a greater story.

By demonstrating, through a close reading of their myths, that the pre-Christian pagans of Greece and Rome not only intuited the nature of good and evil, the reality of human sinfulness, and the need for sacrifice to atone for that sinfulness but desired, without fully understanding why, a closer intimacy with the divine, the apologist can invite story-loving millennials to examine their own intuitions and desires. While bearing witness to the great truth that Jesus fulfilled both the Old Testament Law and prophets and the highest yearnings of the pagan peoples, myths speak to that within the human psyche that longs to be a part of what Samwise Gamgee calls "the tales that really mattered."

- Louis Markos, Professor in English and Scholar in Residence at Houston Baptist University

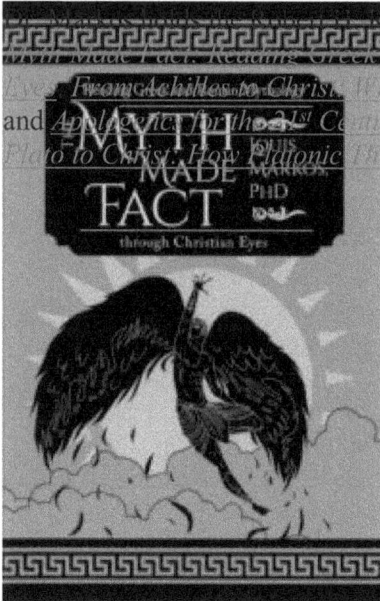

...ay Chair in Humanities; his 21 books include _The Myth Made Fact: Reading Greek and Roman Mythology through Christian Eyes_, _From Achilles to Christ: Why Christians Should Read the Pagan Classics_, and _Apologetics for the 21st Century_. This summer, IVP will publish his _From Plato to Christ: How Platonic Thought Shaped the Christian Faith_.

Wednesday, May 5, 2021: When I lived in Pennsylvania, I dated a gal named Rose Alaimo. Although she would go to vet school, her first love was music. We ended up going our separate ways more than fifteen years ago, but she's always kept a warm place in my heart, and her music is really taking off. She's got her own YouTube channel, and her songs get a lot of rave critical reviews. So happy for her. I was just listening to a bit of her music; it's always lovely to hear.

Finished watching a documentary on Doc Severinsen, the longtime band leader on the *Tonight Show*. Into his nineties, he's still going strong, doing what he loves—music—and always working on making it better. Inspiring.

Got a start on my upcoming apol day presentation on the history of the moral argument. Also reviewed a piece today for *Phil Christi* on divine commands that made much of Wielenberg's claim that DCT suggests that, unless God hasn't issued us a command to do, it would be morally okay to take a nap instead of lifting our finger to avoid a thousand Holocausts. A number of problematic issues. I'll write them up tomorrow and put my comments here.

Truth be told, I have been a bit down for several days. Nothing debilitating, just a low-level chronic state. Although things are marginally better with TJ, we're not talking and praying regularly any more, which makes me sad. I had come to rely on his encouragement and support in the ministry, and without it I have yet to regain my emotional balance.

Thursday, May 6, 2021: I wanted to wake up to some encouragement today, and I did! Jerry Bogacz and his wife want to donate another $500 to the Center! Wow, just blown away.

So here was my response to the *Phil Christi* piece:

I appreciate the chance to review this piece. It's a start to a discussion of these matters, but not much more as it stands. There are simply far too many important questions and potential objections that go unexplored. It seems to have been written hastily, isn't steeped enough in the literature, and at numerous points seems brimming with unearned confidence, if not a thinly veiled sense of

218

impatience at the whole conversation. As such it doesn't merit publication, to my thinking. I will try to identify some of the many ways in which it would need to be bolstered and extended to make anything approaching an original contribution to the literature.

One might begin by distinguishing between a weak and strong version of DCT. A weak version might simply affirm the conditional that: If God commands X, then X is morally obligatory. That version implies no such exclusivity as Wielenberg and this piece are insistently adamant to discuss. The version they are pointing to instead is a strong version, something like God's commands are the *only* thing that can make something obligatory. This deductivist rendering surely was not the main point Craig was trying to emphasize. His point was that a theistic explanation provides a more robust account of moral obligations (and values) than Wielenberg's account does. There is little recognition in either Wielenberg or this piece that Craig's tactic in the debate under discussion was thoroughly abductivist; instead there is an intentional effort to saddle him with the most problematic implications of a strongly deductivist account.

There is also a much larger context to all of this. Craig largely follows Robert Adams in affirming an 'is-of-identity' between God and the good. Although Adams gravitates toward a theistic Platonic account, Craig shies away from Platonism; but either way their DCT is predicated on God as the good. This identity is not designed to go the radically Ockhamistic route, but to show an essential dependence relation of morality on God. DCT for Craig, therefore, is his tentative account of moral obligations, but divine commands don't reside, on his view, at the foundation of all moral realities. For present purposes, the point is that to relegate all of this important background to irrelevance is hardly fair to Craig. DCT is one among other fine-grained theistic ethical accounts. In the context of this debate, Craig tried to fill in some details about how morality essentially depends on God, and he happened to go in the direction of DCT with respect to moral obligations; but in light of his overall ethical theory encompassing matters both axiological and deontic, it seems clear that DCT is just one part of it, and arguably not the most central. Identifying God as the good and locus of objective moral values is likely the more central conviction. I also suspect, again following Adams, that if DCT were shown inadequate he would abandon the theory to the next best one on offer. He just happens to think, for a variety of principled reasons, that DCT is currently the best theistic ethical theory, and best theory overall, on offer among the plethora of options—Platonism, Cornell realism, divine will theory, divine desire theory, divine motivation theory, natural law, etc.

This reminds me of an important point to emphasize at this juncture. The author of this piece helps himself or herself to assuming moral realism as true. Craig would agree, as would Wielenberg, and me too. But there is a large and growing literature on moral scepticism, moral constructivism, error theory, moral anti-realism, expressivism, etc. that should be at least acknowledged. When it's treated as "obvious" that one should prevent the thousand Holocausts by lifting one's finger, perhaps it would be good at least to point out that a great many philosophers would demur. For example, those who don't believe in objective moral obligations in the first place! The author of the piece treats not only moral realism as obvious, but Wielenberg's granular account; this is more dogmatic than principled. A great many naturalists harbor much scepticism about Wielenberg's approach, which seems to many as both metaphysically and epistemically indulgent. Repeated claims that Wielenberg's assertions are obviously true doesn't make them so. What is true is that Wielenberg makes appeal to what most right-thinking persons would affirm, but this arguably has as much to do with the Judeo-Christian context of our culture in which it's been steeped for centuries than anything like an intuition that Wielenberg's alternative account of moral obligations is correct. Supposing it is indeed obviously true that we should prevent the Holocausts when we can do so with minimal effort—which I agree with—simply underdetermines the foundations of moral obligations; and any suggestion to the contrary is tantamount to sleight-of-hand. It seems practically unphilosophical to rest content with what amounts to Wielenberg's *lack* of explanation on this score.

Let me elaborate on that point, because it is easily misunderstood. One way to depict what seems to be Wielenberg's mistake here is to point out what he's suggesting, namely, he is insisting that that which is to be explained is also the explanation. However, what seems obvious is that the explanandum on offer does not, indeed cannot, suffice for the explanans. That one should engage in the basic action of raising one's hand or finger to accomplish the mediated action of preventing a thousand Holocausts is without dispute, as far as I'm concerned—contra the myriad skeptics about objective moral facts. The question next to be pursued, then, is what provides the *best explanation* of this nonnegotiable moral fact—the topic of this debate was couched in IBE. The fact itself is not the explanation, but rather veritably cries out for an explanation. Wielenberg does not provide one, but instead rests content insisting the fact itself is obviously true. It likely is—as a moral realist I would entirely concur we should prevent the Holocausts—and the more obvious it is the more pressing becomes the matter of identifying its ontological foundations, since the more likely it seems able to reveal aspects of ultimate reality. Wielenberg's modus operandi here is reminiscent of Lewis's example of someone, when asked about why something happens in an athletic competition, merely points to one of the rules of the game, when the question instead was instead about why one should play the game at all. The notion that there exist abstract truths like "it's morally obligatory for humans to lift their finger to prevent a thousand Holocausts" is a theory, even it's not much of an explanation and one that seems especially unlikely in light of various debunking objections that theism can solve much more handily than can

Platonism; but Craig would rightly point out that the existence of a personal and loving God who created us in his image and designed us for various purposes and whose nature is perfect provides the arguably better and more robust explanation for why such a truth obtains rather than such impersonal Platonic truths existing in metaphysical limbo and with little authoritative purchase on how we ought to live.

Which reminds me of another recurring problem that's common nowadays. That there would be moral reason to lift one finger and stop the Holocausts is undoubtedly true. Moral reasons can emanate from axiology alone. But moral reasons in and of themselves don't necessarily constitute moral obligations. Wielenberg recognizes this, punting to Parfit's minimalistic requirements for reasons adding up to moral obligations. But moral obligations have quite distinctive features that Wielenberg tends to dismiss. A. E. Taylor, John Henry Newman, and plenty of other luminaries from the history of the moral argument have identified such features. What Wielenberg and those of his ilk do is domesticate moral obligations, overlooking their distinctive features in the process. It's an exercise in intellectual virtue to cultivate a close and careful analysis of the nature of the evidence. An insistence merely to domesticate moral duties in an effort to provide a more palatable explanation of their authority—by replacing talk of their authority with mere "reasons for action," for example—will undoubtedly give solace to those averse to invoking a theistic explanation. But watering down the evidence in such a way fails to do justice to the moral phenomena in need of robust explanation. This is likely the reason why Wielenberg is so willing to say that there are all manner of ways in which duties can be generated; he's predicating his whole analysis on a domesticated account of what such duties require. By radically lowering the bar, he can settle for smaller explanations; but this resembles special pleading more than a little. That this author is so deeply convinced by Wielenberg's analysis is his or her prerogative, but I am left wholly unconvinced.

Regarding whether Wielenberg's Holocaust thought experiment is a counterfactual, which the author denies, it is very difficult to imagine how its import would not be considered as such by one who believes in or is entertaining the hypothesis of something like Anselmian theology. (This isn't question-begging, contra the author's suggestion that Craig was arguing in a circle; the author seems to confuse Craig's argument at points with his laying out his theory; the author, on the other hand, does seem guilty of question begging at a few junctures.) A world in which taking the nap instead of preventing those Holocausts requires the theistic ethicist and divine command theorist to imagine a world in which God's commands wouldn't entail doing the obviously right thing. If such a world were possible, that would show that DCT is quite a flawed view. But no right-thinking DCT'ist, and certainly not Craig, would think such a world *is* possible. This isn't ad hoc; it's a robust account of why in all possible worlds such a necessary truth would obtain.

The author of this piece seems a bit confused on this score. The epistemic method here is to start with some nonnegotiable moral fact or duty—like the wrongness of taking that nap in that circumstance described by Wielenberg. That becomes nonnegotiable. We are surer of that than we are any particular meta-ethical account of where duties ultimately come from, as it should be if we are going to take moral evidence as potentially veridical of aspects of ultimate reality. Epistemology is bottom up, and the moral premise needs to be strong. Then we seek to find the best explanation of such a duty. Divine commands, it can be argued for a variety of reasons, may well and arguably does constitute such an explanation. We then at least tentatively infer to it as the likely true explanation. Whether it's the *only* explanation, or *only possible* explanation, are additional questions, but beyond the standard of proof within this particular debate's parameters. Craig's point in this debate is that divine commands are plausibly the best explanation—or, even less ambitiously, the better explanation than Wielenberg's. Wielenberg's, in truth, is no explanation at all—just brute facts existing in metaphysical limbo, having precious little purchase on our lives, and reflective of precious little about the nature of reality. Wielenberg's thought experiment requires the DCT'ist to imagine a scenario that he has excellent reason to think is a counteressential—a world in which the God of perfect love, divine impeccability, and omnibenevolence would issue no commands that would entail preventing those Holocausts. One like Craig instead thinks that the clarity with which we can apprehend objective moral values and authoritative moral duties requires an explanation good and expansive and powerful enough to undergird their reality. This leads him, by turns, to a robust theistic ethical theory that has no need to domesticate moral duties or settle, like Wielenberg, for merely appearing to provide a good explanation.

All in all, the questions underlying this paper are far bigger and more difficult than the author of this piece seems to want to concede, settling instead for a largely superficial analysis that, as it stands, adds nothing at all to the literature that I can see.

Friday, May 7, 2021: We live in crazy times. Transgenderism is becoming the new orthodoxy; the mere expression of reservations about the rapid trajectory toward its unquestioned acceptance is tantamount to heresy. All sorts of new orthodoxies are enforced in the public square. Meanwhile my people bow their knee to the likes of Tucker Carlson on Fox News, whose behavior is just disgraceful. His reflections on the covid vaccination, for example, are reckless in the extreme: using rhetoric drenched with innuendo and exploiting selective evidence, pandering to anti-vaxxers, giving solace to conspiracy theorists while adept at generating outrage. Concerns about public health and seeing reasonable precautions during a pandemic are cast as fear mongering, lack of faith, or worse.

In ever so many ways, on the political right and left, we are witness to what an erosion of moral foundations looks like. It does not mean morality goes away, but rather narrows and gets focused like a laser beam conflagrating everything in its path. Alan Jacobs recently wrote, "When a society rejects the Christian account of who we are, it doesn't become less moralistic but far more so, because it retains an inchoate sense of justice but has no means of offering and receiving forgiveness. The great moral crisis of our time is not, as many of my fellow Christians believe, sexual licentiousness, but rather *vindictiveness*. Social media serve as crack for moralists: there's no high like the high you get from punishing malefactors. But like every addiction, this one suffers from the inexorable law of diminishing returns. The mania for punishment will therefore get worse before it gets better."

It's almost six and the guys will be over soon. Just a brief addition to what I wrote earlier. Good day for the Center. MB had a great chat with Jan, who has all kinds of ideas for promotion of the Center. Jan's enthusiasm is contagious! More details to follow; Jan's supposed to be writing me an e-mail with details. Also, Craig sent in his class notes for the moral argument class. They look wonderful, all 22,000 of them. The idea occurred that once I write my notes, with an eye on his to avoid redundancy, perhaps we could publish them together. I floated the idea to Craig, and he said he had had the same idea. So that's a real possibility. Exciting stuff! We also procured some more permissions on the pop culture articles, but the big asks are still to come—Open Court and Wiley Blackwell. Still no word from Liberty University Press, but hopeful. I'll be quite relieved once we get that permission, though. We also sent a contract to Keith Loftin for his edited collection on education.

Saturday, May 8, 2021: I wrote Jan a thank you note for her exciting talk with MB yesterday. She wrote this delightful e-mail in reply:

> Yay!!!! Oh that makes me so happy.... but in truth, I don't know exactly what it was, either (I'm laughing, it was such a great conversation, I so enjoy talking to you both) □
>
> Let's see, we talked about Public Relations and I shared a bit about what it is that public relations does, with some ideas to put forth to you both for your consideration (PR has been my job for 15 years now, in all of the industries I've worked in, so if anything in there can benefit the Center, let's do it!). The short version is that PR is a relational pursuit that focuses on outreach, relationship-building, and strategic integrated communication. It is NOT marketing - it's about

truth telling, not selling, and is focused on people. Public Relations professionals typically do a lot of media outreach (including writing and distributing press releases), executive media preparation and engagement, speech writing, and so on. We get messages out, messages like, it occurred to me as I was recruiting the girl who works at the coffee shop where I get a morning latte on occasion for the moral apologetics certificate program (and holding up the line without shame!) - the Center exists and it is awesome and here's why! Once developed, these messages can be pooled to pull when you are courting donors, want to provide an update to donors/supporters, all that kind of good stuff.

Also, Public Relations professionals are advisors. It's our job to submit ideas to you and rationale for those ideas, but the leaders ultimately decide whether those ideas fit the vision. Zero ego! So we chatted about some ideas there, which I'll put in that separate email, such as lifting information from the newsletter and putting it into a press release that we could send out through HBU. I'm a press release writing ninja, it's true (I'm laughing), so why don't we start sending them out from the Center?! Never know what will happen, but it's easy to build a media list, a church list, etc., and start transmitting information (and people like press releases on websites and in donor outreach packages, they are received as evidence of professional credibility).

We talked about some of the last year at Liberty, and Marybeth expressed a desire to speak publicly and more openly about some of the things that happened. I really want to speak life into her on this front, because she can and she should and I feel in my bones that she will! All will come in time, I feel certain, especially because her testimony has had such a powerful effect on me and on other women in her classes. I know she needs to speak widely, it blessed me when she did, so I'm a cheerleader of all that God places on her heart.

We talked about local churches. I need to get some logistical info from you all so I can pitch you to my connections, but I'll put that in another email, too......

Oh! I know a wonderful woman in Houston named Misty Phillips. She runs Spark Podcasting, a Christian group that is amazing, growing every week, and has a big reach with an annual conference, weekly training, and so on. Rumor has it that you have a podcast in development, so this is a connection that needs to be made! I'll send an initial email this weekend to get that introduction.

Also! I'm updating my will in "coincidental-but-its-God" timing, and I'm putting the Center in it. Don't get too excited, you might get $9 if the Lord calls me home, but only He knows ☐ I didn't intend to share that information with her, but the Spirit told me to.

Also also, Marybeth shares my opinion, and William Lane Craig's (you know, for

224

whatever his two PhDs are worth ☺), that you are the leading mind in the moral argument. She mentioned that your humility makes that a bit of a foreign realization to you (I'm using my words here), but that she is excited to see how God is positioning you both with her recent assignment as Department Chair and everything else. She also shared that you started working with the moral argument in undergrad, which is incredible. Bottom line, it is a privilege for me to be here at a time when God seems to be rocketing your work for His glory. All around you see His use of you, as well as your obedience. Thank you.

God lifts himself through you, Dave. He prepares the way. (those are not my words).

Back to my words - THANK YOU for the good wishes! I can't believe graduation is nearly here!!! I'm jamming on the thesis now, this whole thing has been so much fun.

Hope you are enjoying an absolutely wonderful day ☐ So much more to come!

With gratitude and hugs,
Jan

I also wanted to knock out my monthly WB piece so it wouldn't be hanging over my head, so I adapted a portion of my *Phil Christi* review. Chris liked it, and has canceled this week's roundtable question, so I'm done with WB for the month. Here is the piece:

Lifting a Finger to Prevent a Thousand Holocausts

Erik Wielenberg has suggested that it's obvious that it would be morally right, indeed morally dutiful, to lift one's finger if, by engaging in this basic act, one could immediately perform the mediated act of preventing a thousand Holocausts. As such he finds dubious the suggestion that morality requires God. We can often have all we need to apprehend our moral obligations simply by looking at, say, the needless pain we could easily avoid. I'm going to talk about this objection to theistic ethics generally and divine command theory particularly.

Most divine command theorists nowadays follow advice that William Alston gave some years ago to delimit divine command theory to a theory of moral obligations. One like Robert Adams builds his divine command theory on his theistic Platonic account of the good. Steve Evans constructs his divine command theory on his natural law view of the good. And in fact most contemporary divine command theorists follow suit, confining the relevance of divine commands to their theory of duties, and not extending it to a theory of moral goodness.

Now, a criticism such as the one that Wielenberg advances largely assumes something like moral realism. Some things are just obviously good, or obviously bad or even evil. I think this is true. Such obviousness, however, underdetermines the ultimate nature of moral goodness or badness, as well as the nature of moral obligations and their authoritative import. Of course, too, there is a gradually growing crowd of thinkers who are sceptical about robustly objective morality. From error theorists to expressivists, constructivists to anti-realists, they question how genuinely obvious are many of our moral convictions. In this way Wielenberg seems to help himself to the salient vestiges of moral objectivity that still prevail in our culture, when a large reason for their prevalence is the set of influences historically wielded by the Judeo-Christian tradition. A great many naturalists harbor much scepticism about Wielenberg's approach, which strikes them as both metaphysically and epistemically indulgent.

Wielenberg assumes as obvious not just moral realism per se, but his own fine-grained account of it, but there is little hope, to my thinking, to infer his perspective from clear-eyed recognition of objective moral facts alone. His effort to do so strikes me as sleight-of-hand. Supposing it is indeed obviously true that we should prevent the Holocausts when we can do so with minimal effort—which I agree with entirely—this simply underdetermines the foundations of moral obligations. It seems practically unphilosophical to rest content with what amounts to Wielenberg's lack of explanation on this score.

That there would be moral reason to lift one finger and stop the Holocausts is undoubtedly true. Moral reasons can emanate from axiology (moral value) alone, but moral reasons in and of themselves don't necessarily constitute moral obligations. Wielenberg recognizes this, punting to Parfit's minimalistic requirements for reasons adding up to moral obligations. Moral obligations, however, have quite distinctive features that Wielenberg tends to dismiss, and give us reasons for action, rather than coming into existence when enough reasons to act add up. A. E. Taylor, John Henry Newman, Steve Evans, and plenty of other luminaries from the history of the moral argument have identified such features—their connections to guilt, punishment, their overriding authority, and the like. What seems all the rage nowadays is to domesticate moral obligations, overlooking their distinctive features in the process.

It's an exercise in intellectual virtue to cultivate a close and careful analysis of the nature of the evidence. An insistence merely to deflate moral duties in an effort to provide a more palatable explanation of their authority—by replacing talk of their authority with mere "reasons for action," for example—will undoubtedly give solace to those averse to invoking a theistic explanation.

Watering down the evidence in such a way, though, fails to do justice to the moral phenomena in need of robust explanation. This is likely the reason why Wielenberg is so willing to say that there are all manner of ways in which duties can be generated. He is predicating his whole analysis on a domesticated account of what such duties require. By radically lowering the bar, he can settle for smaller explanations.

My preferred epistemic method is to start with some nonnegotiable moral fact or duty—like the wrongness of taking a nap instead of easily avoiding all those Holocausts in such a circumstance described by Wielenberg. That seems nonnegotiable. We are surer of that moral duty than we are any particular meta-ethical account of where duties ultimately come from, as it should be if we are going to take moral evidence as potentially veridical of aspects of ultimate reality. Epistemology is bottom up, and the moral premises need to be strong. Then we seek to find the best explanation of such a duty. Divine command, it can be argued for a variety of reasons, may well and arguably does constitute such an explanation. We then at least tentatively infer to it as the likely true explanation. (Others, convinced that morality essentially depends on God, might opt for a different specific account of the shape of that dependence—divine desire, divine will, divine motivation, etc.) When it comes to the battle between, say, divine command theory and atheistic Platonism, the divine command theorist can argue that divine commands—issued by a God plausibly and for principled reasons thought to be loving, just, good, etc.—are the better explanation of duties than merely brute facts existing in metaphysical limbo, having no real purchase on our lives, and reflective of precious little about the nature of reality.

Wielenberg's thought experiment requires the DCT'ist to imagine a scenario that he has excellent reason to think is a counteressential—a world in which the God of perfect love, divine impeccability, and omnibenevolence would issue no commands that would entail preventing those Holocausts. Count me among those who consider that the clarity with which we can apprehend objective moral values and authoritative moral duties requires an explanation good and expansive and powerful enough to undergird their reality. At any rate, this leads me, by turns, to a robust theistic ethical theory that has no need to domesticate moral duties or settle for the mere appearance of providing a good explanation.

Sunday, May 9, 2021: TJ and I plan to talk later in the week, so that's good, and today I sent Dr. Craig's lecture notes to the moral apologetics students. That was the only work I did; it was Mother's Day. MB and I had breakfast at Cracker Barrel and a nice seafood lunch. Trying to rest today; the next three weeks are going to be a whirlwind. Last week of term, plus my last week to prepare for the moral apologetics class before it starts. Glad Craig goes first. My work is definitely cut out for me. Not entirely sure I'm up to it all. Wish I could break free from the emotional downness, which has been fairly chronic a few weeks running, and hardly conduces to focus, which desperately need.

One can keep a journal about a particular day. It will record the day's events, but only some. Laura Ingles Wilder said that everything she wrote was the truth, but she didn't tell all the truth. A sequence of events might be an entirely accurate chronicle, as far as it goes, yet do nothing to capture the real mood of the day, its prevailing spirit, though that feature may well be by far the most salient part of the week or season, at least for the writer. Today, for example, has seemed to me a day of darkness, a somber, sober occasion all through. I have been altogether unable to extricate myself from the doldrums, to get out from under a dark, oppressive cloud. The day's events can be dutifully, factually recorded and all those redolent subjective factors seamlessly filtered out.

Keeping a journal in this sense is like writing history. From the myriad of details to include, it offers but the slimmest sliver, rife with curated meanings, an act of the selective imagination. Inveterate story tellers, we weave tales to impose an order, to concoct a narrative that makes sense, to find something coherent, discern a guiding motif, an integrating structure, a significant plot or trajectory. Books are usually far better than their corresponding movies, but life is infinitely richer than books. Not always more enjoyable, by any means. It can be excruciating, dripping with regrets, riddled with angst, haunted by all manner of specters. It has its moments, this earthly pilgrimage, no doubt, but the trials and travails are inevitable. We are not yet home, when our tears will be wiped away. This whole life can feel like a night when weeping endures, awaiting morning and a baptism of joy. In the interim it can be hard to see clearly when our eyes are filled with tears.

Monday, May 10, 2021: It's just before 9 in the morning, and I've been hard at it for several hours. A number of to do's this morning, and now I'm diving into the real work. This is going to be a busy day and week, but it has the potential to be very productive. This morning I listened to the story of Samuel being directed to choose Saul as King. Feeling much better today. My spirits seem finally to have lifted considerably. My lamentations for the moment seem to have subsided.

It is now later in the day, and oh boy, was I right! What a day! Just incredible! Where to begin? We heard from Liberty University Press—they agreed to hand the rights back to *Lewis as Philosopher*. We heard back from Bill Irwin after telling him of our plans for *Telling Tales*, and he gave us his enthusiastic support and needed contact information for folks at Open Court and Wiley Blackwell. MB had the idea to have both Jan and Delia over during the intensive, which is a lovely idea. And Jan was put in touch Jerry Johnston at HBU and they are going to coordinate press releases about the Center. She's also working to put us in a podcast network (on her dime) and to get us speaking invitations at churches. Incredible the work she's doing for us! Marybeth and I are just marveling at all that's happening before our eyes—we feel like we're riding a wave of momentum that we didn't generate. This really is of God, we are convinced. Dean Kowalski also signed off on our using a few pieces from UPK Press. Just amazing! And other than all of that, it was also a mightily productive day to boot, though I need them all week to be ready for next two.

Here was the relevant e-mail from Jan:

Happy Monday, Team Baggett!

A few misc questions.....

1) First, I would like to talk to my local church contacts about having you all out to speak, including my church. Is there a fee? How far are you willing to drive? Do you have a minimum audience size? Are you available for specific lengths of time, or in specific formats? Is anything special required to host you in terms of av or other requirements? Do you have preferred links, videos, flyers, etc. that you would like me to share with the churches when I introduce the idea? Is there anything else I need to know, to pitch the churches? Thank you!

2) I spoke with Misty Phillips, founder of the Spark podcasting collaborative, on Saturday. Here is the website to learn more - https://www.sparkmedia.ventures/. Misty is local to Houston and absolutely amazing. I was referred to her through a friend and was just getting my feet wet in the Spark community in 2020 when God said "stop! Go to school! Learn apologetics so you have something correct and effective to share □ " Anyway, she is putting together a package membership for the Center for Moral Apologetics team to have access to the trainings, weekly calls, and her and her husband directly for guidance and IT support. <u>Who do you want on the account?</u> Recommend both of you and Jonathan, if you see him helping with uploading or content planning in the future.... anyone else? I have access to the trainings through my own account so that's covered. Membership is a gift from me to the Center, so no worries on that front. Misty feels as I do, that there is a good future in this relationship for Kingdom work. We're excited to see what it is. Low-hanging fruit, my experience was that the collaborative looks first to the Spark community for guests for their own podcasts, and Misty is GREAT about advertising her podcasters, so I think we can gain some good traction there for word of mouth beyond the immediate world of apologists, AND they're amazing with all things IT related, which will inevitably come up if they haven't already.

3) Would it be alright with you if I reached out to HBU and asked to preserve access to my hbu email in order to better support the Center? Assuming I am accepted into the DMin program I will start classes again in the fall, but I'd very much like to use it for Center business so HBU staff and students can find me in the email directory if need be... .I'm a little worried they'll shut it off after graduation.... not a huge deal, but it would be nice to have that consistency. Thank you!

4) Can't wait for moral apologetics class next week!!!! Dave, you mentioned in your last auditors email that some students are already submitting questions.... would it be helpful if I kept a running list of questions that students bring up throughout the class? It could be good fodder for blogs, podcast topics, etc. and an overall good way to demonstrate your responsiveness to students to a wider audience if we make mention of it on social media (i.e., "last week a student asked us XXXXX. Check out this blog for answers, stay tuned for the next class, submit your own questions," whatever we want our calls to action to be.)

I'll keep you posted as I connect with Clay over at HBU public affairs. I was very encouraged by the general tone of that email train to "remember we have all of these resources that can help the Center, just let us know." Oh, we *will* let them know, with gratitude ☐ ☐ ☐

Hope your days are progressing wonderfully!

Tuesday, May 11, 2021: Had an early morning zoom session with Phil and Mike Devito, who will be helping with the tech side of the moral argument class. Mike's a former apol student here and former NFL player for the Jets. Really great guy. Zoom room tour scheduled for Friday late morning.

Marybeth put this on FB today: "Moral Apologetics Press is pleased to announce that we have signed Keith Loftin to publish an edited collection of essays promoting the value of Christian liberal arts education. The title is *Rekindling an Old Light: The Virtue and Value of Christ-Shaped Liberal Arts Learning*. Contributors include Paul Gould, John Mark Reynolds, Travis Dickinson, yours truly, and more. This volume promises to be a tremendous asset to the church, and we are thrilled to help get its message out to the world! Thanks to Keith for his hard work in making this book a reality."

I really need to knock out grading term papers for my online course and my apol day presentation today, if I'm going to stay on track to get everything done on time over the next several days. Feeling an inordinate amount of pressure. Adam Johnson just wrote saying Kregel had yet to issue him a contract for his book, and that if they didn't he'd go with us. I'm sure they will, but it was nice to hear.

It's now the evening and I'm happy to report that I finished today's two big tasks. Term papers graded and Apol Day presentation in the bag. I decided in the latter to stop at Lewis and sum up the findings by pointing to three broad sorts of moral arguments, make people aware of the upcoming Certificate program, and suggest, for those interested in reading more about the history of moral apologetics, to take a look at Jer's and my book.

Marybeth sent out the last permission requests—to the University Press of Kentucky, editor Jorge Gracia (for the *Passion* piece), Open Court, and Wiley Blackwell. If we get these, we are good to go!

Wednesday, May 12, 2021: We enjoyed a nice Toasted Yolk breakfast, though I couldn't sit at my favorite table. I mentioned over breakfast a tweet MB had written about having "no regrets" about having Nathaniel at 20 and relying, for a season, on some governmental assistance. We discussed the point of it and how it might or would be perceived by some—on both sides of the political aisle. It was more emotional of a discussion for her than I had anticipated, and I almost wished in retrospect I hadn't broached the topic. But then again, perhaps it served a purpose. I know she still has lots of painful memories to process from those tumultuous and trying years. Interesting how on occasion we're reminded that, before we ever met, we had each lived quite few years and through quite a bit of life.

Wrapped up my preparation for the Dallas church presentation by late morning, then turned my attention to Craig's class notes for next week. I'm going through them carefully, recording copious notes with every scrap of insight I've got; about a third done at this point, and have called it a day. Tomorrow I'll try to churn through the rest. Then I can start writing my own notes to be delivered the week after next. It is such a joy going through Craig's thought process; we agree on a great deal, but the differences I think can help, when fleshed out, fill out a fuller, richer picture. And speaking of Craig, I had sent him our admittedly "goofy" promotional video for the class, and he finally responded with this, just this: "Goofy is right!" So far two think it's because they think he thought it funny, and two think he was unamused. I'm the undecided tie-breaking vote.

The Univ. Press of KY gave us permission to re-use the pieces published with them for *Telling Tales*. Still waiting to hear from Open Court and Wiley Blackwell. MB made reservations for an N. T. Wright talk June 19th at the Lanier Library (for us, Jerry Walls, and Nathaniel), and I accepted an invitation to write an article for the journal *Perichoresis* on evolutionary debunking objections to moral knowledge, due March 15. Other than that I did a little more chipping away at grading for the online course. Good, productive day, I think. Now plan to relax for a little while and get ready for bed. Oh, Brian Chilton wrote something for our site, and JP finalized a Mailbag answer of mine as well.

I had put my computer away, but at 6 pm this evening I was scheduled to speak with Adam Johnson. Wonderful talk, as he's trying to think about his future. A most exciting thing: he asked me, if Kregel is okay with it, to write the foreword to his book! Just delighted to be asked! Really cutting-edge work as far as I'm concerned.

Thursday, May 13, 2021: Today is the day I hope to hit the rest of these Craig notes hard. MB is working on her apol day presentation for this Saturday. Whereas I'm talking about the history of the moral argument, she's talking about winsome apologetics. Some recent events—including one with a previous HBU apol student—have really driven home the importance of her topic, for sure. Going for jugulars needs to be replaced with some serious bridge building.

MB and I worked hard at Panera; I still have about fifteen pages of Craig notes to get through. Intense work, but worthwhile. I am seeing numerous ways I can augment what Craig has done.

Today the CDC lifted the requirements of masks for those who've been vaccinated; good news.

I went to bat on FB for a friend (Rob Gagnon) who'd gotten a three-day suspension for posting an article FB didn't like. After getting lambasted by a former HBU apol student who seemed to miss the point, I wrote this: "The content of the article Rob posted isn't the point, but the principle of folks having the freedom to say and share things that we may or may not agree with. I think there's significant danger of a slippery slope when we work hard to find subtle reasons to justify what amounts to unprincipled censorship. Not everything is allowed or should be allowed in the public square, I get that. But when what's genuinely worth relegating to the periphery or to silence altogether gets conflated with what's simply not to our personal liking, we're on the wrong road. At a time when speech codes are getting increasingly enforced, and new orthodoxies are beginning to hold sway with draconian results, it's wise to take notice and take a stand. I tend by nature to be radically averse to most conspiracy theories; this isn't that. Nor am I looking for excuses to be outraged. This is about vigilance to preserve space in the public square for the expression of our God-given mental freedom."

Friday, May 14, 2021: So I joined a gym yesterday and today (it's before 6 am) I'm about to go for the first time…. Just got back. Learned a few machines at the gym, and then went for a pleasant walk at the park afterwards. Donald Williams published a review of Melton's *Wrackturn Method*—in the persona of Screwtape, of course. I need to finish getting through Craig's notes, but feel like not working. But I have no choice; need to shower and get to work.

It's nearly supper time now. Sadly I had a hard time motivating myself to continue going through Craig's notes, but something good did happen today. MB and I were just invited jointly to do the Strauss lectureship in October at Lincoln Christian University. That is really cool! Here was the invite from Rich Knopp:

> I submitted your name for consideration for our James D. Strauss Lectureship…. I've just been asked to follow up with you to see if it's possible for you (and perhaps your wife) to come for the lectureship this October. It's currently scheduled for Tues-Wed, Oct 12-13, though we might be able to move it a week earlier if necessary.

Ideally, we'd like both you and your wife to participate, but we don't have a great deal of remuneration to offer. I think we're in the $1500 range plus travel. In the past, we've had a 40-minute Tuesday morning presentation at our university chapel time, a lunch Q&A, a 60 minute Tuesday evening presentation plus Q&A, and a 45 minute Wednesday morning presentation with brief Q&A. If possible, Zach and I would also love to do a recorded interview with you while you're here. (*Room for Doubt* will help sponsor the lectureship.)

In terms of a possible theme and session titles, we're open to suggestions. From my perspective, topics of current cultural relevance that would have a relatively broad audience appeal would be great. While something more specific in moral apologetics would be good, including a session on the general value and application of apologetics would be good as well. Tuesday morning would have more undergrads, while the Tuesday evening and Wednesday morning audience would have proportionally more seminarians and off-campus guests. If your wife is able to come, you could divvy things up however you want and even do a tag-team of some sort. (We've never had two people do the lectureship, so there's no precedent to break.)

Please give the lectureship prayer consideration. We'd love for you to come if possible. Let me know if you have any questions or suggestions.

In Christ, Rich

P.S. James D. Strauss taught theology & philosophy at Lincoln's seminary from 1967-1994 and died in 2014. He was the reason I went to Lincoln as an MDiv student back in the 70's, and he had tremendous influence on my personal and professional life. The lectureship is named in his honor.

Saturday, May 15, 2021: Today was both graduation and Apologetics Day. Didn't attend graduation, but did give a talk at the conference, both me and MB. Talk went pretty well, and so did MB's, after she got over her jitters. WLC got back to us today and shifted the date of his visit so we can tell Lincoln yes and stick to their preferred dates. I'll do that Monday. Exhausted; going to bed at 7.

Sunday, May 16, 2021: It's about 3:30 in the morning. Woke up early and haven't been able to get back to sleep. Will likely get some more rest before long, but thinking about yesterday's conference, especially the in-between times. Need to get cards to hand out; it might serve double duty, too. Not only will it make more aware of the Center and such, it can also be a means of drawing certain conversations to a close when the time is right and folks aren't quite getting that that moment has arrived. As an introvert I have to guard my time a little closer in some of those social situations.

Two conversations stand out yesterday—both with atheists who were in attendance. Well, at least one atheist and another guy who said he wasn't a Christian. Both were big fans of Jordan Peterson. The strong empirical emphasis and privileging of psychological categories seem to be hallmarks of some of these young fellows for whom Peterson seems to stand as a sort of heroic figure. I don't blame Peterson; I think he's a very interesting fellow, but man alive, is he ever able to ignite loyalty among certain of his ardent followers. They treat his words as practically sacrosanct. Odd phenomenon.

Monday, May 17, 2021: This morning MB and I told Lincoln we accepted their invitation to do the Strauss lecture. Then I got grades in for the spring term and turned to finishing Craig's notes. I should later write a little blog called "What I Learned from Teaching with William Lane Craig." In short, a lot! The discipline of his mind; the systematic approach; the richness of analysis. Just remarkable.

I was nervous about the first day of the intensive with Dr. Craig, but it went pretty well save for some challenges associated with technology. Craig was visibly impatient with some of the technical difficulties, but wrote me after class and admitted he should have handled it better. I thought that was really neat.

Tuesday, May 18, 2021: Class went very well. Dr. Craig was terrific. I spoke up a bit more during class, and handled the last half hour again fielding questions. Some of the questions were very difficult, and I suspect just difficult for us as human beings. We run into limits in our understanding. Sometimes I know in academic settings there's a temptation to make the discussion overly technical as if what's under discussion is primarily an academic exercise. I wish I could find ways to encourage folks to realize that our goal is to proclaim the name of Christ and not lose sight of that in the quest for intellectual clarity.

Halfway through class I received an exciting e-mail! Here it is:

Dear David and John,

I'm delighted to report that your proposed anthology on the Moral Argument has been enthusiastically accepted for publication. Everyone thinks it will be an excellent addition to OUP's list and we are all looking forward to working on it with you.

I am now in a position to send you a contract. For that purpose I will need:

Home addresses for both of you.
An estimated word count, including notes and bibliography: 250,000 words?
A delivery day: January 2025?

As soon as I hear from you on these points I can have the contract drawn up and will send it along. I couldn't be more pleased at the prospect of publishing this important work.

One small suggestion: I assume that you thought to title the book "An Anthology on…" because OUP already publishes a book entitled "The Moral Argument." I suggest that a much better solution would be to call it: "The Moral Argument for the Existence of God: An Anthology." Sound okay?

All the best,

Cynthia

What a remarkable answer to prayer! When I came to Houston last July I didn't have a single book contract. Now I have three—phil theo with Ronnie, the 4th in the tetralogy, and now this collection with Hare. In addition, MAP is working on the new edition of *Lewis as Philosopher* and, additionally, *Telling Tales*. I've done one journal, and I'm nearly half done another, and MB and I are going to try to snag a contract to edit *Ted Lasso and Philosophy*.

Wednesday, May 19, 2021: Today is MB's and my anniversary. Nine years. Incredible! We're at Panera early to do work; both tired. Stormed all night long and neither of us got great sleep. Still very rainy and overcast; not the prettiest day. But a wonderful day of celebration. Also hump day in the first week of this intensive. I need to get some clarity about what I want to share next week.

Class went well. After Craig's lecture I shared with the class a few reflections about the need for us all to remember that what we are doing is not merely an intellectual game, but ultimately for the purpose of using these resources to reach people with the good news of the gospel. It can be tempting to make the intellectual inquiry purely an end in itself. I also shared more details about our website and HBU's Center for Moral Apologetics, inviting them onboard to catch a vision of its importance and mission.

In the evening we discovered that our air conditioning had stopped working, so we ended up staying at a hotel. It is supposed to be fixed tomorrow morning.

Thursday, May 20, 2021: Class went very well today, despite that I had a severe back pain, likely related to stress. Craig discussed the abductive version, which I enjoyed a great deal. Fortunately, I felt like the questions at the end I had to field went well, too. The air conditioning was fixed by the time I got home. John Hare at last acknowledged he was happy to hear the news about the OUP Collection, so that should soon be good to go, contract in hand.

Friday, May 21, 2021: Last day of the week. Delightful class, good question and answer period. Thrilled to get done with the first week. Craig is a machine. Mike DeVito is a delightful host; meeting him has been a real treat of the course. MB and I enjoyed a lovely dinner at PF Changs. Lovely day and lovely evening. Mightily relieved. Even though I'll be the one teaching next week, I think in some ways it'll be easier than this week. At least if I fall on my face WLC won't be around to see it. He really is wonderful, though after he left for the day I assured the students they don't need to aspire to be him—just themselves. He's an inspiration we would all love to emulate, of course, but it's important that folks remember they're not called to be anyone but themselves. The body of Christ has lots of different parts.

Saturday, May 22, 2021: It's a little after 2 am. I went to sleep pretty early, and I'll be going back to sleep. But awake for a few minutes, and still feeling good about yesterday and wrapping up that first week of the intensive. It was a lot harder than people realize, I'm quite sure. To be asked questions at the end on anything and everything is quite a challenge. So grateful God helped me get through. I have not been journaling much only because I have such little left after class and class prep. But since Rob hung out a few extra days, we are planning on dinner and a movie tonight, which is a nice bonus since I had thought last week would be the last for a while.

Jan Shultis wrote this during the course of the day:

Good morning!

I am SO EXCITED for this book! [I had told her about the prospective book with Craig based on the moral argument course.] What a wonderful idea. It is a privilege to help in any way that I can.

To start, I'll run through the videos and type up the questions as stated by students in class. I'll also note where you and Dr. Craig have slightly different approaches.... that could be super interesting for a Q&A section.

I think we have a large enough class that we can extrapolate some statistically significant trends from any patterns in the questions. Selfishly, I would like to go through this exercise to be able to use this data to inform my blogs for moralapologetics.com. It struck me during the lecture on Day 3, when Dr. Craig touched on psychopathy, that to properly present moral injury may require presentation of more robust mental/behavioral health education than I initially anticipated. PTSD, for example, often mirrors psychopathy, and both can inhibit acceptance of the moral argument. (I tossed some comments in the chat to see if anyone had a mental health background and wanted to talk further, but no takers, which doesn't necessarily mean anything but is interesting.) It also struck me that there may be collaboration between the Center and other departments at HBU through the moral injury lens (all those young people at graduation last weekend with counseling degrees - they need more info about moral apologetics!), and we can better make the case if we've got some info on trends from this class.

All that to say..... yay! Sign me up for question duty! I'll have something to you by the week after class ☐

Jonathan, it is a delight to be in touch again! Looking forward to all that is to come ☐

With gratitude,
Jan

By the late afternoon I thought it best to cancel my dinner plans with the guys. Just too much work to do. Swamped with work to finish my prep for the upcoming week. But the good news is that if I keep my nose to the grindstone I should be able to finish much of the potential book with Craig.

A few days ago MB sent this letter to Scott Hicks at Liberty. A tough but necessary word:

Scott,

As I finish up my first year at a new institution, I have thought quite a bit about my seventeen years teaching at Liberty. The following reflections are a distillation of those thoughts, which I offer for your benefit as well as for the sake of Liberty's faculty and students. You'll do with them what you will, but I hope that some needful, though difficult, word will penetrate.

By summer of 2019—especially in the wake of the callous Divinity School terminations—I knew that leaving Liberty was essential for my spiritual and emotional well-being. The culture there had become too toxic to remain. It's a place that sadly has come to be defined by duplicity, oppression, and greed. I thank God every day that he delivered me, but I also regularly pray for those who remain, first for those who faithfully serve God and bring light to the darkness but also for those like you who perpetuate the dysfunction.

You have been ensconced in this sick system for so long that you may have fully embraced as truth the lies that govern it and might struggle to recognize yourself in what I share below. It's up to God to stir your conscience, but the truth of your condition will break through whenever the pieces don't fit, anywhere where the cracks in the façade show, anytime where your stated words and underlying desires mismatch. Speaking as someone now on the outside, I can say that those moments are in fact ubiquitous.

Being in a healthy environment has thrown into considerable relief the damage done to me through the years and to so many by you and the rest of your administration. It's your choice what your legacy will be, but from an employee's perspective, I'll say that great leaders seek the good of those they lead, recognizing that good proliferates and produces a yield immeasurable by the dollar. Small men grasp and seek to control, ironically destroying the very thing they seek to gain. I am glad to be done with such men.

It is empowering and enlivening to work alongside those who wish for your success and who support your flourishing. It is soul-crushing and debilitating to be treated as a cog in the machine, excisable if deemed costly or inefficient.

It is inspiring to teach at a school that values education and discipleship and allows those humanistic aims to drive programs and policies. It is dehumanizing and demeaning to succumb to the whims of an administration that monetizes curricula and exploits instruction for financial ends.

It is edifying to dwell in a community that truly believes Christ is Lord and allows that truth to shape their collective practices. It is revolting to inhabit a barren shell that projects an appearance of godliness for marketing's sake but denies its power.

I realize that to have gotten to the point you are at, holding employees' livelihoods and welfare hostage to your own ambitions, your soul must be callous indeed. But I hope it's not so callous that you cannot sense the spiritual danger you are in, so fully embracing corruption, dishonesty, and power and attempting to baptize the love of money as wise stewardship.

Even as you've twisted biblical mandates to serve indecent purposes, I pray that some of its truths have broken through: be not deceived, for instance; God is not mocked. If you still adhere to scripture at all, you must know that you will reap what you sow. It's profoundly naïve for you to have seen those fallen leaders before you--disposed of when no longer useful, ousted for being inconvenient, destroying themselves with their own decadence.

How in the world can you even begin to imagine you will escape such a reckoning? I sincerely pray that you re-appropriate the truth of scripture before you experience that inevitable and painful fall and before you cause more harm to those under you and to the cause of Christ in your misrepresentation of him.

The beautiful thing is that there is grace for you. In confession and repentance, God can redeem and restore what sin has wrecked.

May God break your heart to heal it.

Marybeth Baggett

Sunday, May 23, 2021: Need to work all day today to get to where I need to be for class this week. We're at Panera early after breakfasting at Toasted Yolk. Working on the heart of the moral argument material—intrinsic human value, essential equality, human dignity, basic human rights, guilt and moral freedom, the category of evil, the argument from rationality, etc. If I can wrap up what I want to do today, lectures should be sketched out through Thursday. This has been an extremely intense period of work. Productive, but exhausting; I'm thoroughly in work mode, though, for now, despite the tiredness. I can sleep next weekend. (Actually when I do fit sleep in, it's quite deep sleep.)

Monday, May 24, 2021: After getting to Panera early, by around 10 am I finished editing my notes for the day, which now gives me some extra time to keep working on my notes for Thursday and Friday. Feeling a bit of a breather.

Well, class was a major challenge. Lots of tech problems. Hard to feel comfortable teaching. Ah well. Perhaps the occasional price to pay to be able to hold a class with this many good folks from all over the world. Want to sleep.

Tuesday, May 25, 2021: Covered moral realism today in class—and error theory, constructivism, and expressivism. Went very well. Limited questions a bit so it would seem a bit less like a game show.

Wednesday, May 26, 2021: Another very good day of teaching as I discussed moral facts and moral knowledge. Just two days to go before this intensive is in the bag.

Thursday, May 27, 2021: Great day in class discussing moral rationality and transformation!

Friday, May 28, 2021: Last day of this two-week intensive. Incredible to have arrived here! There were some days when I felt like I couldn't make it! So grateful to God for sustaining me and giving me the strength to get through. I don't think there's been a bad day. Both Mondays posed some technical challenges, but that is all. The questions have been manageable, and the lectures decent. The tone of the class is delightful. So very grateful for how things have gone. Better than I could have hoped for or expected. I may put my lecture note into the journal, but they remain a work in progress. I've been busy enough to have little time or energy left over each day for the journal, but after today that should change. Feeling great relief. It's now 4:30 am and I'm up to give it one last mad dash to the finish line by wrapping up today's lecture. Quite a bit of work left to do on it, but hopefully I have the time. Overall this has been nothing less than magical.

Saturday, May 29, 2021: I think I neglected to mention that about a week back Nick Henretty sent me a sample audio chapter from Elton's book and it was terrific. I hired him for 300 dollars to tape the whole book. Excited about that prospect! Just got off the phone with Elton; delightful chat. His planned procedure for a second heart stint proved unnecessary.[16]

In the afternoon Marybeth and I watched a documentary on Billy Graham. Pretty well done; fascinating life! Still remember when I taught one of his grandchildren in VA who could have been his twin.

Fun time with Rob and Jerry in the evening. Rob's going back to PA for the summer in a few days; I'll miss him. Brother by another mother.

---

[16] Here are all the class videos from the last two weeks:
Monday: https://youtu.be/0O3-hwdUWIs
Tuesday: https://youtu.be/KsWtct49w08
Wednesday: https://youtu.be/S2yyWEN-i94
Thursday: https://youtu.be/IovIubhY0NU
Friday: https://youtu.be/JFeu7mHkTrc
Monday: https://youtu.be/nslj0rxHxz8
Tuesday: https://youtu.be/8iomf0Og7NI
Wednesday: https://youtu.be/vDFGoYiGQfQ
Thursday: https://youtu.be/f5RIAu8iyg8
Friday: https://youtu.be/i9dtSp5zGOM

Received a personal note from a former HBU MAA student Zak Schmoll, who'd purchased and read my first year journal about the Center: "Just wanted to drop you a quick note about your book regarding the creation of the Center for Moral Apologetics. Your honesty and transparency are remarkable, and I appreciated them so much. You laid your heart out on those pages and shared your fears. I am so excited to see what the Center continues to become, but I just wanted to thank you for being so real. I don't know that I would be as brave as you are (I don't share my emotions very well, especially in journal entries that will become public), but I was greatly encouraged by your example. Hope you are well! –Zak" He also put a nice note on FB about it. Unexpected entirely and very sweet!

Sunday, May 30, 2021: Very nice day of rest for me and MB! Early afternoon watched fun Harrison Ford movie, then took a sweet nap. Feeling good!

MB's been feeling under the weather for a few days, so while she was still napping this afternoon I cooked a bunch. When she got up and came into the kitchen I told her I'd made chicken, salmon, steamed vegetables, spinach with garlic, etc. About three quarters through my description I heard her fiddling with something behind me. I turned to see she had just about opened her new box of Frosted Mini-Wheats. "You're gonna have cereal, aren't ya?"

About half the kids who'd taken the moral argument class for credit have gotten their work in, and each who has wrote a sweet note thanking me and Dr. Craig for the class. Very encouraging!

In the early evening I felt some motivation to work on the prospective book with Craig, then wrote him: "Dr. Craig, I have written a draft of the introduction to the potential book of ours, and put your notes and mine, along with the intro, into one document. I'm planning on doing a bit more editing on my part tomorrow and then send along what I've got to give you an idea of what it would look like. I'll be chipping away at the questions and answers portion of the book--transcribing your answers, digging up answers we've given in various venues, answering questions from this class, etc. I think it's shaping up nicely! You'll hear from me tomorrow. Of course it will be your prerogative to nix the whole deal if you so choose.

"The second week went pretty well, I think. Following you isn't easy! ☐"

To which he responded like this: "Glad to hear it went well and am anxious to see what you come up with! I certainly want this project to go forward and would have at most suggestions for improvement. For example, if you discuss the historical background of the argument, then the brief remarks that I made on that head could be eliminated or blended with what you say. The book does not need to have to hermetically sealed halves."

To which I replied like this: "Yes, having written my notes with yours in mind, I tried to augment and supplement what you had to say, and made numerous connections with your notes from the first week. I think it's a good sign that several students said they thought the two sets of lectures nicely blended and overall gave a fuller treatment. I'll send it along tomorrow for your perusal!"

What I didn't tell him was that the document as it stands is about 60,000 words, before any questions and answers have been included. I'll likely edit mine down a bit, but it looks likely the book will end up around 80,000 words now.

Monday, May 31, 2021: Last day of May. All the assignments have come in from the moral apol class; grades are due tomorrow. MB and I went for a walk this morning. Today I'm hoping to semi-finalize the document to send to WLC; hopefully he'll go for it and we'll be on a trajectory to publish our lectures. Despite a nap yesterday and a good night's sleep, feeling sluggish. May need to ease back into my work after the last few crazy weeks. Planning to organize my books here at home; they been scattered too much of late, especially because of all the trips to Panera with various handfuls of them.

Jan Shultis sent her first blog in for the site today. Looks quite interesting! She's had a lot of energy working for us lately—a blog, work on logos, business cards, putting us in touch with a podcast group, putting us in touch with churches, preparing to issue press releases, etc. Wow!

Tuesday, June 1, 2021: Last full day of MB being here before going to Lynchburg. Sure gonna miss her. In the morning I finished up the grading for the May intensive and wrote the class some general observations. Beginning now to chip away at some of my to-do's that had to be deferred until now. Slept like a rock again last night; I think my brain is still recovering from the frenetic couple of weeks. I think I'm going to ask Ronnie and the press if they'd be alright replacing me as his co-author on the phil theology book with Chris Reese so I can maintain my focus on moral apol. MB and I saw "Dream Horse" late afternoon; a real feel-good movie. Before that I edited a few pieces for the site, one by Jan and another by my old friend Sloan Lee; both good.

Wednesday, June 2, 2021: MB and I had breakfast at Toasted Yolk, then I took her to the airport. It's now midafternoon and she's boarding the plane from Charlotte to Lynchburg. Adjusting to her not being here. Still trying to gear myself up for work. Taking a little time to recover. Ronnie sent along a slightly adjusted division of labor for the phil theology book; looks good:

Introduction

The introduction will provide the reader with a rationale for why this book is needed, lay out the book's methodology, define key terms, and give the reader an outline of the book.

Chapter 1 – Faith and Reason (Dave)

Chapter one will focus on examining the relationship between faith and reason, while also examining the status of epistemic belief in God. It will also accentuate the integrating motif of God's perfect love and goodness as the salient lens of the book's analysis. [Here, we might consider using the moral argument for God's existence as the basis/grounds for the epistemic belief in God. We could also speak a bit about bare natural theology and ramified natural theology, pulling from our *Phil Christi* article.]

Chapter 2 – Models of God (Ronnie)

Chapter two will explore various models for understanding the concept of God and the God/world relationship, while also considering the differences among alternatives within monotheism, namely, Christianity, Islam, and Judaism.

Chapter 3 – The Concept of God (Ronnie)

The focus of chapter three will center on defending the coherence of the Christian concept of God, considering such key attributes as divine goodness, simplicity, immutability, eternity, omnipotence, and omniscience.

Chapter 4 – Divine Providence (Ronnie)

Chapter four will consider the Christian doctrine of providence, examining various models (e.g., determinism, compatibilism, generic providentialism, and Molinism), while also considering divine and human freedom, miracles, and intercessory prayer.

Chapter 5 – Scripture and Revelation (Ronnie)

The purpose of chapter five will serve to examine the rationality and concept of divine revelation, while also considering the authority, inspiration, and truthfulness of the Bible.

Chapter 6 – Trinity and Incarnation (Ronnie)

Chapter six will examine the teachings and claims of Jesus, his deity and resurrection, and his relationship to Jewish monotheism, while also defending the coherence of the Christian concept of the Trinity.

Chapter 7 – Creation, Fall, Redemption (Ronnie)

Chapter seven explores philosophical problems related to the nature and contingency of creation, human fallenness, the nature of atonement, and sanctification.

Chapter 8 – Human Dignity, Moral Transformation, and the Holy Spirit (Dave)

Chapter eight examines the resources within Christian theology for human value, dignity, and worth, while also exploring the relationship between moral transformation and the empowering work of the Holy Spirit in the life of the individual and the Church.

Chapter 9 – Evil, Hell, and Suffering (Dave)

Chapter nine will offer a response to the problem of evil and the problem of hell, exploring the nature of Christian theodicy and defense.

Chapter 10 – Heaven, Resurrection, and Future Hope (Dave)

Chapter ten will round out the book by exploring the Christian doctrines of resurrection and heaven.

Conclusion

Glossary

Bibliography

Subject Index

Scripture Index

Thursday, June 3, 2021: Still not productive yet; hopefully soon. Ronnie and I strategized a bit about our book. Other than that, I took it easy, hoping I bounce back soon. Good prayer and chat time with TJ. He encouraged me to pray an imprecatory prayer regarding Liberty. The place just maddens me. I need to entrust it all to God.

Missing MB but hoping her time in Lynchburg is productive. She sent a pic of our old house, which was a little surreal. I did turn a corner on my eating today, cutting down on carbs almost altogether. Would love for this summer to be show real progress on that front (and exercise) along with writing. Really need to take full advantage of this chance. Knowing that, though, doesn't always conduce to following through; sometimes quite the opposite.

Friday, June 4, 2021: Today I finally was able to go to the Fort Bend library to work. Been here for a little while. Just finished a blurb for Ortlund's book on why God makes sense of life: "Ortlund's considerable talents applied to the ultimate question have yielded an impressive feat and an eminently readable treatise both academically rigorous and deeply personal. Impressively researched and beautifully crafted, the book makes contagious the author's obvious delight at exploring life's mysteries that collectively cast an animating vision of gripping beauty and enchanting transcendence. Without triumphalism it features epistemically modest hearty reasoning that invites readers into a conversation and close consideration of existentially central threads of evidence—from math to morals—that end up weaving a lovely tapestry and a needed corrective to the postmodern fragmentation of truth, goodness, and beauty."

It's about 1:30 in the afternoon now and I'm turning my attention to the book with Craig. Have editing to do and then collating and answering a slew of questions.

Worked until nearly 5 and made good progress on the Craig book, then spent the evening with Rob and Jer. Really hoping to finish up work on the Craig book by the time MB gets back from VA.

Saturday, June 5, 2021: Today was my sister Sandra's and my brother Mark's birthday—they were born a year apart to the day. Didn't speak with either, but posted something on FB for them. Hope they had a good day; miss seeing them in person.

Missing MB today. I spent most of the day working, after chatting with Elton in the morning. Up to about 35 questions and answers for the Craig book, as I'm working through his resources at his site. Have to figure out a way to wrangle this treasure trove of material. I wrote and told Craig I thought the book would likely be closer to 100K words.

Received this sweet note today from Jan Shultis:

Good morning, Dave and Marybeth,

Hope your Saturdays are off to wonderful starts and especially that you are enjoying Virginia and an easy move back to Texas with your son, Marybeth, woo hoo!!!! NOW your move here will be complete ☐

Before blog stuff, I wanted to mention that I just started taking in the material you shared about Liberty this week on Facebook, and I continue to lift you both in prayer, and the faculty and colleagues still there. My heart breaks that you have had to go through this, but you are walking these events with grace, dignity, and candor. Keep walking.... He will resolve this. You are doing a good job.

General blog stuff - God is working on my life and lifestyle, so prayers that I hear correctly and guide my household in His will are very much appreciated. He wants me to work very deliberately in these pieces for moralapologetics.com, more thoroughly than perhaps I ever have. He tells me to arrange the things that support intellectual stamina, such as minding my physical health and my home. He tells me to say "no" to anything that does not support the work at HBU, which includes both doctoral studies and the Center (He says that the job in biotechnology supports the primary work for now, but my spidey senses say that may or may not be a long-term proposition). I feel a bit of anxiety knowing that this is a new phase of life and I have to develop new skills to do what He wants, in this way.... more faith than anxiety, but I'm fighting to keep my mind calm and unworried, if that makes sense. Thank you for listening, and for your prayers.

Okay, now onto the blog! In the spirit of the above, I took a couple of extra days to research every wonderful comment you made, Dave. Thank you SO MUCH for your time and wisdom (and Amazon, for the Jaki books to be delivered soon ☐). Attached is an updated effort, reflecting the following changes:

- I stated clearly that I disagree with the clinician in this dialogue and his views of faith, evidence, and philosophy. I also realized that I can do that - I can say I disagree, in writing. That sounds so silly, I know, but it feels a little bit like a baby apologist growing up ☐
- I removed the reference to Plantinga because I want to read more widely, then come back to Plantinga's book. Craig wrote this in 2012 - Alvin Plantinga's Where the Conflict Really Lies: Science, Religion, and Naturalism | Scholarly Writings | Reasonable Faith - and I don't want to bring up Plantinga until I'm well-read enough to justly take in Craig's criticisms. I am VERY excited by Craig's assessment of where the next generation of philosophers might draw inspiration from Plantinga's book for future work, so I also want to read it again to mine it more carefully for inspiration. When I do talk about Plantinga's book as we go along in this blog series, I want to be able to *do* something robust with it. So for now, I'm going to wait.
- I tightened up the terminology for clarity and per your recommendations.

Standing by for the next round and happy to continue working this until it's a credit to our team. THANK YOU for giving so generously of your time to me.

Oh! Forgot to mention - God also told me to sit down and read the entire Bible, from the beginning, in order, both for me but also for work. I'm doing that, and as of Genesis 3, have insight for the next couple of blogs. I know Genesis is rich in science-y stuff, but still, that made me laugh.... that seems fruitful for just a few pages of study, and I am excited for His instructions ☐ Onward!

With hugs for a happy day,

Jan

Love her enthusiasm and energy and serious effort to discern God's leading! So inspiring! What a blessing to have her onboard.

Sunday, June 6, 2021: Marybeth went to Bethany this morning. That was probably great fun. Then they visited my mom's grave across the street, and now they are at La Villa's. Nathaniel got the Katie Special. Rude. He's also emotionally recovering from having heard I'm not a big fan of *Blazing Saddles*.

Dr. Craig responded to my update with this note: "Very good—and thanks for the excessive praise! In going through the videos I'm deleting a lot of the questions because many were not very good and my answers were lame. So please be selective!" That made me laugh. As it happens, though, I simply have to be selective in light of the abundance of answers he's given to questions about the moral argument over the years. I aspire to be lame like him!

I jokingly put this on FB today: "This living without a wife for a week business is for the birds; I'm just putting that out there. I had 46 years of this aloneness already. I didn't need 46 years and another week. My cats, though undeniably cute, are not nearly as good conversationalists as MB."

Monday, June 7, 2021: MB and Nathaniel are working hard to get ready to move him here. They plan to leave either Wednesday afternoon or Thursday morning.

I worked all afternoon on the Craig book. The manuscript is now around 95,000 words. Hope to cap it at 100K. Getting there!

President Sloan responded to my e-mail update from some days ago in which I told him of the OUP contracts and potential conference. Here is what he wrote:

Dave, thank you so much for this update. These sound like very good projects, and they should definitely bring some visibility to HBU and also shed light on some very important topics. Grateful for your work. Thanks for keeping me posted.

Let's continue to think along the lines of your original endeavors and conversations as well, i.e., seeing if we can cultivate the resources to fund a center on these important matters.
All blessings, Robert Sloan

To which I responded with this:

Will do, Mr. President! Marybeth and I have prayed a lot about the resources issue, and have begun sending out feelers for speaking engagements and the like to generate a buzz. If I may point out just a few of our ongoing initiatives: We have enlisted an enthusiastic graduate student here at HBU (a Naval Academy graduate) with experience in public relations who's going to start in conjunction with HBU sending out press releases about activities of the Center. Marybeth and I are still planning to give a significant gift on her fiftieth birthday, November of next year. We remain confident that this financial piece of the puzzle will fall into place in due course. Working with Phil this summer to glean insight from a fundraising expert. (I admit I'm on a big learning curve on this matter.) In the fall, incidentally, Marybeth and I have been asked to give the Strauss lectures at Lincoln Christian University, where we hope to do more to cast the vision for the Center. All of which to say, the original vision is intact and we remain committed to it, trusting God for the increase.
Blessings in all you do, Dave

And he answered like this:

Dave, thank you so much for this additional update. These are very encouraging developments on several different levels.
God bless you and Marybeth in all your endeavors. Grateful for your work in all these spheres.
Sincerely, Robert Sloan

Tuesday, June 8, 2021: What a day! We found out Nathaniel hadn't taught last year and would need some financial help with the move. We can do that, though he will need to get to the bottom of some of these behaviors. Fitting that today a FB memory came up from nine years ago: "Tonight as I watched my stepson walk across the stage to get his high school diploma, the past 18 years flashed before my mind. When I tried to think back on the many times we must have played catch, gone to a game, watched movies, wreaked psychological damage on one another, and all that other father-son stuff, my mind inexplicably drew a blank. In some sense it all seemed to vanish into this moment. It was almost as if the last 18 years hadn't even happened, that we were strangers who had rather recently met, like the time had passed but in the blink of an eye, and all the moments I must have worried about his future, his maturation, his sexual orientation, had never happened at all. All that mattered was this moment spent anticipating his bright future, assuming the nimrod didn't blow it with boneheaded decisions. Love you, son!"

I worked today a bit on the Craig book and housecleaning, then in the evening accompanied Jerry to Theology on Tap. A really interesting event! Probably sixty or seventy predominantly young people convened to discuss theology. Stimulating and encouraging time! Taylor Neill is on the leadership team; he's my Senior Student Fellow at the Center! Very cool.

Wednesday, June 9, 2021: TJ expressed an openness today to come back to Moral Apologetics! So excited! And some of the other research fellows have hatched a plan for a handbook on moral apologetics. Wow! Just marvelous!

Got confirmation from my dean today that my certificate summer classes, if they make, will count toward load. This bodes very well for my research.

A fourth podcast on Liberty came out today about LU with Gangster Capital, in which MB plays a large role. So proud of her. Erudite, incisive, perspicacious. Recent revelations about Liberty on top of what we already knew have shown me that I'm still getting over the experience. This brought to mind today my impatience with a colleague here at HBU some months ago when he suggested improvements to a syllabus of mine. I had already apologized to him, but I felt compelled to write him again today:

> Jason, I want to apologize to you again for getting angry with you a few months ago when you were only doing your job. I have thought a lot about what happened since then, in an effort to make sense of it. I was disproportionately upset, and I knew it, but couldn't quite figure out why. In today's lingo, I felt triggered for some reason, but wasn't at all sure what the cause was.
>
> In retrospect—and none of this is designed to defend my response, but just to explain it a bit—I think I've had to come to terms with something over the last year since coming to HBU. And this is at the heart of what happened, I think. The last years at Liberty were excruciating, and near the end it was well-nigh intolerable. We have some other friends who left there and liken the aftermath to PTSD. I suspect there's something to it. I had honestly thought when we left I'd left Liberty behind--and though we did physically, the traumatic aspects of the experience have lived with me, and this whole past year I have experienced moments intermittently when things would manifest that genuinely surprised me. I have sadly come to see that some deep vestiges of my time there remain embedded within me. I'm working on getting past it, but it's more than a simple matter of forgiving and/or forgetting. Some real damage was done there by an uncaring and callous administration whose behavior toward and treatment of faculty was inexcusable. By turns the experience was much like one of dehumanization in certain regards. Being there fourteen years gave the operative dynamics of the place a lot of opportunity to seep their way into my psyche, and the process of full emotional extrication and healing is taking more time than I

had realized it would. And sadly, what I did toward you was also inexcusable and disrespectful in the extreme, and I'm ashamed of it.

As I say, when I look back on that innocent e-mail of yours critiquing my syllabus with perfectly legitimate concerns, it dawns that, at the time, without even being consciously aware of it, something about it brought to the surface my rage at Liberty administrators who habitually kowtowed to corrupt senior leadership, treating Jerry Jr.'s every word and dictum as sacrosanct, no matter how reprehensible, and who in the process made for a highly dysfunctional work environment. It had everything to do with this baggage that I sadly brought with me and nothing to do with you at all, even though you were the object of my outburst. Again, I am genuinely sorry, Jason. You didn't deserve it, and nothing like that will ever happen again, I assure you.

Blessings, brother, Dave

Marybeth and Nathaniel are about to hit the road. She's anxious to get back. I've missed her a great deal. Jan wrote us this afternoon with a church speaking opportunity:

Hi, Team Baggett,

Simonton Community Church (42 min from HBU, and my home church) is seeking new relationships with thought leaders in our community, and called me today to ask about your availability - are you all perhaps available Sunday, July 4th, 18th, or 25th to do a one-hour presentation for 75-100ish people (maybe more) on the moral argument? The church is looking both for summer speakers but also to develop a roster of more regular speakers for special workshops and events (Dr. Blackwell has been out multiple times).

You can learn more at simontonchurch.org. SCC is about a 400-member congregation in rural FB County. They are an affluent community church with a higher-than-average educational level, and a strong commitment to Scripture as the ultimate source of wisdom. Lot of engineer types, and a genuine thirst for intellectual development. I have attended off and on for 8 years, and formally joined the church in 2019; my daughter was baptized by our pastors at SCC in the pictures I shared on FB. SCC is also the most committed resource sponsor of The Xena Project, the non-profit ministry I founded (I am speaking at both sermons on July 4th on moral injury, in the context of a covenant partner update from The Xena Project).

The Sunday format is 8:30 service, 9:45-10:45 Bible studies, 11 a.m. service. During the school year they offer as many Bible studies as we can, but in the summer there is one consolidated educational offering.

Fingers crossed that you are available and interested! Once I hear back, I'll do a group email introducing you to Pastor Kenny Johnson, who is very much a kindred intellectual spirit. He's been my biggest cheerleader in studies, and loves to see what books we're reading at HBU □

Thank you!!!! Happy Wednesday □

Jan

Thursday, June 10, 2021: Worked today on the Craig book. Wrote him afterwards:

On track to get you a working manuscript by this weekend, Dr. Craig. It will remain malleable, of course; perhaps some questions in the last section could be eliminated or replaced; some notes will still need filling in; etc. But it'll provide a good idea of what the book would look like.

I had a thought about the conclusion, which we can do later once we decide to move forward and secure a contract. If you'd like me to write it, I could stand back a bit from all our work and talk a little about ways we differ. The main emphasis up until then will not have been on any differences but on the vast areas of overlap and strong points of resonance between us. That's the far more important thing. But having put it off until the end, perhaps (just an idea I'm kicking around) it might be interesting for readers to hear a brief description of points of departure.

To my thinking this might accomplish several things--put such relatively small differences into the larger context of predominant agreement; add a little color and texture to the book; encourage readers to think about the relevant questions themselves (is the counteressential premise in your deductive argument nontrivially true?; might the moral argument gesture to more than mere theism, perhaps something distinctively Christian?; etc.); and it would show readers that we're not shying away from admitting we don't entirely see eye to eye 100% on everything.

That last point might prove helpful, especially for me, so that I don't come across as capitulating to your authority, which is something of a temptation, admittedly! Anyone who knows me knows the respect I have for your work, as so many do. You have an incredible influence on the apologetic community, and sometimes I want to tell my students it's okay if they do something other than defer to or quote you! □ I think it's good for the apologetic community to see that as philosophers we don't always have to be lock in step on every fine-grained and relatively peripheral point—and, importantly, that the moral argument goes through without such unanimity. Like I say, just a thought! Feel free to nix it!

I hope to send you the manuscript and proposal on Saturday. This has been a ton of fun to work on, just a real joy and privilege.

Best, Dave

Craig wrote back a gracious note in which he said he'd prefer my telling him personally where I think he's wrong since he considers me the authority; ha! I assured him it's less a matter of my thinking him wrong and more a case of a few technical vexed questions on which reasonable folks can disagree. But I'll have to find the right way to nuance the conclusion if I go this way; we'll figure it out soon, I'm confident.

Friday, June 11, 2021: I neglected to share yesterday an e-mail I received about how to qualify to train chaplains. Here it is:

Dave,

You once mentioned the desire to investigate the possibility of endorsing military chaplains.
I have attached a copy of the current DoD Instruction on such matters (DoDI 1304.28).

Below are addresses and links for you and your team to start gathering the requisite background and guidance for attempting to become an "official" ecclesiastical endorser.

CAPT William S. Riley, US Navy
Executive Director, Armed Forces Chaplains Board
OUSD (P&R) MPP - AFCB
4000 Defense Pentagon (Rm 2D580)
Washington DC 20301-4000
Email: osd.afcb5120@mail.mil

Link: https://prhome.defense.gov/M-RA/Inside-M-RA/MPP/AFCB/
Ecclesiastical Endorsing Agents: https://prhome.defense.gov/M-RA/MPP/AFCB/Endorsements/

Please let me know how else I can be of assistance!

Very Respectfully,
LT Billy Hardison
Command Chaplain

I worked hard throughout the day and sent Craig the manuscript of the book and a tentative book proposal. It's about 95% done, close enough for us to secure a contract. Earlier today, I think it was, Craig sent out a Newsletter for Reasonable Faith that touched on the class:

> May was highlighted by team-teaching a two-week course on the moral argument for God with Prof. David Baggett at Houston Baptist University. Although I have defended the moral argument for God's existence in debates with secular philosophers like Paul Kurtz, Walter Sinnott-Armstrong, Louise Antony, and most recently Erik Wielenberg, I had never actually taught a course on this argument, as I have on the kalām cosmological argument and the argument from fine-tuning. But Dr. Baggett, a widely published expert on the moral argument, invited me to join with him in teaching this course, and it was a privilege to do so. I taught virtually via the Internet, while Dave was on location. In addition to the students at HBU attending in person, we had around 50 students joining us online, not only from around the US, but also Canada, New Zealand, and Australia.
>
> I was pleased at the enthusiastic response of the students to the lectures. I think that the moral argument is widely misunderstood in various ways, and having those misconceptions cleared up, especially in the Q &A times, really made the light come on for many of these students. I think that they began to see the true strengths of an ethics that is grounded in God rather than a secular view. All the lectures were video-recorded and after editing will eventually be available on YouTube. Even more exciting, Dr. Baggett proposes that we combine our lectures, along with a substantial Q & A section, into a joint book on the moral argument! That would be a wonderful ministry tool.

Saturday, June 12, 2021: Marybeth and Nathaniel got home today at long last. I finished cleaning the house first, and had dinner ready for them when they arrived. Later we went to Nathaniel's apartment, where I'd picked up the key earlier. Nice little one-bedroom. His two crazy cats, Jasper and Sonny, will enjoy it. Nice that he's little more than five minutes away. Hope the move is a new chapter for Nathaniel.

Tomorrow Nathaniel has some hired help to assist unloading the truck. I'm planning on taking the day off, for the most part, then hitting it hard again on Monday—lots to do this summer, and it's just begun.

Sunday, June 13, 2021: Marybeth is over at Nathaniel's, and the two helpers they hired should be arriving any time. The truck will be unloaded, and about eight boxes of books we gave to Nathaniel will be returned to us, most for Marybeth. They will go to our shelves over at school. Not planning on any other work today. We will lunch with Nathaniel after the move. Need to gear up for a big week of work; I'll be working on three different books from here until the end of summer: the 4th in the tetralogy, the Collection, and phil theo with Ronnie. (If the Craig book is a go, I'll find myself simultaneously collaborating on books with Gary Habermas, Jerry Walls [twice], Marybeth, Ronnie Campbell, William Lane Craig, and John Hare.) Love having a clear purpose in the summer. MB and I might wish to go see a movie this afternoon. *Cruella* looks fun, and Nutter suggested Billy Crystal's new movie. Sure am glad Marybeth is home, missed her immensely, and praying that this is a clean slate and new beginning for Nathaniel, some bad habits left behind and replaced with much healthier ones. For his sake and ours! Tentatively hopeful. God is good; his love is so much greater than our sin.

Monday, June 14, 2021: Busy day! Started by going to the gym early, listening to scripture, and giving feedback on two blogs. Then MB and I went to the library to work. I sent out invitations to Hare, Crosby, and Copan for the Collection. Hare said yes to write a chapter on Kantian moral faith; still waiting to hear from the others. We also helped Nathaniel get new tires in the course of the day, and MB challenged him to think more about what happened last year. Craig got back to me and suggested a more integrated book; I told him I think I could do that; actually an exciting prospect. And TJ and I talked and prayed, and he's back at Moral Apologetics! Just sent him an invitation to replace me as Executive Editor of MoralApologetics.com. If he accepts, I'll share more of my logic in conferring this offer in my upcoming contribution to the newsletter. Good day! (He soon accepted and I know he'll do a bang-up job!)

Tuesday, June 15, 2021: I wrote TJ today with some information about the website as he takes over, and also introduced him to Jan and vice versa. Other than that I have been at the library extending more invitations for folks to work on the Collection. I asked Angus Menuge, for example, to write on debunking objections. I also used a big white board to organize the chapters and help me to get my mind around the whole project. It is thoroughly engrossing, occasionally daunting, but exciting. About to extend a series of very important invitations: Craig, Pruss, Moreland, Evans, Adams, Idziak, Rist, etc. By day's end I got Hare, Menuge, and Moreland onboard, a few others pending. Making progress. Just takes time to do this job right. Nathaniel was incommunicado today, apparently uninterested in giving us updates on the job search. Unfortunate. After working MB and I caught *Peter Rabbit 2* at the movies, which was harmless fun.

Also reworked the Craig book proposal on the basis of a more integrated structure that looks like this: (1) History; (2) Moral Realism; (3) Deductive Argument; (4) Abductive Argument; (5) First Half of My Abductive Case; (6) My Second Half; (7) Nontheistic Explanation; (8) Q & A. Definitely think we are getting there!

Wednesday, June 16, 2021: I set out to get the Craig book in good enough shape to send out with the proposal, and finally managed to send a revision to Craig. Here's what he wrote in reply:

> Man, you are so much more *tüchtig* than me! I still have yet to go through the first draft.
>
> Let me say, however, that I trust your judgement. But I'd like you to remove the encomium from the book's introduction. You are the anchor man for this book, not I. Moreover, your name should go first, having alphabetical priority. The Origin Story is better placed in a Preface to the book. I suggest you begin by describing your expertise, as you do later, and then pulling me in subsequently.
>
> Chap 1 could then combine the structure of the moral arg with the historical background into one chapter.
>
> Bill

Tüchtig means "proficient." I looked it up. Ha! Well, I told him "Will do!"

I also filled out some paperwork for the big grant we're applying for to put on a major conference on moral apologetics here at HBU that was due today. Now I need to fill out the proposal for the grant itself.

Nathaniel has yet to apply for any jobs. MB and I trying to figure out what to do about that.

Thursday, June 17, 2021: TJ agreed to counsel Nathaniel a bit over the phone and that happened today, which was a good sign. Nathaniel also signed up for a temp agency, another good sign. And MB took him to the Urgent Care to get checked out—and perhaps prescribed some anti-depressants, which would be a third good sign. She was also going to take him shopping so he won't have to eat out every meal. Baby steps; perhaps all of this will help generate some positive momentum moving forward. It's now nearly 5 in the afternoon; I'm in the library working on the grant proposal due this upcoming Monday. Asking for 30,000 dollars to subsidize a major conference at HBU on the moral argument within a few years. Currently writing out answers to questions like "project narrative," "plan of action," and "product."

Friday, June 18, 2021: Yesterday ended up a good day for Nathaniel, I think. He did some shopping, saw a doctor, arranged for some anti-depressants, spoke with TJ for a bit, and spent the evening with us. Marybeth helped him throughout the day; hopefully he's getting oriented and situated and will soon be fully on his feet. Folks need a little help sometimes. I'm so proud of how MB is handling this latest challenge. Such a wonderful mother.

With Marybeth's help today I finished up a draft of all the grant stuff and sent it in to the grant consultant. I'll get that gal's feedback and then finalize stuff by Monday. Here is what I came up with for a portion of it anyway (and now after sending out a few more Collection invites and tweaking the Craig book, we're going to some movies!):

AMOUNT: $30,000

PROJECT TITLE: Moral Apologetics Conference & Collection

PROJECT ABSTRACT (400 words): This project is designed to address the pressing question of the foundations of ethics, no merely theoretical matter but one of profound practical and existential import. Ethics includes moral goodness in terms of both that which is intrinsic value and that which is good/best for human beings. The range of ethics robustly and realistically construed runs the gamut and traverses a wide territory, and the question to be explored concerns which worldview provides the most comprehensive and compelling account of the full range of moral phenomena in need of explanation. This exploration broaches the topic of theistic ethics versus secular ethics and the relative merits of the moral argument for God's existence. In the past decade or so there has been an appreciable resurgence of interest in this argument. When asked which argument from natural theology has the most potential, Alvin Plantinga said the moral argument; and when William Lane Craig was asked which argument has the most effect on college campuses when he engages in debates about God's existence, his answer was the same. Despite the fact that there have been numerous books covering one dimension of the moral argument or another, there is no single collection in print that navigates the whole ground and consolidates and integrates the diverse work that has been done. This project has for its aim a conference that will rectify that situation, culminating in a major new collection of nearly thirty fresh articles on the moral argument that will collectively cover the whole territory—from its venerable history to the alternatives to moral realism, from debunking objections to the problem of evil, from axiological to deontic matters, from epistemological to rationality and performative variants of the moral argument, from diverse theistic ethical accounts to critiques of secular and naturalistic efforts to explain the range of moral phenomena, and from non-Christian ethical accounts to distinctively Christian ones. The academic conference will feature the best theistic thinkers on the moral argument coming together to share their insights and findings, generating the most expansive and rigorous academic treatment of the moral argument for God's existence to date. The attendees—from Hare to Moreland, from Menuge to Craig, from Evans to Idziak to Zabzebski—will share drafts of their chapters in progress that will, when completed, be combined into a major edited collection, the first of its kind, already under contract with a major university press.

PROJECT NARRATIVE (3000 characters): The project began with implementing a longstanding vision to procure a book contract for a collection on the moral argument. It has been a real gap in the literature for a while now, especially with all the recent developments. There has been work in a cluster of closely related areas germane to theistic ethics and moral apologetics. In terms of historical recovery of the work done on the moral argument by luminaries through the centuries, work devoted to defending moral realism against objections and arguing in its favor, critiquing error theory, constructivism, and expressivism in various forms, explicating and defending a variety of theistic ethical accounts, laying out the rich range of moral phenomena in need of robust explanation, critiquing alternative nontheistic and non-Christian accounts of ethical foundations, and extending the moral argument beyond bare or generic theism to something more distinctively Christian, work has been done in each of these areas. What had yet to be done, however, was for all of this work to be consolidated and put into one accessible volume in order to give readers the full picture of where the discussion on the moral argument as a whole currently stands. So Yale's John Hare and I pitched the proposal for such a volume to Oxford University Press, and it was accepted with enthusiasm. As soon as that piece fell into place, we knew we wanted to apply for a grant to facilitate an academic conference that the contributors to the collection could participate in, reading drafts of their developing chapters. The synergy that could result from this collection of the best thinkers in this field doing cutting-edge work that is able to be integrated for the united purpose of advancing discussion of theistic ethics and this centrally important aspect of natural theology is most exciting. The conference will be an opportunity for iron to sharpen iron and for the participants themselves to become more fully aware of the way in which the varied pieces of this puzzle can come together to advance the case for the explanatory power of theism generally and Christianity particularly to account for a full range of ethical realities. The conference will be a boon and a blessing to the HBU campus, the larger community, and the whole academy as this community of scholars pool their efforts to showcase the level of rigor that's possible in explicating and defending the moral argument for God's existence. Having heard one another and benefited from the Socratic dialogue and give-and-take at the conference, the participants will be all the better able to finish their work strong, contributing to a better overall result when the collection is published. That volume will then have the potential to be widely disseminated, used in classrooms, and ignite interest in the moral argument for a whole new generation of thinkers and scholars and for many years to come, setting the bar higher than it's been set before when it comes to this particular discussion that is arguably of greater importance in our current cultural moment than ever before.

PLAN OF ACTION (3000 characters): John Hare and I are currently extending invitations to the best scholars we can think of to contribute to the collection. The end result, we are convinced, is going to be an unprecedented pool of talent directing their prodigious skills to zero in on a particular argument for God's existence from a number of mutually enforcing directions. Although in one sense the moral argument is *one* argument, in another it is a *variety* of arguments—ontological and epistemic, performative and rational—that are interconnected in several complicated ways. One of the tasks of the conference and collection will be to accentuate the internal cumulative case that is possible when it comes to the moral argument. Another will be to help more scholars and prospective scholars, not to mention informed lay people and various practitioners, to see the need for an active community of moral apologists, philosophers, Bible scholars, literature experts, historians, social scientists, and theologians working diversely but in tandem to do justice to the richness of this material and ongoing research agenda that has only begun to show its potential. After finalizing the best list of contributors we can, we hope to be able to extend to them an offer to attend this conference at HBU, site of the newly formed Center for Moral Apologetics (which I direct), all expenses paid—their room, board, travel, etc. This will be to help ensure as wide participation among the contributors as we can generate. If possible we would even like to offer a small stipend to each participant for their valuable time and contributions, but that may or may not be financially feasible. If we could at least fully subsidize their trips to Houston it would help ensure a thriving and memorable conference that can strongly establish HBU as a central hub of cutting-edge research on the moral argument and inspire scholars there and elsewhere to see more clearly the arena of theistic ethics and moral apologetics as a viable and vital research agenda. The conference and subsequent collection will be a powerful testimony to HBU students, scholars and students elsewhere, the wider Houston community, and the church and society as a whole that the evidential significance of morality is strong and a real clue about the nature of ultimate reality, rightly imbuing believers with greater confidence in the rational defensibility and practical power of their principled convictions.

PRODUCT (1500 characters): Besides the conference itself, which will be a powerful outreach both to the HBU and wider community, the conference will end up having a quite palpable product: a 250,000-word collection on the moral argument that fills a vitally important gap in the literature. Oxford University Press was enthusiastic in its offer of a contract for John Hare and me to edit the volume, admitting that there was nothing like it in existence and acknowledging the power such a volume would possess to advance serious work in this area. We are convinced that the resultant volume will be a very welcome publication, one sorely needed in the field at this time, for several reasons, one of which is because there are several classes for which such a text would be a welcome textbook—where there is currently no such text. Our rationale is to bring together, in one conference and then in one volume, a comprehensive synthesis of the current thoughts regarding what may seem the disparate field of theories, concepts, arguments, and monographs devoted to various facets of the moral argument and allied topics. Here is what one reviewer wrote concerning the book proposal: "The moral argument has become a hot field in apologetics, and this book speaks directly to a need in the market—and a want. As I said above, if the book is sculpted to be high on readability, this will augur well for marketing and sales, it seems to me. I recommend that Oxford definitely offer to publish this text. It is a wonderful proposal and fills such an important niche, just as the proposal claims. Bravo!"

I wrote Brian Chilton, such a kindred spirit, this little rant today about a FB status we both saw the other day lamenting so much preaching on God's love (because, after all, God's also holy, just, etc.): "I think of a loving parent, and it reminds me that love isn't indulgent or ultra-permissive. A loving parent doesn't let a child do anything they want; that's unloving, not loving. Love disciplines, chastens, holds accountable, desires the best for the child, etc. (As well as shows mercy, grace, provides help, and so on.) Who would say, 'A parent is loving BUT also exercises discipline'? If someone does say that, it's obviously confused. There's not so much as an implicit tension between such things. There's no such thing as loving a child too much; 'inordinate love' is actually not loving the child properly. Too many Christians are buying into a degraded notion of love as maximal indulgent permissiveness; what's needed is not less an emphasis on love, but the right understanding of love, which includes desiring the best for the beloved, God's chastening his children, and the like. That fellow the other day was deeply confused, but sadly such confusions are legion nowadays, even among leaders who are as pedantic as they are dogmatic on such issues. Here's another chronic confusion: God doesn't want us to be happy, but holy. Wow. Of course God wants us holy, but God also wants us to be happy, because he loves us and this is what we were meant for: the joy that comes from loving God and neighbor. It's so problematically simplistic. The biblical relationship between holiness and happiness is deeply nuanced and richly textured; ultimately we have principled grounds for believing in their perfect airtight connection. Way too much biblical material we ignore if we piously emphasize holiness to the exclusion of the joy for which we were created. Again, otherwise this sentiment capitulates to the poor understanding of happiness we find in our society's degraded depiction of it. What about the joy of the Lord is my strength? Or seek first God's kingdom and his righteousness and all these things will be added to you? Or the glory to come will make all the present sufferings be forgotten? Or the biblical theme of shalom, or the unspeakable joy to come when we behold the beatific vision? Sanctimony, inauthenticity, and superficiality far too often are the earmarks of popular theology today, sadly. Don't get me started on 'everything happens for a reason.' ☺ Anyhoo, I'm preaching to the choir, I know!! Love ya, bro."

Saturday, June 19, 2021: Had a hard time handling the Nathaniel situation today. Had felt pushed to my limit already, and now this. Ugh. Hoping he turns a corner soon. We offered him to cut eleven hundred dollars from what he owes us as long as he gets a job by this Friday. We will see.

Had to do a Roundtable Discussion about goodness for the WB today; here it is:

The topic of goodness, like that of truth and beauty, is of infinite richness, particularly if the good and God himself are as intimately tied together as one like Augustine thought. If God himself is the ultimate good, then it makes perfect sense that it's no easy matter to say just what goodness is, for the ultimate good would be nothing less than God himself, who defies our finite understandings and escapes our ability fully to define or comprehend. This is why Robert Adams suggests that, if such a picture is remotely accurate, we should retain a "critical stance" toward various and sundry accounts of goodness, because they are unlikely to be the whole picture.

Nowadays goodness tends to be treated in more domesticated and deflationary ways. Goodness is that which conduces to our flourishing, we hear it said, or goodness is what promotes social harmony. Or, following Aristotle, goodness is said to pertain to the function of something. A good car provides reliable transportation, for example. For a long while now, though, I have thought such an Aristotelian depiction of the good inseparable from a more Platonic conception—what is is good for us as human beings, for example, seems impossible to divorce from what is good in and of itself.

Although it makes sense to say that something is good to the extent it performs its function, a further question then always should be asked: Is that function a good thing? This is an especially important question to ask if we wish to think about moral goodness in particular. Of course goodness is broader than moral goodness, but moral goodness is a quite important part of goodness. And in fact, in many contemporary discussions, quite a bit of confusion reigns when it comes to moral and nonmoral goodness.

For example, we often hear that pain is bad, and surely it is. But it's not morally bad per se. It is nonmorally bad. What's morally bad is the needless infliction of pain for no good reason. It tends to be people who are morally good or morally bad. Immanuel Kant recognized this distinction when he distinguished between badness and evil. In plenty of contexts these terms are used interchangeably, but he used the distinction to highlight the difference between something that produces bad consequences and something distinctively and robustly, even perniciously, immoral. Inadvertently missing the nail with the hammer and hitting my thumb instead is surely the former, but hardly the latter.

Students sometimes insist on the need for a pithy, succinct account of goodness, but I suspect such a request is more difficult than it may seem. Besides getting clarity on whether the goodness to be defined is axiological or metaphysical, moral or nonmoral, and whether it's what's good in itself or good for us, still other questions press. Suppose we try to make our task simpler by delimiting the discussion to what is morally good for us. Rather than settling the matter, that step only raises new questions to consider. What sorts of creatures are we? What is good for us vitally depends on anthropology, who we are. It also depends on what range of goods there are. Is what is good for us merely the meeting of our physical needs—or are we spiritual and affective, aesthetic and relational beings as well? Is our deepest good fellowship with God and learning to love God and neighbor as ourselves? Is that the richest source of our deepest joy? Christianity would suggest just such an answer.

Besides questions of anthropology, answers to what ultimate goodness consists in also depend on the nature of ultimate reality. This means that one's conception of God is also at play here. A warped understanding of who God is will invariably diminish one's conception of ultimate goodness. So to insist that we provide a quick and easy answer to what goodness is without realizing that the right answer

depends on both an accurate picture of who we are and who God is will relegate one's answers to superficiality. Few topics are handled so poorly without due consideration of issues of transcendence and the sacred.

As a moral apologist I find the topic of goodness endlessly fascinating, for a number of reasons, one of which is that, like beauty, there is something ineliminably experiential about it. Those without the requisite taste of goodness in their lives are less likely to be moved by something like a moral argument for God's existence, just as those without the requisite experience of beauty are less likely to be persuaded by an aesthetic argument.

This is also why it is a powerful reminder to prospective apologists, as they strive to be salt and light in this world, to offer not just arguments but their very lives as evidence of the truth of the gospel. Like Fred Rogers would often say, our job is to make goodness attractive. And here again we see the truth that goodness and beauty are, as Plato could see, flip sides of the same coin. For goodness is, by its very nature, beautiful, which is why we find ourselves so drawn to it (and them).

I recently heard it said God doesn't want us happy, but holy. I think such a sentiment is deeply misguided. Surely God wants us holy—as he is holy. He's in the process of sanctifying us through and through, making us good, the people we were meant to be, the distinctive reflections of Jesus that God had in mind when he created us. But in that sanctified life, the joy of the Lord is our strength; there's the deepest fulfillment of which we are capable, the richest joy we can experience as we allow the divine life to take hold within us. We are made for fellowship, and we are told that the glory to come will render all the present sufferings insignificant by comparison. We are meant for goodness and holiness, it's true, and these do have a sort of primacy over happiness, but ultimately there is not the slightest tension between them. Rather than mutually exclusive, they are ultimately of a piece. We were meant for both goodness and eternal joy. The beatific vision for Christ followers could produce nothing less.

Sunday, June 20, 2021: This was supposed to have been the weekend for the NT Wright lecture at the Lanier library, but it was cancelled because of covid and travel restrictions. Instead it became a weekend of rest as I tried to bounce back from the Nathaniel debacle. MB spent time with him today laying some things out; she thought it was a good conversation. Time will tell. Surely hope so. Tomorrow I need to wrap up the grant proposal and submit it, and then, as time allows, finalize the Craig book to submit for a contract. Crazy summer; unrelenting. This afternoon MB and I relaxed with some Lupin; good show. Today was Father's Day. MB and I for several such occasions did a trip to DC. Not as practicable anymore.

Monday, June 21, 2021: Finished the grant proposal and sent it in. Boy, oh boy, what a harrowing experience. Paul Copan got back to me and accepted my offer to write on the problem of evil in the OUP Collection. So, so far, I have Moreland, Copan, Menuge, and Hare. Progress is a bit slower than I'd hoped it would be, but the grant proposal slowed me down quite a bit. Hopefully this week I can make a huge stride on enlisting more contributors as well as wrap up what I need to on the Craig book so we can send it out to prospective publishers. By mid-afternoon I got Steve Evans onboard; he'll be writing on the features of moral duties and the issue of accountability. And at just before 4 pm I wrote Janine Idziak.

Tuesday, June 22, 2021: Woke up to find that Idziak had accepted my invitation, expressing an interest in either DCT or divine desire/will theory. I told her I would prefer if she would take the latter; awaiting confirmation. But this means we have six in place, not counting me—though where I'll fit in remains to be seen. I think this means we're a quarter there. Making progress.

Yesterday on the grant application I identified Angus Menuge as the fellow to write an external letter in support of the grant. Here's an e-mail reply I got from Angus about it:

Dear Dave,

On the first question, of course, yes, I can write an outside reference supporting a grant for the conference you describe. Just let me know to whom I should address it, and I will get it done.

On the chapters, a couple of thoughts:

262

As I have done a series of previous works on the evolutionary debunking argument, it might be easiest for me to build on these.

I certainly can also do another chapter on human worth/dignity, but a couple of thoughts:

(1) If you haven't already got him for another chapter, Paul Copan would do a fine job here;
(2) If you'd specifically like an argument rooted in a personalist understanding of human dignity, Michał Rupniewski of the University of Łódź is interesting: he very much supports the personalist approach, and though he thinks it can be defended without explicit appeal to God, he might well be amenable to arguing that nonetheless theism provides the most natural worldview for explaining and justifying the personalist understanding.

One other suggestion for a different chapter:

I happen to know that Stephen Parrish has been working on a new book on meta-ethics, and he has some interesting and novel arguments against the kind of "atheistic moral Platonism" espoused by Wielenberg etc. His argument has nothing to do with the evolutionary debunking arguments but rather depends on primary ontology. His approach is to show that what people like Wielenberg need is "brute necessities," but that this is an incoherent idea, and that once one analyzes the ontological requirements for objective moral demands, only theism can deliver. Just a thought, so no worries if it doesn't belong.

Angus

Spent all morning extending invitations to participate in the Collection, or at least inquiries to see if folks might be interested. Trying to get Wolterstorff's e-mail address; have written Murphy, Ebels-Duggan, Layman, Cuneo, Flannagan, Pruss, Adams, Ritchie, Crosby, Linville, Craig, Zabzebski, Kinghorn, and Anne Jeffrey.

Wednesday, June 23, 2021: Murphy turned me down, Ebels-Duggan is a possibility if I'm open to a reprint, Flannagan agreed to do both error theory and DCT, Pruss turned me down, Linville agreed, Craig turned me down, Zagzebski is a long shot. Finished the Craig book revisions, writing this foreword:

PREFACE: *Origin Story*

Some years ago a well-known Christian philosopher gave a piece of advice to budding apologists, namely, to specialize. I remember being struck by the advice, and I decided to heed it. I had had a number of philosophical interests, but for about as long as I can remember the topic of God and ethics captured my imagination.

On occasion I have wondered what contributed to that interest. I could be wrong, but I trace my own interest in issues of ethics to three important influences early in life. I have written about them elsewhere, so I won't elaborate, just mention them. All of these influences had wielded a mesmerizing effect on me before I was so much as six or seven years old.

One was watching Mister Rogers as a boy. When his show went national in the tumultuous year of 1968, I was in his original demographic, turning three by the end of that year. Fred Rogers was a soft-spoken man who touched generations with his warmth and gentleness. He made goodness attractive.

Another formidable influence was being raised in the camp meeting tradition. There was a time when a significant percentage of Americans was involved in camp meetings. Although their popular had waned by the time I was born, my upbringing continued to be steeped in this vintage piece of Americana that impressed on me from a very young age God's desire that we be not only forgiven for our moral failures, but deeply transformed.

A third influence was seeing a television commercial when I was very young that was encouraging watchers to contribute to the work of a relief agency. Indelibly etched into my memory until this day from that television spot is the image of an obviously needy child handed some food. It profoundly moved me, and I remember having the thought that there was something undeniably lovely and fitting about meeting the needs of a child in that way. So powerful was the recognition that I had the thought that nothing would ever persuade me otherwise. I was that sure of it. From then until now anything less than robust moral realism has had little draw for me.

In college I was initially planning to study math and physics, but then discovered philosophy, and eventually changed my major. It was ethics in particular to which I was drawn, and sometime during my undergraduate years I came across the Euthyphro Dilemma for the first time. It was advanced as an argument against the idea that morality finds its locus in God, which strained my credulity from the start. I didn't know exactly what to say about it, but I knew I wanted to think about it some more.

After college and seminary I started my doctoral work in philosophy at a highly analytic program at Wayne State University, and I knew from day one I wanted to write my dissertation on the Euthyphro Dilemma. I studied under some terrific philosophers like Bruce Russell and Mike McKinsey, Larry Lombard and Larry Powers, and wrote my dissertation on the Euthyphro Dilemma.

Initially that dissertation was going to feature a chapter on a moral argument for God's existence, but that chapter didn't make the final cut.

However, a few years later my friend and former seminary professor Jerry Walls turned the dissertation into a book and published *Good God: The Theistic Foundations of Ethics*, and the chapter on the moral argument made an appearance. The formulation of the moral argument at that point remained, however, a bit sprawling and lacking in focus. So Walls and I decided that we needed to extend the work. Having defended theistic ethics against various objections, we recognized the need to critique a variety of secular efforts to ground morality, so we ended up writing another book, *God and Cosmos: Moral Truth and Human Meaning*.

By then the vision of a tetralogy has crystallized in our minds, so the third in the series was a comprehensive history of the moral argument, and we are currently working on the fourth and last book in the series defending moral realism.[17] Between the second and third books in the tetralogy my wife Marybeth and I wrote a more popular version of the moral argument in *The Morals of the Story: Good News about a Good God* (IVP Academic, 2018).

Through the years I have had occasion to mix it up with some secular folks on the topic of God and morality—from Erik Wielenberg to Julian Baggini, from John Shook to Matt Dillahunty, and just recently the distinguished John Hare from Yale and I have been contracted to edit a major Collection on the moral argument.

In 2020 my wife and I moved from Virginia to Texas to teach at Houston Baptist University, where she's now a professor of English and cultural apologetics and I am a professor of philosophy and director of the newly formed Center for Moral Apologetics. (I will discuss the Center more in the conclusion of this book.) This role has opened yet new doors to work on the moral argument, and in May of 2021 I was able to co-teach a course with William Lane Craig at Houston Baptist University. Craig was the very one whose advice to budding apologists had led to my focusing on the moral argument. Our class was on the moral argument for God's existence, and taught as a two-week intensive. He taught the first week, and I the second. The experience was rich, meaningful, and memorable. Former NFL player and HBU alum Mike DeVito hosted the first week, and my wife Marybeth Baggett hosted the second.

Along the way I suggested we might combine the notes he used for the course with the notes I planned to write for the course, and then augment our lectures with answers to various questions. I broached the topic and Dr. Craig was game. Since he was open to the idea, after getting the notes he planned to use I wrote mine in such a way as to avoid too much overlap and to make our lectures cohere and augment one another's.

---

[17] David Baggett and Jerry L. Walls, *The Moral Argument: A History* (New York: Oxford University Press, 2019).

The book you hold in your hands, then, is the product of this course we jointly put together, though after a significant revision. In Professor Craig's portion of the lectures, first he discussed his well-known deductive version of the moral argument, focusing primarily on objective moral duties and values, and then canvassed an abductive version. He has employed both forms of argumentation in his dialogues on the subject, having debated the likes of Shelly Kagan, Paul Kurtz, Sam Harris, Erik Wielenberg, and others.

Both the students and I greatly enjoyed Dr. Craig's systematic approach; his is an impressively architectonic mind that zeroes in laser-like on the topic. The discipline and depth, and texture and tone of his lectures make either listening to them or reading them a great pleasure. Obviously, in an intensive course of this nature, there was much that could not be discussed at great length, but within the parameters imposed by the class he did an impressive job both giving the lay of the land and sharing a range of insights to enable students a solid grasp of the material. I greatly enjoyed listening to his lectures, learning a great deal from them, especially from the chance to see him apply his prodigious gifts to this topic about which I feel passionately.

In my own lecture notes, I originally tried filling in some details in such a way as to ensure that my notes would dovetail and cohere with his without redundancy. The four topics I covered during my lectures were the history of the moral argument, a defense of moral realism, a four-fold moral argument, and nontheistic alternative accounts of morality. Again, time constraints required that the treatment be fairly aerial at numerous points, more suggestive than exhaustive, but our hope was that both sets of lectures, especially when combined with a set of questions and answers, would provide for readers a robust foundation for further exploration and analysis in this vitally important area of natural theology.

In a book panel discussion of *Good God* about a decade ago, featuring Craig, Walls, and me, along with Paul Copan, Craig and I locked horns on deductive versus abductive formulations of the moral argument. Ironically it was Craig, once more, who had influenced me greatly on the matter of abduction. I had heard him defend the historicity of the resurrection with an abductive argument some years ago that got me thinking along those lines in my own moral argument. Although we dialogued in that panel discussion over the relative merits of the two forms of argument, what became clear is that we agreed on much more than we disagreed.

So this recent course we were able to teach together enabled us to pool our efforts and synthesize our work, resulting, we think, in a fuller and richer picture. Our work features many points of resonance, so to our thinking this made worthwhile the juxtaposition of our approaches. After initially putting our lectures side by side, we then came to see the potential for a more robust integration. Especially since our ideas resonate and augment each other's in so many ways, the material lent itself to a more integrated presentation than originally envisioned. So what follows is that intentional effort to forge a united and collaborative analysis. Different formulations of the moral argument are hardly at odds, in tension, or engaged in a zero-sum game. They rather complement and supplement one another in interesting ways.

The course required four books:

(1) Adam Johnson, ed. *A Debate on God and Morality: What is the Best Account of Objective Moral Values and Duties?* (Routledge) ISBN: 0367135647

(2) *Is Goodness without God Good Enough?: A Debate on Faith, Secularism, and Ethics*, edited by Nathan L. King and Robert K. Garcia (Rowman & Littlefield) ISBN: 0742551717

(3) C. Stephen Evans, *God and Moral Obligation* (Oxford: Oxford University Press, 2013) ISBN: 9780198715375, and

(4) David Baggett and Marybeth Baggett, *The Morals of the Story: Good News about a Good God* (IVP Academic) ISBN: 0780830852079

Because this book is the organic product of a single course, it is appropriately judicious in its ambitions. This material could have easily lent itself to a much longer volume, but we wanted, in this book, primarily to offer readers a basic understanding of the moral argument, to offer them a chance to see the lay of the land so they could feel more confidence to navigate it better, and to clear up a number of recurring and needless confusions that tend to surround the moral argument. The footnotes can direct readers to more detailed and fleshed-out discussions at numerous junctures.

Thursday, June 24, 2021: Today I wanted to finish two tasks: review a book proposal for Peckham's new book series, which I did, and write my WB piece for the month, which I started but didn't wrap up. It's the first step in my prep for what I hope to do next weekend at Jan's church; here's a bit of what I wrote:

In Lewis's *Til We Have Faces*, to have a face in the full sense means to acknowledge all of who we are. We are both made in God's image, but also sinners in need of grace. The former is essential to us; the latter is contingent. The way to authenticity and true identity is to grab hold of our identity as God's image bearers, renouncing the works of darkness to which our sinful bent inclines us. This is the way to the deepest fulfillment for which we were made, the most authentic self we can be.

In this God-formed identity there is both *solidarity* and *individuation*—we all of us have been made after God's likeness; this is something we all share in common as human persons. Yet at the same time each of us is unique, in the true sense of the word, unrepeatable, sui generis. Every one of us is called to inhabit a particular portion of the body of Christ; each of us is called to do the good works that God prepared beforehand for us to do. And for those who avail themselves of God's overtures of love, are reconciled to him, and saved to the uttermost, one day on a white stone their true name will be revealed—a secret between each of them and God. That name will be no merely arbitrary moniker, but a reflection of who God intended them to be.

In the evening Craig sent our book proposal to his agent Steve Laube, a Christian literary agent, suggesting he find a Christian publisher other than IVP. I had discouraged IVP Academic because of their bad track record getting my books into big bookstores. But then Craig mentioned Baylor University Press, which is a bit odd to my thinking, since they wouldn't get the book into Barnes & Noble or the like, either. Oh well, we will see.

Friday, June 25, 2021: C. Stephen Layman turned down the invite to the Collection, but in a remarkable series of e-mails something like a dream team became a possibility. Zagzebski said probably, Adams said to write him again in a year, and Wolterstorff said he'd think about it. That was tremendously exciting. Spent the afternoon trying to make progress on the upcoming WB piece/church presentation, a revised version will likely make an appearance in the book with Craig. A bit slow going, but perhaps I'm getting there. In the evening Jerry and I ate dinner and watched *American Beauty*, while MB and Nathaniel went out to eat and watched a movie in his apartment. Earlier in the day Nathaniel had another counseling session TJ, and the *Ragamuffin Gospel* arrived at the house from TJ for Nathaniel. I made Jonathan the General Editor of MAP today, and the paperwork arrived in the mail effecting the transition of MAP from an LLC to a nonprofit; by coincidence, Hare's and my new OUP contract for the Collection arrived in my inbox. Quite a day!

Saturday, June 26, 2021: Wasn't up to work today; just hit a wall, so decided to take the day off. It was nice. One little bit of work was interacting with Terence Cuneo, who seems open to writing a chapter on error theory. I just have to figure that out, since Flannagan had expressed interest in that chapter. So I floated some possible resolutions to Cuneo, and we'll see what he says. Hopeful we'll have him as a contributor, which will be huge.

MB and I rewatched much of *American Beauty*, doing a lot of commentary as we went along. It dawned on us that the movie has a tendency to fragment truth, goodness, and beauty in its myopic exaltation of beauty, which as a result seems not even to get the beauty part right. There are lots of appearance/reality distinctions in the movie, and the underlying theme is to "look closer," an encouragement of attentiveness with which I resonate and concur. But the sort of attentiveness counseled is problematic at points. Although the movie has some real highlights and delightful, well-nigh priceless moments, its heavy-handed and ethically dubious subversive subtexts undermine its quality, to my thinking. And the insufferable earnestness of the "solution" it offers at the end leaves much to be desired.

A couple other features of the day were these: my chat with Elton, and our evening with Jan. Elton shared some insights about the way Jesus had to come to terms with a certain loneliness or aloneness—scripture says he was amazed at the unbelief of his family; and in Gethsemane he couldn't count on his disciples for the prayer support he asked for. Those he should have been able to count on often proved unreliable. His family at one point even tried taking him home, thinking he had lost his mind. And of course on the cross he felt abandoned. Surely part of the sufferings by which he learned obedience involved certain successive realizations of what he was called to do that left him feeling isolated and misunderstood.

The evening with Jan and Kalyn was very nice. For nearly four hours we spent time getting better acquainted, sharing our visions, exploring the area of overlap between our calls to ministry, and praying at the end of our time together. Jan's story and background are fascinating; an Annapolis grad, she's been on two tours of duty overseas, has all sorts of real-world experience, and brings to the table a plethora of gifts and talents. She is a visionary, one who abounds in enthusiasm, and feels strongly called in the direction of addressing moral injury. Of course the Center is most prominently about exploring and explicating the goodness and love of God—not just God's *existence*, but *nature*. In short compass we found that one succinct and pithy way to capture the connection between our respective visions is that moral injury is the problem, while God's goodness is the solution.

Sunday, June 27, 2021: Largely took the day off. Listened to scripture in the morning, after church Marybeth and I fit in a nap. I did do a little work, mainly logistical work as director. Counseled TJ a bit on how best to help Jan see ways her work and that of the Center's can dovetail; elicited help with promoting books with MAP; encouraged JP on some ways in which to advertise our publications better; wrote the agent who's offered his services to me and MB and said we're interested and would like to chat on the phone when he gets a chance (same agent as Craig's and Pearcey's); and wrote an e-mail to Jason Sudeikis's managing firm to inquire if he may be willing to write a foreword for a book on Lasso and Philosophy. In the evening we watched a documentary on Mike Wallace and took a drive with Nathaniel that was a bit discouraging; he still seems slow to hustle getting a job and adamantly intent to talk about trivial stuff. It left MB down afterwards. Perseverance is hard sometimes.

Monday, June 28, 2021: Finally wrapped up this month's WB piece, then MB and I caught a movie and relaxed a bit:

The Haunting Value of Persons

A growing conviction of mine is that one's anthropology is heavily shaped by one's theology—one's view of persons is largely a function of one's view of God. This isn't to say that atheists can't have a working theory of persons or anything like that; indeed, we will see in a moment that their ability to do so is vitally important. Still, it is to suggest, among other things, that a high view of God tends toward an exalted view of persons, and a low view of God results in an emaciated understanding of them.

Of course this raises questions about what's meant by a high or low view of God, and exalted versus emaciated views of people. I'll have a few things to say about the former, but I'll mainly focus for now on the latter. Among the constellation of concepts associated with a high view of persons I would include the following: human beings are no garden-variety thing; they have great intrinsic worth and value. They are the legitimate bearers of fundamental rights; they should be treated with respect and dignity; there is something sacred and unspeakably precious about them, each and every one.

I suspect that this is part of the treasure of moral data that calls for adequate explanation, so I'm inclined to think it apologetically significant. Of course, at the same time, it's likely that the Christian worldview has contributed to my view of persons as so valuable and precious. So can I have it both ways, and suggest both that Christianity contributes to a high view of persons and the value of persons evidentially points to God and Christianity?

I suspect so, if there's at least a hint or echo of recognition even among unbelievers that people have great intrinsic worth, inherent dignity, and the like. This would helpfully suggest that all of us, believers and unbelievers alike, have access to a general revelational insight that there is something exceedingly special about human persons. Then special revelation can come along and perform what John Henry Newman called the ampliative function of accentuating such a truth and providing even more principled grounds for believing it to be so and finer-grained accounts of why and how it is true.

One need not be a believer to believe in basic human rights, but the more obviously true it is that such rights exist, the more pressing the question of what it is about reality that explains them in a deep and robust way. Grotesque human rights violations are so egregious and they grate against us at such deep levels because we intuitively and viscerally recognize that people should not be treated that way. Among what Steve Evans calls the "natural signs" that point to God is human dignity and worth, and Evans agrees with Nicholas Wolterstorff that belief in the value of human beings undergirds the conviction that we possess "natural right" as humans that arguably hold prior to any governmental fiats conferring such rights. They are moral rights, not merely legal ones; the legacy of one like Dr. Martin Luther King, Jr. highlights the primacy of such basic moral and human rights.

270

Perform an experiment and ask a secular friend if he or she believes in such rights, and especially if your interlocutor suspects you may have your doubts because of their unbelief, be prepared nine times out of ten for an indignant response otherwise. "Of course I believe in them, and I don't need to believe in God in order to believe in them," and of course they are right. Belief in God is assuredly not the key, but real explanatory depth and power may well require nothing less than God himself to undergird such important truths adequately. Why would such truths obtain in a naturalistic world, or a world in which we are all inexorably determined to behave just as we do, or a world in which people are just complex collocations of atoms and nothing more? The great utilitarian Jeremy Bentham thought the notion of basic human rights nothing but "nonsense on stilts."

The apprehension of such truths doesn't explain why they obtain; they may be *self-evident*, but they are not *self-explained*. Was Bentham right, or are rights something with which we have been endowed by our Creator, or something else? Such pressing questions remain for our consideration, and to leave them forever unaddressed bespeaks a lamentable lack of intellectual curiosity. Like the great German philosopher Immanuel Kant argued, people have *value* and *worth*, but not a *price*. There is an inherent dignity to persons that we deeply recognize, and it cannot be quantified or reduced to a dollar amount; there is something about it that is intangible, literally priceless. And somehow we know this, down deep, though we can forget it, or perhaps intentionally repress it, which brings us to an important point. For, if we can so readily recognize the value of persons, why do we so casually repress it?

A high view of persons is consistent with recognizing our capacity for wrongdoing and even malicious evil. The long history of cruelties and indignities imposed by persons on persons is evidence for something like the depraved moral condition in which we find ourselves, and there are few better examples than the temptation to engage in dehumanization and demonization of those we want to rationalize hideously mistreating. We have seen this pattern recur time and again: to name just a few, with the Nazi depiction of Jews, the ugly history of American chattel slavery, and, more recently, with the intellectual contortions of denying the humanity of unborn children to justify their wholesale slaughter. Even in such paradigmatic instances of reprehensible mistreatment, though, we see on ready display the perceived need to deny the humanity of the victims first. This is mistakenly thought to make it okay; somehow we would otherwise know the behavior is beyond the moral pale.

Austin Farrer was a friend of C. S. Lewis's who, in his own work, had for one of his main points of emphasis the value of persons. In one of his books he asked readers to consider the way we normatively ought to think about other people. It is of great importance, he argued, that we value them rightly, that we think about others in such a way as to regard them properly. The only limitation that such deep regard for others should encounter are those that cannot be avoided. Such regard should be at once so pure and so entire that it leads to a sort of frustration. This frustration derives from the incompleteness of our definition of those we so regard. Thinking of our neighbors in too garden variety a way cannot sustain the esteem we intuitively think they deserve. The conclusion to which Farrer felt compelled is that what deserves our regard is not simply our neighbor but God in our neighbor and our neighbor in God.

As David Bentley Hart says, the evolution in moral thought that enabled us to see the sacred and beautiful qualities in the Downs syndrome child, the aged, and the exile was a function of Christian influence. Only a myopic view of history fails to see the revolutionary force of Christianity in generating such moral insight. The longer I live, the more convinced I become that the important moral datum of the enchanted value of persons is best explained by nothing less than God himself—his creating us in his image, for reasons and purposes, his loving each of us, differently but infinitely. This challenges me each day to remember its profound implications. For example, the only real way to authenticity is to grab hold of our identity as God's image bearers, renouncing the works of darkness to which our sinful bent inclines us. This and only this path is the way to the deepest fulfillment for which we were made, the most authentic self we can be.

Another implication is to remember, as Lewis once put it, that there is no ordinary human being. "There are no ordinary people. You have never talked to a mere mortal. [I]t is immortals whom we joke with, work with, marry, snub and exploit—immortal horrors or everlasting splendors. This does not mean that we are to be perpetually solemn. We must play. But our merriment must be of that kind (and it is, in fact, the merriest kind) which exists between people who have, from the outset, taken each other seriously—no flippancy, no superiority, no presumption."

In our God-formed identity there is both *solidarity* and *individuation*—we all of us have been made after God's likeness; this is something we all share in common as human persons. Yet at the same time each of us is unique, in the true sense of the word, unrepeatable, sui generis. Every one of us is called to inhabit a particular portion of the body of Christ; each of us is called to do the good works that God prepared beforehand for us to do. And for those who avail themselves of God's overtures of love, are reconciled to him, and saved to the uttermost, one day on a white stone their true name will be revealed—a secret between each of them and God. That name will be no merely arbitrary moniker, but the deepest reflection of who God intended them to be all along and from the start.

Tuesday, June 29, 2021: Spent most of the time at the library reading the book on shame. About forty pages left to read, then I can try to write the review. If this week I could finish that and knock out this Sunday's presentation, that would be good. After this upcoming Sunday MB and I are going to take a few days at Galveston. The shame book is enabling me to understand some important insights on the matter. I'll share more of those soon. Jonathan sent us some potential covers for our book *Telling Tales*, and we finally decided on one we liked. MB is hard at work getting the book together, planning to use it in a fall class. Adam Johnson told me that the foreword for his book will be due around the beginning of August.

Wednesday, June 30, 2021: MB and I started today to give 100 bucks a month to World Vision to help with poverty and such. Had been on my mind for a while, and we can easily do it. JP sent us a seal for the Center for Moral Apologetics, each piece of which symbolizes something vitally important; very cool! John Hare wrote to say he's had an ear infection but hoped to get the contract in soon. MB and I spoke with our prospective agent in the late afternoon and, after asking him some questions and being satisfied by the responses, told him we were ready and enthused to sign on. I wrote the first draft of the CT review of the book on grief. And MB made good progress on *Telling Tales*. Amazing day! Toasted Yolk may even have made an appearance. Nathaniel also seemed open to the possibility of picking up a paralegal certificate; good sign. Here's the CT draft:

For Shame: Rediscovering the Virtues of a Maligned Emotion, by Gregg Ten Elshof (Zondervan)

When he was a schoolmaster at the Downs School in the Malvern Hills, 1933, W. H. Auden found himself sitting with three fellow teachers when he was suddenly overwhelmed by the sense that all their existence somehow had infinite value and that he loved them for themselves. Immanuel Kant said people have worth and value and dignity, but not a price. Austin Farrer wrote of God in our neighbor and our neighbor in God. There is an inherent dignity to persons that we deeply recognize, and it cannot be quantified or reduced to a dollar amount; there is something about it that is intangible, literally priceless. On a Christian conception, people are creations of God, made in his image, fashioned after his likeness, and they are loved by God, perhaps each of us differently, but all of us infinitely.

Human beings are intrinsically valuable in excelsis both in the aggregate and individually, but to say we are morally valuable is not to suggest we are morally good. Malcolm Muggeridge once said that the depravity of man is at once the most empirically verifiable reality but at the same time the most intellectually resisted fact. Clay Jones writes that all of us, in the right circumstances, are "Auschwitz-enabled." We both *feel* guilty for our wrongdoing, and we *objectively speaking* are guilty, and a significant part of the good news of the gospel is that there is a solution to the problem of our "dear self," as Kant called it, or our being "curved inward on ourselves," as Luther put it. Several luminaries from the history of moral apologetics—from John Henry Newman to A. E. Taylor—have spilt considerable ink exploring and explicating the revelatory features of the phenomenon of guilt, the felt feeling of which can make us cognizant of transgressing a moral standard or law, something each of us does with disappointing regularity.

Elshof's marvelous monograph is less about guilt, however, than its often neglected sibling shame. His laudable effort constitutes a lovely philosophical exercise of exploring the concept and dynamics of shame. By making important connections and drawing fine-grained and textured distinctions in the process, the work results not just in enhanced conceptual clarity, but penetrating psychological, philosophical, and ethical insight. Eminently skilled at clarifying conceptual confusions, unearthing underlying assumptions, and exposing unprincipled conflations, Elshof exhibits a good philosophy teacher's knack for thick, apt, and telling illustrations. Rife with perspicacity and uncommon common sense, appropriately circumspect and judicious, the book's patient and careful analysis provides a partial antidote and useful corrective for rushed analysis and shoddy, sloppy, superficial thinking. As countercultural as it's courageous, it argues that to grasp the import of shame we must achieve something of a golden mean between the Scylla of excess—*chronic shame*—and the Charybdis of deficiency: an individualist-fueled *shamelessness*. Losing the capacity for shame or to blush is far from virtuous, yet sadly, sanguinely quotidian and ubiquitous in the contemporary moment.

Shame can pose a serious threat to the belief that God loves each one of us, that we can be reconciled with God and others, and that we are valuable and worthwhile. Shame has more to do with who we are than just what we have done. And so it can be particularly damaging if we allow shame to detract from recognizing the value we have in God, which it can all too easily do. If we become convinced that we are useless, that our lives are pointless, that we as people lack value, it becomes exponentially harder to see ourselves as creations of God with infinite dignity and value and worth. For just such reasons, many end up thinking that all shame is bad—nothing but a toxic emotion.

This is especially true of undeserved shame. Ours is sadly a society in which certain people—those who have been sexually abused, those with visible disabilities—carry a stigma and are often, for no fault of their own, riddled with a sense of shame. The solution, Elshof argues, has to be communal—usually involving someone with social capital to spare conferring honor on them. If you have never seen it before, watch a 1981 YouTube clip of Mister Rogers hosting a ten-year-old wheelchair-bound Jeffrey Erlanger. They had originally met five years before, and Rogers remembered him and invited him to his *Neighborhood.*

Fred would later say that these unscripted ten minutes were his most memorable moment on television. It is deeply moving, and if there's any doubt as to why, I might suggest that it has to do, at least in part, with this matter of shame.

What makes those ten minutes of television so undeniably magical is that they are a simply profound microcosm of the divine love that deigns and condescends to broken and marginalized people and, in the process, exalts them, replacing shame with honor, beauty for ashes. Like Mister Rogers did for Jeffrey—who was on the stage years later to confer on Rogers his Lifetime Achievement Award—this is a means by which to make goodness attractive, which is an important part of our job description as Christians as we learn to love God and our neighbor.

There is also deserved shame. If I do something shameful, I should feel shame. The suggestion is not that anyone should let shame decimate their sense of self or think of themselves as unredeemable, nor that we should engage in the practice of shaming. That is different, and incompatible with loving our neighbors as ourselves. But if we don't feel at least some shame for doing something genuinely shameful, then we are being shame*less*, and that is not a good thing. Elshof underscores that from Aristotle to Aquinas to so many others in the history of philosophy and theology, the capacity to feel shame has been thought to be a virtue, and the loss of the ability a vice. It is only more recently that as a society we have started to think otherwise, cast shame as categorically toxic, and attempt to be rid of it altogether.

The pages of scripture are replete with narratives of honor and shame. The prodigal son, for example, is a young man who did shame-worthy things. He felt shame, and he deserved to, and he couldn't fix it on his own. He needed someone to confer on him the honor he had lost, like his father did, and like our Heavenly Father does. As Elshof beautifully puts it, "The maker of heaven and earth is in a full sprint—robes and all—to embrace you, kiss you, put a ring on your finger, and throw a feast in your honor. Whatever the opinion of the company you keep, you are of immeasurable value to the One who matters most. You are so valuable that the God of the universe suffered the indignity of limited human form, betrayal, public humiliation, and naked crucifixion to rescue you not just from guilt, but also from the shame of your condition, all to enjoy an eternal life of friendship and communion with you."

Elshof deserves accolades for redemptively accentuating such philosophically powerful, psychologically sound, and biblically consistent truths about the maligned emotion of shame.

David Baggett, Philosophy Professor & Director of the Center for Moral Apologetics, Houston Baptist University

Thursday, July 1, 2021: Good day; generated a draft of Sunday's talk, and chatted and prayed with TJ. Lots of great stuff going on. Each day seems to bring new blessings regarding the Center. MB and I enjoyed dinner and a movie with Nathaniel in the evening. After some more revisions I'll share Sunday's message, which I think adds an important twist to the moral apologetics material.

Friday, July 2, 2021: Here's the final draft for Sunday's message:

The Haunting Value of Persons

It is a real pleasure and joy to be with you today to talk about moral apologetics, and if you are unclear about what moral apologetics is, let me get to that with a story. When the great poet W. H. Auden arrived in the United States with Christopher Isherwood in January 1939, he was not religious, and he had not been since he was thirteen at Gresham's School in England. Os Guinness says that two experiences stood out among those that jolted Auden into rethinking the matter of faith. The first had been earlier in 1933, when he was a schoolmaster at the Downs School in the Malvern Hills. Sitting with three fellow teachers, he was suddenly overwhelmed by the sense that all their existence somehow had infinite value and that he loved them for themselves. Years later he described this experience as a "Vision of Agape" (Love).

The second experience came in New York two months after he had written the poem "September 1, 1939." He was in a cinema in Yorkville on the Upper East Side of Manhattan, which unbeknown to him was still largely a German-speaking area. Eager to follow news of the course of the war, he went to see *Sieg in Poland* ["*sieg*" means victory], a documentary of the Nazi invasion and conquest of Poland, in which S. S. Storm Troopers were bayoneting women and children, and members of the audience cried out in support of their fellow-countrymen, "Kill them! Kill them!"

Auden was horrified. One thread had always linked his successive convictions— a belief in the natural goodness of humankind. Whether the solution of the world's problems lay in politics, education, or psychology, he believed that once the problems were addressed, the world would be happy because humanity was basically good. Suddenly, however, as Auden watched the S. S. savagery and heard the brutal response of the audience, he knew he had been wrong. With everything in him he knew intuitively and beyond any doubt that he was encountering absolute evil and that it must be judged and condemned absolutely. There had to be a reason why Hitler was "utterly wrong."

These two experiences helped him realize that he needed a better understanding of the value of persons and the existence of evil. He probably also had to rethink this idea that people are good if his beliefs were going to align with reality. And this is moral apologetics; in short compass moral apologetics is aligning our beliefs to correspond with reality, especially as revealed by the unshakeable truths of morality. Think about the examples from Auden: human beings are valuable, perhaps infinitely valuable; at the same time, we are not intrinsically good; there is something morally broken about us; and some things are just flat wrong, even evil.

Intrinsic Value of Persons

This is by no means an exhaustive list of moral realities on which to base an argument for God's existence, but it's a good start. For time constraints let's focus in even more and choose just one of these to think about for now: the intrinsic value of people, perhaps even something like the infinite value of people. I don't mean that we are morally good, but we are valuable. Immanuel Kant had a way of talking about this issue: he said people have worth and value and dignity, but not a price. There is an inherent dignity to persons that we deeply recognize, and it cannot be quantified or reduced to a dollar amount; there is something about it that is intangible, literally priceless. And somehow we know this, down deep, though we can forget it, or perhaps intentionally repress it. We can forget that it is true of others, and we can forget that it is true of ourselves.

What I find especially exciting about this particular piece of moral evidence is that many of our unbelieving friends themselves intuitively recognize its truth. At least at moments they are often able to see that people have great intrinsic value and dignity. They may not know why—just as they may not know why we have moral obligations, or that people are of equal moral worth, or that basic human rights obtain—but they can recognize the truths themselves. Otherwise, something like the moral argument could not get off the ground, because the moral argument appeals to just such moral evidences, but fortunately God has made all of us as human beings able to apprehend such truths.

Think about the Nazi depiction of Jews, the ugly history of American chattel slavery, and, more recently, the intellectual contortions required to deny the humanity of unborn children to justify their wholesale slaughter. In such paradigmatic instances of reprehensible mistreatment, we see on ready display the perceived need to deny the humanity of the victims. This is thought to make it okay; we would otherwise know the behavior is beyond the moral pale. Even at our worst, you see, we somehow recognize the value of humans, and to rationalize our behavior we deny the humanity of the victims—just as Goebbels' propaganda did the same of the Poles. I suspect general revelation alone gives us reason to think human beings are intrinsically valuable, sacred, and the legitimate bearers of human rights. What such recognitions should then lead us to do is ask what it is about reality that explains such truths. Why is it that people have such great intrinsic dignity and value?

Now, its very obviousness might be thought to imply that we need not search for a more ultimate explanation. If it's that obvious, why ask why? But this is to confuse the matter of the truth of the thing with our knowing it to be true. We may be able to recognize that something is true without being able to explain why. This is the difference between something being *self-evident* and something being *self-explaining*. Or philosophers might say it is confusing ontology (what is real) with epistemology (our knowledge of what's real). So even unbelievers can often grasp that people have mysteriously great intrinsic value, but this piece of moral evidence cries out for explanation.

As Christians we have terrific reasons to think it's indeed true that human beings, each and every one of them, have great value, perhaps even infinite value, as Auden sensed that day in the Malvern hills. Austin Farrer was a friend of C. S. Lewis's who, in his own work, had for one of his main points of emphasis the value of persons. In one of his books he asked readers to consider the way we normatively ought to think about other people. It is of great importance, he argued, that we value them rightly, that we think about others in such a way as to regard them properly. Such regard should be at once so pure and so entire that it leads to a sort of frustration. This frustration derives from the incompleteness of our definition of those we so regard. Thinking of our neighbors in too casual a way cannot sustain the esteem we intuitively think they deserve. The conclusion to which Farrer felt compelled is that what deserves our regard is not simply our neighbor, but God in our neighbor and our neighbor in God.

This gets us to the heart of why we know as Christian believers that people are of infinite value. They are creations of God, made in his image, fashioned after his likeness, and they are loved by God, perhaps each of us differently, but all of us infinitely. The longer I live the more convinced I become of the revolutionary nature, for each of us, of coming into a deep understanding of God's love.

I used to teach a lot of seminary students and found on numerous occasions that these same folks willing to get up and preach God's love on Sunday harbored doubts about God's love *for themselves*. Another example is my stepson Nathaniel, who's here today. His biological father hasn't played much of any role in his life, which is horribly sad, and it's sometimes tempting for Nathaniel to think that this is how God is—maybe God isn't really loving after all. A line from *Fight Club* strikes him, from the character of Tyler Durden: "Our fathers were our models for God. If our fathers bailed, what does that tell you about

God? … You have to consider the possibility that God does not like you. He never wanted you. In all probability, he hates you."

Sadly, Nathaniel's situation is far from anomalous—so many kids today lack a loving father in their lives, and tragically many of them may doubt God likes them, much less love them. But of course this is also deeply confused, giving bad earthly fathers far too much power—the power to condition our theology rather than good theology being the yardstick. On occasion we have tried to use humor to address this. My wife was with Nathaniel in church one day when they were singing a song about God's love for everyone, and it was all very moving hearing about God's love for all, when she leaned over and whispered to him, "Except you." Now that seems cruel, and hilarious—but I actually think is a powerful use of humor to charm and disarm and help someone see something important from a fresh perspective. There is simply nothing more important than seeing the love of God. It's who he is.

Understanding God's love is a process. Recall Paul's prayer for the Ephesians—that if Christ dwells in their hearts through faith, then they, being rooted and grounded in love, will have power, together with all the saints, to comprehend the length and width and height and depth of the love of Christ, and to know this love that surpasses knowledge, that they may be filled with all the fullness of God.

I find it most instructive, by the way, that when we think about the deepest reasons for the value of persons, it ends up invariably pointing us past humans to the real source of their value: God himself. And not just that—it points to who God is. God is love; in the triune relationship God is by his nature love—perfect, eternal, necessary love. The matter of *who God is* is just as important, if not more important, than merely *that God is*. The good news of the gospel is never merely that God exists, but that God loves us, even likes us, he has made provision for our salvation, and wants us to experience abundant life and fruitful service and the deepest fulfillment imaginable. The better we understand the love of God, the better able we will come to understand the value of those made in his image. A low view of God results in a low view of people; a high view of God results in the right view of people. Our theology conditions our anthropology, inevitably. It's one of the reasons why theology matters a great deal—and not just to appreciate the concepts in our head, but appropriate them in our hearts.

With this in mind, listen to these words of C. S. Lewis: "There are no ordinary people. You have never talked to a mere mortal. [I]t is immortals whom we joke with, work with, marry, snub and exploit—immortal horrors or everlasting splendors. This does not mean that we are to be perpetually solemn. We must play. But our merriment must be of that kind (and it is, in fact, the merriest kind) which exists between people who have, from the outset, taken each other seriously—no flippancy, no superiority, no presumption."

We all of us have been made in God's image; in this there is solidarity. At the same time, each of us is unique, in the true sense of the word, unrepeatable, sui generis. Every one of us is called to inhabit a particular portion of the body of Christ; each of us is called to do good works that God prepared beforehand for us to do. And for those who avail themselves of God's overtures of love, are reconciled to him, and saved to the uttermost, we are told in Revelation that one day on a white stone their true name will be revealed—a secret between each of them and God. That name will be no merely arbitrary moniker, but the deepest reflection of who God intended them to be all along and from the start. Their deepest and most distinctive identity. We live in a time when issues of identity are much discussed, often in the most simplistic and superficial of ways, but our deepest sense of identity can be found only in our God-given callings and vocation. We look for it elsewhere in vain.

A few quotations come to mind that drive home this point about the uniqueness of each person. First, in his 1940 novel *The Power and the Glory*, Roman Catholic author Graham Greene charges his readers to recognize and respond rightly to the intrinsic value of each person: "When you visualized a man or woman carefully, you could always begin to feel pity—that was a quality God's image carried with it. When you saw the lines at the corners of the eyes, the shape of the mouth, how the hair grew, it was impossible to hate. Hate was just a failure of imagination." And second, from the Christian novelist Marilynne Robinson: "Any human face is a claim on you, because you can't help but understand the singularity of it, the courage and loneliness of it."

I like that. By the way, though I don't have much time to explore this just now, the face seems particularly important to our identity and personhood somehow. C. S. Lewis recognized this in his greatest novel *Till We Have Faces*. Interestingly enough, in more than one language, etymologically personality is tied to the face, and sometimes even a mask. There is something ineliminably personalist about the face; it's far easier to be cruel to those who remain faceless; this is often, I suspect, why online activity can be so acidulous and vitriolic. No face, no humanity. In *Till We Have Faces*, to have a face in the full sense metaphorically means to acknowledge all of who we are, the good and the bad, the honorable and the shameful.

Once more, the way to authenticity and true identity is to grab hold of our identity as God's image bearers, renouncing the works of darkness to which our sinful bent inclines us. This is the only path to the deepest fulfillment for which we were made, the most authentic self we can be. Kurt Vonnegut captured the moral of his novel *Mother Night* with these words: "We are what we pretend to be, so we must be careful about what we pretend to be." In his chapter called "Let's Pretend" in *Mere Christianity*, Lewis talks about putting on Christ as like putting on a mask that, by the time it's removed, the face has conformed to. This is the right form of pretending, you see; the right sort of mask, one that makes us more of what we were meant to be, not less.

There is ever so much more that could be said about the intrinsic value and inherent dignity of persons, but I should move on. Before I do let me add one word about special revelation. General revelation can show us that people have value, but the special revelation we have received through scripture amplifies the message. And this accounts for why the evolution in moral thought that enabled us to see the sacred and beautiful qualities in the Downs syndrome child, the aged, and the exile was largely a function of Christian influence. Only a myopic view of history fails to see the revolutionary force of Christianity in generating such moral insight.

Just one quick corroborating word on that, from atheist Jürgen Habermas from his *Time of Transitions*: "Universalistic egalitarianism, from which sprang the ideals of freedom and a collective life in solidarity, the autonomous conduct of life and emancipation, the individual morality of conscience, human rights and democracy, is the direct legacy of the Judaic ethic of justice and the Christian ethic of love. This legacy, substantially unchanged, has been the object of continual critical appropriation and reinterpretation. To this day, there is no alternative to it. And in light of the current challenges of a postnational constellation, we continue to draw on the substance of this heritage. Everything else is just idle postmodern talk."

Though Valuable, not Good

We are each of us uniquely made in God's image and loved infinitely by God, but we are also sinners in need of grace. We are valuable, but not particularly good. Malcolm Muggeridge once said that the depravity of man is at once the most empirically verifiable reality but at the same time the most intellectually resisted fact. Clay Jones writes that his study of numerous atrocities throughout history has demonstrated to him that unspeakably cruel and hideous behaviors are not the exceptional anomaly, but the norm for garden-variety, run-of-the-mill people like you and me. All of us, he says, in the right circumstances, are "Auschwitz-enabled."

All of us have three deep existential moral needs: to be forgiven our wrongdoing, to be changed, and ultimately to be changed to the uttermost, perfected, and this is the basis of a whole different talk I give about the way that Christianity meets each of these deep needs impeccably well. This leads to a version of the moral argument that points not just to theism but to Christianity in particular.

Yes, we are guilty—we both *feel* guilty for our wrongdoing, and we *objectively speaking* are guilty. This is obviously a perfect prelude to proclaiming the gospel, but I'm not going to couch it in those terms today, but do something else that is just as important but not talked about nearly as much. It adds a new wrinkle to the moral apologist's case.

I will say just this much about guilt and sin, though: Our having been made in God's image is *essential* to us, whereas our sinful state is merely *contingent*. In other words, more central to our identity is that we have been created by God in his image for reasons and purposes, than that we have fallen into sin and are in need of forgiveness. We can be forgiven and saved through and through so our sins need not define us; but we cannot help but be partially defined by having been made in God's image. So that is a hopeful reminder.

The Maligned Sibling of Shame

As I say, though, I am going to talk about something different from guilt for now. I want to talk about its often maligned sibling shame, because I am increasingly convinced that we need to talk about this topic more than we do. Shame can pose a serious threat to the belief that God is good, that God loves each one of us, that we can be reconciled with God and others, and, most relevant for present purposes, that we are valuable and worthwhile.

Whereas guilt reveals that we have morally transgressed, shame has more to do with who we are, not just what we have done. And so it can be particularly damaging if we allow shame to detract from recognizing the value we have in God, which it can all too easily do. If we become convinced that we are useless, that our lives are pointless, that we as people lack value, it becomes exponentially harder to see ourselves as creations of God with infinite dignity and value and worth. It's for just such reasons that, for many, believers and unbelievers alike, the temptation is to think that all shame is bad—that it's nothing but a toxic emotion. Guilt might be fine; we can ask forgiveness and such and get past it; but shame is thought to just saddle us with negative emotional baggage and so there is no good reason for it.

In some cases, this is obviously true. Victims of abuse may feel great shame over what happened to them, even though they did nothing wrong. That is undeserved shame, and the problem is not theirs. It's all of ours; we need to listen to such victims, not sideline them, nor silence them, but give them a voice and really hear them. I will give you another example of undeserved shame in just a moment.

But there is also deserved shame. If I do something shameful, I should feel shame—if I were the abuser of that victim we just discussed, for example. I don't

282

mean to suggest that anyone should let shame decimate their sense of self or think of themselves as unredeemable, nor that we should engage in the practice of shaming. That is different, and little compatible with loving our neighbors as ourselves. But if we don't feel at least some shame for doing something genuinely shameful, then we are being shame*less*, and that is not a good thing. From Aristotle to Aquinas to so many others in the history of philosophy and theology, the capacity to feel shame has been thought to be a virtue, and the loss of the ability a vice. It is only more recently that as a society we have started to think otherwise, casting shame as categorically toxic, and attempting to be rid of it altogether. Again, if the shame is undeserved, that is a problem we all need to address; but when shame is deserved, feeling the shame is a step to healing. When I wrap up in a moment, I will give you an example of deserved shame and the proper response to it.

Let's start with an example of undeserved shame.
https://www.youtube.com/watch?v=Q3vp-EXQ5Rs

If you have never seen that before, it was a 1981 YouTube clip of Mister Rogers hosting a ten-year-old wheelchair-bound Jeffrey Erlanger. They had originally met five years before, and Rogers remembered him and invited him to his *Neighborhood*. Fred would later say that these unscripted ten minutes were his most memorable moment on television. It is deeply moving, and if there's any doubt as to why, I might suggest it has to do, at least in part, with this matter of shame. Ours is sadly a society in which certain people—those who have been sexually abused, those with visible disabilities—carry a stigma and are often, for no fault of their own, riddled with a sense of shame—a loss of social standing, and a resultant tendency to shrink and hide. It threatens their sense of humanity. The solution has to be communal—usually involving someone with social capital to spare conferring honor upon them.

And that is exactly what makes those ten minutes of television so undeniably magical. It is a simply profound microcosm of the divine love that deigns and condescends to broken and marginalized people and, in the process, exalts them, replacing shame with honor, beauty for ashes. Like Mister Rogers did for Jeffrey—who was on the stage years later to confer on Rogers his Lifetime Achievement Award—this is a means by which to make goodness attractive, which is sort of part of our job description as Christians. It's how to love God, and our neighbor.

And now an example of deserved shame. The pages of scripture are replete with narratives of honor and shame, from Adam and Eve to the story of the prodigal son and lots in between. You know the story of the prodigal son. He insists on his inheritance ahead of time and engages in profligate spending and living, bringing shame on himself and an almost complete loss of social standing as a result.

Finally, he repents and comes home, and the father, seeing him far off, comes running to him with a kiss and embrace. Here is a young man who did shame-worthy things. He felt shame, and he deserved to, and he couldn't fix it on his own. He needed someone to confer on him the honor he had lost.

And this, my friends, gives us as believers a simply wonderful opportunity. All of us, whether we have social capital to spare or not, are in a position to remind those around us that each and every person is loved and pursued by the God of the universe. The maker of heaven and earth is in a full sprint—robes and all—to embrace you, kiss you, put a ring on your finger, and throw a feast in your honor. Whatever the opinion of the company you keep, you are of immeasurable value to the One who matters most. You are so valuable that the God of the universe suffered the indignity of limited human form, betrayal, public humiliation, and naked crucifixion to rescue you not just from guilt, but also from the shame of your condition, all to enjoy an eternal life of friendship and communion with you.

If there is any doubt that this is what the life and work of Jesus was all about, recall the OT passage that inaugurated his public ministry in Luke, from Isaiah 61: "The Spirit of the Lord GOD is on Me, because the LORD has anointed Me to preach good news to the poor. He has sent Me to bind up the brokenhearted, to proclaim liberty to the captives and freedom to the prisoners, to proclaim the year of the LORD's favor and the day of our God's vengeance, to comfort all who mourn, to console the mourners in Zion—to give them a crown of beauty for ashes, the oil of joy for mourning, and a garment of praise for a spirit of despair."

Saturday, July 3, 2021: Over pizza and wings last night Jerry and I watched *Fight Club*, which he didn't enjoy as much as he had before. Funny I adduce a line from it in tomorrow's talk. Today I plan to review those pages a few more times and tweak my CT review, and that's pretty much it. (I've now done that and put the revision into an earlier submission.) Talk Sunday but come Monday it's vacation for a few days, likely my only of the summer. Looking forward to the biography of Lucille Ball, *Ball of Fire*, I'm planning to peruse at the beach.

This morning I heard this from Richard Swinburne: "Dear David, Thanks for the invitation. You are right that I am sympathetic to a version of an argument from our knowledge of morality to the existence of God, but only one which by itself would add a fairly small amount to the probability of God. However, I don't think I have anything very new to say about it. In any case, I am very full up with commitments for the next year or so - half a book co-authored with someone else, and at least two hoped-for projects of my own. So, I must say no. With apologies, and best wishes for your volume – Richard"

Just sent this letter to the Gangster Capitalism folks whose recent episode on Liberty was a disappointment:

Hi folks,

I'm Dave Baggett, and I used to teach at Liberty. I've been enjoying your podcasts on Liberty and I'm convinced you're doing a great deal of good. For the most part I've thought them really well done, and I'm glad you're doing them. My wife Marybeth is someone you interviewed and she's made several appearances in the podcasts, which has also been great fun to hear.

So I hope you believe me when I say that, for the most part, I think you all have done a marvelous job, when I share just a few reservations about the latest episode on race and gay issues. It's not coming from a place that's defensive about Liberty; quite to the contrary, I'm thrilled I'm gone and don't miss it one bit, and I think it's deserved nearly all the diatribes and negative press it's been getting. I wish it would get more.

You should also know that I have never been even slightly tempted to leave my faith behind because of what Liberty does. Anyone in the church should be disabused quite quickly from thinking that all who name the name of Christ are faithful representatives of Christianity. Without exception any abhorrent behaviors among them are instances of departures from Christian faith, to my thinking, so I have never identified with those who leave faith behind because of the failures of believers. I do sympathize with their struggles, and often feel for them, but leaving their faith behind is just a step with which I don't at all resonate. It makes no sense to me at all except as a psychological necessity predicated on wrongly assuming that all Christian leaders live perfectly in line with Christian doctrine.

Okay, now for the reservations that i had about the last episode. A traditional Christian conviction, based on biblical teaching, is that same-sex sexual practice is not what God intends for human beings. For those who take biblical teachings seriously and authoritatively, this is hard to get around. Arguments against homosexuality can be constructed from natural law, too, but with certain limitations, but the biblical witness is arguably quite clear from start to finish that this behavior, regardless of orientation, is morally proscribed.

I say this because nowadays it's often suggested that biblical teaching is ambiguous on the matter, and I know some people think this is so. But in my studies of the subject, I just disagree. Right or wrong, though, there are plenty of Christians (the vast majority of Christians throughout history, for example) who have understood the Bible to teach that homosexual practice is wrong and not to be encouraged--likewise with adultery or promiscuity or pride or gluttony.

285

Identifying such sins aren't meant to shame people who engage is such practices; the gospel is good news, not bad--the message is that there is forgiveness for our sins and deliverance from their power.

Now, it's true that some folks, including some at Liberty historically, have understood deliverance in terms of conversion therapy. Personally I rather doubt this tends to work. Some people, it would seem, have intractable same-sex tendencies, but I don't think that vitiates the biblical teaching, which is about behavior, not inclination.

The latest documentary, though, really didn't make many strides for a nuanced analysis of any of this. It cast Liberty (and evangelical Christianity in general) as homophobic. I know to be disparaged in those terms nowadays practically functions as a mic-dropping conversation stopper, but any serious effort to understand Christian theology on this matter simply can't with intellectual integrity rest content with so superficial an analysis.

Luke Wilson's contributions to the documentary were more than a little disappointing. He invoked the notion of "shame" and cashed it out in terms of opposition to gay practice. Since "shame" involves implicating one's whole sense of self (and not merely one's actions), Luke cast opposition to gay practice as tantamount to opposition to gay persons since their identity is equivalent to their sexual orientation and thus opposition to their whole sense of self. This is a deeply mistaken, potentially manipulative way of casting the discussion, stacking the deck in one direction, and dismissing with a quick wave of the hand 2000 years of orthodox Christian teaching. Personally I simply don't think one's sexual orientation constitutes an essential part of one's identity, any more than my heterosexuality does.

Even if not essential to us, it can still be part of who we sense ourselves to be, true, but for a gay person to cast anyone who is morally opposed to the practice of homosexuality as guilty of shaming or homophobia is a question-begging approach that shuts any substantive discussion down.

But nothing was said to challenge his exceedingly one-sided perspective, nor was any reservation expressed about eliminating Liberty's tax-exempt status because of its official stance against homosexual practice. But this logic would apply to any and all evangelical or Roman Catholic (or other religious) institutions for taking a stance that for a very long time and for what are thought to be deeply principled reasons has been held. This just strained my credulity to the breaking point. What of issues of religious freedom? Because public support of same-sex practice has changed over the last few decades Christian schools are no longer entitled to retain orthodox Christian teachings on this score on pain of risking their very existence?

Perhaps you think so, and you're of course entitled if so. Perhaps you think opposition to gay practice is any form is homophobia and problematic shaming and should be proscribed by law just as segregationist practices are. Again, if so you're entitled to such a view.

Such an approach certainly came through in the documentary, but it made me sad, because I think it undermined the whole series. You went from talking about greed and corruption at Liberty to what amounted to a frontal assault on a traditional Christian conviction expressed in broad enough terms to apply to pretty much any and every evangelical and Roman Catholic college in existence. And you seemed to intimate that anyone who retains a traditional Christian stance on homosexuality--including the vast majority of people you've been interviewing all throughout this series--is homophobic and tantamount to something like a racist, thus eroding the credibility from which much of the purchase and force of your series derives. I think the unfortunate result was ineffectual overreach.

A better approach would have been to point out the poignant tension between so occasionally harsh and unloving a stance on homosexuality with the license afforded their long-time precedent to live a debauched lifestyle.

Again, I have so much appreciated all the previous installments, and certain aspects of the latest one, but I thought this overreach I'm describing was an unfortunate misfire that did more harm than good.

Thanks for listening,
Dave

Sunday, July 4, 2021: Spoke at Jan's church; it was a fun event. Nice response by lots of folks. Jan spoke in the main service; she's a marvelous communicator. It's now 2:30 in the afternoon and we're planning on heading over to her house before too long.

Monday, July 5, 2021: MB and I headed to Galveston for a little vacation. Lunched at Fisherman's Wharf, which was wonderful as always. Then we visited Galveston Book Store, where I found AE Taylor's book on Aristotle. After checking into the hotel, I read about fifty pages of Ball on Fire, which I enjoyed greatly. Sleep was a bit fitful. We're right on the Gulf. Nice little pool I enjoyed in the afternoon.

Tuesday, July 6, 2021: Enjoyed the pool some more this afternoon, and MB joined me. While we were in there, a young Hispanic dad came with his daughters to swim. It occurred that such simple, garden-variety moments today will be the magical memories of those girls for the rest of their lives. I told the father so, and he heartily agreed. Jerry's son Johnny asked me and MB to proof his new novel and offer him feedback, and we told him we would. Set in Wilmore, it should be lots of fun, I think.

Earlier today I got great news: John Crosby accepted my offer to write a chapter for the Collection. We also got a rejection from Baylor for the moral argument argument book with Craig; our agent Steve forwarded us this:

Dear Steve,

Thanks for your patience as my team and I have deliberated over this proposal. As expected, it is nothing short of impressive; Dr. Craig and Dr. Baggett bring to bear the full weight of their philosophical and theological acumen to this perennial subject of ultimate concern. We appreciate and sympathize with how this project clearly distills a complex argument in such a way as to be accessible to students and, potentially, laypersons. With that said, we still feel that the apologetics angle of the book puts it a bit too far afield from our areas of expertise and our editorial profile. A Christian publishing house such as Baker or Zondervan would I think provide a much stronger platform for the book to reach its target readership and a potential wider audience.

We do hope you and the authors understand. We are grateful for the opportunity to consider this proposal; please express our sincere thanks to both Dr. Craig and Dr. Baggett.

All the best,
Cade

Wednesday, July 7, 2021: Marybeth and I got up and had a nice McD breakfast while looking at a pretty and choppy Gulf of Mexico, then went back to the hotel room where I felt inspired to write Jonathan Falwell a letter, then we packed up and headed home, grabbing lunch at Chili's along the way. In the afternoon Jerry Walls told me he's got into a new experimental treatment program for Parkinson's which is really hopeful, and he also persuaded me to do a podcast in the spring with the Sarah gal from Theology on Tap. Early this morning we listened to the last Gangster Capital podcast, which inspired the letter, as follows:

Hi Jonathan,

I hope this e-mail finds you well.

You have probably listened to the *Gangster Capitalism* podcasts about Liberty; if you haven't, I would encourage it. Although they misfire at points, sometimes pretty badly (especially in the penultimate episode), at other times they do a nice job highlighting some of the many very deep problems at Liberty. I wrote them about their episode on racial and gay issues; their treatment of the latter, in particular, as I told them in no uncertain terms, was deeply misguided. They simply didn't seem to give even the most casual glance at traditional Christian teachings on sexuality, and their agenda was on ready display that, sadly, detracted from their overall investigation of Liberty. I could imagine plenty of evangelicals simply writing the whole thing off because of that episode, which I think would be unfortunate. Some discernment may be needed to separate the wheat from the chaff, so to speak, but there's plenty to learn from listening to the series.

I start by making that point because of the central role you continue to play at Liberty. I thought it most interesting the way they chose to end the last episode (and thus the whole series)—and it was by mention of you. Perhaps, they said, you'll be one to shine light in the darkness, or you'll be the one to "light the match" if Liberty gets too far off track. I'm sure, if you listen, you'll aspire to the former, and I hope God strengthens you to shine that light. What I feel impressed to say to you, though, is that the latter option does not just apply to Liberty going to the left, going liberal, going PC, etc. In truth I don't see that happening. The faculty of Liberty alone would prevent that contingency. The faculty is made up of wonderful people, committed Christians, who have tremendous wisdom and integrity. The administrators don't need to keep them in line; they need to let the faculty do their thing. Something like the Falkirk Center (now called the Standing for Freedom Center), or the shenanigans of the Liberty-supported hack Todd Starnes (a man who has a patent lack of integrity), or a thoroughly corrupt executive committee on the Board, or the miserable excuse of a provost Scott Hicks (about whom I have heard a plethora of stomach-turning horror stories about how he treats people in cruel, dehumanizing, and manipulative ways) are the problem, not the solution. And they certainly aren't the ones to tame the faculty or keep the faculty in line; the faculty, for the most part (except for certain sycophants among them who had actually believed that your brother was leading the school in a godly fashion) are the ones who should be able to lead the way here. They are what's salvageable about this school moving forward.

Liberty is not going to go to the left. Steps continue to need to be taken to be vigilant it doesn't happen, I don't deny, but there are much bigger temptations unique to Liberty. Liberty's biggest threat doesn't come from liberalism; it comes from the temptations of greed, corruption, and power. I like your brother, and he was kind to me while I was there, but it's pretty clear that liberalism wasn't his problem, and in this sense he represents the temptations to which Liberty as a whole is most susceptible. It was the corrupting influence of money and power that led to his downfall. And with Liberty's resources, size, worldly success, power, and influence, it too is most particularly susceptible to the corrupting influences of these factors. A myopic insistence on steering clear of liberalism and secularism is having the pernicious effect of turning a great many of Liberty's students in the direction of the left, at best, and secularism and rejection of faith, at worst. There is something exceedingly ridiculous about that trend, I readily admit; personally I've never been remotely tempted to reject Christianity because of the conspicuous failures of ostensibly Christian leaders. It makes less than any sense to me to respond negatively to darkness by embracing yet more darkness, but this is largely a function of immature Christians not knowing best how to process what they too often see at Liberty.

When I heard you at the end of the podcast make mention of the concerns folks had that Liberty would go liberal, PC, etc., and that if so you'd be the first to light the match to burn the place down, I have to confess it strained my credulity more than a little, Jonathan. Your dad put in place the safeguards to make such a contingency most unlikely. Your words sounded to me worse than straining for a gnat. They sounded like straining for an imaginary gnat. And you know the next part. While swallowing a camel, or in this case, with what's been happening at Liberty for quite a while now, swallowing a thousand camels. Where do we begin? The grotesque avarice of the place? The fact that the president was a money-grubbing voyeuristic cuckold, and his wife a sexual predator, including of a Liberty student? An executive board filled with people of shoddy character? A provost who is among the most mean-spirited and cruel people there is? Wringing faculty dry? Demoralizing faculty and staff on a regular basis? Silencing any voices of dissent even when the dissenters are speaking obvious truth? Propping up a perverse and pernicious radio personality and subsidizing his work right there on campus? Eliminating programs crucial to a university without hesitation because they don't turn a profit—when the school is veritably rolling in gobs of cash with plenty to spare for far less noble ends?

To say you'll be the "first to strike the match" if the school goes liberal is a cool mic-dropping sound bite, but it's vacuous. It's just vacuous, man. It's straining at an IMAGINARY gnat; you're saying you'll do something when a contingency arises that simply won't arise. (Or at least is EXCEEDINGLY unlikely.) But look at what has actually happened! The school your dad founded has exhibited treachery, corruption, debauchery, greed, hubris, deception, and the list goes on and on. But people are approaching you with the concern it might go liberal? Really? Have they been paying attention? Is there no concern about these other sins? Is the idea that the only moral temptations come from the left? Again, this is nothing but straining at an imaginary gnat while swallowing a bunch of camels. Honestly, where was the prophetic voice when it was needed to stand up to the corruption? The unprincipled and vicious non-renewals year after year? The decimation of the SOD or School of Education? The nastiness of flex? The viciousness of a Godwin or Hicks? The dehumanizing practices, the rabid

290

avarice, the ungodly greed, the astounding pride? It was crickets man. So your words now strike me as vacuous and insincere.

This speaks loudly to many of our students that the leadership of Liberty is not about the truth, but about a narrow agenda willing to overlook vast swaths of reprehensible behavior. If it comes from the right (and I say this as a conservative guy—who even voted for Trump twice), the idea is that no harm can come from it. According primacy to the bottom line, not out of financial necessity but to amass more wealth for itself and suck all the oxygen it can from the arena of Christian higher ed, that's fine. Exuding pride and arrogance rather than seeing itself as one among other Christian colleges with a shared mission, that's fine. Rewarding a reprobate at the helm who's wont to show up for work drunk with 2.2 million dollars a year, that's fine. Covering up rapes on campus to project a false impression about campus safety and keep the dollars flowing, that's fine. Egregiously watering down standards for online classes in order to add to the coffers, that's fine. Propping up horrible and sinful leaders as long as it maximizes the bottom line, that's fine. Wringing faculty dry and daily undermining their morale until they can stay no longer, that's fine. Cutting programs that no self-respecting Christian college should ever consider cutting in order to make yet more money--that's fine. No match in sight. Not a peep of opposition. No prophetic voice then.

Just as long as we don't go liberal.

If you're going to show light in the darkness, Jonathan, you need to see the real sources of the darkness in the context of Liberty. I hope you do.

Best, Dave

Thursday, July 8, 2021: Today was a truncated day in certain ways; we had to leave the library early because MB was interviewing Mary Jo Sharp. I was also supposed to pray with TJ but he had to cancel because church issues arose. At the library I wrote back and forth with Anne Jeffrey and Robert Garcia. Anne will likely take the Goodness chapter in the collection, and Robert a chapter on Lewis, which I agreed to add, removing the Buddhism chapter. I also wrote Crosby and he wrote me back a nice note. On a lark I also wrote Oliver O'Donovan and Charles Taylor; nothing to lose! In the process of trying to locate John Rist's e-mail address. Also wrote the Jewish and Muslim scholars Hare suggested. MB finished up work on *Telling Tales*; quite an achievement. Finished a letter of recommendation for Jeremy Neill, who's been nominated for a teaching award. Great guy; hope he gets it.

Friday, July 9, 2021: Charles Taylor graciously turned my request down to write the foreword; not a surprise, but it was nice to hear from him. Terence Cuneo suggested a few possibilities of contributors: "Before I forget: have you contacted either Kevin Vallier or Chris Eberle about this project? Kevin has some really interesting Trinity-based metaethical views (none of his work on this has been published, to my knowledge) and Chris has done some work on theistic ethics as well. His most recent work is on the ethics of war, but it's deeply informed by his theistic commitments." I should probably make a list of folks who've been suggested; Anne has some coming, Menuge mentioned a few, and now Terence, maybe a few more.

MB and I have been praying for Nathaniel along the lines of spiritual warfare. It's hard to know how to pray for him sometimes in light of the fact that God presumably won't override his free will, but there are still plenty of important fervent prayers to pray. Among them that he could find victory over the dark forces assailing him. She spent the evening with him and they had a good talk while Jerry came over for dinner and a movie. Before the movie I showed him the clip of Fred Rogers testifying before Congress about PBS funding; Jer had never seen the clip before; remarkable example of powerful Aristotelian rhetoric—logos, pathos, ethos. Always such an edifying inspiration to revisit.

Jonathan Falwell never answered my e-mail from a few days ago. Nor had he answered MB's e-mail from some months ago. I have little confidence he's the solution to Liberty's ills. I imagine it's psychologically challenging for him to take seriously how off track parts of that place have gotten. All the more reason someone not named Falwell should probably be put in charge.

Otherwise spent the day reading Jonny Walls' novel *Summer of Trouble*; here's the feedback I offered him a little before midnight:

Jonny,

Just finished your novel! Wow! Loved it! What an amazing achievement. The book has a remarkably fun and attractive tone to it. You have a simply great way with words, and the book is filled with quite a number of poignant observations along the way. Chockful of very clever turns of phrase—like "family room of objections" to name just one of a veritable plethora—the book has a charming way of relishing simple moments and exploring various attempts to capture them in an assortment of ways, via memory, mental notes, pictures, and the like.

Your background with moviemaking comes through in a number of places, lending itself to several very cool insights and an impressive and impeccable attention to detail. I told your dad there's something almost Twainish about much of this—small town charms, boyhood hijinks, etc. You seem to remember marvelously well what your experiences were as a teenager, capturing them just so well. Such a way with words—some passages are simply nothing less than beautiful; and several scenes were so flawless and fluid I almost forgot I was reading about them and just felt like I was there. You also capture things about KY and Wilmore that somebody only could with extensive lived experience in that habitat and a rare eye for detail you clearly have.

What consistently impressed me was your almost effortless tendency to be uproariously hilarious. I lost count of the number of times the book simply made me laugh out loud. The first vomiting scene made me laugh for probably two minutes straight. Oh my word! I don't know if a book has ever made me laugh that hard! The transparency and playful self-deprecation is often beyond priceless. Truly, yours is a really distinctive and very likeable voice here. The book is by turns dramatically poignant, extremely thoughtful, and simply hilarious; it's consistently creative in excelsis. Although it's true that my knowledge of the context enhanced my appreciation, I'm also convinced that this background is unnecessary for folks to appreciate it even if they know nothing of Asbury or Wilmore. There's plenty of the universal in the particulars!

I was struck by several recurring themes. To mention just a few: perspective—a teen's perspective, perspectives from a higher vantage point spatially, differing perspectives of the same event among different people, younger versus older self's perspectives, the relativity of up and down, etc. And of course another recurring motif is one of memories and nostalgia, and perhaps more primordially and existentially, of existence and rich experience. The mystery beneath the surface of things—whether your town, the ocean, or the allure of a girl—is another theme that recurred and resonated nicely throughout. The mysteries of time, of course, are also huge: how it can seem to speed up and slow down, how it can't be captured, how eternity is especially beyond our ken, at least most of the time. You're your father's son, most certainly! (And your spot-on depictions of each of your family members was such a treat and joy for me to read!)

Loved the many callbacks you did as you went along, and especially appreciated the playful juxtaposition of very adult and insightful reflections about life, meaning, personhood, etc., on the one hand, with the winsome mindset of an adolescent, on the other. That was quite delightful.

The ending did not disappoint. It was quite powerful, and the way you handled the processing of the pain of your parents' divorce was really done well. Nothing maudlin or self-victimizing about it, but real and undeniable nonetheless.

I really, really, really enjoyed this! I think you have prodigious talents to write great fiction, man! I can't tell you how impressed I am. This was a real treat, from beginning to end. I think you've found your calling!

Thanks for letting me take a look! Kudos!!

Blessings,

Dave

Saturday, July 10, 2021: MB wanted to interview me today about the writing life for the class she's putting together for the MA in apol program. Here are the questions she wanted to ask and answers I wrote out, though I didn't look at them when she interviewed me:

1. How do you understand the writer's vocation? How should one's Christian faith inform or shape that vocation? What about the apologist's task—how should that color the way an apologist approaches writing?

    > Not every apologist is called to write, but presumably if you're pursuing a Masters in Apologetics, the likelihood is that writing will play an important part in your ministry, which is I suppose to say that writing may well be part of one's God-given vocation. The trick is to figure out the calling specific to you, and then know that if God calls you to write, he'll make it possible. Our part is to put in the work—acquiring expertise, thinking hard, reading widely, and working on the craft of writing, and it is a craft. God may give you the gifts and calling, but that doesn't mean you don't have to work on it. This is one of those cases where faith without works is dead. God calls us to be faithful in practicing the gifts he's given us. Personally I wouldn't first and foremost think of yourself as a writer, but as, say, an apologist. In other words, it's the content that matters most. The style is in service to promoting that content. It's not about showing people how good or talented you are; it would be better if you gave a good argument in bad writing than a bad argument in good writing, but it's best to be able to write good arguments very well. This is a way to integrate truth and beauty. And though we should work hard, always strive to remember that ultimately our trust is not in our preparation and hard work, but in God to give the increase.

2. Can you talk a little about your own approach to writing? What kinds of projects do you take on, and where do you find inspiration for them? How do you get started and keep going? Do you have any kind of routine you enter into—such as in terms of scheduling your work, setting up your writing environment, seeking feedback from others, or anything else that's relevant?

    > I rather doubt anyone wants to emulate my method of writing. It's like a wrestling match punctuated with periods of self-doubt and invariable debilitating recriminations for not reading enough or working hard enough, followed by flurries of activity and often periods of inactivity that gives me yet more reason to doubt myself and beat myself up. This is a restaurant you don't want to see the kitchen of. I'm exaggerating just

a little in order to emphasize that the writing process can be very difficult and challenging. It's messy, not unlike life. I suspect it is for everyone, so it's good for you to know that, because if your expectation is that writing isn't messy, and it turns out that it is, you might be tempted to give up. But it's actually par for the course. I'd rather not share any specific routine that works for me, because each person needs to find what works for them, and we're all different. I will say that I do best when I find a block of time to work on a project so my attention isn't overly fragmented in a bunch of different directions. Maybe that works for some, but not for me.

3. What are some of the biggest challenges in undertaking this work? How do you overcome them? What temptations are unique to the writing life (specifically of an apologist)? How do you resist them?

    You may find yourself thinking, what do I have to say that hasn't been said before? This pressure to be original is common among prospective writers. But there's a paradox here. The more we think about being original, usually the less original we become. But the more we're focused on doing what we feel God has laid on our hearts to do, and to do it in the power of his anointing with all of our energy and effort, creativity just sort of naturally emerges. Again, keep the focus off yourself, your gifts, your productivity, your reputation, and focus on the ideas themselves. God has something unique and distinctive to say to and then through each of you. Find that voice, that theme, that motif, and if you experience is anything like mine, it will enable you to see everything through that lens and what you'll have to say will be fresh and important. There are specific good works that God has prepared beforehand for you to do, and he delights in being a lamp to your feet. Don't obsess about finding your voice or path; do what God impresses you to do, faithfully and rigorously, and see what God will accomplish through it.

4. What role do spiritual disciplines play in preparing or sustaining you for this work of writing? How do you see the ministry of apologetic writing interacting with your own spiritual formation?

    In apologetics it's especially important that we cultivate not just a rigorous mind but a warm heart. Our job is to reflect Christ and love our neighbor; yes, give an answer for the hope we have within us, but unless we first show that we really have that hope and that God has touched our lives, people will often not be very interested in asking us any questions at all. Often what makes apologists especially effective is not merely what they say but who they are, and it comes through, either in our speaking or our writing. So assigning a high priority to prayer and scripture study and fellowship with other believers isn't just important in and of itself, though of course it is; it's also highly useful in making us effective apologists.

5. What is your most pressing piece of advice for students in HBU's Apologetics MA program?

> Cultivate epistemic humility. I see altogether too much of this: let's talk about the cosmological argument. Yes, no problem, here's the argument, neatly laid out in discursive format, and here's a few objections. Moreover, here are good answers to those objections, usually quoting William Lane Craig, and done. All of that's fine as far as it goes, but the problem is that it doesn't go very far. It's a good and indeed crucial first step to understand an argument clearly and be able to lay it out— identifying premises and conclusion, defining your terms, defending premises, anticipating and answering objections. But none of that means you've really lived with the argument long enough to make it your own. If you see it merely as a weapon with which to bludgeon the head of your opponent, you forget that the purpose of apologetics is to win people, not simply win arguments. Rigor is important, but involves quite a bit more than parroting your favorite apologist. Don't lose your epistemic humility; and the more you learn the material, I promise, the bigger the temptation will be to forget humility. But nothing will detract from your effectiveness at persuasion faster than arrogance.

Sunday, July 11, 2021: New pastor at Sugarland United Methodist church started today—an Asbury seminary grad. He graduated six years after I did, so I didn't know him. Good message, and I like him. Unpretentious, self-deprecatory, and insightful. I hope to write him and tell him about the Center for Moral Apologetics. In the afternoon MB spent some time with Nathaniel. They looked up exactly how much money he had left in his account, and did follow up calls to some places he'd applied to. He scored an interview for Tuesday on one of the calls. Some good things happening there, but the challenges that come from Nathaniel's being so slow to get his act together continue to wear on us. Both MB and I have so much work to do, and this is an unexpected and very draining challenge contending with Nathaniel's needlessly dire situation. Hard to make sense of, but as the message in church this morning reminded us, life will feature fiery trials through which we can be changed for the better. Hard to see at the moment, but we're trying to hang tough and not lose heart.

Got a follow up from an old student, Chris Underwood, who had earlier expressed some interest in helping us advertise Moral Apol stuff; he realized it wasn't the right gig for him, but he gave some advice:

> My only thought is that advertising on YouTube is your best path forward. YouTube skews heavily male, and towards young men who want to engage with topics more thoroughly than other forms of media.

The Christian YouTube channels that do well attract a lot of the bright young minds perusing the inter webs. I think based on your email, you guys are doing everything you can to reach the University audience who would be inclined to consider your resources already.

If you check out YouTube, I especially encourage you guys to connect with Pastor Mike Winger. He has almost 500,000 YouTube followers, and his channel is absolutely phenomenal for discussing challenging biblical topics in compassionate and thorough ways. He's passionate about leveraging social media for the Gospel and apologetics, and he has videos and training materials for other Christians to maximize YouTube.

I think he would be a great partner for advertising, not to mention if he has books he wants to publish.

It just dawned on me I forgot to copy and paste the Center's newsletter from a week ago:

Moral Apologetics

Monday, July 11, 2021: Got up early, read scripture, and went to the gym. I really need to go more regularly to work out. My mom would always say she wanted to live long enough to raise her kids. I want to live long enough to do the work God's called me to do. Going to the gym should help.

A little after 9 this morning MB and I got to the library and I made some good progress on a chapter in the philosophical theology book I'm doing with Ronnie Campbell. The chapter is the first in the volume, on faith and reason, with a moral apol theme, which will run throughout the book. After we got home we received two exciting things in the mail: a moral apologetics cup, part of the new stock of swag on sale in the Moral Apol store, and a hard review copy of *Telling Tales*. Looks great! MB deserves all the credit.

Tuesday, July 12, 2021: A year ago today was our last full day in Lynchburg. So odd a year has passed. In some ways it seems longer, in other ways shorter. Finished a draft of ch. 1 of the philosophical theology book. Feeling decent about it.

Heard back from Jonathan Falwell:

Hi David, thanks for your email.

I do want you to know I have always appreciated you and your work at LU. I recognize your concerns about LU and I intend to do whatever I can to ensure LU is all God intended for it to be. And to be fair, regardless of any safeguards my dad may have put in place while alive, it would be naïve to believe they will stand in perpetuity without someone continuing to fight for those safeguards. That is what I intend to do.

My statement regarding the place going "left" has nothing really to do with the idea of politics. My statement, and if the podcast was honest and played the entire clip, went on to say moving away from the Gospel, the Scriptures, etc., that I would "light the match." My intention was then, and still is today, to keep this place focused on honoring Christ in EVERYTHING it does.

LU has a difficult year. But I believe God's best is yet ahead and I will do anything in my power to protect what my dad spent his life building through the clear calling and power of God. I hope you will continue to pray for God's best at LU considering you too have spent so much time in helping to build this great university.

Please know I am always a phone call away if you ever need anything. God's blessings on you and your wife in your important ministry work.

Jonathan

Here was my reply:

Thanks Jonathan, I appreciate the note, especially knowing you were under absolutely no obligation to respond to my strongly worded e-mail. I was at the ocean when I wrote it, which lent itself to a bit of bombast.

I do hope and pray for Liberty's best, although I don't mainly associate that with the biggest numbers or endowment. An environment that doesn't give PTSD to those in its employ, that holds leaders accountable to biblical standards, that releases former employees from bogus non-disclosures, that effects a clean sweep of the executive committee on the Board, kicking Todd Starnes as far off campus as possible, replacing an inordinate money lover in the office of the Provost—these are the sorts of steps I'm earnestly hoping for. I don't see God's best for this school without some hard choices, and I'm praying those in a position to effect such significant changes will find the will to do it.

When my wife and I saw you in the Lynchburg airport in December of 2019, we were returning from having interviewed at HBU. We had already decided that, without or without offers from elsewhere, we were going to leave Liberty at the end of that school year. Fortunately we got the offer, and were able to go. We had already seen far too many troublesome things, well before the disasters of this past year. Boz Tchividjian was there on that flight as well, and he too had decided to leave that same year. What we saw in the last year was not anomalous, but the inevitable manifestation of a great deal of preexisting corruption that had gone unchecked for far too long. I suspect the lack of accountability in evangelical circles is part of the subcultural challenge Liberty faces to fix its course. Really hoping that the next president is someone with gravitas, impeccable integrity, and an inspiring vision of Christian higher education.

My respect for your dad is stratospheric; you have a wonderful heritage. I know you want to honor that heritage. May God give you wisdom and be a light to your path.

Blessings,
Dave

Wednesday, July 14, 2021: A year ago today was the middle day of our drive to Texas, when we went from TN to around Louisiana. Lots has happened in the last year, and the recent stuff with Nathaniel has been mightily stressful. I've been feeling the stress in my body. I'm about to go to the gym to help alleviate some of that stress. When I woke up this morning, though, I felt like God gave me an assurance he will help me wrap up the chapters for the phil theology book in short order, which was encouraging. Writing it through a moral apologetics lens, as Ronnie and I agreed to do, is proving a fertile approach. It's now a little after 2 in the afternoon and I'm working on chapter 9 of the phil theology book, the chapter on hell, suffering, and the problem of evil. Coming along well. Now it's nearly bedtime; the chat with Kedric at 5 went well. Insightful young fellow.

Thursday, July 15, 2021: So this is the day one year ago we got to Houston. And today was also the day we got our official invitation to do the Strauss lectures! Here's the e-mail:

> Dear Drs. Baggett,
>
> It is with great pleasure that I invite you to present the 2021 James D. Strauss Worldview Lectureship at Lincoln Christian University.
>
> This lectureship honors the legacy of Dr. James D. Strauss, who is credited with bringing the concept of "Biblical worldview" to the LCU campus. This annual lectureship endeavors to reinforce Dr. Strauss' defining Scriptural verse: "to bring every thought captive to Christ" (2 Cor. 10:5) by inviting some of the finest minds in the Christian world to address a wide variety of disciplines, especially in the areas of Biblical studies, including theology, philosophy, apologetics, and contemporary culture.
>
> This year's lectureship is scheduled for Tuesday, October 12, as follows:
>
> | | | |
> |---|---|---|
> | Lecture 1 | 9:00 am | Hargrove Chapel |
> | Book Talk/Q & A Session | 12:00 pm | Dowling Auditorium |
> | Lecture 2 | 3:00 pm | Dowling Auditorium |
>
> In appreciation for serving as this year's lecturers, we will present you with a speakers' fee of $1500 (total) and cover any reasonable travel expenses.
>
> I would appreciate if it you would please reply with a formal acceptance of this invitation and, as soon as it is convenient, provide me with a title or theme for the lectureship as well as an indication of how the two of you would like to share the lectureship assignments (one lecture each with both of you participating in the noon interview?).

Blessings,

Peter A. Verkruyse, Ph.D.
Interim Vice President of Academics
Professor of Communication Studies

Marybeth wrote this back on our behalf:

Thank you so much for this invitation, Dr. Verkruyse. We wholeheartedly accept and are very much looking forward to our visit to your campus.

Our theme for the lectureship will be "Coming to Life." We will divvy up the lectures as follows:

I will handle lecture #1. The title of that talk will be "Taking Sin Seriously: Lessons from Flannery O'Connor."

David and I will cover the 12:00 hour together. That talk is entitled "*Till We Have Faces*, Self-Knowledge, and Learning to Die."

David will do lecture #2 with a paper titled "Shame and the Haunting Value of People."

Please let us know what else you might need from us at this point. Again, we are grateful for this opportunity and look forward to our visit.

Marybeth

Really blessed time of talking and praying with TJ from about 5 to 7. Great things happening in a number of aspects of the moral apologetics ministry. So glad I gave him his leadership position!

I have stayed up too late, but at least did this; my sister on FB had written this post:

How is it that you could Love someone more than anything in the world, you would give up your life for them but still the streets win. The streets could care less for you, the so called friends could care less for you, the dope don't Love you but they still have more power than the ones that love you more than anything. How can you even compete with that, how do you fix it? It doesn't matter how broken your heart is, the streets still win. What do you do next? 😢 It's a lie when they say "Love conquers All."

I responded with this:

Whether it's a *lie* to say "love conquers all" largely depends on what one means by "conquer." If it's taken to mean that love can ensure particular results despite

301

people's free will, then it's pretty clear it doesn't conquer all. Unrequited love exists, after all. And loved ones suffer from horrible and deleterious addictions contrary to the earnest wishes of family and friends. So that's a fairly naive construal of what conquering amounts to; it would require that love vitiate meaningful agency. But might there be some other ultimate sense in which love wins? I suspect so. God's love conquered death, for example, in the resurrection. There's a richer and more nuanced way in which something can be affirmed about love's ultimate victory, though it leaves open the possibility, if we are meaningfully free, that some might choose to turn their back on light and life and love, and the result would be tragic. Presumably God loves everyone, right? Yet do some go to hell? Some suggest no--they are called universalists. But the more common traditional view in the Christian tradition is that universalism is false and some do sadly and tragically end up experiencing damnation. Is this a "defeat" of love? Again, much depends on what we mean by the relevant terms. If love is offered and obstinately rejected, and, with the love, joy and peace and fulfillment, the loss of all those things is the result. That seems less like the defeat of love, though, than the intentional and deliberate, repeated and ultimate rejection of love. The choice of darkness over light, and death over life, doesn't veto love, but rather sadly closes its heart to love. But love doesn't give up, even when it can seem hopeless. Like faith and hope, love endures.

Friday, July 16, 2021: Paul Gould wrote us and agreed to write a foreword for *Telling Tales*, which is quite cool. It's currently a little after 9 in the morning. Washing clothes before heading to the library. Feeling a bit tired today; hopefully I'll wake up more fully soon.

I admit that I'm struggling today with what to do about Nathaniel. Last night we spent some time with him, and he pridefully shared a fight he had had with his uncle some time back on the issue of professional sports guys taking the knee during the national anthem. I found it annoying, and it just reminded me of how he seems to stand foursquare about so much of what I hold dear. He supports abortion, celebrates sodomy (which the Bible calls an abomination), etc. It's tempting to think his values disqualify me from ministry. Many say adult children who rebel don't disqualify a parent in ministry. Maybe. Doesn't make me feel much better.

Just don't know what to do with any of it. Tears me up, honestly, and not infrequently of late makes me apoplectic. But expressing my angst about it to MB just puts her in an impossible situation. Really not sure what to do about any of it. What does love look like in a case like this? Hard for me to know A recurring piece of advice is to let go of our adult children, realizing they have free will in the matter. But Nathaniel resides in a sort of intermediate limbo zone in which he remains highly dependent on us. He's a kid when he wants to be, and an adult when it's convenient. I find myself very angry with him, and have to figure out what to do with this anger. Angst over it all pretty much took away any chance to be productive today, and I cancelled the evening with

Jerry. Just not up to socializing. Definitely feeling the weight today of being a failure as a stepfather. If I can't be effective at persuading my stepson, why think I can persuade anyone else?

Watched a neat little video today of Ben Witherington explaining why he's not a Calvinist. Good stuff. He points out that in the Bible there are just three nouns used to identify God—there are various adjectives but just three nouns—and they are light, love, and life. He considers this quite significant, as do I. He fairly rejects each part of the Calvinistic TULIP.

Saturday, July 17, 2021: Slept pretty well last night; got up in the middle of the night for a little while, which has happened quite a bit recently, but was then able to go back to sleep and get enough rest, I think. Spoke with Elton in the morning and shared with him my concerns about Nathaniel. We talked about when the open rebellion of a child is a disqualification for ministry, and about the relative wisdom of my talking more with Nathaniel about our ideological differences.

Elton cautioned me not to be motivated by concerns about my own sense of failure as a parent, a temptation to which I know I'm susceptible. It kills me I have been unable to persuade him when this is the work I do. He seems so much more influenced by the current trends of what's PC and "woke," by entertainers and comics and musicians, than he is by me, but Elton suggested, for the most part, in the context of the relationship, I set it aside. He said there are two important questions to bear in mind: do I have a voice with him (not just generally but specifically regarding these issues), and will using the voice be likely to do more good than harm? Perhaps all things considered I've said my piece and I should refrain from pushing things further, but man alive is it exasperating holding my tongue. Had a good conversation with MB about it all. No answers, but it was good to talk it out a tad.

For lunch today MB and I went to the same Fadi's we visited when we interviewed here a year and a half ago. We hadn't been back since. My memory failed me, as I was convinced it was on the other side of the highway. Before lunch I opened up quite a bit with MB about what it is about the Nathaniel situation that's getting to me. It's quite complicated, needless to say. One recurring motif seems to be the ambiguity of the situation. He's a boy and a man; responsible for himself and not; under our jurisdiction and not; unable to care for himself and able to; my son and not. Makes it hard to know how I fit into the picture, and what traction I can have.

We are currently this afternoon in the library, where in vain I'm trying to motivate myself to write. Meanwhile MB is making progress with a program to do the index for *Telling Tales*.

Sunday, July 18, 2021: Five things I miss since moving to Texas: camp meeting, King's Island, pool with Nutter, apple orchards, and Peaks of Otter. Well, a sixth: the doctoral classes.

This morning I wrote this to the moral apologetics team:

Hi Team! Blessed Sunday! Marybeth and I were just praying for the moral apologetics ministry in all its various dimensions, and for each one of you on the team—that God's hand of blessing would rest upon you, that each of you would be anointed for the tasks that God is laying on your hearts and empower each of you to do the good works for which he intended you. We are so grateful for each one of you, and truly exciting things are happening. We are praying for God to purify our heart and keep them pure as things develop and grow and good results continue to come about.

This morning we were listening to the CT podcast on the dissolution of Mars Hill subsequent to Mark Driscoll's "fall," and it reminded us of exactly what we don't want. When the time comes for me and MB to hand the reins of moral apol over to others, we want the ministry to continue unabated, stronger than ever. We want it to depend on us in no way at all; of course, though, we want to be faithful and effective in all that God has called us to do in the meantime. Recently we already handed over some leadership roles to Jonathan and TJ, making Jonathan the General Editor of Moral Apologetics Press and TJ the Executive Editor of MoralApologetics.com, and we have felt nothing but abundant confirmation that these were the right steps. They bring an energy, enthusiasm, and expertise to these roles that will propel these initiatives forward, and it has also helped free us up for projects of our own. Just so excited at all that God is doing. Speaking of which, a smattering of examples:

Stephen is on the cusp of generating curriculum on moral apologetics; JP continues to be the Managing Editor of the site and is now the General Editor of the Press; proposals have already begun to start coming in for the Press (please pray we have wisdom to know which ones to pursue; we'll have to be selective and discerning); Marybeth and Jonathan have been wrapping up our collection of essays on pop culture and philosophy (we asked Paul Gould to write the foreword and he agreed), and she's now cracking the nut on how to use programming and elbow grease to generate an index, which bodes well for future book projects in the series; TJ's initiatives in charge of the site are exciting and are sure to yield a great many dividends—such a joy to have him back and in this role; Dave & Jan are hard at work on a Dictionary of Moral Apologetics—what a cool project—fun, fun fun—so grateful for their initiative and enthusiasm; Brian Chilton is now such a valued member of the team, and feels inspired to work on his Masters in Philosophy to enhance his grasp of moral apol and the tools of philosophy in this work; Marybeth is going to be the editor of a new book series we'll be launching at Moral Apologetics Press on apologetics and pop culture (analogous to philosophy and pop culture), an idea whose time has come and

God has granted us the tools to spearhead; we are awaiting news on whether we received the 30,000 dollar grant we applied for to put on a major conference on the moral argument here at HBU; in connection with that conference John Hare at Yale and I have gotten an OUP contract for a major edited collection on the moral argument (among folks onboard already include Hare, Moreland, Copan, Garcia, Jeffreys, Evans, Zagzebski, Crosby, Flannagan, Cuneo, Ebels-Duggan, Idziak, Linville, and others; please pray as I fill out the rest of the slots—Wolterstorff and Adams haven't said yes, but they haven't said no!); Ronnie Campbell and I are writing an introduction to philosophical theology with a moral apol emphasis; Jerry Walls and I are working on our book on moral realism, the fourth in our tetralogy; the Center's Student Fellows program will be starting here at HBU this fall; the Certificate program in moral apol will begin next June (please pray I finish a draft of the moral realism book by then); and we are working to figure out how to crack the promotion/advertising nut for books with the Press (please pray to that end). That's just a partial list of all that's going, folks. God is really powerfully at work. I can hardly believe it. The image often comes to mind of a blessing too great for us to contain.

The most important thing of all, friends, is that we incline our ears to God's voice and remain vessels through whom God can operate freely. It's God who will give the increase. Fundraising remains a big need for the Center, and Marybeth and I have no training for how to do such things. But with every other challenge we face, our prayer is that God directs our steps and that he provide the increase. Our trust is not in strategies and methods, though we're not averse to them; faith without works is dead. So we'll do whatever he directs us to, at least hopefully, but our trust is in God to open the doors and pour out his blessings.

If we could somehow eventually generate enough money to pay you all for your efforts, and bring you to Houston if you wanted to come, and endow a Chair in moral apologetics at HBU, and build a building on campus for the Center—where we could all work together to generate curricula, speak to churches, generate podcasts, offer workshops, teach classes, write books, run the website, house the Press, etc.—I'd love it, more than words can express. If we can never raise enough funds to all of that, that's fine too—as long as we do anything and everything it is God's calling for us to do. This is why it remains vitally imperative for us all to hear what God's saying and how he's directing, and for each of us individually and all of us together to have a heart to obey all that God directs us to by his empowerment. If he calls us to do it, he'll enable us to do it. Let's keep bathing every part and person of this God-given initiative in prayers, my friends.

Today, though, on this blessed Sabbath, we can simply stop and marvel, and rest in God's finished work, realizing it's not on us, but on God.

Richest blessings, Dave

After church, which Jerry attended this week, Jerry, Nathaniel, Marybeth, and I piled into the car and went to Galveston for the day to enjoy a look at the ocean and a nice lunch at Fisherman's Wharf. Delightful time. Lots of great fun.

Monday, July 19, 2021: Finished the chapter on the problem of evil and got going on the chapter on resurrection and heaven. MB and I saw a silly movie in the afternoon. Felt a lot of burden to pray about a number of matters.

Tuesday, July 20, 2021: I asked MB this morning what her life mission was, and she said helping people understand what it means to be made in God's image. This covers her love of literature and obligations we have to one another. Mine might be helping people see that God loves them. Also occurs to me that I should write a book called *Your Good is Too Small*.

Wednesday, July 21, 2021: Not much to report about today; I largely took the day off and thus took a break from working on the philosophical theology chapters. Continuing to pray hard about the grant proposal, but haven't heard a thing about it.

Thursday, July 22, 2021: Organized my books upstairs to facilitate finishing up the footnotes in the phil theology chapters. Made some progress on the notes, but not as much as I'd hoped. Nice breakfast at Toasted Yolk with Nathaniel and MB, and a long conversation with Cathy Chulis, the first in about a year.

Friday, July 23, 2021: Finished finalizing the draft of my four chapters on phil theology, but still plenty of notes to fill in. Gonna try to wrap those up tomorrow. Dinner at PF Changs with Jer and we're planning to see a movie tomorrow night, when Jan and MB are out to dinner.

Pruitt asked me this question:

Hi Dr. Baggett,
I hope you are doing well!

Got a question for you. What would you say is the relation between the good and love?

A couple of thoughts for context.

It seems to make sense that we can say something about what the good is like. I agree with what you said in various places that we can't really define the good exhaustively. But on the other hand, does it make sense to say that we can discern certain features of the good? To me, that seems like an intelligible question. But when I try to be precise about it, it's hard. For example, if I say that good is selfless, is that right? If we think God is identical to the good, should I be saying that God is the good *and* that God is selfless so that God is identical to both? Not that God is good and that *means* he is selfless?

If we think that good is recognizable, then it would seem to follow that we can discern what the good is like. When I observe a selfless act, I can say "that is a good thing to do." But again, the precise connection is a little mysterious to me. Is being selfless merely associated with the good and evidence of its presence or is it a feature of the good itself?

And if it is a feature of the good, how do I make sense of that idea? Goodness is a property distinguishable from the property of being selfless. Should we think of the good as *containing* all these other properties, like selflessness? Or maybe we should think that ultimately there really is no distinction between being good and being selfless, that in God there is a sort of synthesis of all goods? Would that imply that "selflessness" is not a "real" property, but should be translated into something like, "selflessness is when someone reflects the character of God in a specific way, namely they act as God would by regarding others before themselves." Then, selflessness is a *way* of being good.

That sort of option seems to make the most sense to me. But at the same time, there does seem to be a threat of, by collapsing all distinctions, making the good unintelligible.

What do you think?

Here was my attempt at a rather quick reply:

JP: I think these are very challenging questions. Even saying "God is the good" is a bit mysterious, but I'm determined to keep saying. I think of God as the ultimate good, and, following Adams, other goods good in virtue of relevant resemblance to the ultimate good. But God is also, practically by definition, worthy of worship. When I'm good, I'm not worthy of worship. Somehow it's important, it seems to me, that we maintain a distinction between the Creator and created things. At most, unless God directly expresses his goodness through us, our goodness is limited, impure, fragmentary, partial, etc.

On selflessness, one might wonder what such a trait really means. The Bible tells us to seek first the kingdom of God and his righteousness, and then "all these things" shall be added to you. Getting those other things added is definitely in our self-interest. Rather than being selfless when we put God first, it seems like it's the best way to do what's best for oneself. This isn't being selfish; it requires not putting oneself first; but the result is definitely what's in one's self interest. Is selflessness not putting oneself first? If so, that makes pretty good sense. But then there's something of a disanalogy between God and us, since God, being God and all, sort of comes first, and rightly so. Now Jesus was willing to humble himself and give up his rights as divine in the incarnation, and that could be said to be selfless, I suppose, although he also kept his eyes on the glory to come. In general, depending on what we mean by selflessness, we need to be careful, because God does want us to be happy, and I don't think he minds if we want to be happy, just so long as we don't privilege it over other things that ought to have primacy.

Some of your questions are nitty gritty metaphysical questions to which I'm unsure of the answers, admittedly. I'm not altogether sure we can find the fine-grained analyses you're after. Maybe we can, though, not sure. I'm just pretty sure I'm not the guy who'll figure it out. J
Another word on the earlier stuff—worship is a good thing for us to do, since we're creatures. But not a good thing for God, since there's nobody God should be worshiping. Another wrinkle. Our being selfless (say, let's define it as not generally putting oneself first), let's say, is a good thing. I think that means it has the property of being good. Good seems more basic somehow though, right? So the property of being selfless itself has the property of being good. Perhaps not the property of being good simpliciter but the property of being good when instantiated by creatures like us. As to how to root that in God, I'm not altogether sure what to say about that, since this is one of those trickier cases where there seem to be some important disanalogies between God and us. But perhaps we could say something like this: God is the ultimate orderer of values, one of which is that creaturely beings should be selfless in important respects; the created order having been made like this, when a human person doesn't put himself first, but rather privileges others, this is the way in which such a creature ought to behave ("ought" in the general value-theoretic sense, not the strict deontic sense). So the relevant value is rooted in the created order as God intended it and is in some ultimate sense dependent on some aspect of God (his will, nature, character, etc.).

I definitely agree we can say all sorts of things about the good. What I resist is ever thinking we have a complete bead on it, since that would require nothing less than getting to the bottom of God. But I don't think implies we can't say a great deal about the good—just probably not a large percentage of all that's true about it.

These are deep and mysterious waters; precision, owing to our epistemic limits and seeing through a glass darkly, is sure to be hard to come by not infrequently.

I prefer a resemblance relation to a containing relation when it comes to the infinite versus finite goods. Craig would say God is the good, by which he'd mean there's no abstract thing called goodness; the good is concrete—God himself. One day I'm determined to get clarity on such matters.

All for now!
djb

Saturday, July 24, 2021: I was able to finalize the four chapters for Ronnie's book and send them over. I should have probably added some more footnotes, but I figure I can do that later if need be. In the meantime I can set that project aside and do what I can on the tetralogy before the summer is through. God blessed the efforts to get over this hump, though, for sure.

Sunday, July 25, 2021: This morning MB got an e-mail from Jan about her plans to pursue a PhD in theology from Durham. This was a bit of an about face from her plans to get the DMin from HBU. TJ and Jerry, it appears, encouraged her to go in this other direction. My feelings are distinctly mixed. Of course it's her prerogative to do this, and maybe this is how God is leading her, but it leaves me wondering about her commitment to HBU and the Center. Going this direction will invariably be a major time commitment for her.

But ultimately our trust is in God to bring us all we need at the Center. Whether that includes Jan or not, God will be faithful to provide. MB and I prayed and talked about it this morning quite a bit, and we both came to peace about it. We are going to redouble our efforts praying for HBU and the Center, especially the fundraising piece. That's something of a microcosm of the challenge of trusting God, because it's an area where I'm acutely cognizant of my inability to crack this nut by my own resources. The experiences at Liberty, though, heavily shaped our attitudes toward money. I simply have to believe that our trust is in God, not money. We have to believe before the money comes. God has given enough reason to believe in the vision of this Center and what he wants to do through it. We are called to walk by faith, not by sight, hoping that in time God gives the increase and sends us all the help we need, the donors big and small, the students, the folks who need to come alongside of us to help.

MB and I decided to turn at least a portion of each Sunday into a mini-prayer retreat for the department of apologetics, HBU, and the Center. I also think I want to spend time walking the campus, and all around the campus, interceding on its behalf, asking God to do what only he can do. To give the increase. To bring something from nothing. To make the Center a reality. This is where I am called, and I want to be true to that calling. Make me faithful to the vocation to which I have been called, dear God. Help me to walk by faith and not by sight. Make me bold to pray as I ought, refusing to let go of the horns of the altar until the answer comes. Root out anything from within me not in accord with your perfect plan for me. Work repentance deep within my heart for anything unpleasing in your sight. Give me clear marching orders in perfect alignment with your will and desire for me. May all I say and think and do be pleasing to you and bring glory to your name. Help me to walk in the path as you illumine it before me and not allow me to depart or deviate from it even a little. Live your life through me, I ask, in Jesus' name. Accomplish your plan here at HBU, in Houston, and in the Center for Moral Apologetics, I beseech you, dear God. In Christ's name, amen.

Monday, July 26, 2021: Today I need to write the foreword for Adam Johnson's book. It's a little before 10 in the morning and we are at the library.

Later in the day. TJ is leading a second meeting of the editorial team for MoralApologetics, even as I write this. I did the foreword and finished by about noon; yay! Went like this:

It is an exciting time for moral apologetics. Work on theistic ethics and versions of the moral argument for God's existence in recent years has experienced a major resurgence. Deductive, inductive, abductive, natural-signs-theoretic, and confirmation variants of moral arguments have been advanced using the technical machinery of analytic philosophy. Correlatively, a whole range of theistic metaethical accounts have been delineated and defended—from natural law approaches to divine command theories, from divine motivation to divine desire accounts, from divine will to divine motivation analyses, and more besides.

The common chord struck by so many of these diverse approaches has been the nagging suspicion and principled case for an ineliminable dependence relation of morality on theism. Into this burgeoning literature Adam Johnson's significant contribution, a divine love theory, is a welcome addition, augmenting and supplementing many prior approaches, occasionally breaking prior paradigms, eminently worthy of a seat at the table. Johnson has done an admirable job here of laying out a fresh variant of theistic ethics, assigning primacy to the love of God as illumined by the perichoretic relationship featured in Trinitarian monotheism. This makes the project cutting edge and superlative, featuring a metaethics that sports numerous strong explanatory features and entails among other things that God's commands are not arbitrary but a function of God's desire for us to enjoy the deepest aspect of reality: the love of the Trinity.

Johnson's book adds important texture to the recent work extolling and explicating the explanatory benefits of Anselmian theology in the realm of ethics and metaethics. Anselm himself was both a proponent of greatest being theology and distinctively Christian theology. In that vein, Johnson has extended the work of moral apologetics to something beyond generic, thin, or bare theism to something thicker and specifically Christian. The idea of using distinctively Trinitarian resources in this way makes for a fascinating project generative of fresh, solid insights that comprise genuine contributions to the literature. If something in even the vicinity of his argument goes through, it pushes in the direction of classical theism, generally, and Christian theism, specifically, providing a robust account of a range of important moral phenomena, likely a better explanation than the salient alternatives on offer.

A luminary from the history of the moral argument, John Henry Newman, spoke of the ampliative function served by special revelation. Unapologetically tapping into specifically Christian theology arguably yields important dividends. The way, most centrally, Johnson uses Trinitarian theology to give a finer grained account of Robert Adams' theistic adaptation of a social requirement model of moral obligations is genuinely perspicacious—just one of many examples of his innovation.

The scholarship and research of this extended essay is top-notch, delving deeply into two separate literatures: one in theology pertaining to the Trinity, and another in ethics and meta-ethics. The range and breadth of the scholarship is impressive, the depth of Johnson's grasp on both sets of material fantastic, as is his facility in their interaction, synthesis, and rapprochement. The quality of the case is at a very high level, the writing a thing of beauty, and the result is a joy to read. Readers may not agree with every ancillary point along the way, but the central integrating thread of his argument strikes me as fundamentally right. Of this I am sure: the work is not responsibly ignored, and the investment of time closely and carefully reading and considering it will be time well spent.

Also sent in my July WB piece a few days back; here it is; my dignity of persons kick is still going on:

Dignity, Not Price

When the great poet W. H. Auden arrived in the United States with Christopher Isherwood in January 1939, he was not religious, and he had not been since he was thirteen at Gresham's School in England. Os Guinness says that two experiences stood out among those that jolted Auden into rethinking the matter of faith. The first had been earlier in 1933, when he was a schoolmaster at the Downs School in the Malvern Hills. Sitting with three fellow teachers, he was suddenly overwhelmed by the sense that all their existence somehow had infinite value and that he loved them for themselves. Years later he described this experience as a "Vision of Agape" (Love).

The second experience came in New York two months after he had written the poem "September 1, 1939." He was in a cinema in Yorkville on the Upper East Side of Manhattan, which unbeknown to him was still largely a German-speaking area. Eager to follow news of the course of the war, he went to see Sieg in Poland ["sieg" means victory], a documentary of the Nazi invasion and conquest of Poland, in which S. S. Storm Troopers were bayoneting women and children, and, to Auden's horror, members of the audience cried out in support of their fellow-countrymen, "Kill them! Kill them!"

These two experiences helped him realize that he needed a better understanding of the value of persons and the existence of evil. He also had to rethink this idea that people are good if his beliefs were going to align with reality. Aligning our beliefs to correspond with reality, especially as revealed by the unshakeable truths of morality, is key to thinking theologically. Take the examples from Auden: human beings are valuable, perhaps infinitely valuable; at the same time, we are not intrinsically good; there is something morally broken about us; and some things are just flat wrong, even evil.

This is by no means an exhaustive list of moral realities on which to base our thinking about nature and existence, but it is a fruitful start. For now let's focus in even more and choose just one of these to think about some more: the intrinsic value of people, perhaps even something like the infinite value of people. I do not mean to suggest that we are morally good, but we are valuable. Immanuel Kant had a way of talking about this issue: he said people have worth and value and dignity, but not a price. There is an inherent dignity to persons that we deeply recognize, and it cannot be quantified or reduced to a dollar amount; there is something about it that is intangible, literally priceless. And somehow we know this, down deep, though we can forget it, or perhaps intentionally repress it. We can forget that it is true of others, and we can forget that it is true of ourselves.

What I find especially exciting about this particular piece of moral evidence is that many of our unbelieving friends themselves intuitively recognize its truth. At least at moments they are often able to see that people have great intrinsic value and dignity. They may not know why—just as they may not know why we have moral obligations, or that people are of equal moral worth, or that basic human rights obtain—but they can recognize the truths themselves. Otherwise, something like the moral argument could not get off the ground, because the moral argument appeals to just such moral evidences, but fortunately God has made all of us as human beings able to apprehend such truths.

Think about the Nazi depiction of Jews, the ugly history of American chattel slavery, and, more recently, the intellectual contortions required to deny the humanity of unborn children to justify their wholesale slaughter. In such paradigmatic instances of reprehensible mistreatment, we see on ready display the perceived need to deny the humanity of the victims.

This is thought to make it okay; we would otherwise know the behavior is beyond the moral pale. Even at our worst we somehow recognize the value of humans, and to rationalize our behavior we deny the humanity of the victims— just as Goebbels' propaganda did the same of the Poles. I suspect general revelation alone gives us reason to think human beings are intrinsically valuable, sacred, and the legitimate bearers of human rights. What such recognitions should then lead us to do is ask what it is about reality that explains such truths. Why is it that people have such great intrinsic dignity and value?

Now, its very obviousness might be thought to imply that we need not search for a more ultimate explanation. If it's that obvious, why ask why? But this is to confuse the matter of the truth of the thing with our knowing it to be true. We may be able to recognize that something is true without being able to explain why. This is the difference, as H. P. Owen was wont to point out, between something being self-evident and something being self-explaining. Or philosophers might say it is confusing metaphysics (what is real) with epistemology (our knowledge of what's real). So even unbelievers can often grasp that people have mysteriously great intrinsic value, but this piece of moral evidence cries out for explanation.

As Christians we have terrific reasons to think it is indeed true that human beings, each and every one of them, have great value, perhaps even infinite value, as Auden sensed that day in the Malvern hills. Austin Farrer was a friend of C. S. Lewis's who, in his own work, had for one of his main points of emphasis the value of persons. In one of his books he asked readers to consider the way we normatively ought to think about other people. It is of great importance, he argued, that we value them rightly, that we think about others in such a way as to regard them properly. Such regard should be at once so pure and so entire that it leads to a sort of frustration. This frustration derives from the incompleteness of our definition of those we so regard. Thinking of our neighbors in too casual a way cannot sustain the esteem we intuitively think they deserve. The conclusion to which Farrer felt compelled is that what deserves our regard is not simply our neighbor, but God in our neighbor and our neighbor in God.

This gets us to the heart of why we know as Christian believers that people are of infinite value. They are creations of God, made in his image, fashioned after his likeness, and they are loved by God, perhaps each of us differently, but all of us infinitely. There are few things as revolutionary, for each of us, as coming into a deep understanding of God's love—not just of others, but of you.

Tuesday, July 27, 2021: Stayed at home today and wrote a few blogs. Here's one for a Patreon piece for the WB:

Errors Come in Pairs

313

Having been delivered from a toxic and traumatic work environment, sometimes I find myself wondering how I should think and pray about my previous place of employment. The potential problem with indulging righteous indignation is that the ratio of righteousness to indignation might be altogether too small. Recently a leader at the institution wrote and expressed the hope that I would continue to pray for them, especially, he wrote, since we had devoted so much time and energy to the school.

I do pray for the place, and I pray for God's best for it, but what exactly that looks like is hard for me to say. It seems to me that some hard decisions need to be made about the leadership, the growth strategies, the treatment of its employees, its academic vision, and the like. It is hard, as I pray, not to see mainly the school's deficiencies and problems, and this poses a temptation for me.

C. S. Lewis once said that errors come in pairs, and he was right. When we see a problem, or a whole slew of problems, with an institution, a church, an outfit of any kind, and it bothers us viscerally, strains our credulity, and raises our hackles to the breaking point, we want to see justice prevail, the problems acknowledged and addressed forthrightly, the dysfunctia rooted out. But in our zeal to see things set right, we can be tempted to sacrifice love at the altar of righteousness.

The story of Jonah going to preach to the Ninevites never ceases to challenge us. The reason he didn't want to go and preach there was because he was afraid that God, in his love, would show them mercy. The worst case scenario for Jonah was that his preaching would prove efficacious, the Ninevites would repent, and God would be gracious to them, which is exactly what happened. And then Jonah pouted about it afterwards, his lust for just desserts dissatisfied. He wanted to be the prophet who called down God's judgments, not see them have a change of heart, return to God, and find forgiveness and healing.

When indignation trumps righteousness, we can fall into the same trap.

Or think of the elder son in the Prodigal Son story. His profligate younger brother returns and is thrown a party, and the older brother resents it, forgetting how much he had received and was still receiving from his father. Or think of the Pharisee and the tax collector. Despite his righteous acts, the Pharisee had lost sight of his own ongoing dependence on God's grace and mercy, losing the humility he needed to react to sinners with compassion rather than contempt.

Sometimes Jesus is thought to have lowered moral standards, but in fact he often elevated them. But there is an explanation for the confusion; there was something distinctive about his ministry that some interpreters mistakenly think involved a lowering of standards. What was distinctive was, as Robert Gagnon puts it, his incredibly generous spirit even toward those who had lived in gross

314

disobedience to God for years. In fact he did not merely wait for the lost to come to him; he went actively in search for them, with neither contempt nor condescension.

The example of Jesus provides a wake-up call to those in the church on both sides of the theological aisle. Gagnon again:

> For liberals who think that an aggressive outreach to those on the margins of society entails acceptance without transformation and a diminishment of the church's moral standards, Jesus' ministry provides incontrovertible proof that the church can practice radical love without sacrificing "one iota or one letter stroke" from God's demands for righteous conduct. For conservatives who think that upholding holiness means complete separation from and contempt for the wicked of the world, Jesus' ministry demonstrates that righteousness can be wed with love. When either love or righteousness is sacrificed, the church proclaims a truncated gospel.[18]

I think my prayers for my old school to repent are fine, but without minimizing the wrongdoing or injustice that grieves me, I must not allow the speck in their eye to lead to a log of judgmentalism in my own. I need to be sure that I retain an earnest desire to see them repent. More than a desire for retribution or just desserts, the disposition of my heart, if it is to be like Christ's, should be free of contempt or condescension, filled with the gratitude and humility that come from remembering that I, too, stand under perpetual grace. Otherwise my indignation can serve as a barrier to repentance. Then and only then can I have the eyes of the father of the prodigal straining to see, and a heart poised to embrace, the prodigal after returning from far off.

I also wrote another piece, this one for the Roundtable Discussion on the WB—on the topic of which book had the biggest influence on us as either an apologist or Christian philosopher:

The Book that Influenced Me the Most

When I was in college I first encountered the Euthyphro Dilemma in an early Socratic dialogue. The Euthyphro Dilemma—not the "Urethra Dilemma," as one student wrote in a paper—is the challenge, to put it in modern terms, of whether God commands something because it's moral or something is moral because God commands it. It fascinated me from the start, and I knew I wanted to think about it quite a bit more. I found it endlessly engaging, and though I thought there was a good answer to it, I didn't quite know what it was.

---

[18] Robert A. J. Gagnon, *The Bible and Homosexual Practice: Texts and Hermeneutics* (Nashville, TN: Abingdon Press, 2001), 213.

After switching majors from physics to philosophy, I had occasion to think some more about the Dilemma, and the connections between God and morality more generally, but it was while subsequently attending Asbury Seminary that I found the chance to think about it in much greater depth. Studying with Jerry Walls, in particular, furnished me the opportunity, and so as a seminarian I was able for the first time to start writing about it. Admittedly I was only getting started; some of my lines were less than memorable—"God is at least as much God as a circle is a circle," for instance. (Let's never mention that again.)

By the time I finished seminary I knew I wanted to earn a PhD in philosophy, and I knew from day one that I would write my dissertation on the Euthyphro Dilemma. The work of Robert Adams had been important to me already, but I heard he was working on a big book on the topic of God and ethics. Serendipitously, perhaps providentially, as I was in the throes of writing my dissertation, his book was published in 1999. *Finite and Infinite Goods: A Framework for Ethics* did not disappoint and proved to be a treasure trove of goodies.

I had been working on my doctorate and dissertation at Wayne State University, a bastion of analytic philosophy. Alvin Plantinga had started his career there after Yale; he describes coming up with the central idea of *God and Other Minds* in a dingy parking lot on Wayne's campus. I'm quite sure I have found myself in that dingy parking lot; if not that one, plenty of others. But by the time I came around there were no believers on faculty in the philosophy department. There are now, once more, but not when I was there. My friendship with fellow believer Sloan Lee while there was a lifesaver.

I did the bulk of my study of ethics there under the tutelage of Bruce Russell, a very good philosopher but a committed atheist. He was fair, and he taught me a lot—as did plenty of others on faculty from Herb Granger to Michael McKinsey, Larry Lombard to Larry Powers. The work in ethics and analytic ethics was done with Bruce, though, and fairly all of the reading I did seemed divorced from anything like theism. This bothered me, because a longstanding conviction of mine had been that morality robustly and rightly construed almost certainly broached central matters of worldview and was more plausibly at home in a theistic world rather than an atheist one. The rigor and analytic machinery were a thing to behold, crucial to learn, but sometimes the aridness of it all felt like a lifeless desert, leaving me feeling parched.

I still vividly recall an afternoon in a library on campus, dutifully reading through an anthology for class, coming across George Mavrodes' "Religion and the Queerness of Morality." It was nothing less than exhilarating, an oasis and stream in the desert. At long last I had found someone who spoke my language and saw ethics the way I had for as long as I could remember. But that was just a prelude or precursor. Thanks to the resurgence of interest in Christian philosophy, I gradually began to come across more profoundly good work in ethics and metaethics by Christian thinkers, along with unbelievers who took theistic claims seriously. Finally, at last, when Adams' magnum opus came out, it was a rigorous, book-length treatment of a whole range of moral phenomena, the whole discussion structured by a (Platonic) theistic paradigm—more theistic than Platonic. I remember long nights spent reading the book, enraptured by its every page, mesmerized by it, inspired by it, like practically nothing else I had ever read. It ushered me into a whole new arena, and I knew my work would never be the same.

Among other things, what a tremendous confidence booster it was to see a world-class philosopher at the top of his game, an unapologetic professing Christian believer, so forthrightly and intelligently bring his theistic convictions to bear in his work. Mine was a context where the reigning view and undeniable subtext so often was that theism is suspect and God is for the credulous. I know I should have known better already, but sociological forces in a context like that are strong. I know plenty of professing believers, facing such explicit or implicit resistance and condescension, who simply stop bringing up their faith in those environments. Maybe religious conviction in our culture remains a majority view; it is often a distinctly minority one in secular philosophy departments, a dynamic that can wear down one's defenses and over time prove oppressive and daunting. Sometimes a single flicker of light in such darkness is priceless. *Finite and Infinite Goods* was that flicker for me—at the time it felt like a ball of fire. To this day I remain more grateful than I can put into words.

Invariably the book's timing and epic quality meant it would have a significant impact on my own developing views, and sure enough, it has continued to wield an ongoing influence on me until this day. I count it one of the very best books on theistic ethics and moral apologetics—John Hare's more recent *God's Command* is the only other contemporary book in its league on the subject, as far as I am concerned.

Sometimes scholars might wonder if their work is read, and whether it has an impact. The sort of training and rigor it takes for a book like this one to be produced means it loses lots of its readers. In a constantly hurried, harried culture, it does not garner lots of tweets or Facebook likes; nothing viral about it. Adams is no pop cultural ion, nor counted an internet celebrity of note or social media superstar. His is a long, slow, and challenging book (as are his others, like his treatise on Leibniz), but so eminently worth the effort to wade through and digest carefully, rife with substance, replete with insight, redolent with wisdom. A weighty exercise in culture making, it prodigiously impresses without trying to.

Despite that it does not have thousands of reviews on Amazon, and likely never will, Adams' book will continue to have a longstanding influence for generations to come. Like relentless drops of water gradually cutting rock, its

317

influence will eventually and ever so incrementally percolate down and make its difference felt; only a furtive glance at its ultimate payoff will be seen in our lifetimes. Like A. E. Taylor's *Faith of a Moralist* or John Henry Newman's *An Essay in Aid of a Grammar of Assent*, *Finite and Infinite Goods* is a classic; it explores matters that matter most and will be sure to stand the test of time and endure well after the entertaining ephemeral voices of fame have been long silenced.

Wednesday, July 28, 2021: Up early, and hopefully will be hitting the gym soon. Yesterday was a pretty relaxing day. It was nice to take a day off without spending the whole day obsessing I wasn't working, which doesn't tend to be restful in the least. But I was able to enjoy it instead on this occasion, which was great. Today I would like to wade into the debunking material in order to make some progress on that chapter in the moral realism book. I also need to write Rist and spend time praying about who else to invite onboard the Collection.

Thursday, July 29, 2021: Productive day! I wrote Melissa Cain Travis to see if she'd be okay with my advocating for her at HBU to get reconnected. We're going to do a zoom chat this evening. I asked TJ if I could become the Book Review Editor at the site, and he said yes, and then TJ agreed to do a review of Zak Schmoll's forthcoming book on disability and the problem of evil and JP agreed to do a review of Anne Jeffrey's book on God and morality. I also wrote Brian Chilton about doing reviews on the books MB suggested on abuse.

Then I wrote the following e-mail to all the MA in apol students:

Hi all, all of you are residential MA in apologetics students at HBU. I have touched base with some of you already, and now I want to reach out to all of you.

As the Director of the Center for Moral Apologetics here at HBU, I'm excited to announce a new initiative that will get underway this fall, and to invite each of you to participate in it. Each of you is invited to become a Student Fellow of the Center. I have asked Taylor Neill to be the Senior Student Fellow who'll help me lead this initiative, and he has graciously agree. We would relish each of you to assume the role of a Student Fellow.

Taylor and I still have to figure out how many meetings there will be this upcoming school year. We don't want it to be too prohibitive a time commitment, but at the same time we'd like for it to be a substantive part of your education here at HBU. The content of the meetings will vary--maybe one evening we'll watch a debate on the moral argument and discuss, another evening Taylor will hold a discussion of moral realism, etc. This first year I'd like to be pretty heavily involved myself; on nights I'm not there, Taylor will be in charge.

318

As I envision it, each meeting will have four components: fellowship, prayer, service, and an educational component. The fellowship will be designed for us all to get to one another better and form more of a community. The prayer will be designed to lift up your burdens in prayer and contribute to our being a community with one another. The service component will just be a brief reminder that talk of ethics should be conjoined with active steps taken to serve others (we'll just talk about ways in which this is already being done and new ways that are available—even if it's just handing out water to homeless folks). And then the bulk of time each meeting will be spent learning the tools of moral apologetics.

When I'm there leading discussions, I'm leaning toward giving y'all a working outline I have (about 30 single spaced pages) canvassing the whole territory of moral apologetics—all things related to moral arguments for God's existence and goodness. Of course this is the central focus of the Center, as we wish to make HBU the hub of cutting-edge work in this area from a variety of disciplines. The Center itself may offer opportunities for service for those who are interested. (I can discuss that later.)

As I see it, being a Student Fellow gives you two major advantages: a stronger sense of community with your fellow students in the program, and an opportunity to learn the tools of moral apologetics--without spending an additional dime. It's all on the house, gratis, just for you. These resources, I am convinced, are really crucial to be an effective apologist today, and I want to give you all I can within the time constraints of our gatherings. This is why I felt called to HBU—to do this work, and to prepare and equip a new generation with these resources and this material with which I've lived for thirty years.

I'm currently under contract for my fourth and fifth books with Oxford University Press on the topic of the moral argument for God's existence, William Lane Craig and I are attempting to secure a contract for a collaboration on the subject, and I'm excited to see the Center here at HBU grow. Your participation in the Center and in this initiative is a crucial step in that process.

So, once more, I hereby invite each of you into this initiative. If you have any interest, please let me know! (I know several of you have already expressed interest, but feel free to write me again, and anytime, any and all of you.)

Please give this your prayerful attention, and if you know of any students who might be interested in this outside of the MA in apol, please do me a favor and let me know their names. Thanks!

Dave B.

TJ sent an e-mail out in the afternoon to the Moral Apologetics team to bring everyone up to date on the latest developments:

Good afternoon, team!

I wanted to update you on a few important items related to MoralApologetics.com.

1. Marybeth has discerned that the Lord is directing her toward laying aside her role as Associate Editor at the site due to other demands related to HBU and the Center. She will continue to contribute as she has opportunity (and will certainly have her hands full keeping Dave in line!), but she will no longer serve in an official editorial capacity for the site. We are all so blessed by her, and wish her only the most success in her pursuits. Thank you, MB! Blessings to you!

2. Dave (the Dr. Dave B., not the almost Dr. Dave O.) will now serve as the Book Review Editor for the site. He'll take the lead on finding books to review and reviewers to write the reviews. So grateful to have him back in the mix, and don't be surprised if he taps each of you at some point to do a review! (He's already drawn me in, and I suspect JP will not be able to resist him for long!)

So grateful for each of you, and may God continue to bless MoralApologetics.com!

T. J.

Friday, July 30, 2021: Today has been a bit of a struggle. Some weight of heaviness hangs in the air. MB and I both feel it. We prayed about it, but it persists. Could be the result of lots of things, or the cumulative effect of a number of challenges. Today, for instance, was the day I figured I'd hear if we got the grant, but no news. Trying to trust God, and not just for particular results, but it is hard. I have no earthly clue how to raise money for the Center, and ours is an environment where the soil to do such work seems as hard as it's parched. Probably shouldn't have but cancelled prayer time with TJ this afternoon; just was not up for it. Nor for time with Jerry this evening; I postponed that until tomorrow evening. Hard to shake this dispiritedness. I decided to tell Jerry I didn't have the emotional bandwidth to meet in August, which is quite true.

Saturday, July 31, 2021: Rob's birthday today. Last evening realized I had a niece's husband who is an avid, rabid anti-vaxxer. Hard to take. The disappointment I felt was surprising for being so visceral. How to confront such self-satisfied irrationality is baffling to me. Trying in vain to convince him showed me that I seem to be dealing with a fair amount of anger—a recurring feeling of frustration. I just seem so ineffectual. I can't persuade my ignorant nephew of basic medical facts; I can't persuade my stepson to take Christianity more seriously; I can't figure out how to raise money for the Center. The frustration leads to anger, and it grows worse. Not hearing on the grant proposal by the deadline surely didn't help. Tough moment.

A challenge for historians is to know the zeitgeist of a prior moment in history. It may not be readily evident from consideration of salient events themselves. For example, at this particular juncture of history, if I were to back up and examine it, there's a pervasive sense of tension in the air. We were emerging from the pandemic, and then variants began to arise, especially this highly contagious "delta" variant, and now it's spreading, especially among the unvaccinated, like veritable wild fire. This is exacerbating tensions between those who think getting vaccinated is a good idea, and those vociferously opposed for a whole range of reasons from mistrust of government, rhetoric about freedom, claims the vaccines are experimental, fears of side effects, etc. Somehow this has gotten politicized—a slice of conservatives distinctly among the anti-vaxxers, most liberals strongly in favor. Though more conservative than liberal, I definitely side with the vaxxers right now, though for the life of me I can't see any connections to politics, not any principled ones anyway. In fact it seems to me that the pro-life person should stand with the vaccine, since there's ample reason to think that it's highly effective at stemming the tide of the pandemic. Second and third waves spurred by variants have historically been the worst. So anyway, the anti-vaxxers think the vaccine represents all that's wrong with the nation, and the vaxxers have a very hard time understanding such perspectives, and tensions seem to keep escalating between these camps. I had an unpleasant "conversation" myself with a niece's husband yesterday that went exactly nowhere good—he's a rabid opponent of vaccination.

Anyway, all that to say that this is a very real operative dynamic in the air nowadays. It contributes all the more to the difficulty of civil discourse and building bridges. The conversation with my nephew, though annoying, didn't bother me as much as noticing that my sister had liked his original anti-vax post, which bothered me a great deal. If this issue didn't involve putting lives at risk, I probably wouldn't care, but it does. This is exactly one of the reasons for the intractable conflicts; each side thinks something vital is at stake. Personally though, the anti-vaxxers in general strike me as incorrigible, ignorant, and defiant, not at all averse to employing the language of abortionists to justify their stupidity, irresponsibility, and life-threatening recklessness.

Jan wrote us some e-mails today—good stuff happening. She's writing a press release, trying to get action from HBU, working on generating more speaking engagements for us, compiling resources on moral injury, continuing to transcribe questions from the moral argument class, etc. She's a marvel and a dynamo.

Sunday, August 1, 2021: So today is the Sabbath, and I'm looking forward to resting. Nathaniel will come by after church to cook stir fry and watch the latest episode of Ted Lasso with us. Sundays are supposed to dedicated to prayer in a special way, so looking forward to that later with MB. I continue to find fascinating why some folks are adamantly opposed to getting the vaccine. I'm tempted to compile a list of all the various reasons people give. Elton encouraged me to try to understand their position better despite my strong disagreement, which is a good idea.

Mark Ragsdale, for example, a former student from Liberty, gives this set of reasons: "1. By medical definition it is not a vaccine. 2. By medical definition diagnosis are not cases. 3. By that aforementioned, deaths are overblown and survival rates are under blown. 4. Diagnoses are not based upon any identification of a pathogen, only inflammation. 5. Inflammation is attributable to multiple causation, before, during, and after this issue. 6. 45k to 65k annual deaths via flu have surprisingly gone unreported. 7. I have lost dear friends to COVID that had the vaxx. 8. The authorities vacillate in their reports. 9. Unfettered immigration does not match the narrative. 10. Fear has historically been used by governments to control the populous. 11. Anyone who kills babies should not lecture me on the Decalogue as Harris did."

Looking at his list, here are a few thoughts: (1) By medical definition it is not a vaccine; not sure what that means. (2) Unsure what this means. (3) Deaths from the virus are overblown and survival rates underblown? What's the evidence for this? (4) Diagnoses based on inflammation only? That seems quite unlikely to me. (5) Inflammation attribute to multiple things—a point relevant only if point 4 holds, which I doubt. (6) A bunch of annual flue deaths have gone unreported—maybe the idea here is that some with the flu died because of that instead of the covid? (7) Anecdotal. How old were they? What are their names? (8) Which reports? (9) There's an inconsistently between the covid policies and not cracking down on immigration—that may be true, but it would suggest the need for tighter immigration policies, nothing against vaccination. (10) Fear has historically been used by governments to control the populous, perhaps, but most of what he seems to be doing is tapping into fear. (11) Pretty clearly an ad hominem fallacy.

All in all this is pretty dismal reasoning, embarrassingly bad. Yet this guy is getting a doctorate in apologetics. Wow.

According to the CDC a vaccine is this: A product that stimulates a person's immune system to produce immunity to a specific disease, protecting the person from that disease. Vaccines are usually administered through needle injections, but can also be administered by mouth or sprayed into the nose. They come in different varieties: prophylactic vaccines (that work by exposing healthy individuals to a weakened pathogen, or parts of it, in order to trigger a protective immune response), post-exposure vaccines, and therapeutic vaccines. Therapeutic vaccines aim to teach the immune system how to destroy a pathogen or other disease-causing entity (e.g. cancer cells) by introducing an antigen associated with it. But rather than training it against new pathogens, the goal of therapeutic vaccines is to persuade the immune system to fight harder against an existing illness.

Here's the difference between a vaccine and a non-vaccine medication: "Vaccines are a specific type of drug which teaches the immune system how to defeat a disease. Importantly, once this education has taken place, 'memory cells' persist in the body, ready to initiate a rapid response if the pathogen is encountered again. This means that a vaccine can prompt long term protection against a disease, although sometimes multiple doses are needed to make sure this protection appears in all recipients. Some vaccines also require booster doses over time to ensure that enough well-functioning memory cells are present. A drug also helps the body to fight a disease, or lessen the symptoms associated with it – and it may even do so by influencing the immune system – but it doesn't aim to cultivate this immune memory."

So why does Ragsdale insist that the covid vaccine isn't a vaccine? Here's a guess: The best prophylactic vaccines also block transmission of that pathogen to other people, by preventing it from gaining a foothold in the body and replicating, a phenomenon called *sterilizing immunity*. And recent tests indicate that the covid vaccine, while greatly reducing transmission, doesn't prevent it altogether. By the definition here, though, this doesn't stop it from being a vaccine, but just renders it not as good a vaccine as one, all other things being equal, blocking transmission better. If this interpretation of his idea is right, he seems to be treating complete prevention of transmission as a necessary condition for a vaccine, which seems likely wrong. At the least it could be said it's a highly idiosyncratic usage of the term, since we customarily speak of a vaccine being effective to some degree or other, and it's usually always less than 100%.

By coincidence just this morning, as I was writing this, MB got a horrible message from her mother decrying MB's pro-vaccine stance. That her mom would basically put her own anti-vaxx stance above this relationship staggers the mind. The lunacy quotient right now is just through the roof.

Monday, August 2, 2021: Relaxed a bit today and decided to cut way down on caffeine and carbs. Hadn't been feeling very good lately, and it's' important I adopt a healthier lifestyle. Heard from agent that Baker seems to taking a serious look at the book with me and Craig.

Tuesday, August 3, 2021: Woke up to two things, one good and one not so good. The grant was turned down, not unexpected at this point. C'est la vie. And MB finished all of her final revisions on *Telling Tales*. Looking great. Just waiting at this point on Paul Gould's foreword and a couple blurbs. Later in the day Paul Gould sent us his wonderful blurb for TT (we will revise it slightly):

William Kent Kruger's *New York Times* best-selling book *This Tender Land* (2019) opens with this arresting thought:

In the beginning, after he labored over the heavens and the earth, the light and the dark, and land and the sea and all living things that dwell therein, after he created man and women and before he rested, I believe God gave us one final gift. Lest we forget the divine source of all that beauty, he gave us stories.

In the span of a few sentences, Kruger suggests a theology of story. Stories are a gift, like everything else, from God. As such, we should expect to see God in stories too. And I'm not just thinking about the latest "Christian" movie or novel. No, if God has gifted us stories, then we should seek his divine clues in all stories—or at least all the good ones.

Stories help us see. And they teach about deep truths—including about the true story of the world. But there is a tension today between what we might affectionately call "High Culture" and "Pop Culture." The intelligentsia tell us there is no story alive and inviting. The true story of the world is more mundane, more this-worldly, more secular. But that story—and those individual stories build on that story—are rather boring. If we pay attention to the stories we love—the ones we read and re-read, and the ones we watch and re-watch, we learn something startling: they are suggestive of something transcendent, something other-worldly, something enchanted and mysterious.

So, there is a tension between what we are told by the intelligentsia and the deepest longings of the human heart. It seems when we think about the stories we love, that our hearts long for more. Our hearts long for a story alive and inviting, a story that names us, even. It seems then, that we find clues about that true story of the world—"Intimations of the Sacred"—in Pop Culture; in the tales we tell.

If we pay attention, these stories we love are a kind of divine clue, awakening us and setting us on a journey of discovery. Ultimately, if faithfully followed, they point us to the point of all good stories: Jesus. But we need guides. I cannot think of a better pair of guides than Marybeth and David Baggett, that dynamic duo of literature, art, story, and philosophy. You are in for a real treat. In *Telling Tales*, our faithful—and funny—guides take us on a tour through some of our most beloved stories—from Kurt Vonnegut to Ted Lasso, Harry Potter to The Hunger Games, pointing out along the way rich insights about faith and truth, hope and goodness, love and beauty.

I'm kind of impressed with the Baggetts. They watch a lot of good television. And they read a ton of great books. And they know literature, philosophy, pop culture, and theology. They are the perfect guides to help us see the divine voice in the text and on the screen. Listen, along with them, for the voice of God in story.

May you enjoy this rich book of adventure and folly, comedy and tragedy, love potions and Shadowlands, theology and philosophy, Jesus and journey. And then thank the God who gives us all things, including story, to remind us of his beauty.

Wednesday, August 4, 2021: We woke up in Austin and made it to a little diner for breakfast. No success finding an English breakfast, alas. Then we saw UT-Austin, which was pretty. Austin is a hip place. I joked Lansing's a poor man's Austin. On the way home I got quite emotional struggling with what I had to do in the fall—teach three classes, including a time-intensive medieval course, assist Craig, try to write, and raise money for the Center. Not to mention the Strauss lectures. Felt overwhelmed, and cried a bit.

Before going home we visited Nathaniel and a guy from a local school—North American University—called to arrange a meeting with Nathaniel to discuss his teaching. I had a chance to chat with the fellow and told him to let me know if he needed a philosophy teacher. Turns out he does! Despite all my busy-ness, I told him I might be interested. Then, after getting home, my dean suggested that they give my medieval class to someone else to give me a chance to create a new course on theistic ethics and moral apologetics. I wouldn't have been able to do otherwise. I jumped at the idea. So now I'm thinking I'll teach two classes for North American and create this class, which should generate five or six thousand dollars, which I can give to Center. So my schedule became more workable and I made some progress on fund raising. We'll see how it goes.

Thursday, August 5, 2021: Hard time getting motivated today to do any serious work. Had a doctor's appointment early on and was put on a new medication to control my A1c better. In the afternoon the car acted up and we're trying to get to the bottom of that. Nathaniel was offered the chance to teach three college classes in the fall, which is great for him. I have an appointment in the morning to see if I might wish to take a class or two at the same place.

I wrote my dean this e-mail today:

Phil, hey man. Wanted to tell you about two quick things. First, though, thanks so much for your good idea to defer a class until the spring. Getting rid of Medieval freed me up to do what I need to do in the fall, including putting together the new course, coordinating the Student Fellows, chip away at publications, etc. I had been really stressed about the schedule, so this helps immensely.

Perhaps it's not my place, but you had asked for suggestions for folks to come in and teach in apol, folks who have something of a platform. My suggestion, for what it's worth, is Melissa Cain Travis. I know she left HBU and that there were tensions, but I think we can easily understand why. The rule had come into place that put a ceiling on her advancement, and though she had earned a PhD and worked and advocated hard for HBU, others (not all of whom had earned a doctorate--nothing against MJ, I love her, but just speaking objectively here) were grandfathered in and granted an exemption to the rule. I bring Melissa up just because she really does strike me as a person HBU should want to keep around in some capacity. She's come to my mind on many occasions, and I'm open to its being a nudge to say something. She's very sharp, a good teacher, passionate about apologetics, and loves HBU. Although she can't come and teach on campus, she's still fairly local and, my guess is, would be happy if HBU did what it could/needed to to invite her back. I'd love to see it happen. She's good people. I encourage it. Anyway, for what it's worth.

Second, I want to tell you something that nobody else knows. I know fundraising is a big concern around here. Totally get it. Of course I also feel peculiarly ineffective at it, as it's simply outside my wheelhouse. I've hoped and prayed for speaking opportunities where I can cast a vision for the Center in the hopes of generating a buzz and such. And maybe that will still happen. A few doors have opened, but nothing to write home about. So we're a year in and I'm feeling distinctly loserish about my success so far on that specific score. I know we have those upcoming zoom meetings in which we'll learn strategies and such about fundraising. But perhaps it would be good for you to know MB's and my plans concerning what we intend to give to HBU. On her birthday next year, in November, we're planning on personally giving 50,000 dollars to the Center. But that's not the big thing.

When we die, we're going to give all but 50,000 dollars from the estate to the Center. That's anything remaining in retirement, our house, and any money we might get from insurance. We'll be putting this into our will soon. Potentially this is upwards of a million dollars.

I just wanted you to know this in order for you to know that we really are committed to fundraising, even though I don't think it's my first calling here or anything I'm particularly good at. I still do hope God raises up donors to the Center big and small, but do know that this is something on which MB and I have agreed. We agreed on this some time ago but haven't shared it with anyone. Despite HBU's struggles, we love the school and deeply believe in its leadership and mission. Of course I don't know when we'll shuffle our mortal coil, or details about end-of-life expenses. Still hoping MB writes a bestseller one of these days. ☐ I'm sure I will bite the big one well before she does. I turn 56 this year;

she's only 48. But we're committed to this. Nathaniel will be given 50K but that's it. We don't think it would do him any favors to get much more.

Things are better where Nathaniel is concerned, by the way. He was just officially offered today to teach three English classes in the fall at North American University locally. So things are looking up there. He's already in a much better place emotionally.

Best,
Bag

Friday, August 6, 2021: This morning Nathaniel will come by the house; we need to use his car until ours gets repaired this afternoon. So we'll take him to work and have access to his car. I have an appointment at 9 am.

The appointment went pretty well. I'm inclined to take the intro phil course and use the money, 3K, for things in the house we need—bathroom repairs, grill, speakers, and new chair. About to write Larry there to tell him. Early afternoon TJ and I had a nice time of chatting and praying.

Later I reconsidered, and had to write Larry again:

Larry, please call me Dave.

Listen, man, I am really sorry to do this. This evening as I was trying to hammer out a schedule for the intro phil class I felt my stress levels going through the roof. I really wanted to do this class, and really wanted to work with you, but I'm afraid I'm having to come to terms with my limitations. This term, in addition to teaching my full-time schedule at HBU, I've also been tasked with generating a new online course they want to run in the spring. In addition, I'm starting a new initiative of Student Fellows for the Center I run, and that project will involve meeting with them four or five times over the course of the term. Plus I remain under pressure to do fundraising for the Center, which is something I feel is altogether outside my wheelhouse, but I know I have to crack that nut and do what it takes to make it happen. And on top of all of that I'm under four book contracts at the moment, two with Oxford University Press.

As I was working on the course for you this evening, it began to dawn on me that I simply can't get the job done in the midst of all of this crazily hectic schedule. I went to bed and told Marybeth that I could almost feel a sense of panic welling up within me, and we both figured that, if this is so, I had better reconsider. I'm so, so sorry to be unable to do either of these courses. I suspect I still think of myself as a younger man than I am, when I could burn the candle at both ends and be resilient to bounce back no matter what. My bounce back-ability quotient,

I'm realizing, has undergone a serious reduction. As much as I really despise having to do this, I have to back down. Again, my sincerest apologies for this. This afternoon, though it was a tough call at the time, I was inclined to think I could bear down, pull out the stops, and just do it, but this evening, as the weight of the term bore down on me and the implications of my decision crystallized, I found myself experiencing radical second thoughts that I cannot honestly repress. And I figured I should tell you as soon as possible.

I joked with my wife that I wish God had told me no clearly this afternoon, but then admitted that perhaps he did and I wasn't listening. ☐ I really wanted to do this. I believe in your mission; you were inspiring.

One of the hardest things about this is letting you down, my good man. You were nothing but a joy and a treasure; both my wife and I absolutely loved your spirit. As I said earlier, you were the biggest selling point of all.

I truly wish you all the best as you continue to perform so excellently in your role there at NAU. I'm so glad our paths crossed, and once more I'm so sorry that I have to bow out. If I can do anything to help you find a suitable replacement, please let me know. Perhaps a different HBU philosophy person might be able to do it? Don't hesitate to ask for my assistance to find someone if that might help.

Every best wish, Dave

Saturday, August 7, 2021: Graduation was held today. Marybeth attended, while I finished getting the house ready for the party afterwards. Besides us, Craig Evans, Nancy Pearcey, Phil Tallon, Jan Shultis, Jerry Walls, Nathaniel, and the Catchings were in attendance. Went on for some time; folks seem to have a good time. Nancy shared some really interesting things about nonheterosexuals, 80 percent of whom don't identify as exclusively gay, but rather as bisexual. In the evening MB was feeling a bit vulnerable having had folks in the house, but I assured her that things had gone really well. Long social engagements are just a bit rough on us introverts. This evening I also shared with her my own struggles with sanctification of late, and she prayed for me. God's calling us both to trust him more, I'm convinced.

Sunday, August 8, 2021: Feeling like we're turning a spiritual corner, and glad for it. We went to Toasted Yolk this morning for a lovely breakfast, and we're planning on doing some serious praying today. Among topics I wish to pray about: filling out the rest of the contributors to the Collection, the Student Fellows initiative, work on the realism book, the contract for the Craig book, and we should pray for the Mitchells at Liberty, who just lost a daughter. MB's requests concern the Strauss lectures, the fall semester, her desire to write, Nathaniel's finances, and trusting God as she should.

Monday, August 9, 2021: Finished my summer fun book on Lucille Ball yesterday. Enjoyed it, but lots of it made me sad. Woke up early this morning and went to the gym to exercise. Then made a healthy breakfast. It's now a little before 9 in the morning and we hope to hit the library before long. MB's making coffee; although I have cut down on my caffeine of late, I may just have some. I've begun reading *Till We Have Faces*, a simply amazing book, and MB is reading *Jesus and John Wayne*; neither of us is impressed with the latter—lots of broad-brushing and going after low-hanging fruit.

Early afternoon. Been working on the debunking material. Challenging stuff. But I need to master this. MB is frustrated and feeling inadequate to some of her tasks. Tough time. Wrote Taylor Neill and suggested we zero in on a date for the first meeting of the Student Fellows.

Sometimes I have to remember not to grow weary in well doing. This life beats you up quite a bit. Because of some aspects of my upbringing, I'm especially sensitive to certain sorts of criticisms, and I'm in a field in which criticisms are fairly common. This wears me down over time, and tempts me to wonder what the point of it all is—and whether it's worth it. All the expressions of insanity and irrationality lately have only bolstered my feelings it makes much of a difference. It's as if people are hell-bent on believing what they want to, the evidence be damned. We were probably told not to grow weary in well doing for good reasons.

Tuesday, August 10, 2021: Marybeth has some meetings today. I'll be staying home and working on the debunking chapter, hopefully. Nathaniel's appointment with his psychiatrist went well; he got the medication prescription he needed, and his vitals are much improved. Going to the gym regularly has helped, and he seems appreciative. I hope he always remembers the lessons of this summer: the importance of community, the power of truth and of perseverance, what a good momma he has. Rather than going to Theology on Tap tonight, the three of us enjoyed Fadi's for dinner, the same one MB and I went to on our interview. After dinner I gave a bit of feedback to TJ on his dissertation proposal and to Brian Chilton on his review of Wade Mullen's book. Late in the evening I applied for an IHS Sabbatical grant for Fall 2022 to work on the moral realism book without interruption.

Wednesday, August 11, 2021: Want to get some good work done today on the debunking chapter. And want to learn to trust God more. I believe, Lord, but help my unbelief. It's almost noon now and we are at the Sugarland library. I briefly thought of writing a review on the Lucy book I recently finished, but then thought better of it. Speaking of reviews, Brian is happy to revise his review of Mullen. He's got to realize that language of *forgiveness* and *moving on* is often exploited by abusers. I also shared with him this paragraph I have in a footnote in the book with Craig: "An important caveat here involves situations of chronic abuse that have stripped people of dignity, marring their sense of self. Here real work may be needed to address the situation to enable victims to see themselves as undeserving of such ill treatment, for their temptation may be to internalize the attitudes of their abusers. Insisting too quickly on victims in such dire circumstances of brokenness simply to forgive without first seeking restoration of a sense of their dignity as having been made in God's image can inadvertently do harm and perpetuate real dysfunctia, rather than conduce to healing and restoration. This is an ongoing research agenda at the Center for Moral Apologetics, involving interdisciplinary conversations between, for example, philosophers, theologians, and social scientists—and canvassing such challenging psychological issues as PTSD, predatory relationships, and moral injury."

I wrote this short bit on the Lucy book for FB: "In between my serious work I fit in reading a book just for fun this summer, finishing it yesterday, called *Ball of Fire: The Tumultuous Life and Comic Art of Lucille Ball*, by Stefan Kanfer. It is always fascinating to find out more about the real person who, before, was always just a public figure I assumed I knew more about than I actually did. I never realized all the serious struggles she endured, how hard she had to fight to pursue her dreams, how many glass ceilings she had to shatter, how insecure she was that she would lose what she had after she'd achieved remarkable success, how troubled her marriage with Ricky was, what an accomplished actress she was. It was also fascinating to read what led up to their iconic show, all the obstacles to overcome, all the pessimism about its prospects for survival, all the naysaying and second guessing and twists and turns along the way—knowing all the while that, while readers know the outcome, none of the players at the time did. All the innovations, all the departures from the norm, were a big risk and hardly a guarantee of success. I also enjoy watching someone find their voice, exercise their gifts, and finally operate on all thrusters and showcase their God-given talents honed to near perfection. But ultimately, like so many comics, her genius was inextricably tied to enormous pain and loss, grief and betrayal, and especially as the book wore on, much about her life was heartbreaking to read. In ever so many ways she was a paradoxical figure, as the book nicely illustrates. Quite an interesting read. I found this commentary on 'I Love Lucy' especially intriguing: 'Ricky symbolized how the world was supposed to run. Lucy was that absurdist factor of modern American humor—the irrational force which cannot be anticipated.'"

Thursday, August 12, 2021: Today the book with Craig should receive a verdict from Baker. Yesterday our Baker guy inquired through my agent about my online presence. I answered his questions and then asked Celeste and TJ and JP to effect some changes to make my presence a little stronger out there. I saw the latest entry in the handbook Dave and Jan are working on; I think they need to streamline the work and pitch it at a more elementary level. What they are doing will quickly reach a point of diminishing returns. It seems of late that lots of burdens seem to be wearing on me. I need to hang in there and keep going. My sleep last night was fitful. Today we have a meeting online to discuss fundraising—Phil and I and a few others. The afternoon online training on fundraising was useful.

Friday, August 13, 2021: I awoke this morning with a notion to change the name of the Center from the Center for Moral Apologetics to the Center for the Foundations of Ethics. I think it's a little easier for some to understand who aren't familiar with apologetics, and it's less off-putting for those who associate apologetics with negative connotations. Here are the five reasons I sketched to my dean for the change:

1. I think changing the name of the Center to the Center for the Foundations of Ethics puts its finger directly on a key and fraught cultural issue that many people recognize, namely, the erosion of those foundations and the importance of contending for them well and rightly. The new name more succinctly connects with the Center's cultural mission.
2. "Apologetics" is a term that for some is immediately off-putting, smacking more of unprincipled advocacy than a principled search for truth. Although I don't share the sentiment, I don't think it's altogether uncommon, and a name change could help mitigate those perceptions. We will continue to use the term in our work, though it need not always occupy center stage.
3. The task of the Center is broader than merely apologetic; it involves a measure of polemics, theology, epistemology, metaphysics, counseling, evangelism, teaching, preaching, exegesis, cultural analysis, political philosophy, literary studies, history, etc. The name change helps broaden the mission out and lends itself to an explicitly multi-disciplinary approach. The new name thus functions as a more effective umbrella phrase for this fuller range of activities.
4. For what it is worth, I think the name change helps with branding when it comes to fund raising. Rather than needing to convince people of the value of promoting the resources of a variety of moral arguments for God's existence, we can go straight to the importance of discussing the foundations of ethics. This can and often does include an element of evidential support for theism and Christianity, for both God's existence and goodness, but it also involves a defense of robust moral realism, on which such arguments are predicated. Strictly speaking, though, this is less a matter of apologetics than one of metaethics. The name is thus both more accurate and inviting.
5. I could be wrong, but I'm finally of the view that the new name would convey more gravitas in the public square and imagination.

The homework for the next fundraising training session will involve laying out the vision for the Center, which should be a great exercise. Good prayer time in the morning with TJ. Great to catch up, and he liked the name change idea. At the library I finished Fraser's first chapter again, taking copious notes (first writing them out and then typing them up) and started hammering out a power point presentation to get my mind around the material better. Nathaniel joined us and we went to see "Free Guy" and had dinner at Fudrucker's. MB wrote a book review today on *When Narcissism Comes to Church* for our site, which I lightly edited before we sent it in.

Saturday, August 14, 2021: Challenging day. Hard to get motivated. I've mainly spent my day reading TWHF after chatting with Elton this morning. Energy low. Discouraged, hard to know why. I think one factor may be that I just seem to have too much on my plate and I don't know how I can do it all. MB and I are about to hit the hay early; it's barely 6, and listen to an adaptation of *A Canticle for Leibowitz*.

Sunday, August 15, 2021: MB and I were up a few times during the night, sometimes at the same time. Chatted a little here and there, and then this morning both were awake by 7 or so and spent time chatting, praying, and listening to scripture. Gonna be a great day! Nathaniel came over and we had some great stir fry and then watched the Christmas episode of season 2 of *Ted Lasso*. Later in the day I asked Jan Shultis to consider writing (for the site) on Afghanistan, where she served, especially now that Kabul has fallen to the Taliban. The people in Afghanistan desperately need prayer; a human rights debacle is in the midst of unfolding there.

Monday, August 16, 2021: Worked at the library and made good progress reading TWHF and working on the debunking chapter. Should be hearing any day now on the Baker proposal. CT sent a few small revisions on the book review for the book on shame, so that's in the bag.

Tuesday, August 17, 2021: We worked in a little café in Katy. More progress on debunking, and started reading Ruse's *Taking Darwin Seriously*. For fun I did an experiment for a few days by this time, challenging anti-vaxxers to back up their views. Not many good arguments on offer. Scheduled the first Student Fellows meeting for September 2 at the house. Helped Brian Chilton finalize his review of Mullen.

Wednesday, August 18, 2021: Reads lots more of TWHF. Closing in on it. Twain scholar and FB friend Hal Bush died, sadly, never recovering from his horrible fall. MB had a bunch of meetings at school today as a run up to the semester.

Thursday, August 19, 2021: Jan's piece on Afghanistan went up on the site today. Very good. That's shaping up into a major human rights nightmare over there. Horrifying. We're working again on the Certificate paperwork; fortunately, MB is helping. Hate that stuff with a passion. We heard from Baker and they turned down the morality book with Craig. Had had a sinking feeling about it, so not surprised.

Decided to knock out this month's WB piece today:

Perhaps Let's Not Be Outraged All the Time

I take on today's topic with some fear and trembling, because of how easy my voice could just add to the cacophony of cultural conflicts already raging. It's still worth the risk, I think, because of the challenges we face in this fraught cultural moment. I am writing primarily to fellow Christians, and my basic appeal is that it would do us good not to be quite so perpetually outraged by the goings on of this world.

This is of course far from remotely suggesting that there are no appropriate causes of outrage. In fact, there's enough fodder out there to fuel outrage most all the time. Examples are legion, and I need not offer a litany here. In fact, doing so would immediately invite scrutiny about what most raises my own ire—is it children's gender getting changed or the events of January 6? For the moment let's not dwell on the particular examples, because I suspect the sociological phenomenon we are experiencing transcends party lines. And there are professing Christian believers who are so caught up in various culture wars, from one side of the aisle or the other, that this is what they are becoming known for more than anything else.

My suggestion is not that we avert our eyes from those parts of our moment that deeply disturb us; we can and should retain a rigorously honest appraisal of what is happening around us. But what I would like to respectfully suggest for my fellow believers is that they heed the words of scripture anew from Philippians 4:8: "Finally, brothers and sisters, whatever is true, whatever is noble, whatever is right, whatever is pure, whatever is lovely, whatever is admirable—if anything is excellent or praiseworthy—think about such things." This isn't myopic or Pollyannaish, but a matter of intentionally filling our minds with things that are true and noble, right and pure, lovely and admirable, excellent and praiseworthy. We are to keep such hopeful matters as a significant focus of our attention and imagination.

Just a few verses earlier, perhaps not coincidentally, Paul had written, "I plead with Euodia and I plead with Syntyche to be of the same mind in the Lord." This reminds me of another verse, from John 13:34: "By this everyone will know that you are my disciples, if you love one another." I used to wonder, when I heard that verse, "But aren't we supposed to love everyone?" The recent divides I have seen, however, *among Christians*, on various political matters has helped me to see that even loving our fellow believers is challenging enough. And if we can't get that requirement down, I doubt we'll have much success loving those with whom we don't agree about faith at all. It's undoubtedly interesting, though, I think, that John says that it's our love for one another that will enable onlookers to know we are Christ's disciples.

What are some of the salient features of having the same mind in the Lord? The context offers a nice list. Euodia and Syntyche had contended at Paul's side in the cause of the gospel. Then Paul immediately counsels his readers to rejoice in the Lord always, and then reiterates that advice. Our gentleness is to be evident to all, in recognition of the nearness of the Lord. We are to be anxious for nothing, but with prayer and petition, and thanksgiving, make our requests known to God. And then we are promised that the peace of God, which transcends all understanding, will guard our hearts and minds in Christ Jesus.

Are we known for our love for one another? For our sharing the same mind in Christ? For our gentleness and freedom from anxiety and a peace that transcends understanding? When professing believers are breaking fellowship over whether the coronavirus vaccine qualifies as a vaccine or not, something has gone seriously awry. Rather than loving one another and being of one mind, too often, in our divisive moment, believers can hardly treat one another with minimal civility. Instead of being countercultural, we are too often lock in step with it, yielding predictable results in both ethics and epistemology.

On the matter of ethics, consider how we treat others, and mistreat those with whom we disagree. What used to be friendly political jousting now takes on a religious hue, and many are not content merely to express disagreement. Those with whom they disagree have to be cast and castigated as evil incarnate, as if we wrestle not against spiritual forces of darkness, but flesh and blood. I also wonder how much of the animus is motivated by the old mistake of looking most ultimately for political solutions to what at root are spiritual problems.

Regarding epistemology, how do we process evidence? Believers should be cultivating tools for properly assessing arguments, following evidence where it leads, not developing reputations for incorrigibility and obstinacy in the face of compelling evidence to the contrary of their pet theories. It was eye-opening of late to be involved in a few discussions and being defied by folks closed to good evidence for reasons to change their mind. It was a little crazy-making, and hard to process. The experience certainly left me wondering if this is how that person interacted with unbelievers—with similar dismissiveness and condescension. How often have I fallen into that trap? I rather doubt that to be a pattern that will convince the world we are Christ's disciples.

A large part of the wisdom of biblical counsel on these matters is that we not give ourselves over to hopelessness and despair. The life, death, and resurrection of Jesus makes this possible, indeed our mandate. Somehow, through it all, we can trust and, in our own faithful ways, big and small, build toward a world redeemed, in which light outshines darkness, hope defeats despair, and life conquers death.

Rejoice in the Lord always. I will say it again: Rejoice!

Friday, August 20, 2021: Looks like the TN event is shaping up—a lecture on debunking arguments and also a panel discussion with some fellows, including Russell Moore, to be held at the biggest church in TN. Wow! Neat. At present it looks like the panel discussion is going to cover the most pressing perceived scientific challenges to faith. I'm guessing evolution, age of the earth, the historical Adam, debunking, transgenderism, same-sex attractions, etc. Other relevant issues might include science-based epistemologies, the distinction between science and scientism, arguments from design, and the theologial foundations of science.

Michael Ward got his Lewis essay in for the Lewis as Philosopher book, so now just waiting on the Addison's Walk paper and Lazo's piece. I also just sent to the website my blurb on Tawa Anderson's *Why Believe*.

Finished reading TWHF for the third time. So interesting how many times the theme of shame recurs.

Saturday, August 21, 2021: Pretty good day of thinking about TWHF some more. These are my thoughts on the overall logical line of the novel I want to use to structure the paper, with lots of details able to filled in:

Ugly. Not her fault. Shame. Recurring theme in TWHF. Not just in the east. Plenty in west too. Aristotle for example. Undeserved. Often thought of as toxic. (Maynard, book I reviewed, Bradshaw, TED talk, etc.) But what she does with it is important. She allowed bitterness to grow. Came to see herself as the perpetual victim. And this resulted in the consumption of others. Love that was mostly hate. How others served her purposes. And without realizing who she was on the inside, she didn't know herself, and this made it hard for her to realize who God is. Thinking of herself as better than she was didn't make it easy for her to believe in a good God. In fact, just the opposite. She was actually hateful, and she projected that hatred onto God. This is a particular example of a general phenomenon: that ethics can serve as a foundation for our metaphysics. Lotze's dictum. The question becomes one of the lens through which we see the world. She was wearing a mask, not just to conceal her physical appearance from others, but to conceal her inner brokenness from herself. We need to come to terms with our sinfulness and brokenness. We have an almost infinite capacity for rationalization. We make so many excuses, we tell ourselves false narratives, we rationalize our misbehavior. And the better we make ourselves feel about ourselves, often the worse of God we think. It's often said it's easy to believe in a loving God—it wasn't for Orual. It's not easy to be in the presence of real love when one's heart is filled with hate. We need to stop being curved inward on ourselves and open ourselves to others, and this can be a painful process (O'Connor). This can begin to open our eyes to see others as we ought, and to love others as we ought, and ultimately to see God's love. Much of the hiddenness of God is a function of our brokenness. (It's a mercy; we wouldn't be able to handle it.) We lose the eyes with which to see God at work, to sense his presence, to know his love, as we hold obstinately to sins—even if those sins are what we somehow down deep think are what we need or deserve, perhaps because of undeserved shame that's been heaped upon us. Though the shame might have been undeserved, our behavior that results might be shameful indeed. It's our response that matters so very much. To come to have a face is to face who we really are, and it require that we lay down our arms, our excuses, our rationalizations. We needn't be defensive. God's not interested in condemning us, only pointing out that we're in need of forgiveness and healing. God doesn't want us to stew forever in shame or writhe in guilt, but to repent, so that his grace can forgive us our sin and heal us of our shame. An important part of our healing will be to see God for who he is—fascinans and such. (Otto) Your God is too small. Holy, worthy of awe, mysterious; also, unspeakably loving, more beautiful than we can imagine, etc. And he wants to fix our ugliness and brokenness and make us into something beautiful. Holiness and wholeness are inextricably linked; sanctification can be thought of as the beautifying of our souls. God's love for us has the implication of making us the best version of ourselves, rather than Orual's twisted love that more about control and domination than flourishing. Coming to know ourselves is valuable, no doubt; finally knowing who God is, that's priceless. There is nothing more revolutionary than coming to apprehend the love of God.

Sunday, August 22, 2021: Nathaniel over; we're about to have stir fry and watch Ted Lasso. This morning MB and I spent time talking and praying about HBU. What we're coming to terms with is that HBU is very much a work in progress. It's a youngish school still going through a lot of growing pangs and, despite being in a rich town like Houston, it has a lot of struggles to make ends meet. It's a school in serious need of some major financial breakthroughs. But what we find heartening is the solidity of its foundations. Incompetence may be an issue, but at least corruption isn't. It has a world of potential, and we just have to bide our time. We lament the way efforts to effect positive changes are often met with a lot of resistance, or at least a lot of needless bureaucracy.

At any rate, MB and I have decided that what we need to do is seek renewal within ourselves. Whether our efforts at HBU succeed or not, we are to live in victory. We need to get into the center of God's plan and stay there, seeking first God's kingdom and righteousness, entrusting to God all the rest.

An example of outrageous red tape is the latest list of anticipated questions the Certificate program needs to answer—from Phil's assistant:

1) Change the date on Form A at the very beginning to a more current date.
2) Change the launch date to Summer 22 (Form A beginning; Form C, 1.B; Form E)
3) Did the Apologetics dept take a vote on this? It would be good to include that if they did. If not, we may need to circle back on that.
4) I think you should be prepared to give evidence that you can attract 20 students in the first class. Given where are current student numbers are, this number is quite large.
5) Form C, 2.B: state here that the SCT approved. If the Center for Moral Apologetics has board members that you consulted, or any other experts in the field you spoke with about the program, make sure to mention that here. If not, that's fine.
6) Form C, 3.G: this statement doesn't align with current HBU credit hour policy. See here: https://www.hbu.edu/publications/provost/HBU_Credit_Hours_Definition_Policy.pdf. It sounds like you are proposing a hybrid style, in which case, you need to say that more clearly.
   a. It is stated that the courses will meet in three-week formats, two hours a day, five days a week (Form C, 4; Form E). This does not fit the current HBU summer schedule which offers classes in 5-week for residential and 8-week for online. Have you received approval for this schedule from higher-ups? If not, we will need to get it before making this ask. But the easier solution is to follow the standard HBU schedule.
      i. We used to offer a 4-week session but that has been removed I believe. This suggests that the movement is toward bringing everything in line.
   b. I don't know that you need to say in this proposal that it will meet for two-hours a day, five days a week. Stating this in the proposal may lock you into a certain pattern.
   c. Have you considered offering these classes at night? Theology offers night classes in the 5-week session that meet twice a week for four hours each time. Depending on what kind of student you are trying to attract, you may find that working folk can't do this because it meets during the day. Offering it at night may open up some options.
   d. I think you should anticipate questions about what you mean when you say 'and extensive reading and interaction during the rest of the two-year-long program' (Form C, 3.G).
      i. Will you be asking students to do things outside of the assigned term time (whether 3 or 5 weeks)?

ii. If so, how will this affect their grade? Remember grades must be submitted at the end of each term.
7) Form C, 5.A: You should state here what resources the library has that already support the program to show that we have sufficient holdings. Dean Riley may be able to help: https://hbu.edu/academics/moody-library/library-faculty-and-staff/.
8) Form C., 5.B: This statement is confusing. Is the program being offered in multiple modalities: in-person synchronous; remote synchronous; asynchronous; and online (you checked the online option at Form C, 1.E.)?
   a. Will you be creating online courses for this certificate? If so, will these also run in the summer or another time? Have you talked with the online folk to see if they want the certificate?
   b. I don't think there will be support for a truly asynchronous modality (distinct from online). I think that was a modality tolerated because of Covid but not one the university wants to see as a permanent option.
   c. If remote synchronous is the vision, then we should meet with Rita Tauer. SACSCOC has issued new guidelines about this modality.
9) Form C, 4: I fully understand why Dave is listed as the main instructor, but I think it would strengthen the proposal if one or two other faculty were also listed as possible instructors. Not only does it show wider support for this in the department (possibly university if any philosophy folk are listed), but it avoids awkward questions about what happens if Dave isn't available to teach.
10) Form F: does this need to be filled out or is this material from some other proposal?
11) Other questions:
    a. Will regular apologetics students be able to take these courses? Will they have to take all four, or are they able to just take what interests them? Will they be required to submit an essay about why they should be admitted (Form E)?
    b. Have you considered embedding this as an option within the MAA, as you may do with the Inter-cultural material. Something like an MAA with a certificate in Moral Apologetics? You mention this in Form E, but I think it worth spelling out more. If you make it an option for an embedded certificate, then a degree plan would need to be created, which can be done as part of the revisions you will be working on this semester with the Apol dept.
    c. How does this impact the current Apol course offerings, if it does at all? Will you be reducing the number of courses current available, or will this be expanding the number available?

In my mind, the most important issues are the credit hour definition (point 6) and modality (point 8).

In terms of procedure:
1. I think we should ask Rita or Lisa, our Accreditation folk, to review this first. Based on what you are envisioning, we will want specific directions about the following:
    a. The schedule for 3-week classes. If this is the direction, Phil probably needs to ok this with the Provost as well. This is a big ask, I think.
    b. Modality, esp. if remote synchronous is on the table. We need to find out what we have to say for SACSCOC.
    c. It is my understanding that certificates do not need SACSCOC paperwork, but we need to confirm this, esp. if you are thinking remote synchronous.
2. Once they are happy, then it would go to Graduate Council since these are graduate courses.
3. If they approve it, then it moves on to Academic Affairs.

I need to meet with Rita/Lisa soon so I can help facilitate anything that we need their feedback on.

At any rate, maybe this sort of stuff is unavoidable, but it's just exhausting. At least at times it feels like the school tries way too hard to make needed changes possible. The apologetics department online is strong, but residentially is very weak, so arguments along the lines of "this isn't how it's usually done" carry far more weight than they ought.

Monday, August 23, 2021: First day of faculty orientation today. A little hard to take, some of the focus on fiscal responsibility and such. I don't want to be negative, but Christians, if they care about making a difference, had better take seriously the study of the humanities, irrespective of whether or not it generates a robust bottom line.

Wrote about 2000 words today on TWHF; coming along nicely. JP wrote and asked me a question about extending the rationality to Christianity. Afterwards I wrote him this:

JP, just a quick follow up. I could imagine someone saying that the appeal to Christian theology borders circularity. If, that is, we assume Christianity is true, then something like total depravity follows, God and the good are tightly connected, we've all sinned and fallen short of the glory of God, etc., and rejection of God is tantamount to rejection of moral light. But is this an argument for the truth of these Christian teachings or an assumption of their truth--on Christianity? Probably more the latter. It leaves one wondering if what's going on is apologetics or theology. I suspect there's at least some of the latter. This isn't necessarily a bad thing, the circularity might not be vicious; but it's a reminder that there can be a bit of a tradeoff--the more fine-grained our theology, the more we might be able to explain, but it's predicated on the assumption of the truth of that theology. It's an extension of the conversation, I'm convinced, but not wholly in the direction of apologetics alone. There's an importation of a real element of theology into the analysis. Unless you think you have good reasons for disagreeing with this point, it's entirely permissible, it seems to me, that you simply acknowledge it (or something in its proximity) somewhere in your work, to whatever extent and in whatever fashion you deem appropriate.

Tuesday, August 24, 2021: Jonathan got back to me with this quite good response; I think he's going to be able to defend his dissertation quite able:

> I get that one could push the objection that I am just assuming its true then concluding it is. Really, I agree with everything you said. But I am not sure that the hypothetical objection is all that worrisome. I think in reality, by using abduction, I am not assuming it is true. I only hold it out as a hypothesis that might be true. If I have to assume more, that is a real burden in terms of explanatory power. Whatever is assumed has to pay off at least what it costs in terms of its added complexity.
>
> I think one problem that I face, and it's bit different from the circularity problem, is that the hypothesis can become so complex that is very hard if not impossible to judge whether all the assumptions actually do pay off.
>
> There is a lot of theology, I think. But I think theology works in terms of explaining how it is that the hypothesis is internally consistent, how it makes sense on its own terms. One could say that I am defining the terms so that they fit the facts, but I think that would still be different than circular reasoning. It would be ad hoc and a defect in the explanation. To the extent the hypothesis is ad hoc, it is a bad explanation.
>
> But the way I see it right now is that my dissertation offers a complex, but internally consistent explanation of some key aspects morality. It is likely not possible to judge its explanatory success with any real precision. There are so many assumptions and they go in so many directions. Nevertheless, I think the explanation is clear enough that one can get at least a *sense* or an inkling of its overall fit with the moral facts considered.
>
> So I think its coercive power is very weak. It is very suggestive. In *God and Cosmos* I think you really achieved a very coercive argument, not in the negative sense that Nozick talks about. But in my mind, the overall effect of that argument was very powerful and hard to resist the conclusion. I genuinely think it is hard to

be a moral realist and an atheist after reading God and Cosmos. I think the conclusion of my dissertation is probably pretty easy to resist and that's because of all the assumptions. I'm okay with that. If it just points to the power of a fully developed Christian explanation of morality, then I'll be satisfied. I am pretty sure we're on the same page on that. I think I only say that now because it is part of how the aim of the dissertation has been refined for me in the past few months.

Anyway, I also don't really have a problem with casting the dissertation as theology over apologetics. But in my mind is still is an apologetic argument, just one with a limited force. Perhaps it has a sort of aesthetic force, but it is a different force, for sure, from *God and Cosmos*.

Totally open on this. Let me know what you think!

Wednesday, August 25, 2021: Today has been a day of faculty orientation stuff. In the morning session Dr. Sloan talked about the new Ten Core Convictions of the university. They are these: (1) God, Creator of a Good and Knowable World; (2) Plan of Restoration; (3) Importance of Human Agency; (4) Renewed People; (5) Mandate to Understand the World; (6) Learning and Teaching as Discipleship; (7) Marriage, Gender, and Life; (8) Governmental Institutions; (9) Christian University; and (10) Mystery of Unity in Christ.

The Christian university idea struck me. It got me to thinking about why I'm at HBU. Honestly I have harbored a number of doubts of late that I'm in the right place. Is this where the Center should be? Are there unique things a Christian university does that the Center requires? Am I called to the Christian university? I have felt so called for a long while now, but lately things have felt different. It's hard to feel like I fit in here at HBU. I'm a philosopher in the School of Christian Thought—I don't get half their jokes about the Bible. I end up spending much more time than I'd prefer doing things that any adjunct could do. Perhaps I should become more steeped in the history of this school. Honestly I don't know much about it. Perhaps God had reasons for sending us here of which I remain largely unaware.

In my college meeting it was announced there are going to be various initiatives to cultivate community. Students have been asking "for more spiritual life centered in the school, more opportunities to gather outside of class, and more contact with professors." I'm hoping my Student Fellows initiative will help scratch some of that itch. College-wide there will be some initiatives—Monday seminar and coffee time; Wednesday PB&J lunches; and weekly prayer times on Mondays at 11 am and Tuesdays at 6 pm—but this Center initiative will hopefully yield important fruit as well. They also want us to meet up with advisees once a term, do an online get-together for online classes once a term, create virtual office hours for online classes, and hold office hours, even if all our classes are online. Perhaps I should schedule that once a week or so.

341

Before leaving campus my dean Phil Tallon and I had a nice conversation. He gave me updates on a few matters about which I'd inquired, and he encouraged me to apply for the presidential grant to help subsidize the conference on the moral argument. We also talked about MB's prodigious leadership skills. Good talk!

Thursday, August 26, 2021: We had an apologetics department meeting in the morning, which was good. We talked about how it would be helpful if we could hire a PR person who could intentionally put the content of our work as department members on social media. Putting that burden on us is just too much. We talked as well about whether or not to rework the program. I shared my concern about the over bifurcation of the two tracks. We'll see what happens.

After the meeting we were going to head to Galveston but we decided we weren't up to it, so perhaps we'll just hang out here today, maybe catch a movie and nice dinner, and head to Galveston tomorrow. Later now; we saw "Stillwater," a slow but decent movie, then went to Melting Pot. Lovely!

Friday, August 27, 2021: Marybeth and I had planned for a little Galveston getaway but I'm just not up to it. Too close to school. But still hope to fit in some relaxation and decompression before school starts Monday. And definitely lots of prayers. I need peace going into a busy time, letting things play out in due course as they need to. I can't get it all done in a day. In the morning MB and I prayed together, committing the new term into God's hands, and, in MB's case, about her mother, to whom MB sent a note yesterday. Still having a hard time coming to terms with summer's end.

Saturday, August 28, 2021: MB and I have prayed a lot today, and other than that I'm relaxing and continuing to gear up for the term. A bad-looking hurricane named Ida is predicted to make landfall around Louisiana pretty soon. When Monday comes, here are some of my priorities: fundraising, Strauss lectures, online class, creation of new class, Student Fellows meeting on TH.

Sunday, August 29, 2021: A fellow from England had written me with some questions a few weeks back. Finally got around to answering him; here's my reply:

Andrew, you have been a saint awaiting my reply; so sorry for the delay. Here we go:

1. Where does Lewis most completely state his argument from morals?

2. From what I understand, he thought the objectivity of moral value to

be an absolute?

3. I wonder, are there contemporary ethicists who advocate similar binding positions?

4. And / or — thinker / philosophy who deny this is true and argue value is subjective?

In terms of (1), the clearest version of the moral argument Lewis provides is in Book 1 of *Mere Christianity*. HIs argument for the Tao in Abolition of Man might be taken to suggest we don't need God to undergird morals, but I think that's a misreading; it's rather, most essentially, a set of considerations to take morality as axiomatic. But this is fairly needed FOR the moral argument.

In terms of (2), I don't think Lewis was averse to using the idea of "absolute," though nowadays that terms is often maligned. It can mean slightly different things. Minimally it might merely suggest objective moral truths. More ambitiously it might be taken to suggest rules admitting of no exceptions, and though some objective moral truths admit of no exceptions--the wrongness of child torture for fun--most do admit of some exceptions, arguably anyway. Lying to the German soldiers to protect innocent Jews during the Holocaust, for example.

Ethicists who affirm moral realism affirm the existence of objective moral truths. Among contemporary ethicists, some are realists, but realism has come under a lot of criticisms, and there are alternative positions often advocated--error theory, expressivism of various stripes, constructivism, sensibility theory, etc. But a strong strain of realists remains active. I'm definitely in that category, and most theistic ethicists are. But notable secular folks are too--from David Enoch to Russ Shafer-Landau and plenty besides. (These usually tend to be Platonists of one form or another.) Your use of the term 'binding' is interesting--it's a pretty good way of capturing the notion of strong prescriptive authority for morality, which I think is best accounted for by realism; less-than-robustly-realist ethical positions tend to be more adept at explaining the appearance of such authority than actual moral authority.

Regarding (4), plenty of contemporary ethicists end up suggesting that morality is subjective. They can do this in various ways. Some might say morality is essentially subjective and that's why there's no truth to the matter. Others point to subjectivity--especially intersubjectivity, subjective appraisals that for various reasons tend to be common among most people--that approximates something objective. There are various degrees of subjectivity among ethicists, in other words. They don't all gravitate straight to error theory. All of which to say, the picture can get very complicated pretty fast. Of course one big trend among a number of contemporary physicalists is to cast as "bad" something like pain or social disharmony, objectively identify patterns of behavior that produce these, and then say those behaviors are objectively bad (for demonstrably leading to pain, social disharmony, etc.). I consider this to be a bit of sleight-of-hand, though, as it overlooks a main crux of the issue, namely, binding authority. What most of our secular friends have done is invert the picture, it seems to me, replacing moral authority with a consideration of "reasons for action," predicated on taking as fairly axiomatic certain states of affairs (being pain-free, social harmony, and the like). (The mistake I see in this methodology is mischaracterizing something like pain as not just nonmorally bad, but morally bad; it's morally bad needlessly to inflict pain, but pain per se is morally neutral and bad, but only nonmorally.)

Hope some of that helps at least a little!

Best, Dave

Monday, August 30, 2021: Today has been a wonderful day. It's currently a bit past 11 a.m. I slept well last night and woke up just shy of 5 a.m. Went to the gym and had a nice workout, then Nathaniel showed up and we shot baskets for probably 45 minutes or so. I encouraged him to use his good mind to read the Bible imaginatively—not unlike how he likes to think hard about something like *Ted Lasso*. We also chatted about Kobe Bryant's work ethic, founded on principles that can be applied by folks in different professions. After that MB and I read some from Richard Foster's *Celebration of Discipline*, which I'm enjoying immensely! Especially what he has to say about how the disciplines can be means of grace by which God effects changes within us that we can't simply volitionally choose to make happen on our own. He's also good at distinguishing between eastern and Christian conceptions of meditation; the latter does not sacrifice our sense of selves and is about more than merely emptying our minds. After wrapping up other morning chores, MB and I got to the office just after 9, where I wrote my online class and am now doing the reading for the week from Gould and Dew's intro to philosophy. Jamie had asked me to do that book with him, but I was too busy; they did a great job, though. Also filled up some more space on my book shelves, so that's looking at least marginally better, though still plenty to fill. Had a nice chat with Jeremy Neill, who suggested I might speak with Chris Hammands (sp?) in Government about fundraising for the Center.

Tuesday, August 31, 2021: Last day of August. The month seemed to move slowly, but here we are, and strangely enough we're now just three weeks until autumn. Still very hot in Houston. Marybeth taught her first classes today, and she says they went very well. First meeting of the Student Fellows is in two days.

Wrote out a brief outline for TH:

Student Fellows Meeting #1, September 2, 2021

Center for the Foundations of Ethics (formerly Center for Moral Apologetics)

I.   Preliminaries
   A. Get acquainted
   B. Prayer
   C. Service (possibilities include writing something for MoralApologetics.com or a file for the Center)
   D. Story of how we came here and the vision for the Center

II.   Four-fold goals for the Center:
   A. Defend moral realism;
   B. Defend theistic ethics
      1. Defend against objections
      2. Positive reasons in favor
   C. Critique secular (and, to a lesser degree, nonChristian religious) ethics; and
   D. Learn the history of the moral argument

III.   A Bit of Logic
   A. Challenges we face; role of rhetoric (logos, ethos, pathos)
   B. Definition of argument
   C. Deduction—distinguishing feature
      1. Modus Ponens (a implies b, a, so b)
      2. Modus Tollens (a implies b, not-b, so not-a)
   D. Induction—distinguishing feature
   E. Abduction—distinguishing feature
      1. Pool of explanation candidates
      2. Use criteria to narrow the list (criteria like explanatory scope and depth)
      3. Infer to the truth of the best explanation
   F. Arguments don't always have to be formally stated

IV.   Versions of moral arguments

V.   A Four-Fold Moral Argument (*share outline*)
   A. Moral Facts
      1. Objective moral values
      2. Objective moral duties
      3. Free Will
      4. Moral Rights
      5. Moral Regrets, etc.
   B. Moral Knowledge
   C. Moral Transformation
      1. Forgiveness

2. Change
3. Perfection
4. Shame
D. Moral Rationality
1. Fulfillment
2. Virtue

{What are any questions that you might enjoy our exploring together this year related to MA?}

Wednesday, September 1, 2021: In the morning TJ and Tom Morris both wrote and said something nice about my piece on outrage. That was nice. Truth is, I've been so discouraged lately, and I wrote Tom and shared that. He wrote this eminently sweet reply:

If you ever feel down and need to talk, we'll zoom or phone ANY TIME.

We're needed more than ever.

And we do have to engage in self-care in order to be our best for others as well as for our mission.

I'm as proud of your work as I could possibly be. And I do think you and I are friends in a way that isn't replicated by any of my "actual" grad students. So you never missed out on anything. They did!

TM

Late afternoon I got President Sloan's reply to Phil's having passed along my request to change the name of the Center. Phil had shared my rationale with Stan and Dr. Sloan, and Sloan replied like this: "I'm certainly OK with the change and appreciate the rationale."

I had a conversation with my old friend Ginger in which I was quite unsuccessful convincing her of an epidemic of irrationality in the evangelical subculture right now. That was less than encouraging, but the other two developments of the day were most encouraging and edifying indeed.

Thursday, September 2, 2021: Came with MB to school today in order to work in my office for three hours or so. Did a bunch of meditative prayer early this morning; seemed to help. Takes practice. Want to get better at it. Foster is definitely helping.

Listening to the Bible and theology talks on offer so far at HBU has been useful. The connection between justification and sanctification is closer than I had realized; Jesus' ascension is relevant to the culmination of the sanctifying process; and to have been made in God's image—seen most closely in Jesus—is not just a thing of the past but also constitutive of our teleology. And part of that teleology is meant to address not just our guilt, but our mortality, which reminds me of mortality putting on immortality. Indeed, in TWHF, our mortality is something of a source of shame. Or maybe I should ask Kugler about this. Is our mortality more associated with our guilt than our humanness?

Stan replied today to Phil's e-mail about the name change of the Center like this:

Phil and Dave,
Dr. Sloan has already approved, and that is all you really need.

How do you see this name change (which sounds a bit like a mission change to me also) will impact your programming, your scholarship and writing, your partnerships, your donors, your ability to recruit and retain students, your interdisciplinary collaborations on campus, your curriculum impact, etc.? How long as the Center for Moral Apologetics existed (informally, on the web, through newsletters and other writing)?

Thanks, Stan

To which I responded like so:

Hi Dr. Napper,

The name change won't change the mission or vision of the Center, so far as I can see. The notion of moral apologetics points to the evidential significance of morality—and the argument(s) suggest that various moral phenomena have as their best explanation theism generally and Christianity particularly. If such arguments hold water, it's predictable if those theistic foundations are ignored and thus, at least in the popular imagination, degrade and erode, that there will ensue something of a crisis in ethics. If we're right, we can't do away with the foundations and ultimately still retain the same level of commitment and conviction in objective moral truth—which includes such matters as the intrinsic value of persons, the dignity of individuals, authoritative moral obligations, basic human rights, and so on. I think there is ample evidence of this phenomenon in our culture. The name change puts front and center a discussion about the foundations of ethics, without tipping our hand that the way in which we will argue that the best account of those foundations is a theistic one. It's rather an invitation to folks to have a dialogue about what the best account is of those foundations, once we take seriously the task of paying careful heed to the moral evidence in need of explanation.

So apologetics remains a crucial part of the mission, but from the start ours—at the website MoralApologetics.com, which has been in operation for about 8 years now—has been an intentionally interdisciplinary approach. We tap into a bunch of disciplines in order to do moral apologetics as we envision it. Arguing for moral realism, defending theistic ethics against objections, giving positive reasons to take the theistic foundations of ethics seriously, recovering the rich history of the moral argument--all of these are among the tasks of the site and Center, and by turns these tasks draw on psychologists, historians, theologians, Bible scholars, philosophers, literature experts, and more. Perhaps most fundamentally, the quest of moral apologetics raises the question, what does the evidence suggest are the best grounds for moral objectivity? In that sense replacing the name of the Center changes very little, but what changes are effected are, I think, largely positive. Some people are unfamiliar with the notion of apologetics, for example, or think it carries largely negative connotations. There's no good reason I can see why we need to saddle ourselves with those disadvantages when it can be easily avoided.

Once the name change is official, I'm planning on doing a few small tweaks to the overall mission and vision statement of the Center, but no substantive changes will be called for. Programming, scholarship, and writing won't much change, except perhaps to free up contributors from thinking they always have to be explicit and on-the-nose with apologetics references. In terms of partnerships and donors, we're hoping and thinking the name change will help with branding, since many nowadays will readily see the need for the issue of eroding moral foundations in our society to be dealt with systematically and programmatically. I can't foresee much of any change in the effort to recruit and retain students in the Certificate program starting this next summer. The appeal will be the same; the four-course sequence will remain the same; the content will be the same. Interdisciplinary collaborations on campus, if anything, will only be strengthened by the name change, it seems to me. No curricula changes that I can foresee.

To answer your question, the Center officially kicked off last school year when Marybeth and I left Liberty after a combined 31 years to come teach here and start the Center—after I had been in discussion with Dr. Sloan about such a prospect for about two or three years. The moral apologetics ministry through our website had been in operation for about seven years by that point, but the Center officially began Fall 2020. The work I've done on the moral argument began, I suppose, with the publication of the book I co-wrote with Jerry Walls in 2011, *Good God*. We're now working on our fourth in a tetralogy on moral apologetics with OUP, and I'm under contract for another OUP book with Yale's John Hare, a large anthology covering the whole terrain of the moral argument. At any rate, I hope this helps clarify a few matters.

Best,
Dave

It's later in the day now, and I did decide to go ahead and write Chris Kugler about my question. Here's what I wrote him:

Chris, hey there. I have a quick question about your talk from the other day, which, again, I enjoyed very much. I was wondering....in your estimation, is there anything from I Cor 15:53 (about the perishable putting on the imperishable and mortality immortality) that's relevant to what you were getting at in the "something more going on than forgiveness of sins" in Christ's redemptive work? (I was thinking it bore some resemblance to what you'd said about overcoming the divine/human divide.)

The reason I'm asking is that I have an upcoming talk I need to do on CS Lewis's *Till We Have Faces*, where a theme of shame is predominant (just as much if not more so than forgiveness), and it's interesting that a few times our "mortality" is cast as something essentially shameful. I'm wondering if there might be any biblical grounds for thinking this is so--and if your speculations might prove relevant to this verse, I'm wondering if that might help.

At any rate, that background aside, any thoughts on this? Or do you think I Cor 15:53 is exclusively tied up with the forgiveness/guilt theme?

Sorry for my amateurish question; you Bible guys are way ahead of me on all this stuff. If my question makes no sense, feel free to ignore me and we'll never mention this again. ☐

And his encouraging reply:

David,

Thanks for this. Yes, I think that's exactly right. And, yes, that's more or less what the relevant verses in 1 Cor. 15, and, actually, 2 Cor. 4, are about. Of course, redemption from sin and corruption takes center stage in scripture itself and thus is, of course, central; but, there are also indications—and you pick up on some of those with immortality swallowing up mortality—that, *even if Sin had never been a problem*, God was going to have to do *something* to make mere creatures fit for eternal fellowship with the creator. I hope that makes sense.

Blessings,
ck

It's now 5:15 pm and we're just fifteen minutes away from the first Student Fellows meeting of the (newly renamed) Center for the Foundations of Ethics. MB's picking up some copies from Kinko's and the pizza.

It's now nearly 9. The meeting went pretty well, though it left me feeling drained and vulnerable. Just an occupational hazard of being an introvert. But I do think it went decently.

Friday, September 3, 2021: For some reason I felt emotionally down today, and have felt this way ever since last evening's meeting. Not sure why. I felt a little rusty, not having taught in person for a while, and one fellow left early, which made me feel a bit self-conscious. Been having such a challenging time getting over this chronic melancholy lately. Didn't do much work today, but did read Bart Campolo's piece he wrote prior to his de-conversion about the limits of God's grace. I resonate with much of what he wrote, but I think he took a needlessly tendentious tone toward orthodoxy—or perhaps just mistakenly identified orthodoxy with something like Calvinism. I ordered the book he did with his dad, and two other books: Melissa Cain Travis's book on science and the mind of the Maker, and a 500-page history of fifty years of HBU's history. Wondering if I might find something in that history that confirms HBU's the right place for the Center. Also wrote John Rist today with an invitation to join the Collection. Still have a dozen slots to fill for that volume.

Saturday, September 4, 2021: Woke up to some very exciting news! John Rist wrote back and, at the age of 85, agreed to write the chapter on moral realism in the Collection!! Woohoo! Marvelous. Assuming I take one of the remaining chapters, I have just ten slots left to fill. The eleven remaining slots are precursors to Kant, from Newman to Farrer, contemporary voices, expressivism, constructivism, moral knowledge, natural law, Cornell realism, Hinduism, Islam, and Christianity. Ideas to pursue: Scott Smith, David Horner, Angus Ritchie, European guys, write Baylor gal, Beckwith, suggestions by Moreland, Cuneo, etc.

On FB today there was a throwback post from seven years ago to the day: "Thankful for two former students, Delia Ursulescu and Jonathan Pruitt, for spearheading our new website on moral apologetics. Before long—we'll need a bit more time—we hope it to be the main hub for resources on all aspects of moral arguments for God's existence—from a survey of the relevant literature, a defense of an array of theistic ethics from various objections, critiques of naturalistic ethics of every stripe, a chronology of the history of moral arguments, and efforts to refute moral anti-realism. A one-stop shop for all this and more. These former students are both brilliant and have been more than generous with their time already, and they share the vision for a site like this. Very grateful for them both."

Sunday, September 5, 2021: Up early, about to spend some time in prayer. Later in the day now; good day with Marybeth and Nathaniel. Lots of fun watching Lasso. But later in the day the little baby kitten Nathaniel had taken in died. It was hard on him, but I was proud he tried. Marybeth and I took the little body to the vet place. Sad. Another painful reminder the world isn't yet what it's supposed to be.

Monday, September 6, 2021: We treated Nathaniel to breakfast at Toasted Yolk this morning, knowing he was down from yesterday. We tried to buoy his spirits a bit. Later we took a day trip to the Woodlands, eating at Landry's and spending time at Barnes and Noble out there. I picked up a book by a Jewish writer, rabbi Jonathan Sacks, about ethics entitled *Morality: Restoring the Common Good in Divided Times*. The winsome and well-written book had some quite interesting features, not least the way in which religion was portrayed as relevant to morality in certain clearly specifiable terms—primarily sociological ones, in my estimation. The way the metaphysics of the matter gets rendered superfluous and relegated to the back seat (at best) tends to leave me skeptical. Such an approach strikes me as an over-deference to the demands for neutrality and a projection of objectivity in the public square when discussing so delicate and potentially divisive a subject. Still, the book is worth a careful look and seems to have a great deal of merit.

Tuesday, September 7, 2021: Got to work in earnest today on the new online course in moral apologetics I'm putting together. For required books I chose *Good God, Morals of the Story, The Moral Argument,* and *God & Moral Obligations*. I also chose this list of recommended readings:

RECOMMENDED READING

John E. Hare (2001), *God's Call: Moral Realism, God's Commands, and Human Autonomy* (Grand Rapids, MI: Eerdmans). ISBN: 0802849970

John Hare (2002), *Why Bother Being Good? The Place of God in the Moral Life* (Downers Grove, IL: IVP). ISBN: 9781610970501

John E. Hare (2015), *God's Command* (Oxford: Oxford University Press). ISBN: 9780199602018

John E. Hare (2009), *God and Morality: A Philosophical History* (Oxford: Wiley-Blackwell). ISBN: 9781405195980

Erik J. Wielenberg (2014), *Robust Ethics: The Metaphysics and Epistemology of Godless Normative Realism* (Oxford: Oxford University Press). ISBN: 9780198714323

R. Keith Loftin, ed. (2012), *God and Morality: Four Views* (Downers Grove, IL: IVP Academic). ISBN: 9780830839841

Robert K. Garcia and Nathan L. King, eds. (2009), *Is Goodness without God Good Enough? A Debate on Faith, Secularism, and Ethics* (New York: Rowman & Littlefield). ISBN: 9780742551718

Russ Shafer-Landau (2003), *Whatever Happened to Good and Evil?* (New York: Oxford University Press). ISBN: 9780195168730

John M. Rist (2002), *Real Ethics: Rethinking the Foundations of Morality* (Cambridge: Cambridge University Press). ISBN: 9780521006088

C. S. Lewis (2015), *Mere Christianity*, Book 1 (New York: HarperOne). ISBN: 9780060652920

(In retrospect I realize now I should have included Robert Adams' *Finite and Infinite Goods*.)

Later in the afternoon I was able to finish Week 2 assignments for the course—list of course goals, a description of each weekly unit and a selection of each week's readings and, when applicable, videos to watch and such.

In the evening, in conversation with MB, we came up with an idea about the apol conference in the spring, which will be held at the Woodlands United Methodist Church. In my special talk about the Center, we intend to make the theme something like "The Wesleyan Roots of the Center for the Foundations of Ethics at Houston Baptist University."

Wednesday, September 8, 2021: Up very early, around 3:30 am, and hoping to get some work done on Week 3 assignments of the course creation, and on grading for my online course.

Turned out to be a very productive day, making significant progress on the online course. Still doing the narrated power points of Week 3.

Thursday, September 9, 2021: Continued building this online course on the moral argument. The big-eyed kitty in the yard seems gradually to be building trust. Second day in a row I went to the gym to work out; good thing. Received in the mail Melissa Cain Travis's book on science. Would like to find the time to read and review it for the site. It's a little after 7 in the evening now; winding down fast.

Friday, September 10, 2021: Had an exchange with a FB friend today. He wrote me this:

> Dr. Baggett, hello again. I just finished listening to your lecture uploaded on the moral apologetics youtube channel. I enjoyed it to my core. I especially liked the way you showed that something is missing on the evolutionary account "truth". I loved it. Thank you so much for that. There is one thing that I like to hear more about, and I know from what you have told me that is part of your upcoming book on dealing with anti-realism. The whole lecture seems to be around the premise that we trust our intuitions and that they yield to some things being intrinsically valuable, and from there the whole case is launched. You

352

emphasized that if there are no intrinsically valuable things, then morality cannot even get off the ground. Therefore, I would be delighted to hear you talk more about reasons to trust our intuitions in those matters and how to respond to challenges on trusting them. I have read several articles and books on the matter, but there seems to be a whole lot of epistemology regarding basics belief, foundationalism, internalism vs externalism and so forth when we take that route that, we are almost at the edge of our capacities to argue about. Hence it becomes controversial and I do need help as a Christian to navigate it all. I have my feet wet, but I am still learning to swim those waters. Again, thank you so, so much for your work. May the Most High bless you greatly and the influence you have on my life. Thanks!

I replied:

Yeah, these are good questions and deep waters. The book we're writing now should definitely help. Just a few quick things or now. Audi has done good work on intuitionism; might want to take a look at his stuff. Also, God can reveal his truth to us in a number of ways, I figure--scripture, intuitions, conscience, cultural teaching, reason, general revelation, etc. Most people are more sure of at least some core moral convictions than they are of any arguments to discard them. But this is a challenge we'll hear about more and more, especially because of so-called "debunking objections" based on evolution. We're planning a chapter on that in the new book. Your question, I suspect, ultimately has more to do with reasons to believe in moral realism than just intuitions specifically. There you might look at the work of Cuneo, Shafer-Landau, and Enoch, if you haven't already. Blessings!

Then he wrote this:

Thank you so much. I am an ardent Christian moral realist for sure, thanks to pretty much all those names you mentioned. I do incline towards divine command theory. Where I have issues mostly is in handling objections to moral intuition, and often it comes down to those epistemological deep waters I mentioned. For instance, the problem of two or more people having contrary intuitions, I understand that such at best may bring relativism in the question, but does not defeat that there may still be moral truth, but it does bring a problem on how to arrive at those truths. Which in turn turns the tables on arguing for why trusting intuitions or think you got the right ones, but jot the person who has the contrary ones. A lot of the challenges I do think have a J.L. Mackie flavor into them. But seems to me that inevitably arguing at this level, involves some degree of getting acquainted with issues behind moral knowledge, which in turn opens a can of worms regarding knowledge in general, Gettier issues, internalism/externalism, and so forth. And that is an enormous ocean for me still. I incline towards foundationalism and internalism, but still there are some challenges to resolve; which I would love if they are more watered down since I am not a philosopher per se. But train myself in apologetics. In any case, that's the type of things I struggle with.

Then I replied like this:

Yeah, good struggles. I might suggest not overdoing the intuitions, since they've fallen on hard times lately. I'm inclined to think we should have supreme confidence only in a rather narrow range of intuitions. On most vexed matters, we have to appeal to a whole lot more. Regarding Mackie, we discuss him a lot in the upcoming book. Interesting to note how all three of the "queerness" objections he raises can be handled pretty well by theism--by his own admission. He was also, I think, wrong to impose on the realist the need to defend a special set of cognitive powers to apprehend moral truths. Theists are no worse off than any moral realist, and I think we're in a better position. Again, Mackie admitted that if God indeed exists this is so. Of course he was skeptical that God does exist, but I don't share his skepticism. Good luck!! Keep thinking hard!

Saturday, September 11, 2021: Ran into a bit of a wall working on the online course, but that's okay. It was September 11, 20 years to the day of the great tragedy. A day for sober reflection. A day when we saw religion skew ethics horrifically.

Sunday, September 12, 2021: Relaxed and enjoyed the day with Marybeth and Nathaniel. The stir fry was great, and the latest Ted Lasso episode superlative! They know what they're doing. Hopefully we'll get that book contract! Read a chapter of Travis's book; she's very clear and sensible; should be helpful preparing for the spring event in TN.

Monday, September 13, 2021: Churned out the Provost Grant Proposal for the conference I'd like to do; here it is:

Provost's Excellence Fund Grant Proposal (2021)

Name of Project: The Foundations of Ethics

Name and Title of Project Lead: David Baggett, professor of philosophy, Apologetics Department SCT, and Director of the Center for the Foundations of Ethics, Houston Baptist University. E-mail: dbaggett@hbu.edu. Cell: (434) 534-4525

Name(s) and Title(s) of Project Collaborators (if applicable): Dr. Jerry Walls, Scholar in Residence and professor of philosophy, Philosophy Department,

HBU; Dr. Marybeth Baggett, professor of English and cultural apologetics, English Department (& Chair of Apologetics Department, SCT), HBU; Dr. Robert Gagnon, professor of theology & New Testament, HBU

Project Narrative –

Description of project: This project is designed to address the pressing question of the ultimate foundations of ethics, no merely theoretical matter but one of profound practical and existential import. Ethics includes moral goodness in terms of both that which is of intrinsic value and that which is good/best for human beings. The range of ethics robustly and realistically construed runs the gamut and traverses a wide territory, and the question to be explored concerns which worldview provides the most comprehensive and compelling account of the full range of moral phenomena in need of explanation. This exploration broaches the topic of theistic ethics versus secular ethics and the relative merits of the moral argument for God's existence. In the past decade or so there has been an appreciable resurgence of interest in this argument. When asked which argument from natural theology has the most potential, Alvin Plantinga has said without hesitation the moral argument; and when William Lane Craig was asked which argument has the most effect on college campuses when he engages in debates about God's existence, his answer was the same.

Despite the fact that there have been numerous books covering one dimension of the moral argument or another, there is no single collection in print that navigates the whole ground and consolidates and integrates the diverse work that has been done. This project has for its aim, firstly, a conference that will start to rectify that situation by culminating, secondly, in a major new collection of nearly thirty fresh articles on the moral argument that will collectively cover the whole territory. From the venerable history of moral apologetics to the alternatives to moral realism, from debunking objections to the problem of evil, from axiological to deontic matters, from epistemic to rationality and performative variants of the moral argument, from diverse theistic ethical accounts to critiques of secular and naturalistic efforts to explain the range of moral phenomena, and from non-Christian ethical accounts to distinctively Christian ones, the scope of the conference and volume will be expansive and exhaustive.

The academic conference will feature the best theistic thinkers on the moral argument coming together to share their insights and findings, generating the most elaborate and rigorous academic treatment of the moral argument for God's existence to date. The attendees—from (hopefully) Hare to Moreland, from Menuge to Rist, from Evans to Idziak, from Crosby to Zabzebski—will share drafts of their chapters in progress that will, when completed, be combined into a major edited collection. The collection will be the first of its kind, and it is already under contract with a major university press.

With a notable gap in scholarly examination regarding the whole terrain of the moral argument, this proposal centers on a longstanding vision to publish contemporary work on the topic of the foundations of ethics. A plethora of work exists in areas germane to theistic ethics and moral apologetics, but the vision of the present work will consolidate findings in all of these areas, which is currently not anywhere on offer:

(1) Historical recovery of the work done on the moral argument by luminaries through the centuries, including such powerful Christian thinkers as William Sorley, A. E. Taylor, Hastings Rashdall, and many more (Jerry Walls and I have published *A Moral Argument: A History* (OUP, 2019));

(2) Defending moral realism against objections and arguing in its favor;

(3) Explicating and defending a variety of theistic ethical accounts (see Walls' and my *Good God* (OUP, 2011));

(4) Laying out the rich range of moral phenomena in need of robust explanation;

(5) Critiquing alternative theistic and non-Christian accounts of ethical foundations (see Walls' and my *God and Cosmos* (OUP, 2016)); and

(6) Extending the moral argument beyond bare or generic theism to something more distinctively Christian.

The result will be an accessible volume designed to give readers the full picture of where the discussion on the moral argument as a whole currently stands. Oxford University Press has accepted the proposal for this Collection submitted by Yale University Divinity School's Dr. John Hare and me.

This grant proposal project will plan, execute, and evaluate an academic conference in which some or all of the contributors to the collection will participate. The synergy that will result from the conversation between these premier world-class scholars in this field is sure to advance the discussion of theistic ethics and this centrally important aspect of natural theology.

The conference will be an opportunity for participants to become more fully aware of the way in which the varied pieces of this puzzle come together to advance the case for the explanatory power of theism generally and Christianity particularly to account for the full range of ethical realities. The conference will be a boon to the HBU campus, the larger community (the fourth largest city in the U.S.), and the whole academy as this community of scholars pool their efforts to showcase the level of rigor that is possible in explicating and defending sturdy theistic foundations for ethics.

Having heard one another and benefited from the Socratic dialogue and give-and-take at the conference, the participants will be all the better able to finish their work strong, contributing to a potent overall result when the collection is published. That volume will then have the potential to be widely disseminated, used in classrooms, and to ignite interest in the moral argument for a whole new generation of thinkers and scholars for many years to come, setting the bar higher than ever in this particular discussion that is arguably of greater importance in our current cultural moment than ever before.

John Hare and I are currently extending invitations to the best scholars we can think of to contribute to the collection. We already have about fifteen significant scholars onboard who make up a veritable "who's who" in this field. The end result, we are convinced, is going to be an unprecedented pool of talent directing their prodigious skills to zero in on a particular argument for God's existence from a number of mutually enforcing directions. One of the tasks of the conference and collection will be to accentuate the internal cumulative case that is possible when it comes to the moral argument. Another will be to help more scholars and prospective scholars, not to mention informed lay people and various practitioners, to see the need for an active community of moral apologists, philosophers, Bible scholars, literature experts, historians, social scientists, and theologians working diversely but in tandem to do justice to the richness of this material and ongoing research agenda that has only begun to show its potential.

After finalizing the best list of contributors we can, we hope to be able to extend to them an offer to attend this conference at HBU, site of the newly formed Center for the Foundations of Ethics (which I direct), all expenses paid— their room, board, travel, etc. This will be to help ensure as wide participation among the contributors as we can generate. A thriving and memorable conference can help establish HBU as a central hub of cutting-edge research on the moral argument and inspire scholars here and elsewhere to see more clearly the arena of theistic ethics and moral apologetics as a viable and vital research agenda. The conference and subsequent collection will be a powerful testimony to HBU students, scholars and students elsewhere, the wider Houston community, and the church and society as a whole that the evidential significance of morality is strong and a real clue about the nature of ultimate reality, rightly imbuing believers with greater confidence in the rational defensibility and practical power of their principled convictions.

Alignment with University mission: Of late I have been enjoying reading _An Act of Providence: A History of Houston Baptist University, 1960-2010_, and just today I read the new _Ten Pillars_ document from start to finish. In addition to being a Christian university generally, HBU has a particular narrative and history, shaped by its background and context, contributing to its particular mission. A holistic understanding of the biblical narrative functions as a central unifying purpose and singular vision of the university, and it's a school intentionally built on those ancient foundations. As Dr. Sloan writes, "[O]ur ability to weather fierce storms depends upon solid foundations." Pillar 7's focus on life and marriage, gender and humanness, for one, assumes not just the reliability of special revelation, but even more fundamentally robust moral realism, an assumption increasingly challenged in today's cultural climate. Moral apologetics offers principled reasons to believe in sturdily objective moral truth, for their theistic foundation, and for seeing the limitations of treating God as eliminable when accounting for such important truths as binding, authoritative obligations, enduring human value, essential human equality, and the like. A conference at HBU and major resultant book dedicated to exploring these principled reasons can help this institution fulfill its distinctive mission for standing for truth, goodness, and beauty in a society often wont to subject these classical transcendentals to deflationary and reductionist analyses. The purpose of this conference and the ensuing book can, among other things, serve as an antidote to the erosion of moral foundations we so often see today by pointing to their ancient and truest source.

Strategic plan and purpose of Provost's Excellence Fund (Christian worldview integration, cross-disciplinary integration, student success, or institutional efficiency): Among the ways in which this initiative would serve the strategic plan and purpose of this Fund, (1) students would be offered a shining example of world-class Christian scholarship to be inspired by and to emulate; (2) it would help with the fundraising efforts and mission of HBU's Center for the Foundations of Ethics, Philosophy Department, Apologetics Department, and the SCT more generally; (3) it would heighten the profile of HBU as a leading place of cutting-edge work and research in apologetics (broadly construed) and philosophy; and (4) it would forge deeper collaborations between four departments and two colleges here at HBU.

Desired outcomes: Besides the conference itself, which will be a powerful outreach both to the HBU and wider community, the conference will end up having a quite palpable product: a 250,000-word collection on the moral argument (co-edited by an HBU professor) that fills a vitally important gap in the literature. Oxford University Press was enthusiastic in its offer of a contract for John Hare and me to edit the volume, admitting that there is nothing like it in existence and acknowledging the power such a volume would possess to advance serious work in this area. Our rationale is to bring together, in one conference and then in one volume, a comprehensive synthesis of the current thoughts regarding what may seem a disparate field of theories, concepts, arguments, and monographs devoted to various facets of the moral argument and allied topics. Here is what one reviewer wrote concerning the book proposal: "The moral argument has become a hot field in apologetics, and this book speaks directly to a need in the market—and a want. As I said above, if the book is sculpted to be high on readability, this will augur well for marketing and sales, it seems to me. I recommend that Oxford definitely offer to publish this text. It is a wonderful proposal and fills such an important niche, just as the proposal claims. Bravo!"

Timeline: What we are envisioning is to plan well enough in advance to ensure that this conference is done well and right. Holding the conference this school year would be too rushed, so we are thinking the ideal time table would feature the conference at the earliest to be held spring of 2023, the second half of next school year. This would give us ample time to make preparations, arrange the speakers and accommodations, accord all the relevant details due diligence, and ensure the participants enough time to generate solid drafts of their contributions.

Possible challenges or obstacles: Another reason for holding the conference next year is to make it less likely that ongoing challenges posed by covid don't stand in the way of a successful conference. Other than that, I cannot think of any other likely challenges or obstacles to overcome.

Criteria for evaluating success: (1) a robust and well-attended conference; (2) engaging the imaginations of students interested in pursuing the study of apologetics and philosophy from a Christian perspective; (3) a superlative collection emerging from the conference and published by OUP, making a significant contribution to the literature and conversation; (4) HBU coming to be seen as a leading institution of higher learning for focused and rigorous study in these areas.

Possibilities for continuation or expansion if proposed project is successful (if applicable): Insofar as the conference and book can help contribute to HBU becoming a venue of cutting-edge research on the moral argument, the Center will continue to spearhead initiatives building on the momentum produced by these initiatives as it strives to cultivate a community of students and scholars from various disciplinary perspectives engaged in this work so vitally important both perennially and specifically to our cultural moment.

Project Budget –

Salary (student workers, staff support): $500

Travel: $10,000

Room/Board for Participants: $3,000

Supplies and equipment: $500

Other: $1,000

TOTAL PROPOSED: $15,000

If HBU puts $15,000 toward this initiative, I am committed to raise or donate at least another $5,000 in order to make the conference everything we envision it to be, and ensure inclusion of everyone we can accommodate who is contributing to the book and has an interest in attending and participating.

: Kyla Ebels-Duggan (Northwestern), Robert Garcia (Baylor), Terence Cuneo (Vermont), Angus Menuge (Concordia), Paul Copan (Palm Beach Atlantic), John Rist (emeritus Cambridge), Anne Jeffrey (Baylor), John Crosby (Franciscan University of Steubenville), Steve Evans (Baylor), John Hare (Yale), David Baggett (HBU), Matthew Flannagan, Janine Idziak (emeritus Loras College), Linda Zagzebski (Oklahoma), J. P. Moreland (Biola), Mark Linville (Faulkner), Len Goodman (Vanderbilt)

Tuesday, September 14, 2021: Classes cancelled today owing to a tropical storm hitting Houston. I was able to finish the WB roundtable piece:

Quest for Immortality

Some years ago I had the pleasant experience of using for a textbook Clifford Williams' fine book on existential reasons for belief in God, and found the volume to be tremendously insightful. It's one among other books in recent years that have intentionally tried to stretch the apologetic quest beyond the confines of an overly narrow empiricism or epistemology. Such existential and experiential reasons should usually be thought of as supplemental sorts of confirmations that augment an evidential case, but sometimes the reasons arguably carry evidential support of their own. For example, I have used the example of the way our deeply felt existential moral needs for forgiveness, change, and ultimate perfection can be used in a performative variant of the moral argument, and there are plenty of other examples as well. My WB colleagues are talking about their own particular examples of existential reasons, and the one that I will consider is our longing for immortality.

Sometimes moral arguments try to show that God exists, but Immanuel Kant also gave a famous version of the moral argument that attempted to demonstrate the reality of immortality. It went something like this: since we can never achieve the "holy will" that God alone possesses, the best we can do is progressively approach it—*asymptotically*, to use a concept from mathematics—getting ever closer but never fully arriving. The process can never be completed, so if morality is to taken with full seriousness, we need to posit the existence of an unending afterlife.

As arguments go, it leaves something to be desired, although I suspect it does capture something of some importance. Even subsequent to the day of Christ Jesus, when the good work that's been begun within us will be completed, likely involving an experience of the beatific vision and complete conformity to the image of Christ, there remains a dynamism to our heavenly state. Presumably even then, and forevermore, we can and will grow deeper into ever more loving relationships with God and others. This picture reveals some of what is wrong with thinking that the new heavens and earth might end up ever being

360

monotonous or boring. To the contrary, it is a place of the most active and abundant life possible.

A picture of the heavenly state as one of irremediable ennui came at the culmination of the television show *Good Place*, which depicts (in hilarious fashion) something of a secular picture of an afterlife in which there is the prospect of an unending existence. The show's secularity manifests in its commitment to what Charles Taylor calls the "immanent frame," which inclines the modern mind to find fulfillment without recourse to any transcendent source. At best love relationships between people are thought of as our highest good, and this is just what we find in the *Good Place*. In this way the show confirms Ernest Becker's conclusion that the modern relationship is all that's left for those who believe in the "death of God." But such relationships (even between Eleanor and Chidi) fall short and fail to satisfy, unsurprising because, as Becker puts it, "No human relationship can bear the burden of godhood."

The Christian vision is different, featuring a never-ending source of joy, an ultimate good big and transcendent enough to satisfy forever. Eternal joy is not an oxymoron, or contradiction in terms, because there's an ultimate good, a perfect and perfectly loving and holy God, it will take all of eternity to worship and adore properly—a process that will literally never be accomplished and over with. The problem with secular pictures is that their good is too small. This world alone is not enough.

Hearing of immortality, or eternal life, usually raises the specter of something of unending quantity, which is perfectly natural. Biblically, however—especially in places like the Gospel of John—eternal life is, additionally, associated with a qualitative aspect as well. This is why it actually makes good sense to say that in a real way eternal life has already begun in the lives of believers. There is obviously a glory to come that we have yet to enter fully into, but even now we can catch furtive glimpses and momentary glances, as the kingdom of God seeps and shines through and occasionally irrupts even in the most seemingly pedestrian of life's events.

While recently rereading C. S. Lewis's *Till We Have Faces*, something stood out for the first time. When Orual (Maia) discovers Psyche alive, Psyche describes what had happened to her. At one point Psyche says, "When I saw West-wind I was neither glad nor afraid (at first). I felt ashamed."

"But what of? Psyche, they hadn't stripped you naked or anything?"

"No, no, Maia. Ashamed of looking like a mortal—ashamed of being a mortal."

"But how could you help that?"

"Don't you think the things people are most ashamed of are the things they can't help?"

"I thought of my ugliness and said nothing."

What stood out in this remarkable passage was our mortality as a source of shame, and the way the work of Christ takes away both our guilt and our shame—both deserved and undeserved.

I can't help but wonder if there isn't some biblical precedent to such a notion. I Cor. 15:53, for example, speaks of the perishable putting on the imperishable and mortality immortality. Before Adam's fall introduced death, life might have gone on indefinitely, but there was still a susceptibility to sin that needed to be rectified.

As my colleague Chris Kugler wrote to me, "Of course, redemption from sin and corruption takes center stage in scripture itself and thus is, of course, central; but, there are also indications—and you pick up on some of those with immortality swallowing up mortality—that, *even if Sin had never been a problem*, God was going to have to do *something* to make mere creatures fit for eternal fellowship with the creator."

Jesus fixed the sin problem by going to the cross, but he also fixed this vulnerability within us, making possible the removal of the shame of our mortality. This is why the beatified state will be even better than a restoration of Eden.

I also sent Chris Reese my September WB piece that looks like this:

The Big Ghost, Thor, and the Self

The fourth chapter of C. S. Lewis's imaginative *The Great Divorce* features the Big Ghost, formerly a man, now an insubstantial wisp of a ghost, a transparent phantom pursued by one of the solid people under whose tread the earth seemed to shake. In contrast the Big Ghost and other inhabitants of the heaven-bound bus from hell had trouble walking at all, for to their feet the blades of grass in this strange land seemed as sharp as diamonds. The Big Ghost had already been told he didn't have to leave this place, but was free to stay as long as he pleased, and his pursuer confirms it by offering to accompany him on his journey into the high country.

The Big Ghost is appalled when he recognizes the bright person following him, a solid spirit jocund and established in its youthfulness, for the spirit is none but Len, who as a man had murdered their mutual acquaintance Jack. To the Big Ghost Len is still nothing but a bloody murderer, while he himself had unjustly been relegated to haunt the filthy, macabre streets of Dark Town. The Ghost is incredulous that Len is in this place of light instead of him. Len deserves punishment and should be riddled with guilt and shame, yet seems entirely delivered from them, which viscerally grates against the Ghost. Len the substantial spirit's entire orientation contrasts with that of the self-consumed, paradoxically insubstantial Ghost. The bright spirit assures the Ghost, "I do not look at myself. I have given up myself. I had to, you know, after the murder. That was what it did for me. And that was how everything began." The event in Len's life that had served as the catalyst for repentance and deliverance from self-consumption is, to the Ghost's undiscerning eyes, a cause for nothing but unrelenting condemnation.

The forgiven spirit is not at all interested in vindicating himself, whereas the Ghost is interested in nothing but trying to vindicate himself. "I done my best all my life, see? I done my best by everyone, that's the sort of chap I was. I never asked for anything that wasn't mine by rights." The Ghost doesn't see that his very effort at self-vindication is a manifestation of his focus on self that prevents him from the necessary process of losing his self in order to gain it. Comparing his behavior with those of others, he thinks he comes out smelling like a proverbial rose, and thus demands nothing but his rights, without realizing that, as the bright spirit says, "I haven't got my rights, or I should not be here. You will not get yours either. You'll get something far better. Never fear." But it's as if their frameworks of understanding are so different that the wisdom the bright spirit is trying to share doesn't even register to the Ghost, smacking of inverted or perverted truth, as he remains consumed with indignation that he would be put below "a bloody murderer" like Len.

The irony is palpable that the insubstantial Ghost, unable to move a blade of grass even when exerting all his strength, continues puffing himself up. Refusing to give up his self-focus, he's relegated to becoming ever less substantial, while insisting on the sort of chap he is, how he only wants his rights, and refusing anybody's bleeding charity.

Elsewhere in Lewis's writings he laments the diminution of meaning the word 'charity' has undergone. Traditionally it wasn't merely benefits conferred on the less fortunate, but one of the theological virtues, an orientation toward others rather than oneself, putting the needs of others before one's own, esteeming the other better than oneself. "Ask for the Bleeding Charity," the spirit exhorts the Ghost. "Everything is here for the asking and nothing can be bought." But the Big Ghost will have none of it: "I don't want charity. I'm a decent man and if I had my rights I'd have been here long ago and you can tell them I said so."

Undeterred, with mirth dancing in his eyes, the bright spirit points out that the Big Ghost, as a man, didn't actually do his best and wasn't so decent after all. "We none of us were and none of us did," but he assures the Ghost it doesn't have to matter now. Once more, the offer of hope sounds to the Big Ghost like nothing but condemnation from a worse sinner, and he won't countenance it.

In a sense the bright spirit admits it's worse than that, that his murder of Jack wasn't the worst thing he himself had done during his life—that he had murdered the Big Ghost in his heart for years while they lived as men. This is why he was sent to him—to ask for forgiveness and to be his servant as long as he needed one, longer if the Ghost pleased. The Ghost bristles at any suggestion of his own shortcomings, insisting that they are his own private affairs, to which the bright spirit replies, "There are no private affairs," we're all tied in an interlocking web of mutuality; an insight lost because of the Ghost's inflated sense of self.

Relishing the chance to refuse the offer, content with his diminished state, insistent on his rights, the Big Ghost tragically chooses hell over heaven. Unwilling to give up his life, he loses it, still unable to bend a blade of grass for being so diminished and insubstantial.

Here I cannot help but contrast the Big Ghost with Thor. In the first movie, the initially brash and arrogant Thor is cast out of Asgard and stripped of his powers, and subsequently unable to lift his hammer, no matter how hard he tries. In a sense he's like the Big Ghost, too weak and diminished to move a small stone or leaf after disembarking from the bus. When Thor was banished, his father, before casting the hammer to earth as well, had said, "Let him who is worthy possess the power of Thor."

At the climax of the film, a matured, heroic Thor becomes willing to give up his life to save others. He offers his own life to spare the rest, and then, after a moment when it looks like his brother might relent, Thor is killed. And it is just then that the hammer, miles away, takes off and flies in a fiery trajectory into the hand of a revived Thor. Having given up his life, he found it. Having been unable to so much as move the hammer, now he can wield it with splendid force. It is a great scene, resonating with a universal truth: life is found when we are willing to lose it.

Of course Thor is no real god. As Captain America says, after all, "There's only one God, and I'm pretty sure he doesn't dress like that." The essence of salvation, on a Christian picture, is not about obtaining a ticket to heaven, or saving your cosmic rear end from getting flames on it, but about deliverance from the tyranny of self, from a hell locked from the inside, from sufferings intrinsically connected to the inevitable product of consumption with self. To be saved to the full is to be made able to love God and others with all of our hearts, to find deliverance from an inward orientation that forever blocks us from the life that only comes when we are willing to give up our own. It is not about being good enough, but realizing that none of us is very decent, and we can do nothing to purchase this life. We can only receive Bleeding Charity from nail-pierced hands.

Wednesday, September 15, 2021: Today I wrote a proposal for consideration by our homeowner's association:

PROPOSAL FOR COMMUNITY MITIGATION EFFORT
TO ADDRESS FERAL CAT POPULATION

Since moving to Pagoda Drive in July 2020, my wife and I have noticed five or six local feral cats in the neighborhood. On the assumption that this isn't the whole set of feral cats on our streets, the number is liable to be considerably more, and prospects for even more if some of the females get impregnated.

In the interest of reducing innocent and needless animal suffering and avoiding seeing more feral cats added to the population, this proposal is designed to address both concerns. Its goals are these:

(1) To ensure that the feral cats are adequately taken care of in terms of food and water;
(2) To prevent the cats from adding to their population;
(3) To provide for an at least moderately warmer location for the cats to stay when the weather turns unseasonably cold during the winter months.
(4) To ensure cats are given flea treatments, necessary shots, and a sterilization procedure.

The plan involves these steps:

(1) Each block providing several inexpensive cat shelters for the cats to avoid the worst of the inclement weather;
(2) To get the female cats spayed and the male cats neutered;
(3) To get the cats needed shots and flea treatments;
(4) To domesticate any of the feral cats able to be domesticated;
(5) Providing enough food and water that the cats need.

This plan is not as prohibitive as it might at first seem. Here are the steps needed to implement the plan.

(1) Establish a community fund (to which giving is voluntary) from which to draw to pay for local cats to be spayed or neutered, necessary shots, and flea treatments.
(2) Ask for volunteers to procure from the animal shelter a cat cage so that the cat, after getting collected, can then be taken in to be spayed or neutered and given a flea treatment.
(3) Ask for at least a few volunteers each block to leave out fresh food and water every day for the cats.
(4) Ask for a few volunteers on each block to purchase an inexpensive cat shelter for a cat to remain when the weather is brutally cold; such shelters often cost less than $100.

My wife and I are willing to volunteer to spearhead this effort among those in our homeowner's association. If anyone would like to help me spearhead the initiative, I would be happy for the help, though it isn't necessary. My wife and I put out fresh food and water daily already, and we are willing to purchase three cat shelters.

Those who wish to contribute to the Fund, once we establish it, can do so on a purely voluntary basis. Not everyone would have to contribute as long as some percentage (perhaps ten percent) do so voluntarily.

Likewise not everyone need try to domesticate a stray, collect one for sterilization (and shots and flea treatments), or put out fresh food and water daily. So long as at least some consistent (rather small) percentage of animal-loving residents are willing to do so consistently, we should be able to handily reach the goals of this initiative.

Respectfully submitted,

David Baggett, PhD, Professor of Philosophy, Houston Baptist University

11510 Pagoda Drive, Stafford, TX (434) 534-4525

dbaggett@hbu.edu

Thursday, September 16, 2021: Up early, currently 5 am. I think I'll head to the gym so I can be back in time for MB to head to class. Hopefully will make a lot of progress today on wrapping up the narrated power points for the online course I'm building.

Friday, September 17, 2021: Yesterday and today I managed to just about knock out this online course. Lots of momentum. Fun evening with Rob and Jerry.

Saturday, September 18, 2021: Nice chat with Elton this morning, and this afternoon I wrapped up the Week 4 assignments for the online course. About all that's left is the faculty guide and the rubrics. Writing a letter of recommendation today for Michael Keck; he's applying to lots of big schools. He's got a tremendously bright future. Got this question in an e-mail today:

Hello Dr. Baggett!

I started reading God and Cosmos today and came across the brief discussion regarding supererogation in the introduction to chapter one. Though I have heard of the distinction between moral rightness and moral goodness, I have never heard it labeled as supererogation. If supererogation is defined as the performance of more work than duty requires, how are we to reconcile this to the fact that we are sinners who can never be perfect? Also, doesn't Jesus teach that our good works are merely what is due of us? The distinction between right and good says that moral goodness doesn't imply obligation, but don't we have a moral obligation to do good? I have always had no trouble holding to the distinction between moral value and moral obligation until it being explained under the label of supererogation. Certainly there has to be good answers to the objections raised against the right/good distinction! Could you help me with my sagging confidence in this distinction? Any help at all would be very appreciated!

Thank you and God bless you,
Cayden Diebold

To which I responded:

Hi Cayden! You ask a good question, and you're in good company. Guys like Luther and Wesley were skeptical there's any such thing as supererogation. But I think there's a bit of an equivocation here. Going above and beyond the call of duty is hardly to make God beholden to us in any way. There's a profound sense in which nothing that we do compares with what God is due or with what we ought to be willing to do in service to him.

But to my thinking there's a great deal of sense to be made of talking about going above and beyond our call to duty, nonetheless, at least in a fallen world like this. Our energies are limited, and it's simply not the case that we are obligated to do every good thing we could do. We'd end up doing nothing else. I don't think God's demands on us are that onerous and impracticable. My going to the food kitchen five days a week to help out would be a good thing, but it's not necessarily something I'm obligated to do. It's surely not obligatory simply because it's a good thing to do.

So I use the notion of supererogation to refer to good things to do that aren't obligatory. As a divine command theorist, I'm inclined to think we're obligated to do things God communicates to us to do. The status of a prospective action as morally good is not in and of itself enough to make it obligatory, on my view. That doesn't mean we shouldn't do it; in many cases we have plenty of moral reasons to do it, but just not the sorts of reasons that come from an action being morally obligatory.

Now, you might say we "ought" to do good, and that's true, but the notion of oughtness doesn't always refer to moral duty. Sometimes for example it can refer to nonmoral duties, or in this case to moral reasons apart from moral duties. But if God commands us to do something, I'm inclined to think we have a moral duty, which adds to the moral reasons and makes our failure to perform the action morally blameworthy. My not going to food kitchen five days a week is not morally blameworthy, even though it would be a potentially morally good action to perform and an action for which I can adduce solid moral reasons to perform.

And that's why I think retaining the category of supererogation in our moral theory a useful thing.

But as I say, not everyone agrees--including some big names in church history! ☐

Blessings,
Dave

Sunday, September 19, 2021: Spent an enjoyable afternoon with family watching the latest Lasso episode, and spent time reading from Travis's book on science and the Campolos' book about Bart's pilgrimage. Might wish to do a series of blogs on the latter, and a review for the site on the former. Some good prayer time with MB.

Monday, September 20, 2021: Woke up around 3 and really prayed hard about the Center, Strauss lectures, my online course, fundraising, etc. Really trying to relinquish my cares and concerns into God's hands. Prayed especially hard for peace, joy, and victory. Then got up around 3:30 and did the weekly announcement for the online course and graded discussion boards from last week. About to head to the gym in a few minutes. During office hours today I'm hoping to wrap up work on the online course creation, which will free me up to get back to work on the Strauss lectures. Exciting!

Tuesday, September 21, 2021: Planning to finish the Campolo book today. Lots of fodder for good discussion. Planning to chat and pray with TJ at 2; it's currently almost noon, and I have three outlines left to look at, and then some final revisions on the online course construction. Hoping by 2 to be done with all of that, which will leave just the Keck letters to write and two colleagues' evaluations. Then I'll be in a position to get busy on the Strauss lectures once again.

Wednesday, September 22, 2021: Got up in the middle of the night and did the Keck letters and finished revising the online course. Fasting one meal today, and I chose breakfast. Getting to work now; it's a little after 10 am and I've been chipping away at the Logic Primer I want to put together for the apologetics students. Doing that has gotten me interested in doing a WB piece on Wesley on logic. His Sermon #70 on the importance and limits of reason, his "Address to Clergy," and his *Compendium on Logic* are good fodder for a little piece. An online student in my Faith and Reason course wants to chat a bit about the course because he seems to be struggling a bit.

About to quit work for the day. I've made some progress on the logic primer, a blog about Wesley on logic, and wrote the first Campolo blog for our site. Wrapped up the evals for Mary Jo and Nancy, and so tomorrow I should be able to dive back into TWHF. Excited! Here's the Campolo blog:

Response #1 to *Why I Left, Why I Stayed*, by Tony and Bart Campolo

The name *Tony Campolo* invokes quite a bit of nostalgia for me. Like many church kids, I grew up watching the animated Christian sociologist/evangelist, always struck by his humor and energy, his insight and erudition. While attending Asbury Theological Seminary in the late 1980's and early 1990's, a friend and I read several of his books together, each in turn, taking the time to discuss them together as we did. Occasionally we may have balked a bit at some of what we read, a rhetorical flourish, something a tad hyperbolic here, a hint of needless iconoclasm there; but for the most part we enjoyed his passion, personality, and prodigious gifts a great deal.

This made it all the more fun when we were able to see him speak in person outside Lexington, Kentucky before I left that area for good. If memory serves, he spoke in the same church where my seminary graduation would be held pretty soon thereafter. I still remember how he effortlessly held the capacity crowd in his hand on the day he spoke. His charisma was contagious, and I distinctly remember thinking that if he misused his considerable gifts he could do real damage. I have often said that he's one of the three most gifted communicators I have ever seen (along with James Robison and Tom Morris).

It has been some years now since I have read any of his work, but I recently purchased his latest book because the topic was irresistible. His son Bart has lost his faith, after having served in ministry for many years. And the evangelical father and humanist son have written a book together, called *Why I Left, Why I Stayed*, a friendly conversation on the topic of Christianity published by HarperOne. I had had an interest in the book for a while, and finally ordered it, then read it through pretty quickly.

As I read the engaging and irenic dialogue, it spurred a lot of interest within me and served as fodder for a good deal of reflection. So the thought occurred it might be worth the trouble to blog a bit about each of the chapters. Tony and Bart take turns writing chapters, so the first chapter is by Tony, the second by Bart, and so on. In subsequent posts I will take each chapter in turn and discuss its contents, sharing some of my own reflections the chapter inspired as we go.

The nature of their close relationship makes for compelling reading. So often it's hard for people of diametrically opposed worldviews to remain civil while discussing their deep differences. Tony and Bart are determined to do so because of their long and close familial relationship, and because it's important to find good models of such difficult conversations, it's worth considering for that reason alone. As the culture wars have ramped up, suspicions of those with whom we disagree have elevated to often alarming levels, exacerbating and intensifying the chasms and divides between those with conflicting perspectives. The casualty of such tensions is often substantive dialogue, which is a real shame. This book can help serve as a partial corrective to this lamentable state of affairs and a better way forward.

As the Preface notes, the Campolos are not unusual; many Christian parents are struggling, both emotionally and spiritually, because their children have left the Christian faith. So often the result is one of tension, acrimony, and alienation, and they hope to show a better way. "Hopefully," they jointly write, "this book models a graceful way to process what has become an increasingly common crisis, while also serving as a safe forum for those struggling with doubts and questions about the Christian faith." They aim to heed the apostle Paul's advice to be kind, tender-hearted, and forgiving to one another, and this is laudable indeed.

The poignant Foreword to the book was written by Peggy Campolo, husband to Tony and mother to Bart. Although she's heartbroken that Bart has lost his faith, she's also proud of him for being authentic and transparent about his convictions, especially in light of the painful price they have exacted. She retains the belief that God is still involved in Bart's life, just as God was, by her own admission, at work within her for a long time before she realized it.

One last preliminary: I am intrigued by the more social scientific tenor of much of the conversation. Tony has a PhD in and a career teaching sociology, and he often brings to bear insights from a range of thinkers—from Durkheim to Heidegger, from Freud to Maslow—with whom I don't interact very much. This adds a texture and richness to the conversation I find enjoyable and enlightening. Obviously, I cannot help but reflect on what they talk about from my own background and professional training in analytic philosophy, but I think the resulting interdisciplinary nature of the conversation should prove both interesting and illuminative.

If folks decide to read along, I might suggest you get a copy of their book and read each chapter with me as I go along. Doing so would probably enhance your enjoyment and ability to add to the conversation.

Thursday, September 23, 2021: MoralApologetics.com put up a piece by Tony Williams on guilt, and someone responded on FB they didn't see how it served as evidence for God. I wrote this reply:

The piece is about a particularly poignant moral phenomenon, namely, guilt. We all of us seem to have a deep existential moral need to be forgiven. We have feelings of guilt, which most of us, at least on occasion, tend to connect with an objective condition of guilt. If such guilt is not merely a false appearance, it raises the question of how to deal with it. Christianity offers a good explanation of why we both feel and are guilty and how we can be forgiven. Obviously this is just a short blog, but I take it to be suggesting that the reality of moral guilt, on reflection, points in the direction of God. Steve Evans might call it a "natural sign," fulfilling the Pascalian constraints of being both universally accessible and easily resistible. Of course some might suggest that more needs to be said to lay all this out, and that's true, but blogs are usually meant to be more suggestive than anything. The phenomenon of guilt is quite interesting and I suspect that it would do us all good to be carefully attentive to its salient features. It's easy to be in too big a rush and miss its significance. In his classic Gifford lectures *Faith of a Moralist*, A. E. Taylor, for example, identified such features of guilt as these: (1) it involves a sense of condemnation for ourselves and our actions, so it's different from mere discontent with our surroundings; (2) its indelibility, or power of asserting itself with unabated poignancy; (3) the regular attendance of a demand for punishment; (4) a particularly polluting quality; and 5) the sense that it's the very foundation of our moral personality that's somehow poisoned. A visceral recognition of a deep sense of guilt is ubiquitous. This raises the question of how best to make sense of such a phenomenon, and how best to deal with it— really to explain it and not just explain it away. A Christian solution involves forgiveness from the One before whom we are guilty, not to mention deliverance from shame that can cripple us, sinful patterns that can hold us in bondage, and hope for ultimate deliverance from moral brokenness altogether. Again, all of this is cursory, but the basic idea is that such good answers to these practically universal, deep existential moral needs makes Christianity more likely than it would otherwise be--even if taken by themselves they don't make Christianity or theism more likely true than not. In this sense, as I see it, the blog is in the spirit of something like Book 1 of *Mere Christianity* and chapters 5 and 10 of John Henry Newman's *Grammar of Assent*.

Friday, September 24, 2021: I chipped away a little on the TWHF piece and also wrote the apol department about the possibility of a logic primer. Got some good and useful feedback which should help me refine the proposal.

Saturday, September 25, 2021: Nice breakfast with MB and Nathaniel, then a nice chat with Elton. He and I talked about a number of things, including the temptation as we get older to rest more content than we should in the face of guilt for chronic patterns of wrongdoing. He also gave me advice on how to navigate department politics when it comes to the logic primer initiative: make clear I'm not suggesting they've done anything wrong heretofore; stress the varied backgrounds of our students; this is to address a situation that couldn't have been foreseen before; it's not about keeping people out of the program but enhancing the experience of those already in it; be sure to argue for the benefits of the plan; etc.

Sunday, September 26, 2021: A good day with the family. Nice meal with MB and Nathaniel and an episode of Ted Lasso, though it wasn't the best episode. Actually it was rather bad in a couple respects; ah well, c'est la vie. I didn't put any work in today; wanted to make it a day of rest.

Monday, September 27, 2021: Good work day. Held office hours and was able to make serious strides on the TWHF piece. Also attended Jason Mattson's afternoon talk on the apostle Paul's attitude toward death. Depending on which passage, he says different things, with both comparisons and contrasts with prevailing philosophical views about death that were in the air. Should hear on the grant by the end of the week. Praying for God's will to be done.

Tuesday, September 28, 2021: Today's biblical passage covered the armor of God. What a great passage. The belt of truth. Breastplate of righteousness, protecting our hearts. Feet shod with the preparation of the gospel of peace—wherever we go we take the gospel of peace. Shield of faith, blocking things shot our direction. Helmet of salvation, protecting our minds. The sword of the Spirit, which is the Word of God. Pray at all times in the Spirit, stay alert, intercede for the saints. Sometimes I think my main job anymore is to be a cheerleader—encouraging others to reach their potential, exercise their gifts, doing the good works to which they're called. Rather than waiting on others to encourage me, make me an encourager of others, dear Lord, entrusting my future and whatever you have left to do through me into your hands.

Wednesday, September 29, 2021: Did a podcast with Brian Chilton today about moral apologetics. Here are the questions he sent and answers I had jotted in advance:

1. What is the basis for moral apologetics? That is, what does the moral argument set out to do?
   Moral arguments for God's existence highlight the evidential significance of morality. From basic human rights to essential human equality, from binding moral obligations to intrinsic human worth, morality raises questions about what it is about reality that explains these vitally important truths.
   An important key to doing moral apologetics well is a willingness to take the evidence seriously. No reductionist and deflationary accounts of morality can do justice to the nature of the profound moral truths we most all of us take for granted. They call for serious explanation, and attentiveness to the nature of the evidence can help us see that.
   Something we can do from the outset, though, to facilitate good discussion is not always insist on using language like apologetics and argument. Simply helping

people to think about the nature of right and wrong, good and evil, vice and virtue, can sensitize them to the significance of these realities and get them reflecting about the human condition and ultimate reality.

Three basic tasks: (1) defend moral realism; (2) defend theistic ethics; and (3) critique secular alternatives.

2. In your research, you trace the history of the moral argument. Who are the earliest moral apologists?

Immanuel Kant is often cited as the first proponent of the moral argument, giving two quite significant moral arguments to show that the postulation of God's existence is eminently rational—an argument from grace and an argument from providence. But even before Kant there were precursors—WLC points to Plato as something of the original moral apologist. But of course Plato is also connected to a big challenge to theistic ethics we'll see in a moment. But beyond him there are important elements in Aristotle, and later during the Middle ages guys like Augustine and Aquinas, Ockam and Scotus, and later such Frenchmen as Descartes and Pascal, and yet later Berkeley and Butler, the British John Locke, and Scottish philosopher Thomas Reid. But then most all of those influences really came into focus with the work of Kant, which really initiated the subsequent to come on the moral argument.

3. Who are some of the most important moral apologists--that is, outside of Dr. David Baggett?

Well, after Kant I'd include such names as John Henry Newman, William Sorley, Hastings Rashdall, A. E. Taylor, and then of course C. S. Lewis, a distinctly modern figure, and his argument from Book 1 of Mere Christianity. A number of contemporaries have done wonderful work on the argument—from Steve Evans to Paul Copan, Matthew Flannagan to Mark Linville, Angus Menuge to Angus Ritchie, John Hare to Robert Adams, William Lane Craig to JP Moreland, Austin Farrer to Steve Layman, Jerry Walls to Scott Smith. It's an exciting time to be a moral apologist.

4. Can you describe the Euthypro Dilemma? What is the best solution to the dilemma?

Sure: in contemporary terms, is something moral because God commands it or does God command something because it's moral? So we have two options, and each one is thought problematic. If something is moral because God commands it, what if God were to command something horrific, like child torture? Would it become moral in virtue of God's commanding it? That seems troublesome, to say the least. But if God commands something because it's moral, that makes morality seem to exist independently of God, which is something many if not most traditional theists would resist. So there is this challenge to connecting up God and ethics.

I'm inclined to distinguish between values and duties, or the good and the right. The axiological matter of goodness or values I see rooted in God's essential nature, and the deontic matter of moral rightness, especially moral obligations, I see as rooted in God's commands. But one can be a moral apologist without being a divine command theorist, though I happen to be one. It makes sense to me that God would have the requisite authority to generate moral obligations by commanding us to do certain things. But of course because God is essentially loving and such, there are some commands he never would and never could do, because it would be tantamount to denying his own nature. This matter of who God is is just as important for the moral apologist than the fact of God's existence.

5. Can you explain your version of the divine command theory?
   I largely follow Robert Adams' theistic social theory of moral obligations, according to which God's commands constitute moral obligations. Some versions of DCT have it that God's commands cause obligations, but I tend to take divine commands as the very same as moral obligations. God's commanding something for us to do invests in what's commanded a new moral quality of rightness and obligatoriness. The action may well have already been morally good—this is usually the case—but since not all actions that are good are also obligatory, we need a way to delimit which among those actions are good to perform are also dutiful, and on my view divine commands do the trick. But DCT has a bad rap in lots of circles, so usually there's a slew of objections that need to be anticipated, and various DCT'ists have spilt quite a bit of ink trying to answer them.

6. You use the abductive approach to moral apologetics. Can you explain the abductive approach and its benefits?
   Well, the nature of the evidential connection, if there is one, between morality and God can be depicted in different ways. Evans speaks of natural signs— widely accessible and easily resistible evidence, and he thinks certain moral facts are natural signs that gesture toward God, but not necessarily in such a strong sense as to render anyone who might wish to resist patently irrational. Presuppositionalists might wish to argue that God is the only possible explanation of certain moral facts, but that goes beyond what I try to do. Deductivists might wish to suggest that the existence of various moral truths entails God's existence, but I don't tend to do it that way, either, though in some contexts I can certainly understand why some might wish to take such a route. Inductivists suggest that various moral truths might increase the likelihood of theism, either by a lot or a little. I tend to go an abductive route—an inference to the best explanation. I start with various moral phenomena—facts like objective moral values and duties, intrinsic human worth, essential human equality, moral knowledge, moral transformation, moral rationality, and so on. I take a really close look at the evidence, not rushing it, but really trying to apprehend its significance. Then I construct a pool of potential explanation candidates, then we

use a principled set of criterial to narrow down that list to the best explanation among the alternatives. Ultimately, I think the case can be made that theism is the best explanation, but of course in a conversation with a particular person, I usually don't try to cover all that ground, but might just focus in on a comparison of a theistic explanation with whatever that person might wish to suggest functions just as well if not better as an explanation—social contract theory, utilitarianism, or what have you. As I see it an abductive approach lends itself nicely to a communal approach that puts a lot of focus on shared common ground, and I needn't insist that someone who might find reasons to resist it are flat irrational or incorrigible. This stuff is hard, and it takes serious thinking to penetrate some of these mysteries.

7. You, WLC, and Plantinga have all noted the power and impact of moral apologetics. Why is it such a powerful argument?
    I think we all have a visceral recognition of moral truth and of its significance. It says something important about the world. It's a window of insight into reality. WLC says on college campuses it's the most effective argument he gives, and Plantinga has said he thinks it's the best argument in natural theology. I'm not interested in this matter of which argument is the BEST, since no one argument can be expected to do all the work that needs to be done, but it's an important argument because it points not just to God's reality but to God's essential goodness, and it has the potential to both persuade the mind and touch the heart.

Thursday, September 30, 2021: Zoom session with the WB guys. We're going to try adding two new folks and extend our reach with more videos featuring interviews and the like. Gavin Ortlun and Melissa Cain Travis. I wrote Melissa and she's considering it. Wrote a few new blogs on the Campolo book. Here's the second installment:

Reflections on *Why I Left, Why I Stayed*, by Tony and Bart Campolo, Part 2

Back when I saw Tony Campolo speak in person, he got the crowd laughing right off the bat. In his characteristically animated and rapid-fire diction, he practically yelled that physicists tell us that the faster to the speed of light an object travels, the more mass it obtains. Then, mischievously looking over at the corpulent pastor, pausing for comedic effect, he added, "Pastor, you're not fat! You've just been moving too fast!"

All these years later, it is admittedly a little surreal reflecting on a book that Campolo has written with his son who's lost his faith. Last time we made brief mention of the foreword that had been written by Peggy Campolo, Tony's wife and Bart's mom, which reminds me of a humorous anecdote about her too from a long time back. When she was staying at home raising the kids, she would grow weary of being asked what she did for a living, so rather than keep answering that she was a homemaker who had elected to stay home, she took to giving this for an answer: "I'm socializing two Homo-sapiens in Judeo-Christian *values* so they'll appropriate the eschatological *values* of utopia. What do you do?" They would often blurt out, "I'm a doctor," or "I'm a lawyer," and then wander off with a dazed look in their eyes.

Nobody was laughing, though, Thanksgiving evening in 2014 when Bart, in his old three-story house in an "at-risk" Cincinnati neighborhood, told his parents that he no longer believed in God. The first chapter of *Why I Left, Why I Stayed* is Tony's poignant account of that evening. Bart had long served in ministry, doing outreach to the poor and proclaiming the Christian gospel alongside his famous father, and had exerted a significant impact in the lives of many. This made all the harder for his dad to reconcile what he was hearing. It was overwhelming and painful, leaving Tony reeling, feeling "bewildered and unsure."

After the excruciating conversation, Tony and Peggy spent a lot of time praying, determined that they would love their son unconditionally just as he was. Of course, though, this didn't mean Tony wouldn't try to get to the bottom of some things. He had questions. *What had led to his son's decision? Could he get Bart to reconsider? Had Tony failed somehow as a father?* Before long an editorial in *Christianity Today* suggested that if Tony hadn't focused so much on social issues and concerns for the poor, Bart might not have departed from the faith. Tony admitted this was painful to read because it made him doubt he had been a good father. In subsequent posts we will take up this topic in some detail.

Soon after that fateful Thanksgiving, Tony booked a weeklong speaking tour in England, and Bart happily agreed to tag along so they could spend time in substantive conversation. And so, in a succession of English parks and cafes, they shared with one another their innermost feelings and most deeply felt convictions. In our cultural moment, such candid, caring conversations are often hard to come by, riddled as it is with so much divisiveness and animus, tendentiousness and acrimony, among those with conflicting worldviews. But this is a father and son determined to forge such conversations.

This very dynamic is one of the features of the book—that came out of those conversations—I find most compelling: the model it provides for such challenging but valuable discussions. In both its spirit and execution the book is an eminently attractive picture of familial commitment despite deep differences, the diametric opposite of and efficacious antidote for our reigning, pervasive, and far too unimaginative "cancel culture."

At this juncture and on this note, I might anticipate an objection among some of my evangelical friends. Tony Campolo himself, though respected greatly by many, has been fairly written off by others, including by some close friends of mine. The reasons are various, and some of the concerns altogether legitimate—from Campolo's rabid commitment to the Democratic party, to the change of his stance on gay marriage, to what was likely a fair bit of dissembling and disingenuousness on the matter of homosexuality for quite some time before officially "changing his mind."

376

We will have occasion to discuss all of these matters in subsequent entries. Bird by bird. For now, though, we might ask readers to suspend some of those judgments, hold them in abeyance, and simply empathize a bit with an evangelical father who had to come to terms with a painful situation, and who then had to think hard about how best to show his son love despite a crushing turn of events. It is a situation the vicinity in which any of us is liable to find ourselves, and it would do all us all good to give it some thought.

The penultimate paragraph in Tony's opening chapter struck me as especially interesting. He began it this way: "The world doesn't need any more theological polemics or debates about the truth of Christianity, and this book certainly isn't trying to be either of those." That said, though, he immediately admitted he's always trying to make his best case for following Jesus. This introduces a fertile topic for an entry of its own, so the next blog will pick it up here, exploring this matter of what the role of arguments for the truth of Christianity realistically is and isn't. By way of a tantalizing preview of coming attractions, for some assistance we will appeal to a few insights from none other than the inimitable John Wesley.

Friday, October 1, 2021: Today was the day we were to hear about the grant proposals, but I didn't hear squat, and Hartenburg heard he received a grant, so it's not looking good. Bummer. Ah well, here is the third Campolo blog.

Reflections on Why I Left, Why I Stayed, by Tony and Bart Campolo, Part 3

The previous blog ended on the note of discussing what can be realistically expected of arguments for the Christian faith. Recall that Campolo, at the end of the first chapter of the book he co-wrote with his son Bart, had written, "The world doesn't need any more theological polemics or debates about the truth of Christianity, and this book certainly isn't trying to be either of those," despite that he immediately added that he always does try to make his best case for following Christ.

On the surface there seems to be a potential tension between Campolo's claims: that we have no need for theological polemics or debates about the truth of Christianity, on the one hand, and that he nevertheless feels compelled to make the best case he can for following Christ, on the other. Perhaps what explains the apparent tension between these claims is that Campolo is intentionally casting polemics and debates with a negative connotation, but this is worth pointing out because not everyone construes polemics or debates in a negative way, nor should they.

Debates held with mutual respect and a commitment to rigor can be a highly effective way to foster substantive dialogue; in some ways, Campolo's protestations to the contrary notwithstanding, there is an undeniable element of debate contained within this book. Each Campolo is making his case, after all, explaining his convictions, pointing to evidential considerations to make them plausible, underscoring perceived weaknesses of opposing views, and the like. This is essentially what a debate involves. That it can be done civilly and, in this case, even lovingly, with as much commitment to listen as to talk, only shows that debates need not be an unfriendly and inherently negative activity, nor need be construed in that way. If speaking the truth is love has primacy, each participant in a debate of this nature, in a real sense, should be rooting for his opponent. We wrestle not against flesh and blood.

For many readers of the Campolo book, after all, while deeply appreciating the irenic tone of the volume and the model the discussion provides of how to disagree agreeably, may well also be genuinely interested in weighing the relative merits of both sides in their own efforts to discover the truth and achieve greater clarity. Debates may be more pointed and adversarial than plenty of other dialogical exchanges, but they can surely serve useful purposes. Some might suggest we don't need less of them (much less no more of them!), but a great many more, at least done well and right. I suspect the resistance to debates among many is because they often tend to be more about projecting appearances of victory and orchestrating mic drop moments than a genuine, mutual, and humble quest for the truth.

Likewise with polemics. In fairness it is likely Campolo was intentionally exploiting the common depiction of polemics as largely adversarial and predominantly confrontational. But colloquial employment of the locution doesn't determine the essence of the referent. Lexical definitions themselves often don't provide as penetrating insight into a word's meaning as does careful conceptual analysis. Polemics in the realm of theology might pertain to arrogating or appropriating, say, a secular thought pattern, category, or story to a Christian application; or in the realm of dialectics, polemics often pertains to fine-grained discussions about which specific theology might be most in evidence—in an effort, for example, to adjudicate between Christian or Islamic theology. Since Bart by his own admission considers secular humanism his new religion, a polemical component to the discussion is practically unavoidable. This is a perfectly legitimate and valuable exercise with little to no hint of any intrinsically negative implications. The aversion plenty of kind-hearted persons to interpersonal conflict is laudable, but it shouldn't mean we don't see the value of iron sharpening iron. Not all ideas are equally good or defensible, penetrating or veridical. Of course in practice, as Tony and Bart admit, conversations of substance about significant differences calls for an abundance grace to keep the wheels turning.

Context can usually make clear whether one means by polemics its denotation or connotation, and it's fairly obvious that Campolo was gesturing toward the latter.

Fair enough. I'm not trying to strain for gnats here or be unduly nitpicky. Still, my point is this: contending for the truth ineliminably involves, by turns, both apologetics and polemics, rightly understood and properly practiced. To say we need more of neither in a book preoccupied with the propriety or lack thereof of believing the truth claims of Christianity strains credulity at least a little.

I considered perhaps trimming the present point a bit for fear of belaboring, but then thought the better of it, because I think there is an important point to emphasize here. Even etymologically "polemics" is connected to war, so this might be thought to confirm the fraught connotations of the term, but we can go to war with people or with ideas. Clearly Tony is not at war with his son, but there is a clash and conflict of worldviews here, and that's okay. It shows we don't have to make it a battle between persons; we can keep the conflict at the level of ideas, which is practically a lost art in our cultural moment. Seeking to root out bad ideas is a noble and needed venture, and thoroughly biblical. 2 Cor. 10:4-5 says this: "The weapons of our warfare are not the weapons of the world. Instead, they have divine power to demolish strongholds. We tear down arguments and every presumption set up against the knowledge of God; and we take captive every thought to make it obedient to Christ." And in fact Tony, to my thinking, marvelously models this approach throughout the volume.

Allow me now to back off from the specifics here in order to deal with the more pressing and general question all of this broaches: the relative importance of reasons and rationality in Christian conviction. Again, Campolo himself tries to make the best case for following Christ, as he does impeccably throughout this book. Still, perhaps what he's getting at in distancing himself from any overly strident model of discourse here are what he recognizes to be some limitations to reason, limitations that reason itself might help us grasp. Perhaps these words by Campolo a few sentences later confirm this reading: "While I understand that Bart's faith probably won't be restored by my arguments, I hope they at least help him stay open to what ultimately must be the work of the Holy Spirit." And of course he also hopes his arguments will model for other Christians a way to keep the communication lines open with nonbelieving loved ones, a way that is both wholly loving and respectful without compromising the gospel.

For help in understanding both the purpose and limits of reason and rationality when it comes to matters divine, let's briefly consider a few points from John Wesley's sermon entitled "The Case of Reason Impartially Considered." Having taught Greek, logic, and philosophy at Lincoln College at Oxford, Wesley was clearly a man who took argument seriously, and he lamented when anyone under-appreciated reason. Here is what he wrote near the end of this sermon to such people:

Suffer me now to add a few plain words, first to you who under-value reason. Never more declaim in that wild, loose, ranting manner, against this precious gift of God. Acknowledge "the candle of the Lord," which he hath fixed in our souls for excellent purposes. You see how many admirable ends it answers, were it only in the things of this life: Of what unspeakable use is even a moderate share of reason in all our worldly employments…. When therefore you despise or depreciate reason, you must not imagine you are doing God service: least of all, are you promoting the cause of God when you are endeavouring (sic) to exclude reason out of religion.

Wesley says more in that vein, and it is most inspiring, but in fact at least half of the sermon is directed at those who over-value reason, assuming it is replete with powers of which in fact it's quite bereft. Specifically, Wesley points out three central realities that reason alone cannot generate or guarantee, contra those in his day (and ours) who so lionized the power of reason as to form expectations

that go beyond its capacities. First, reason cannot produce faith. "Although it is always consistent with reason, yet reason cannot produce faith, in the scriptural sense of the word. Faith, according to Scripture, is 'an evidence,' or conviction, 'of things not seen.' It is a divine evidence, bringing a full conviction of an invisible eternal world."

Interestingly, while discussing this first point, Wesley spoke of a personal confirmation of this limitation of reason. He tells of having heaped up the strongest arguments that he could find, in ancient or modern authors, for the existence of God, and then finding there was still room for doubts that reason is powerless to quench. He challenges readers to do the same, setting all our arguments for God in an array, silencing all objections, and putting all their doubts to rest. The result is that they may repress their doubts for a season, but "how quickly will they rally again, and attack you with redoubled violence." This does not show that faith is irrational or unprincipled, but rather that reason alone is not its ultimate source or locus. Can reason alone, for example, illumine what happens after the grave, satisfying our curiosities and banishing our fears? Hardly. The best unaided reason can do is suggest that death is, as Hobbes put it on the precipice of shuffling his mortal coil, "a leap in the dark," whatever bravado we might wish to project to conceal our intractable existential angst.

Second, reason alone cannot produce hope in any child of man—scriptural holiness, that is, by which we "rejoice in hope of the glory of God." Where there is not faith, there is not such hope; and since reason is impotent to produce the former, likewise the latter. At most but a lively imagination or pleasing dream resides within rationality's lonely grasp.

Third, reason, however cultivated and improved, cannot produce the love of God, for it can produce neither faith nor hope, from which alone such love can flow. It is only when we "rejoice in hope of the glory of God" that "we love Him because He first loved us." Cold reason can produce merely fair ideas, drawing a fine picture of love, but "only a painted fire." Beyond that reason alone cannot go.

Some other resultant limitations of reason include virtue and happiness. Those without the theological virtues of faith, hope, and love can experience pleasures of various kinds, but not the sort of happiness for which we were made—merely shadowy dreams of ephemeral pleasures fleeting as the wind, unsubstantial as the rainbow, lacking satisfaction.

"Let reason do all that reason can," concludes Wesley. "Employ it as far as it will go. But, at the same time, acknowledge it is utterly incapable of giving either faith, or hope, or love: and consequently, of producing either real virtue, or substantial happiness. Expect these from a higher source, even from the Father of the spirits of all flesh. Seek and receive them, not as your own acquisition, but as the gift of God…. So shall you be living witnesses, that wisdom, holiness, and happiness are one; are inseparably united; and are, indeed, the beginning of that eternal life which God hath given us in his Son."

Campolo and Wesley, both of them, recognized the importance of reason and its limitations, and depicted faith as a gift of God. In subsequent posts we will have occasion to speak in more detail about what each of them means by this, and whether or not their views converge. But for our next post, we will move on to Chapter 2: Bart's story of his deconversion, how he left.

Saturday, October 2, 2021: Nice chat with Elton at 9. Today I mainly tried getting through my grading for my online class so I can turn back to the Strauss lectures. But I couldn't finish. Got wore out in the afternoon. Will have to finish on Monday. Glad there's still another week before that trip. Collaborated with Nathaniel and MB to strengthen the Lasso proposal.

Sunday, October 3, 2021: Finalized the Lasso proposal, and took a day off from work. Nice time with the family.

Monday, October 4, 2021: After exercising I put in a pretty long day wrapping up the grading on those dang online papers. Still have DB's and shorter essays to grade, which I hope to knock out tomorrow so I can turn back to Strauss. Want to wrap up TWHF and put it into MB's hands, then turn back to my afternoon paper. MB and I have been enjoying a series of Ken Burns documentary episodes on Muhammed Ali. I floated to TJ the idea we just have a chat on the moral argument at his church, and he loved the idea. Gave some thought today to writing a book on logic for apologists. Submitted the revised proposal to Irwin, who told me by evening things were looking good. We are planning on submitting it in a week, after the last episode of the season. Fit in a movie in the late afternoon—the prequel to *Breaking Bad*.

Tuesday, October 5, 2021: The list of grant winners was sent out, and like I already knew ours wasn't one of them. It is admittedly deeply discouraging, and of course makes me just want to quit. But I will not quit. If God doesn't choose to give the increase to our Center and this initiative, then it wasn't of him. If it is, then he will, and I needn't sweat it. I'm just a temporary steward of the thing. The temptation to quit is pernicious cowardice. Nothing worthwhile is easy. Nothing. I give you my disappointment and frustration, dear Lord. Take it and use it and accomplish your purposes. Spent the day grading discussion boards and then getting the TWHF paper in shape; sent the latter to MB mid-afternoon for her to tweak and finalize; she'll be the one reading it. Early evening we went to see *God's Not Dead 4*, which I rather enjoyed. They still have a tendency to characterize the opposition in overly stark terms, but there was actually much about the movie I thought rather well done. I'm sure my mother-in-law would buy into all of it without recognizing any even potential hyperbole, and my stepson wouldn't buy any of it. But the truth is neither all nor nothing.

Wednesday, October 6, 2021: Today is the day I want to really start getting my afternoon Strauss lecture into shape. Hopefully that will happen!

Thursday, October 7, 2021: Marybeth is working to finalize her papers for the Strauss lectures. I'm trying to conserve my strength for the busy days ahead.

Friday, October 8, 2021: Nice evening with Rob and Jerry. After I'd put the brakes on some of the political discussion the week before, I was glad that they felt free to talk about politics a bit this evening. It was a good time. Bill Irwin continued to tweak the Lasso proposal a bit to get it into top-notch shape.

Saturday, October 9, 2021: Elton and I had a nice conversation in the morning, and throughout the day Marybeth and I read to each other our papers and practiced getting our pronunciations and emphases just right.

Sunday, October 10, 2021: MB, Nathaniel, and I watched the last Lasso episode of season 2, and I tweaked the Lasso proposal one last time and sent it to Bill. Marybeth read her paper to Nathaniel, then we printed up hard copies of all three Strauss lectures. We went to bed knowing we're getting on a plane in the morning.

Monday, October 11, 2021: We got up and were finalizing our prep to go to the airport, then got a text telling us our flight was cancelled. We went to Denny's and got another message about the replacement flight. We were about to confirm until we saw that the flight was for the next day—the very day of the Strauss lectures! So at Denny's we prayed, and while MB was praying the idea occurred to me that we should simply drive. And so over breakfast we decided we would do just that, and drive to Lincoln, Illinois. The rest of the day was spent in the car. Six hours in Texas, through Arkansas, then Missouri. Right after seeing the St. Louis arch we stopped for the night. It was pretty late, and we still had a few hours to go. But a very good trip, with just two brief patches of traffic. God was gracious, and the drive gave us a chance to reflect on a lot of things and practice our papers some more.

Tuesday, October 12, 2021: We hit the road when it was still dark and drove to Lincoln, arriving about forty-five minutes before MB's paper. Before the paper Zach and TJ showed up, which was great, and I met Rich Knopp in person for the first time, along with Hannah, the IT gal who helps *Room for Doubt* out. MB's paper on O'Connor went very well, and since it served in lieu of chapel that day, attendance was great. That first paper was in the chapel building, and the later papers in Restoration Hall. MB read the lunch talk, and then I fielded questions, which had more to do with moral apologetics than with TWHF, perhaps owing to not a lot of folks having read the novel. It was funny MB cried a little during her reading of that paper. Zach, TJ, and Rich fellowshipped with us between papers. I read the afternoon paper and then fielded some questions. All in all we thought the papers went very well and were well received. It was great to see Zach having found a home at Lincoln Christian. He's clearly the heir apparent of *Room for Doubt* in Rich's eyes; hopefully that will work out. As tuckered as we were, we attended a big dinner that evening, and that was the end of the Strauss stuff. MB especially slept quite well that night! I had trouble sleeping; perhaps too much caffeine that day. Around midnight or 1 in the morning I tried catching up on e-mails, and graded some paper outlines for my online course.

Wednesday, October 13, 2021: For breakfast we went to Rich's house, where Paula had made a lovely breakfast. Zach and his girlfriend were there. Good discussion over breakfast about a number of matters, including guilt and shame. We also shared our idea of printing the three lectures in a little booklet through our press and sending them some offprints, of which Rich and Zach seemed appreciative. After breakfast we taped a segment for *Room for Doubt*—Rich, Zach, MB, and I. That was a lot of fun, and I was able to plug the ministry there, Rich's book, and Zach's book too. I tended to hit themes, while discussing their books, I'd hit in the blurb and foreword, respectively. Then we hit the road to West Frankfort, IL, the town of TJ's church. In the 7 pm service TJ and I did a fun taped conversation in front of the adults who were there that evening, a good crowd. Got to lay out the vision for the Center. Really sweet church folks, and I beat TJ in a game of HORSE in the gym afterwards, but a close game!

Thursday, October 14, 2021: We got up at the hotel and packed up, yet again, making it to TJ's just before 9. Saw their lovely home and played with their cat, then enjoyed some coffee and donuts. After that MB got set up in the basement to do a podcast on Ted Lasso. CT had contacted her to see if she'd be interested and she jumped at the chance, doing a great job. During that time TJ and I went to visit with his mom, and I met his oldest sister there too. That was great fun, then I saw TJ's dad's grave (and those of some other family members), his childhood home, his childhood church, and the church he pastored before the present one. When we got back to the house I played both of his boys in ping pong, beating one and getting beat by the other. Lots of fun; the kids are sweet. And we anointed Amy, TJ's wife, with oil and prayed for her healing. For nine months now she's been afflicted with a condition that just won't go away, baffling the doctors.

Then TJ, MB, and I went to an apple orchard, which no fall without is complete. During the drive there TJ shared that he felt motivated to write Dr. Sloan and inquire about raising a portion of his own salary should he be able to come to HBU to teach and help build the Center. A great idea, as far as I'm concerned. By the time we got back to the house it was time to hit the road—4 pm. We went two and a half hours before getting a hotel in northern Arkansas. Just after midnight we awoke and listened to the podcast MB had done earlier on Thursday. Earlier in the evening we got this exciting message from Bill Irwin:

Buck,

It looks good for Ted Lasso. See correspondence below.

T

Hi Bill,

Many thanks for sending this over; I've read through and quite agree, it certainly is a winner! I've learnt a bit about Ted Lasso and can see it's a great fit for the series, I think David is a great candidate as editor, and his proposal is nice and thorough, and the ToC shows a great breadth of topics.

Next steps will be me to add this to the queue of proposals to present to our editorial board for approval to contract (I have a handful on my plate at the moment) but I should be able to get back to David with the good news and contracting details in the next 2-3 weeks, hopefully!

All best and thanks,

Will

Assuming that contract comes through, it will be my fourth contract (not counting Moral Apol Press books) since arriving in Texas. Another marvelous blessing. We hope to add MB's name to the book later.

Friday, October 15, 2021: Lots of driving today; finally stopped near Lafeyette, Louisiana, about three and a half hours from home. Got an invite to participate in a faculty deal in the spring involving a one-course release. That should mean all I teach in the fall is moral apologetics, along with helping Craig out in his one-hour class. Speaking of Craig, after getting to the hotel this evening, I received this e-mail from him:

Dear Dave,

In writing my systematic philosophical theology, I have now moved on to a discussion of God's attribute of goodness, and I would like to ask for your advice.

In this section I want to address, first, the question of the relationship between God and the good/right. I figure to defend divine command theory.

I'd also like to say something, second, about the nature of God's goodness. I recently read two articles, one by Laura Garcia and one by Jordan Wessling, both defending what Wessling calls the Identity Thesis, namely, that God's moral character is reducible to the single attribute of love. I was reminded of Robert Adams' version of divine command theory, according to which our duties are constituted by the commands of a loving God. It seemed to me incomplete because it leaves out of account the justice of God, and so I amended his account to speak of "the commands of a just and loving God."

It seems to me that the attempt to reduce God's entire moral character to love is the unfortunate vestige of classical, 19th-century liberal theology, which scorned the wrath and justice of God. I noticed that Wessling admits that his account is incompatible with divine retributive justice that is not redemptive of the sinner. My work on the atonement has convinced me more than ever that retributive justice is essential to the moral character of God, and so I'm going to resist this reductionism.

One problem with my formulation, I have been told, is that whereas being loving is not itself a moral property, justice is. So by saying that our moral duties are constituted by "the commands of a just and loving God," I am caught in a vicious circle, using a moral property to ground a moral property. This is not entirely obvious to me, but I wonder if there is a morally neutral equivalent to retributive justice that I might ascribe essentially to God. For example, God is necessarily such as to give people what they deserve. That is a morally neutral description of retributive justice. I've searched for a word for this, for example "the commands of a retributing and loving God." But that sounds awkward. Less awkward, but rather frightening, would be the description "the commands of an avenging and loving God." That would be very bold, but maybe boldness is called for here!

A third question that I think I need to explore is the coherence of divine goodness and freedom. As you may know, William Rowe and others have mounted a very plausible challenge to divine freedom on the basis that a morally perfect being must always do the best. If there is no best, then he is paralyzed, rather like a moral Buridan's ass! Laura Garcia seems to think that one can avoid this problem by denying a duty theory of divine morality, which would be a welcome escape route, but it's not clear to me that the objection relies upon duty theory rather than simply God's moral perfection.

Anyway I'm writing to you to ask for your help in directing me to resources on these questions. What have you written about these questions that I might read? Are there any other essential works I need to read? Notice that I am not here interested in a moral argument for God's existence, but simply in a theistic moral theory.

Thanks so much for your expert advice,

Bill

Saturday, October 16, 2021: Got home at 9:30 am, then we picked up Nathaniel for breakfast. After that I unpacked a bit and collapsed in bed for several hours. It's now 3:15 and by sixty-five minutes from now at the latest Jerry and Rob are supposed to be here. Meeting some friends of Jerry's for dinner at 5.

Sunday, October 17, 2021: Today we spent a lot of time with Nathaniel, sort of a late birthday present. Took him to lunch at Cheesecake Factory, then to a movie, then to dinner at Fadi's. I turned down Chad Gross's invitation to do a discussion with an atheist on God and ethics. Just too much on my plate. Things have really piled up because of the trip. The next two weeks are nightmarish in terms of workloads. But hopefully I'll get through, a day at a time, bird by bird.

Monday, October 18, 2021: Did a bunch of errands today, including a response to Craig, as follows:

> Hi Dr. Craig, thanks for writing me this. These are challenging questions! I'd like to write more about these matters than I have. I'll be happy to share a few thoughts anyway, and perhaps at least a few sources, but my research in these specific areas hasn't been as fine-grained as would be most helpful.
>
> So you want to address, first, the question of the relationship between God and the good/right and defend divine command theory. Yes, so the DCT is our account of the right. The question of goodness and values is something else, and here there are different possibilities, as you well know. The theistic natural lawyers give their account of the intimate relationship between God and the good, the theistic Platonists their account, etc. The notion of God as the good— an 'is of identity'—is the view to which you and I both gravitate, I think (which is of course altogether consistent with predicating perfect, necessary goodness of God—AC Ewing pushed this point heavily). I tend to call this theistic Platonism, but you may prefer to shy away from any Platonic reference. But that's how Adams characterizes his view of the good on which his DCT is predicated. Steve Evans readily acknowledges such approaches, but doesn't tend to take that route as much as talk about what's "good for us," and then connects up those goods to God in particular ways. (At the Plantinga-fest at Baylor you and I went to, I asked Plantinga a question about goodness, and he quickly moved to the matter

387

of "what's good for us," which left me slightly disappointed.) One of the things that's best for us, of course, is a relationship with God.

Although I'm not averse to this more natural law type of an approach, there seems something deeply right about God being the ultimately good himself. I often suspect that these more Aristotelian and Platonic approaches can be reconciled—I did a paper at EPS about that some years ago I no longer have. God IS the good—*and* is perfectly self-exemplifying and so IS GOOD, indeed the paradigm of it—and God also functions at the foundation of all those things *good for us*, and what's best for us is what's *intrinsically good*. This is where that aspect of a Platonic picture often works so nicely, according to which God is the ultimate (and in Adams' language infinite) good, and other lesser and finite goods relevantly resemble God and derive their goodness from such a resemblance. At any rate, it doesn't seem to me as Christian theists we are forced to choose between these differing approaches to the good. They seem deeply connected.

You would also like to say something, second, about the nature of God's goodness. A point from Adams that always strikes me as deeply correct and insightful along these lines is this: If God indeed is the ultimate good (which you'll recall he characterizes along the lines of excellence and in terms broader than the merely moral), then we should always retain something of a critical stance when it comes to filling in the content of the good. We are unlikely ever to have a complete bead on it, just as God himself remains beyond our ken in various respects. God *is* the good, after all; if that's right, this makes sense. Of course it also reveals what we might call an intensely personalist account of the good—no mere state of affairs or something like that, but a person, or triune picture of persons. Anyway, the portion on goodness in *Finite and Infinite Goods* is worth reading and rereading, of course.

You tell me that both Garcia and Wessling defend the Identity Thesis, the idea that God's moral character is reducible to the single attribute of love, and you have a certain reservation about that because it seems incomplete. This is something I've thought about but haven't written much about. At some point I'll hopefully do more writing on it, but here are a few thoughts for now anyway, for what they are worth. I understand your concern, but I don't think love does leave out of the account the justice of God, at least if we understand love rightly. I think the notion that it does concedes too much to degraded conceptions of love so common nowadays. For example, suppose I were to say that parents should be wholly loving toward their children, and I get this response: "But they should also be solid disciplinarians." I think that response mistakenly assumes that love and discipline are at odds. In fact, of course, love should discipline on occasion. It's the unloving parent who doesn't. Similarly with God, who chastens whom he loves.

I don't see the problem with assigning primary and central importance to love when it comes to God's character, but rather with the degraded, deflated, desiccated picture of love people often use when they say *God is love*—as if God's just a benighted avuncular figure who wants us to be happy in superficial ways. Love led to the cross; literally hard as nails. So you may be right that the attempt to reduce God's entire moral character to love is the unfortunate vestige of classical, 19th-century liberal theology that scorned the wrath and justice of God, but my analysis is that the error isn't the "reduction to love" but the *operative degraded conception of love*. Indeed this is the very reason I'm uncomfortable with language of *reduction* here. My suspicion is that God's love is the most expansive, all-encompassing thing there is, and that if it doesn't entail such things as damnation for the obdurately unrepentant, it's at least absolutely consistent with it. This is why I often express misgivings when folks use the locution "but" when they say something like, "God is love, *but* he's also holy (or just or what have you)," as if there's anything like the remotest tension between God's love and his justice or holiness. I think doing away with this misconception is crucial.

The Bible itself uses language like "God is love," so I'm wondering here if there's some slippage in language. To say "God is love" may or may not be reducing God's moral character to love, it seems to me. Perhaps it's designed instead to say, among other things, that God's love is so central, so primordial, so much a picture of who he essentially is, that nothing else about him can be understood properly apart from his love—including his sovereignty, his holiness, and his justice. When I say that God is good, and the Good, I'm also suggesting very much like that. And again, when a liberal thinker appeals to God's love to justify a permissive sexual ethic or universalism, I'm inclined to talk about the aspects of love that don't always result in warm fuzziness—accountability, wages of sin freely chosen, need for repentance, what happens when folks resist God's overtures of love to the bitter end, etc. Again, for anyone who scorns God's wrath and justice, I am convinced that the problem is not their *focus* on love, but their *definition* of love.

The most challenging issue in this vicinity, which you put your finger on, I think, is retributive justice. Sure, some would say, God chastens those he loves, and allows us to go through painful things so we can benefit by them, but what about hell? It is literally beyond redemption. And does the atonement feature something like God's punishment of sin at its heart? Like you, I'm inclined to think it does, but what of hell? More recently Kevin Kinghorn and another guy have written a book arguing that even hell can be explicated in terms of God's love, which I think is a cool effort. I need to go through it more carefully, but the piece of their case about which I remain a bit skeptical is their rejection of retributive justice. I think there's a better way to go than eschewing the category.

Some weeks ago, while out driving, the thought occurred to me that perhaps retributive justice just is giving people what they most ultimately choose to worship, or something like that. And so if their choice is darkness and sin, then hell might represent God honoring their choice, a function of God recognizing the value of the agency he inculcated within us. This is of course in the vicinity of some C. S. Lewis stuff, but I think there's something to it. So how about this for a neutral characterization: *God honors people's choices by giving them what they ultimately choose to give themselves over to.* I think that's better than that he gives us what we deserve, because, thankfully of course, he surely doesn't do that for those who avail themselves of his grace. For the redeemed, they choose to give themselves to him, and he gives himself to them—life and light and love— and of course their very choice to give themselves over to him was made possible by his first loving and pursuing us (a necessary condition, not sufficient, contra the Calvinists—who by the way relish to talk about the limitations of God's love). For the unredeemed, despite God's overtures of love and offers of salvific grace, they choose darkness instead, and are finally given what they "want." Of course they don't want all the resultant consequences, any more than someone who wants ice cream incessantly and consumes it to his heart's content doesn't want the resultant heart disease. (Now I'm feeling a bit guilty; moving on!)

I don't know if my suggestion for a neutral equivalent is helpful or not, but if it's right, then I think we can see, once more, that God giving us over to what we choose to worship is consistent with his loving us. He honors our choice. Those who end up in hell will have been offered the gift of faith, but they turned it down, and the result is the logical outcome of rejecting the only true source of happiness there is.

So personally I don't feel the need to include the reference to "just" in the description of the sort of God that makes sense of DCT and doesn't fall prey to various criticisms. I might just refer to a "good God," or, occasionally, I might say "loving God," but I probably shy away from the latter unless I have enough time to clarify that I don't mean love in a degraded, permissive sense. I should probably wage this battle more, because 'love' is certainly a term we don't want to see lost to irremediable fuzziness. I suppose if you don't insist on "just" it would help get you around the trouble you mention, if what you say is right. Like you, though, I'm not convinced. Maybe I'm a bit obtuse, but why justice is a moral concept and love is not is unclear to me. At any rate, I'm comfortable with *love* as a sufficiently expansive and inclusive penumbral term to use in this context so long as it's clear what's meant (more the biblical conception of love than today's poor counterfeits). But if you feel like you want or need to add something else, I might suggest my idea about God honoring our choice about what we choose to worship—but personally I think I'd simply include that addition in a fuller description of what love involves. Love allows another to turn their back. This makes hell the ultimate unrequited love. I'm afraid language like "avenging," though technically accurate, quickly reaches a point of diminishing returns by reinforcing in the minds of some (perhaps many) that God's justice is in tension with his love. I wouldn't risk it, but you're nothing if not bold! ☺

More briefly, a third question that you think you need to explore is the coherence of divine goodness and freedom. I very much doubt there's always a "best" course of action for God to pursue. The notion that this leaves God paralyzed strains my credulity. I think a reminder that the deepest biblical notion of freedom there is involves freedom from sin, and in that sense all of God's choices are maximally free. I also suspect in a vast range of cases, at least, God has prerogatives. You and I have both endorsed that notion—say, with regard to how much God chose to tell us to tithe. If that decision is *not* an inexorable function of his character (which seems likely), neither does it seem like a determined choice based on what's somehow "best." Surely God retains prerogatives at least on occasion, it seems to me; to me that principle seems more obvious than the conjunction that God can choose only the best and that if there's no such thing he's paralyzed. Maybe I need to read Garcia's piece, but I don't see the connection to duty theory. In fact you and I both incorporate an element of divine latitude in at least some divine commands—as Ockham did with the second table of the Decalogue—and Hare, Adams, and Evans follow suit.

I'd encourage you to write John Hare about this at Yale. And Adams too, of course, and maybe Evans. They are all still active, amazingly. Evans and Hare of course are contributing to my collection (I'm editing with Hare) and Adams hasn't yet said no! If only that bold, well-known apologist near Atlanta would reconsider! Gonna be epic! And I still have slots open. ☺

Blessings,
Dave

Tuesday, October 19, 2021: Marybeth and I finished the paperwork for the certificate program. That was important. Got the paperwork finalized for Arthur Schneider's thesis project as well, along with a number of other items on the to-do list as I keep trying to get back caught up.

Wednesday, October 20, 2021: Wrote two blogs today and then took our car in for work to the tune of 1200 bucks. Ouch. But grateful for God's bountiful provision. The blogs were for the WB, one on TWHF, one on conducting spiritual conversations with family over the holidays. Arranged for Jonathan Pruitt's dissertation defense on Nov 22nd. Bill Craig wrote me this:

Dear Dave,

You'll remember that I wrote you about my concern of reducing God's moral character to love. I wanted to amend Adams' account of moral obligation by saying that our duties are constituted by the commands of a *just* and loving God. Well, I am re-reading *Finite and Infinite Goods,* and I was utterly shocked by what I read in chapter 11, section 2 on Divine Commands and the Role of Obligation. There he says in footnote 10:

> The importance of God's justice for the grounding of a divine command theory is rightly
> emphasized in MacIntyre, "Which God Ought We to Obey and Why?" It was wrongly neglected in some of my previous papers on divine command metaethics.

Gasp! He affirms that one important excellence of God's nature is justice. Moreover he addresses the question of circularity by saying that he is using a "thin theory" of justice which does not presuppose moral obligation. We can think that God is just even though he has no superior over him imposing duty on him and sanctioning him.

This is exactly what I wanted to say!

Bill

Thursday, October 21, 2021: Today I need to finish preparing for this evening, the second meeting at our house of the Center's Student Fellows. I'm working on a handout listing ten examples of discursive moral arguments of various sorts, from Swinburne's P-inductive epistemic argument to Evans' natural signs approach. Bill Craig wrote me again today:

Dear Dave,

I hope that you do not mind my pestering you as I continue to read Adams' work as part of my section on God's goodness.

In his chapter 12 Adams presents what he calls Abraham's dilemma:

(1) If God commands me to do something, it is not morally wrong for me to do it.
(2) God commands me to kill my son.
(3) It is morally wrong for me to kill my son.

To my surprise Adams chooses to reject (2). I have followed Philip Quinn in rejecting (3).

But Adams argues that one could never be justified in believing (2). Our conviction of (3) is so powerful that we should call into question any ostensible divine revelation commanding us otherwise. So God did not in fact command Abraham to sacrifice Isaac.

Adams' response seems to me to confuse justification and truth. Even if we could never be epistemically justified in believing (2), that does not show that (2) is false. Maybe someone will always be more certain that something is morally wrong than that God has commanded him to do it, but it does not follow that God has not commanded him to do it. The Bible clearly states that God commanded Abraham to do it, even if it leaves us wondering how Abraham could be so certain of that fact.

Moreover, Adams' position brings general revelation into conflict with special revelation. He thinks that our moral knowledge is a result of God's general revelation. But then what is his view of the clear scriptural teaching that God did command Abraham to sacrifice Isaac? Doesn't he have to deny both that God gave a special revelation to Abraham and that the scriptural account is special revelation to us? I wonder what that implies for his doctrine of biblical inspiration.

How would you resolve Abraham's Dilemma? Do you think that God has the authority to command us to do something that would be wrong in the absence of a divine command?

Bill

My response:

Hi Dr. Craig, you can write anytime; I can't imagine I'd ever characterize it as your pestering me! □

I think Adams' view of scriptural authority is a bit compromised. I'm virtually certain that he has embraced a permissive sexual ethic when it comes to homosexuality, for example. I think he sees himself in the mainline liberal tradition on such matters. So that's part of what's going on there, I think. (I appreciate his metaethics beyond words; not so much some of his applied ethics.)

In *Good God* we argued that there's an important distinction between a command that is *difficult but not impossible* to square with our best moral intuitions, and one that's *flat impossible* rationally to square with them. I suspect for Abraham,

393

who was still learning who God is, the command to kill Isaac qualified as belonging to the former category, at least at that stage of salvation history.

Kierkegaard, I think, traversed the hermeneutical gap between Abraham's situation and our own too hastily, thinking we're basically in the same epistemic boat as Abraham. If God told us to kill our son, we'd be obligated, that sort of thing, necessitating a teleological suspension of the ethical and all that jazz. But owing to some significant differences between the two contexts, I think that we'd indeed always have better reasons to think we missed God than that God told us to kill our own son.

But that doesn't mean God couldn't tell us to kill our son, right, though it would put us in an epistemic pickle. It might be true that God tells us to do such a thing, but if we couldn't be in a good enough epistemic position to know that he's told us, then we'd be justified to believe that he didn't tell us. Even though he did. That poses a rather bad epistemic problem for us, I think.

Again, this doesn't apply to Abraham's situation, but it would apply to our own, if we think God has told us to do such a thing. Or to change the example, if someone told me that they think God's told them to kill their son, I'd tell them I think they missed God. Is it possible that they heard God right? I suppose I might say it's conceivable enough, but I'm not sure it would be possible at this point, at least not without some overriding moral justification. Perhaps God knows that the killing would avoid some far worse evil? That might make sense. So, yeah, maybe I'd say it's possible. But again, it's problematic epistemically, because I think we'd have better reasons to assume the message wasn't really from God. So, if that's right, although it would be true that God commanded it, and presumably dutiful, we'd also be justified, and perhaps obligated, not to perform the action because we have reason to think we missed God. And this would lead to a conflict of duties. So that's tough. Perhaps I could say it was hard but not impossible for Abraham to square with his ethical knowledge, but it would be exceedingly even harder for *us* to do so, even if not utterly impossible. Even if our believing God were to issue us such a command doesn't pose a *logical* problem, it certainly seems to generate something of an intractable *practical* one.

Of course that particular scenario, for us, is farfetched. What I mainly want to say is that God can indeed give us specific commands to obey. Like to help a particular homeless person or something. And I think such commands would be authoritative and generate moral duties. Which is to say I don't agree with Adams (I suppose) that all of our moral knowledge comes from general revelation. Seems like a command to a specific person at a specific time could transform an imperfect duty to a perfect one.

Does Adams say that all of our moral knowledge comes from general revelation? I haven't read that last bit of *Finite and Infinite Goods* on epistemology in a while. I should reread the whole book soon. I seem to recall his talking about the need for sensitive exegesis or something along those lines.

Anyway, to answer your last question, I'd pose the question in terms of badness rather than wrongness. Can God command us to do something in some sense bad? I say yes. What I think God can't do, because of his essentially loving nature, is command us to do something irremediably evil—like torture children for fun or something like that. And the algorithm for where to draw the line between the two (something in some sense bad versus something irremediably bad) involves asking whether we can imagine a scenario in which the command in question might be thought morally justified. This is how I square the conquest narratives with God's goodness, but rule out something like double predestination. A modicum of reflection generates potential reasons for the former; I have never thought of any way the latter can make sense of God's essentially loving nature.

The reason I prefer couching the question in terms of badness instead of wrongness is that wrongness means a duty not to do, and presumably as a DCT'ist that means for us that God's already issued a command prohibiting it. And once more that leads to the intractable epistemic problem of figuring out that the command is a genuine one since it's already proscribed. If a good sign of authenticity is whether an alleged command is consistent with what God's already told us, a command at odds with a previous command gives us reason to think the "new command" isn't a genuine one.

I don't know if any of that helps, but it's great fun to think about! You're doing great work, and as always you inspire me!

Blessings,
Dave

I also wrote Tom Morris today to express some of the frustrations I was feeling this morning:

Hey there, Thomas V. Morris!

Found myself thinking of you. Perhaps for this reason: when we came to HBU we took a big financial hit. We never made money like you made money out there on the lecture circuit, but we did quite well at Liberty. Notwithstanding the voyeuristic cuckold at the helm and the corrupt senior administration and complete lack of what it means to be a real university, Liberty did pay well, and MB and I together made slightly over 200K a year when we left. Coming to HBU we asked for 75K and a 3-3 load. They offered 70K (total) and a 4-4 load for each of us. I have one course reduction for leading the Center for the Foundations of Ethics, and she has two course reductions for being the apologetics dept chair and an online coordinator. But between research, teaching, and administration, we're as busy as ever, but now making substantially less than we used to. We were doing fine until my stepson Nathaniel moved here over the summer. MB flew to VA and helped him drive here in June, but two days before they left there to come here he finally told us the truth. Rather than teaching high school last school year, he had lost his job and sat on his butt all year and burned through all his savings. So we had to bail him out to get him here, which cost several thousand dollars. We were just bouncing back until yesterday when we got slammed with a 1200 dollar car repair bill. We had it, but it's taken away our margin again.

We'll be fine financially, but that's not the main thing that's getting to me. It's the incessant busyness. I really want to do serious writing and research in ethics but it's so exceedingly difficult to find the time. Especially during the school year, so many things eat away at one's time. i was looking forward to a lighter schedule coming here, especially with the low pay they were going to give us, but I feel as busy as ever, and I'm just not as resilient as I used to be. Can't burn the candle at both ends anymore. And as I get older I worry I'm not going to do the work I really feel called to do. The dumb pay makes it much harder now to purchase the books for research I'd like to, but again, it's mainly the time. And I'm starting a certificate in moral apologetics this summer that's going to take up six weeks of my time--during the summer, which has always been the best time to write. So I worry that's going to cut into my research. So I don't know, there are days when I worry it was a mistake coming to HBU. Although they gave me the title to lead the Center, pretty much all the growth is on me to create--fundraising, etc. There was just a big competition for a grant--the school was giving out ten of them, between 5K and 10K each. 32 folks applied, I was one of them. I wanted to put on a big conference on the moral argument that would culminate in the OUP book John Hare and I have a contract to edit. Thought I had a real shot at it, but, once more, no dice. The school hasn't given me a space for the Center, they haven't devoted a dime to the Center, they just put pressure on me to get it all done. And all of this is so much outside my wheelhouse. I'm a friggin' ethicist, not a businessman.

Anyhoo, i thought of you because I know you've gone from making serious money to making a whole lot less because of circumstances beyond your control. Are there days this gets to you? On most days I'm fine, and hold discouragement at bay. But this morning it hit me fresh. Time keeps marching on, and sometimes I fear I won't do the work I'm meant to do. I'd rather hoped at this stage of my career some things would fall into place and become easier. Instead it seems like I'm just starting out, having to prove myself all over again, not to mention being as busy as ever and having less resources (time, energy, money) than I used to. I know I should be grateful for the many blessings God's given me. It's a lot, and maybe I'm being a brat. But some days, man. Some days.

Best, Dave

Here's the piece I sent to TJ and Jonathan for the site, an adaptation of the handout I'll be using this evening with the Student Fellows:

A Dozen Moral Arguments

The Center for the Foundations of Ethics at Houston Baptist University exists to generate a community of scholars devoted to exploring the rich resources of moral apologetics. Moral apologetics has for its focus the evidential significance of moral realities of various sorts. On occasion such evidence can be put into premise/conclusion format. The following is a non-exhaustive list of moral arguments hammered into discursive format, in an effort to show some of the range of possibilities in two senses:

First, there is diversity when it comes to the *moral phenomena under consideration.* Second, there are several ways in which to *couch the evidential connections*—from natural signs to induction, from deductive to abductive formulations. Obviously, all of these arguments invite critique and critical scrutiny; the purpose of this list is not to settle such matters, but simply to provide some examples of possible arguments. The footnotes have been kept to a relative few, but point to some of the complexities involved in the analysis of such arguments, and a few of the salient sources.

Immanuel Kant: *Arguments from Grace and Providence*

Argument from Grace:

1. Morality requires us to achieve a standard too exacting and demanding to meet on our own without some sort of outside assistance, resulting in a "moral gap."
2. Exaggerating human capacities, lowering the moral demand, or finding a secular form assistance are inadequate for the purpose of closing the moral gap.
3. Divine assistance is sufficient to close the gap.
4. Therefore, rationality dictates the postulation of God's existence.

Argument from Providence:

1. Full rational commitment to morality requires that morality is a rationally stable enterprise.
2. In order for morality to be a rationally stable enterprise, it must feature ultimate correspondence between happiness and virtue.
3. There is no reason to think that such correspondence obtains unless God exists.
4. Therefore, rationality dictates the postulation of God's existence.[19]

---

[19] See John Hare's *Moral Gap: Kantian Ethics, Human Limits, and God's Assistance* for these formulations.

Henry Sidgwick: *An Argument Based on the Dualism of Practical Reason*

1. Morality can be made completely rational only if a complete harmony between the maxim of rational self-love and the maxim of rational benevolence can somehow be demonstrated.
2. If God exists, we may legitimately infer Divine sanctions such that there is a complete harmony between rational self-love (one's interest) and rational benevolence (universal happiness).
3. If we can legitimately infer that there is complete harmony between rational self-love and rational benevolence, morality can be made completely rational.
4. Therefore, if God exists, morality can be made completely rational.[20]

C. S. Lewis: Argument from Book 1 of *Mere Christianity*

1. There is a universal Moral Law.
2. If there is a universal Moral Law, there is a Moral Law-giver.
3. If there is a Moral Law-giver, it must be something beyond the universe.
4. Therefore, there is something beyond the universe.

Austin Farrer: *An Argument Based on Human Worth/Dignity*

1. Human persons have a special kind of intrinsic value that we call dignity.
2. The only (or best) explanation of the fact that humans possess dignity is that they are created by a supremely good God in God's own image.
3. Probably there is a supremely good God.[21]

Alvin Plantinga: *A Moral Obligations Argument*

1. If there are objective moral duties, then God exists.
2. There are objective moral duties.
3. So, God exists.[22]

Richard Swinburne: *An Inductive Epistemic Argument*

1. Humans possess objective moral knowledge.
2. Probably, if God does not exist, humans would not possess objective moral knowledge.
3. Probably, God exists.[23]

---

[20] This formulation has obvious limitations. Even if we affirm that morality can be made completely rational, it doesn't logically follow that God exists. It is probably best interpreted either inductively or abductively.

[21] This formulation is not directly from Farrer, but Farrer focused heavily on the value we should recognize in our neighbor for being made in God's image.

[22] See my article on this argument in Walls and Dougherty's *Two Dozen (Or So) Arguments for God.*

[23] Find Swinburne's discussion in his *Existence of God.* He thinks of the argument as a P-

C. Stephen Evans: *Natural Signs Approach*

1. Natural signs satisfy the Pascalian constraints of wide accessibility and easy resistibility and dispose us to believe in God.
2. Human value and authoritative moral obligations function as moral natural signs.
3. Therefore, human value and authoritative moral obligations dispose us to believe in God.[24]

William Lane Craig: *Value and Duties Argument*

1. If God doesn't exist, then objective moral values and duties don't exist.
2. Objective moral values and duties do exist.
3. Therefore, God exists.

C. Stephen Layman: *Authority of Morality Argument*

1. The overriding (or strongest) reasons always favor doing what is morally required. ("Overriding Reasons Thesis" (ORT))
2. If there is no God and no life after death, then ORT is not true. ("Conditional Thesis")
3. Therefore, either there is a God or there is life after death in which virtue is rewarded.
4. If (3) then God exists.

Mark Linville: *A Deductive Epistemic Argument*

1. If evolutionary naturalism (EN) is true, then human morality is a byproduct of natural selection.
2. If human morality is a byproduct of natural selection, then there is no moral knowledge.
3. There is moral knowledge.
4. So, EN is false.[25]

Baggett/Walls: *A Four-Fold Abductive Cumulative Argument*

---

inductive argument, increasing the likelihood of theism somewhat, without making it more likely true than not (though the argument might be part of a cumulative case that does do the latter). Angus Ritchie gives an epistemic moral argument in his *From Morality to Metaphysics: The Theistic Implication of Our Ethical Commitments*.

[24] Find Evans' argument in his *Natural Signs and Knowledge of God*.

[25] Find Linville's argument online here: https://appearedtoblogly.files.wordpress.com/2011/05/linville-mark-22the-moral-argument22.pdf. That article also features critiques of the standard substantive ethical theories of egoism, utilitarianism, and virtue theory with respect to intrinsic human worth.

1. Moral facts[26], moral knowledge, moral transformation, and moral rationality require robust explanation.[27]
2. The best explanation of these phenomena is God.
3. Therefore, God (probably) exists.[28]

The meeting with the Student Fellows went well. Salina, Alfred, Hunter, and Taylor showed up, and afterwards MB helped with advising. Some good discussion of a range of moral arguments.

Friday, October 22, 2021: Last night's meeting of the Student Fellows was great fun, and MB did good advising afterwards. Just touched base with four more I'm supposed to advise who still may need it. Finished a blog on Campolo today, and it looks like this:

Reflections on *Why I Left, Why I Stayed*, by Tony and Bart Campolo, Part 4

"Those who have deconstructed their faith or significantly revised their sexual ethic seem to have one thing in common: They're angry." This was sent to me by a friend who knew I am reading the book by Tony and Bart Campolo, but I have to admit that Bart does not seem to match this description. He does not appear to be angry at all, but rather cheerful and downright chipper, despite that he has pretty much deconstructed his faith and significantly revised his views on sexual ethics. Perhaps he is concealing his anger, perhaps my friend is wrong, or perhaps Bart is, if not unique, at least anomalous. I am unsure, but he at least does not obviously fit into the category my friend describes.

I thought about this as I reread Bart's opening salvo in the book, a chapter entitled "How I Left: A Son's Journey through Christianity." The chapter is characterized by none of the animus and stridency so often associated with those who vocally reject their faith. It is rather an eloquent, lucid, and engaging exposition of his trajectory first into faith, and then out of it. Growing up as Tony's son, Bart makes clear, posed no obstacle to becoming a Christian. He always admired his dad, and thought that Tony made the Christian life seem like a huge adventure. The problem, though, at least until high school, Bart just didn't believe in God. Since his mother and sister, during that time, had no faith to

---

[26] Among relevant moral facts we discuss are moral goodness per se (objective values), human moral worth, binding moral duties, moral freedom, moral regrets, etc.

[27] Moral transformation and moral rationality correspond to the two Kantian arguments above, and to the two aspects of Kantian moral faith: (a) that morality is possible (and we emphasize three existential moral needs, namely, to be forgiven, changed, and perfected) and (b) that morality is a fully rational enterprise.

[28] See *God and Cosmos: Moral Truth and Human Meaning* for a fuller explication of this approach. For a slightly more accessible discussion, see *The Morals of the Story: Good News about a Good God*. For a much more comprehensive history of moral apologetics, see *The Moral Argument: A History*.

speak of, either, "In our family, the real religion was kindness. As long as I was nice—and especially nice to people on the margins—I was fine."

Things changed in high school, though, as Bart became part of a dynamic Christian youth group. He enjoyed the fun and relished the fellowship, and before long, though he still didn't believe in God, he really wanted to "because I wanted to become a full member of the most heavenly community I'd ever seen." So when he was asked to receive Christ as Savior, he didn't hesitate, and soon became active in evangelism and social outreach himself. From the start he saw following Jesus mainly about systematically transforming the world for the better. The new community helped forge his sense of identity and focused his energies. From the beginning, though, he struggled with the Christian narrative—from the creation story in Genesis to the resurrection of Jesus to the apocalyptic prophesies of Revelation. The supernatural aspects of the faith seemed to him the price of admission, not the attraction.

Tony Flew once said Christianity dies the death of a thousand qualifications. Bart describes his gradual loss of faith over the next three decades as dying a death of a thousand cuts—and ten thousand unanswered prayers. Seeing the hardships and sufferings of kids in a day camp in Camden, New Jersey was one of the first of those cuts. One encounter in particular stands out. Shonda, the mother of one of those kids, had grown up in church but was raped when she was nine years old. When she later asked why God had not protected her, her Sunday school teacher explained that God was all-knowing and all-powerful, so since he did not stop the attack he must have allowed it for a good reason. The real question, the teacher went on, was what Shonda could learn from the experience that would enable her to better love and glorify God, and it was at that point Shonda lost her faith.

Bart admits that, when he heard this, his own theology was much like that of the teacher's. His view of divine sovereignty made God seem like a cruel tyrant, at least where Shonda was concerned. For his theology included both that God didn't intervene to save Shonda from the rape and would relegate her to hell for her resulting unbelief. This led him to alter his theology, and this is, to my thinking, one of the most interesting and informative features of his story. For Bart's alteration of his theology was perhaps justified; there are indeed, say, construals of divine sovereignty that stand in great tension with an essentially loving God. Tweaking one's theology along the way can be an altogether appropriate and necessary thing to do, but Bart seems to interpret it as choosing to believe what we want to believe, rendering theology altogether malleable. In this case, he saw what he was doing as "dialing down God's sovereignty" and "dialing up His mercy." "For the first time in my Christian life, without consulting either my youth leaders or my Bible, I instinctively and quietly adjusted my theology to accommodate my reality." I might suggest, though, that Bart's interpretation of what he did is a bit misleading. What he did instinctively may well have been justified, and deeply consonant with the biblical depiction of God as wholly good and loving.

Instead Bart describes that event as the "beginning of the end" for his faith, which I cannot help but think unfortunate and needless. Because he thought that what he had been willing to do involved a compromise of biblical commitment, and unprincipled theological accommodation, it led to a slippery slope culminating three decades later, as he puts it, with "literally nothing left of my evangelical orthodoxy." What I suspect happened is that some of the later accommodations he was willing to make were, indeed, from the vantage point of orthodox Christianity, unprincipled capitulations. But because Bart saw himself doing that from the get go made the subsequent steps easier to take, without realizing that along the way he crossed a line. His initial concession when it came to jettisoning a particular view of sovereignty did not qualify, as far as I'm concerned. As Christians we're committed to the teachings of scripture as sacrosanct, not every last particular interpretation of such teachings with which we were raised or happened to acquire along the way.

Indeed, right after telling Shonda's story, he talked about his friendship with two homosexual roommates at Haverford College, and how for a while he struggled to reconcile the Bible's clear injunctions against homosexual behavior with his dawning realization that his gay friends' "sexual orientation were no more chosen than my own." In the end, he found that none of his interpretative solutions satisfied both his friends and his own evangelical sensibilities, and he concluded that he had to choose between them. The next entry will take up this issue in more detail.

Saturday, October 23, 2021: Marvelous chat with Elton this morning, followed by a great talk and prayer time with TJ. I had started a letter to the moral apol team before chatting with TJ, then tweaked it afterwards. Here it is:

Hey Moral Apologetics Team!

I woke up this morning with all of you on my mind, and the desire to touch base and provide you all an update on what's going on with us and the Center, which has now been renamed the Center for the Foundations of Ethics. Marybeth and I are fresh back from our time at Lincoln Christian University in Illinois, where we were able to see Zach Breitenbach and TJ's haunt three hours south, where we were able to spend time with him, his family, and his church in West Frankfort, IL. Such a delightful time; it was a little bit of heaven on earth. TJ and I have been discussing the prospect of inviting Zach onboard to help us here at Moral Apologetics; it looks likely to happen soon. We're confident he'd made a valued member of the team.

In the Strauss lectures we gave at LCU, Marybeth read her paper on Flannery O'Connor, especially "Good Country People" and "A Good Man is Hard to Find," and the topic of sin. Then we did a joint paper on *Till We Have Faces* and the dangers of self-deception, on warped views of God, and on a morally robust epistemology. Then I gave a paper on guilt, shame, and human dignity. Turnout was good, especially at Marybeth's erudite and perspicacious paper (as it was the convocation hour), and questions and discussion were good. Wonderful people up there in the Restoration tradition, such kindred spirits, and the Christian fellowship was eminently sweet. Meeting Rich Knopp in person and seeing *Room for Doubt* up close in operation were a great and exciting privilege. Seeing TJ, who came up to LCU for the lectures too, is always such an unmitigated joy, although his older son's beating me at ping pong nearly made me change my worldview. His church folks were simply delightful.

As it happens, the morning we were due to fly up to IL our flight was cancelled, and the replacement flight was the next day—the very day of the lectures! So we had to call an audible and drive the 16 hours up to IL, and then back. The day we got back, after close to forty hours in the car all told, I took a long, hard nap and then, with Jerry Walls and Rob Gagnon, made my way to the Lanier Library here in Houston to hear a lecture by John Warwick Montgomery. The talk was surprisingly simple, truth be told; we all left a little disappointed by it. It almost seems like he hasn't much kept abreast of the more recent developments in apologetics. But c'est la vie. Still neat to see a legend, and we were able as well to see my *Worldview Bulletin* buddy Paul Copan, which is always a treat.

On the moral apologetics front, thanks to you all for the bang-up jobs you are doing. The site seems to be thriving all the more, and I'm so proud of and thankful for you all. Moral Apologetics Press is about to release Marybeth's and my *Telling Tales: Intimations of the Sacred in Popular Culture*, and, corresponding with that release, launch a new book series of which Marybeth will serve as editor. The series will be about Apologetics and Popular Culture, and we envision a series much like Bill Irwin's Wiley Blackwell series on Philosophy and Popular Culture. Folks will be invited to submit proposals to edit a book on some piece of pop culture, and then elicit chapters by folks in the field. We've been surprised that this niche hasn't been filled before, and we are now, with the Press, in an ideal situation to take advantage of that and fill the need. Jonathan continues to lead the Press impeccably well and there are a number of other exciting projects in the works—so many that we're veritably bursting at the seams. (Speaking of Irwin's series, incidentally, it looks likely that Marybeth and I are about to procure a contract to edit *Ted Lasso and Philosophy* with Wiley Blackwell. When we were at TJ's house, MB did an interview with *Christianity Today* on Ted Lasso using TJ's equipment in his basement.) So many good things are happening! Still, there remain challenges and discouragements, but we're keeping our eyes on the prize, casting our bread on the waters, and trying not to grow weary in well doing.

Something of vital importance is in the works of which you should be apprised. As my department chair, Marybeth just turned in all the official paperwork for the Certificate in Moral Apologetics that we hope to see get underway in June. This will be a two-summer program, two classes each summer. Each class will run for three weeks, two hours a day, five days a week. The four classes will correspond to the tetralogy Jerry and I have written (well, we're wrapping up the fourth now)—theistic ethics, critique of secular ethics, defense of moral realism, and the history of the moral argument. This summer's two classes will be a defense of theistic ethics and a defense of moral realism, if everything gets approved.

But this is a major prayer request: all of this needs to be approved by HBU, and we're trying some innovative things that some could balk at, and some ambitious things that get some people nervous. We're also functioning under the constraint that if we don't get at least ten students enrolled, it won't run. So they're not making it easy for us. I don't want to entertain worst-case scenarios, but needless to say, if this isn't approved it would constitute a major setback, and leave us frankly rather reeling at that turn of events. Hopefully it will all go through smoothly and we'll be good to go by this summer. But please, please pray to this end—there is a Grad Council meeting Friday, Nov 12th at 2 pm Central. And if all of that goes through, as we are tentatively hopeful it will (though we've been told it's no foregone conclusion), pray additionally for our first crop of students. I'm hoping for twenty, and to cap enrollment there. But ten is the absolute minimum to make it workable. Please pray, folks, as never before, as this is an absolutely crucial piece of the puzzle.

The night before last we had the second meeting in our home of the Center's Student Fellows made up of present MA in apol students, so that's coming along. So between the site and Student Fellows, the certificate and Press, exciting stuff's in the works. I was also able recently to redo the online course offered here at HBU on moral apologetics and theistic ethics. In the spring I'll teach that online for the first time. That course sort of puts all four of the components of the Certificate into one class, obviously in abbreviated format. And I continue to fill slots in the anthology on the moral argument I'm co-editing with Yale's John Hare for OUP.

I am more and more convinced that the Foundations of Ethics is one of the most important battlefields in our cultural moment, and that the Center is uniquely poised to make a significant contribution to that discussion, in a way at once both rigorous and irenic, redemptive and restorative, winsome and powerful. I remain convinced that each of you has been providentially made to be a part of this initiative, and I'm greatly looking forward to seeing what God has in store for us all. Thanks to Jan's initiative, MB and I will have another opportunity to speak in a church in November (on the same day Jan is preaching there) here in town. Marybeth will do the speaking on this occasion, which should be a marvelous experience. We continue to pray for God to open such doors for us to share the vision and mission of the Center and of HBU.

I was about to send this e-mail to you a bit ago, but then TJ and I had our weekly chat and prayer time, and he shared some exciting developments relevant to the aforementioned prayer requests. He and Tony are planning on enrolling in the Certificate program, which is mightily helpful, because I can start compiling a list of potential folks interested in the program. This should help us make our case come Nov 12th. My dean has told me as much, so this news from TJ was great news indeed. If I might ask the rest of you, if there is anyone that you know who has expressed even the possible interest in signing up for the Certificate program in moral apologetics, might you pass those names along to me at your convenience. It could really contribute to making this dream/vision an actuality.

(If any of you are personally able/interested to participate, I think it would be a really good thing in terms of bringing you up to speed on the resources at our disposal in moral apologetics that we are here to apply/promote/translate in our work. I'd ask that you prayerfully consider it.)

Aslan's on the move!

Richest blessings to each of you,

Dave

Sunday, October 24, 2021: Most of yesterday was utterly consumed with grading, since the grades for my Faith and Reason class are due by tomorrow. But by evening I was able to submit them, so that class is in the books. This morning I received an e-mail from Jonathan Pruitt saying he's interested in signing up for the Certificate program here at HBU. He has to win Sara over; she's been so exceedingly patient as he's wrapped up his degree. Hope it works out. So folks interested so far are TJ Gentry, Jonathan Pruitt, Tony Williams, Curtis Evelo.

This morning I put this message on FB:

So the Center for the Foundations of Ethics at Houston Baptist University is excited that a new Certificate program here will be going up for approval in Graduate Council in just a few weeks. The program will feature a four-course sequence over two summers, starting this summer, if all gets approved. Each summer will feature two classes.

The four courses will correspond with Jerry Walls' and my tetralogy on the moral argument--a defense of theistic ethics against various objections and positive reasons to accept it; a critique of secular (and certain religious) ethical theories; the fertile history of the moral argument; and a sturdy defense of moral realism.

Readings will range from Robert Adams to John Hare, C. Stephen Evans to Angus Ritchie, Immanuel Kant to John Henry Newman, A. E. Taylor to William Sorley, C. S. Lewis to H. P. Owen, Erik Wielenberg to David Enoch, Russ Shafer-Landau to Richard Joyce, Hastings Rashdall to Arthur Balfour, and plenty besides, including a whole range of contemporaries working in the field from Mark Linville to Angus Menuge, C. Stephen Layman to Linda Zagzebski, and many, many more.

The first two courses this summer will be on moral realism and a defense of theistic ethics. The courses will each run for two hours a day, five days a week, for three weeks, and they can be taken remotely. (Some details have to be hammered out and approved in the upcoming meeting, so more details will be forthcoming; some will wonder, for example, if they can take the class and watch the lectures later; that's one of the details that has to be approved. I should know all of those details soon; the meeting is Nov 12th.)

The hope is to cap enrollment at 20 students, so that they can do it together and form a community of learners over and between the two summers. It's a new and fresh model we'll be using in various ways. I'll be leading each of the courses, but I'm liable to tap into the expertise of colleagues like William Lane Craig, Robert Gagnon, Jerry Walls, Nancy Pearcey, Craig Evans, Lou Markos, etc. We will open applications once it is all approved, but I was wondering, for those interested, if you would jot me a private message to let me know. That would be helpful.

The main purpose of the program is to provide a chance for a deep dive into the moral argument—its history, formulations, resources, literature—in an effort to train premier moral apologists discontent with reading just a book or two or taking merely one class or part of a class on it. There's simply far too much here for a cursory and superficial treatment. We think such a Certificate program is an idea whose time has come, and one that's vitally important and needed in our cultural moment.

I urge those potentially interested to let me know (in a private message)—and to give it your prayerful consideration.

Throughout the day some more folks said they were potentially interested in the Certificate.

Monday, October 25, 2021: Stayed home today in preparation of Bill Craig's online course on the historical Adam beginning this afternoon at 3:30. In the meantime I'm making sure everyone in the course, both those officially enrolled and those auditing, have access to the zoom link, the syllabus, and a daily reading list Dr. Craig wanted me to distribute. Now I have to set up the new online course on Apologetics Foundations. Another new person expressed interest in the Certificate. So that makes 11 and counting:

Matthew Winter (chapter director of *Reasonable Faith* in Helsinki), Tyson Smitherman, Tim Stratton, Holli Frazier, Jeremy Huntington, TJ Gentry, Jonathan Pruitt, Tony Williams, Curtis Evelo, Santi Rangel, Mike Harper. (Later in the day, another: Brandon Basse. 12!)

This afternoon Marybeth and I intend to write up an announcement launching the new series on Apologetics and Popular Culture that MB will be editing. Between that helping Craig with his course, big day, including a big day for the Center!

Wrote Michael Ward early this afternoon:

Hey Michael!

Hope you're well. I had a thought and wanted to pass it along. As the leader of this Lewis Center here at HBU, might you be willing to consider something like this? A little baby Certificate program on Lewis—maybe just reading some number of books by and about Lewis and listening to some number of lectures—designed for high schoolers—at least in the United States, but maybe from all over. And maybe more than just high schoolers. Lectures could be taped—by you, Markos, Walls, etc. (I'd be happy to help if you'd be interested)—and there could be a set reading list. Once up and running it wouldn't require much maintenance, but it would be a neat way for high school kids, say, to earn a college credit or two and be able to put it on their college applications--and of course to learn some Lewis along the way. It might also implant HBU in their minds as they're considering where to go for college. They could learn about Lewis as a literary scholar, as an apologist, even as a philosopher. I can't help but think something like this, over time, could really be a draw, especially with the sort of scholars you could tap into here at HBU, and of course with you at the top of the list.

Anyway, just an idea wanted to throw out there for your consideration! Appreciate you, man! Looking forward to that Lewis movie soon; we got our tickets!

Blessings, Dave

After Craig's class Stan Napper e-mailed and encouraged me to apply again for the grant next time around! Exciting!

Tuesday, October 26, 2021: Biggest challenge today was a rabid young earther in Craig's class whose style leaves something to be desired. I didn't want to just shut him down, and I wanted to protect Craig, but the students need some protection too. I don't think anyone wants him to be silenced or begrudges his presence or involvement or conviction, but the disrespect he shows to Craig is hard to take.

Wednesday, October 27, 2021: I think we found an amicable solution to the YEC proponent. Time will soon tell! Craig decided to teach on God and time in the spring. Crazy week! It looks like my schedule may get adjusted to something a bit more realistic—two classes per term—giving me a fighting chance to write more. And it looks likely our base will increase to the 75K we originally asked for.

Thursday, October 28, 2021: Good fourth day of Craig's class. Interesting issue of discussion: the way we need to do good hermeneutics first, then look at science. And remember to distinguish belief in the inerrancy of scripture from belief in the inerrancy of one's hermeneutic. Looks like I'll speak in Feb in Nebraska for *Ratio Christi*, that chapter of which just filed a suit over the school's unwillingness to support that student group. Then in March speak in TN. This evening in prayer MB and I remembered how we had felt an impression before moving here: just like when the ancient Israelites still had battles in the promised land, there would be battle here in Houston, but ones we can hope to see victory in as we depend on God.

Friday, October 29, 2021: Wrapped up the Craig class, and got news that we are getting the Lasso and Philosophy contract. Went over the call for papers and sent it back to Bill. That will go out next week. Also managed to write a fifth Campolo blog:

Reflections on *Why I Left, Why I Stayed*, by Tony and Bart Campolo, Part 5

Our previous installment ended with mention of the example of homosexuality as a theological topic about which Bart Campolo changed his mind. After defending for a while what Bart thought was (*and thinks is*) the biblical proscription of homosexual behavior, his relationship with some gay friends led to a change of mind.

In order to understand the trajectory of his thought, we need to examine with some care exactly what transpired here. He admits that for a while he struggled "to reconcile the Bible's clear injunctions against homosexual behavior with my dawning realization that my gay friends' sexual orientations were no more chosen than my own." But eventually none of his interpretive solutions were satisfactory both to his friends and his own evangelical sensibilities, and, he writes, "I knew I had to choose between them."

Bart's story is similar to and different from Tony's change of mind on this issue. Although Bart refers later in the book to his dad's famous decision to support gay marriage, Tony himself doesn't refer to it in the book. But on June 8, 2015, Tony released this statement, which I will cite in its entirety:

As a young man I surrendered my life to Jesus and trusted in Him for my salvation, and I have been a staunch evangelical ever since. I rely on the doctrines of the Apostles Creed. I believe the Bible to have been written by men inspired and guided by the Holy Spirit. I place my highest priority on the words of Jesus, emphasizing the 25th chapter of Matthew, where Jesus makes clear that on Judgment Day the defining question will be how each of us responded to those he calls "the least of these."

From this foundation I have done my best to preach the Gospel, care for the poor and oppressed, and earnestly motivate others to do the same. Because of my open concern for social justice, in recent years I have been asked the same question over and over again: Are you ready to fully accept into the Church those gay Christian couples who have made a lifetime commitment to one another?

While I have always tried to communicate grace and understanding to people on both sides of the issue, my answer to that question has always been somewhat ambiguous. One reason for that ambiguity was that I felt I could do more good for my gay and lesbian brothers and sisters by serving as a bridge person, encouraging the rest of the Church to reach out in love and truly get to know them. The other reason was that, like so many other Christians, I was deeply uncertain about what was right.

It has taken countless hours of prayer, study, conversation and emotional turmoil to bring me to the place where I am finally ready to call for the full acceptance of Christian gay couples into the Church.

For me, the most important part of that process was answering a more fundamental question: What is the point of marriage in the first place? For some Christians, in a tradition that traces back to St. Augustine, the sole purpose of marriage is procreation, which obviously negates the legitimacy of same-sex unions. Others of us, however, recognize a more spiritual dimension of marriage, which is of supreme importance. We believe that God intends married partners to help actualize in each other the "fruits of the spirit," which are love, joy, peace, patience, kindness, goodness, faithfulness, gentleness and self-control, often citing the Apostle Paul's comparison of marriage to Christ's sanctifying relationship with the Church. This doesn't mean that unmarried people cannot achieve the highest levels of spiritual actualization – our Savior himself was single, after all – but only that the institution of marriage should always be primarily about spiritual growth.

In my own life, my wife Peggy has been easily the greatest encourager of my relationship with Jesus. She has been my prayer partner and, more than anyone else, she has discerned my shortcomings and helped me try to overcome them. Her loving example, constant support, and wise counsel have enabled me to accomplish Kingdom work that I would have not even attempted without her, and I trust she would say the same about my role in her life. Each of us has been God's gift to the other and our marriage has been a mutually edifying relationship.

One reason I am changing my position on this issue is that, through Peggy, I have come to know so many gay Christian couples whose relationships work in much the same way as our own. Our friendships with these couples have helped me understand how important it is for the exclusion and disapproval of their unions by the Christian community to end. We in the Church should actively support such families. Furthermore, we should be doing all we can to reach, comfort and include all those precious children of God who have been wrongly led to believe that they are mistakes or just not good enough for God, simply because they are not straight.

As a social scientist, I have concluded that sexual orientation is almost never a choice and I have seen how damaging it can be to try to "cure" someone from being gay. As a Christian, my responsibility is not to condemn or reject gay people, but rather to love and embrace them, and to endeavor to draw them into the fellowship of the Church. When we sing the old invitation hymn, "Just As I Am", I want us to mean it, and I want my gay and lesbian brothers and sisters to know it is true for them too.

Rest assured that I have already heard – and in some cases made – every kind of biblical argument against gay marriage, including those of Dr. Ronald Sider, my esteemed friend and colleague at Eastern University. Obviously, people of good will can and do read the scriptures very differently when it comes to controversial issues, and I am painfully aware that there are ways I could be wrong about this one.

However, I am old enough to remember when we in the Church made strong biblical cases for keeping women out of teaching roles in the Church, and when divorced and remarried people often were excluded from fellowship altogether on the basis of scripture. Not long before that, some Christians even made biblical cases supporting slavery. Many of those people were sincere believers, but most of us now agree that they were wrong. I am afraid we are making the same kind of mistake again, which is why I am speaking out.

I hope what I have written here will help my fellow Christians to lovingly welcome all of our gay and lesbian brothers and sisters into the Church.

410

Obviously, there is a great deal to unpack here, but for now I will point out one significant similarity between Tony and Bart, and one significant dissimilarity. The similarity is that, for both of them, their decision was importantly spurred by personal friendships they had formed with practicing gay people. The difference I wish to highlight, however, is important. Bart came to think of the effort to square such acceptance with biblical teaching as futile, ad hoc, and unprincipled. Tony instead argues that a solid biblical interpretation can be rendered according to which gay practice is morally permissible. This is no small difference. Although they both end up condoning gay practice, their respective rationales for doing so, despite a surface resemblance, remain starkly different.

Bart remained dissatisfied with an interpretation of scripture that allowed for gay behavior; he thought scriptural teachings were pretty clear that gay sex was unholy and immoral. With this pronouncement he disagreed, so for him the decision to accept gay practice as normative required a rejection of biblical authority—"inerrancy," as he puts it. Tony's decision is different. He claims he came to think that the Bible is not *rightly interpreted* as proscribing gay practice. So in principle Tony can continue to affirm biblical inspiration, but simply deny that the Bible teaches that homosexual behavior is wrong.

Recall Tony's words: "Rest assured that I have already heard – and in some cases made – every kind of biblical argument against gay marriage…." Tony thinks the Bible, "rightly divided," simply does not teach that gay practice is wrong. Bart thinks it does. They both wish to accept gay behavior as normative—though they often couch it in terms of people being born with gay proclivities, with the apparently hidden premise smuggled in that proclivities to do X make X morally permissible, which is obviously rather problematic. But, importantly, they differ on what the Bible teaches here. Since Bart thinks the Bible teaches against gay practice, he rejects biblical authority; since Tony thinks the Bible is consistent with gay practice, he can be gay-affirming while continuing to embrace biblical authority.

So two distinct questions need to be identified here. One is *what the Bible actually teaches about homosexuality*. This interpretive matter is the "hermeneutical question." The other is *whether that teaching is reliable*. This is the "inspiration question." Bart and Tony disagree on both questions. The vast majority of Christians in the history of the church would have agreed with Bart on the hermeneutical question, and with Tony on the inspiration question. Of course this means they would also have disagreed with Tony on the hermeneutical question, and disagreed with Bart on the inspiration question. Truth isn't simply settled by a vote, of course, so the next installment will continue this discussion by elaborating on the hermeneutical question.

Saturday, October 30, 2021: Tried to relax today after this exhausting week. Rob and Jerry will be coming over tonight, but it's nearly 2 in the afternoon now and I need a major nap. So I've cleared my to-do list and I'm about to saw some logs. The previous day I got this e-mail from my provost Stan Napper:

Phil and Dave,
Please accept this e-mail as an introduction to Dr. Joe Thomas, Director of the Admiral James Stockdale Center for Ethical Leadership of the United States Naval Academy. I was introduced to Dr. Thomas through Robert Miller, a friend and a donor of HBU, who suggested that the goals of the Stockdale Center might align with the mission of HBU. You can see below how I, very generally, summarized your roles and efforts at HBU.

Dr. Thomas has agreed to introduce you to some of the key faculty and leaders of the Stockdale Center. My hope is that you would be able to find points of genuine intersection and agreement, that would lead to exchange of presentations, sharing resources and content, and at a minimum some mutual respect and awareness.

Joe,
Thank you for our correspondence to date, and I hope you and your colleagues will find a beneficial relationship with my colleagues at HBU.

Blessings, Stan

Stan,
Let's do that. On our end Prof Chris Eberle and Prof Ed Barrett are probably the perfect contacts for such a discussion. If you send an introductory note to your folks, I'll loop in ours.
All the best, Joe

Very Respectfully,
Joseph J. Thomas Ph.D.
Director,
VADM James B. Stockdale Center for Ethical Leadership
United States Naval Academy
(410) 293-6085, jjthomas@usna.edu

Joe,
I am very sorry that we keep missing each other. I reviewed the material you sent (the Moral Deliberation RoadMap). I can see how it would prompt

conversations and help crystallize decision-making in hard circumstances.

HBU's Center for Moral Apologetics engages in similar conversations. See https://hbu.edu/school-of-christian-thought/related-student-organizations/center-for-moral-apologetics/ The director of this center has recently proposed a name and focus change to the "Foundations of Ethics."

What are the chances that you or someone from the Stockdale Center could visit HBU to give a talk on the roadmap, either in person or through Zoom? And I wonder if we could identify someone at your campus and someone at HBU who could pick up the conversation where you and I left off (or where we had wanted to begin). On our end, I would recommend either Dr. Phil Tallon, our Dean of the School of Christian Thought (and an apologetics scholar) or Dr. David Baggett, who directs the center I mentioned above.

Blessings, Stan

Sunday, October 31, 2021: A day filled with much rest. I couldn't generate the strength to go with MB and Nathaniel to the movies in the afternoon. The knee is hurting a lot; I may need to go to emergency care soon.

Monday, November 1, 2021: Tried to get my blood checked for an upcoming doc appointment, but the gal who does it wasn't there. I did, though, afterwards go to emergency care. The location of the knee pain made the nurse practitioner think it a torn meniscus. I joked on FB I've told a few I have a torn hibiscus. My sister Sandra was diagnosed with covid; *so* glad she's vaccinated! And Nathaniel was told he would be offered a full-time position of lecturer (with benefits) at NAU. Grateful! A good day of dealing with lots of loose ends—I can feel the schedule lifting a bit.

Tuesday, November 2, 2021: Taught on Sherlock Holmes in MB's detective fiction class. Went okay. I think it could have gone a little better, but I was a bit groggy from the pain medicine, despite sleeping like a rock all night. But went decently, I think. Sweet class. In my office at school afterwards I signed the *Ted Lasso and Philosophy* contract with Wiley Blackwell; Marybeth and I are slated to edit it together. Fun; our fourth book together.

Wednesday, November 3, 2021: In the evening Rob Gagnon, Jerry Walls, and I went to see "The Most Reluctant Convert," the story of C. S. Lewis's conversion amid the towering spires of Oxford. Great fun. My colleague Michael Ward did a fine job playing the role of an Anglican priest.

Thursday, November 4, 2021: Today was a very difficult day. Tumultuous day at Liberty with a big press conference highlighting the need for more accountability. We saw a dead cat in the street that had been hit by a car. I didn't have the heart to look too closely, but Big Eyes (pregnant) kitty hasn't shown up all day in our yard, and I worry it was her. I'm heartbroken. Two students in the historical Adam class complained to my dean about the final exam being too hard, without first talking to me, reminding me that teaching is sometimes a rather thankless job.

And before any of that I had a long chat with TJ about the struggles I've been facing lately coming to terms with aspects of HBU. We're just eight days from the Grad Council meeting to move the Certificate program forward, and a few months from giving the school a major financial gift to help with the Center, but we're riddled with doubts we're in the right place. Praying desperately for clear direction. Just a tough, tough day. Not to mention that the "full time position" Nathaniel was offered at NAU pays 20K annually (and carries a 5-5 load). Ugh, and argh. Some days take more intentionality than others to count our blessings. Are we on the cusp of good things, or is a major change in direction called for? Hard to know sometimes.

Friday, November 5, 2021: Feeling a bit exhausted. Trying to fit in some rest. Marybeth wrote her swansong piece in her advocacy for Liberty:

A Time to Speak: Standing for Real Freedom at Liberty University

Last summer, I was in Houston when I heard the news of Jerry Falwell, Jr. being put on leave. The next few minutes were a rollercoaster of emotions. Shock, elation, relief, hope: the usual suspects after long waiting and praying for positive change to come at Liberty University. For those outside the Liberty bubble, it's well-nigh impossible to understand the stranglehold Falwell had on the institution and just how extraordinary and sudden his change of fortunes felt. It seemed nothing short of a miracle.

But there was also a deep grief that unexpectedly overtook me. I sobbed intensely and uncontrollably. For a brief instant, I wondered if our move had been premature. Should we have continued to abide the toxic conditions at the school in anticipation of this moment? Had the tipping point for renewal finally arrived?

It was an excruciating but necessary decision to leave Liberty. Staying there had become spiritually and emotionally corrosive, even if our ties to the school remained strong. Combined, my husband and I had invested over thirty years in the students and purported mission of the institution. But by the day, the effects of its corrupt leadership and culture became increasingly unbearable, as Falwell weathered scandal after scandal and the board repeatedly refused and resisted their responsibilities to hold him accountable.

What was valued, abided, and accommodated by leadership had sunk deeply into the very DNA of the institution at all levels. Dishonesty, mistreatment, apathy, posturing, competition, cold calculation, manipulation, and spite all fit comfortably in an abusive ecosystem that projected the appearance of godliness but time and again denied its power.

Then came the decimation of the School of Divinity in 2019, where a dozen or so veteran faculty members were handed non-renewals (for supposedly financial reasons) with only a month left on their contracts. That was the same year Falwell gained a million dollar pay increase, doubling his already exorbitant salary. David and I knew then that we could not stay, even if it meant walking away from our academic vocations. It didn't, thank God, but at that crucial crossroad, we had no idea what the future held.

Despite the upheaval our decision entailed, I knew that we were the lucky ones. So many before us were unceremoniously shoved out the door after years of faithful service, cast aside without their consent, without prospects and—due to coercive NDAs—without a voice. So many others remained under the thumb of crooked administration, unable to leave for a variety of reasons and trying to do good in a culture dead set against it.

With this year's revelations, the most vulnerable and maligned victims of the school have come streaming out of the woodwork—those previously unknown who endured the worst that Liberty enabled. Thanks to Gangster Capitalism, Julie Roys, and others, we have heard countless tragic stories of harassment and abuse, assault and objectification, silence and shame, with all avenues for recourse shut off to the victims. Those voices hint at even more wounded whose anguished tales have yet to be told.

This week's events suggest the dam might be breaking. Positive change might yet be possible. The press conference and rally with Rachael Denhollander pressured President Jerry Prevo and the executive committee to verbally commit to a truly independent investigation with a report to be made public. Time will tell if they follow through, but if they do not, pressure will only increase and something will eventually give.

It's hard to envision what justice looks like when an institution casts a long shadow of abuse and mistreatment, with untold casualties who have wounds of various stripes that go back years, even decades. How in the world can all that has gone wrong at Liberty University be fully appreciated, let alone be set right? How can each victim, whose individual experience was personally devastating and utterly dehumanizing, ever be given his or her proper due, their dignity restored? Is it even possible? Joel 2 promises that God will restore the years that the locusts have eaten, but from the muck and mire of Liberty, amid the fields ravaged by the profit-driven locusts, that seems little more than a pipedream.

While still on the inside, I struggled with these same questions. I felt so powerless to make any real positive difference. What good I aimed to effect felt so insignificant. And I daily questioned my motives and wrestled with the institutional realities: Did I stay at Liberty out of fear or pride? Was my presence there a vote of public confidence in those I knew to be unfit? Was I propping up and enabling a sinful system that routinely wracked havoc on so many lives and regularly damaged the church's witness? Did I compromise my integrity to retain my standing?

Even now, on the outside, I see these answers only through a glass darkly. But what worries me more is the subtle warping influence that such an environment may have had on my sense of right and wrong, good and evil. What troubles me is how I and others may have consciously or unconsciously justified the goods offered by the school as a trade-off for the ills, as though righteousness is zero-sum game, subject to human calculations.

Ursula Le Guin's short story "The Ones Who Walk Away from Omelas" asks readers to consider exactly such a scenario. Le Guin paints an alluring picture of a stunningly beautiful city, filled with pleasure and plenty, apparent joy and riches untold. Omelas has often reminded me of the façade of Liberty University with its glittering buildings and bright white pillars, its ever-increasing endowment. There is, as you may imagine, a catch. Someone always pays for that opulence. In Omelas, we learn, there is a child locked away in a cellar, mistreated and isolated, left to its squalor and suffering. And yet the happiness of the city is (mysteriously) utterly dependent on this child's "abominable misery" as Le Guin puts it.

Everyone in Omelas knows this. How they respond is the question. Do they put the child out of their minds and continue to enjoy the festivities? Do they rationalize that the happiness of the many outweighs the agony of the one? Do they attempt reform, despite the clear warning it will never come?

Some, of course, leave, as the story's title makes plain. I must admit that such an option has always unsettled me. For similar reasons, I was reticent to leave

Liberty, despite knowing of its deep-seated problems, its own sinister secrets. Leaving felt like surrender to the darkness. It may have meant no longer participating in a system that oppressed another, but neither was I helping them.

As I reflect on Le Guin's story now, in light of current conditions and a possible reckoning at Liberty on the horizon, I realize there's another way to understand her project, one that's completely compatible with clinging to and fighting for the good, true, and beautiful.

Those who walk away from Omelas, I have come to realize, are walking away from the corrupt transaction that it offers. They are saying no to the Faustian bargain of ease and comfort and resources galore that come at the cost of another person's well-being and dignity. They are, in fact, squarely facing the truth and standing up for it by refusing their part in an oppressive and repressive system and turning down ill-gotten gain. Accommodation, no less than enablement and abuse, makes possible all manner of evil, as the reporting out of Liberty this year has shown. The ones who walk away renounce such accommodation.

At this pivotal moment for Liberty University, may there be a flood of passionate, principled men and women who follow that lead. Sanguine contentment with the status quo should be unthinkable. Instead, let those still at the school be compelled by courage and love to speak up and out.

My own season of public advocacy on behalf of Liberty's victims and stakeholders is drawing to a close. The current tumult provides an opportunity for remaining community members to step up, to embody the righteousness that God demands. Now is your moment. Speak the truth in love and trust God to transform your restored liberty and simple acts of obedience into mighty prophetic voices.

Saturday, November 6, 2021: Graded the first discussion boards and met with Ken, a guy on the Homeowners' Association Board—about the feral cat issue in the neighborhood. He's a kindred spirit.

Sunday, November 7, 2021: Gained an hour with Daylight Savings Time over the night. Also trapped a possum. Ken will be picking it up late morning to put closer to the bayou. Before trapping the possum we trapped Big Eyes, but I let her go. Yes, Big Eyes! After missing her for three days, we were delighted to see her show up, though no longer pregnant. We're trying to locate the babies. We've set up a place for the babies on our back porch, and have on order two outside cat houses. Teaming up with Kan and his wife is a joy. Finally feel like we're doing something to help. MB and I have floated the idea of co-teaching a course on *Till We Have Faces* in the fall, an interdisciplinary deep-dive into the novel.

Monday, November 8, 2021: Full day so far, and it's not yet noon. We were able to send the 8000-word essay on *TWHF* to Zach for the upcoming *Perichoresis* issue. That felt good. And we had to hurry and ask the apol department to approve a change to the degree plans for the apol programs in order to help ensure the success of our Certificate initiative at Grad Council on Friday. Here's the e-mail I sent to the department after MB broached the topic and asked for a vote:

> Apol colleagues, if I might interject a word regarding this matter, I'd like to reiterate the point that the goal of this loosening of electives is to take the path of least resistance to get the Certificate in Moral Apologetics up and running. We had originally envisioned not adding the courses in the Certificate as electives because the point of the Certificate initiative was to reach (and generate) altogether new students rather than already existing HBU students. Expansion was a primary goal from the start. But to fulfill all righteousness with SACS, going that route and not making these electives, we've been told, is dicey, costly, and work prohibitive, and the better way to go is just to add the Certificate classes to the electives and effect on paper a revision to the degree plans (this elective initiative). In terms of the two tracks, cultural apol students are probably not nearly as likely as the phil apol students to opt to take any of the Certificate classes. And the probability is that only one or a few or the phil apol students will avail themselves of the classes. I certainly wouldn't expect that this change would detract from enrollment in any of the cultural apol classes. Both the content and particular innovations involved in the Certificate program make such a contingency unlikely—as we're intentionally targeting completely new HBU students and not any of the existing students (who can take the catch-all course on moral apol already on the books if they're interested). So I hope and honestly urge the department to see its way to approve this change. I am not planning on pushing any of the Certificate classes to residential advisees to satisfy a stray elective requirement; what we are hoping for instead is a cohort of 20 students (primarily if not exclusively all new students) who will take all four Certificate classes together and, over the course of the two-summer program, form something of a community of like-minded budding moral apologists. In that way it's its own thing, appearances to the contrary because of today's vote notwithstanding.

> Thanks, Dave

I also finally got around to responding to some questions left over from William Lane Craig; here was my e-mail to him:

> Hi Dr. Craig,

> I've been slammed with stuff since your course ended, so I'm only now rounding back to address your questions. There are three items to cover—one a holdover

from the early discussion about God commanding something wrong. Then a response to the e-mail of yours I include below. And finally your question about nomenclature in connection with Adams' equation of God and the good.

One of the things you wrote on Oct 21 was this: "You raise a really good point about God's commanding us to do something wrong implies that He has already given a previous command forbidding it! So we would be recipients of contradictory commands, which is very problematic. *I wonder if God's specific command might overrule His more general command.*" (Italics added.)

Regarding that last sentence, my gut reaction is to distinguish between two cases. Suppose God were to issue a command to me to give 20% of my income to the church instead of 10%. I would see that as consistent with his nature and I'd take that to be a case where God's specific command overrides the more general command. But I think it's different when God's putative specific command lowers the bar on the more general command. If I were to think God told me to do something in violation of a clear command that he's given, I think that's one of those cases where we should say, "Well, you missed God, then, because he's not going to tell you something contradictory." I fear that according primacy to the particular command in such cases would be highly problematic. In the former case God requires *more*; but in the latter, *less*, and that's when we should let the explicit general commands assume priority.

I'll come back to the e-mail below, but first let me discuss your question about nomenclature. On Nov 2, you wrote the following:

> I'm looking for an alternative to "Theistic Platonism" as a label for Adams' view that God Himself is the Good, the paradigm of moral value. "Divine Virtue Ethics" suggests itself, since moral virtues are grounded in God as their exemplar. Then one's meta-ethics could be construed as the conjunction of Divine Virtue Ethics + Divine Command Ethics.

> This might seem inadequate, since Adams construes God's goodness to be much more than moral goodness. But insofar as my interest is only in moral goodness, would this be a good name for the view? What nomenclature do you and others adopt rather than Theistic Platonism? Is there an accepted term?

I don't know of an accepted term or phrase here. In truth I've tended to call Adams a theistic Platonist (more theist than Platonist, as Adams puts it), and I've let that suffice. Since he construes finite goods as good insofar as they resemble the ultimate good (God), that's another feature of a generally Platonist picture, so I figured deferring to him on this score worked pretty well. You could call the specific conflation of God and the ultimate good as "exemplarism" or something like that, I suppose, but you could, if you'd like, it seems to me, stick with "theistic Platonism," distinguishing it from the sort of Platonism with which you have so many qualms. One minor concern is that you distinguish your position from that of Zagzebski's divine virtue ethic.

Finally, regarding your e-mail, it went like this:

> I wonder if you're familiar with Daniel Hill's *Divinity and Maximal Greatness* (New York: Routledge, 2005). It's a very sophisticated treatment of divine attributes, including divine goodness. Hill provides the following explication of maximal goodness:
>
> (D6.1) For every being, x, x is maximally good if and only if it is the case that, with respect to the set, S, of actions within x's power, know-how and opportunity,
>
>> (i) if there is one member of S, A, better than every other member of S, then x performs A;
>> (ii) if there is a sub-set of S, S', such that for each member of S' no member of S is better than it, then x performs a member of S';
>> (iii) if, for every member of S, there is another member of S that is better (or less bad) than it, then x performs a good member of S if there is one.
>
> As I think about this, it seems to me that (ii) should read "such that no member of S is as good as it." For if the members of S and S' are equal in value, why would x have to choose from S'? To require him to choose from S', wouldn't all the members of S have to be morally inferior to some member of S'?
>
> Hill's explication would allow us to respond to William Rowe's argument about the incoherence of perfect goodness and divine freedom, for it allows that if there is no best action to perform, then x simply performs a good action.
>
> More generally, what do you think of such an action-based account? It might seem prima facie inconsistent with Adams' Platonistic theism, which thinks of divine goodness in terms of excellence rather than good actions. But it occurs to me that (D6.1) doesn't really define maximal goodness but simply provides truth conditions for the claim that "x is maximally good." Compare the following explication of "p is true": for any proposition p, p is true if and only if God believes that p. That doesn't tell us what truth is, e.g. correspondence with reality; it just states adequate truth conditions for "p is true."
>
> Hill himself goes on to grant that one could claim that the primary loci of goodness are agents, not actions, and claim that every divine being is

perfectly good if and only if he has the greatest possible class of virtues and no vices. That definition seems more in line with Adams' view. But if I'm right, one could say that "*x* has the greatest possible class of virtues and no vices" if and only if (D6.1).

What do you think?

Thanks for asking for my thoughts on this. This is neat! I have not read Hill but I'd like to, for sure. I tend to agree with your analysis on every point. Your revision of ii sounds right to me for just the reason you adduced, and it seems to provide resources for answering Roe.

More generally, there is indeed something about this action-based account that strikes me as wrongheaded. I agree it's less a matter of definition of ultimate or maximal goodness than potential entailments of ultimate or maximal goodness.

I also have a great deal of sympathy with the notion that the primary loci of goodness are agents rather than actions. Following guys like A. E. Taylor, William Sorley, and others, I tend to think goodness most primordially is a property of persons, and only secondarily a property of actions, which indeed seems quite consistent with a thoroughgoing personalist account of goodness, i.e., in line with Adams. And your conjecture that "x has the greatest possible class of virtues and no vices" just in case D6.1 seems right, especially if we construe D6.1 more as a truth condition than a definition or analysis.

I don't feel like I said anything too helpful here! But such as it is, there ya go!

Blessings, Dave

The apologetics department unanimously passed our efforts to change how the electives work, which cleared the way for us to add the certificate classes to the list of electives. This should make Friday's meeting a whole lot smoother. The SCT is now voting on it, and votes of YES are streaming in.

Tuesday, November 9, 2021: Went to the knee doctor and he thinks I have arthritis in my left knee. I asked for the MRI because I'm a bit skeptical. I may have a little, but the pain is primarily to the right of my knee cap, not beneath it. So we'll see. Praying for God's healing touch. Walking is such a wonderful gift; the prospect of losing such an ability is horrifying. The vote in both the apol dept and the SCT was an overwhelming show of support. We are just about ready for Friday's meeting!

On the feral cat front, so far I've trapped two possums, which Ken relocated, and one beautiful female black cat, that's now fixed and resting in the animal shelter until we release her on Friday.

Wednesday, November 10, 2021: Early in the morning I answered an e-mail from someone named Matt Hartman, a Duke grad with whom I've corresponded before. He has a great interest in the Certificate program. So names of folks who have expressed interest now include Matt Hartman (Duke grad), Matthew Winter (chapter director of *Reasonable Faith* in Helsinki), Tyson Smitherman, Tim Stratton, Holli Frazier, Jeremy Huntington, TJ Gentry, Jonathan Pruitt, Tony Williams, Curtis Evelo, Santi Rangel, Mike Harper, and Brandon Basse. This makes 13!

A student in the one-hour Craig class of which I was the teacher of record is vocally balking at the requirements, thinking them prohibitive. I offered a slight adjustment but still required 17 pages of writing, but he plans to appeal to admin. It's his prerogative. This gives us a chance to work through a genuine difference of opinion in an irenic and kind way. Hoping for an amicable solution and the wise adjudication of administration.

This was my effort to write a 250-word abstract for the *Perichoresis* article on TWHF:

Till We Have Faces is a retelling of the Cupid/Psyche myth with a few twists, namely, a nonstandard narrator and the inability of Psyche's sister, Orual, to see the palace. Both innovations lead the reader to understand better some of the dynamics at play in Orual's effort to disrupt Psyche's happy life with her husband/god. The inability to see, on Orual's part, at first suggests that the nature of the story is primarily one of epistemology. What is it that can be reasonably known or inferred? Digging deeper, however, reveals that the epistemic elements are actually penultimate, and that instead the book bolsters an ethically robust epistemology. Who we are deeply affects what we can see. Before Orual could apprehend the nature of the gods, she had to be brutally honest about who she herself was. A victim of abuse who was constantly shamed for reasons beyond her control, she is a sympathetic character in several ways, but she gradually moves from being victim to victimizer, treating others as means to her ends, and, in the case of Psyche, "loving" her in a way that was more hate than love. Self-knowledge was needed for Orual to apprehend the truth. Her treatment of Bardia, Batta, Redival, and especially Psyche was not as pure and altruistic as she had thought. She had to come to terms with the ugliness within herself, and her penchant for consuming others, before she could hope to see the beauty and love of the gods for what they were.

Thursday, November 11, 2021: Today at 11 am TJ and I plan to pray. At 1:45 I hope to speak with my dean about tomorrow's Grad Council meeting. At 5 I do a zoom session with Kedric. At 7 MB is leading an advising info session via zoom for HBU apol students. Busy day! Tomorrow, though, is a huge day. What Grad Council decides is simply momentous. Just sent this e-mail to my Moral Apologetics Team:

Hey Team! Hope you are well.

If I could ask for your prayer support, tomorrow is the single most important day yet regarding the Center since we got to HBU. It's a Grad Council meeting on the Certificate in Moral Apologetics. Either they will approve it and we'll be good to go this summer with the first two classes, or they'll nix it. We are tentatively quite hopeful all will go well, but we have been told it is no foregone conclusion that they will approve it. In some ways the deck is stacked against us. The last Certificate program the School of Christian Thought advanced didn't pan out. Students enrolled in a Certificate program don't qualify for student loans or scholarships through HBU. There's always fear we won't attract a large enough interest. Etc. Lots of fine-grained questions can be raised that are nearly impossible to answer ahead of time sans a crystal ball.

On the other hand, this will be an opportunity to cast a vision for the Certificate and the importance of this training at this fraught cultural moment. Thirteen people have expressed strong interest in participating, and we haven't even begun to advertise (as we are waiting for approval before proceeding). If all goes well, we are about to embark on a major matching fund-raising campaign, and we will hold a fundraising event during the apologetics conference in the Woodlands later this school year. I firmly believe that the step of this Certificate could be a major stride for the Center and our mission as we continue to aspire to train premier moral apologists and to make HBU the central hub of cutting-edge work in this vitally important field. We could well be at a crucial juncture, the precipice of God's visible conferral of his blessing on this whole initiative.

Please pray that those on the Grad Council will sense the importance of this work and will show a spirit of collaboration and cooperation rather than needless obstruction. Pray for a healthy spirit to permeate the place tomorrow. Pray that they be motivated by courage and faith rather than fear and reticence. Pray above all that God's will would be accomplished here. And please pray for me and Marybeth, and our SCT advocates Jason Maston and Adam Harger, that God will give us the words to speak and an anointing with which to speak them in his power. We need tact and diplomacy, discernment and sagacity. Please pray to this end. And pray that we have peace that surpasses understanding and a hope that won't disappoint; this has been a tumultuous last few weeks here. And long-term, pray for sustainability, fund raising, and the right students in the Certificate program, if you would. Thank you!! Appreciate each one of you so much!

Blessings, Dave

Friday, November 12, 2021: Today's the day of the Grad Council vote on the Certificate program. It's currently 11 am. The meeting is at 2. It's by zoom. It's admittedly hard for me to focus on anything else beforehand. This is huge. I know I have got to trust God no matter what, but boy, it's hard for my mind not to wander and imagine the worst case scenario here. I need to be intentional to focus on good stuff, and the prospects of things going well. Chances are it'll go through with little resistance. They have something like 18 action items for the meeting; they probably don't want to belabor things unnecessarily.

It's now a tad past 5 pm. We are a go! Faculty council unanimously passed the Certificate initiative! Woohoo!! What a relief. After MB shared it on FB, someone contacted her who's definitely interested, making 14. One James Lopez (jadlopezd@gmail.com). My work's cut out for me; in seven months I teach my first intensive in the Certificate.

MB's last piece on Liberty has yet to be picked up for publication, which is a source of discouragement for her. Hopefully it'll happen soon. Her resultant melancholy on that matter has put a bit of a damper on this evening's celebration.

Saturday, November 13, 2021: Still basking in the afterglow of yesterday's victory. Feel a palpable sense of relief. MB also heard from Julie Roys that she intends to publish her piece tomorrow, so that's great news, and represents the bookend of MB's public advocacy regarding Liberty. A real turning of the page. MB is going out this evening with her detective fiction class, which should give me the evening to get some more work done. I have a few projects that have been held in abeyance for a week or two.

Sunday, November 14, 2021: At WordServe church out about a half hour today, both Jan Shultis and Marybeth were able to speak, in consecutive services. MB delivered a light version of her talk on Flannery O'Connor from the Strauss lectures. Afterwards we went to a barbecue restaurant for lunch. It's nearly 1 now and we're home, and MB and I are planning a nap and relaxing day of rest.

Monday, November 15, 2021: Had trouble sleeping last night, so a bit groggy today. Trying to do some grading for my online course. Boy this term has worn me down. Prayer with TJ was neat. This is the week he's devoted to writing full-time his dissertation for Liberty. Some months ago I awoke one morning with a strong sense that this dissertation of his would constitute something of a working blueprint for the mission of the Center moving forward. He seems well on his way, and he's also keen on generating study guides to accompany our various books on moral apologetics. Such a kindred spirit and dear brother.

Tuesday, November 16, 2021: Finished two blogs—one for the WB, and another on Campolo. Also responded at some length to a critic of a WB series. Here was the Campolo blog:

Reflections on *Why I Left, Why I Stayed*, by Tony and Bart Campolo, Part 6

Last time we distinguished between the interpretive and inspiration (or inerrancy) questions when it comes to biblical teachings on homosexuality. We saw that Bart and Tony disagree on both. Tony thinks the Bible is authoritative but that it does not teach that homosexual behavior is wrong; Bart thinks the Bible does teach that it's wrong, but that the Bible isn't authoritative. In this blog we will pause long enough to consider some more the interpretive or hermeneutical matter of whether the Christian scriptures teach that gay and lesbian behavior is in fact sinful. I tend to agree with Bart that the Bible does in fact teach that the Bible morally proscribes homosexual behavior.

As this is a large question of biblical interpretation on which no small amount of ink has been spilt over a long period of time, I will endeavor to delimit what I have to say to matters that have specific connections with the sorts of considerations that convinced Tony to adopt a progressive and permissive interpretation of scripture on this vexed matter. Recall he characterizes the position at which he's arrived, after what he characterizes as a long period of ambiguity and deep uncertainty, as full acceptance of gay couples into the Church who have made a lifetime commitment to one another.

The deepest underlying and prior question, to Tony's thinking, is this: *What is the point of marriage in the first place?* Here he bifurcates the options into these two categories: An Augustinian depiction of marriage as having for its sole purpose procreation, on the one hand, and a view that recognizes a "more spiritual dimension" to marriage, on the other. According to the latter view, God intends married persons to help actualize in each other the fruit of the Spirit; marriage is primarily about spiritual growth.

He admits that a large factor that convinced him to change his mind was his experience of spending time with gay couples, and he thinks it's high time for the exclusion and disapproval of their unions by the Christian community to end. He invites others to join the battle against making them feel like they are mistakes or not good enough for God "simply because they are not straight." As a social scientist, he is convinced that sexual orientation is hardly ever a choice, and he takes as a cautionary tale common stances in the past justified at the time by an interpretation of scripture we later came to reject.

Let's consider the fundamental question as far as Tony is concerned: What is the point of marriage in the first place? It seems fairly obvious that Tony's treatment of the issue of procreation in marriage casts this dimension in extremist fashion, namely, that procreation is the *only* value or purpose of marriage. That is arguably something of a straw man. It simply doesn't follow from procreation not being the only purpose of marriage that it isn't essentially tied to its nature.

Three main sources have proven themselves helpful to my own analysis of this issue. First, the book *What Is Marriage?* by Robert George, Ryan Anderson, and Sherif Girgis, who argue for an understanding of marriage according to which its essential nature is "a comprehensive union: a union of will (by consent) and body (by sexual union); inherently ordered to procreation and thus the broad sharing of family life; and calling for permanent and exclusive commitment ... a moral reality: a human good with an objective structure, which is inherently good for us to live out." This *conjugal* view of marriage (one rife with spiritual import), in contrast to a *revisionist* view that eliminates the procreative component from the picture altogether, seems to me to make considerably better sense of the purpose and point of marriage. It includes reference to procreation but not in the one-dimensional way that Tony willfully paints it.

Second, I would point readers to this article by longtime Asbury College President and Old Testament scholar Dennis Kinlaw: "Homosexuality Calmly Considered: A Theological Look at a Controversial Topic." It's well worth a careful read.

Third and last, but certainly not least, I urge those interested in the issue of what the Bible teaches on this matter to look at probably the best single volume on this issue—written by my friend, Bible scholar Robert Gagnon—entitled The Bible and Homosexual Practice: Texts and Hermeneutics. The most important issue about this whole matter, from a Christian perspective, is what the Bible actually teaches—this is the heart of the interpretive matter under discussion. That the Bible has been misinterpreted before, as Tony points out, is undoubtedly true, but relevant to the present discussion only if the traditional interpretation of scripture on homosexuality is mistaken. Pointing out such a possibility is no argument that it's the case. That this debate involves an important exegetical question makes clear that the question isn't merely one of take-it-or-leave-it. There is such a thing as rightly dividing the word of truth—and wrongly dividing it. It strains credulity to think that Tony has done his due diligence in this matter when a book like Gagnon's goes unaddressed by him.

Rather than discussing a mere handful of biblical texts, Gagnon's treatment is comprehensive, careful, and exhaustive. It ranges from the witness of the Old Testament, the notion of going "contrary to nature" in early Judaism, to the witness of Jesus and of Paul and Deutero-Paul. With the mind of a top-rate scholar and heart of a pastor, Gagnon also considers the hermeneutical relevance of the biblical witness and anticipates and answers a wide range of objections. I urge those who wish to understand biblical teaching on this question to read this book.

Notice Gagnon's reference in his title to homosexual *practice*. The concern is not one of *orientation*. Fallen human beings are filled with all manner of inclinations for wrongdoing without that fact implying anything about what's morally normative. The issue is behavior, not predilections or proclivities, trials or temptations. For Tony still to conflate these matters, after orientation versus practice have been carefully distinguished time and again, makes one wonder how ingenuous he's being.

Not coincidentally, the same question haunted him during the years he half-heartedly feigned his official resistance to gay practice in various debates. With his pro-gay wife he would appear, offer weak, fideistic-seeming arguments against homosexual practice, and allow her to give her best arguments in favor of it. Another time he actually joined with Gagnon and argued against homosexual practice against two opponents who took an affirmative position, and conducted himself in such a way that Gagnon personally challenged him afterwards by pointing out the obvious: Tony didn't believe what he was claiming to believe, even then.

On this issue, then, Tony's ostensible "change of mind" does indeed seem to fall prey to Bart's depiction of it elsewhere in their book: Tony has chosen the interpretation of the Bible on this matter that he wants to hold rather than adopt an interpretation based on solid principles of exegesis and hermeneutics. It's difficult to see how this qualifies as studying to show himself approved as a workman who need not be ashamed.

Wednesday, November 17, 2021: My mom would have turned 94 today. Miss her.

This was my response to the WB commenter:

Recently we at the *Worldview Bulletin* did a series on so-called existential reasons to believe, using Clifford Williams' book Existential Reasons to Believe: A Defense of Desires and Emotions for Faith as something of the impetus for our reflections. We divided the labor by Paul Copan discussing the universal experience of human guilt and the inability to escape from it apart from a gracious God who forgives. Paul Gould examined the human need for a deep and expansive life, which, he argued, is best explained by being made for God and to thrive in his creation. And I explored the human desire for immortality and how the Christian worldview meets this need in a marvelous way. What Williams' book makes clear is that, though such arguments can supplement and buttress evidential considerations, they are not sufficient in themselves to make the full case for faith. So from the start, using Williams' approach as our springboard, there was an implicit limitation to the arguments on offer. They were but a part of a much bigger picture.

A reader named Wayne offered some critiques of what we wrote, which we appreciate, and I thought I'd take a moment to offer a few replies, for what they're worth. His first concern was to stress that the human desire for immortality is not universal. "Many people including myself have no problem with ceasing to exist when we die, after all we will be unaware."

There are two questions here: the empirical matter of how widespread such a desire is, and what if anything the widespread desire for immortality might suggest about reality. Surely the desire for immortality is not universal; there are some if not many who would claim indifference on the matter, or even a preference for mortality. I have recently seen in more than one piece of fiction the idea recur that what gives life meaning is the fact that it comes to an end, for example. But of course "some" or "many" is consistent with a relatively small percentage of people. I don't claim any particular expertise on the matter, but a desire for immortality is quite common even if it is not universal. Not much rides on its being universal for present purposes. Mercy on the oppressed isn't universal, but that doesn't mean it isn't proper. Something can be a ubiquitous human desire and still admit of some exceptions.

Setting the question of universality aside, is there any existential or evidential significance to the widespread phenomenon of the desire for immortality among human beings? Again, the suggestion is not that such a desire entails or provides a knock-down argument for its truth, but rather that it's a significant existential feature of the human condition, and a desire that, as it happens, the Christian worldview impeccably satisfies. If there are other reasons to take the truth of Christianity seriously (which we believe there are), this additional consideration may well add something to the overall case. So considerations of immortality may well have apologetic significance. In this life, for example, there is often a conspicuous disconnect between virtue and happiness; the scales of justice often go unbalanced; nothing like perfect joy is achieved; nothing like total holiness is found. For most people, this life leaves us wanting more. Christianity teaches that this desire is no Pollyannaish pipe dream, but a veridical hope that won't disappoint.

Secondly, Wayne asserted that the "nearly universal experience of human guilt" is a phenomenon mostly associated with Christianity, because that is the way Christians have been taught. This is an eminently interesting critique, and it reminds me of something that the great Roman Catholic philosopher and famed student of Wittgenstein, Cambridge philosopher Elizabeth Anscombe, once wrote in a piece called "Modern Moral Philosophy." There she argued the concepts of moral obligations, and the sort of distinctive guilt we feel for violating them, as these developed in the western world, were a function of our theological heritage. Such binding duties and resultant guilt made sense in a world in which God and authoritative divine commands is taken seriously, but not otherwise.

Baylor's Steve Evans challenges Anscombe on this score, though, by pointing to what we can learn about guilt and our moral duties by a careful examination of the four features that stand out to Evans as comprising moral obligations: (1) A judgment about a moral obligation is a kind of verdict on my actions. (2) A moral obligation brings reflection to closure. (3) A moral obligation involves accountability or responsibility. (4) A moral obligation involves holds for persons simply as persons. Interestingly enough, contra Anscombe, Evans then shows that all four of these features can be found in the ideas of Socrates, who obviously predated Christianity. This is significant in showing that the notion of duties as verdict-like and rife with authority, whose violations rightly lead to ascriptions of moral guilt, are no mere function of special revelation, but arguably a part of general revelation. Thus they potentially can stand in an evidential relation to an instance of special revelation like the deliverances of Christianity.

Most all of us seem to have a deep existential moral need to be forgiven for wrongdoing. We have feelings of guilt, which most of us, at least on occasion, tend to connect with an objective condition of guilt. If such guilt is not merely a false appearance, it raises the question of how to deal with it. Christianity offers a good explanation of why we both feel and are guilty and how we can be forgiven. Might this point in the direction of God generally or even Christianity particularly? Perhaps so. Evans invokes the notion of a "natural sign" here, fulfilling the Pascalian constraints of being both universally accessible and easily resistible.

The phenomenon of guilt is quite interesting, and I suspect that it would do us all good to be carefully attentive to its salient features. It's easy to be in too big a rush and miss its significance. In his classic Gifford lectures *Faith of a Moralist*, A. E. Taylor, for example, identified such features of guilt as these: (1) it involves a sense of condemnation for ourselves and our actions, so it's different from mere discontent with our surroundings; (2) its indelibility, or power of asserting itself with unabated poignancy; (3) the regular attendance of a demand for punishment; (4) a particularly polluting quality; and 5) the sense that it's the very foundation of our moral personality that's somehow poisoned.

A visceral recognition of a deep sense of guilt is ubiquitous. This raises the question of how best to make sense of such a phenomenon, and how best to deal with it—really to explain it and not just explain it away. A Christian solution involves forgiveness from the One before whom we are guilty, not to mention deliverance from shame that can cripple us, sinful patterns that can hold us in bondage, and hope for ultimate deliverance from moral brokenness altogether. Again, this is quick and cursory, but the basic idea is that such good answers to these practically universal, deep existential moral needs makes Christianity more likely than it would otherwise be—even if taken by themselves they don't make Christianity or theism more likely true than not. In this sense, as I see it, it is in the spirit of something like Book 1 of *Mere Christianity* and chapters 5 and 10 of John Henry Newman's *Grammar of Assent*.

Third, is God needed for a deep and expansive life? Wayne is skeptical. He says that when he thinks about the history of the world and tragedies that befall so many innocent people, and God's apparent unconcern, he's concluded that "I should just get on with life, accepting that God may be watching, and accepting that if we actively love one another, we are satisfying the stated requirement of loving God." Loving one another, he thinks, makes sense, but loving God is a much more mysterious notion.

I think Wayne is certainly right that there is a great deal of mystery associated with God. We see through a glass darkly, and his ways are above our own. But something I might resist is the implicit tension or contrast between loving God and loving our neighbor. From the earliest pages of the Old Testament the commands to love God and neighbor are inextricably tied together. I might suggest that the way to learn to love God is to start by trying to love our neighbors as we ought.

This reminds me of a passage I recently read by Tony Campolo in *Why I Left, Why I Stayed*. He was relating a conversation he had had with some students at the University of Pennsylvania years ago, in which he had argued that we can meet the resurrected Jesus, who can enable us to overcome the feeling of alienation that plagues our existence. He was asked how, and this is what he said:

> "Jesus can be found exactly where He said," I told them. "He told us that He did not dwell in temples and churches that we build in His honor. Instead, He encouraged us to look for Him in one another. He said, 'You are my temples; I dwell in you.' What I am trying to say is that the Jesus who incarnated God two thousand years ago is mystically present and waiting to be discovered in every person you and I encounter. I am claiming that every one of us is a priest who can communicate Jesus to those whom we meet, and that those whom we meet are priests who can communicate Jesus to each of us. Consider the very obvious fact that all of us are aware that there is something sacred in every other person. Something about each of them makes us believe that each is of infinite value and worth. Usually we do not bother to name this sacred presence we encounter in others, but we know it is real and that it requires respect."

Rather than arguing that God is not mysterious, perhaps I'm rather inclined to argue, in the spirit of what Campolo just said, that loving our neighbor is a more mysterious thing than we might think. Presumably love is more than just a biological event in our brain; there's something about it that is transcendent, bursting the confines of a material world alone.

430

An Oxford contemporary of C. S. Lewis, Austin Farrer, similarly spoke of the regard we should have for other persons. Thinking of our neighbors in too garden variety a way, apart from the element of transcendence we can discern within them, can't sustain the esteem we intuitively think they deserve, he argued. The conclusion to which Farrer felt compelled is that what deserves our regard is not simply our neighbor but God in our neighbor and our neighbor in God.

As Christians we also speak of the need for God's grace truly to love our neighbors as we ought. Our neighbors, like ourselves, aren't always easy to love. By God's grace we can better and better love as we ought. In all of these ways, starting by loving our neighbors is a great place to start, and we would submit that in that very process we discern inklings of something yet more ultimate.

We applaud your efforts to discover the truth, Wayne, and we are honored to strive doing so alongside of you. Thanks for the feedback.

Thursday, November 18, 2021: Talked to an undergrad group at the University of York in England today via zoom about *Good God*. Nice discussion. They asked good questions, several about the problem of evil.

Friday, November 19, 2021: Saw *King Richard* today, a marvelous movie about the father of the Williams sisters. Really moving and touching. In partial celebration of MB's birthday tomorrow, she, Nathaniel, and I are going to see the new Vonnegut documentary this evening. *Unstuck in Time*, it's called. Then MB and I are going to Galveston for the weekend, and plan a prayer retreat while there.

It's later now; we just got home from the documentary, which I enjoyed a great deal. Remarkably creative mind Vonnegut had. Especially inspiring was all the labor he poured into *Slaughterhouse-Five* to get it just right. Heartening to know a great writer had to do plenty of trial and error, rewrites, etc. As I gear up to write the realism book, it was a good word to hear.

This week marked the end of MB's public advocacy for victims at Liberty with her piece published by Julie Roys. And in three days, this upcoming Monday, with Pruitt's dissertation defense, I'll be closing my last door with Liberty as well. Fitting, and high time. Our future is in Houston; Lynchburg is in our past.

Saturday, November 20, 2021: MB's 49th birthday. Headed to Galveston for the weekend. Fish, Gulf, and prayer. I wrote this on FB:

Today is my wife Marybeth's birthday, and I want to take the occasion to talk about her a bit. We have been married for close to ten years now, and I've only begun to understand some of her depths. Nobody makes me laugh harder, and every day with her is an adventure.

Because she is so unassuming and such a genuinely sweet and guileless person to the core, she can be all too easy to underestimate. But beneath her kindness, gentleness, and amiability, she's tough as nails—tenacious to fight for what's right and against abuse and oppression of various stripes, passionate about seeking justice, courageous to take what she knows is a principled stand, whatever the cost.

She has the most remarkable (and occasionally maddening) knack for understanding narratives; many a time while we are watching a movie she'll casually share an insight about what's to come that, as soon as I hear it, I know is right, and I'm as impressed by her as annoyed I didn't see it coming. She's like a story savant. It's of course part of what makes her teaching so delightful.

She has a talent for words that's obvious to everyone. Her pursuit of the right way of putting something is relentless. She's shown me both what great writing looks like and what it requires to generate.

She's taught me what it means to be in touch with one's emotions in a healthy way. One of the reasons I pursued philosophy, I know now, was a tacit mistrust of emotions, mainly because growing up I so often saw them manifested in unhealthy ways. Marybeth has shown me a better way—both giving emotions their due, and telling them just where their jurisdiction ends.

Her administrative gifts are as legion as they're prodigious; so often I watch her operate in her gifts and I simply find myself marveling at what she can do.

Her ability to viscerally connect with others is one of her central defining traits. No doubt it's related to a pre-marital evaluation a counselor administered to us that revealed that her capacity for empathy is simply stratospheric, off the charts. (As mine rivals that of a psychopath, that's another area in which she's helped me along quite a bit.) Her heart for God, most of all, and, for organically related reasons, for victims, the voiceless, and the marginalized, in particular, is capacious.

Marybeth inspires me simply all the time, and every day I count myself exceedingly blessed to share my life with her.

I love you, my sweet, smart, amazing, and altogether lovely wife, and I hope today is your best birthday celebration yet.

Sunday, November 21, 2021: We came home and continued the prayer retreat from there. Prayed hard about the future, about Nathaniel, about the Center, and the like. Felt like real work was accomplished.

Monday, November 22, 2021: Jonathan Pruitt defended his dissertation today. He did a fine job. His work extends the moral argument to Christianity. Feeling bummed afterwards that my direction of dissertations has come to an end. Here's a FB post I did reflecting on it all:

> Finished directing my last PhD dissertation for LU today—as Jonathan Pruitt deftly defended his dissertation extending the moral argument to Christianity in innovative ways. Hearty Congrats to Jonathan, who's been my right-hand man at MoralApologetics.com since its inception nearly eight years ago. It was a thrill to see all his hard work and his family's sacrifice pay off, fitting that Jonathan was my last student to direct, and that Ronnie Campbell was a reader on the committee, whose dissertation several years ago was the first I directed. (The other reader today was my mentor and buddy Jerry Walls.) And there were four dissertations in between Ronnie and Jonathan (Robinson, Fraser, Jordan, and Obanla), but today's was the last.
>
> A significant chapter has ended. Distinctly mixed feelings. I have an avalanche of regrets about and issues with that school, mainly with its senior leadership, but teaching in that program was one of the great and unmitigated joys of my life, generating a slew of memories and rich experiences I daily cherish. I was able to do courses on Newman and the history of the moral argument, on secular ethics and religious epistemology, on Lewis and Nietzsche, on religious ethics and moral realism, and plenty more besides. Leo Percer gave me the freedom every semester to teach whatever I wanted; it was a simply glorious gig, filled with classes of eminently bright and industrious students with a love of God, passion for ministry, and hunger for knowledge. I can only hope that one day I'll have a comparable set of opportunities.

I also asked Jonathan to post my blurb or Gavin Ortlund's new book, *Why God Makes Sense in a World that Doesn't*: "Ortlund's considerable talents applied to the ultimate question have yielded an impressive and eminently readable treatise that is both academically rigorous and deeply personal. Impressively researched and beautifully crafted, this book makes contagious the author's obvious delight at exploring life's mysteries, and it casts an animating vision of gripping beauty and enchanting transcendence. Without triumphalism it features epistemically modest yet hearty reasoning that invites readers into a conversation and into close consideration of existentially central threads of evidence—from math to morals—that end up weaving a lovely tapestry and providing a needed corrective to the postmodern fragmentation of truth, goodness, and beauty."

Tuesday, November 23, 2021: I'm still emotionally reeling a bit from the realization that my days of teaching and directing doctoral students are over, at least at Liberty. But HBU doesn't seem to be in any rush to create a doctoral program I can teach in. I guess there are days I worry my best is behind me—my best writing, my best teaching, and so forth. This is probably lack of faith on my part, but walking by sight is awfully easy. Recent events have reminded me of some of the cost of walking away from Liberty, despite the advantages. Invariably mixed bag.

Wednesday, November 24, 2021: Good prayer time with TJ today, and later in the day he wrote a letter to Dr. Sloan, which went as follows:

> Good evening, Dr. Sloan.
>
> My name is T. J. Gentry, and I am a close friend and ministry colleague of Dave and Marybeth Baggett. For quite some time, I have felt a growing burden to approach you and share what I believe is something the Lord has laid on my heart about my vision and hopes for becoming a part of the HBU family. I ask that you charitably indulge my coming to you in this manner, as I do not intend to be presumptuous in any way, but I feel that the time has come to reach out to you.
>
> I am a southern Illinois native, having been raised in a Christian home and receiving a call from the Lord to Christian ministry at the age of nine. I began preaching at age fourteen and have served for the last thirty-seven years variously as youth pastor, evangelist, church planter, pastoral counselor, Army chaplain, senior pastor, Christian school teacher and headmaster, apologist, and professor. Over those nearly four decades of my ministry life, God has blessed me with wonderful and enriching educational opportunities, both formal and informal, and especially in the formal realm over the last twelve years. At the age of forty I entered graduate school and have since completed five master's degrees and three doctorates. I am currently finishing my fourth and fifth doctorates with graduation for both expected in May of 2022. I do not share that to draw unwarranted attention to myself or to boast even remotely; what I have is from the Lord and I know it. However, by describing my academic journey over the last twelve years I am better able to explain why I am contacting you.
>
> In 2016 I began studying under Dave as a PhD student at Liberty University. Our first encounter was in a Religious Epistemology class, and I was deeply impressed by the Spirit during that class that Dave and I had been brought together by the Lord for a deeper, lasting purpose. He expressed the same sense, and in the summer of 2017 he and Marybeth approached me about joining the work of MoralApologetics.com as a contributor and associate editor. I was delighted to do so, as I had long found the integration of philosophy, apologetics, theology, and pastoral ministry to be of foremost importance and an ever-growing interest in my own life. It was one year later that the three of us joined

with a few others for a time of prayer and reflection in their Lynchburg home concerning the hopes of establishing what has now become the Center for the Foundations of Ethics at HBU.

As Dave and Marybeth discerned the call to leave Liberty and join the HBU family I was part of a small cadre of close prayer warriors and supporters and have since become the executive editor of MoralApologetics.com and a senior fellow of the Center. As testimony to my commitment to integrating moral apologetics and related ethical concerns into my ministry work, I have written a book on preaching and moral apologetics, a dissertation on evangelizing Mormons using moral apologetics, a thesis on Thomas Aquinas and moral apologetics, a dissertation on the centrality of ethical concerns in exegesis in Philemon, a dissertation on ethical leadership as modeled in the Epistle of Jude, and I am currently writing my dissertation for the PhD in Theology and Apologetics at Liberty on the centrality of Dave and Jerry Walls's four-fold moral argument as it relates to pastoral ministry in the areas of evangelism, preaching, and counseling. Dave has shared with me, and I agree that my dissertation at Liberty is likely to serve as something of a blueprint for the applied aspects of the work of the Center for pastors, counselors, chaplains, and those involved in church work, campus ministry, and other types of practical ministry. To say it plainly—my heart beats with the vision of the Center for the Foundations of Ethics at HBU, and I would very much like to find a way in God's providence to devote my full-time efforts to supporting that vision and the broader mission of HBU.

Also, beyond my ministry experience and education, I have extensive experience in marketing and fundraising as part of the various bi-vocational seasons in my ministry life. I have led sales teams, directed large staffs, served in command chaplain roles in the Army, spearheaded the start of a Christian school, began church-based ministry training programs, founded a counseling center and an apologetics ministry, and succeeded in several fundraising campaigns with church and community supporters. Indeed, God has blessed me with a diverse background since calling me those many years ago, and I believe he is calling me to bring those skills, educational credentials, life experiences, ministry years, business and leadership acumen, and passion for colaboring with Dave to HBU.

I am asking you, Dr. Sloan, to prayerfully consider if there might be a place for me in the HBU family. My wife of twenty-six years and our five children (two married) are all seeking to know what God has next for the Gentry family, and we would very much like it to be serving alongside of and capitalizing on the synergy created by Dave and I working together at HBU. To that end, I have included a copy of my curriculum vitae for your consideration, and I would love the opportunity to talk and pray with you about how the Lord may be bringing me to your team at HBU.

Sincerely and with great appreciation for your vision and wisdom,

T. J. Gentry, DMin, PhD, PhD

Thursday, November 25, 2021: Nice Thanksgiving day of celebration. Nathaniel came over and we had a good family time. Dr. Sloan wrote TJ this back:

> Dr. Gentry,
>
> Thank you for this gracious email and prayer request. As you know, these matters can be a drawn out process, but I am certainly grateful that you put this before me. I do promise to give this consideration, but that of course may not be quick. I also want to involve what a few others in the process. As you will understand, financial constraints are also part of the issue.
>
> Thank you for your humble willingness to serve the Lord and your desire to be at HBU. I am blessed and encouraged by your commitments. I'm sure Dave and Marybeth would be blessed to have you nearby.
>
> Blessed Thanksgiving to you and yours. Sincerely, Robert Sloan

Friday, November 26, 2021: Woke up with this idea I shared with Dr. Craig in an e-mail:

> Dr. Craig,
>
> Happy Thanksgiving!
>
> I woke up this morning with a thought about our collaboration on the moral argument. We're both involved in other things at the moment, as previously discussed, so this would be for a little down the line after I finish the fourth in the tetralogy.
>
> Still, here goes: my thought was Baker. They seem to do a really nice job with their covers and promotion. I've never worked with them before. I was reminded of them when I received a copy of Gavin Ortlund's new book. Looks really sharp.
>
> Regarding the project itself, I'm thinking of doing a rewrite of the whole thing, from beginning to end, using your material, my material, and select answers to questions that you have offered at your site. Rather than a separate section on questions and answers, I'm thinking of including the gist of some of those answers in the analysis itself at appropriate junctures.

This version of the book would feature our shared voice throughout, rather than alternating voices, and it would be an intentional effort at a more truly and deeply integrated picture of our approaches. I think it would be a great deal of fun to do once I have the chance to set myself to it. i would generate the draft; you'd just have to offer feedback once the whole thing is done.

If you'd like, I can revise the proposal and then, if you're open to it, we can ask Steve to float it to Baker. Although the prospect of writing a book with Cambridge or Oxford with you on this topic is exciting, and at first I was thinking we should do that, a Baker book would likely lead to a wider readership.

Anyway, just a thought. I think what got me thinking along the lines of a yet deeper integrative approach were the plethora of resonances between us I discerned as we taught that class together in May, and I'd like our book to do justice to that dynamic.

Best, Dave

He wrote back and said he was game! I then wrote our agent and shared the idea with him. Other than that this morning, I wrapped up a second installment on *TWHF* for the WB. MB and I also went to Kelly's for a delicious breakfast—a veggie omelet with an avocado and an orange.

Later in the day now. I redid the proposal and aimed it right back at Baker; here was the opening page of it:

What follows is a book proposal specifically tailored to Baker Press, after an earlier version of the proposal was rejected. We had been hopeful of a contract with Baker, and were disappointed by the initial rejection, but it has had the effect of making us rethink the book we would like to do. Rather than floating our proposal elsewhere, we have reworked the proposal in the hopes of getting you to reconsider it. Still confident it is a very good fit with Baker, we would thus like to offer for your consideration a substantially revised proposal for our book.

Having co-taught a Masters level course at Houston Baptist University on the moral argument in May of 2021, our original idea was to publish our elaborate notes on the course. At first the idea was juxtaposing our respective lectures, but then we thought we could effect a measure of integration; the resulting proposal, however, still featured largely alternating voices. We had also planned on including a series of questions and answers for the last part of the book, but on additional reflection we thought better of it, and we see our way forward now for a much more holistic and integrated treatment.

In the new volume we envision, our earlier notes will serve not as our draft, but as the springboard for a fresh, robust revision, from beginning to end, written not with two voices, but with one. Moreover, rather than a separate section on questions and answers, we will incorporate relevant insights from those answers into the body of the text at appropriate junctures. The result, we are convinced, will be a seamless and integrated, comprehensive and holistic treatment of the moral argument incorporating and extending the full panoply of insights we have garnered on the subject over the last few decades of work in this area.

To ensure a single voice, I (Dave) will effect this muscular revision, and will set myself to this task as soon as I'm done with the current book I'm writing with Jerry Walls for OUP, the fourth in our tetralogy on the moral argument. One of the contributing factors that made me see the potential of this wholesale rewrite was what I came to grasp while co-teaching with Craig: a plethora of deep, heretofore unmined resonances between us on the moral argument. It was our differences that had previously been at the forefront of my mind, and there are ways in which our treatments do diverge and deviate.

What I came to see, though, is that, in nearly every case, our differences don't divide us, but rather offer an opportunity for a richer and more comprehensive overall treatment of the subject. Together our cumulative moral argument, encompassing deductive, inductive, and abductive elements, and touching on the good and the right, moral knowledge, and both aspects of Kantian moral faith, is stronger than either of our arguments taken by themselves. What is needed, therefore, is not simply showcasing to some measure their rapprochement, complementary natures, and mutually enriching features, but an intentional and sustained effort to accentuate their comprehensive integration. Doing justice to this dynamic from the beginning to the end is exactly what we aim to do in this proposed volume, in an effort to write the definitive volume on this topic to date.

Saturday, November 27, 2021: I woke up with a strong impulse to pray this morning—for Nathaniel, Marybeth, the Center, HBU, and other things too. Lots of strong and hopeful intercession, for which I'm grateful. I'm currently trying to get some grading done this afternoon, but earlier I was able to write my seventh blog on the Campolo book:

When I first started this series about Tony and Bart Campolo's book, I figured I'd do a blog per chapter, but I've been going at a slower pace than that. The richness of the material requires it. I now need to do a third blog on Bart's first contribution to the chapter, "How I Left." What we have seen is that Bart, owing to various experiences, began to see his confidence in his Christian convictions erode. His friendships with some gay friends made him lose confidence in biblical authority, for example, which we've already discussed a bit. And similarly he rejected his belief in the doctrine of hell.

I suppose belief in hell isn't exactly an essential Christian belief, in the sense that, presumably, Christians can be universalists. At least when it comes to human beings, then, they might think hell remains empty. What their view is of fallen angels, Satan, etc. would be another matter. But the point is that one doesn't have to believe that anyone goes to hell in order to be a Christian. That said, though, traditionally most Christians have endorsed some doctrine of damnation, and there seem to be solid biblical reasons for doing so. So in this blog and the next I'd like to reflect a bit specifically on Bart's reasons for rejecting the doctrine and why I do not find his reasons compelling, but rather confused.

Bart writes that while his commitment to Jesus' teachings about loving relationships and social justice grew stronger, the content of his faith kept shrinking. The intensity of his commitment to effect good in the world was increasing, but his confidence in traditional Christian beliefs was lessening. This included the doctrine of hell, which was "long gone by then," thanks, he says, "to Shonda and a host other Shondas we got to know."

Shonda, recall, was the mother of one of the kids in the day camp he helped run in Camden, New Jersey. She had been raised a believer, but at the age of nine, tragically, she was gang raped by a group of young men. When she asked why God hadn't rescued her, her Sunday school teacher explained that because God was all-knowing and all-powerful, he could have stopped the attack, which meant that he must have allowed it for a good reason. "The real question, the teacher when on, was what Shonda could learn from the experience that would enable her to better love and glorify God." At which point Shonda said she rejected God forever.

What Bart admits was that his theology at this time wasn't much different from that of Shonda's Sunday school teacher. "Indeed, I believed that God was sovereign, and that anyone who didn't accept Jesus in this life was going to hell afterward, which made God seem like the cruelest of tyrants, at least as far as Shonda was concerned." It struck Bart as absurd that an all-powerful, all-loving God would willingly fail to protect an innocent little girl in this life, and then, when she couldn't trust Jesus as a result, "doom her to eternal damnation in the life to come." So absurd, in fact, that Bart decided to think otherwise.

Note that it wasn't at this point Bart rejected faith altogether. Rather, he "instinctively and quietly adjusted" his theology to accommodate his reality. He decided that God wasn't actually in control of everything that happened in this world after all, and then he decided that there must be "some kind of back door to heaven reserved for good people who didn't manage to come to Jesus before they died."

There are (at least) two important issues to discuss here: divine sovereignty and the doctrine of damnation. For the rest of this blog I intend to discuss the matter of divine sovereignty, and in the next blog the matter of hell.

I find it supremely telling that Bart's adjustment to his theology regarding sovereignty was to choose to believe that "God wasn't actually in control of everything that happened in this world after all." This is a very important point, because it reveals that Bart's operative conception of sovereignty was a conception that would arguably make God the author of sin. To believe that God is in utter control of everything that happens is the view of meticulous providence, but to my thinking there is little reason to believe any such thing, and a number of reasons to disbelieve it. All that happens is within God's permissive will, surely, but to put God's agency at the center of all that happens yields unpalatable results and goes beyond biblical teaching.

Once more, there are two questions regarding such a doctrine. Does the Bible teach it? And is the Bible reliable? I don't think the Bible teaches it, and most Christians do not. When a group of men gang rapes a child, did God somehow cause that to happen? Surely not. Now, it's true that some would affirm that God *does* cause such things to happen. John Piper has said as much, as has a certain stripe of other Calvinists. But I find such theology fundamentally mistaken, if not pernicious. And if it *is* mistaken, the question of whether the Bible is accurate in teaching such doctrine doesn't even arise.

Here's an interesting insight. Some have suggested that it was the liberal and progressive aspects of Bart's upbringing that made him so susceptible to losing his faith. I doubt it. I'm rather inclined to think it was the ultra-Calvinist-sounding nature of some of his convictions. And notice this by way of confirmation: Bart himself, when he adjusted his theology on sovereignty, admits in retrospect that this "was the beginning of the end for me." He identified Christian theology with something like extreme Calvinism and meticulous providence, and when he rejected the latter, it put him on a road to reject the former and lose his faith altogether. What makes this as needless as it's tragic, to my thinking, is if the original conflation of Christianity with meticulous providence was mistaken in the first place. It was.

Among the many problems with such theology, in my view, is that it renders the problem of evil intractable. Making God the ultimate author of sin and of the most heinous acts of cruelty and injustice and abuse is hardly consistent with God's essential nature of love. Rather than conducing to finding a practicable solution to the problem of evil, it exacerbates the problem to the point of rendering it intractable. Rather than saying the possibility of such things tragically happening is introduced in a world in which God confers meaningful

440

freedom that can be horribly abused, it makes us say silly things like God must have wanted *the rape itself* to happen for some reason. It's both bad theology and bad philosophy.

So Bart's mistake was not, I would submit, the rejection of meticulous providence, but his identification of such hideous theology with Christianity. If there are other accounts of divine sovereignty that don't yield such unpalatable implications—accounts entirely consistent with sound principles of biblical interpretation—then it's altogether rational and principled to reject something like meticulous providence. Indeed, I think it's rationally, ethically, and exegetically incumbent on us to do so. It's no unprincipled theological accommodation; it's doing good theology, refusing to treat as sacrosanct a rather obviously wrong interpretation that represents a minority view in the history of the church to begin with.

Bart admits to dialing down God's sovereignty and dialing up His mercy. I don't think he was wrong to do so, starting as he did with his warped and inhumane understanding of sovereignty. Sadly, he is hardly the first to abandon faith because of a clear-eyed recognition of the morally distasteful implications of such hyper Calvinism.

In the next installment, we will take up the matter of damnation.

Sunday, November 28, 2021: Wrote this update to the moral apol team today:

Hi Apologetics Family!

I hope your Thanksgiving weekend was a blessed time.

Congratulations to our own Jonathan Pruitt, who successfully defended his dissertation on the 22nd. He will be graduating in December with his doctorate in apologetics and theology, having defended an innovative dissertation extending the moral argument beyond theism to something more distinctively Christian. Cutting-edge stuff. So happy for and proud of him! It's been a joy working with Jonathan since the inception of the website, and I look forward to many more years of collaboration. Now I just have to figure out how to get him and his family to Houston!

How about an update? In all honesty I think we're quickly approaching a Gladwellian tipping point when we're going to see just a surge of creativity and productivity come to fruition in a number of converging areas. The website is really flourishing under TJ's leadership and JP's management. So many thanks to you all for your consistently quality contributions. Speaking of TJ, he's now in the throes of writing his dissertation on an application of the principles of moral apologetics to such arenas as preaching, evangelism, and counseling.

Moral Apologetics Press is neck high in contracts and, over the next several months, will be churning out several books germane to our mission—books by TJ, Elton Higgs, Daniel McCoy, and others. Among the books will be a published version of the Strauss lectures that MB and I did at Lincoln in October (when we got to hang out with Zach and TJ), with a foreword by Rich Knopp. Nick Henretty is on the verge of producing an audio version of Melton's *Wrackturn Letters*.

The Certificate program, as you know, has been approved by Grad Council and, subject to the president's and provost's signatures, will be good to go. We are about to launch a $50,000 matching campaign leading up to the start of the Certificate program. The money should help with student scholarships and other initiatives. We are trying to arrange a physical fundraising event at the Lanier library in Houston around May with, perhaps, Steve Evans from Baylor as the speaker. We will hopefully get the president of HBU to hand the Center a big check on that day (the final tally of the matching campaign) to let people see exciting things are happening.

We are about to officially release Marybeth's and my *Telling Tales: Intimations of the Sacred in Popular Culture*, and two points in that connection are important to emphasize. First, all proceeds from sales of that book will go toward the Center, and, second, the book's release will correspond to the launch of a new book series of which Marybeth will be the series editor. This series will be on Apologetics and Popular Culture, patterned after the various Philosophy and Popular Culture series. It will involve folks sending to MB pitches for edited collections on some piece of pop culture, chapters devoted to accentuating apologetic aspects of the movie or television show under consideration, written in the spirit of the show or film and in an accessible and engaging manner.

Speaking of philosophy and pop culture, MB and I were able to procure a contract with Wiley Blackwell to edit Ted Lasso and Philosophy, which keeps our connection to that whole endeavor initiated by my old King's College buddy Bill Irwin. Regarding other contracts, Ronnie Campbell and I are wrapping up our book on philosophical theology with a moral apol twist (with B&H). Jerry and I are at work on the fourth in our tetralogy—I'll be in the throes of debunking objections to moral realism over the next few months. John Hare and I are still editing our big collection on the moral argument—still need prayers to finalize my list of contributors (a project to which I hope to return over Christmas vacation). And William Lane Craig and I are trying to secure a contract (with Baker and other presses) for a collaborative book on the moral argument. In our revised proposal we're suggesting a wholesale integrated rewrite in one voice from beginning to end.

On the encouragement of our provost, we will be applying for a $15,000 grant from HBU to put on a major conference on the moral argument in conjunction with the aforementioned OUP Collection in progress. That would be huge, and could really help put HBU on the map on this issue.

So lots and lots of exciting things are happening, and that's not even everything. We so appreciate each member of the team, and we're excited about moving into the future. Thanks for all your efforts and your consistent prayers for God's blessings on the ministry. If you could be in prayer especially for fundraising efforts and for the right students in the first cohort of the Certificate program, we would greatly appreciate it. From day one we have always had a poignant cognizance that if anything good was going to happen here, it's God and only God who will be the one to give the increase. And please let us know the prayer requests on your hearts; we want to uphold you all in prayer on a regular basis.

Blessings, Dave

Monday, November 29, 2021: Wrote my 8th Campolo blog this morning:

As promised, this blog will now explore the doctrine of damnation, the logic of perdition, the terrifying and much-maligned notion of hell. Bart seems to have interpreted scripture along the lines of meticulous providence, which understandably and invariably encountered insuperable difficulties in the context of brutal human experience. He admits that his theology before losing his faith was not much different from that of Shonda's Sunday School teacher, which is a sad commentary about the quality of his theological sophistication at that stage. For someone with his strong ethical sensibilities and soft heart, he was, in retrospect, eminently ripe for walking away from his faith.

He had believed that "anyone who didn't accept Jesus in this life was going to hell afterward," and this would include one like Shonda unless she changed her mind about Jesus. He writes, "To me it was absurd to think that an all-powerful, all-loving God would willingly fail to protect an innocent little girl in this life, and then, when she couldn't trust Jesus as a result, doom her to eternal damnation in the life to come. So absurd, in fact, that I decided to think otherwise."

After rejecting meticulous providence (mistakenly taking this to involve eschewing divine sovereignty), Bart then "decided there must be some kind of back door to heaven reserved for good people who didn't manage to come to Jesus before they died." Once more Bart effected this maneuver with at least a tacit sense that doing so constituted a departure from orthodoxy—simply a decision he was undertaking on his own, a deviation from biblical teaching.

443

Again, there are two issues at play here. Prior to asking whether the Bible's teaching on this matter is accurate, the question is whether or not Bart's interpretation was right. If it wasn't, the question of whether such an interpretation is accurate does not arise. Bart's confidence in his biblical interpretation is strong—far too strong—and in light of his moral sensibilities and personal experience, he simply thought he needed to reject biblical inspiration and adopt views at variance with biblical teaching.

A far preferable methodology, to my thinking, would have been to subject to much greater critical scrutiny some of his narrow biblical interpretations. But as we have seen, he equated such an effort with theological accommodation. Surely this is a danger; indeed, I have suggested that Tony's change of mind on the issue of homosexuality is a paradigmatic example, which seems to be Bart's view as well. But there is a distinction between principled theological adjustment and unprincipled accommodation, a distinction often seemed lost on Bart because of his failure to subject to adequate scrutiny his biblical exegesis.

So there seemed to form in Bart's worldview a perfect storm: the conjunction of treating his biblical interpretations as sacrosanct, interpretations often predicated on ultra-Calvinism and meticulous providence, a failure to distinguish between principled and unprincipled theological adjustments, and his largely laudable moral sensibilities. Frankly what would have been surprising is if he *didn't* end up losing his faith given this cacophonous cocktail.

As time went on, Bart says that, by a certain point, belief in hell was "long gone." But what *was* his doctrine of hell, exactly? It was not simply based on the notion that salvation is ultimately only available because of Christ, but something like that conviction conjoined with a host of add-ons. Not only must one accept Christ to avoid hell, for example, one must accept Christ *in this life*, without exception. Bart could have rejected, or at least questioned, the latter without rejecting the former. For example, what happens to the unevangelized subsequent to their death? Even Billy Graham admitted he wasn't sure, and not because he harbored doubts that salvation was only through Christ.

Moreover, by Bart's admission, he began looking for a back door to heaven reserved for good people who didn't manage to come to Jesus before they died. I'm not entirely sure what Bart means by "good people," especially if all of us as human beings are sinful and in need of salvation. If he means people who haven't definitively rejected Christ in this lifetime, but who for one reason or another didn't explicitly accept him, I'm eminently open to such a possibility. I think many Christians are. It seems to be an arguable entailment of God's love. This is no "back door," or unprincipled theological accommodation. It is, though, a rejection of an ultra-fundamentalist epistemology, a Calvinist paradigm of soteriology, a meticulous providence view of divine sovereignty, and presumptuous theological add-ons.

Not every view with which we have been raised needs to be treated as a sacred cow, a nonnegotiable, sacrosanct tenet. There is a huge distinction between a hermeneutical commitment to the reliability of scripture, on the one hand, and a treatment of each of one's own biblical interpretations as inerrant, on the other. The latter bespeaks a profound lack of epistemic humility.

Belief in biblical inspiration means that its truly nonnegotiable and crystal clear teachings are to be accepted as altogether reliable. But it assuredly does not entail that we assume as beyond criticism our biblical interpretations on every ancillary, peripheral, or secondary question that might arise. The Bible makes clear that salvation is ultimately only through Christ; this is properly treated as a nonnegotiable piece of orthodoxy. Various presumptuous and fine-grained conjectural add-ons are not.

C. S. Lewis's *Great Divorce* offers a way to understand hell that doesn't depict it as simply the ultimate torture chamber for those who unluckily failed to accept Christ in this life or who happen to rejected a garbled, twisted, or degraded picture of Christianity. It is rather a morally robust picture of damnation as the tragic consequence of a clear-eyed rejection of every last overture of God's love, where, as in Dante, one's sufferings are intrinsically connected to those sins one refuses to let go of until the bitter end. I mention thinkers like these not to treat their fictional pictures as gospel truth, but to showcase intriguing possibilities for how to think maturely about substantive matters of theology.

In his *Exclusion and Embrace*, Miroslav Volf reflects on the apparent tension between a God who loves us enough to die for us and a God who would relegate us to hell. Among his many insights is this one: "God will judge not because God gives people what they deserve, but because some people refuse to receive what no one deserves; if evildoers experience God's terror, it will not be because they have done evil, but because they have resisted to the end the powerful lure of the open arms of the crucified Messiah."

Tuesday, November 30, 2021: So far this morning I shared Marybeth's e-mail to Lanier with Steve Evans, and hammered out a 12-page talk for the *Ratio Christi* meeting tonight. The talk is an abbreviation of the big paper on *TWHF*—with a central focus on shame. It's later now—the talk went really well, with a good question and answer period afterwards. Bill Scott wrote me this just now: "I wanted to say that your lecture tonight was absolutely wonderful. It was as moving as it was pragmatic. I learned so much tonight. The student feedback has been tremendous so far as well. You touched the hearts of many. Thanks for all you guys do, Dr. B. Truly a wonderful night." That was very sweet. Grateful to God, as I wasn't feeling the best about the talk beforehand. Encouraging night for sure.

Stan Napper wrote this to TJ today:

Dear. Dr. Gentry,

President Sloan forwarded your message and request to me for review. We are honored that you value the mission and accomplishments of HBU and would consider joining us. I don't believe I have ever met someone with five earned doctorate degrees. Your model of life-long learning is an inspiration.

I imagine that your life and teaching would also be an inspiration to our students. Your collaboration with Dave and MaryBeth would also exemplify the type of scholarship and engagement that I personally value. We have a great faculty in the School of Christian Thought, but as for our current situation, I believe that all of our instructional and scholarship needs are being met. As the new D.Min grows, and as a renewed focus on recruiting pays off, we may need to add faculty in the next few years, but I can't see it for FY23. I am grateful for your interest and will try to keep it in mind in case our situation changes.

Blessings,
  Stan

After writing to TJ a short encouraging letter, it was still on my mind, so I write him another note: "Still thinking about this letter from Stan. I'm not surprised, in light of his number-crunching tendencies. He's not the visionary here. Sloan is. I don't think it was a mistake you wrote, nor do I think the timing was a mistake. I think it was just right. Things, I think, are about to take off. That's the tipping point I referred to the other day. You'll be poised this way to be brought in at just the right time. Let's double down on prayers for donors, students, exponential growth for the Center, etc. Miracle times are quickly approaching, I sense. This is all in God's hands. All of this was God's idea, not ours. It's on him to show up and make it happen, and I think he will. Be encouraged, my brother! Love ya, buddy."

Wednesday, December 1, 2021: Heartbroken to see a FB friend's daughter at 17 had collapsed two days ago and brain scans reveal no activity. Cannot imagine. When we're told that the glory to come will make the present sufferings pale by comparison, when such sufferings include something like this, is nothing less than unspeakably remarkable.

Updated list of folks interested in the Certificate (15 total so far): Robert Brunner (robertbrunner@rocketmail.com); James Lopez (jadlopezd@gmail.com); Matt Hartman (Duke grad); Matthew Winter (chapter director of *Reasonable Faith* in Helsinki); Tyson Smitherman; Tim Stratton; Holli Frazier; Jeremy Huntington; TJ Gentry; Jonathan Pruitt; Tony Williams; Curtis Evelo; Santi Rangel; Mike Harper; and Brandon Basse. On the phone today my dean mentioned we could still put off the first run of the Certificate classes until summer of 2023 if I so chose. I appreciate the latitude, but I'm thinking this summer is the time to hit it.

Thursday, December 2, 2021: So today is 12/02/2021. It's both a palindrome and an ambigram. Also, unrelatedly, a bit of a discouraging day, owing to two recent HBU decisions. Suffice it to say they were both financially motivated decisions that, where we were concerned, was a bit disheartening and demoralizing. So it goes.

In other news, this considerably more positive, Adam Johnson from Nebraska finalized the dates I'm going there in March. I'll fly out March 29 and fly back March 31. As *Ratio Christi* is in litigation with the university over Audi's visit last spring, I told Adam if they don't get university funding, and they pay for the hotel and plane ticket, I'll speak gratis. The two talks I'll be giving are these: "Does the Existence of God Help Explain Moral Knowledge?" and, for RC, a repeat of this week's talk: "The Solution to Shame: Reflections on C. S. Lewis's *Till We Have Faces*." The dates I'm going to TN are March 17-18. There I'll give a talk on debunking objections and be part of a panel on scientific challenges to faith.

Today was most definitely a day of several earnest prayers of lament and some quite fervent intercessory prayers. For example, that HBU not fall into the trap of thinking small; that they jettison the tightfistedness that may seem to benefit them in the short term but is bound to hurt them deeply in the long haul; that unhealthy dynamics at the school are healed; that MB and I put our trust wholly in God and not in men to see an increase and the fruition of our labors; that we not resent HBU if they don't get with the program to our satisfaction; that what surely seems like their motivations of fear be replaced with robust, principled, biblical faith as the institution moves forward, shattering paradigms in preparation of God's miraculous provision; that we allow God to do a new work within us when we encounter heart-wrenching disappoints, which we invariably will; that MB in particular remain attentive to some cautionary tales and teachable leadership moments/lessons, especially if her sense of more leadership opportunities to come is accurate.

Friday, December 3, 2021: MB and I had a nice breakfast and then a delightful prayer time. During the afternoon prayer and chat time with TJ, something remarkable may have happened. I can hardly believe it! While we're talking he shares about an admin post at HBU, a Director of Student Conduct position, and inquires whether or not he should apply to get into the HBU ecosystem. I tell him I think it's a great idea, and while we're on the phone he e-mails Stan about it. While we're still on the phone, Stan replies enthusiastically and asks for his vita. Not only that, TJ knows a multi-millionaire pastor in the Houston area and, if he so chooses, could possibly augment his income by assisting him in the pastorate—while this fellow, fresh from having received a huge inheritance, is looking for a worthwhile cause to donate to! Wow! Just wow!

Saturday, December 4, 2021: Other than chat with Elton and read a bit of Harman, didn't do much today. Elton and I lamented the often poor art displayed in Christian films nowadays. Restful day. Purchased a reader at the CVS—basically just magnifying glasses—to facilitate reading. Will need to ratchet up my reading regimen in the next few months. MB and I also got our covid booster shot. She also got a flu shot; I already had mine. Jonathan Pruitt told me his degree was conferred yesterday. I wrote him back and said it's time for us to pray hard about his next step, and that I'm hoping for Houston. "Time for the team to get together," I wrote. He doesn't know of the very real prospect of TJ heading this way before long. We also finished listening to the last CT podcast on Mark Driscoll. It dawned on me today, not for the first time, I should try my hand at writing a CT piece on the Center. Definitely feeling like this term needs to end, but still two weeks left. It was well-nigh exhausting.

Sunday, December 5, 2021: After getting preternaturally tired last night, I woke up in the middle of the night for about four or five hours. I've been dragging much of the day, and am running a bit of a fever. It's now nearly six in the evening and I look forward to bouncing back from this booster. MB and I are now watching the second episode in the *Pride and Prejudice* mini-series with Colin Firth. In the late afternoon I got invited to speak at Ratio Christi at Texas A&M this spring. I told them April would probably be best. Exciting doors opening!

Monday, December 6, 2021: I wrote this e-mail to Jan Shultis today:

Jan, I hope you're well!

Hey, I'd like to touch base with you on a few matters pertaining to your work and our work. A few ideas have occurred, and I thought it would be good to share them.

Your Xena project is one of the most remarkable ministries out there, and we want to do anything we can to highlight its importance and need. You had and have a powerful vision for a needed ministry and you've been doing, from all I can tell, a simply remarkable job reaching out to veterans, first responders, law enforcement workers, and the like to meet them at desperate points of need. My admiration for such work is through the roof.

What I often try to think about and get clarity on is the connection between your work and ours, in an effort to forge more connections between them. I know there are connections, and your cast of mind seems to see those connections instantaneously. But sometimes I'm slower on the uptake and have to think a lot harder about it. ☐

As I see it, the work of your ministry is largely a hands on, very practical effort to meet people's needs. Which is beautiful and eminently laudable and important.

The work of the Center, as I envision it, is generally more theoretical. I see it as filling a need that has heretofore not been addressed: providing a hub of cutting-edge work on the foundations of ethics from a theistic and Christian perspective. People search in vain when looking for, say, a job teaching philosophy or theology to find a position whose specialization includes the religious foundations of ethics. There are jobs in applied ethics, business ethics, medical ethics, sometimes normative ethics or Kantian ethics, and of course a whole range of jobs in areas like queer theory, feminism, Marxism, postmodernism, existentialism, etc. But anything like a position, much less endowed Chair, in theistic ethics is just not out there. Once in a blue moon there's a position in metaethics on offer, but for an avowed theist to snag such a position is quite rare. Establishing an endowed Chair in moral apologetics is one of the eventual goals of the Center, but of course it would require that we can generate the money for it. But in the meantime what we envision is cultivating a community from an array of perspectives that works on a rich variety of aspects of moral apologetics--defending moral realism, defending theistic ethics against objections, giving positive reasons to think that morality evidentially points to God, the history of the moral argument, pointing out the deficiencies of purely secular ethical approaches, etc.

We do hope to cultivate openness to more practical dimensions of the work by giving attention to ways in which training in these areas can help evangelists, pastors, teachers, counselors, leaders, chaplains, etc. I see those as sort of spokes emanating from the central hub.

Although I encourage practical outreach among, say, the Student Fellows for the Center, the primary focus of the Center, as I think of it, is not in the arena of making ethical decisions or getting over ethical hurts, but something prior to all of that--namely, getting clarity into the foundations of ethics. Why is anything morally obligatory at all? Is it possible that we become people of virtue? How is it we come to acquire knowledge of ethical truth? What's the solution to our guilt and shame? Is morality an essentially rational enterprise? How does God make sense of important moral categories?

It's especially matters metaphysical and epistemic that occupy our attention, although I want all sorts of folks involved in the exploration, not just philosophers. We want social scientists, theologians, Bible folks, literary experts, etc. At least that's what I like to envision in my head.

We're making progress bit by bit in moving in these directions, but my point is that what I see the Center primarily concerned about is insight into the foundations of ethics and the ineliminable role God plays in making sense of its various features and dimensions.

So I look at you and I see a tremendously brilliant person with a big heart for ministry. You put a high priority on practical ministry, but you also aspire to write--and you're a beautiful writer. But the writing, though it may have implications for practical ministry, is writing, after all, which in and of itself is more theoretical than applied. That comports with the Center's emphasis. And the category of moral injury is clearly at the center of your concerns. You're writing your dissertation on moral injury, which I think will be tremendous. I'm still learning what this is all about. I'm confident there are a number of organic connections between moral injury and God--and thus between your work and that of the Center's. I'm hoping to understand more and more of that.

When I listen to you describe the practical ways of addressing moral injury, it's deeply moving--and no doubt a work of the church being God's hands and feet in this world. But I admit I remain on a learning curve trying to see the connections between such practical work and our inquiry into the foundations of ethics. Again, my inability to see something with crystal clarity is no indication it's not there to be seen; it's more about my own limited perspective. Until a year ago, for example, I hadn't much seen or thought much at all about the connection between moral apol and the issue of shame, but several events conspired over the last twelve months or so to open my eyes to a whole new rich area of exploration and overlap, involving a bit of intersection between theory and practice. I'm hoping for the same on this issue.

So I wanted to share all this with you to let you know I continue thinking about all of this in an effort to understand it better--and undoubtedly as I do I'll have more and more insight into God bringing you into our lives, an act of providence of which I have no doubt! My guess is there are all sorts of fertile overlaps between our respective callings and vocations that remain to be discovered.

I found myself recently struggling to understand something else that all of this reminds me of. You'll recall Stan Napper, the provost at HBU, putting us in touch with the folks at the Naval Academy involved in creating a "moral map." It sounds like some sort of elaborate algorithm for figuring out how to make ethical decisions in difficult circumstances. And in Stan's mind, he was thinking that perhaps there was some amount of dovetailing between such work and that of the Center. As a science guy, he has a tendency to accord primacy to the practical and quantifiable. I think this has led, on a few occasions, to our rather talking past each other.

Honestly, I've thought about it a lot, and I rather doubt there's a great deal if much of any real overlap. And again, maybe I'm wrong, but it struck me as apples and oranges. I suspect the work by the Academy folks has a lot of connection with most ethical centers out there that tend to be more practically oriented than ours. But the Center here pertains to the theoretical foundations of ethics. Is there such a thing as binding morality in the first place? And if so, does God have something to do with it? Those are the sorts of questions that interest me as a philosopher. Not what's some decision-making process for making ethical decisions in some specific fraught situation? It just doesn't seem inherently connected enough. With moral injury, I retain the conviction we can find connections, but in this other situation I'm rather skeptical. What they're dealing with is hardly unimportant, but it's just a quite different animal.

I bring it up because I thought I might suggest that your applied work with Xena may be more closely connected with what they're doing, and that if you wish to follow up with them to forge a collaboration or closer connection or even just a conversation--especially with your history with Annapolis--I'd encourage you to do so. I've largely drawn a blank seeing much of a connection between their work and ours, and honestly I just don't have the time or energy to devote more time thinking about it. We've got our own thing going, and figuring out its connection to what seems like a rather different thing being done at the Naval Academy just stretches me beyond my limits. I'm sure what they're doing is terrific, and I'm not uninterested, but it's sufficiently beyond the confines of my wheelhouse that I thought it better to pass it along to you in case you have any interest in pursuing a discussion with them. I share, again, Stan's letter below if you do.

Anyhoo, that issue was secondary. Mainly I wanted to share with you my ongoing effort to see more clearly connections between your passion and the topic of your dissertation (I guess they call it a thesis over there!) and the work of the Center. I look forward to our ongoing conversations about this important matter as you progress with your exciting research.

Blessings, my friend,
Dave

Here was Jan's excellent reply:

Hi, David (and Marybeth :)),

Thank you so much for the gift of your time and thoughts. This email is extraordinary, and I am grateful.

Thank you, too, for your kind words and support across the board. I thank all of my guardian angels for bringing you both into my life.

To cut straight to the Center, bottom line is that the call on my life is to pray, think, write, and I've known that for some time. Though moral injury is the area of my dissertation, there is another area of passion that perhaps more neatly fits into the Center's mission. I think I'm your first theological scientist (that's a thing

I just made up, but it sounds fancy, right?!). I have a 30,000-word book on stem cells coming out at the end of the month that is heavy on issues of human dignity, and am turning my masters thesis that MB supervised (regenerative medicine as a moral argument for God's existence) into a Templeton Foundation application. I want to dig heavily into our obligations surrounding co-creation and *imago Dei* as a foundation from which to base our bioethical decisions about clinical research in regenerative medicine (I submitted a paper to the Center for Bioethics and Human Dignity just last week on some of these topics for consideration for their June conference.) Much of this research is also required for my dissertation, and God seems to want me to stay working in clinical research for the time being, so I'm flowing with this, not fighting it, and His hand is everywhere, quite quickly. It's exciting, and I hope a good way to extend visibility for the Center. I know it's a little dicey now because we don't necessarily have science editors, but in doing research for this book I have reviewed more scientific literature than I even had the vocabulary to comprehend a year ago. Now I do believe I can position some pieces for the website that are sufficiently researched to justify any scientific claims with scientific literature..... would work in this vein support the Center?

Switching gears, I do believe that moral injury has a place in the Center's work because it is simply a slice of the larger "shame" picture. I think that the Center should include work in moral injury because shame/moral injury is something that separates. My stance here is both a professional and personal one - remember, I did not buy into the moral argument at all when I first heard it, because moral injury stood in the way. Shame is the first consequence of sin, the original separation, the thing that makes all of this work around ethics even necessary. People need to be taught how to think and talk about shame, including moral injury as a specific manifestation of shame. Of the questions that you listed in your initial email, these strike me as extremely important with regard to moral injury:

- Why is anything morally obligatory at all?
- Is it possible that we become people of virtue?
- What's the solution to our guilt and shame?
- Is morality an essentially rational enterprise?

Of these, I think the third is the most profound point of intersection for research - and if we can answer that, we can provide hope for the morally injured (aside: Lewis found a solution in Christ, and then through his work. That's why he's the subject of my dissertation - not because he's THE C.S. Lewis. Because he found an answer to that third question, and left us enough of a body of work, personal letters, etc. that we have some tools to figure out how he did it.).

On a related note, I am thrilled to reach out to the Naval Academy and will do so after some prayer; thank you so much for that license! I do see quite clearly the relationship between the two organizations. The Naval Academy has their ethical map and there is value in it. But they are sending leaders into the military force ill-equipped in this sense. Young military leaders *need* the work of this Center, of your Center; tired war dogs need this Center once they've seen the world and all of the questions are swirling. We don't need to be taught what to do, we need to be taught how to think. The Academy knows that more is needed, which is why they fund the Stockdale Center, but they don't know what that thing is or why..... they're grasping, from their growing Chaplain corps to a growing number of counselors to the Stockdale Center. They need the Center for the Foundation of Ethics as you are building it, because there can be found *actual* answers. It's going to be quite a ride to leverage all of this apologetics training into showing it to them, one interaction at a time, but wow, would it have reach if a relationship could be built! I am happy to pursue that conversation as just me, the sum of all of these experiences, if that is alright with you, and let's see how the relationship develops.

A personal note, which I share in hopes that you will remember my heart and see these as heartfelt truths, not complaints.... I have prayed for years to be free of The Xena Project. My heart is actually not in hands-on ministry at all. The Spirit used XP to bring me to Christ and it does good work, not the least of which is giving me "street cred" from which to write and stories worth telling. It has shown me many things, most of them questions around human dignity, that need to be talked/written about, and I will spend the rest of my life doing just that. But for however long I am there, the long-term vision of that organization is to become a think tank that uses the immediate area as a giant laboratory to test ideas and approaches. I think as it's Founder I will always talk about it, promote it, share what the Spirit revealed to me through it, but I rejoice as God removes me from it, piece by piece. Many others there do feel strongly called to hands-on ministry, and they are wonderful. They are far better suited than I ever was, and it's fantastic.

I could happily talk to you, and listen to your thoughts, for hours and hours and hours. I feel like I'm rambling and do not want to use up your time, especially near end of semester, but I very much look forward to your thoughts if you have time to offer them again..... thank you so much for talking to me :)

With gratitude, love, and lots of hugs,
Jan

On a not unrelated note, I really began in earnest putting together the fourth in the tetralogy today, compiling drafts of various of its pieces and locating the introduction I had written some time back. Hopefully I'm on my way! I double checked the book proposal and it appears I had said we'd turn it in January 2023. That gives me just a tad over a year, if I'm to get it in on time. We'll see.

Tuesday, December 7, 2021: An eventful day. Plane and hotel reservations for Nebraska trip ready; told Adam Johnson I'd cover my hotel as a gift to his ministry. We visited with a new MA in apol student and her parents here in our home, which was delightful. She's impressive—Kaitlyn Moss is her name. Poised to start going through Fraser's dissertation again. I worked a bit on the new manuscript. Arranging the Center to host Mike Austin for a talk in the spring (along with Evans). Baker is going to take another look at our proposal in the editorial meeting next week—I think it's much more hopeful this time around. We're trying to make the back cover of *Telling Tales* look just right with a blurb or two and our bio's. And last but not least, MB wrote the announcement launching our new book series on Apologetics and Popular Culture. Here it is:

Apologetics and Pop Culture, A Series from Moral Apologetics Press

Series Editor, Marybeth Baggett

Moral Apologetics Press is pleased to announce plans for a new series, Apologetics and Pop Culture. Individual volumes in this series will engage with artifacts from popular culture to dig deeper into weighty matters of worldview, philosophy, and theology, an approach modeled after St. Paul's posture at Mars Hill reported in Acts 17. There the Apostle mines the rich cultural landscape of the Athenians to draw out nuggets of truth about God and human existence, to correct misconceptions, and to bring his audience to repentance and Christian faith. The Apologetics and Pop Culture Series aspires to these same goals.

Much like the Philosophy and Pop Culture movement inaugurated by William Irwin, this Moral Apologetics project provides a means for readers and writers alike to engage in substantive conversations based on pop culture relics that allow for a pre-existing connection. Television shows and movies occupy much of our time, and when we look closer as this series aims to, we find that they are rife with philosophical, theological, and apologetic significance. Apologetics and Pop Culture seeks to make possible apologetics at its best, through friendly conversations built on shared grounds.

Although not itself part of the series, David and Marybeth Baggett's collection, *Telling Tales: Intimations of the Sacred in Popular Culture*—**now officially launching!**—provides the template for the Apologetics and Pop Culture series. All proceeds from *Telling Tales*, and a portion from all the books in the series, will support the work of the Center for the Foundations of Ethics at Houston Baptist University, including scholarships, conferences, and lectureships.

Call for Proposals

The Apologetics and Pop Culture series is seeking proposals for books that fit the spirit of the project as described above. A successful proposal will be for an edited collection of new essays by a variety of contributors, where individual entries center on a unifying pop culture element (television show, film, band, artist, director, etc.).

These submissions should come directly from prospective editors of such volumes and should include the following:

- 25-30 potential topics with memorable titles for corresponding chapters
- Explanation of why the artifact would serve as a good starting point for apologetics arguments or discussions
- Justification for their role as editor, including their qualifications
- Current curriculum vitae
- Discussion of why the project would be marketable or of reader interest

Interested editors should also keep the following in mind while crafting their proposals:

- While contributions can be sophisticated or high brow, an intentional effort must be made to make the material accessible to the wider public
- Volumes in the series should have 20-25 chapters of 3,000 to 4,000 words each
- The writing of the volume should be punchy, engaging, pithy, memorable, and fun, written in the same vein of the cultural artifact under discussion
- Contributors generally need a graduate degree, preferably with a track record of previous publications; contributors with enough interest but not much experience may be paired with a more seasoned collaborator
- Even though this is an initiative of the Center for the Foundations of Ethics at Houston Baptist University, many and varied apologetics methods are acceptable and encouraged for use in such volumes. These include, but are not limited to, literary or imaginative apologetics, comparative religions, cultural apologetics, scientific apologetics, philosophical apologetics, historical apologetics, moral apologetics, and more

Proposals should be emailed to the series editor, Marybeth Baggett, at mbaggett@hbu.edu

Wednesday, December 8, 2021: Today was an interesting day. Last week, after some disappointments at HBU, I wrote the president of SAU and expressed openness to going elsewhere. Today I heard back from him:

> Your inquiry comes at a time where I am curious of God's leading. We are in conversation currently with a couple of donors in hopes of creating a Center for Christian Apologetics at Spring Arbor University. The idea behind our center would be to aid all disciplines at SAU in understanding and teaching with a framework of Christ as creator, redeemer and reconciler of the world (which we do very well already). As our students graduate and head around the world, we

Sunday, December 12, 2021: Jonathan tells us we're ready to launch *Telling Tales*, perhaps tomorrow. MB, Nathaniel, and I watched the *Muppet Christmas Carol*. Becoming something of a tradition. I was glad to see it includes Scrooge's breaking off the engagement early in life, which I think is a crucial part of his story. Busy week of grading coming up, but the end of the term's in sight. Ratio Christi barbecue tonight at Lou's, but we're not up to it. Just wore out from the term. Likewise with get-together at Sloan's house tomorrow. Part of not overly wanting to fraternize with HBU folks right now might be related to some of the struggles I'm having making sense of aspects of our being here. We see through a glass darkly, though, and are called to walk by faith, not by sight. Do I just persevere despite my inability to understand everything about being here? Is there something wrong, or is this just par for the course? Am I just to keep casting my bread on the waters?

Monday, December 13, 2021: Wrote this for the WB today:

Pride and Prejudice & *King Richard*

Marrying an English professor is bound to have its effects, and in my case it certainly has. I rather doubt I would have gotten around to the quirky writings of Kurt Vonnegut as soon as I did, if at all, without Marybeth's deep interest in the fellow. But recently I made it through what may be his best book, in the estimation of many, *Slaughterhouse-Five*.

It is quite a prodigious literary achievement, integrating a largely real-life heart-breaking account of war and tragedy (culminating in the firebombing of Dresden, which even Winston Churchill in its immediate aftermath expressed grave doubts about) with elements of time travel, science fiction, and plunger-looking aliens for whom a human's urination habits are the stuff of endless entertainment. The book has several laudable features worth noting—from its reflections on free will to the dignity of persons, and from its delicious humor to its deft playfulness with the mysteries of time—but it's the juxtaposition of the serious and silly, in particular, that struck me as especially intriguing. The farcical and fun elements make the medicine go down smoother; the overall effect is a powerful, fascinating, and memorable one.

As much as Vonnegut's book mesmerized my attention, it isn't the one I'm conferring top honors on for the year, but I mention it because, surprisingly enough, it was what led me to the book that gets the nod. In many of his books, and certainly in this one, one of Vonnegut's charms is his penchant for a nonlinear way of telling a story. After reading *Slaughterhouse-Five*, as a result, I found myself with a hankering for something a bit more straightforward.

In years past I had tried my hand at Jane Austen's work, but had never quite been able to sustain my interest long enough, so I thought it might be the occasion to try again. This time did the trick. I started reading *Pride and Prejudice*, and just couldn't stop. As Tolkien's *Lord of the Rings* eventually drew me in with its lush descriptions of nature and scenery, *Pride and Prejudice* enchanted me with its marvelous dialogue, each piece of which strikes me as a miniature artwork, their exquisite assemblage a masterpiece. It takes more than a modicum of patience, and a little getting used to, but once immersed in it, the book becomes an irresistible page-turner and aesthetic delight. The taste for it, once acquired, becomes a voracious hunger for more. The protracted love story it tells is also, though doubtless reflective of another time, as timeless as it is unspeakably romantic, until at long last it matures and comes to fruition.

There is just ever so much about Austen's marvelous novel deserving accolades and appreciation—the breathtaking dialogue, the masterful use of language, its rich motifs of appearance versus reality and value versus price, its implicit Christian themes that are never heavy handed, including infusions of grace from unexpected places. The 1995 BBC mini-series is a wonderful adaptation, but, for no fault of its own, cannot compare with the novel itself punctuated with its priceless and comedic, ironic and opinionated narrative voice.

It is an interesting phenomenon the way some books may fail to appeal to us at one point in our lives, but veritably leap off the pages at another time. I remember having that experience years ago with C. S. Lewis's *Till We Have Faces*. After a few unsuccessful efforts to read it, a time came when it simply burst to life before my eyes. It was there to be discovered all along, waiting patiently for me to develop the ears with which to hear it. Likewise with *Pride and Prejudice*. I might suggest, if there's a great book you've tried in the past to get through but to no avail, you might be ready to give it another shot.

As for the best movie, I'll mention a film I saw recently that I found very moving: *King Richard*. It's the story of the father of Venus and Serena Williams, and how, against impossible odds, he pursued a dream of his daughters becoming the best in the sport. Knowing the end of the story, we can hardly call his animating vision nuts, but it certainly seemed so at the time. Against all odds, it happened. Tennis fans the world over would eventually see these two sisters go head to head in the finals of Grand Slam tournaments like the U. S. Open, the Australian Open, and on the fabled lawns of Wimbledon. The movie is a remarkable underdog story about the power of persistence and of a dream.

I relished one line perhaps most of all. As she was a bit older, Venus was the first to break through to the pro's. Serena watched from the sidelines, biding her time, and celebrated as Venus met with success. Discerning some of the challenge this posed to her, Richard walked over to Serena at one point and offered this prophetic encouragement: "Venus is going to be the best in the world. You are going to be the best ever."

Tuesday, December 14, 2021: Chipping away at grading today, and making progress in my math book of the year, *The Universe Speaks in Numbers*. When I was a boy I wanted to pursue math and physics, and didn't change my mind until college. Sometimes I regret not having double majored in philosophy and mathematics, but I wimped out. The tension in theoretical physics between experience and thought parallels, it seems to me, a similar tension in ethics between empiricists like Jonathan Haidt and theoretical ethicists like, say, John Hare or Robert Adams. I definitely lean toward the latter, but nowadays the former seems to attract considerably greater attention. When we build ethical theory, though, for example, we choose to employ some rather universally applicable criteria for what constitutes solid theory. A book vindicating ethical theory might be useful—not one that reduces it to what we mean by our terms, not one content with doing applied ethics, nor one that settles for psychological insights, but theory that takes seriously the most distinctive and telling features of morality.

Wednesday, December 15, 2021: Today is my 56th birthday, and it's a banner day for the Center. Official launch day of both *Telling Tales* as well as of our new series on Apologetics and Pop Culture of which MB will serve as editor. Exciting stuff! Folks are being sweet on FB. Since the editorial board at Baker is meeting sometime this week to consider our revised proposal on the moral argument, this week has the potential to be simply huge. Just spend the day enjoying being with MB, and in the evening had dinner with her and Nathaniel at PF Changs. Nice day.

Thursday, December 16, 2021: Should hear soon from Baker. Exciting. Praying for God's will to be done. Good prayer time with TJ; we're trying to discern God's direction. Saw a meme on FB today that went like this, a quote from John Frame: "God has the sovereign right to do as he wishes, and no other explanation is necessary." I responded like this: "I don't disagree with Frame on this score, but notice that some might read it as suggesting that God might well will anything at all since divine sovereignty is unconstrained altogether. But if God, as the Bible says, can't deny himself, sin, etc., then there may well be constraints internal to his nature, which are actually marks of his perfection and worship-worthiness. In other words, as long as we don't assume something like absolute radical voluntarism that vitiates our ascriptions of goodness to God of any determinate content, I would agree with Frame. Otherwise I would respectfully demur."

Friday, December 17, 2021: Well, today has been interesting. I see that Stan told TJ they'd hired "just the right person" for the position he'd applied for—and it wasn't TJ. Argh. But we're trying to trust God. I suggested TJ get one of his rich friends to offer a donation to the Center contingent on TJ getting to help run it. Before hearing from TJ, I was already struggling a bit emotionally after reading my book on math and physics. Since I had wanted to pursue such disciplines all growing up, sometimes I lament I didn't stick with it. Can't help but feel the contrast between esteemed scientists and mathematicians and one like me, working in ethics, thought by benighted freshmen they can take down with vacuous skepticism.

But MB encouraged me and suggested that it will likely be my books rather than HBU than affirm my gifts and calling. It is admittedly hard being at an institution that doesn't seem to have much appreciation for the work. Stan's decision didn't help. Nor does the school's giving exactly nothing toward the Center, nor carving out a space for it. On some days it's more of a battle than others not to grow weary in well doing. Hoping to hear from Baker today, but nothing yet. Fit in some grading; inching closer to the deadline on Monday. Graduation has been moved to this evening, in about three and a half hours. Still believing God will act, Aslan's on the move, and the moral apol team somehow will be able to come together. Trusting God, or trying to. I believe, Father; help my unbelief.

Saturday, December 18, 2021: Finished *Pride and Prejudice* at long last. What a simply delightful novel. I want to start a literary journal to record insights relevant from literature to my work—thick illustrations of important ethical concepts and such. It will prove especially important, I think, to the collaboration with Craig. Haven't yet heard from Baker; not sure what that means, but I remain hopeful. Spent much of the day grading. Just have one discussion board and about twelve essays left to grade, and I'll be done. We postponed our trip to the comedy club; a maelstrom was raging around the time we were planning to leave. We watched *Mother Night* instead.

Neat conversation with Elton today. He mentioned a piece he'd read by a lady mathematician, who spoke of the need for abstractions in her field. Numbers themselves are abstractions. He then made an application to the notion of goodness. We can talk about good individual things, but goodness itself of necessity is an abstraction, and a needed one if we wish to talk about good things in the first place.

Sunday, December 19, 2021: Nice day fellowshipping with Marybeth and Nathaniel, and with Rob and Jer in the evening. The guys and I ate steaks Nathaniel made and watched *It's a Wonderful Life*. Lots of fun and laughs. Won't see Rob for a month. Ten more essays to grade, which I'm planning to do in the morning. Grades due at noon, then

Christmas break rather officially commences. Seven or eight chapters into *Sense and Sensibility*. Still no word from Baker or my agent.

Monday, December 20, 2021: Got my grades in. Feels good. Now it's time to throw myself into my vacation work. Looking forward to making progress on the book. I've been missing Virginia lately quite a bit. Far superior weather, lovely scenery, better coffee houses. Miss the mountains. Wanted to be here when I was there, and now I have to resist wanting to be there while I'm here in Texas. Certainly don't miss Liberty, save for the healthy remuneration, but definitely miss Virginia. Job at Virginia Tech recently posted; tempting to apply, but my chances of getting it would be small. Besides, it wouldn't much conduce to building a Center. Just want to know if HBU is the right place to build it.

My agent told me he didn't hear from Baker on Friday, and now doubts we'll hear before the holidays are over.

I seem called on time and again to give up power. To live the cruciform life. It's hard, so hard. Yet giving up power is at the heart of the cross.

I'm profoundly disappointed in HBU right now. Profoundly—as in words fail. Is this the right place for the Center?

On another note I want to get a journal and make it into a literary journal—in which I record insights germane to my work in moral apologetics.

I wish by now I'd have written my way into the job I want.

Struggling to know how to cast the vision for moral apologetics—the vital importance of exploring the foundations of ethics. A piece for CT? I just don't know.

Tuesday, December 21, 2021: I felt so good yesterday morning, waking up with a clean slate, ready to tackle the vacation projects. I even mentioned to MB at breakfast how good I was feeling, unencumbered by any pressing burdens. I also mentioned that, whenever this happens, it's usually short-lived. And sure enough something happened yesterday, yet again, that threatened my equanimity and, once more, made me wonder if HBU is the right place to build the Center.

Part of the challenge in building the Center is that doing such a thing is so different from what else is out there. An illustration. One might review the philosophy jobs currently on offer, especially those touching on ethics, and here's what he would find: jobs in feminist philosophy, African philosophy, philosophy of gender, Indian philosophy, empirical ethics, ethics of technology, philosophy of race, indigenous American philosophy, environmental ethics, digital ethics, queer legal theory, animal ethics. There's usually a smattering of jobs mentioned in normative ethics and meta-ethics, but for an avowed theist to be seriously considered for the latter, he or she would likely have to be very, very good, and in most cases not overly forthright about their theological commitments. Anything like an explicit commitment to do such work through a theistic lens, especially a Christian one, is almost certainly tantamount to a disqualification.

There is just nothing of the kind when it comes to the Center as I envision it. But as a result I feel like so many of my efforts go against the grain and face a really challenging uphill battle. If someone wants to build, say, a seminary, that's a daunting task, and certainly one that's worthwhile, but at least it has the advantage of people understanding the point and purpose of such an institution. But a Center concerning the foundations of ethics? Not so much. Yet it's the latter that is currently not in existence and yet vitally important to fill a gaping hole. We already have seminaries, for example, especially in this country. Perhaps as many as can be realistically sustained and filled with students, truth be told. We don't, however, have a central hub of cutting-edge research in moral apologetics and the foundations of ethics, perhaps in part because its financial benefits aren't obvious. The Center is not designed to capture a slice of some preexisting market share or pool of prospective students.

I also find myself desperately wanting to be free to do the work I feel called to do. I would relish the chance to be my own boss, without the need to attend silly, time-consuming, energy-depleting meetings, parties, functions, gatherings. *So* not my thing! They drain me as an introvert. Just excruciating. Getting browbeaten for my lack of extroversion surely doesn't help. I just want to do the work and good works I've been tasked to do, and lose myself in the labor, socializing with a relative few of my own choosing as I go along. I don't get why I need to project gregariousness and ebullience; it's all dissembling and disingenuous. I want to work for God and not for men. I came here with a vision, a dream, yet after arriving have felt so often like an agenda not of my own devising gets imposed on me from without, and efforts of my own get stymied and thwarted with remarkable casualness and an air of presumption, at least when they are not simply overlooked, ignored, or trivialized.

I was so grateful for the deliverance from Liberty, more than words can say, but now I find myself wondering more often than I'd prefer if HBU is the place that will sustain the vision of the Center after I am gone. I harbor doubts, which breaks my heart. No place is perfect or ideal or optimal, I know, but what to do with these nagging, recurring, chronic doubts is the question. Are they a deal breaker and sign to look elsewhere? Or rather a temptation to diverge from the path that God has provided, best resisted for all I'm worth?

Started reading *Gaudy Night* this morning with some green tea; Dorothy Sayers was a marvelous writer. Susan Haack, I think it was, wrote an essay on the novel, thinking it highly philosophical. Looking forward to seeing ways this is so.

Shared what I'd written earlier this morning with TJ, and he just wrote this marvelous encouragement back to me:

Thanks for sharing this, brother. I delighted and winced as I read it; delight because I LOVE the way you write, and wincing because I acutely feel the same pain you feel. I suspect it is our brotherly bond and the same burden I share for the vision God has given you. Truth be told, again and again I have found myself in the last days wrestling with the thought that my calling in all this may be by way of helping you pioneer, like the point of the spear in military lingo, the work of the Center in a place (perhaps building it ourselves by the grace and power of God) that is—from day one—grounded on a clear and concise mission that is insulated as much as possible from the mission drift so often foisted upon such undertakings by the very matters you lament in your entry above. We are called to this. We are most certainly called to this, and this vision will not be stymied by anything or anyone out of sync with the Lord's calling for us. This I believe. To this I am committed with every fiber of my being.

Mid-afternoon I got back to work a bit on the Collection, writing Scott Smith and David Horner at Biola, Oxford's Mark Wynn, William Lane Craig (one more time), and extending another invitation to Nicholas Wolterstorff, who hadn't altogether turned me down before. These are the chapters that still need to be assigned: Precursors to Kant, From Newman to Farrer, Contemporary Voices, Expressivism, Constructivism, Moral Knowledge, Natural Law Theory, Cornell Realism, Hinduism, Islam, Christianity.

Wednesday, December 22, 2021: Last night and again this morning I feel like God at long last gave me a deep sense of assurance that HBU is the right place for us. Not just to have come to, but to remain. So, that prayer having been answered, I'm diving in! This morning I extended additional invitations to contribute to the collection to Frank Beckwith, Christian Miller, and Matt Jordan. Matt and I will be chatting on the phone before long. TJ and I will be praying within the hour.

And I just wrote Phil Tallon this letter:

Phil,

Merry Christmas, my friend! Hope you and the family have a wonderful celebration.

To keep you in the loop, I'm about to start a matching fundraising campaign for the Center. Since MB and I are planning to give 50,000 dollars before the end of the school year to the Center, it'll be a 50K matching campaign. Hopefully this will be successful and lend itself to some lectureships, conferences, scholarships, etc., especially with the Certificate program coming up. I'll be trying again, at Stan's recommendation, for the grant from HBU to do the conference we want to do in the spring of 2023. I also am planning to bring in two speakers for events this spring: Mike Austin and Steve Evans. Mike was going to be in town and asked if HBU wanted for him to speak; I told him we'll pay him 500 bucks to speak. We're trying to arrange a date. He's the president of EPS right now. And Evans of course teaches at Baylor and I want to bring him in sometime in April for a big talk. The Center will pay for all the expenses. We have some money to draw on already, plus we'll be doing fundraising plus giving money ourselves, so it should all be handily covered.

Prayers appreciated as we embark on all this. I know it's been a long time in coming, but it's taken a little while to get our ducks in a row.

Best, Dave

In the early afternoon TJ and I prayed, and it turns out that we had both sensed an impression about HBU. In his case, it was that he felt God told him that he wasn't going to take him out of the church altogether in bringing all this about. In other words, that TJ was to continue to pastor. TJ didn't know what this meant exactly, but when combined with my message, it was exciting. For if we are to remain here, then maybe TJ could come to this area without having leave pastoring. Then, as icing on the cake, during the call I got a text from MB in which she shared a message from Melissa, who asked if we know of anyone who might be interested in taking a teaching pastor position in the Woodlands. While we were on the phone, TJ followed up with Melissa, and now he's sending her his CV and a tape of his preaching, and she'll pass it along to the church. If TJ were to take a position like this, it would introduce a veritable world of opportunities, not least chances for the Center to extend its reach into local churches. Exciting times! God's at work.

David Horner is going to write for the collection, though he has to decide on which chapter. Smith likely will, but is still deciding. WLC turned me down, and still waiting to hear from Jordan, Miller, Wynn, and Wolterstorff. I also extended invitations to Christian Miller and Frank Beckwith, and they both accepted! Christian will write on constructivism, and Frank on natural law. Woohoo! This leaves nine chapters remaining. I just wrote a follow-up to Robert Adams, and then forwarded it to John Hare so he'd have a good update.

This was Frank's reply:

Hi David. Good to hear from you.

Thank you so much for the invitation. I'm honored!

Given the timetable you mention—18 months—I accept!

The issue you're asking me to write on is one that I've always wanted to address directly in full swoop. I allude to it in a recent piece I published in *Religions* earlier this year (https://www.mdpi.com/2077-1444/12/6/379/htm), but I've not really dealt with the rigor it deserves. There are three different folks to which I'd like to respond: (1) naturalists, like Johnathan Haidt and Michael Ruse, who have the right intuitions about the primary precepts of the natural law but deny the God on which it depends, (2) Christians, like Karl Barth and Carl Henry, who think that natural law theorists are saying that God is unnecessary for the natural law (which, at least in the Catholic tradition, is not true), and (3) new natural law theorists, like John Finnis and Robby George, who play down (contra Aquinas) the role of eternal law and divine law in the reality and inadequacies of the natural law.

Hope you and HBU are doing well.

I've been meaning to drive down visit you guys, but Covid hit.

Take care,

Frank

In the evening Dave Horner decided to take the first chapter, on the precursors to Kant. This is great; I love the idea of this guy leading off the collection. Marvelous. So we're down to eight slots to fill, which includes the Hindu and Islam chapters. So six slots not counting those. Wrote Robert Adams once more this evening just in case. Man would it be terrific if he took the last chapter?! One can dream. I had assumed I'd take whatever the last chapter that was left open (of course neither the Islam or Hinduism chapter), but who knows? If someone like Wolterstorff or Adams wants the last available one, I'll rest content writing the introduction and conclusion!

On another note, an e-mail from Jerry revealed he has covid. And he was here Sunday night, so both Rob and I were exposed. So far Jer's symptoms have been mild. He's vaccinated but not boosted. Nor is Rob boosted, though he's vaccinated. MB and I are both vaccinated and boosted. Nathaniel is scheduled to get boosted tomorrow.

It's 8 pm, and I just got word that Scott Smith is onboard the collection to write the moral knowledge chapter! What a banner day!

Thursday, December 23, 2021: Robert Adams replied and asked a few questions about length and deadlines, then said he's thinking hard about doing it. I'm hoping he takes the very last chapter—on extending the moral argument to Christianity. What an amazing thing that would be!

Nathaniel came over and we all watched *Die Hard*, which was fun. I also noticed in the course of the afternoon that Joan Didion died. I had seen a documentary on her within the last year, and there was a lot about her I liked. After Nathaniel left I read her essay "On Morality," I think it's called. Much to unpack there; something to affirm, some to challenge. I may do that either for the WB or MoralApologetics.com. In the late evening I did this month's WB post. And MB purchased for me today the journal I wanted to start recording insights germane to my field from the arena of literature. Should prove a boon. Before bed I wrapped up another chapter of *Gaudy Night*. And also before bed I threw caution to the wind one more time and asked Al Plantinga to write a short foreword to the collection.

Friday, December 24, 2021: Christmas Eve. Quite a year this has been! A hectic spring term, co-teaching with Craig in May, getting three books contracts, Nathaniel moving to Texas, MB becoming department chair, *Telling Tales* getting put together, and the list goes on. More died in the US from covid in 2021 than did in 2020. This morning MB, Nathaniel, and I enjoyed a trip to Toasted Yolk, where we had some great conversation, including about Joan Didion's "On Morality." After getting home MB and I discussed it some more, after she read it. She made the point that Joan seemed to have misunderstood conscience along purely solitary and unverifiable lines. I think I want to do a longer piece on Didion, Twain, Swift, Austen, and Vonnegut. A section from the latter's *Palm Sunday* is relevant by way of comparison with Joan. Loving this new notebook interfacing literature and ethics!

In the afternoon heard from Wolterstorff that he needs a week to think about joining the collection, so I sent him an update. And I got an e-mail from my agent that he sent to me and Bill Craig—looks like we're going to be given the Baker contract! The last few days have just been amazing! Wow. Blown away. Looks like they're only giving us 100,000 words, though, not the 120,000 we put in the proposal.

Heading out at 7 this evening for a Christmas Eve church service.

Saturday, December 25, 2021: Nathaniel came over early in the morning, and I awoke to the smell of bacon, eggs, and biscuits, bringing to mind those mornings I would wake up in my grandmother's house in Tennessee as a kid. We had a lot of fun hanging out all day, discussing a big range of topics. I read Swift's "Modest Proposal," and was mightily impressed by the satire. Apparently there are three sorts of satire; I wrote them down in my literary journal. Good satire, it would seem, require a solid moral foundation; similarly Lewis says Austen's social commentary did as well; but this is just what seems lacking in Didion's "On Morality"—despite the legitimacy of some of her beefs. Marybeth and Nathaniel worked on a puzzle together, and all of us watched *The Man Who Invented Christmas*. Quite a good Christmas movie about the creation of *The Christmas Carol*, of course taking all manner of artistic license and creative liberties. William Lane Craig acknowledged getting the e-mail about our prospective contract with Baker. Although he didn't gush, or mention Christmas, he used an exclamation mark, which is always an exciting, veritably momentous event. Before Nathaniel left, he and I thought and talked a lot about the novel I'm interested in writing. He seems quite interested, especially in the prospect of helping me structure the plot and then perhaps being the one to turn it into a screenplay.

Sunday, December 26, 2021: MB and I enjoyed a nice church service at 10, then Nathaniel came over and we enjoyed a meal and a movie. He and I continued to kick around ideas for the prospective novel, filling in details about the characters. MB seems a bit down and can't seem to get out of this funk. We prayed in the evening about several of the issues she's confronting: Nathaniel growing up, rising to the occasion, and figuring out this job situation; the tragic, needless, and traumatic conflict with her incorrigible mom; some of the challenges at HBU. I hope and pray tomorrow is a better day for her. Now that the Christmas celebration days are over, tomorrow is really the first day we need to dive in with all we've got. I know if she doesn't manage to get some clarity she wants on being department chair over break and doesn't get her Vonnegut book proposal done, she's going to be really down on herself. Hoping and praying for the breakthrough she needs soon.

I also wrote Brian MacPherson, an old Michigan buddy, this afternoon. I hope I hear back and get from him a robust update of what he's been up to. We have largely fallen out of touch for twenty years. He was an important and enjoyable friend around my last years at Wayne, very encouraging and helpful; many long hours spent discussing philosophy and life. We even did a road trip to Wilkes-Barre (and NYC) after I got the King's job. He's a good philosopher and talented teacher; a graduate of McGill who wrote his dissertation on advanced logic. He had started doing medical school classes; I'm most curious how far he ended up pursuing a medical degree. A Canadian and only child, he lost his elderly parents some years back. He's written back and we've had a nice exchange getting caught up. He's wrapping up another doctorate, this time in integrative biology!! Fantastic.

Before bed I wrote this letter to a Hindu ethicist with some Oxford connections:

Hi Dr. Ranganathan!

I hope this e-mail finds you well.

I am writing to inquire to see if you might be interested in contributing a chapter to an anthology that Yale's John Hare and I are editing for Oxford University Press.

The book is on the foundations of ethics, and it's fairly expansive in scope. We look at the history of moral arguments, deficiencies of secular ethics, ways in which moral truths of various sorts may essentially depend on the divine, etc.

The final section of the book moves beyond theism per se into more fine-grained accounts of specific religious persuasions. There will be a chapter on Judaism, another on Hinduism, another on Islam, and one on Christianity.

I'm looking for an author of the chapter on Hinduism, exploring connections between ethics and Hindu thought. From a look at some of your work, I'm thinking you may well be the perfect candidate to write on this with your background, training, and written work.

What we're looking for is someone who unapologetically wants to argue that morality, in one way or another, points evidentially not just toward a divine or transcendent source generally, but more specifically toward Hinduism, however tacitly or indirectly (or overtly and directly).

I realize this topic deserves a book-length treatment rather than just a chapter, but such as it is, this will be such a vitally important contribution to the whole book.

Lots of folks have signed on to write a chapter already, including: David Horner, Kyla Ebels-Duggan, Robert Garcia, Terence Cuneo, Christian Miller, Angus Menuge, Paul Copan, John Rist, Anne Jeffrey, John Crosby, Steve Evans, Scott Smith, John Hare, Matt Flannagan, Janine Idziak, Linda Zagzebski, Frank Beckwith, JP Moreland, Mark Linville, Len Goodman. Nicholas Wolterstorff and Robert Adams are considering joining the project, and will let me know their final verdict any day now.

The chapter would be between 7500 and 8000 words and would be due in about a year and a half.

I would really appreciate your giving this your serious consideration! I think you would make a fabulous addition to the project. Thanks ever so much for your time.

Best, Dave

Put this on FB, too: "Got in contact with a friend from twenty years ago this evening, after we'd largely fallen out of touch for all that time. What a joy. Life is such, I know, that some friendships are bound to fall by the wayside, but this was a fellow whose generosity around the time I was finishing my doctorate and entering the job market was incredible. Having traversed such a path himself some years before, he offered advice, encouragement, and a ton of practical help. I remember that he arranged a mock interview to help me prepare for an upcoming interview, and we would spend just hours and hours discussing life and philosophy. He was a caregiver to two elderly parents, now gone, and endured a lot of hardships through the years. I regret we fell out of touch, but it was heartening this evening to see that, with but a little effort, our friendship could be fully revived and restored."

Monday, December 27, 2021: Delighted this morning to see that an HBU online student named Michael gave 500 dollars to the Center. It was entirely initiated by him! I hadn't gotten around yet to writing the fundraising letter. Incredible, and most encouraging!

I think we have an outside leak that explains the higher water bill we received recently. Contacted a plumber. We need a few plumbing jobs in and around the house to be done, anyway, and before it gets cold it would be prudent to get taken care of.

Finished going through Fraser's first chapter on debunking, on the empirical premise of the evolutionary debunking objection. That topic should be my first in the chapter. Also, books that should prove helpful include the following: Ruse's, *The Universe Speaks in Numbers*, Joyce's two, Plantinga's on science, Melissa's, and Craig's on the historical Adam. Hoping tomorrow is a good day of research and writing.

Struggled getting going today, putting this bit of funny on FB: "On the verge of a major and daunting writing assignment, I find that I simply HAVE to do something else first, namely, find out the meticulous details of the lives of each and every cast member of the 1960's *Batman* show. Burt Ward, Adam West, Yvonne Craig, et al. For some reason this is the single most important thing I've ever had to do all of a sudden in all my born days. Unsure how much depends on the red wheelbarrow, but I'm pretty sure EVERYTHING depends on this."

Have yet to hear back from a Muslim or Hindu scholar, though I've written several. No response from McGrath or Wynn, but hoping. Still waiting on Adams and Wolterstorff, and praying!

Just decided to throw caution to the wind and try something new:

Hi Dr. Shafer-Landau,

I'm writing to make an inquiry of you. To begin with, I admire your work in ethics, particularly your defense of moral realism. I heartily concur with so much of my analysis, and I consider you to be one of the best in the business.

I'm a philosophy professor in Texas, and I'm under contract with Yale's John Hare to edit a book on God and ethics. It's a largely sympathetic treatment of the subject, and I realize that this isn't quite your view, despite your moral realism. But still, I thought I might make of you an inquiry to consider writing a chapter in the book.

Here's why. We're dividing the labor of the book up in a particular way. So there's a section on moral realism in which someone will argue for moral realism in one chapter, but others will take on error theory, constructivism, and expressivism. Your friend Terence Cuneo is writing the chapter on error theory, for example, despite that he'll have nothing to say about God in his chapter.

Chapters in which aspects of morality will be suggested evidentially point to God will be in other sections of the book. There's a fair bit of interesting work done on that topic out there, and we were glad to see that Oxford University Press agreed to give us this chance to showcase it.

Inclusion of someone like you in the project would be helpful for lots of reasons, including to show that there are good reasons to entertain reservations about something like expressivism that can be shared by both avowedly theistic moral realists and nontheistic moral realists.

We have a solid lineup so far. David Horner, Kyla Ebels-Duggan, Robert Garcia, Terence Cuneo, Christian Miller, Angus Menuge, Paul Copan, John Rist, Anne Jeffrey, John Crosby, Steve Evans, Scott Smith, John Hare, Matt Flannagan, Janine Idziak, Linda Zagzebski, Frank Beckwith, JP Moreland, Mark Linville, Len Goodman. All of these have signed on.

Robert Adams and Nicholas Wolterstorff are also considering writing a chapter, and they will let me know soon.

SO....here is the deal. We're closing in on filling all the slots, but I need someone top-notch to write the chapter on expressivism, mainly a chapter that underscores reasons to think it's not as good a metaethical theory as moral realism. And honestly, I can't think of anyone better than you, if you'd be willing.

It would of course be made very clear that you're not in sympathy with every chapter or the overall thrust of the book. Your part would be a critique of expressivism, which would not be tantamount to putting your imprimatur on the other arguments in other chapters. They are all fair game deserving of their own critical scrutiny.

So that's my inquiry and invitation to you! Again, I so appreciate your work! And either way, thanks so much for your time!

(By the way, the essay if you choose to write it would be due in about a year and a half and you should aim for about 7500 to 8000 words.)

Best,
Dave

Tuesday, December 28, 2021: Arranged for a plumber to come tomorrow morning. Hoping it isn't too expensive. Wrote my ninth Campolo blog, and got to work on my moral realism book, starting with how moral realism should be defined. Here's the Campolo blog:

Reflections on *Why I Left, Why I Stayed*, by Tony and Bart Campolo, Part 9

I have now done several replies to just one chapter, Bart's chapter explaining how he left the faith, so I had better do one more post about that chapter and call it done. We have seen how Bart gradually moved away from various of his religious convictions—some orthodox, some he merely thought orthodox, for reasons that were sometimes a matter of capitulation to other influences, and for other reasons which were arguably not a matter of capitulation or compromise at all, but quite principled. What conduced to a slippery slope, however, was his unwillingness to make those very distinctions.

On top of his struggles with issues like the moral propriety of gay sexual practices, the doctrine of damnation, and divine sovereignty, he had a life-transforming experience when he endured a terrible, life-threatening cycling accident in Cincinnati. Later on, in retrospect, he took three big lessons from the crash. First, "I learned that my core identity—my essential self, if you will—is all in my head…that my individual personality, mind, heart, and soul are all contained in my brain." [Here he points to the work of Malcolm Gladwell and David Linden to the effect that our judgments and desires are largely controlled by the release and absorption of certain chemical in our brains in ways our conscious selves only vaguely understand; for a solid response, see here.] Second, he suddenly knew he would die one day. And third, when he dies, including his brain, he will vanish forever. "Like it or not, this life is the only one I've got."

What he calls lessons are probably better thought of as inferences that he makes on the basis of what he considers good evidence. Of course, though, plenty of believers think there are intimate, organic connections between body and soul without inferring that the latter is finite, and their convictions are not without evidence, too—such as a range of highly evidenced out-of-body experiences that defy naturalistic analysis (see here). That we are going to die is a sober fact that all of us, believers and unbelievers, have to come to terms with.

But Bart's elaborate assertion without much of an argument that we just are our bodies and that, at death, we cease to exist is a quite ambitious metaphysical claim, radically underdetermined by the evidence he adduces.

When Bart shared his newfound conviction that nobody survives past physical death with his wife, he discovered this was something she had come to believe herself for some while. He realized that, if they're right, it wouldn't entail God's nonexistence, but steeped as he was in evangelical theology, he took such a fact about the finality of death as reason to disbelieve in God. "As far as I was concerned, if there was no afterlife, there was no good and just God, which reduced the teachings of Jesus to an odd mix of delusional metaphysics and commonsense wisdom about the benefits of virtue."

This was both sobering for Bart as well as animating, motivating him to figure out a new way to live. Despite his change in worldview, some things remained the same. For example, he retained his commitment to build warm and loving communities, to social justice, to education and the arts, and to believing that sacrificial love is the best way to live. Their worldviews had changed, but not their values. He gravitated to what he thought were scientific explanations and logical arguments, but also yearned for something of a "new gospel."

This he found in secular humanism and his new hero, Robert Ingersoll, a 19-century politician and orator. "What struck me most when I started reading Ingersoll…was his deep and obvious commitment to love as the ultimate hope of humanity, and his great eloquence in communicating it…. [T]he surest path to true happiness is to concern yourself with the happiness of others. He instantly became my role model as a secular humanist evangelist."

For now I will reply just to this last point about the correspondence between love and happiness. I have written quite a bit on this topic, as have many other moral apologists through the centuries. Not only is Bart right, in one sense, he's more right than he knows; and in fact he's implicitly furnished us with the resources for a variant of the moral argument for God. This is the argument from providence, as John Hare calls it, and it goes something like this: Full rational commitment to morality [or a life of love] requires that morality is a rationally stable enterprise; in order for morality to be a rationally stable enterprise, it must feature ultimate correspondence between happiness and virtue; there is no reason to think that such correspondence obtains unless God exists; so rationality dictates the postulation of God's existence.

Without theism and a providential God at work ensuring ultimate and airtight correspondence between a life of love, on the one hand, and happiness, on the other, there will invariably be points of disconnect when the virtuous life of love, far from conducing to happiness, will result in far more misery than happiness. Theism, though, salvages the rationality of morality. This was an insight that Sidgwick, Kant, Reid, Locke, and others have spilled a great deal of ink on through the centuries. If Bart is looking for an argument, I might point him in this direction.

As much as I am loath to do this, because I don't want this to seem a diatribe against Bart, it's worth noting that such an argument would be unlikely to speak to Bart, because he actually isn't committed to anything like the rationality of morality. Indeed, he has given up that there is anything objectively binding about morality at all. He has abandoned moral realism, by his own admission.

So his ongoing commitment to, say, the value of a life of love, is predicated on a divorce of fact and value. Whatever sense in which such a life, at least in general, is a better choice is purely practical or pragmatic. He seems to replace the "delusional metaphysics" of Jesus with no relevant metaphysics at all—just a choice on his part to live in a way that he thinks will conduce to happiness. As a philosopher I find this wholly inadequate and, frankly, profoundly unphilosophical. In some ways he remains, I think, his father's son— content with sociological analysis, which is often fine as far as it goes. But it's no substitute for robust philosophical reflection. It's no surprise that plenty of other atheists would find there to be little compelling reason to be committed to living such a life; if Bart wants a worldview that actually puts love front and center, not just contingently but essentially, perhaps he should reconsider the faith he left behind.

To read more about the argument from providence and the television show *The Good Place*, see here.

To read more about the natural human desire for immortality, see here.

Wednesday, December 29, 2021: This question was posed to the WB:

Hey Guys,

Just want to say thank you to all of you who put out the *Worldview Bulletin*. You are all doing a fantastic job of equipping others to defend and live out the faith.

I have a question. I feel like it's a "John the Baptist" question "is He the one or should I expect another?" It's not that type of question, but I am a bit embarrassed to ask it as a pastor. I am sure this is not an original thought, but the thought came to me that (I have worked with youth all my life predominantly)— that something needs to click in the heart and mind of a young person when it comes to viewing God and Christ—their faith needs to move from only the "subjective" to also the "objective." What I am saying is that they need to see God as being objectively real and true and not just a matter of faith or a preference or something that could be true for them but not for others.

Now as soon as I say that —I am wondering (and here's the question) if philosophically I can say that—that God's Existence is objectively true. I know that we Christians hold that He is ultimate reality but I sense that non-believers would say we believe that but it is subjectively true (at least I think one would say that). What I am trying to ask or state is—that our culture since the Renaissance or the Enlightenment (you would know) or so has really moved matters of faith from objective truth to subjective truth and this thinking is deeply ingrained in the culture so much that most young people just accept it to be true and what I am asking is can I confidently get up and say that young people (especially Christian young people) need to begin to see God as objectively true—how do I do that without violating philosophical foundations?

I hope that makes sense. Sorry for taking so long to get that out—can you help me here? Or direct me to something that might address this.

Thanks

Tony

I offered this reply:

Tony is right, I think, to notice that it's common nowadays to associate faith with something like epistemic deficiency. "I may not have good evidence to believe it, but I have faith anyway," that sort of idea. Or Twain's charming depiction of faith as believing what we know ain't so. Such a notion of faith is consistent with a strong sense of subjective certainty, however misguided, and unfortunately some interpret the Bible as encouraging faith of just such kind. I don't tend to see it this way, thinking that faith thus construed is overly fideistic for my taste. More importantly, though, it strikes me as a departure from the biblical picture of faith, not to mention the *knowledge* we can have of God's goodness and grace.

I remember in seminary one of our assignments was to do a big word study of "faith," and the takeaway was largely this: biblically speaking, faith is trust in God's faithfulness. Now, when we look at the biblical narratives what we usually find, especially, say, with the people of Israel, their calling to trust God was not to exercise blind faith, but rather to remember his long track record of faithfulness and respond accordingly. Likewise in our lives, the longer we live, the more and more evidence we have not just of God's existence, but of his goodness and love and trustworthiness. Time and again he has demonstrated his faithful provision. So each day it seems like God's track record of faithfulness grows longer, and thus our faith yet more evidenced and principled, at least normatively, and figuring in the inevitable undulations of our spiritual lives.

I do suspect there is something about "not seeing" in our exercise of faith. Suppose we encounter a situation in which we need God's provision of some sort—an instance in which God needs to demonstrate the sufficiency of his grace, or manifest his deliverance in some way. Suppose we then come before God in prayer and ask for his help and intervention. What we may not and likely will not see from the start is the form of God's answer to the prayer. It may come in a predictable way, or it may show up in an altogether different form from what we had imagined or expected or hoped—like God's refusal to remove the thorn in Paul's flesh but promised to use it for his glory. Recognizing that we're saddled with those sorts of limitations is a useful reminder that we shouldn't presume too many of the specifics of how God may answer our prayer. Such are paradigmatic times when walking by faith and not by sight is the wise course.

But what faith essentially involves is abiding trust in God's steadfast faithfulness, and such faith, rather than being at odds with the evidence, or mutually exclusive with knowledge, is something for which our evidence is excellent. We have historical, scientific, biblical, and philosophical reasons to believe in and know God's reality and his worship-worthy essential goodness and perfect love. We also have, the longer we walk with Christ, an increasingly long list of occasions when God has demonstrated his love and abundant provision for us. Our trust in God's faithfulness has precious little to do with epistemic deficiency; rather, the more evidence we have of God's power and sufficiency, the stronger our abiding trust in his faithfulness should be. The stories of God's faithfulness in the lives of the ancient Israelites in the OT and the church in the NT are the even deeper theological grounding for such confidence, which the liturgies of the church and our study of scripture remind us of over and over.

So when appropriate, I try to challenge the narrative that depicts faith in a way that's nothing but capitulation to an "Enlightenment" portrayal of faith as absence or paucity of evidence. The biblical definition of faith is the diametric opposite. And once we habitually bear that in mind, we can even take the inward assurances of the Holy Spirit of God's reality and provision and love as more than merely subjective experiences, but rather as something we have good grounds for taking as altogether veridical. indeed, I suspect those quiet moments of spiritual intimacy and inward assurance are potentially examples of the deepest form of knowing—knowing not just that God is real, faithful, loving, etc., but knowing God himself.

Thursday, December 30, 2021: New Year's Eve Eve. Started the day with scripture reading and a trip to the gym. Got a second opinion on a water line in need of fixing at the house. What a blessing it was 2300 dollars less than the first!

God has been good to us. I feel like, in just the past few weeks, he has given me a deep assurance HBU, despite its problems, is the right place for the Center. Looking forward to seeing what God has in store for the year ahead. The theme of this year has been casting bread. The year was filled with doing so much of this. To change the metaphor, this year featured planting many seeds, and I'm hopeful it won't be long before we start seeing a mighty harvest. Mark Wynn contacted me this morning with an interest in the last chapter in the collection. If Adams turns me down, I told Wynn it's all his.

Friday, December 31, 2021: New Year's Eve! Great chat and prayer with TJ this morning. Much discussed the future of the Center, and especially what happens after I step down. Most geared around the roles of TJ and Jonathan. Being the youngest, Jonathan would be best to take over from TJ after he takes over from me. We prayed about this as well. I'm confident these two right hand men will take the Center in the right direction when those times come.

Steve Parrish wrote and took on the Contemporary Voices chapter. This surprised but delighted me. Also chatted with Matt Jordan on the phone and he's seriously considering the chapter covering moral arguments from Newman to Farrer. He'll let me know soon. Having penciled Bonevac in for Cornell realism and myself in for expressivism and Adams for the last chapter, that just leaves the Hinduism and Islam chapters. If Adams says no, I can put Wynn there. If Adams says yes, I can ask Wynn to collaborate with me if McGrath isn't keen on doing so himself.

Here is the fundraising letter we put out late yesterday:

$50,000 MATCHING FUNDRAISING CAMPAIGN FOR THE CENTER FOR THE FOUNDATIONS OF ETHICS AT HOUSTON BAPTIST UNIVERSITY

It scarcely goes without saying that moral foundations in our country and in this current moment are eroding and degrading all too fast. The Center for the Foundations of Ethics at Houston Baptist University seeks to address this trend and offer a positive and well-reasoned vision for believing in enduring moral truths built on ancient foundations that are altogether sure and trustworthy. The Center, we believe, is an important piece of what Andy Crouch calls culture making, an institution that will be around well after we are gone and that will continue to make a great impact. Our hope is to establish a central hub of cutting-edge research in moral apologetics and the foundations of ethics.

In its inaugural year, the Center has overseen a great many initiatives along these lines, with many more in the works. Here is a small sampling of the Center's activities:

Under the new leadership of executive editor TJ Gentry and managing editor Jonathan Pruitt, MoralApologetics.com is doing better than ever generating solid content.

We have also expanded our Moral Apologetics team to include as associate editors at the site and/or research fellows at the Center Zach Breitenbach, Jan Shultis, Brian Chilton, Stephen Jordan, TJ Gentry, Jonathan Pruitt, David Ochabski, and Tony Williams. Pending approval by the president and provost of HBU, the Center saw passed a Certificate in Moral Apologetics, hopefully to begin June of 2022.

Moral Apologetics Press, in just the next few months, will be publishing a number of volumes under Jonathan Pruitt's leadership: my journal of my second year as the Center director chronicling its ongoing development and maturation; our Strauss lectures called Coming to Life; Daniel McCoy's book on Buddhism and Christianity; Elton Higgs' collection of Twilight Musings; a few books by TJ Gentry; and a collection of Worldview Bulletin articles. Additionally, Marybeth Baggett has assumed the series editor role for a new series on Apologetics and Popular Culture, and Marybeth and I published our Telling Tales: Intimations of the Sacred in Popular Culture.

In another significant development for the Center this past year, Marybeth and I were privileged to give the Strauss lectures at Lincoln Christian University, where Zach Breitenbach and Richard Knopp, kindred spirits both, are doing stellar work with Room for Doubt.

This school year the Center also initiated a Student Fellows program run by Taylor Neill and me here at HBU featuring about a half dozen meetings throughout the school year.

Additionally, my research and writing has born much fruit. Ronnie Campbell and I got a contract with Broadman and Holman for a forthcoming book on philosophical theology. Jerry Walls and I have a contract with Oxford University Press for the fourth in our tetralogy on God and morality—a book on moral realism. Yale's John Hare and I have a contract with OUP for a significant collection on the moral argument, with contributions from leading scholars in the field. Marybeth and I have a contract to edit Ted Lasso and Philosophy for Wiley Blackwell, and just a few days ago William Lane Craig and I were informed that Baker will be offering him and me a contract to write a book on the moral argument.

Additionally, the Center is currently planning a number of activities over the near year. Mike Austin will be speaking at HBU in the spring of 2022, and Baylor's Steve Evans in the fall of 2022. We are also hoping to put on a major conference on the moral argument in the spring of 2023 at HBU in conjunction with the collection that Hare and I are editing, culminating in the publication of that volume.

Owing to a $50,000 gift to the Center, we are now in a position to do a matching fundraising campaign to support the continued work of the Center. All donations will support the Center's goals of generating a diverse community of scholars at work in the arena of the foundations of ethics and the moral argument(s) for God's existence. Specifically, financial gifts will be used wholly for such purposes as scholarships for students enrolled in the four-course Certificate of Moral Apologetics, conferences, and invited speakers lecturing on God and ethics.

We are earnestly praying that God blesses this ambitious effort to raise money to help build the Center, forge this important community, and advance cutting-edge work in the area of theistic ethics and moral apologetics. There is no other outfit or institution quite like this one, and the fruit of this ministry has only just begun bearing great fruit.

If you want to contribute to a bulwark against encroaching secularism and equip voices to articulate with rigorous minds and warm hearts the love of God, the goodness of the gospel, the enduring value of persons, deliverance from guilt and shame, the evidential significance of moral truth, and the transcendent foundations of ethics, please consider contributing to this important ministry.

Submit tax-deductible gifts through the HBU online giving form (select "Additional Giving Opportunities" and designate Center for the Foundations of Ethics from the pop-up list). You may also mail contributions to the following address (with Center for the Foundations of Ethics in the memo line): HBU Advancement Lockbox, PO Box 4897, Dept #527, Houston, TX 77210.
(https://securelb.imodules.com/s/1761/lg21/form.aspx...)

Finally, for any brave of heart who muscled through this volume—like Zak Schmoll, bless his heart—please remember it was primarily designed to chronicle a year's worth of the history of the Center, which is at this juncture inextricably tied to my own history. Reading it straight through is quite the achievement, forcing you to endure way too many of my idiosyncrasies and way too much of my incessant whiny-ness. That said, if you did it, I hope you found some encouragement in it. It's basically a peak into the kitchen in a restaurant. I hope it doesn't spoil the meal! In truth I hope it's a narrative that makes clear, despite my inconstancy and frequent faithlessness, God's enduring goodness and love, power and provision, constancy and faithfulness.